INTRODUCTION

Never before in the history of the cat fancy has a breed taken over the hearts and homes of so many people so quickly. Word of this new and fascinating breed is sweeping the world, and Ragdoll breeders are having trouble keeping up with the demand. The Ragdoll is the gentle giant of the domestic feline world, and, as you will see, the perfect cat for the 21st century.

This book is written for new or potential Ragdoll owners, those who already own and love their Ragdolls, and those simply interested in learning more about this incredible breed. We have also attempted to make this book breeder friendly, as the ultimate authority on your Ragdoll is its breeder.

Blue mitted male Ragdoll kitten. Photo by Muncy Smith.

The Ragdoll cat of today was developed from the unlikely combination of three feral cats in Riverside, California. Lots of stories have been told about the origins and characteristics of Ragdolls, but one common thread runs through them all: the purebred Ragdoll cat owes its existence to a woman named Ann Baker and a female cat named Josephine.

Josephine was a feral cat living in a cat colony on the property of Ann Baker's neighbor. She had become somewhat tame while being nursed back to health following an automobile accident. It was Ann Baker who recognized special qualities in Josephine's subsequent litters and obtained a female kitten from one of Josephine's litters, naming it Buckwheat. Buckwheat was a black self female, meaning that she was solid black. Ann Baker's neighbor also kept one of Josephine's kittens, a pointed male with white mittens named Daddy Warbucks. Ann Baker obtained a daughter of Daddy Warbucks and Josephine, Fugianna, who was the first bicolor Ragdoll. Using the stud services of her neighbor's cat, Daddy Warbucks, Ann Baker used these cats to establish the Ragdoll breed.

Ragdolls have become the fastest growing and most lovable breed of cat ever developed. Owners readily admit that they are captivated by their Ragdolls' sweet temperament, beautiful coat, generous size, and big blue eyes. Each of the following chapters will introduce you to one important aspect of Ragdoll ownership, from understanding special Ragdoll traits to selecting your Ragdoll, from making your home "Ragdoll friendly" to caring for your Ragdoll's health, and from breeding to showing your Ragdoll. As Ragdolls can live to be twenty years old, you will have many years to discover for yourself exactly why Ragdolls are held to be such a special breed by those who know and love them.

WHAT'S SO SPECIAL ABOUT RAGDOLLS?

THE RAGDOLL PERSONALITY IS PURRFECT

A more loving cat you'll never find. Ragdolls are strictly indoor cats that love and depend upon their owners. In exchange, owners receive an endless supply of love and affection from their Ragdolls. Many Ragdoll owners have compared their Ragdoll's personality to that of a loyal canine. Ragdolls are eager to interact, and there are numerous accounts of Ragdolls fetching their favorite toy, learning how to shake hands, and sitting up on command.

The Ragdoll personality is characteristically warm and friendly. Your Ragdoll will want to be with you all the time. You'll be met at the door when you arrive home and followed around the house, even into the bathroom. When taking a shower, expect your Ragdoll to watch and wait patiently for you right outside the shower. As you push aside the curtain or shower door, you'll see your Ragdoll looking up at you with those big blue eyes. Your Ragdoll will be curious and eager to meet and greet guests to your home.

If you want a lap cat, the Ragdoll is for you. Ragdolls need their owner's attention and lots of love. If not on your lap, your Ragdoll will be lying nearby. Very few breeds of cat offer the

A nicely marked seal bicolor male at six months of age. Photo by Terry Sharkey.

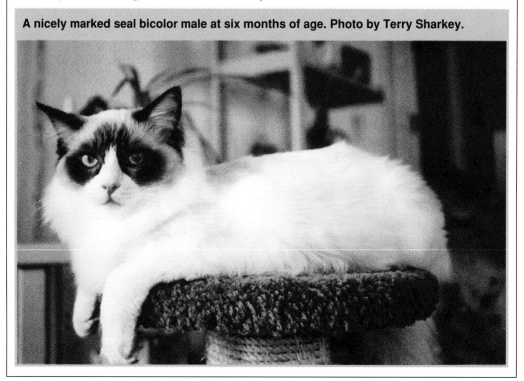

intimate companionship characteristic of the Ragdoll. Persians are purchased for their beautiful coats. Maine Coons are purchased for their large size. Siamese are purchased for their blue eyes. Himalayans are purchased for their dramatic color points. Ragdolls are purchased for their purrfect personality. As a bonus, you get a beautiful coat, large, stunning blue eyes, calm laid-back personality, and the classic pointed pattern—all together in one fabulous package called the Ragdoll.

THE RAGDOLL VOICE IS QUIET

Ragdolls go about their daily activities with little vocalization. They don't meow insistently like some other breeds, but Ragdolls can be trained to respond to your voice. When Ragdolls do vocalize, their voice always reflects the way they are feeling.

Each separate Ragdoll vocalization expresses a different emotion. If your Ragdoll is feeling happy, you're likely to hear a short, upbeat meow. Turn toward the "meow," and your Ragdoll will be looking at you intently. Your Ragdoll just wants a little attention. When your Ragdoll is feeling lonely, you will hear a longer, more plaintive meow. You can be certain that you are expected to stop what you are doing, pick up your Ragdoll, and administer a good snuggle. If your Ragdoll takes a nap and awakens to find that you have left the room, it will pace the house crying for you. At times like this,

A seal mitted Ragdoll named Dolly with a young member of her human family. Well mannered children go nicely with gentle Ragdolls. Photo by Susan Nelson.

it is best to call out to your Ragdoll so that it can find you. Your Ragdoll will run to you, craving companionship. When your Ragdoll is feeling sleepy and wants to curl up in your arms, you could be blessed with a purr that ends in a trill or a chirp. If it's your bedtime, too, your Ragdoll will curl up purring on your chest or snuggle up beside you. What a lovely way to go to sleep. In the morning, your Ragdoll will chirp happily to you when it realizes that you are awake.

THE RAGDOLL LIVES ONLY INDOORS

Ragdolls belong indoors.

Whether you have a studio apartment or a mansion, your Ragdoll will be at home indoors with you. Ragdolls are reputed to be so docile that they will not defend themselves from other cats and animals. They are so beautiful and friendly that they are susceptible to being "catnapped." Outside cats can spread diseases to your Ragdoll. Keep your Ragdoll indoors to protect it from harm.

THE RAGDOLL IS EASY TO TRAIN

When you get your Ragdoll kitten at eight to sixteen weeks old, it should already be litter box trained. Often, Ragdoll breeders report that kittens are using the litter box by four to five weeks of age. This attests to their ability to learn quickly by imitating their mother's behavior.

Your kitten should be trained to a scratching post by the time you bring it home. Cats scratch and manicure their claws when they are feeling good. So, you don't want to jump up and yell "No" if

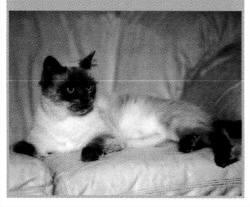

Desilu, a blue colorpoint. The large blue eyes are a hallmark of the breed. Photo by Susan Nelson.

your Ragdoll forgets to use the scratching post. You'll only succeed in upsetting it and making it run away from you. Instead, if you find your Ragdoll scratching a forbidden spot, just walk over calmly and pick it up in a matter-of-fact manner while saying "No," bring it to the nearest scratching post, and begin demonstrating what you want by scratching the area yourself. Your Ragdoll will very often begin to imitate you. To help with this training, provide more than one permissible scratching area. Be especially careful to have a scratching area close to where your kitten sleeps, as it will want to scratch upon awakening. With Ragdolls, this training is fairly easy to accomplish.

Ragdolls have a playful nature. Many Ragdoll owners have reported that their Ragdolls are actually able to learn to fetch. If your Ragdoll has a favorite toy such as a knotted shoe lace or any easy-to-carry object, your Ragdoll may retrieve it when it is thrown across the room. Sometimes, your Ragdoll may come up to you with a toy as if it is begging you to play fetch. Take advantage of this natural behavior and toss the toy. See what happens. If your Ragdoll brings it back, toss it again.

When your kitten is small, you need to teach it patience. Ragdolls are docile by nature, but, like any cat, they need to learn patience. When you are holding your kitten, it is important that you—not it— make the decision as to when it gets let down. If a Ragdoll is

Will the "real" Ragdoll please stand up? This seal mitted male seems surprised to be caught by the photographer! Photo by Eva Davis.

allowed to get down anytime it wants to, it begins to think that it is in charge and will become difficult to handle when it reaches, say, fifteen pounds. In order to avoid being used as a launching pad, this is also the time to teach it to expect to be placed solidly on the ground rather than letting it leap from your arms. So, if your Ragdoll struggles to get down, firmly and lovingly maintain your hold until *you* decide that it's time to place it on the ground. Talk gently to your kitten during this time. Patience must be taught at the earliest possible age, preferably two to four months old. Once your Ragdoll is past this age, the training is more difficult, and it will take rewards, such as a special treat, to encourage patience.

THE RAGDOLL IS A SPECIAL COMPANION

From their laid-back personalities and quiet voices to their playful nature and craving of attention, Ragdolls are special, loving companions. Whether you adopt one, two, or half a dozen, your life will be filled with a special warmth because of their presence.

SELECTING YOUR RAGDOLL

RAGDOLL COLORS AND PATTERNS

The standard Ragdoll comes in four colors and three patterns; and all Ragdolls have blue eyes and a soft, non-matting hair coat. Kittens' coats may not be as soft as adults' coats, as kittens go through a four- to six-month growth cycle that usually alters the hair coat's texture. Each Ragdoll color and pattern is discussed below. Some breeders are presently working to add new and unusual colors to the breed standard, and these are discussed later in this chapter.

Note the nice ruff, which is the collarlike projection of fur around the neck, on this seal mitted male. Photo by Gary Strobel.

STANDARD COLORS

All Ragdolls are pointed cats. This means that they have color on their ears, faces, legs, and tails, with a much lighter, contrasting body color. Ragdolls come in four standard colors: seal, chocolate, blue, and frost (sometimes called lilac).

Seal Ragdolls have points that are a deep seal brown. Their bodies should have fawn to cream color shading, although some may have darker shading. Their nose and paw pad leather should be a deep seal brown.

Chocolate Ragdolls have points that are a light milk chocolate color. Their bodies should have ivory to cream shading. Their nose and paw pad leather should be what some have called a "burnt rose" tone. However, the chocolate Ragdoll is not yet standardized, and there is still discussion among breeders as to what comprises a true chocolate. Some chocolates have darker nose leather, and this is permissible.

Blue Ragdolls have points that are slate blue to silver, with a generally gray appearance. Their bodies can be ivory to bluish white. The nose and paw pad leather should be slate blue.

Frost Ragdolls have points that are lilac to pinkish beige. Their bodies should be milk white, and the nose and paw pad leather should be pink to lavender.

STANDARD PATTERNS

The three standard Ragdoll

patterns are colorpoint, mitted, and bicolor.

Colorpoint Ragdolls have darker color on their ears, face, legs, feet, and tail. Their body color is lighter than their point color. The chest and chin are usually lighter in color but are closer to the body color.

Mitted Ragdolls are identical to colorpoint Ragdolls, except that they have white paws, chin, and chest. Their front paws have little white mittens. On their back legs, the mittens extend halfway up their legs, becoming white boots. Their bodies, with the exception of their white chin and chest, are at least a shade lighter than their point color.

Bicolor Ragdolls have darker color on their ears, face, and tail. However, a bicolor's face is characterized by a white, inverted "V." The stomach, all four legs, the feet, and ruff are white. The body color should be at least a shade lighter than the point color, and the bicolor Ragdoll may have various markings of white and color patches across the back. This distinctive appearance sets the Ragdoll apart from all other breeds. The bicolor's nose and paw pad color is pink.

A Ragdoll's weight can range from 12 to 20 pounds. This blue colorpoint male is a very large example of the breed. Photo by Susan Nelson.

NEW AND UNUSUAL COLORS

In the spring of 1997, the Ragdoll Fancier's Club International voted to accept the lynx pattern and the red color. The lynx pattern does not affect the four colors or the three basic patterns of the Ragdoll. It merely adds a striking striped effect to the face, legs, and tail, in addition to contrasting white on the inside of the ears. This pattern was present in Ann Baker's early breedings, but she sold these kittens to other breeders, who began to reintroduce it just a few years ago.

Colors to look for due to the acceptance of the red are the tortie point and flame point. Ragdolls with this red gene are presently in development. Tortie points have a tricolor, somewhat mottled appearance to their point markings, while the flame points have a reddish hue to their points.

It is the authors' opinion that whatever new colors are developed, the Ragdoll should remain a large, pointed cat with blue eyes and a non-matting hair coat. And the Ragdoll personality should never be compromised. As is the case with all of the major breeds, these new colors will probably eventually be accepted and standards set by the majority vote of Ragdoll breeders.

FINDING THE PERFECT RAGDOLL
Go to Local Cat Shows

There are many ways to find your perfect Ragdoll kitten. One good way to get started is to go to local cat shows. Usually, there will be at least one Ragdoll entered. Sometimes, there may be no local cat shows in your area or no Ragdolls entered in your local shows. If this is the case, skip to the next paragraph. However, if you are lucky enough to be able to attend a show where Ragdolls are being exhibited, talk to the people showing the Ragdolls and find out who their breeders are and if they are happy with them. This is a good way to get to see Ragdolls as well as talk with people who actually own them. However, don't expect to be allowed to hold or touch the Ragdolls, as it is not proper etiquette at a cat show to touch, or even ask to touch, other peoples' cats. This is because of the risk of spreading disease from one cat to another.

Read the National Cat Magazines

Another way to find your perfect Ragdoll is to get a copy of one or more of the following magazines: *Cat Fancy*, *Cats Magazine*, or a yearly publication called *Cats U.S.A.* Look at the breeders' directories located at the back of these publications, and locate the breeders nearest your home. If there are no local breeders, contact the ones nearest to you. Be aware that shipping kittens is not at all unusual. And Ragdolls' temperament enables them to take shipping in stride.

A lilac (frost) bicolor with a beautiful, soft, non-matting coat, as all true Ragdolls have. Photo by Gary Strobel.

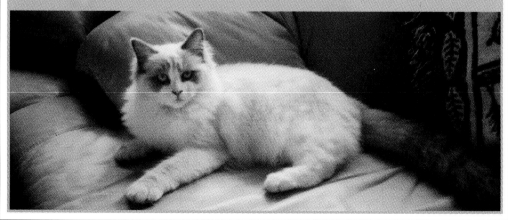

Connect with Breeders on the Internet

The Internet is also a good way to find Ragdoll breeders near you. Using the larger search engines, simply type in "Ragdoll Cats." You will find a wealth of information, including breeders located near your home.

Check out Several Catteries

Once you have a list of breeders in mind, make arrangements to visit as many catteries as you can. Although it is often difficult to resist buying the first kitten you see, try to wait until you have had a chance to check out several catteries and meet several breeders. However, many a beautiful kitten has been purchased on the first visit. Sometimes, a kitten may be sold if you delay purchase, as Ragdolls are very popular and usually in short supply. Yet, you can take your time in making a selection, as Ragdoll breeders generally plan litters so that they will have kittens available on an ongoing basis. If you are patient, they will be able to supply you with the Ragdoll of your dreams.

In some areas, breeders may be few and far between, in which case you may want to be prepared to leave a deposit on the color and pattern of your choice. Some patterns and colors may not be readily available, and you will need to place a deposit to reserve your Ragdoll. Remember, you are searching for a companion for the next fifteen years or more. Be selective, and be willing to wait for what you want. You owe this to yourself and your future companion.

A lilac (frost) bicolor being carefully assessed by a judge. Going to shows is one good way of obtaining information about where to select a Ragdoll kitten. Photo by Kathy Lam.

When visiting catteries, there are several things to keep in mind. Plan to visit only one cattery or breeder per day, to prevent diseases or germs being spread from cattery to cattery. When you arrive at a breeder's home, look to see whether cats are roaming freely about the house. If so, this is a good sign. Make sure the premises appear and smell reasonably clean. Remember though, that the breeder cannot control when a cat might choose to visit the litter

A three-week-old litter of Ragdoll kittens eager to start exploring their world. Photo by Susan Nelson.

box. Check whether the cats are outgoing or run away from you when you try to pet them. Observe whether the general appearance of the cats is healthy. Red eyes? Sneezing? Runny nose? Ribs showing? Bloated stomach? Excessive scratching? Dirty ears inside? All of these conditions are signs of possible problems.

Although some breeders may not have you visit the youngest kittens in the "queening room," the room where the kittens are born and spend their first three weeks of life, the breeder should be willing to share with you the rest of the cattery. Don't be afraid to ask to see the mother and father of your prospective kitten and where the breeding males are housed. If the breeder has nothing to hide, there should be no problem with allowing you to walk through the cattery.

While you are visiting catteries, do not forget that the breeder you choose must be someone you feel comfortable talking to, as you may wish or need to contact him or her with specific questions throughout your Ragdoll's lifetime. Breeders appreciate notes and pictures telling them how your Ragdoll is doing and what sorts of behavior and tricks your Ragdoll has learned. When you purchase your kitten, you and your breeder are beginning a relationship spanning fifteen to twenty years.

THE PURCHASE CONTRACT

Each breeder has a purchase contract. The main components of a purchase contract are the health guarantee, the vaccination records, and the agreement to have the kitten spayed or neutered.

Two of the first purebred Ragdoll flamepoints in the world. They were bred from original stock of Ann Baker. Note the almond-shaped eyes and Ragdoll muzzle. Photo by Susan Nelson.

The health guarantee is of primary importance. Most breeders guarantee their kittens to be healthy and free of parasites, such as fleas, ear mites, and round worms, at the time of pick up. In order to protect yourself and ensure your kitten's ongoing good health, most breeders would like to have you visit your veterinarian as soon as possible after the kitten goes home, usually within seventy-two hours. You might want to arrange to stop by your veterinarian on the way home from the breeder's with your kitten. This way, your kitten won't need to be removed from its new environment during the critical first week of settling into its new home.

Reputable breeders will also guarantee their kittens against genetic problems for at least the first year. Some breeders will put restrictions on declawing kittens. Others will restrict to whom and where the kitten goes in the event that you can no longer take care of it. These are all individual differences between breeders. And most of these requests are reasonable. If you have any questions or concerns about the contract, discuss them with your breeder, as your breeder will give you the rationale for these restrictions.

Some contracts may address the issue of whether to vaccinate your kitten for feline infectious peritonitis (FIP). This vaccine is controversial due to its use of a modified live virus. Some breeders fear that the administration of this vaccine could infect the kitten with FIP. However, most veterinarians believe the contrary. As with all purebred cats, it is best to err on the side of caution, as administering the FIP vaccine could void the health warranty.

Since Ragdolls are strictly indoor cats, their chance of being exposed to this virus is minimal. Follow your breeder's advice, as most veterinarians are not familiar with Ragdolls because they are still relatively rare.

When you pick up your Ragdoll kitten, your breeder will give you a written record of its first vaccinations. Bring this with you to the veterinarian. The most common vaccinations that your kittens should have had are the three-in-one distemper vaccine, with or without *chlamydia*. Each breeder will have his or her own personalized vaccination protocol. In general, however, your kitten will have had its first distemper shot between the ages of six and eight weeks old, the second between the ages of eight and twelve weeks old, and at least one or two more distemper shots after twelve weeks of age. Yearly boosters must be given.

The feline leukemia vaccine should not be given until at least twelve to sixteen weeks of age. There is also controversy surrounding this vaccination. Ragdolls are indoor cats and their chance of being exposed to this virus is minimal. Therefore, some

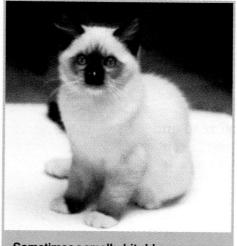

Sometimes a small white blaze appears on the nose, such as the one on this seal mitted male Ragdoll. Photo by Marcella Frenken.

breeders question taking the risk, as any vaccine can have side effects. In any case, *all vaccines* given to Ragdolls must be killed virus vaccines. Do not allow your veterinarian to give anything else. Each time you bring your Ragdoll in for shots, remind your veterinarian to give killed vaccines *only*. A good veterinarian will welcome your reminder. If you board or show your Ragdoll or have an indoor-outdoor cat living with your Ragdoll, this greatly increases the chance of harmful viruses entering your home, in which case the risk of vaccine side effects is likely outweighed by the risk of contracting a serious virus.

When purchasing your Ragdoll, you will be asked to neuter or spay any kitten that will not be used for breeding. You will be asked to pay a much higher price for breeding and/or show-quality Ragdolls versus pet-quality Ragdolls. Females that are not spayed run the risk of uterine infections called pyometra after several estrus cycles. Males that are not neutered may spray pungent urine on furniture to mark their territory. Unneutered females may spray urine to attract a mate.

Generally, neutered cats enjoy a longer life and better health. Most breeders request that female Ragdolls be spayed between the ages of four and seven months. Males should be neutered when they are a bit older, usually not before seven months. If your breeder does not have a preference, talk it over with your veterinarian. Most breeders will withhold registration papers until receiving written proof from a veterinarian that your cat has been spayed or neutered. This proof can usually be supplied by furnishing your breeder with a photocopy of the paid invoice from your veterinarian.

Be certain that you read and understand the purchase contract before you purchase your Ragdoll. Some contract terms can be individually negotiated with the breeder. Don't hesitate to ask questions and get answers. A good breeder will not be reluctant to discuss any contract term with you.

YOUR RAGDOLL'S PAPERS

When the kitten that you select was born, the breeder filed a litter registration form with the appropriate cat association. When you take your kitten home, either you will be given a form to fill out and send to the same cat association, along with the registration fee, or you will be told that the registration form will be given to you upon proof of neutering or spaying. The form will have a place on it where the breeder can restrict breeding and showing. Some breeders will not

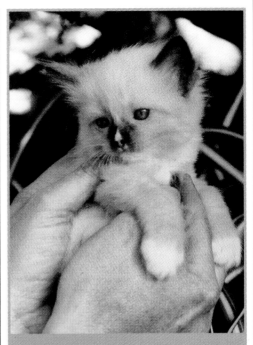

The "hour glass" blaze on this six-week-old seal mitted male is very distinct. Photo by Muncy Smith.

restrict showing pet-quality Ragdolls in the alter class, and you should ask your breeder's policy before you buy. If you do not plan to show your Ragdoll, you are not required to register it. However, the fee is minimal; and if you should ever want to show your kitten, registration is required. So, you might as well obtain your Ragdoll's final registration papers at the earliest opportunity.

ONE RAGDOLL OR TWO?

Ragdolls easily adjust to multi-cat households. You may select one kitten and decide later to add a playmate. Or you may select two kittens at once. If you decide on a solo kitten, it will quickly adjust to your schedule. There is also a chance that a solo kitten will

Owning two Ragdolls is twice as fun as owning just one. Additionally , they can keep each other company when you are not at home. Photo by Elsa Brent.

bond with you more strongly. If you later add a new kitten, they will probably have an adjustment period of about one to two weeks. During this time, they may hiss a bit at each other to establish dominance. This is normal feline behavior; however, you should carefully monitor your kittens during this time to be certain that they are adjusting well. If they hiss more than you would like, give them a break from each other for a few hours daily by letting them play in different rooms. You will be rewarded for your patience when you see them playing happily together.

Most breeders suggest that you purchase two kittens at the same time. That way, your Ragdoll will have a companion even when you must be away at work, running errands, or on vacation. Unless you are at home nearly twenty-four hours a day, there is a chance that a solo kitten, after being taken from its litter mates, could be lonely and stressed. Two kittens are double the fun and double the love, and you will have double the enjoyment watching them roll and tumble, groom each other, and sleep nestled together. The choice is yours.

Unlike other kittens, two Ragdolls will generally play quietly together. They will not climb draperies or tear up your home; thus, they are great for even small apartments. Either way, after selecting one kitten or two, you won't want to miss the experience of having a Ragdoll in your life.

HOW TO MAKE YOUR HOME RAGDOLL-FRIENDLY

ELIMINATE HAZARDS IN YOUR HOME

Before bringing your Ragdoll home, examine your home from the perspective of a tiny kitten. Getting down on your hands and knees may seem silly, but it will help you to realize what may present a hazard to your Ragdoll. Remember, your little Ragdoll is full of curiosity and anxious to explore its world. He or she will find any crack or crevice and climb in. There will not be a square inch of your home that is not left unexplored. Therefore, it is your responsibility to assure that your new kitten's home is safe.

Hazards include electrical cords, open toilet seats, unattended flames on stoves and candles, hot liquid in potpourri bowls, hot stove burners, wall or space heaters, fans, open oven doors, open refrigerator doors, open dishwasher doors, open trash compactors, open clothes dryers, unattended dishwater and bath water, all cleaning supplies, tiny objects that could be swallowed, open fireplaces, open

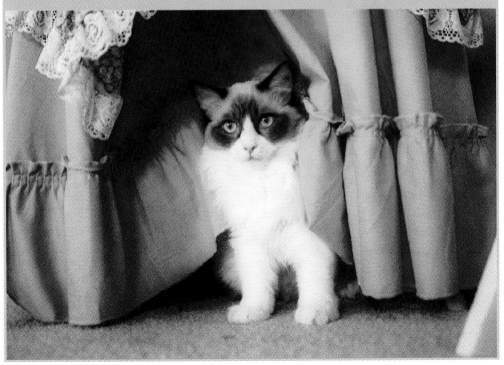

Grand Champion Ragmeister's Blueberry Sharkey, a chocolate bicolor. Photo by Terry Sharkey.

windows, loose window screens, balconies, electric paper shredders set on automatic, thread, string, rubber bands, ribbon, yarn, and sharp objects such as broken glass, discarded staples, needles, pins, feathers bitten from kitty toys, and knives. Beware of store-bought cat toys with small parts that can tug off and be swallowed. Be careful when closing open drawers, as kittens love to crawl inside and behind them to explore. If you have any doors on rollers, be especially careful to check that your kitten is not behind them when you close them, as toes, paws, or tails can be crushed or worse. Be especially careful with

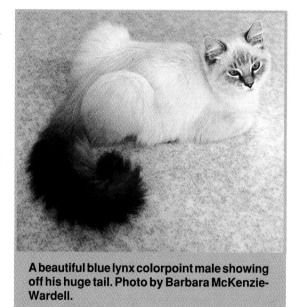

A beautiful blue lynx colorpoint male showing off his huge tail. Photo by Barbara McKenzie-Wardell.

what you use to decorate for any holidays that you observe, as broken glass ornaments and small parts that can be chewed off could be deadly to your Ragdoll.

The injuries resulting from the above hazards can be heart wrenching. Kittens can get severe electrical shocks and/or burns and die from biting into electrical cords that are not covered with foam insulation tubes. These tubes, which are available at most hardware stores, have slits along the length of the tube. The slits allow easy insertion of several electrical cords into one tube. Drowning can occur when a kitten falls into an open toilet, bath, or sink of dishwater. Flames, space heaters, hot liquid, open oven doors, and hot stove burners can catch fur on fire, burn right through the skin, or cause severe blistering of tender paw pads. Open appliance doors can cause suffocation if closed without checking for kitty. Kittens have been killed when clothes were quickly thrown into a clothes dryer and the drying cycle started. Paws can be caught and cut in electric fans and paper shredders. Since cats have little spines on their tongues that force them to swallow whatever they get even partially inside their mouths, they can swallow staples, pins, thread, and myriad other objects. Once inside the digestive tract, these objects can pierce the intestine or twist up inside the bowel, causing an obstruction. Household cleaners can be licked up or transferred to the kitten's mouth by self-grooming after the kitten walks across a surface cleaned with a poisonous substance.

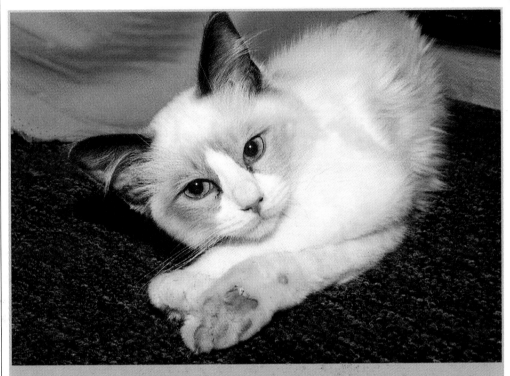

A lilac (frost) bicolor female posing for a cameo. In bicolors, the chest, stomach, legs, feet, and ruff are white. Photo by Susan Nelson.

Check all labels; if you see that any label has a poison control telephone number listed, don't buy it. Finally, many cats have been maimed or died falling through open windows and loose window screens; many more have died because their owners never realized that they would jump from an open balcony. An additional hazard is living plants. Before exposing your Ragdoll to any indoor or outdoor plants that you may already have in your home, consult a good gardening book to determine whether they are poisonous. If in doubt, bring them to your local nursery for identification. Never purchase cut flowers that are poisonous, as cats will sample vases of flowers. If you do have any poisonous plants, replace them with silk plants. Nothing is more heartbreaking than watching a pet suffer from an accidental poisoning that could have been prevented.

Although our list of hazards may seem quite lengthy, you must protect against all of them. If you do, you will save your kitten potential injury and yourself trauma and unexpected veterinary bills.

IT'S EASY TO ACCIDENTALLY STEP ON A KITTEN

Your new Ragdoll will tend to want to be with you all the time and is very easily stepped on. You will be amazed at how quickly a kitten or grown cat can silently move from one area of a room to a

A blue bicolor male. Note the well-defined color of the ears, mask, and tail. Photo by Pauline Somers.

point right under your feet without your realizing it. Crushing a Ragdoll's leg, or worse, is not something you want to experience. Therefore, always be cautious walking when there is a kitten in the house. They can dart underfoot from behind sofas and tables when you least expect to see them. They also can dart underfoot in an attempt to race you to the top or bottom of the stairs. Be especially cautious when sitting at your computer or desk, as your Ragdoll will have a tendency to lie under the chair, either beside the leg or against the wheel caster, in an effort to be close to you. If your Ragdoll sleeps with you and you need to get out of bed in the dark, it is best to shuffle your feet as you walk. An ounce of prevention can save a huge veterinary bill.

RAGDOLL-FRIENDLY TOYS

Ragdolls need toys. They need a wide variety of toys that can be rotated on a weekly basis, or else they will become quickly bored by them. However, Ragdolls are not "picky." They will play with anything from an empty cardboard tissue tube or empty thread spool to a wad of paper or expensive store-bought toys. Many an expensive toy has been purchased only to lie dormant as a kitten chooses the crumpled-up piece of paper instead. But toys are a necessity if you want to keep your Ragdoll from making up its own games using your things.

The main thing to consider when selecting toys for your Ragdoll is whether parts can break off and be swallowed or whether the toy itself is so small that it could possibly be swallowed or lodged in the mouth or throat. Never let your Ragdoll have unsupervised access to toys with feathers, string, yarn, or ribbon. If the toys that you purchase come with bells, either cut them off or stitch them down securely. Better yet, save these toys for interactive play. Also, it is best to cut the tail off those cute, little furry toy mice. The tail can be bitten off and swallowed. Care in toy selection will eliminate potential hazards.

Since your Ragdoll most enjoys your company, be certain to have several interactive toys in reserve. These are toys on a string or piece of elastic or toys suspended from a wand or "fishing pole." To avoid frustrating your Ragdoll, let it "catch" the "prey" about every third time you entice it to pounce. Start out slowly, quicken the pace, and taper it down again before putting away the interactive toys. This will let your kitten or adult Ragdoll burn off any excess energy and become even more relaxed than usual before it's time for bed. Since all felines are nocturnal, you will need to help your Ragdoll adjust to your schedule, and a nightly play time will do the trick. Your Ragdoll is an indoor cat and depends upon you for stimulation and exercise. Be certain to keep the interactive toys in a closed closet when not in use, as interactive toys tend to have feathers, string, and bells attached to them.

Kittens love boxes, any boxes. Try cutting out holes in a couple of places and putting a terry cloth towel inside the box and/or a safe toy or ball. Your Ragdoll will enjoy jumping through the holes, playing with the toy, and relaxing inside the box. A shallow box can be made into an inexpensive "kitty tease" by putting a couple of jingle balls inside, taping the box securely closed, and cutting out small circles and squares for your Ragdoll to reach through to bat at the balls.

Paper bags from the grocery store or mall also can provide hours of fun for your kitten or adult Ragdoll. Be certain to cut through any handles so that your Ragdoll doesn't accidentally slip its head through the handle and get caught. As with human children, kittens should never be allowed to play with plastic bags.

One of the all-time favorite toys that your kitten will love is a large, donut-like toy with an accessible ball that your kitten can bat and watch as it rolls around inside the track. It will also enjoy playing the game with you.

Kitty condos and cat towers are wonderful playthings that can double as sleeping quarters. They come fully carpeted or partially covered with sisal rope. Unlike carpet, sisal rope is easily replaced if it begins to look shabby from nail grooming. Towers using only carpet tend to be torn to shreds as time goes by. Offer your kitten a wide variety

Seal mitted male patiently awaiting the return of his owner. Ragdoll cats will often meet you at the door. Photo by Susan Nelson.

of toys to choose from, and let it decide its favorites.

HOUSEHOLD PLAY AREAS

Some Ragdoll owners set aside a room in their home as a designated playroom. It can be your bedroom. This room is used when the owner is away. It usually contains a litter box in one corner, dry food and water as far away from the litter box as

Scratching posts are essential in any household with a cat. The one shown here features both carpeting and sisal. Photo by Carla Applegate.

possible, a wide assortment of toys, a scratching post, and a cat bed. When your kitten is young, it is important to have such a semi-confined area to leave it in when you are away so that it can't get lost or wedged somewhere in your home and separated from its litter box.

SHOPPING LIST FOR YOUR FUTURE RAGDOLL

Obtain the following items for your kitten before bringing it home, and both of you will be happier for it.

Cat Carrier

Think safety first, and buy a sturdy carrier for your Ragdoll. Don't get one to fit your kitten, get one to fit a twelve-to-twenty pound cat. This means a carrier of medium size, as you will want to use it in the future to take your cat to the vet or shows or out for a drive or on vacation. A carrier will prevent your kitten from getting

under the gas or brake pedal while you are bringing it home from the breeder. It is will also protect your kitten from injury when traveling with you. Put a nice, warm blanket or towel on the bottom of the carrier to make your kitten's trip home cozy. Either wedge the carrier between the seats or wrap the seat belt around it and lock the seat belt into place. If the seat belt will not stretch around your carrier, tie the seat belt to the handle on top of the carrier. In the unlikely event of an accident, an unsecured carrier could be ejected from your car.

You need not keep a litter box in the carrier with your Ragdoll, but on trips of more than two hours, you may want to stop and offer it an opportunity to use the litter box. We have found that keeping a litter box on the floor of the back seat is a big help when traveling with our Ragdolls. We stop the car, get into the back seat with our Ragdoll, close the car doors, and open the carrier door. Our Ragdoll comes out for a stretch, and we simply place it in the litter box. We give it a chance to relax for about five minutes and offer a little food and water. If it doesn't need to use the litter box after five minutes, we place it back into the carrier and offer it another opportunity an hour or two later. We never drive with a cat loose in the car.

When not in use, we leave the carrier sitting in the house with

and litter scoop. Start with a small, low-sided litter box that your kitten can climb into easily. You may choose either pressed paper, regular clay or clay clumping litter, or one of the many wheat or corn pellet-formed litters that are now available. Generally, kittens prefer the finer, sand-type litter as opposed to chunky litter. Ask your breeder what type of litter the kitten is used to, as this will make the transition to your home easier and

A lilac (frost) bicolor female named Misty. The Ragdoll mask appears in the shape of an inverted "V" and extends to the outer edge of the eyes. Photo by Susan Nelson.

the door open in a cozy spot and place a soft terry towel inside. That way, our Ragdolls get used to napping and relaxing inside their carriers. So, we never have a problem putting our Ragdolls into their carriers for trips to the veterinarian or cat shows. If you bring out the carrier only when it is time to go to the vet, you will find your Ragdoll putting on a quick disappearing act as soon as it sees you with its carrier.

Litter Box, Litter, and Litter Scoop

The next most important purchases are the litter box, litter,

prevent most accidents. If you decide to change litters, gradually add it to the litter box until the old litter is completely displaced. As your kitten grows, you may want to increase the size of the litter box. If your kitten desires privacy or tends to scratch litter over the sides of its box, get a covered litter box. We have found a sturdy metal scoop to be most serviceable. A small bathroom mat in front of the litter box helps lessen litter tracking. Pet stores also carry a rubber mat designed for this purpose. Whatever litter box and litter you choose, proper

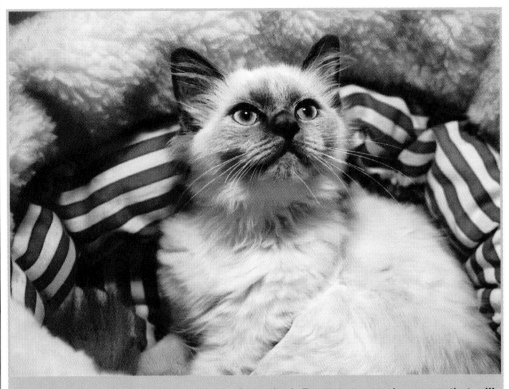

Your Ragdoll will appreciate a nice, soft cat bed. Be sure to purchase one that will comfortably accommodate your kitten when it is fully grown. Photo by Susan Nelson.

litter box maintenance is a basic requirement for a healthy, happy Ragdoll.

We have a hint for optimal litter box maintenance that you may choose to try to prevent any litter box odor problem from developing. It takes a bit more time, but it is well worth the effort. Once you find a litter pan and litter that your Ragdoll likes and readily uses, keep the litter box and litter clean by following these suggestions. At least once each month, depending upon the type of litter that you use and the number of cats that you own, empty and throw away all litter. Scrape the bottom and sides of the box clean. Take the box outside and rinse the bottom pan with pressurized water from the garden hose. Place about a cup of regular bleach into the pan and carefully swirl it around to wet the bottom and sides of the pan. Let it sit for about five minutes. Then, fill it halfway with water and rinse once or twice. Dry the box with paper toweling and let it sit in the sun for about 10 minutes. Spray the bottom and sides of the box with a non-stick cooking spray. Let the box sit for about five minutes and wipe down any wet areas. Next, put at least three inches of litter in the pan. The bleach helps cut down on lingering odors, and the cooking spray helps used litter clumps to pop easily from the bottom and/or sides of the box. Twice daily, sift

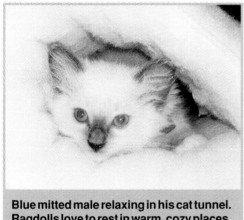

Blue mitted male relaxing in his cat tunnel. Ragdolls love to rest in warm, cozy places. Photo by Susanne Nielsen.

and remove soiled litter using the litter scoop. Add litter as necessary to keep the level at three inches. Try this method and see if it doesn't make a difference.

Bed

In addition to its carrier and any cat tower that you have provided, your Ragdoll needs at least one bed it can call its own. Don't let it choose your favorite chair as its bed. A bed can be as simple as a cardboard box with a towel inside. The day you bring your Ragdoll home, help it adjust by showing it to its bed right after it has been allowed to inspect its litter box. Give it a toy or bite of dry food, pet it, and let it know that the bed belongs to it exclusively. Watch your Ragdoll to see where it prefers to sleep. If it doesn't sleep in its bed but consistently sleeps in one spot, try moving its bed to that spot.

Scratching Post

If you do not have room for a cat tower, you will still need a scratching post to prevent your

Ragdoll from grooming its claws on your sofa. Be certain to get a post that will allow a full-grown cat to stretch out completely and pull vigorously without causing the post to tip over. Be assured that Ragdolls are extremely easy to train to a scratching post. We have found that if we just pretend to scratch the post and encourage our Ragdoll to copy us, the task is accomplished in less than a week. Of course, you must consistently demonstrate the preferred behavior. Demonstrating just one time probably won't be enough for even the most intelligent Ragdoll.

Scratching posts offer hours of healthy exercise and enjoyment for cats and kittens while preventing them from damaging furniture. Photo courtesy of Four Paws.

A lilac (frost) bicolor kitten enjoying a favorite feline pastime—catnapping. Photo by Susan Nelson.

Food and Water Bowls

Your kitten should have its own bowls for food and water. Plastic retains food odors; glass does not. Get three bowls: one for water, one for dry food, and one for wet food. If you have two kittens, they can share for a few weeks, but they should eventually be given their own bowls so that they won't be required to jockey for dominance at the feeding bowl as they grow larger.

Be certain to clean your kitten's water bowl at least daily since food particles will collect in the bottom of it. Since you will be feeding your kitten at least breakfast and dinner, it is easy to remember to change the water twice daily. Your kitten cannot have too much fresh water available. Your kitten's wet food bowl should be washed and *thoroughly* rinsed with hot water when serving each meal. Be mindful that soap residue left on feeding utensils can make any cat ill. Hot water can help to kill bacterial growth on the bowls. Giving each cat its own food and water bowls and keeping them clean prevent disease.

Grooming Supplies

You will want to purchase a flea comb, a metal slicker brush, a high-quality nail clipper, cotton swabs, cotton balls or cotton squares for cleaning nose, ears, and eyes, a toothbrush and toothpaste made especially for kittens, and a gentle shampoo. Your Ragdoll will enjoy the personal interaction of being groomed by you. Begin a grooming routine within the first week and continue it throughout your kitten's life to eliminate parasites, such as fleas, and formation of hairballs in the stomach.

Do not bathe your kitten until it needs it, as the first bath can be very stressful, and you want your kitten's transition to its new home to be as smooth as possible. Occasionally, your kitten may get feces in the hair around its bottom or on its paws. This does not call for a full bath. Simply rinsing the area with lukewarm water by holding the soiled area under a running sink faucet will take care of the problem quickly with little fuss. Save bathing for when your cat's hair coat really needs it.

SUMMARY

By following the suggestions in this chapter, you will provide a safe, fun, healthy environment for your Ragdoll.

CARING FOR YOUR RAGDOLL'S HEALTH

LIFTING YOUR RAGDOLL

All cats have thin skin and fragile ribs and need to be fully supported when lifted up for grooming and loving. Ragdolls are heavy cats and can be injured by incorrect handling. You may have read that Ragdolls will dangle limply if hoisted up under their forelegs. Don't do this to your Ragdoll. The weight of its dangling body pulling against its forelegs and shoulders can cause pain and/or injury. Lifting by the scruff of the neck can cause muscle and skin injury for the same reason. Lifting by grabbing a Ragdoll around the ribs without supporting the hindquarters can injure the rib cage. Lifting under the armpits or by using the forelegs as levers can also cause injury. When picking up your Ragdoll, support the rib cage by placing your hand firmly under it, with one finger between the forelegs pointing toward the chin. At the same time, use your other hand to lift and support the hindquarters. To protect your Ragdoll's welfare, teach your children to lift your Ragdoll only in this manner.

GROOMING

Due to the nature of a true Ragdoll's coat, little grooming is required. However, your Ragdoll will enjoy the personal contact that brushing and combing affords. A weekly grooming

Ragdoll kittens are irresistible. The sweet face of this bicolor lynx is just one reason why Ragdolls are loved so much. Photo by Muncy Smith.

session can be fun for both you and your Ragdoll. We keep grooming supplies in a basket so that they are readily accessible at all times.

Routine grooming includes trimming nails, combing the hair coat, cleaning eyes, ears, and nose, and brushing the teeth. Clip your Ragdoll's nails whenever it is necessary. Use a wide-tooth comb, a slicker brush, and a flea comb to keep your Ragdoll's coat in top condition. Start off with the wide-tooth comb and follow with the flea comb. Use the slicker

Pet shops stock a variety of shampoos that are specially formulated for cats' sensitive systems and that leave a healthy looking coat. Photo courtesy of Four Paws.

brush to fluff up the ruff and tail. Use the cotton swabs and cotton balls to clean eye corners, nose leather, and outer ears. Some people brush their Ragdoll's teeth with special pet toothpaste and brushes. If you regularly groom your Ragdoll, you can easily accustom it to having its teeth brushed. This removes tartar buildup, which can lead to gum disease. Gum disease is not unique to the Ragdoll. It can occur in all breeds of cat. Ask your veterinarian to teach you how to brush, and your Ragdoll will not have to experience being anesthetized and having its teeth cleaned by the veterinarian. Feeding dry food also supposedly helps to prevent and remove tartar buildup.

Finally, it is unusual to need to bathe a Ragdoll, and there is probably no need to do so unless you are planning to enter your Ragdoll in a show. However, some cat owners may wish to give their Ragdolls regular baths. If you want to bathe your Ragdoll, your pet shop can recommend a shampoo specially formulated for cats.

THE BATH

If you bathe your Ragdoll, here are some suggestions. First, increase the heat in the room until it is really toasty. Cats have a higher body temperature than humans and can get chilled easily. If you don't have one, a space heater made especially for the bathroom works very well. While the room is heating, gather pet shampoo, cotton pads, wash cloth, towels, hair dryer, and comb. You will also need a flexible spray shower hose to get the soap off completely. These are available at drug stores.

Although the Ragdoll's coat is not subject to matting as are some other longhaired breeds of cat, occasionally tangles will form here and there. Therefore, before the bath, comb through your Ragdoll's hair coat completely, and remove any tangles by grasping and holding the hair at the base and gently working the hair loose. Never use scissors: even a small nick on a cat's skin can cause big problems because cats have very thin and sensitive skin. Do not skip the pre-comb step, as wet tangles are extremely difficult to remove without damaging the underlying skin. Finally, inspect and clip all claws before the bath.

A great way to accomplish the bath with a minimum of fuss is to put a halter and leash on your Ragdoll the way a professional groomer does and secure the leash to the soap dish in such a way that your Ragdoll can't struggle away from you. But don't secure your Ragdoll near a running faucet. Like any cat, it can be terrified by the rushing water. If you wish, use a small table or box in the tub to raise your Ragdoll to a comfortable working height. Give your Ragdoll a towel or old window screen to stand on so that it won't slip around on the wet sink or tub surface. Any frightened cat that is not being properly managed will try to climb out of a bath by grabbing your chest with its claws, pulling itself over your shoulder and jumping to the floor from your back. To avoid this, always keep one hand on your Ragdoll at all times, and keep it either facing away from you or facing to one side. Don't let it face you. It may try to make a break for it when you least expect it! So, be alert.

Before applying shampoo, you must wet down your cat's hair coat. Cats don't like to be submerged in a sink or tub of water; so don't use this method to wet down the coat. When you begin wetting the hair coat, you will find that it easily repels water, and you must get past this stage before applying the shampoo. Start at the neck and work back

The thick, nonmatting coat makes Ragdolls easy to care for. Just a few strokes with a slicker brush is all it takes to look this well groomed. Photo by Susan Nelson.

toward the tail. While working, talk reassuringly to your Ragdoll. Do not wet the head or face. When wetting down your Ragdoll with a sprayer, keep the spray head close to your Ragdoll's body so that the spray doesn't scare it. If you do not have a sprayer, you will need to pour gallons of warm, not hot, water over and under your Ragdoll to thoroughly wet the coat. A one-quart measuring container can do the trick. Continue to reassure your Ragdoll during this process. A matter-of-fact attitude on your part can be calming. If your Ragdoll begins to shiver, either the room or the water temperature is too cool.

The easiest way to apply shampoo to a wet coat is to dilute it in an empty dish soap bottle before you begin the bath. Dish soap is not appropriate for bathing any cat, so the bottle must be cleaned of any detergent residue. Apply the shampoo, lather up completely, and rinse thoroughly. This step can be repeated if necessary. Unapparent soap residue left after incomplete rinsing can cause itching, with consequent pulling out of the hair coat. Therefore, all soap must be rinsed from the coat by using gallons and gallons of warm water both over and under your Ragdoll, including the underarm and tail areas. During this process, never get

Pet dental products are available for helping to fight plaque, reduce tartar build-up, and control unpleasant breath. Photo courtesy of Four Paws.

water in your cat's ears or eyes. In fact, the only way a cat's face and ears should be washed is with a dampened wash cloth using no shampoo. If you elect to show your Ragdoll, you will learn about "recipes" that others use when doing show grooming. However, the process just described will be more than adequate for any Ragdoll, even show cats.

BRUSHING TEETH

Most Ragdolls don't object to having their teeth and gums brushed. Start this early in their lives, and you will save expensive veterinary bills for teeth cleaning, as your veterinarian must use anesthetic before cleaning any cat's teeth. What can be a simple procedure at home can turn into a major one with all the risks attendant to anesthetics if teeth are neglected. Tartar buildup is not unique to Ragdolls; all cats can get tartar buildup on their teeth.

TRIMMING NAILS

A Ragdoll that has its nails trimmed regularly will sit quietly during the process. Make sure that the clipper is sharp enough to make an even cut.

It is a good idea to check all nails once weekly. Often, owners combine this check with a weekly grooming session. The nails on back paws tend to grow slower than the nails on the front paws and usually need to be trimmed less frequently. With experience, you will notice that not every nail will need to be trimmed each week.

To trim nails, you need only grasp your cat's paw and press down on one toe at a time. The claw will pop out for trimming. There are five nails on each front paw and four nails on each back paw. If you look closely, you will see the pink "quick," which is located inside the base of the nail closest to the paw and is shaped like a tiny claw. The next layer

A blue colorpoint whole (unneutered) male named Prince. He weighs almost 15 pounds. Photo by Susan Nelson.

that you will see is a whitened area that seems to surround the quick. Trim only the clear nail that lies beyond both of these areas and that forms the sharp, front part of the claw. If you cut too deeply, you will cause painful bleeding, just as if you cut into the quick of your own nails. A styptic pencil will stop the bleeding, but you will never need to use one if you are always cautious when trimming nails.

SELECTING YOUR VETERINARIAN

Unless you have a veterinarian that you regularly use and trust or that comes highly recommended by someone you respect, the only way to find a good veterinarian is by trial and error. The two keys to an excellent veterinarian are skill and the ability to communicate.

Before bringing their new Ragdoll home, some people go to the extent of interviewing five or six veterinarians before they decide which they prefer. Others simply choose the veterinarian closest to their home. Whatever

you decide, you should feel comfortable talking to your veterinarian. Your veterinarian should welcome your observations and questions. Don't stay with a veterinarian who discounts your observations or questions. You know your Ragdoll and what is and is not unusual behavior. Most veterinarians, even feline specialists, have never seen or treated a Ragdoll. Don't be easily dissuaded from treatment that you believe would benefit your cat.

The connection between you and your veterinarian should feel close if your Ragdoll is receiving

A close-up of Prince. Note the almond-shaped eyes, long whiskers, and large, oval paws. Photo by Susan Nelson.

ongoing treatment of any kind. If you feel estranged from your veterinarian or suspect that your veterinarian does not really care about you and your Ragdoll, talk your feelings over with your veterinarian; if there is no improvement, go elsewhere. Do not continue with a veterinarian who does not handle your Ragdoll gently or require his or her staff to do so. Most towns have at least a few veterinarians. Large cities have scores of veterinarians. Don't settle for impersonal attention. Both you and your Ragdoll deserve kind, professional, knowledgeable care from your veterinarian.

Ragdolls are a unique breed. They are physiologically similar to other pedigreed cats, but they are not the same as non-pedigreed cats that spring from a huge and diverse gene pool. Many Ragdoll breeders believe that Ragdolls are slow to mature. Many also believe that a Ragdoll's immune system is slow to mature. This needs to be taken into consideration when vaccines are given. Never let your veterinarian talk you into a modified live or live vaccine. Also, don't let more than one vaccination be administered at any one visit to your veterinarian. It may take a little longer for you to obtain all necessary vaccinations in this way, but it will be safer for your Ragdoll. Finally, always be certain that the mildest forms of anesthesia are administered when any surgical procedure, such as neutering, is performed.

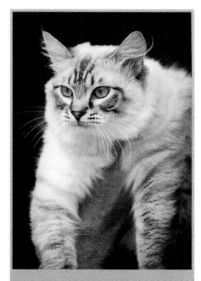

A large seal lynxpoint male named Ragmeister's Diego. Males may be noticeably larger than females. Photo by Susan Nelson.

THE FIRST TRIP TO YOUR VETERINARIAN

Usually, the breeder that you bought your Ragdoll from will encourage you to visit the veterinarian as early as possible. This reassures you that you received a healthy kitten and gives your veterinarian a baseline as a measure during future visits.

The first time that you bring your Ragdoll to the veterinarian, you should ask for a complete examination. This may include taking a viral panel to rule out any possibility that a major feline disease is present. All responsible breeders will have no problem with a viral panel, and some would even encourage you to take this action. Write down any questions that you may have before you leave for the veterinarian's office. Don't rely upon your memory, as it is easy to inadvertently move off a topic before all of your questions are completely answered.

At minimum, your veterinarian will take your Ragdoll's temperature, check ears, eyes, nose, listen to the heart and lungs, and examine the teeth and gums and under the tail. Try to bring a fresh fecal sample so that a worm check can be made; however, worming kittens for round worms is usually routine, even if mature adult worms have

A seal lynxpoint enjoying the afternoon sun. Ragdolls should *never* be allowed outside without close supervision. This male is posing in an enclosed backyard. Otherwise, he stays strictly indoors. Photo by Susan Nelson.

not yet migrated to the stomach. Your veterinarian will request your kitten's vaccination record, which the breeder will have supplied to you at the time of purchase. If your breeder has given you instructions regarding spacing of vaccinations and type of vaccine to use, be certain to give a copy to your veterinarian. When you bring in your Ragdoll for any treatment covered by the breeder's instructions, be certain to reiterate those instructions verbally, even though they are already in the veterinarian's file. This avoids any confusion or misunderstandings that could occur and void your Ragdoll's health warranty.

During any trip to the veterinarian, protect your Ragdoll by using its carrier and securing the carrier to the seat with the seat belt. If the seatbelt won't fit all the way around the carrier, tie the seatbelt to the carrier handle. You don't need to put a litter box, food, or water in the carrier with your Ragdoll. Bring these items with you only if the trip is going to take more than an hour or two. Put a toy or two in the carrier, in the event that you must wait for the veterinarian. That way, you can make at least part of the experience of visiting the veterinarian fun for your Ragdoll.

VACCINATIONS
In general, there are four types of vaccinations for cats: the distemper vaccine, the feline leukemia vaccine, the rabies vaccine, and the feline infectious peritonitis vaccine.

Distemper Vaccine

The distemper vaccine is actually three or four vaccines in one. The three-way killed distemper shot vaccinates for panleukopenia (FPV), rhinotracheitis (FVR), and calicivirus (FCV) viruses. All of these viruses are related to upper respiratory disease, which can cause serious illness in any cat. The four-way killed distemper shot includes the previous three vaccines plus *chlamydia*, which is a type of bacteria that causes infection. As we recommended earlier, all vaccines given to Ragdolls should be of the killed variety only. The three-way killed distemper vaccine can be given as early as six weeks of age, and pregnant females can also be vaccinated with three-way killed distemper vaccine. The four-way killed distemper vaccine is usually not given until kittens are at least eight weeks of age. Some breeders believe that it should not be given until twelve weeks of age. When you pick up your kitten, it will probably have had two distemper

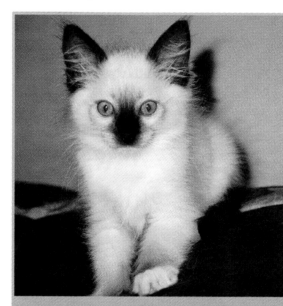

Cheers, a ten-week-old seal mitted male, projects every outward appearance of good health. Photo by Alfred Landegger.

shots. Each breeder has his or her own vaccination regimen. Your breeder will tell you when the next distemper shot is due. You must not neglect to have it administered. Normally, a kitten will have three to four distemper shots as a kitten, with an annual booster.

Feline Leukemia Vaccine

There is some controversy regarding the feline leukemia vaccine (FeLV). There have been reports of adverse reactions by Ragdolls to the feline leukemia vaccine. Many breeders are of the mind that since Ragdolls are solely indoor cats and that the feline leukemia virus is caught from contact with other cats, there is little need to risk using this vaccine. Other breeders believe otherwise. Follow the instructions from your breeder, and discuss this question with your veterinarian. If you plan to show your Ragdoll, you will want to consider obtaining this vaccination. Should you decide to vaccinate for the feline leukemia virus, be sure that the virus is of the killed variety only. The leukemia virus vaccine is usually given twice, at one-month intervals at three to five months of age, with a booster annually.

Rabies Vaccine

Some states require that all cats receive the rabies vaccine, in which case you have no choice but to comply. If you live where the rabies vaccine is not required, most breeders believe it is not worth taking the risk, since your Ragdoll will live strictly indoors. Again, discuss this with your breeder and ask your veterinarian. Rabies vaccine is given at four months of age and annually thereafter.

Feline Infectious Peritonitis Vaccine

At this point in time, there is extreme controversy regarding the feline infectious peritonitis (FIP) vaccine. This vaccine is administered by drops placed on the mucous membrane of the nose and, at present, is available only in a modified live form. Some breeders believe that it actually causes FIP and will not allow you to vaccinate your kitten for it. Once again, we believe that since your Ragdoll is going to be indoors only, the need for vaccination is questionable. Follow the instructions of your breeder, as it may affect your health guarantee if you elect to vaccinate for FIP.

ELIMINATING PARASITES

When you bring your Ragdoll home from a responsible breeder,

This seal colorpoint female is wearing an Elizabethan collar, a protective device used to keep animals from biting and scratching themselves or tearing out surgical stitches. Photo by Susan Nelson.

it will be guaranteed free of parasites. Keeping your home and Ragdoll free of parasites will require a lifelong commitment on your part. Maintaining a parasite-free environment is critical to assure your Ragdoll's continuing health and vitality. There are generally three types of parasites that you must either control or eliminate from your home and cat: fleas, worms, and ear mites.

Fleas

Uncontrolled fleas can pose a serious threat to your Ragdoll's well being. This threat can range from annoying itching and scratching with potential loss of hair coat or skin infection, all the way to the potential of flea anemia, whereby your Ragdoll's red blood cells have been depleted to such an extent by fleas feeding on them that your Ragdoll's life could be endangered. This is especially critical with kittens, but adult cats can also be seriously weakened by heavy flea infestation.

Manual Removal of Fleas

Get in the habit of flea combing your Ragdoll regularly. This way, you will spot any flea dirt or fleas before they become a problem. Check your kitten's gums at least once a week. Pale gums indicate possible anemia from flea bites. If you suspect fleas, part the fur

Seal mitted female kitten. A Ragdoll's coloration is not fully mature until the age of around two years. Photo by Muncy Smith.

on the abdomen and look to see if any fleas run from the light. Don't let this problem get out of hand, as fleas reproduce at a phenomenal rate.

Parasiticides

As of the publication of this book, new and vastly improved technologies have been developed to deal with flea infestation. Your vet can recommend a product that will greatly aid in keeping your home and your Ragdoll free of fleas.

Carpet Powder and Crystals

An excellent product that we use regularly is boric acid powder or crystals, sprinkled onto all carpets and upholstered surfaces and manually worked into the fibers. If you use it, don't forget to apply it under sofas and chairs and under all sofa and chair cushions as well. It is great for long-term flea control. The boric acid works by drying up the egg and larvae stage of the flea. It does not kill adult fleas. For an effective regimen against fleas, one must also treat the pet.

The flea-fighting product recommended by your vet, along with the boric acid based carpet powder or crystals, will rid your house of fleas and keep your Ragdoll flea free and healthy. Flea powders and sprays that are applied directly to the cat's body can cause tremors and drooling, or worse, and we do not recommend that they be used on your Ragdoll.

WORMS

There are several types of worms that could infest your Ragdoll, robbing it of important nutrients. The two most common are roundworms, which live in the stomach, and tapeworms, which live in the intestines.

Roundworms

When your kitten is three to five weeks old, your breeder will administer the medication necessary to deworm your kitten of roundworms. This medication is given at three and five weeks of age. If your kitten develops an extremely bloated abdomen, roundworms can be suspected. Roundworms are so common that it may take several treatments, spaced regularly within the first year of life, to completely eliminate them. Contact your veterinarian for the proper medication.

Tapeworms

Tapeworms live part of their life cycle in fleas. When your Ragdoll ingests a flea, tape worms can be introduced into its digestive system. Tapeworm segments eventually break off and appear as small white pieces of rice on your kitten's stool, rear hair coat, or anal area. Upon close inspection, you may even see these tapeworm segments moving. Once again, contact your veterinarian for the proper medication.

EAR MITES

When you bring your kitten home, inspect its ears. They should appear clean and free of any brown, dirt-like material. Tiny specks of wax are normal, just as with human ears. However, if you notice any dark brown, waxy clumps developing down inside your kitten's ears, suspect ear mites. Ear mites can be confirmed only by using a microscope. Consult your veterinarian for diagnosis and appropriate medication.

SPAYING AND NEUTERING

All breeders will require you to have a pet-quality kitten spayed or neutered at the appropriate age. Generally, a breeder will withhold registration papers until you have provided proof of spaying or neutering.

There is some discussion in the veterinary community regarding the appropriate age at which to spay or neuter kittens. Most veterinarians continue to suggest that kittens be neutered between four and eight or nine months of age, depending upon gender. Since your Ragdoll will not be outside, there is no reason to neuter before six months of age. Early neutering is done only to help control pet overpopulation and is not an issue with Ragdolls, which are kept only indoors. Follow the recommendations of

A blue colorpoint male relaxing on an enclosed patio. Photo by Susan Nelson.

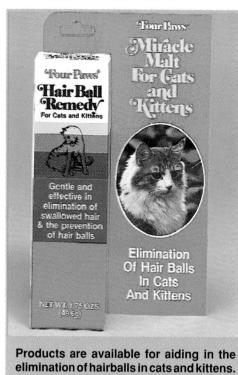

Products are available for aiding in the elimination of hairballs in cats and kittens. Photo courtesy of Four Paws.

your breeder and veterinarian.

COMMON CAT ILLNESSES
Kitty Colds

The most common problem seen in kittens is sniffling and sneezing. If sniffles and sneezing develop, most veterinarians would recommend that a five- to fifteen-day course of mild antibiotic such as amoxicillin be administered to avoid the possibility of pneumonia. Antibiotics will not stop the course of a cold; they will just prevent complications. The sneezing and sniffling should normally run its course within a week to ten days. Always bring a kitten with a cold to the veterinarian for assessment. Keep your kitten warm and away from drafts if it has, or you suspect that it has, a cold.

Diarrhea

Occasionally, kittens get diarrhea. There are several underlying reasons, ranging from the stress of a new environment to a change in diet. If diarrhea persists for more than 24 hours, consult your veterinarian.

OTHER SYMPTOMS THAT REQUIRE A VET'S ATTENTION

As a survival technique, cats are notorious about not exhibiting signs of illness until they are simply too ill to mask them. So, always take loss of appetite or a listless, depressed demeanor seriously. If your kitten exhibits any of these signs, it is best to see the veterinarian without delay.

Despite the ability to mask symptoms of illness, cats can vomit fairly easily. They vomit for any number of reasons, such as lactose intolerance, ingestion of fur in grooming, spoiled food, or overfeeding. This sort of vomiting usually involves a single episode. Often, you will see fur in the expelled stomach contents. If your healthy kitten suddenly vomits a couple of times and/or exhibits listlessness, see the veterinarian immediately.

SUMMARY

Ragdolls are generally healthy and not prone to illness. Monitor their health just as you would that of any small child who depends upon you for survival. Ragdolls provide us with a wealth of love and devotion, and it is only fair that we return the favor by providing a happy, healthy home environment.

YOUR RAGDOLL'S DIET

There are many ways to approach your Ragdoll's nutritional needs; however, it is up to you to ensure that it has a complete, balanced diet.

When you bring your kitten home, you should follow the advice of your breeder and veterinarian regarding diet. If you decide that you want to alter your Ragdoll's diet, you may opt to use only dry kibbled food or a combination of both dry and canned food. We do not recommend feeding semi-moist foods, and we do not recommend feeding solely canned food. You may decide to forego commercial foods and feed rations that you prepare from scratch. However, realize that rations prepared from scratch have little to nothing in common with the undesirable practice of feeding table scraps, and they may lack some dietary requirements. Many fine pet food companies have researchers who do nothing but work to develop food that provides sound nutrition to kittens and adult cats while retaining palatability.

We cannot emphasize enough that your kitten will have been fed a specific diet by your breeder, and you must adhere to your breeder's instructions when you bring your kitten home. Feed only what the breeder has fed, and adhere to the breeder's feeding schedule, at least until your

This seal point female weighs in at 12 pounds, which is the smaller end of the spectrum for a Ragdoll's weight. Note the fluffy bib-like ruff. Photo by Susan Nelson.

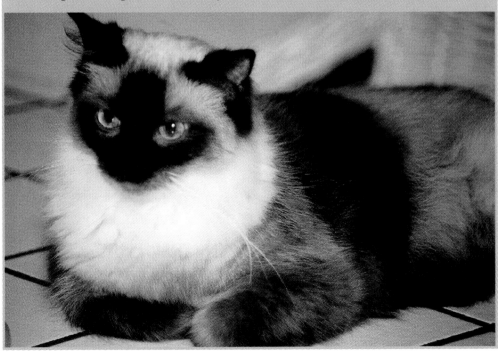

kitten has become acclimated to its new home.

Cats are carnivores. They need protein and fat to thrive. Do not feed vegetarian foods or dog foods to your Ragdoll, as it must have meat-based foods to attain its proper size and musculature. This is especially critical because Ragdolls typically grow to be quite large, usually at least ten to fifteen pounds for females and fifteen to twenty pounds for males. Breeding Ragdolls are generally slightly smaller. Once a kitten is weaned, it no longer requires milk, and some cats may develop diarrhea from drinking milk. Unlike people, cats cannot thrive on anything except a carnivorous diet.

If you want to change the brand of food that you feed your kitten, go to a large pet supply store and read the labels on lots of different brands of kitten and cat food. With dry food, you will see that the protein content varies between brands, and you should select a food with the highest protein that you can find. Protein should be at least 30 percent, preferably higher. Since your Ragdoll must have lots of quality meat and fat to reach its characteristically large size, we recommend that you feed mostly a high quality, palatable dry food. This type of food is highly concentrated, so more nutrients are delivered per bite compared to a similar quantity of canned food. Canned food labels generally list less than 12 percent protein. Take the time to compare labels, and you will see significant variations in protein, fat, and minerals between brands. Select a food that lists meat products within the first few ingredients. However, no matter what new food you intend to introduce, do so slowly, over about a week or two period, to prevent intestinal upsets and diarrhea.

Food also impacts your kitten's dental health. Dry food tends to mechanically remove tartar from the teeth during feeding, and it is best to offer dry food every day.

Whether to free feed or schedule feeding times is a matter of time and preference. We find that our Ragdolls enjoy a light morning and evening treat of canned food mixed with dry kibble, and we leave dry kibble out for free feeding during the day. Canned food can spoil after sitting out for several hours. While your kitten is growing, keep food readily available, and let it consume as much as it will eat. If you do not want to free feed, you must adhere to a set schedule and always be home at regular meal times. This can present a problem for those working outside the home. When feeding on a schedule, keep the food down for at least 30 minutes so as not to force your Ragdoll to eat quickly and possibly just as quickly regurgitate its meal. Either way you decide to feed, it is up to you to ensure that your Ragdoll consumes adequate, healthy rations.

Finally, have fresh water available at all times. Two bowls in different locations will ensure that water will always be available if one bowl should be accidentally tipped over.

INTRODUCING YOUR NEW RAGDOLL TO YOUR HOME

If at all possible, arrange to pick up your Ragdoll at a time when you can stay at home with it for at least twenty-four hours. Staying home for the first forty-eight hours is even better for your Ragdoll.

THE FIRST DAY

When you arrive at home with your new Ragdoll, there are several things you can do to make it feel comfortable, whether it is a kitten, juvenile, or adult.

First, let your Ragdoll leave its carrier on its own. If it is reticent, encourage it with a toy. If it still doesn't want to come out, sit down in a chair where you can see the carrier and where your Ragdoll can see you, and begin reading a magazine or book. When your kitten comes out of its carrier, relax and talk calmly to it. Praise it. Cuddle and reassure it a bit and, then, place it gently into its new litter box. Scratch the clean litter with your finger a few times to give it an idea of what you expect. This may induce the digging response. If your Ragdoll follows this suggestion, praise it.

Next, show your Ragdoll where you have placed its food and water. After your Ragdoll has visited its litter box and food areas, encourage it back to its litter box area by dragging a tiny toy for it to chase. Do this a few times. That way, you are certain your kitten won't get "lost" when

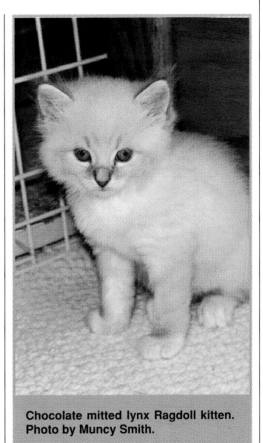

Chocolate mitted lynx Ragdoll kitten. Photo by Muncy Smith.

it next needs the litter box. At first, have the food within 10 feet of the litter box but no closer than 5 feet. Cats, like us, don't like to eat or drink near where they eliminate.

If your Ragdoll eats when you show it to its food area, you can rest assured that you are well on your way to a happy transition. If your kitten is not interested in food, play with it for a while, cuddle it, and try again later. Lavish praise on your kitten during this time.

The main thing that you want to do during the transition period is to show your Ragdoll that you are trustworthy. The number one sign that your kitten is settling into its new home is its willingness to eat. The next most important sign is its use of the litter box. Keep the litter box within your kitten's view. Your house is a big place to your little kitten, and if you do not keep the litter box within easy reach, accidents may happen because your Ragdoll will want to stay with you rather than search for its litter box. Its bed should be within 5 to 10 feet of the feeding area, away from the litter box. Keep a few toys out at all times, and play with your Ragdoll in a way that encourages trust.

A seal colorpoint and a lilac (frost) bicolor rest after a long day of playing together. Photo by Susan Nelson.

If you must leave your kitten unattended during the first several weeks, confine it to either your bedroom or any other room that can contain the litter box, food and water, toys, and a bed. The bathroom is a cold room with lots of slick, hard surfaces, and it may not be the safest place to leave your kitten unattended.

THE FIRST NIGHT

There are two ways to handle the first night. You can let the kitten sleep with you, or you can confine it in its room. If you choose the latter, you might expect to hear prolonged crying, as your kitten only wants to be with you. As long as you have confined it to a safe area, do not be alarmed. Do not respond to your kitten's cries because it needs to learn how to settle itself. If you enter the room frequently to reassure it, you will be training it to continue crying for attention. Eventually, your kitten will fall asleep. When it awakens, it will be anxious to see you. Remember, your kitten has probably never been alone before, and this first night can be difficult for it.

On the other hand, kittens love to sleep with their humans. There are two things to be concerned about when a kitten sleeps with you. First, it will jump down to visit its litter box during the night. You must show it how to get back up on the bed. A stack of books can serve as a "step." Or, you can put a small kitty condo beside the bed. Second, you could roll over and injure your kitten during the night. So, be careful to protect your kitten. Nothing is sweeter than waking up to the bright eyes and tiny purr of a Ragdoll kitten. If you're lucky, maybe you'll even get a tiny kiss on the nose.

THE MULTI-PET ENVIRONMENT

No other cat adjusts as readily to other pets as a Ragdoll. They love cats, dogs, rabbits, and even birds.

When you bring a Ragdoll kitten into a household with existing cats, there will be an adjustment period for the other cats. It is sometimes helpful to keep the new addition in a separate room for a few days. Then, remove it and let the established cats come time goes by, the other cats will begin to accept your Ragdoll. The Ragdoll's loving, non-aggressive nature makes it a perfect cat to introduce into a multi-cat environment. Existing cats will quickly realize that the new kitten is not a threat. However, to protect your kitten from rough play, keep it separately in its room when you are not present to supervise the interactions. Within two weeks, you should expect to see your Ragdoll playing happily with its house mates. Even so, you should continue to confine your kitten when you are out until you are absolutely certain it has

Seal mitted female. Note the clearly defined, evenly matched front mittens. Photo by Susan Nelson.

in to investigate the scent of the new kitten or cat before actually introducing them to each other. Before the introduction, be sure to clip all front and rear nails to avoid any possible injury during the adjustment period. Your Ragdoll kitten will probably attempt to make friends right away, but the other cats will hiss and rebuff it. Don't be concerned, but do not leave established cats alone with your new addition. As been accepted or it is at least twelve to sixteen weeks old and more able to escape or fend off aggression.

Dogs will generally be much more accepting of your new Ragdoll. However, dogs can get too rough. So, allow only supervised play until your kitten is at least sixteen weeks old. When bringing a Ragdoll into a home with dogs, rabbits, or birds, the key thing to remember is that

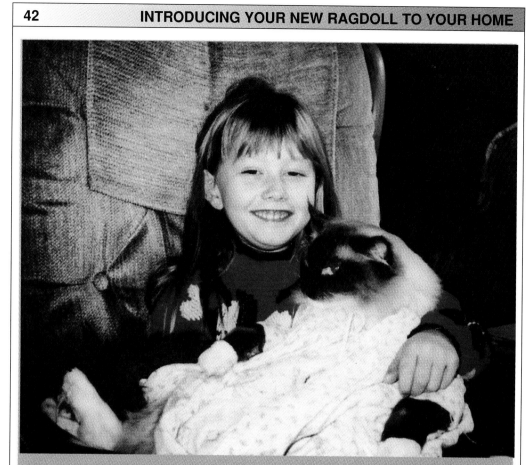

Ragdolls are known for their penchant for snuggling, as this seal mitted Ragdoll named Wally and his young friend demonstrate here. Ragdolls are excellent for children who have been taught how to gently handle cats. Photo by Dodie Strobel.

the Ragdoll does not have the fighting instinct of a regular cat. This leaves it vulnerable to attacks and rough play, which could lead to injury. The safest course is to exercise caution during the introductory period, even following the suggestions outlined above for the multi-cat environment. Many Ragdolls end up regularly napping with the family dog or dogs.

INTRODUCING YOUNG CHILDREN

Young children can also injure Ragdoll kittens by squeezing them too tightly, picking them up incorrectly, or pulling on the head, legs, or tail. When bringing your Ragdoll home, immediately begin to teach your child how to properly handle it. Never let a child pick up a Ragdoll by the neck, leg, or tail. Although a regular kitten or cat may bite or scratch when handled improperly, a Ragdoll may not react at all until it is seriously injured or hurt. It is best to have your child wait until the kitten jumps on its lap for cuddling. Otherwise, the kitten could be injured or frightened by being chased or grasped roughly.

GOING ON VACATION

You will be amazed at how quickly your Ragdoll becomes one of the family. So, you will want to plan carefully for its care when you go on vacation or a business trip. Your Ragdoll cannot care for itself; it depends completely upon you to meet all of its needs.

LEAVING YOUR RAGDOLL AT HOME

If you cannot bring your Ragdoll with you, it will be happiest at home. Never leave a kitten alone for more than twelve hours. An adult Ragdoll can stay alone for a period extending from Saturday morning to Sunday evening, assuming that it readily eats dry food and has at least two bowls of fresh water available at all times. Do not leave out wet food while you are gone because it could spoil and make your cat ill. If you will be gone longer than this, hire a reliable pet sitter. A good friend may also want to take on this responsibility. No matter whether you hire a sitter or use a good friend, a daily visit is essential. Two visits a day is optimum. Be sure to instruct your cat sitter to take some time to comfort and love your Ragdoll, in addition to playing, feeding, watering, and cleaning the litter box. There are trained pet sitters who operate home-based businesses, and you may want to locate one of these individuals. No matter whom you have care for your Ragdoll at home, always leave written instructions and the phone number of your veterinarian in an accessible place.

BOARDING YOUR RAGDOLL

When boarding is the only alternative, try to select a reputable boarding facility that will supply you with several

Purrfectly content...Like many other cats, your Ragdoll may prefer your bed to its own. Photo by Alfred Landegger.

references. Then, check out the references. Don't trust your Ragdoll to a boarding facility that you have not checked out thoroughly. Beware of facilities that cut corners on comfort, feeding, and sanitation. If a facility will not let you inspect the entire kennel, don't leave your Ragdoll.

One of the main dangers of boarding is the transmission of disease between animals. If the facility does not insist that all cats have health certificates with up-to-date vaccinations, don't risk your Ragdoll's health. Also, a well-run kennel, like a well-run veterinary hospital, should not have a heavy litter box odor. The cleanest kennels will have little or no odor. Ideally, you should select a boarding facility well in advance of the time that you will need to board your Ragdoll, and inspect it one more time shortly before your trip.

TAKING YOUR RAGDOLL ALONG

Many Ragdolls have been trained to be wonderful travelers, whether by motor home, automobile, or airline. If traveling with your Ragdoll is in your future plans, accustom it early on to public life. Purchase a halter and leash and gradually let your Ragdoll become accustomed to wearing them. Give it a treat when it maintains a relaxed attitude.

Take it for rides in the car and bring it to visit neighbors and friends. This helps train your Ragdoll to be comfortable in unfamiliar situations. The more exposure you give your Ragdoll, the more relaxed and enjoyable it will be as a travel companion.

Just one note of caution: Don't leave your Ragdoll alone in a car, as it can be overcome by heat prostration quicker than you would believe possible. This holds true for other pets as well.

A Ragdoll quartet: seal mitted, blue mitted lynxs, and seal colorpoint lynx. Photo by Susan Nelson.

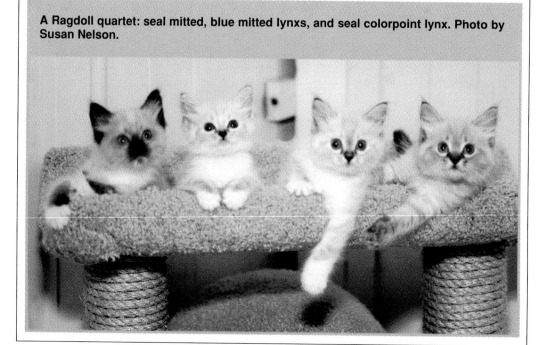

Be certain to bring a supply of your Ragdoll's regular litter, food, and water to prevent bouts of diarrhea while traveling. Pack its favorite toys and blanket or bed. Bring its grooming tools. Make arrangements to stay at accommodations that welcome pets. As soon as you check into your room, hang out the "do not disturb sign" to minimize the chance that a service person may inadvertently let your Ragdoll out while you are at dinner or the pool. Do not leave your Ragdoll alone in unfamiliar surroundings for an extended period of time. Be aware that your Ragdoll may have trouble adjusting its sleep schedule if you vacation in another time zone. Follow all of these suggestions, and you will thoroughly enjoy taking your Ragdoll along on vacation.

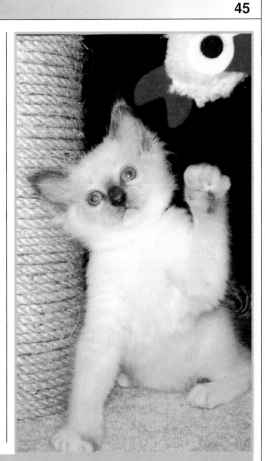

Above: Blue mitted male kitten playfully swiping at a toy. Offer your Ragdoll a variety of toys to keep it occupied. Photo by Susan Nielsen. *Below:* A rare tortie lynxpoint Ragdoll kitten. Photo by Muncy Smith.

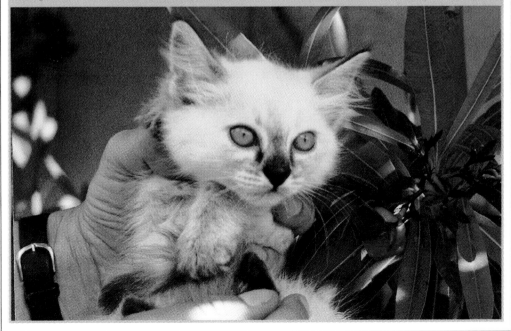

THINGS TO CONSIDER ABOUT BREEDING RAGDOLLS

Breeding Ragdolls is not something to enter into lightly. Although the thought of cuddly kittens playing in your living room sounds tempting, there is a lot more involved in breeding than meets the eye. What follows is a quick breeding overview. After reading the overview, we suggest that you think long and hard before you make any decision to breed Ragdolls. If you do decide to breed Ragdolls, contact the Ragdoll Fanciers Club International (RFCI) for more information and insight into breeding challenges.

Before you decide whether to breed, do lots of homework first. After all, you are going to gamble a considerable amount of money to establish a breeding pair in your home, including all the equipment that you will need, such as a stud cage, queening cage, scales, special diet, license,

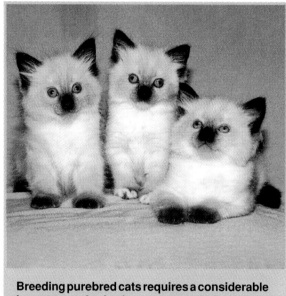

Breeding purebred cats requires a considerable investment in both money and time. It is essential that you carefully weigh all of the factors involved before you make any decisions about starting a breeding program. Photo by Susan Nelson.

cattery registration, and so forth. Therefore, contact a wide range of breeders, and don't be afraid to ask questions. Do not buy from the first breeder that you interview. Talk with veterinarians and discuss the costs associated with breeding complications. Read all the books that you can on breeding purebred cats and feline husbandry in general.

Take your time. Not all breeders will be able to produce the top-quality breeding pair that you must have to establish a reputable cattery. Examine the entire pedigree of each breeding Ragdoll you are considering, and if you do not know enough about the particular Ragdolls listed on the pedigree, ask for the names and addresses of the registered owners, and phone them to discuss their bloodlines. And remember, the relationship that you establish as a new breeder with your selling breeder will be ongoing. You need to feel absolutely comfortable calling your breeder any time of the day or night, if necessary. So, the breeder that you eventually buy from must be someone that you trust to provide you with quality breeding stock and with whom you can communicate easily, without reservation. Anything less will jeopardize your successful entry into breeding.

BREEDING COSTS

When purchasing breeding Ragdolls, you can expect to pay two to three times the amount that you would for a pet-quality Ragdoll. Some breeders believe that whatever your yearly veterinarian's bill would be for one Ragdoll, triple it for a breeding pair. Barring any unforeseen events, such as a retained placenta or difficult birth, both of which require veterinary assistance, the cost of deworming and vaccinating your kittens as well as caring for the general health care of your breeders can be a major expense. When breeding cats, you must feed premium food and supplemental vitamins, which is another cost that must be considered. A preventive flea control program must be maintained and adequate stocks of litter and nursing and weaning supplies must be kept on hand at all times. Failure to provide your breeding cats and kittens with these minimal requirements will negatively impact the reputation of your cattery and you as a breeder. To enhance your cattery reputation, you also must regularly enter your breeding cats and best kittens into cat shows.

Champion Miss Ashley of Ragmeister, a seal mitted female, with Chloe, her six-week-old daughter. Photo by Susan Nelson.

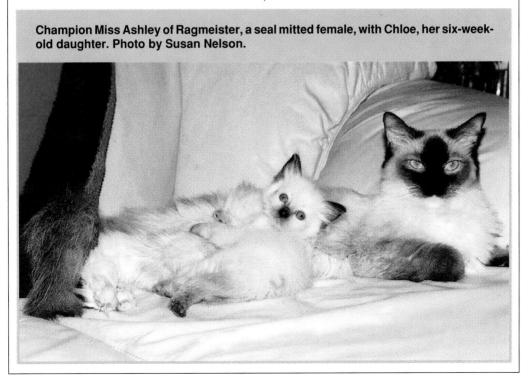

Entry fees, per show, for two cats or kittens and grooming space can add up to a pretty penny, not counting transportation, food, show supplies, and, possibly, motel expenses.

THE BREEDING PAIR

Some Ragdoll associations require you to purchase a breeding pair of Ragdolls before you may ethically breed at all. This can present a real problem to the novice, as breeding males (often referred to as studs or whole males) must be kept isolated to prevent urine spraying in the house, and the spray of a whole male is particularly offensive. Although not all whole males spray, you must have an alternative living quarters for your male should he do so. This behavior may not occur until your male is eight months old or older and becomes sexually active. However, most whole males spend their entire lives in stud cages. Without three or four females to keep company with a breeding male, a solo male in a stud cage leads a bleak existence. Some small breeders solve this problem by introducing a spayed or neutered companion cat into the stud cage. If you plan to do this, it is best to have them grow up together as kittens. In any event, you must enter the stud cage at least once daily to tend to the emotional needs of your stud male.

Whole females (often referred to as queens) can also spray, although their spray is not as pungent. Spraying is a natural behavior of breeding animals, as they use this scent to attract a mate. Whole females will often "call" when they are in heat. This can involve loud yowling and crying all through the night, which is an important consideration for you, your family, and your close neighbors. Regarding such noise, be aware that each time a breeding or rebreeding occurs, the female screams loudly. Your

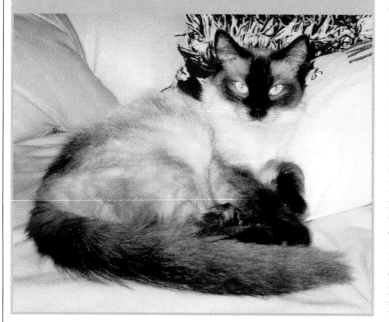

A female seal colorpoint. Ragdolls that are selected for a breeding program must be as genetically diverse as possible. Photo by Gary Strobel.

A blue bicolor queen nursing her kittens. In their first weeks of life, kittens receive all of their essential nutrients from their mother's milk. Photo by Muncy Smith.

family and neighbors may not appreciate this screaming, especially during the early morning hours. Like stud males, whole females require love and attention from you on a daily basis.

If your city or town has special ordinances governing the breeding of animals, unhappy neighbors could attempt to shut down your breeding program, resulting in the loss of your entire investment.

SPACE REQUIREMENTS

As if yowling, spraying cats are not daunting enough, there are critical space requirements when it comes to breeding Ragdolls. As discussed above, you must be able to provide a separate living area for the breeding male, should he be a sprayer. You must also provide a "queening" area in a warm, quiet location of your home for the birth and nursing of the kittens. Finally, you must be able to accommodate toddling kittens in a totally safe space. Proper breeding practices require that queens and their litters be separated from other litters until the weaning stage has passed. If you keep three or four breeding females, this means that you may have to separately accommodate and clean up after as many as four litters at any one time.

TIME REQUIREMENTS

The time required for proper cattery maintenance and breeding saps nearly all free time available and ties you completely to your favorite litter scoop, bleach bucket, and mop. Additionally, if you work away from the home, you may have a difficult time arranging to be present for each birth, but you must be present to provide whatever assistance your queen needs. When each litter is born, there is the possibility that supplemental feedings will be required; and, on occasion, if the queen is not able to nurse her kittens, you must take over the duties of the mother. This involves feeding the kittens every two to four hours around the clock as well as stimulating the kittens to urinate and defecate after each feeding. These complications are unlikely to occur; but, nonetheless, they are possible and must be taken into consideration

Four-week-old seal mitted kittens. Note the fluffy quality of their fur. Photo by Muncy Smith.

Bright-eyed and bushy tailed, a "lotta lynxs" pose for the camera. Photo by Susan Nelson.

A blue lynx bicolor female. The term "lynx" simply refers to the striped pattern, as is evident on this Ragdoll's forehead. Photo by Susan Nelson.

when deciding whether to breed cats. Even if supplemental feedings are not required, kittens must be weighed and examined at least twice each day. Even with this level of care, you can lose a kitten quickly if it becomes chilled, and you may not realize that a kitten is in trouble until it is too late.

When the kittens are being weaned, you must devote additional time to assure that each kitten is adjusting appropriately to its new diet, eating well, and continuing to gain weight. Some kittens refuse to start eating solid foods and if not monitored carefully and fed by hand, they can whither and die before you realize that there is a problem.

Although Ragdolls are inherently sweet and loving, a good portion of their personality development will depend on you spending hours and hours of time socializing them through cuddling and play. Because breeding is so time intensive and your presence is nearly always needed, you will seldom be able to leave the house for longer than it takes to have dinner with friends. All of this omits the twice-daily feeding, water changing, litter box chores, and the additional time that you will need to spend vacuuming,

Vivian, a seal bicolor female. As is true for any other cat breed, Ragdolls selected for breeding must be in perfect health and top condition. Photo by Susan Nelson.

cleaning, and disinfecting your home and the breeding quarters, to ward off disease. All this having been said, breeding Ragdolls can be enormously satisfying.

GENETIC CONSIDERATIONS

If you should decide to breed Ragdolls, it is important that the genetic makeup of your male and female be as diverse as possible. As with any other breed of cat, using animals that are closely related for breeding can cause genetic health problems. Due to the fact that the Ragdoll breed is only about 30 years old, it is especially important not to breed from close genetic lines. If you are unable to obtain a quality, unrelated but genetically

compatible breeding pair from one breeder, that breeder can arrange for another to supply the missing cat.

SUMMARY

You may feel that we have presented an unnecessarily bleak picture of what breeding entails, but we assure you that all of the above topics must be carefully considered before you decide to enter into any breeding program. Lots of people have entered the breeding field and left after only a few months or years when they realized all that it entailed. We want you to know the obligations involved before you invest your time and money into breeding.

SHOWING YOUR RAGDOLL

WHY SHOW YOUR RAGDOLL?

Assuming that you purchase a show-quality Ragdoll, showing your Ragdoll can be some of the most fun you've ever experienced. This is because you will meet some incredibly nice people and have a chance to show off your Ragdoll to others. You will advance the Ragdoll breed by exposing others to this relatively new breed of cat. At the same time, you will have a chance to meet people from all over the country and make new friends in the process. Your Ragdoll may even win a couple of ribbons!

WHAT DO I NEED TO DO FIRST?

The first step on the way to showing your Ragdoll is to obtain what your breeder would call a show-quality Ragdoll. Your breeder should be able to discern whether or not your Ragdoll possesses the necessary show qualities. Depending upon the breeder, you will either need to pay a premium over the standard pet-quality price or agree to advertise the cattery during each show that you attend. This would usually entail putting some of the breeder's business cards on your show cage and making a point of

Co-author Susan Nelson confers with a show judge after receiving a "final" on her seal mitted female named Ragmeister's Dolly. Photo by Kathy Lam.

You will often find your Ragdoll resting in unusual places when your lap is not available, as this seal colorpoint shows us. Photo by Carla Applegate.

telling those who stop to talk with you where you obtained your Ragdoll. When you purchase a show-quality Ragdoll, your breeder will supply the necessary registration paperwork immediately. You will still need to spay or neuter your Ragdoll at the appropriate age, in accord with the purchase contract. Nearly all cat associations require your kitten to be at least four months of age, in good health, tested and free from feline leukemia, and inoculated against specific diseases before you can show it.

HOW DO I FIND OUT ABOUT SHOWS?

There are several different cat associations that sponsor cat shows. You will need to register your kitten in each association in which you intend to show. So, while your kitten is growing, you may want to contact the various associations and inquire about upcoming shows that are being sponsored in your area. You can also look in *Cat Fancy* or *Cats Magazine* to find out about show dates. Decide which shows you want to enter, and mark your calendar. Showing can become very expensive, even if you attend only one show each month, but some shows offer a discounted entry fee if you enter before a specific date. There is transportation expense, and you must eat during the eight to twelve hours that you will be at the show. Many shows will be a good distance from your home. If you need to stay overnight, there will be additional motel and restaurant expenses to consider. For all of these reasons, it is a good idea to find out about upcoming show dates as early as possible.

REGISTERING YOUR RAGDOLL FOR THE SHOW

If the association sponsoring

Seal mitted female. The Ragdoll's large blue eyes are moderately wide set. Photo by Susan Nelson.

the show that you want to enter is different from the one in which your Ragdoll is registered, you must register your cat in the new association. This is a one-time requirement and involves sending a copy of your original registration papers, with a three-generation pedigree, to the new association along with the registration fee. You will receive your new registration papers in the mail, generally within a week or two. Keep them in a safe place along with your Ragdoll's other important papers.

SHOW SUPPLIES
Cage Curtains

When you arrive at the show, you must check in, obtain a show program, and locate the benching cage that has been assigned to your Ragdoll. You will have brought with you the required "cage curtains." At minimum, these curtains must cover the outside and top of your cage, and you need a show blanket or towel for the bottom of your cage. Most experienced show people use only show curtains that also cover the inside of the cage, to protect their cats from cold show halls and any germs that might be on the benching cage wire. You can find the dimensions of the cages on the show's flyer. These are usually standard, so once you have a set of cage curtains, you can use them repeatedly. You can make your own curtains, or you can

The requirements for championship titles vary from one association to another. It is up to you to familiarize yourself with the points required for your Ragdoll to reach each championship level. Photo by Susan Nelson.

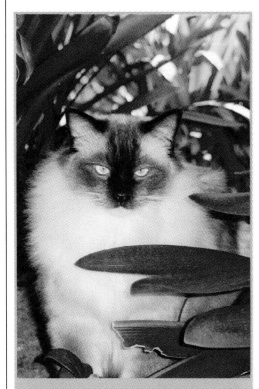

A Ragdoll photographed during a supervised outing in the garden. Photo by Marie Palm.

and can be purchased at pet stores. You will also need small food and water dishes for inside the cage. Take along your cat's favorite food as well as a bottle of the water it usually drinks. You may also want to put in a soft, plush bed or pillow for your cat to sleep on or hide behind. These are available from show vendors, and you can select one that matches your cage curtains if you don't have one when you attend your first show. We have seen exhibitors use a doll bed inside the benching cage, and cats seem to love them. Bring along a couple of your Ragdoll's favorite small toys so that it has something to play with in the cage. There are hammocks and hanging carpeted ledges that you can purchase or make for your cage, and you will see these in some exhibitors' cages when you visit your first cat show. Some cats prefer to lounge on these while waiting to be called to each show ring. Let your fantasy run wild when decorating your Ragdoll's show cage, and you will have even more fun at each show!

Grooming Supplies

Bring your usual grooming aids to the show in your show tote. These will include a wire slicker brush, metal comb, and flea comb. The flea comb's fine teeth are good for completely separating your Ragdoll's fur coat before using the slicker brush to fluff ruff and tail before each show ring. You will also need cotton swabs and/or cotton balls or cotton squares for any last minute

buy a set at most shows, but you must obtain them before your first show. Don't plan to buy them at your first show. Since it is a good idea to observe at least one show before you begin showing, you can use that opportunity to purchase show curtains from a show vendor or get ideas for making your own set.

Cage Supplies

There are a few things that you must have for inside your Ragdoll's show cage and a few things that are optional. You will need to take along a small litter box and the litter your kitten prefers for inside the cage. Small litter boxes are about 12" x 15" cleaning of the ears, nose, or eyes. You will pick up tips from other show people as you become more accustomed to showing. There are lots of powders, sprays, and grooming tricks that you will learn about as you gain more experience.

Disinfectant

Never go to a show without a spray bottle of disinfectant and a roll of paper towels. People may want to pet and touch your Ragdoll, and you have every right to refuse. However, if you would like them to be able to experience a Ragdoll up close, it is of the utmost importance that at least their hands be disinfected before coming in contact with your Ragdoll. You have no idea how many other cats they may have touched, and upper respiratory infections are spread easily at shows. You will see the importance of this measure at every judge's table, as they spray their own hands and clothes as well as the judging platform in between each cat that they handle. You should use the disinfectant frequently at the show as well. It can be purchased in a concentrated form from your veterinarian, who stocks it to use on all hard surfaces before examining the next patient. Simply tell the vet that you want to purchase some disinfectant to use for disease protection while showing your Ragdoll.

Grand Champion Ragmeister's Baby Blueberry Sharkey, a perfectly marked seal bicolor male, catches a few winks during a long day at a show. Photo by Terry Sharkey.

SHOW GROOMING
The Bath

The show bath is required by all associations because your Ragdoll must be absolutely clean and free of any parasites. You can do a simple show bath with a hypoallergenic shampoo or you can do an elaborate show bath with many different steps. The choice is yours. You may want to give a shorter bath the first few

We have already given a detailed explanation of how to bathe your Ragdoll. You will learn more about the show bath as you continue showing and talking with others. You may want to have someone help you give the bath and assist with the drying process. Drying can be accomplished either by placing your Ragdoll in its carrier and blowing in warm air with a hair dryer, or you can hold your

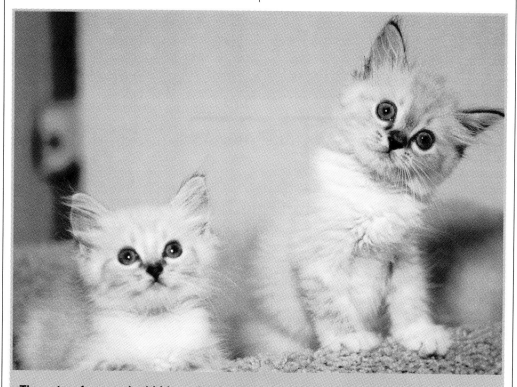

These two four-week-old blue mitted lynxs are the embodiment of a Ragdoll kitten's personality and charm. Photo by Susan Nelson.

times you show so that your Ragdoll becomes accustomed to the process slowly. You will be able to decide what approach you want to take once you have spoken with other show exhibitors and observed your Ragdoll's reaction to being bathed.

Ragdoll on your lap in a dry towel and gradually blow it dry, using a wide-tooth comb to gently separate hair clumps and making certain that your hand is always between the blow dryer and your Ragdoll, to assure that you don't overheat or burn your cat.

Clipping the Nails

All associations require that each nail be clipped before any cat can be shown. We have discussed nail clipping previously. Do not clip into the quick, but make certain that you thoroughly trim the clear area that forms the front of the claw. Your cat may be nervous at the cat show, and it is important that its nails be a length that cannot hurt you or the judges.

that you may observe inside your cat's ears. Do not go any lower than you can see. Some people purchase a special solution at the pet store to use for this purpose.

Cleaning the Mouth

If you plan to show your cat, you should begin a program of brushing its teeth while it is still a kitten. That way, you will never need to scrape tartar from your cat's teeth when preparing for a

Priscilla, a seal colorpoint female. Ragdolls are gentle cats with laid-back personalities. Photo by Susan Nelson.

Cleaning the Ears

Ears must be clean and free of parasites such as ear mites. We have discussed ear mites previously, and it is unlikely that your Ragdoll will ever contract them. A certain amount of waxy build-up is normal, and using a cotton swab, you can gently remove any tiny clumps of wax

show. Simply use a special pet toothbrush and pet toothpaste, and brush as usual. Do not use human toothpaste on your cat's teeth.

AT THE SHOW
What To Do When You Arrive

When you arrive, you will proceed to the registration table

and pick up your "show packet." This packet will include an entry number, which your Ragdoll will be known by throughout the day. Proceed to the "benching area," which is the set of cages where your Ragdoll will be housed for the day, and locate the cage with that number. Immediately write the entry number on your hand, as you will need to refer to it countless times during the day. Begin to set up your cage by putting down your Ragdoll's show blanket or towel, hanging your curtains, and putting out the cage supplies. Place your Ragdoll's number on the front of its cage. Then, place your Ragdoll into its cage, verbally assuring it that everything is fine, petting it in a matter-of-fact way, and letting it

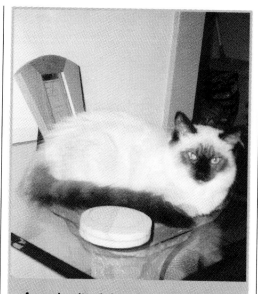

A seal mitted female named Amber. Ragdolls belong indoors. No matter how small or large your living quarters, your Ragdoll will be happiest and safest at home indoors. Photo by Gary Strobel.

This Ragdoll is feeling frisky. Note the huge, fluffy tail typical of Ragdolls. Photo by Susan Nelson.

Lilac (frost) bicolor female. Photo by Kathy Lam.

get accustomed to its new surroundings.

Next, locate your Ragdoll's entry information listed inside the show program, and make certain that each item of information is correct. If it is not, you must speak with the clerk of each ring and request that the information be corrected. Otherwise, you may not be able to claim any winners' ribbons that your Ragdoll may receive during that show. Then, take a few minutes to go over the show schedule listed on the program and determine approximately when your Ragdoll will be called to each ring. No times are listed on the program, and the judging progression depends entirely on when each judge begins and how quickly the judging of each class proceeds. We have found that the best way to keep track of when your Ragdoll must be present at each ring for judging is to circle your Ragdoll's entry class on each judge's schedule; otherwise, the hustle and bustle of the show hall could result in your missing a judging call.

Be aware that unless you paid extra for grooming space, you will need to do most of your grooming in your lap. Bring a towel for this purpose or invest in a portable grooming table. There will be no space for you to spread your things out. The benching aisles are fairly narrow, and you will need to put all of your supplies, carrier, and show tote under the benching table.

The Show Rings

A typical show consists of approximately six rings. Each of these rings is an entire cat show unto itself. There is one judge in each ring, and by the end of the day, that judge will have evaluated all the cats in the show hall. As the day progresses, your Ragdoll's number will be called out over the loudspeaker along with instructions such as, "Cats 19 through 28, this is your first call for ring 3." Quickly back brush and fluff up your Ragdoll and, in a timely manner, carry it to the ring to which it has been called. There will be a cage at that ring with your number on top of it. Place your Ragdoll in the cage and have a seat in the audience section. Try to sit in the front row, in view of your Ragdoll. It will be able to see you, and knowing you are present will provide some comfort if your Ragdoll is a bit nervous. It is also a good idea to sit in the front row because you can hear exactly what the judge is saying. If you listen closely, you will learn a great deal. It is improper to speak to a judge throughout this process, unless you are spoken to first.

Each cat association has its own requirements for champion, grand champion, supreme grand champion, etc. Even the championship titles vary from association to association. It is up to you to become familiar with the points required for your Ragdoll to reach each championship level. Naturally, you must keep track of your Ragdoll's points if you want to claim any of its titles.

When the judging is finished, there will be an announcement that your cat may be returned to its cage. At this time, you must remove the cat without speaking to the judge, and take it back to your benching area. If your cat is lucky enough to "final" in a ring, your number will be called again at some point during the day to return to that ring. Sometimes, the specific numbers are not called. There is simply a general announcement that "Finals are posted in ring 1, please check your numbers." Be

A CFA (Cat Fanciers' Association) judge examining a seal bicolor Ragdoll. Cat shows are informative and fun. They can provide the opportunity for you to share your interest in Ragdolls with other Ragdoll fanciers. Photo by Susan Nelson.

certain to walk to that ring and actually check for your Ragdoll's number, as signs and decorations sometimes will block your view.

It is important that you listen to the announcements all day long and walk to the various rings to check on judging progress. You can check on judging progress by looking at the entry numbers of the cats caged in that particular judging ring, looking up some of the numbers in the show catalog, and deciding what class is being judged at that time.

What the Judges Will Look for in Your Ragdoll

Before the judge even takes your Ragdoll out of its cage, he or she will have made some assessments as far as bone and coat appearance are concerned. When the judge removes your Ragdoll from its cage, he or she will be noticing temperament and weight. Once the judge places your Ragdoll on the judging platform, he or she will carefully check the head for proper conformation and ears for proper placement. To do this, the judge will often use a toy to attract the cat's attention, moving the toy so that the cat's head can be examined from all angles. Eye color is also checked at this time. The coat and overall feel of the body is checked by running the hands over the Ragdoll's body. At this point, the judge may pick the cat up and hold it aloft to examine its face more closely before returning it to its cage. You will see the judge and the judge's assistant making notes about

your Ragdoll. At some point, the assistant will announce that your Ragdoll can "go back."

Cleaning Up and Leaving the Show Hall

Be considerate of the sponsoring cat club and clean up your area before you leave. There are trash cans provided strategically throughout the show hall for this purpose, and cleaning up will be easier if you attend to this task throughout the day. This is particularly important because if the show hall is left in clean condition, the owners will be more likely to rent it out again when that cat club wishes to sponsor another association show. Be sure to get the phone numbers or business cards of people whom you've met at the show, as you may want to keep in touch and discuss upcoming shows and showing techniques with them.

ENJOY YOUR SHOWING EXPERIENCE

We hope that you will enjoy your showing experience. It is hard work preparing for a show, getting up early in the morning, and driving to a show, but we wish that we had the time to enter more cat shows. We have found that the best way to approach showing is simply to prepare thoroughly for each show, get set up quickly when you arrive, and, then, relax and enjoy the camaraderie of being with a show hall full of beautiful cats and bona fide cat lovers!

ABOUT THE AUTHORS

Gary Strobel is a school teacher in Southern California. As a hobby, Gary has been involved with animals and animal husbandry since he was a young boy. Gary started Ragmeister Ragdolls in 1991 with his first female Ragdoll named Lucy, a lilac bi-color. Located in beautiful San Diego, California, Ragmeister Ragdolls has become an internationally recognized and respected breeder of the Ragdoll cat. Gary is dedicated to improving the Ragdoll breed and believes that the special "Ragdoll personality" is the top breeding priority. Gary's love of the Ragdoll breed and his enthusiasm in educating the public in regard to the uniqueness of the Ragdoll was his inspiration for writing this book.

Susan Nelson is an attorney and award-winning wildlife photographer who has owned and loved cats for nearly five decades. She was planning to add either a

Co-author Susan Nelson with Chloe, her six-week-old seal colorpoint female. Photo by Kathy Lam.

Co-author Gary Strobel, center, pictured at a cat show with fellow Ragdoll fanciers Roy and Muncy Smith. The Ragdolls are Ragmeister's Hawkeye, a blue mitted lynx male, and Ragmeister's BJ Honeycutt, a lilac bicolor male. Photo by Susan Nelson.

Himalayan or Maine Coon kitten to her home when an article in *Cat Fancy* magazine about the Ragdoll breed aroused her curiosity. After learning that there were no published books about Ragdoll cats, Susan began searching for information about them. Her search led to Ragmeister Ragdolls of Southern California. There, she met Gary Strobel and discovered that Ragdolls truly do possess unique temperament, size, and beauty. Since that time, she and her husband have acquired three Ragdolls. Susan spends a large portion of her free time showing her Ragdolls and co-authored this book to share her love of Ragdolls.

BETTER·GARDEN·DESIGN
Roger Turner

with line illustrations and
colour photographs by the author

JM Dent & Sons Ltd
London   Melbourne

BY THE SAME AUTHOR

Capability Brown: and the Eighteenth-century English Landscape

First published 1986
© Roger Turner 1986

All rights reserved. No part of this publication may
be reproduced, stored in a retrieval system, or transmitted,
in any form or by any means, electronic, mechanical, photocopying,
recording or otherwise, without the prior permission of
J. M. Dent & Sons Ltd.

This book is set in 10½/12½ Linotron Sabon by
Input Typesetting Ltd, London
Printed in Great Britain by Mackays of Chatham Ltd for
J. M. Dent & Sons Ltd
Aldine House, 33 Welbeck Street, London W1M 8LX

British Library Cataloguing in Publication Data

Turner, Roger
  Better garden design
  1. Gardens—Design
  I. Title
  712'.6   SB472

  ISBN 0–460–04703–5

·CONTENTS·

Note: All metric equivalents are approximate

ACKNOWLEDGMENTS

I would like to thank several of my friends in the Hardy Plant Society for their help, and Mrs Gill Mullin in particular. Thanks are also due to Mr David Allen, Mrs Beth Chatto, Mr Brian Corley, Mr Peter Healing, Mr Preben Jakobsen, Mrs Alvide Lees-Milne, Mr and Mrs Reginald Merritt, Mr and Mrs J. Pomfet, Mr and Mrs Peter Shillito, Mr Jim Reynolds, Mrs Isabel Grindley and to my wife.

PART

1

BEFORE
· WE ·
BEGIN

CHAPTER 1

A Plan of Action

There comes a day, towards the end of October, when wintry weather prevents even the hardiest gardener from pottering in the garden. Then, from the refuge of a comfortable chair, we can at last relax and take stock of the garden. All that remains now is a picture: a view seen from the windows of the house. The riot of colour of July days has gone, and plants that once gave pleasure on individual inspection now merge to form part of the general scene. It is easy to forget that for most of the year this is all we see of the garden, and that even in summer most of us spend more time inside than out.

To many people, especially keen gardeners, the garden means the plants in it. But fine flowers on their own do not make a fine garden, and only if the overall arrangement forms an attractive picture will we get any pleasure from the garden during the long winter months. In Gertrude Jekyll's words:*

> I am strongly of the opinion that the possession of a quantity
> of plants, however good the plants may be themselves and
> however ample their number does not make a garden, it only
> makes a *collection!*

What, then, does 'make a garden'?

A theory of gardening, like all good theories I suppose, would divide the subject into three elements: the visual, the functional and horticultural aspects. It must look good: it must be convenient to use: and the plants must be grown well and be appropriate to their soil and situation; and each of these three elements must make their contribution to the art of garden making.

In the visual side of his art the gardener is not alone. Like the

---

* Gertrude Jekyll *Colour Schemes for the Flower Garden* Introduction.

painter, the photographer, the architect or the designer of stage-sets, the gardener is attempting to create scenes to delight the eye. He has to learn by trial and error, and by studying and appreciating what others have done. In this way he learns how to choose what is good and to discover the means of achieving it. No one is born with perfect taste or with an original imagination: we have to learn by experience; gradually we are able to discriminate and make judgments about what what we see. But of all the arts, I suppose the gardener's is the most ephemeral. Not only are flowers transient and the seasons short, but also a garden takes many years to reach maturity, and needs constant adjustment and creative maintenance to keep it looking right.

There is no mystique about making a garden. It is not a question of green fingers or of hitting on a lucky idea by chance. On the contrary, it is a matter for careful forethought and deliberate choice. No one builds a tower, it is said, without first sitting down and counting the cost. Time spent thinking and planning at the outset is time well spent. Of course, many of us find we have inherited a garden from previous owners, but whether we are re-making from old or whether we are making a completely new garden, we need some kind of an aim, or a scheme: and if not a plan on paper then at least a plan of action. There are some who claim that "design" is not in their vocabulary, but it seems to me only sensible to have some idea what you are going to do before you do it.

A PLAN OF ACTION

It is sensible, too, to tackle the task of garden-making in a logical order. Firstly, as I have said, we must form some idea, or plan, of what we are going to do, and a large part of this book aims to provide some guidance about this. Secondly, we must put our intentions into effect in a methodical manner, and the order is first the bones and then the flesh. By this I mean that we should first form the underlying structure by making the shape of the garden, and undertake any constructional work that is needed. When this is done we can proceed to the planting, to clothe the structure and so put some flesh on the bones of the design. The sequence of operations, therefore, is groundwork, constructional work, preparation for planting, planting, enjoyment.

GROUNDWORK

Any messy groundwork should be undertaken at the outset: any terracing or contouring that requires a mechanical digger; and land drains to improve boggy or waterlogged areas should be put in now. If any earthmoving is undertaken it is important that good topsoil does not become buried under the surface. Nor should poor-quality sub-soil be allowed to come to the surface; it is better to remove unwanted material from the site altogether.

Tall trees can be a problem in small gardens and taking them down is an extremely disruptive process. This is another task best tackled at the start. Any unwanted sycamore or ash tree should be removed as soon as possible: otherwise their seeds will be a recurring nuisance both to you and your neighbours. Like cedars, chestnuts, beech trees and many others, they are far too large for most town gardens. Large trees take vast amounts of water and nutrients from the soil and create problem areas of dry shade where very few kinds of plants will grow. However, if you have plenty of room the shade of a mature tree can be a real asset in the summer. It is not even advisable to keep old fruit trees in an ornamental area of the garden, and certainly you should think twice about making borders beneath them. Picking out windfall apples from amongst roses is no joke, and collecting half-rotten damsons off the lawn is not very pleasant either.

CONSTRUCTION WORK

The third stage is to undertake the paths, walls, paved areas and other "building" work. This can also be a disruptive operation which needs to be done before borders are prepared or planting undertaken. This is perhaps the area of endeavour which will require more careful preparation than any other, and some kind of drawing or paper-work may even be necessary to get the best results.

PREPARATION FOR PLANTING

The fourth stage is to prepare the ground for planting. A careful investigation of the soil should be made, and if it is defective in some way it is worth making an effort to improve it. There is little that can be done to change the acid/alkaline rating of your soil. If you are determined to grow azaleas it is probably easier to move house, since any attempts to create the right conditions on limy soil are just not worth the trouble and expense. But with regard to the texture of the soil, a lot can be done to improve matters and this is certainly worthwhile. Grit or coarse sand added to a clay soil can transform it from a stodgy, clogging mass to a good working medium. On fast-draining, sandy soil the addition of well-rotted farmyard manure or other bulky material with plenty of humus will help to make gardening in such a situation a more rewarding experience.

The introduction of topsoil is often necessary, and care should be taken to ensure that a first-class substance is being supplied: it can easily turn out to be no better than what you have already. Longterm, slow acting fertilizers can be usefully added at this stage, especially on poor soils.

Another major problem to tackle before planting starts is the treatment of weeds. A wide range of chemical weed-killers is available, and every possible effort should be made to eradicate brambles, couch-grass, bindweed (*Calystegia sepium*), docks, ground-elder and horse-tails before planting. Once these persistent weeds get entangled amongst the roots of shrubs or perennials the only answer is to dig up the plant and laboriously remove the weeds from the roots. It is far better to treat the soil thoroughly first; this can mean several applications, possibly using different chemicals for different weeds, and it may take a whole season.

PLANTING

The fifth stage is to undertake the planting, and the right sequence here is to put in the strong functional elements first: screening plants, hedges, trees and the large shrubs. These are all plants that have a definite purpose in the design, or else are so large that they will have a dominant effect. Afterwards we can put in what might be called the decorative infill. All kinds of "plants for pleasure" can go in the spaces left over. And then when all is done, all that remains is to get out the deck-chair, lie back and enjoy it.

But what of the overall scheme, how are we to arrive at what some people call a "design-concept"? This is perhaps the most difficult task of all. What kind of a garden is it to be? A cottage garden, a mini-Sissinghurst, a "room outside", a Versailles *en miniature*, or what? In reality such arbitrary stylistic choices do not have to be made. No one ever starts with a complete blank sheet of paper, with no limitations on what can be done on the site. The style of the house, for example, or its materials are likely to impose some kind of discipline on the design. It makes sense to match bricks to the house, or to match the stone to the cottage. And in a country area the surrounding landscape is bound to have some effect on the style of garden. A heather garden amongst Kent orchards for example is sure to look incongruous.

In new gardens the rectilinear outline of the plot will be painfully apparent, and one of the first tasks will be to find ways of providing privacy, and of softening the edges of the site with greenery, using shrubs, climbers or trees for varied effect. There may be some undesirable features in sight, such as the neighbours' garage or somebody's tatty shed, and in this case a selection of quick-growing shrubs or trees may solve the problem; or alternatively it may be worthwhile erecting a screen which is ornamental in its own right, and in this way the design has commenced.

But the main aim will be to create a restful picture to be seen from the house, not only a blaze of colour in the summer, nor an assortment of "features", but a tranquil scene where the eye can come to rest, a calm retreat from the stresses and tensions of the outside world. To make this picture the perfect English lawn provides the ideal resting place for the eye: smooth, green and the perfect foil for plants of every kind.

At the same time the position of various elements will need to be considered. A paved sitting area – should it be in full sun, in shadow, or in dappled shade? Paths need careful placing: maybe they can lead the eye on invitingly to a further part of the garden; and there are practical considerations too, such as the position of the working areas. Is the nastiest, shadiest corner of the garden actually the best place for the potting and propagation area, if we are going to spend a lot of time there? The far end of the garden may seem the best place for a shed; but although it is as far away as possible, it may still be in full view of the sitting-room windows. If we want to grow vegetables, must they take the traditional bottom-half of the garden and deny us the chance of a longer view from the house?

Maybe we want to make a pool, so that we can enjoy the cool sound of water on hot summer days. Or our view of the garden from a certain position may call for some other kind of focal point or special treatment, or there may be a view, a vista to be made, or "surprises" to be created.

When we come to the planting itself we must take stock of our situation. Is it a sheltered southern garden where we can try all kinds of semi-tender plants, the envy of gardeners in the home counties? Or are we in a frost pocket, or exposed to north and east winds? The choice of the right plants to suit the situation will avoid disappointment later on.

The plants must suit the soil too. Whether acid or alkaline, clay, loam, peat, or sand, the greatest success will be obtained by choosing the plants that flourish in your conditions. A healthy plant is always more rewarding than one which sulks and won't do its best for you. Sunny and shady positions also have to be given due attention. For every situation there is the right plant to fill it. Some plants "flop" attractively onto gravel or paving; others make tough edging plants that can be mown up to and so avoid tiresome lawn edging.

To use plants to best effect visually their shape and texture have to be considered as well as the colour of their flowers. Some plants have scarcely any shape: cranesbill geraniums, for example, are just a leafy mass but others are very distinct: *Thuja orientalis* 'Aurea Nana' for example is almost the shape of an egg, and dome-shapes and columns are quite usual amongst dwarf conifers. Some plants have feathery textures, like artemisias, while others have bold foliage like *Viburnum davidii*.

However, with regard to the scheme as a whole it is best not to attempt too much, especially if space is limited. It is better to do one thing well, rather than several things half-heartedly. Good ideas have to be carried through with conviction if they are to work. One bold effect will have much more impact than several conflicting or hesitant ideas. Above all be consistent.

The Site and its Surroundings

Before we start to do any planning, we may have all kinds of preconceptions about the sort of garden we want to make on our site, and we may have other very definite ideas about what our practical requirements are. But first we need to ask what limitations, or restricting factors, there are on the site which will override anything we want to do with it.

The main limitation, of course, is one of size. When we compare our own gardens with all the great gardens of the past and most of the admirable ones open to view we find that our own are minute in comparison, and that we have to accept the fact that we are working on a totally different scale. What is possible on a vast canvas and what suits a miniature are completely different things, and this is the reason why it is best to aim for one or two simple effects in the garden. Any attempt to cram in a multiplicity of ideas is sure to end in failure. The small size of the garden will also encourage us to be consistent in our approach. Once we begin in a certain vein, certain other things become inappropriate. As an illustration, on formal occasions the clothes we wear are suitably formal, while in other situtations, such as a country walk, or on the beach, other clothes become appropriate. It is the same with interior decoration; success is usually achieved by a determination to exclude anything that does not fit the overall scheme. A good rule is that the details should be made to suit the general idea. For example, a group of heathers and pine trees has one particular kind of atmosphere and it is a totally different one from, say, a walled garden with old-fashioned roses and clipped box hedges; each has its own character. To introduce rocks amongst heathers would seem quite natural, but an irregular scattering of rocks inserted into a walled garden would look quite incongruous. To include too many different kinds of plants and too many different types and colours of building materials can also

9

show a similar lack of singleness of purpose, and produces a restless effect. Some gardens suffer from garden-centre-itis: they have one of everything. Each plant contrasts with the next, with no regard for the unity of the whole. It is one of those cases where "less is more". A little restraint and discipline will achieve a more rewarding result than a policy of "anything goes".

Another limitation on the design of the garden is the existing character of the surroundings. In a rural situation it is a wise precaution to consider the landscape over the fence, and decide whether it should have some influence on the character of the garden. In the small scale landscape of Kent, for instance, with its orchards and hedges, the enclosed character of the garden at Sissinghurst seems exactly right, and indeed it was the conscious intention of its designers to make it appropriate in that way. But I recall the coloured end-papers of a book on conifers which illustrates a garden of heathers and an assortment of green-, yellow- and blue-foliaged conifers; but in the background, with no attempt at screening, is a neighbouring field: a lush green water-meadow with willows in the distance. In this setting the massed heathers seem utterly inappropriate: heathers belong to windswept moors, not to flat, fertile farmland.

The eighteenth century landscape gardeners used to refer to the "Genius of the Place", a phrase that originated from Virgil's *Aeneid*, originally meaning the local deity. But to "consult the Genius of the Place" came to mean what Lancelot Brown described as acquiring "a perfect knowledge of the country and the objects in it", and thus reach an understanding of what it is that gives each landscape its own unique character. An understanding and respect for the local setting is a necessary ingredient for success. It seems only right, for instance, that a precipitous garden in the Lake District should have a character of its own which would be quite different from another garden situated, let us say, by an old mill in a Shropshire valley.

But even if a garden is so enclosed and inward-looking that it can safely ignore its surroundings, there remains the question of what effect the garden has on the surrounding landscape. It has been said that architecture belongs to the passer-by, but there are many places where other people's gardens also belong to the public sphere. Front gardens in the suburbs eventually grow up and almost take over from the houses behind them in creating the street-scene, and considering the quality of the average suburban house this is not a bad thing. In the countryside also garden plantings can have a strong impact on the landscape. There are some situations where to plant yet another row of *leylandii* (the Leyland cypress) is almost an act of vandalism. Some rural areas are

10

peppered with small cottages every half-mile or so (such as the Forest of Dean), and if every cottage surrounds its plot with *leylandii* or the yellowish 'Castlewellan', the whole landscape will eventually change its character, and not for the better.

And for the sake of those who pass by, think twice before you plant a purple-leafed tree. Such trees can be beautiful in themselves, interesting horticulturally and have a place in the garden. But in the English countryside they are just intrusive blobs of colour, which only spoil the landscape. The ideal colour for a tree is green and it is worth remembering that other colours are in fact freaks of nature which have to be artificially propagated to keep them going.

Blue foliage is almost as disturbing. Such trees can be charming in themselves but in the landscape, under a typical grey English sky, blue foliage merely looks dreary.

The safe approach for planting in the context of the landscape is to keep to native trees. Is there any tree more magnificent than a mature oak tree? Of course it is too big for the average garden, but as a more general guideline, aim to plant green trees, with rounded tops. The disruptive effect of conifers with pointed tops can often be seen in the grounds of Victorian estates. Some species of foreign conifers grow taller than our native species and eventually poke their pointed shapes above the general soft line of the surrounding deciduous trees. These tops are then exposed to the wind and often become scrawny and unsightly. The National Trust has now adopted an enlightened policy on its properties of felling such trees as these, which have ceased to have any ornamental value.

In a semi-rural situation or in a village the local materials often predominate and this offers another obvious guideline. The sensible course is to make a virtue of necessity. The use of local stone imposes its own discipline and character: for example, Westmoreland stone in a rockery in a Cotswold village is obviously out-of-place, and yet Cotswold stone tends to flake and disintegrate if used in this way. If you want to grow alpines this may lead to a decision not to make a rockery but to build raised beds with dwarf walls – a use to which Cotswold stone is well suited.

In many cases, the architecture of the house may give some indication about the style of the garden. Again the question of scale must be answered first. Cottage gardens are for cottages, while houses in the grand manner require a suitably grand setting. There should be nothing fussy or mean in the setting of a large house in its own grounds: every element should be generously proportioned. Great Palladian mansions are set off to perfection by vast sweeping lawns and a backdrop of mature trees. The houses and gardens designed by the architect Sir Edwin Lutyens (1869–1944) are an interesting case in point. When, in his early period, his houses were in a kind of Vernacular Revival style, the gardens match them exactly, as at Little Thakeham in Sussex or Deanery Garden in Berkshire. But when his architecture became more grandiose and neo-classical the style of his gardens and terraces did not change to suit. At Ednaston Manor in Derbyshire, or Heathcote, at Ilkley, the terraces in front of the houses seem fussily designed, with their innumerable steps and little walls. Such grand houses would have been set off better by simpler, plainer lines.

But most of us do not live in grand old houses whose style suggests a grand garden to match. We live in average town houses, in comfortable but characterless suburban houses, or in convenient but boring bungalows: not usually because we like the look of them, but because of a lack of any alternative. The design of these houses, we all admit, is weak: it does not inspire us in any particular direction. Almost anything would fit, and even if the house does have any style, the style of the house next door is liable to be quite different.

If this is the case we may feel it is up to us to decide from our own ideas the kind of garden we should introduce to the site. But before we rush into some horticultural preconception, it is advisable to consider the functional needs, such as outdoor living, children's play, washing lines, bin areas and so on, which are discussed in Part 3 of this book, and make sure these needs are catered for, and it is better to make sure the garden is convenient and workable first. There will be plenty of room left for good plants and horticultural interest when these problems are resolved.

CHAPTER 3

Horticultural Preconceptions

Some styles of gardening immediately conjure up an image in the mind, and sometimes one is tempted to adopt one of these as though it was a complete package that would be sure to bring success. Usually these ideas come from seeing the great gardens of the past. We forget that the age that created them has passed and with it have gone all the privileges of their leisured owners who had a small army of cheaply paid gardeners to do all the work for them. It is a nice idea to model one's style on the very best, but first of all one must ask whether the resources are available – not only the finance but the time and effort required to make and maintain this ideal garden, even supposing everything else about it makes it a suitable solution.

One of the things that provokes plenty of admiration in "stately" gardens is a herbaceous border. It looks magnificent from the middle of June to the middle of September, but for the rest of the year what is it? In the winter it is nothing at all, because all the green parts of the plants have died off leaving the roots and shoots dormant under the soil. In spring it is merely a mass of amorphous greenery, which needs weeding, dividing, replanting, staking, tying-back and so on. It is noticeable that herbaceous borders are rarely made where they can be seen from the house, for this very reason. Perhaps the most famous of all herbaceous borders was the one made by Gertrude Jekyll at her own garden at Munstead Wood near Godalming. Although the border is not what it was, it is certainly well documented, with detailed plans and contemporary photographs surviving. But even this one is not visible from the house; it is in its own "compartment" where it can be visited when in its glory or ignored when out of season.

Another kind of gardening which concentrates on plants of only one kind is what the Victorians called a shrubbery. Nowadays it is termed "shrub gardening" or given some other fancy title. The idea of a shrubbery immediately conjures up a picture of grass walks between spotted laurels where the hero of a novel paces up and down in distraught manner. But whereas the aim in the Victorian period was to create sheltered walks where the ladies of leisure could fill in time out of doors, the argument for today's shrub garden is that it is labour-saving and takes very little time to maintain. More significantly for the horticultural trade, shrubs are easy to sell in containers, look attractive at garden centres and can be propagated by the thousand, and bought by hundreds of innocent impulse-buyers on bank holidays and weekends.

The advocates of shrub-gardening conclude that because shrubs are so useful and because many of them are so attractive you must only have shrubs. But to accept such a limitation is a mistake. It is as wrong to have only shrubs as it would be to have only herbaceous plants. Plants should be chosen on merit, to perform a useful purpose, and there is no benefit in straight-jacketing yourself by exluding all but one type of plant. The right plant to do a certain task (such as screening, or ground-cover), to suit the situation (such as limy soil, sheltered corner) and appearance (such as height, colour of foliage, etc.) may well be a shrub, but it may not.

A decision to devote part of the garden exclusively to trees can run into similar difficulties. Sometimes people buy part of a field or a paddock in order to extend their gardens. Unfortunately these are some-times planted as a mini-arboretum with trees of every description, dotted about as if they had been scattered at random by a passing helicopter. The biggest problem with planting tree collections is the difference in size between a freshly-planted sapling and a mature tree. Eventually (and it happens even in the best arboreta) it is discovered that two lovely and equally indispensable specimens have been planted too close; and a decision has to be made: one must go if the other is to show to advantage. There are two possible ways of avoiding this difficulty: one is to plant "fillers" around the tree that is special, which can be felled when the important specimen gets bigger. These fillers can be anything inexpensive or ordinary to fill the gap for the time-being. Another solution, which is possibly better, is to plant a group of trees all of the chosen type and select one of these to fill the entire space in due course. It is important to carry out the planned felling at the right time; (of course sometimes gardens change hands and this plan is forgotten), but the tree will not show its typical shape as a whole if it gets "drawn-up" and becomes all trunk and no crown.

A tree should be planted for a good reason. Perhaps shrubs would do the job better if all we want to do is to fill up spaces between meandering paths. Trees can create shelter; they can be used to mask an ugly building or unwanted view; they can help to hide the exact extent of the piece of ground and screen the boundaries; or to frame a view. It often helps to think about the space left over between the planted areas. Is it a sensible shape? If there is a path, does it lead anywhere? If we think about the effect we want to achieve and the problems we want to solve, rather than fixing on a horticulturally-based idea (be it a shrubbery, arboretum or whatever) we will produce a much more satisfying result. For example, to reduce traffic noise a tall screen may be more effectively provided by very large evergreen shrubs such as rhododendrons than dense tree-planting.

At the other end of the scale are rock-gardens and gardens devoted to alpines. These tiny plants are exquisite in themselves, and it is not surprising that there is a society of enthusiasts dedicated to growing them, but their usefulness in the garden as a whole is limited by their essentially small size. If there is nothing higher than six inches between the house and the back fence, as is the case in one garden I know, then the view from the windows will be that of fence. The impact of an alpine from more than five feet away is minimal and to make an effective garden much larger elements must be used. However, there are many small plants that can be used at the front of the border, especially if the border is edged by paving or gravel rather than grass. They can also look very effective grown in gaps in paving, though too many can be annoying if the area is used for sitting or as a path. They are also ideally suited to troughs, tubs and raised beds, where they can be cossetted and given the conditions they like.

Small rockeries for alpines are not often a success. It is usually all too obvious that a load of lumpy rocks have been introduced and scattered around on the surface of the garden. Real rocks are huge and appear out of the ground like the tip of an iceberg, indicating that there is far more below than above. In the rock garden at Kew, which is one of the few successful ones I can remember, the whole garden has been sunk below the level of the surrounding area, and the ground slopes up steeply on each side of the path. This makes the sudden appearance of rocks, apparently following the contours, seem a realistic possibility. As a rule-of-thumb it is better not to use any rock that has not needed a crane to lift it, and theoretically at least half of the rock should be buried in the ground – but of course that would cost a fortune.

Little remains to be said of other horticulturally-based ideas. Heather gardens have already been mentioned and some people find these interesting in season. Out of flowering season they seem to me most dreary. When the roses in other people's gardens are in full spate and perennials are looking splendid, heathers offer nothing at all.

Conifer gardens were in fashion at one stage and they do offer winter greenery which is some advantage, but apart from that nothing ever happens in a conifer garden. There are no buds, no flowers, no autumn colours to mark the advent or the passing of the seasons. The great variety of strong shapes of conifers also needs careful handling: too often one sees a restless, congested conglomeration of different types of conifer, and a more pleasing effect would be obtained by exercising a little restraint on the number of varieties employed.

Another quite popular idea, which is mainly a matter of horticultural convenience, is to grow plants in island beds of vaguely curved outline. They do have the advantage of being easily worked, since access can be gained from all sides. The scheme at Bressingham, in Norfolk, works fairly well, where there is plenty of space and a large amount of material to be displayed. The island beds there are very long and in many instances consist of the space left over between long winding grass walks. In small, private gardens they are less successful; one difficulty is that such islands seem just to float, as it were, on a sea of grass, not rooted or attached to anything, and a lawn can easily be spoilt by cutting into it in this way. The shape of the lawn will not be satisfactory if it consists merely of what is left over after amoeba-shaped beds have been cut in it. Another problem in small gardens is that it is difficult to create height in an island bed. A tree in an island bed will dwarf the "island": ideally the height of the plants should not exceed the length of the bed, otherwise it looks unbalanced, or top-heavy.

Some people favour the idea of a wild-garden. This is not exactly a horticultural idea, nor is it really an ecological one; but on the other hand it is more than a romantic notion. Apparently it need not mean keeping to British natives, and since most garden plants grow wild somewhere, it seems hard at first to decide how wild-gardening may be defined. As far as I can see, it is a matter of style. The way wild flowers grow in an English hedgerow, or on sunny banks on the edge of a wood is so charming that the apparent simplicity and artlessness seems superior to a conventional garden. Compared with the delicate grace of bluebells and primroses most garden plants seem gross and loud. The difficulty comes in trying to reproduce this natural-looking arrangement in the garden. If we merely dig up a lot of wild flowers (which is illegal in any case), plant them in grass and wait for the result we shall be disappointed. If we happen to have brought the roots of nettles, docks or brambles in with the wild flowers they will soon take over: even grass is too strong a competitor for most flowers. It has to be remembered that in the wild the grass may be stunted by poor, stony soil or be controlled by the regular munching of cows. In fact the whole idea is much more complicated than it seems at first, and to get the desired effect may in the end require more work than a normal garden. But if you have a large meadow to experiment with it may be worth a try. A quite successful example can be seen at Great Dixter in Sussex, but for the average suburban garden or town garden the experiment is best avoided.

It may at first sight appear that the advice given in this chapter is negative, and that I have spent most of it saying "don't", but on consideration you will see that this is not so. The advice is, do not arbitrarily restrict your horticultural palette; make use of the full range of plants that are available and select the best and finest plants for your garden, whether they are shrubs, alpines, perennials or wild flowers.

CHAPTER

4

Stylistic Preconceptions

We are fortunate in this country that a large number of historic gardens have survived almost intact, some going as far back as Tudor times, and the distinct style of these gardens gives them a special charm. It is tempting to want to introduce the style of these gardens to our own, and apply it *en bloc*. My own feeling is that this is fine where it suits the house: a Tudor garden for a Tudor house is perfectly logical, but a Tudor garden for a 1905 spec-builder's semi seems rather silly. The advantages and disadvantages of some styles of the past are worth a brief consideration. I will take the various kinds of formal garden first. The term "formal garden" means those gardens that are characterized by geometrical form: such as straight lines, squares, rectangles, circles and so on.

The Renaissance gardens of Italy have never been successfully transported to this country, although there is no reason in theory why they should not be. Of course, the light is different; in Italy it is bright and clear and shows up the sculpture and stonework to great effect. The astonishing fountains also have a more dramatic effect in the bright sunlight and the cooling effect of water in the heat is something that could not be reproduced in this country. Cool and damp grottos, which provide a few moments refreshment to the ardent garden visitor in Italy also lose their point when transported to our cold climate and become miserably dank and uninviting. But Italian gardens would be nothing without the ornate stonework of their balustrades, steps, fountains and sculpture. Clearly the cost of such garden ornaments is prohibitive today. Italian gardens are essentially architectural: they were built, rather than grown. The horticultural content of most of them is very small; although some are planted with bedding plants, many are content with scarlet geraniums or *Plumbago* in pots, and coloured gravel between the clipped box hedges.

The gardens of the Islamic world are also formal in style. An architectural framework of rectangular compartments, hard surfaces, pools and fountains are essential ingredients of the style. Like the Italian gardens the kind of garden was a response to the climate – an effort to provide a shady cool retreat from the harsh and arid world of the Middle East. Any attempt to recreate such gardens in England is liable to send shivers down the spine on a chilly day: one can reproduce the forms easily enough but inevitably the atmosphere is lost.

The great French gardens were perhaps a little less densely packed with masonry than those of Italy but what they may lack in that respect they make up for in size. What underlay the great gardens of seventeenth century France was a desire to dominate the world with geometry: to be vast in scale was the essential thing. There are several gardens in England which have tried to copy the style, most of which were made in the nineteenth century. Cliveden, in Buckinghamshire, for example, has a very large parterre, but some people think it fails to dominate its setting, which is on rather high ground overlooking a bend of the river Thames, and for this reason it is not a complete success. And which of us today has all those acres to lay out on such a scale?

However, the gardens of seventeenth century England were much smaller, and usually consisted of a series of rectangular compartments. Like their Italian and French counterparts they were planted with clipped box hedges and yew trees clipped into interesting shapes. The amount of good plant material available in those days was limited, by modern standards, and there is every reason to suppose that coloured gravel was often used in these gardens just as it was abroad, to occupy the spaces between the little box hedges.

When formal gardening was revived in the nineteenth century bedding plants were used extensively to make a more colourful picture, a highly labour intensive procedure which eventually became too expensive. The solution adopted at Hidcote in Gloucestershire was to retain a formal arrangement of compartments with beds still edged in some cases with dwarf box, but the borders themselves planted with a profusion of herbaceous material, shrubs, sub-shrubs and annuals, a lively mixture, which contrasted with the formal framework into which it was placed. This was extremely successful, in as much as the horticultural and visual elements were held in balance. This approach was followed later by Harold Nicolson and his wife Victoria Sackville-West at Sissinghurst and by Norah Lindsay in her alterations at Blickling Hall, and by scores of admiring garden-makers in many places since.

One advantage of the style is that the framework of Yew and Box remains green and has sufficient shape to give interest during the winter period. A small garden can be treated as just one compartment or "room", or a slightly larger garden as two or three. The style is perfectly suitable for plots of simple geometrical outline; its shapes are easily appreciated by anyone, while its beds and borders give scope to beginners and keen plantsmen alike. On the other hand it must be remembered that this is an eclectic style, borrowed from the past. While it is perfectly suited to old Cotswold manors like Hidcote, its suitability for the suburbs is questionable.

To some extent style is a matter of personal inclination, and some people think that although formal gardens are clear, intelligible and logical, like all such things they can pall eventually by becoming too obvious. Symmetry has its attractions, but so does an element of mystery. The poet Alexander Pope (1688–1744) ridiculed gardens where

> Grove nods at Grove, each Ally has a Brother,
> And half the Platform just reflects the other.

If every element of the design can be clearly seen from the dining-room window, who will bother to go out into the garden to see it? Even a small garden can be designed to give the feeling there is something more to be discovered, and can give a sense of movement; whereas the formal approach tends to be more static and rests in itself.

There are many styles of gardening in which geometry plays a much less prominent part, and which provide a more natural and less architectural effect. The eighteenth century English Landscape movement is an obvious example. Once again, an important characteristic of this style was the enormous scale of operations, since in many ways it was not so much a way of gardening but more a countryside improvement programme. The whole landscape, as seen from the steps of the great eighteenth century houses, was altered to conform to ideal standards of beauty; eye-sores and utilitarian items were screened and the rest was groomed and improved to achieve visual perfection. Although there can scarcely be anyone who can afford to work at this scale today, some of the same principles still apply. Even in a small plot we may well wish to screen out the world beyond our own fence, and there is no reason why one should not wish to create a green, restful, naturalistic picture in the garden rather than use it as a storehouse of flowering plants.

In the last half of the nineteenth century many Woodland gardens were created to house the vast number of new plant species which were being introduced at that time by plant collectors and travellers. The most colourful of these were the rhododendrons, and the woodland

setting provided just the right amount of shelter and light to suit rhododendrons. Unfortunately insufficient thought was given in many cases
to the layout of paths through such areas of woodland, and in many
of these great collections the paths twist and wind in a way which
completely disorientates visitors, who end up feeling lost and unsure
whether they have seen the whole garden or not. But it is important
for those who are keen on rhododendrons to bear in mind that many
of them can only be grown successfully where there is sufficient shade,
shelter and moisture, which a woodland situation provides.

It is sometimes suggested that the English Landscape style was partly
derived from sketches and descriptions sent back by travellers from the
Far East, since the gardens of China and Japan are also in a naturalistic
style. No-one in the West, as far as I can recall, has made a serious
effort to copy the Chinese style of gardening, but many attempts have
been made to reproduce the gardens of Japan, even though these were
opened to Westerners much later than those of China. The results in
this country have been generally disappointing – and the only one I
have seen in the USA (Golden Gate Park, San Francisco) was no better.
Japanese gardens are so rich and complex and the ideas and concepts
behind them are so deeply imbedded in Japanese culture that it is
virtually impossible for an outsider to make a genuine-looking Japanese
garden. But even if a Japanese designer is used to lay out the garden
initially, as has been done, the garden will still need traditionally trained
Japanese gardeners to maintain it: clipping pine needles, training the
miniature trees, shaping azalea bushes to rounded forms, and so on. It
is said that one Japanese visitor to a so-called Japanese garden in
England, searching for a compliment to his host, remarked "We have
nothing like it in Japan".

It becomes clear, therefore, that to transport a style out of its
cultural, climatic and social setting is extremely difficult: such a project
offers a mine field of possible errors. It is so much safer to stay on
home ground and work in a style we fully understand, one which is
generated by our own climate, our soil, or our own requirements of
day to day use.

A modern style of gardening to suit modern houses has never really
caught on in Britain. But then modern architecture has not been very
popular as a domestic style either. People are happy enough to work
in modern factories, schools and offices but when they get home they
seem to want something with older roots, and something less coolly
and rationally conceived. Another factor is that wealthy families in this
country (who can afford houses and gardens on an enviable scale)
frequently inherit an older property, and those whose wealth is more

21

recent, wishing to appear long-established, prefer to buy an older property rather than commission a new one. Because of the association of ideas, "ordinary" people get the impression that wealth (and therefore, happiness) and a traditional style belong together. So it is that those who can afford to garden on a grand scale (and provoke the admiration of others) usually have a Cotswold manor or a Georgian country house, and a traditional style of gardening is perfectly sensible for them. But vast numbers of people live in modern houses, with modern furniture and have a modern car, and a well-designed garden in this situation should not be historical but should be modern. This has long been accepted in the United States and in South America.

The work of Roberto Burle Marx (b. 1909) in Brazil has been of outstanding importance in developing a style derived from modern painting and suitable to accompany modern buildings, and yet of the highest horticultural significance. In California, designers such as Thomas Church and Garret Eckbo, have also worked in a modern idiom, creating gardens in a climate which allows outdoor space to be considered as an extension of the living space of the house. Unfortunately the climate in this country does not allow this to happen to the same extent. Much as one would like to lie on a lounger by the swimming pool in the sunshine, the amount of time when this is possible is small and it tends to occur at unforeseen moments – never at the weekend it seems. Nevertheless, those precious moments when meals can be taken in the garden are worth planning for, I think. Gardening in this country tends to be considered as an activity, a hobby in fact, rather than a kind of routine maintenance (like dusting or hoovering the house) which is done to provide a pleasant background to family life. But the fact that for most of the summer one can only keep warm outside by moving about is probably the reason why this is so.

A NOTE ABOUT LATIN PLANT NAMES

In the next part of this book we shall begin to discuss plants in some detail. Unfortunately it is impossible to do this without using the names by which they are known to gardeners, and by which they are offered by the horticultural trade, and these names are almost all in Latin.

The need to use these Latin names becomes inescapable for any serious gardener. But don't worry about the pronunciation: even the experts pronounce them differently, particularly in this country. Just make a stab at it and you'll be all right.

Every discipline has its jargon, and the jargon of horticulture is a good deal less frightening than that of computing, economics or even the inside of cars. In any case the jargon in this book has been kept to an absolute minimum.

Plant names follow a very simple system. Every plant has a pair of names, just as people do, only in the case of plants the group name comes first – Smith John instead of John Smith. Many Latin names have passed into common usage, such as Chrysanthemum, Dahlia, Rhododendron, Magnolia, Laburnum and so on, and in these cases the Latin name and the ordinary one is the same. But a second name is used to identify exactly which Magnolia or Laburnum is being referred to. Thus we find, for example, *Magnolia grandiflora*, literally the large-flowered Magnolia, and *Magnolia sinensis*, the Chinese Magnolia. *Magnolia sinensis*, is called a *species*, indicating a *specific* kind of Magnolia. The word 'species' is the same in the singular as it is in the plural. (There is no such thing as a *specie*, a word which sometimes appears in nurserymen's catalogues.) The specific name, in this case *grandiflora*, is always spelt with a small first letter, even if it commemorates someone's name. *Magnolia sargentiana*, for example, refers to Charles Sargent (1841–1927), an American botanist.

Magnolias as a group are referred to as a *genus* (the plural is *genera*.) The first half of the plant name is therefore termed the *generic* name, and is always spelt with a capital letter. Unfortunately the word *genus* is untranslatable: one cannot use the word Family because this is used for the next tier of botanical grouping. The Magnolia Family, for instance, contains not only the magnolias but also the genus *Liriodendron*, the tulip trees. The Magnolia Family in Latin is the *Magnoliaceae*.

This two-name system was first adopted by the famous Swedish naturalist Carl von Linné (1707–78) always known by his Latinised

23

name Linnaeus. Today the naming of plants is governed by an International Code of Nomenclature, which sorts out problems such as which name to use in case of confusion. Supposing for instance two plant-collectors, unknown to each other, discover the same plant species growing in different parts of the Himalaya and each give it a different name: the rule here is that the first published name is the one to be adopted. This is why in botanical books the plant name is always followed by the name of the botanist who published the name and often the date of publication: e.g. *Magnolia grandiflora* L. 1753, which means that *Linnaeus* (L. for short) published the name in 1753. But gardeners don't have to trouble their heads with this kind of detail.

The first published name is adhered to even if it is illogical, unpronounceable, misleading, or mis-spelt. For example, *Larix decidua* literally the Deciduous Larch is very logical but not specific, since all larches are deciduous. Similarly, Philip Miller was mistaken in thinking *Lonicera × americana* came from America, but nevertheless the name must stand. And the genus *Stewartia* commemorates the Earl of Bute, who advised Princess Augusta about Kew Gardens in the eighteenth century, actually he spelt his name Stuart, but *Stewartia* it is.

The Code also sorts out other problems such as when two botanists have inadvertently given the same name to different plants. It then becomes necessary to change one of them. This tends to be annoying to gardeners, but if the botanists have a system it is only sensible for them to stick to it.

Many garden plants have a third name (such as *Magnolia grandiflora* 'Exmouth') and this indicates a plant which has been selected for some horticultural reason. It will have no significant botanical difference, but offers something of value to the gardener. Most of these plants do not breed true from seed, whereas the species does. Such plants are called "cultivars", which is a piece of jargon, short for "cultivated variety". Cultivar names are always placed between single quotes, and are printed in ordinary type, not in italics. Every important word in the cultivar name must have a capital letter, 'Alba Superba', for example. Older cultivar names tend to be in Latin, but more recently Latin names have been avoided in favour of names in modern languages, such as 'Eddie's White Wonder', 'Osakasuki' or 'Boskoop'.

When a plant is a cross between two natural species it is termed a hybrid, and a multiplication sign is placed before the specific name; for example, *Magnolia × soulangiana*, which is a cross between *Magnolia denudata* and *Magnolia liliiflora*. Sometimes, however, the hybridizing may be so complicated or so uncertain that no specific name can be given, at least until the botanists get to work on it, and in such cases the specific name is dropped as, for instance, in *Magnolia* 'Michael Rosse'.

Some plants have a third Latin name as in *Magnolia campbellii mollicomata*, which becomes rather a mouthful. This means that there are significant botanical differences from *Magnolia campbellii* itself (which is called the "type") but not sufficient to justify describing *mollicomata* as a separate species. Instead it is referred to as a sub-species.

A mere handful of horticultural terms have been used in this book. Here are some definitions.

Evergreen means the plant retains its leaves during the winter, whereas *deciduous* means it loses them.

Conifers are trees of basically cone-shaped outline, such as firs, spruces and cypresses; but some such as the pines are not particularly conical, and in fact the term "conifer" is used for any tree which is not a *broad-leaved* tree. Conifers instead have needles (pines, larches, silver firs, spruces) or flattened, scale-like sprays (cypresses, false cypresses, junipers, thujas). Most conifers are evergreen, but some such as the larches are deciduous. Broad-leaved trees may be either deciduous or evergreen.

A *tree* or *shrub* is a plant which has woody stems. The stems of a *herbaceous* plant, however, die down in winter, but the plant survives underground. *Perennial* plants are often herbaceous, in which case they come up every year (with luck!), but some perennials (such as *hellebores*) are evergreen but not woody.

Annuals are sown, grow to maturity, flower, set seed and die, all in the course of one season, or year. *Biennials* are not quite so short-lived: their life cycle spans two years instead of one.

PART

2

LOOKING ·AT THE· GARDEN

CHAPTER
5

Clothing the Boundaries

The first thing we can do in almost any garden is to clothe the boundaries with greenery. In many small gardens it is all too obvious that they consist of a plain rectangular plot, and immediate benefit is gained by planting climbers and shrubs around the perimeter of the garden, and this is best done as soon as possible, because of the time it takes for them to grow.

Of course there are exceptions: some gardens back on to open country, or golf courses or some other feature which is worth retaining. But this kind of situation is unusual: normally the outlook is enclosed, and unless the garden is well planted the view from the house is of the back fence and houses beyond it. There is no satisfaction, in my opinion, in a plot whose limit and extent is so clearly distinguishable and to soften the boundaries with greenery and make them less defined helps straightaway to make a more pleasant outlook.

It is necessary, I think, to have something substantial between one's own garden and the one next door. A chain-link fence is something and nothing; it may keep out the neighbours' dog, if you are lucky, but it does little else. It is worthwhile having a screen which is high enough to provide adequate privacy, in other words one at least five foot six inches (1.7m) high. The sight of next door's washing line, the cauliflowers in their vegetable patch and the feeling that your neighbours' eyes are boring into your back, will be features of your garden, unless you erect a definite barrier between you. It is possible to wear what might be described as mental blinkers and only see one's own patch, but a look through the view-finder of a camera will reveal the true picture – in fact a good photograph of your garden may be impossible if the background is too distracting.

In small gardens it is better not to plant a hedge; not only will it take up useful space in itself, but in addition it may be difficult to provide room between the back of the border and the hedge, to stand and clip it. A hedge draws out useful nutrients from the soil and another disadvantage is that it will take several years to grow, whereas a wall or fence is immediate in its effect. A wall is undoubtedly the best kind of boundary, whether built of brick or, in country districts, of local stone. But the cost of this will admittedly be very high, and many of us are forced to take second best and erect a wooden fence. It is better to avoid the interwoven "larch-lap" type of fence because the only way to prevent these rotting away is to treat them regularly with preservative, and if they are giving support to climbing plants or are hidden by shrubs in the way this chapter envisages, this will not be possible. It is better to have a fence where the timber members are of reasonable thickness, substantial enough to last a few years, such as a close boarded fence, or one made from boards fixed on alternate sides of the support members. For increased durability one must ensure that the posts are well secured into the ground, and that there is a slight gap between the fence itself and the soil so that the timber is not constantly damp. Wattle hurdles also make a good boundary, and are a more pleasing background than an array of geometrical timber members, but they are only available in certain parts of the country. In very narrow town gardens the claustrophobic effect of a tall fence can be reduced by making the upper part of trellis-work instead of solid wood. Climbers can then be induced to grow on the trellis.

If our climbers are to be effective in their task all the year round, a large proportion of them must be evergreen. The choice of evergreen shrubs is bewildering, but in contrast the range of evergreen climbers is quite small. One of the best is Ivy, and although this may sound at first an uninteresting solution there is, in fact, a fascinating range of attractive ivies. The leaves come in a wide range of shapes, and the different kinds of variegation can provide much brighter colours than the normal dark green. One of my favourites is *Hedera helix* 'Buttercup', and on this variety the new leaves are a bright yellow colour which contrasts with the older leaves that are mid-green. 'Cavendishii' is another excellent variegated ivy, with an irregular creamy-yellow edge to the leaves; but this variety is not commonly offered yet. 'Gold Heart', however, is quite easily obtainable, but its stiff habit makes it a little less attractive.

It is important when buying ivies to make sure that they are of the "vining" type, which will climb in the way one expects, and will not be the "self-branching" kind which have been developed for the indoor plant market, and may be reluctant to climb. 'Adam', 'Eva' and 'Harald' are all prettily marked ivies, but they all come into the self-branching category and so are not likely to do what we want in this chapter. 'Glacier' which is a pretty grey-leafed ivy, is also sold in vast quantities as a pot plant, but this is more vigorous and can be used as a climber; unusually severe frosts, however, can damage 'Glacier' – despite its name. For much larger leaves and for covering large areas, there are two excellent forms of *Hedera colchica* (sometimes called the Persian Ivy): 'Dentata Variegata' which has irregular yellow edges to its leaves, and 'Sulphur Heart' which is perhaps more sophisticated with green leaves splashed with lime-yellow in the centre. 'Sulphur Heart' is sometimes sold under the more memorable name of 'Paddy's Pride'. There are two interesting ivies with very dark leaves which are called *Hedera helix* 'Atropurpurea' and 'Glymii'; they are distinctly purple in the winter, but revert to green in the summer; both of them are climbers. Even plain green ivies offer a surprising range of different leaf shapes. The leaves of *Hedera helix* 'Deltoidea', for example, are curiously rounded, and almost heart-shaped: apparently in America it is known as the Sweetheart Ivy; 'Sagittifolia' has arrow-shaped leaves; while 'Pedata' is the Bird's Foot Ivy. 'Green Ripple' and 'Ivalace' are also good distinct forms, but 'Neilson', which is similar and usually offered as 'Neilsonii', is a self-branching form.

For very large leaves the Irish Ivy 'Hibernica', is certainly the most impressive, though *Hedera colchica* 'Dentata' is good as well: like the two variegated forms of the Persian Ivy, its leaves do not have the usual three or five lobes, but come instead to a single point.

The great advantage of the dark green forms is that they provide a perfect background to other plants. Some of these forms have a tendency to revert to ordinary ivy. I find 'Goldheart' does so regularly. Any branch which has done so should be removed straightaway since it will probably be more vigorous than the selected form and is therefore liable to take over.

There is only one other evergreen climber worth growing in small gardens, but it is not very often seen. It is called *Pileostegia viburnoides* and, as with delphiniums and chrysanthemums, there is no common English name; one just has to get used to using the Latin one. This Pileostegia has dark leathery leaves, long and pointed in shape. It has some resemblence to a Viburnum as the second part of the name (the *specific* name) suggests; its white flowers in panicles appear in late summer; it is a plant well worth trying.

There are several evergreen shrubs which can be grown as if they were climbers, and do not mind being clipped back when they reach out too far. Pyracanthas are a good example, and are very useful for this purpose, since they offer flowers and brightly coloured berries in

31

addition to being evergreen. In theory pyracanthas can also be called firethorns, an English name, which is a rough translation of the Latin one. But in practice hardly anyone actually uses this name, and if you do start talking about "Firethorns" to a more knowledgeable gardener he or she will probably give you a rather pitying smile. When selecting pyracanthas it is better to avoid the more bushy species, because the flowers and berries occur mostly on the new growth and if this has to be cut back after flowering there will be no berries in the autumn. Some of the selected forms such as 'Orange Glow' and 'Watereri' are the most likely to be satisfactory, while *Pyracantha atalantioides* will probably be too vigorous since it can form a small tree. In some districts the birds come and strip the bushes of their berries which otherwise would have lasted all through the winter, and in this case one should plant varieties with yellow berries since the birds do not find these so attractive. *Pyracantha rogersiana* 'Flava' or *P.* 'Soleil d'Or' are both good yellow-berried forms.

Cotoneasters can also be grown against a wall or fence. The well-known *Cotoneaster horizontalis* is perfectly happy to be pruned back when it projects too far, and its appearance is so unlike any other plant that it should not be despised for being commonly seen. In November, *Cotoneaster horizontalis* is covered in berries, and is likely to be one of the best things in the garden. There is also a variegated form. Another excellent choice would be *Cotoneaster lacteus* with leathery leaves which are larger than those of the average Cotoneaster. Several other species could be tried, particularly those which are fairly erect in the way they grow, compared with the more common wide-arching kinds. *C. microphyllus*, normally a low-growing species, can be trained to grow up a wall: however it would be happier planted at the top of a retaining wall, and allowed to hang down. There are many other ever-green shrubs that could be trained against a fence or a wall, and slow-growing species which do not require perpetual cutting back are clearly the ones to go for. One I particularly like which I grow in my own garden is *Bupleurum fruticosum*, which has greenish-yellow flowers in July and sea-green foliage, but it does need a little training.

Another unusual shrub which I also grow against a wall is *Itea ilicifolia*, which has slightly spiny leaves and interesting hanging catkins in August and September; they are greenish and between six inches and ten inches (15–25 cm) long. It can be grown free-standing but in most areas it prefers the shelter provided by a wall or fence. If we want a variegated shrub to carry out this task of clothing the boundary the first choice will be the excellent *Euonymus fortunei* 'Variegatus', a very similar shrub to *E.* 'Silver Queen', but one which can be persuaded to climb, though rather slowly.

Walls, and even fences give protection, and for this reason many attractive shrubs which like a sheltered or warm position can be planted on a south facing boundary. Several examples of such desirable, ever-green and flowering shrubs, which benefit from this position, can be found in the genus *Ceanothus*. There are no other large shrubs with such splendid blue flowers, and this makes them especially valuable. Outside of the favoured south west where severe frosts are unlikely, it is best to go for the hardiest varieties, and amongst these are *Ceanothus* 'Autumnal Blue', *C.* 'Delight', and *Ceanothus* × *veitchianus*.

Sometimes one sees *Garrya elliptica* used as a wall shrub, but I do not recommend it for the average garden. Although it is interesting when it produces its strange, grey, tassel-like catkins in January or February, for the rest of the year it looks dreadfully dull and dusty, and eventually grows too large for town or suburban gardens. I would rather give space to *Buddleia crispa* a lovely deciduous shrub which is grown for its almost white foliage. Its pale lilac flowers are not so large nor so overpoweringly scented as the ordinary *Buddleia*. It needs to be tied back if grown against a wall.

Amongst our shrubs and climbers that we plant to clothe and soften the boundary, we shall surely want a proportion of plants with attractive flowers, even though they may be deciduous. Climbing roses will be our first choice as they are the finest of all climbing plants. There are so many different varieties that I cannot possibly make a fair selection here. However, a few names spring to mind which I will mention: rather an arbitrary selection, but all good. 'Albertine', an old favourite, can be relied on to smother itself with scented pink flowers year after year. The overwhelming quantity of bloom entirely makes up for it not being recurrent, and the glossy foliage has excellent cover ability. For continuity of flower there are two good roses with no thorns which does make pruning a more painless procedure: 'Zéphirine Drouhin' is quite a vivid pink, and 'Kathleen Harrop' its paler, shell pink counter-part, which is a little less vigorous, but tall enough for our purpose. For continuity of bloom another good choice would be 'New Dawn'; its flowers are quite a pale shade of pink and fragrant and it also has good foliage; perfect for cottage gardens. Quite a different rose with an old-world character is 'Climbing Pompon de Paris'. It is a miniature rose which has taken it into its head to become a climber. The flowers, needless to say, are like small round pompons, bright pink against dark green foliage. The original miniature dates back to the 1830s, but when the climbing form appeared is unknown. For a north-facing position,

'Madame Grégoire Staechelin' is a magnificent pink rose, and smells like sweet peas.

The only yellow climber I grow is 'Leverkusen', raised in Germany in 1954. The flowers are semi-double, in a pleasant lemon shade that fades to white, but it is less recurrent than I was led to believe. 'Golden Showers' is, I am told, much more reliably continuous. Its flowers are more double, modern in shape, but a pleasing shade of yellow.

'Climbing Iceberg' is a reliable white, the climbing version of the excellent floribunda. For something utterly different in every possible way 'Sander's White Rambler' provides masses of small white flowers, cascading in clusters, in the style of the old 'Dorothy Perkins', with small glossy leaves and good fragrance.

There are a few roses with more unusual colours, and of these I must mention 'Guinée', which is the most wonderful dark red rose there is. It is so dark than it needs a pale background to show to advantage, and its scent is as exotic as the colour. For a curious mauvy-blue colour one should try 'Veilchenblau', which is happy in a shaded position. The older flowers fade to a greyish-lilac colour, and blooms are in clusters, rambler-style.

Of course many shrub roses are perfectly suited to being grown against a boundary wall or fence, but not all are tall enough for our needs. The rugosa group provide ideally dense foliage and of these 'Roseraie de l'Haÿ' (which is double purple-red) 'Sarah van Fleet' (in clear pink) and 'Alba', are splendid examples, and tall enough for our purpose. But there are many other shrub roses which are six feet (2 m) high, with dense foliage and good flowers.

If roses are our first choice for climbing plants of floral value, *Clematis* come a very close second. Again, only a few can be mentioned here, and these will be varieties which are easy to grow. My favourites are the late flowering kinds – the ones which do not start to bloom before July, such as the named varieties of *Clematis viticella:* the deep red 'Abundance', the white 'Alba Luxurians' or 'Kermesina', which is crimson. These have a richness of colour and yet a simple charm which makes them more appealing in some ways than the larger and more eye-catching hybrids. The vexed question of pruning is easily answered for these late-flowering varieties: they should be cut down to about eighteen inches (45cm), or even less, at the end of the winter. The same rule applies to Jackmanii types, such as the rich purple, 'Jackmanii Superba', 'Jackmanii Alba', 'Comtesse de Bouchaud', in soft rose pink, or 'Perle d'Azur' which is pale blue. There are several other attractive named varieties, which are late flowering and can be treated in just the same way, such as the lovely white 'Huldine'; for a sunny position,

'Ernest Markham' which is petunia red; and 'Hagley Hybrid' in dusky pink.

There are two other late flowering species which must be mentioned: *Clematis orientalis*, which is often called the orange-peel clematis, because of the thickness of its yellow petals (although, in *Clematis* the coloured parts of the flower are strictly sepals, not petals). The foliage is ferny and prettily divided, amongst which the nodding flowers appear on their slender stalks. 'Old Man's Beard' of our native hedgerows is a wild clematis gone to seed, and *Clematis orientalis* also has silky seed heads – though much more refined ones than 'Old Man's Beard'. *Clematis tangutica* also has good seed heads, and yellow nodding flowers.

The great advantage of all these varieties of *Clematis* is that they can be grown with and through other plants, so that one can double up on the amount of interest and floral display without taking up any more space in the garden; and there is no fear of a clematis of this type overpowering its companions or host, since every year it will be cut down to size.

The spring-flowering clematis species are even more easy-care: you don't have to do anything with them at all. If they do get completely out of hand after several years and become such a vast tangled mass that something has to be done about it, you should attack them in May reducing them to the required size so they have plenty of time to make new flowering shoots. The typical species is *Clematis montana*, of which *rubens* is a good form. The named varieties come in white or pink: 'Alexander' is white and 'Elizabeth' and 'Tetrarose' are pink. They are all very vigorous and build themselves up into a kind of heap which is useful for smothering unsightly sheds and garages. They are too strong to grow with other climbers or shrubs satisfactorily. They can be trained to grow up into a suitable tree, but it has to be a good strong tree to cope with the stranglehold of these spring-flowering clematis species. *Clematis chrysocoma* is similar to *montana*, and pale pink, and has the advantage of being a bit less rampant.

By all means try the large-flowered hybrids, such as 'Nelly Moser', 'The President' and 'Lasurstern', but they will only do their best if they are carefully pruned, disentangled and selectively cut back in February, frankly a fiddly business, worthwhile for the keen gardener, but too time-consuming for many people.

Another climber which can be grown in amongst other things is *Eccremocarpus scaber*, and since it comes from Chile it is not surprising that it is liable to be killed in a hard winter; however I grew it for several years against a west-facing wall at our previous house, where it twined its way through climbing roses. It produces plenty of seeds so it can be treated as an annual if necessary. The unusual orange tubular flowers are produced over a very long period right into the autumn.

The Golden Hop, *Humulus lupulus* 'Aurea', also likes a warm position. It is grown for the colour of its foliage, and its brilliant yellow leaves look marvellous scrambling over an evergreen shrub, or else combined with a dark green ivy such as *Hedera colchica* 'Dentata'. It is extremely vigorous.

Vines are scramblers as well, which climb with the aid of tendrils, and like the Hop they are grown for the beauty of their foliage. Even the ordinary grape vine *Vitis vinifera* has pretty foliage, but the purple version, 'Purpurea', is more distinctive and looks particularly effective when combined with silver foliage. The most remarkable vine is *Vitis coignetiae*, with huge leaves which turn to every shade of crimson and red in the autumn. It is very vigorous and apt to climb to the tops of trees once it gets going. Closely related to these vines is another beautiful foliage plant, named *Parthenocissus henryana;* this is a most refined climber whose leaves have five pointed leaflets with unusual white veins that are even more prominent in the autumn when the leaves turn bright red.

But there is something else to be enjoyed in the garden besides beautiful flowers and pretty foliage, and this is scent. With many flowers you must put your nose right into them before you can appreciate their perfume; not so the honeysuckles, who generously fling their fragrance into the air, and on balmy summer nights it is quite intoxicating. I don't actually grow any honeysuckles myself, but I do get the benefit of our neighbour's wild one which clambers over the wall that divides us. This is *Lonicera periclymenum*, of which there are two cultivated forms: 'Belgica' and 'Serotina', otherwise known as Early Dutch and Late Dutch Honeysuckle respectively.

Lonicera japonica has the advantage of being evergreen and, as it is rather rampant, it is good for covering unsightly buildings. But it can get out of control and become rather an unsightly object itself and unless you give it an annual grooming it will eventually become an untidy tangled mess. Its flowers are paler than our own native honeysuckle, but they are just as fragrant and occur over a far longer period. The usual form is *L. japonica* 'Halliana', but there is also a pretty variegated form 'Aureoreticulata', with leaves marked with a yellow, net-like pattern. Unfortunately this form hardly produces any blooms – so of course if there are no blooms, there will be no scent.

You cannot have everything in one plant, and so it is that the honeysuckles with the best flowers have virtually no scent: *Lonicera*

× *brownii* 'Fuchsoides', and *L.* 'Dropmore Scarlet', both have more brilliantly coloured flowers than other varieties, first in July and again in the autumn. With bright yellow flowers there are the very decorative *Lonicera tragophylla*, and the closely related *Lonicera* × *tellmanniana*, both of which do best in a shaded position.

Perhaps the best compromise for a Honeysuckle with both flowers and scent is the *Lonicera* × *americana*, a hybrid between two European species. Its flowers are pale pinkish yellow, and are borne in the greatest profusion in midsummer.

Honeysuckles are not the only climbers for a north-facing wall or fence: most of the clematises mentioned in this chapter are perfectly happy with any aspect. Of course there is no reason why clematis and honeysuckles cannot be grown together, either to give two seasons of interest in one spot, or else in flowering together in an exciting combination of colours.

Summer Jasmine also has an amazing scent. If Honeysuckle fills the whole air with its heady sweetness, Jasmine tends rather to make a grab at you as you pass by, smelling like the world's most exotic talcum-powder. Summer Jasmine, *Jasminum officinale*, needs quite a lot of space: this is another plant that is likely to become a big tangled mass of ferny foliage. The flowers are white and delicate, not very remarkable except for their wonderful scent. Winter Jasmine, *Jasminum nudiflorum*, will need some support if it is going to reach any height or provide adequate covering to a fence or a wall; unless it is tied up it flops all over the place. It may be common, but it is also unique in providing its perky little yellow flowers in December and any milder weather later on. Well trained and neatly hoisted up it makes a most graceful display of arching branches.

The climbing Hydrangea, *H. petiolaris*, is happy in sun or shade. Like several other plants in this chapter it may need a little support until it gets into the habit of climbing or clinging, which it does with aerial roots. The flowers are the lace-cap kind, in a greenish shade of white, not very long lasting. Compared with some of the untidy scramblers and sprawlers I have mentioned, *Hydrangea petiolaris* is a paragon of elegance and neatness. There is also an evergreen climbing Hydrangea, a plant not often seen, or offered for sale: *H. serratifolia*. Its flowers are more columnar in shape than those of *petiolaris* but they only appear on the bushy roots lower down, not the climbing ones. It is happy in a shaded position, but nevertheless it is not suitable for the very coldest localities.

Climbers are the most neglected of all groups of plants, and to do justice to the wide range of varieties is not possible in this short chapter.

But their usefulness in furnishing the garden is undeniable. We need no longer be surrounded by a severe, cell-like arrangements of fences or walls, we can transform them with what might be called a "living wallpaper" of greenery, and floral displays of the greatest variety and distinction.

CHAPTER
6

Screening

Having transformed our boundaries with a marvellously varied array of greenery, with flowers of every colour and foliage of every description, there are still likely to be objects in view in most town and suburban situations which are unwanted: an ugly garage or the houses in the road at the back. We are rather an antisocial race, and the art of living together in an urban situation is something we have never really acquired, in spite of the efforts of Modern architects. We prefer the romantic illusion that we are the only ones around; if our home is our castle, set in splendid isolation, then our garden is our demesne, or so we like to think.

There are some cases where no amount of screening can improve the situation. Nearby buildings more than four storeys high require something of the scale of a forest tree to blot them out of sight, and if you do plant such a tree, firstly you have to wait half a lifetime for it to grow, and secondly, the tree will have completely filled the garden by then, and blotted out all the light in the house. Although there are situations like this, where what cannot be put right has to be tolerated, there are many other cases where a quick growing tree will make all the difference to the appearance of the garden. This may be another case where the owner may be able to keep his eyes down and mentally blot out the offending object, but the camera's eye will reveal all.

What we are looking for ideally is an evergreen tree, which is fast-growing, but will not end up too large. Unfortunately there is no such tree that fits this description. The ubiquitous *leylandii*, for example, grows impressively fast, as everyone knows, but it keeps on growing. Some of the earliest specimens are now about a hundred feet (30m) tall, and this means that ours will have to be clipped, which may be acceptable for a hedge but in isolated specimens can only result in ugly mis-shapen trees.

39

Perhaps the fastest of all are members of the genus *Eucalyptus*, of which *E. gunnii* is the one most commonly seen. But these are usually too thin and scraggy to be of any value for screening; in fact they often look so scrawny, with drab, lifeless, adult foliage that they can only be described as giant weeds fit to be pulled out. The way to grow *Eucalyptus gunnii* is to keep it as a bush by clipping it, and so retain the attractive, blue, juvenile foliage, which is so good for flower arrangement. Even so, every twenty years or so there will be an extra hard frost which will kill all the eucalyptuses including *gunnii*.

Most of the conifers normally recommended as fast-growing will become giants eventually. *Abies grandis, Pseudotsuga menziesii* (the Douglas Fir), *Picea sitchensis* (the Sitka spruce) which are all splendid when well grown, can grow three feet (1m) in a year, which should be fast enough for anyone; but since they reach a hundred and fifty feet (50m) in maturity they are no good for average gardens. *Sequoia sempervirens* (the Redwood) and *Tsuga heterophylla* (Western Hemlock) are just as fast, but at a hundred and thirty feet (40m) are probably still too big, and need the right conditions. *Pinus radiata* (the Monterey pine) is fast, and extremely attractive, but still reaches a hundred feet (30m) and so does the Monterey cypress, *Cupressus macrocarpa*.

Almost all the broad-leafed evergreen trees will be too slow-growing. However there are two small but fairly fast trees suitable for milder areas in the south and west: one is *Eucryphia nymansensis* 'Nymansay' which is columnar in shape, and has the additional virtue of good white flowers. It can reach fifty feet (16m) when happy. It is not happy on limy soil, but on moist, acid, shaded loam it makes rapid progress. The other is *Pittosporum tenuifolium* which is usually limited to coastal districts, but is occasionally seen as a bush in sheltered corners of London gardens; flower arrangers rightly admire its unusual crinkly foliage. It forms a neat, columnar tree, in due course.

If our garden is not in a mild district, and is too small for any of the fast-growing conifers, we may decide that a deciduous screen may be adequate. But once again those species which grow fastest are too tall, and most willows, poplars and robinias (the fastest genera), develop into trees of the largest size, and have the added disadvantage of drawing vast amounts of water out of the soil. However, there are one or two members of these genera worth considering.

A good choice for a small but vigorous tree would be the Violet Willow, *Salix daphnoides*. The younger branches of this species are white; but this is only a "bloom" which can be rubbed off, and underneath the bloom the branches are a dark purple colour, hence the name.

Its long, narrow, pointed leaves are blueish white on the underside, and there are good yellow catkins early in the year on male trees. *Salix daphnoides* behaves in the ideal way. It starts off fast, three or four feet a year and then conveniently slows down to about a foot a year, reaching twentyfive feet (8m) eventually. The Bay Willow, *Salix pentandra* is about the same size, and is mainly remarkable for not looking like a willow. Its glossy, green leaves are not long and narrow like many willows, but look as though they ought to belong to an evergreen tree. They are similar to the Bay Laurel but less substantial.

Salix caprea, the familiar native Pussy Willow, or Goat Willow, is slightly taller at around thirty feet (10m) but is hardly decorative enough to be recommended and the smaller *S. caprea* 'Pendula', the Kilmarnock Willow, is an ugly form to be avoided. The Common Osier, *Salix viminalis*, could also be considered, being either an erect shrub or a small tree, not more than twenty feet (6m) high, of vigorous growth. This is another British native, one which has been cultivated because of the use of its stems for basket making. The long narrow leaves have a silvery appearance. The Purple Osier, *Salix purpurea*, is similar in size, but not so silvery, and it may need a little training to develop a trunk, since it is basically shrubby. There is a selected male form called 'Eugenei', sometimes available, whose catkins are a pinkish-grey shade, appearing before the leaves.

But the prettiest small Willow is not perhaps quite so fast nor so short as these. It is a selected form of the White Willow, called *Salix alba* 'Sericea'. Its leaves are really silver, and blown in the wind they make a beautiful sight, especially effective if contrasted with the dark glossy foliage of *Phillyreas* or conifers such as *Libocedrus*. I must also mention the Twisted Willow, *Salix matsudana* 'Tortuosa', which is interesting because of it strangely twisted and spiralling branches. Unlike many plant curiosities it is elegant as well as unusual, and it has the added attraction of being early into leaf and late to lose them – a useful trait when it comes to screening.

Out of the large number of different kinds of Poplar, all of which make rapid growth, there is only one small enough to consider here, and that is the Aspen, *Populus tremula;* even this can reach sixty feet (20m). Robinias, on the other hand, include several smallish trees – all selected, cultivated varieties. The most well known is *Robinia pseudo-acacia* 'Frisia', which provides an amazing splash of yellow. It is better planted as a feature in its own right, and one is enough I think. Some people consider it is becoming so common that it is almost a cliché; however, its critics have to admit that there is nothing else to match it for brilliance. It is not exactly the tree to plant at the far end of the garden to hide anything there, because it is so bright it will 'jump forward' visually, giving a foreshortening effect. Grey foliage trees, such as the willows we have already discussed, are more suitable in such a position. *Robinia pseudoacacia* itself is too large for most gardens and, in this country, too open to be any use for screening. It also has thorns, but one of the cultivated varieties, 'Inermis', has none. Its English name is the Mop-headed Acacia, because of the dense rounded mass of foliage which sits neatly above the plain trunk, just like a railway-modeller's idea of a tree. The density of foliage, however, and the speed of growth make it very suitable for screening. For more elegant foliage one could choose another variety named 'Rozynskyana', which has branches that bend at the tips and long pendulous leaves.

Two highly desirable maples can grow as much as three feet (1m) in a year; both have ornamental bark, or "snake-bark" as it is called. They are *Acer davidii* and *Acer hersii*. Both are of elegant growth and have excellent autumn colour. After a few years growth slows down which is convenient and, although they can ultimately reach fifty feet (15m), they are unlikely to be more than thirty feet high (10m) even after thirty years' growth. The normal green form of the so-called Box Elder, *Acer negundo*, is one of the fastest of the maples. It usually reaches about fortyfive feet (15m), although some specimens seventy feet high (23m) have been recorded. This species is not so decorative as *Acer davidii* or *Acer hersii*, but there are two selected varieties of *Acer negundo* with prettily coloured foliage which are called 'Variegatum' and 'Auratum', however these are slower than the ordinary green-leafed form.

Most of the other deciduous trees with a reputation for speed will eventually become too large. Several members of the Ash genus, for instance, are quite fast-growing, but even the smaller ones such as *Fraxinus ornus*, the Manna Ash can reach sixty to seventy feet (20m). The Dawn Redwood, *Metasequoia glyptostroboides*, has pretty foliage and grows quickly, but this also reaches seventy feet (23m) in time. *Pyrus betulifolia*, whose English name must be the Birch-leafed Pear, is reputed to be a fast-growing small tree but I confess I have not seen it. It is said to be quite ornamental. *Pyrus nivalis* also has pleasant grey foliage, but is not so fast.

At a lower level, bamboos can be useful in small gardens by providing height quickly without initially taking up a lot of space across. They are also evergreen, elegant and distinctive in their growth, which is an added attraction. But in rich, moist soil they soon spread to quite large clumps which may need annual reduction to keep them at bay. The most common Bamboo, and perhaps the one with the broadest leaves, is *Arundinaria japonica*, but I suggest you avoid this one because it usually looks a poor sight in the winter. The best for elegance and non-aggressive behaviour is definitely *Arundinaria mureliae*, which reaches eight or ten feet (2.5–3m) and would make a dense screen to hide a garage or some other unwanted single-story object. *Arundinaria nitida* is also good; elegant, but a little taller and slightly more invasive. I am trying out *Phyllostachys nigra* 'Henonis' in my own garden. This is said to be a decorative plant, as tall as *Arundinaria nitida*, but less invasive.

Sorbaria arborea, in spite of its name, is really an over-ambitious shrub. It is very vigorous, but its foliage is very pretty and it has large panicles of white flowers in July. These do not look so good when they have died and turned brown. I grow both *Sorbaria aitchisonii* and *S. tomentosa* in my garden; they are both a bit shorter than *arborea* which means it is possible to cut the dead flowers off after flowering.

If we have a little more patience, and can afford to wait a little longer, there is quite a wide selection of small trees with dense foliage which will form a perfectly adequate screen given time. Most members of the genus *Sorbus* grow at a reasonable pace, both the Rowan and the Whitebeam kinds, and several ornamental *Malus* (Apple) species and *Crataegus* (Hawthorn) species are also worth considering. For something taller, and extremely dense, *Carpinus betulus* 'Columnaris' and *C. betulus* 'Fastigiata', selected varieties of Hornbeam, could be chosen. Lilac, a favourite suburban tree, is also worth considering for summer screening. It is really a large shrub, and it is best to select a reliable named variety, such as 'Katherine Havemeyer' or 'Souvenir de Louis Spaeth', both of which have flowers of a good rich colour. The pale shades, especially white, are to be avoided; they are beautiful enough in bloom, but look disastrous when the flowers die off in shades of brown.

I am rather against the planting of too many pointed conifers, and the idea of a row of them planted to form a screen does not appeal to me. Many of the varieties which are small enough for the average garden, such as the well known 'Ellwoodii' and a host of others in green, blue or yellow, are so distinct in shape and outline that they need to be planted as specimens for deliberate emphasis. Someone has described them as being like exclamation marks! Too many exclamations together just look silly!!! and too many pointed conifers usually looks restless. I should be quite happy to have a garden without any pointed conifers at all. I do confess to having one or two in my present garden, the best of which is *Cryptomeria japonica* 'Elegans', which I like because of its restrained colour and soft foliage (purplish in winter) which gives it a slightly irregular outline. Large specimens of this variety tend to lean over and get unshapely, but this can be prevented by trimming them now and again, which they do not seem to object to. There are a handful of conifers of looser, softer shape, which I prefer to the usual run, but these are not particularly suitable for using as a screen. If you have space, there is a lot to be said for Yew, which is dense, dark and elegant, and it can be clipped if you decide it is too big.

If we really are prepared to wait for the right effect, and we are determined to have an evergreen screen, there are several good trees to choose from. But by no stretch of the imagination could they be called fast. However, they will at least be effective all the year round. For example there are many ornamental varieties of Holly, and most of these are unlikely to exceed fifty feet (15m) when full grown, and most are much smaller. Some are dark green and glossy like the native Holly; others come in various permutations of gold, cream or white variegation, with or without spines, with or without berries. It is the female forms that have berries, and of these 'Camelliifolia', 'Wilsonii' and 'Pyramidalis' are varieties to look out for, and *Ilex aquifolium* 'Pyramidalis Fructuluteo' and 'Bacciflava' have the distinction of yellow berries. Of the many variegated forms, two wholly admirable ones are 'Lawsoniana' and 'Handsworth New Silver'; both are female and berry-bearing. 'Golden King', despite its name, is also female; while Perry's Silver Weeping Holly, 'Argentea Pendula', is another attractive and distinct variety.

Several other broad-leafed evergreens make desirable small trees, slow-growing though they may be. *Phillyrea latifolia*, for example, resembles a small evergreen oak, but is even darker in colour. Its shape is rounded, usually slightly irregular, but elegant nevertheless. *Ligustrum lucidum*, another attractive small evergreen, is the aristocrat of the privet family – altogether superior to its plebian relatives, the dreary privet bushes of suburbia. In spite of being of tree proportions, the foliage of *Ligustrum lucidum* usually goes right down to the ground, giving the whole plant a round, 'billowing' outline. The leaves are dark and glossy, except for the young growth which is a much paler green; it has white flowers in great numbers in the autumn, and reaches about twenty feet (6m) in height – a little shorter than *Phillyrea latifolia*. There is a good variegated form of *Ligustrum lucidum*, which has the flattering name of 'Excelsum Superbum'.

Pyracanthas are usually thought of as shrubs, but at least one species, *Pyracantha atalantioides*, can be grown as a tree, and I know of one elderly example which is doing very well. This species probably needs a little training to form a trunk, but its eventual height is likely to be about twenty feet (6m). There are one or two cotoneasters that behave in the same way with a little encouragement: *Cotoneaster salicifolia*, for example, which is a rather variable species. Some of the named hybrids, which are classified under *Cotoneaster* × *watereri*, can reach at least twenty feet (6m), such as 'Cornubia', and 'Exburyensis' which are excellent varieties, with a profusion of red and yellow berries respectively.

Cherry Laurel, *Prunus laurocerasus*, is sometimes planted as a screen but I do not recommend it. Left to grow naturally it forms a vast rambling bush twentyfive feet (7.5m) high and thirty feet (9m) wide. To stop it spreading like this it has to be clipped regularly, and its large, firm, glossy leaves look most ugly when cut with shears. Far better to plant a shrub which is more manageable, such as the Portuguese Laurel, *Prunus lusitanica* – this easily reaches twenty feet (6.5m) in height, but doesn't spread out much, and will form a bushy kind of tree if desired. Just because the Victorians planted it to excess in their shrubberies, is no reason to despise this excellent plant with first rate evergreen foliage.

7

Making a Garden Picture

Having surrounded ourselves with greenery, and blotted out as far as possible every unwanted object in sight, the field (so to speak) is now free for us to do something positive. What then shall we make of it? In later chapters we shall discuss the way we use the garden, but before that I want to discover what we want it to look like.

If we don't know where to start, one of the windows of the house will be a good place. We cannot be out in the garden all the time, even if we are the keenest gardeners in the country, and most of us are unlikely to do much outside between October and March. The kind of picture that most people want on their walls is like a moment's holiday: a release from the pressure of the present, an escape from the unending rush, from trivial tasks, or the tedious routine that occupies us. Many great paintings were not designed for this purpose, nor were they intended for a domestic location, they were painted to instruct, to stir the feelings, to encourage piety and so on. It is not surprising, therefore, that many famous paintings are not really suitable for the living room: who wants to look at Goya's "Horrors of War" or Munch's "The Cry", for instance, day after day, or at portrayals of shipwrecks, storms or the dying moments of famous people? These belong in picture galleries or books where they can stir our emotions at the appropriate moment. What we want is a picture that can be enjoyed every day such as a cool still-life, a landscape, or perhaps a portrait of someone we love or admire.

Most paintings are slightly idealized; in other words they depict a slightly improved version of the world. The grass is greener, the sky is more blue, the clouds are perfectly placed in the sky, and every lady has a perfect complexion. A view into the garden, therefore, should be a significant improvement on the "real world": restful, relaxing and soothing to the spirit; something which enables us to look up from the small print that occupies us, or turn away in a tense moment, and offer our eyes an escape into a calm, green and tranquil scene, that presents itself through the windows of the house. Already we have gone some way to create this ideal picture, by eliminating the unwanted elements with a screen of carefully chosen plants; but to be satisfying a picture has to be well-composed, it is not the brightness of the paint that gives us pleasure but the "rightness" of the complete arrangement.

It follows that before we can decide on the content of the garden we must consider its form. Possession of the finest dahlias in town tells us only about the content: it is like the artist telling us he has crimson lake in his paintbox. The problem is to know how to put the paint on the canvas. What we find in most paintings is that some areas of the canvas are carefully detailed, while other parts are relatively plain. If the entire canvas were covered in intricate detail all of equal interest we shouldn't know where to look, but most pictures are not like this. Usually the artist gives loving attention to some areas of detail but leaves other parts plain, and it is often the case that an object of special interest is placed against a background, or foreground, where it shows to advantage without undue competition. Just the same effects can apply in gardening. One can have exciting colours and colour combinations, interesting shapes and so on in the plant material, but to show to advantage there must also be simple, uncluttered surfaces where the eye can rest. Nothing sets off a mixed border of flowers and foliage better than the plain, smooth foreground which a perfect lawn provides.

There is a parallel here with some interesting research which has been done in the United States on the design of offices and, in particular, the best environment for the office-bound executive. One need which has been identified is something called a "visual rest centre". In many working environments these days a view from a window is not possible, but the eye still needs to be able to look away from the taxing detail of the written word on a desk to a more distant, undistracted area. The detailed recommendations resulting from this research include such suggestions as the need for plain surfaces, uncluttered walls, quiet colours and glare-free lighting.

It is clear, therefore, that in our garden picture we have the ideal thing ready made for us. The soft green of mown grass is the perfect colour on which to rest one's eyes: no colour of paving or gravel is so pleasant, nor is there any ground cover to equal it. In natural scenery this kind of surface which is restful, but pleasing, is often provided by water. How many attractive pictures can be created by framing the sparkling surface of water by trees. The landscape gardeners of the eighteeth century were given all the scope they needed to do just this kind of thing, but if we do not have such an opportunity, we can at least make the most of the miniature scale at which we are working. In this country we are lucky: our climate is ideally suited to the success of a lawn; in California or the Mediterranean Region it is a struggle to make one, but for us it comes easily. It is worthwhile, therefore, making the most of something we can do well.

The ideal lawn is perfectly flat and smooth, like an expensive carpet. In a large country garden the outer fringes can perhaps afford to be lumpy and bumpy like a field, but near the house the surface should be carefully graded to eliminate all irregularities in the way of humps, depressions, valleys, banks and twists to create the desired "carpet" effect. In some cases it is impossible for it to be dead level because of the contours, but in such cases it still ought to be an even plane, although set at a slight incline. A lawn, therefore, in all but the smallest of plots, is an indispensable feature of the garden, worthy of as much attention as the border. By this I don't just mean that it should be mown, raked, weeded, fed and fertilized, though it deserves all those. Before all that happens it should be designed, i.e. its size, shape, slope, surface, direction, angle and edges, all need to be thought about. So often the planted areas get all the attention, especially in gardens belonging to keen plantspeople, and the poor lawn is just what's left over, but my advice is to pay attention to the shape of your lawn and let the borders look after themselves.

The way to approach this is to think in terms of spaces, rather than objects. Let me explain this by saying that one should not treat the garden as a *tabula rasa* on which to arrange one's trees and shrubs, as if they were so many ornaments on a shelf. We are more likely to be successful if we think of the garden as a sculptor thinks of his material, carving shapes out of a solid mass. This can be seen plainly in some Italian gardens such as the ones at the Villa Garzoni at Collodi and the Villa Reale at Marlia, near Lucca, where the formal planted areas give the appearance of having been made in a clearing cut in a wood. All round the ornamental areas there is solid *bosco*, out of which the spaces have been carved.

Because the surface of the lawn is something which we can walk about on, it resembles the shape of a room, and in a building it is the shape of the rooms (i.e. the space) which is important to the user, not the thickness of the walls that surround the room. Town planners talk of something called "sloap" which is short for "space left over after planning". In towns we are familiar with the awkward, litter-accumulating corners that seem to occur with every so-called planning improvement. The shape of the lawn or of any other space in the garden is

a) *Correct solution.*
The lawn as a space of
definite shape which is
defined by the borders.

b) *Poor solution.*
The beds and trees are
"peppered" on to the
blank suface of the
garden with no rhyme
or reason to them.

c) *Poor solution.*
The lawn is "what's
left over" after the beds
are made; there is no
focus of interest.

therefore a prime consideration. It must be definite, not haphazard, wayward, nor an afterthought.

In many cases it is a good idea to have a lawn of clear and distinct shape, and the choice of something as obvious as a pure square, a rectangle or a circle is no bad thing. Plants are so irregular and ungeometrical that a shape has to be strong if it is to read when surrounded by all the different sizes, shapes and colours of plants, especially when those plants tend to flop forward and weaken any firm line that may be created between lawn and border. Because of this factor, it is no good attempting anything too fussy or intricate; not only will the effect be obscured by edging plants, it will also be annoying to mow. There are countless good shapes for a lawn, which can be arrived at either by geometry or by the use of simple flowing curves. If we think of the lawn as space enclosed by plants, and treat it as if it was a "room", the effect of this will be to create the impression that we have arrived at something definite and intentional. If it is the beds and borders which have shape and the lawn is what's left over, this will only produce a corridor effect where there is no focus, but the space leaks away into the gaps and the eye is led away into the corners.

In small gardens it is best to have an "open centre"; in other words I don't recommend beds or ornaments placed in the middle of the lawn. There may be a few ornaments good enough for this dominant position – if you can find one – but few beds will look good enough to be placed centrally; rockeries or beds of roses in such a position look simply appalling.

Whether you should go for symmetry will depend on the style within which you are working. Symmetry is formal, and has an air of finality about it: one is reminded of the description of a classical building as one where nothing can be added and nothing taken away without spoiling the whole. However, with a strongly symmetrical scheme it is perhaps harder to go wrong, once you have started, than with a freer, more informal design.

Straight lines have a clarity and simplicity about them and make mowing easy. But curved lines also have a certain charm – they are easy on the eye and blend well with the rounded shapes of plants. Curves should be few, strong and bold like those of the letter S. On no account should one have so many small "ins" and "outs" that a kind of wriggling line emerges; rather there should be gradual curves, if possible not less than eight feet (2.4m) in radius. Sharp points where curves meet straight lines should be eliminated and jagged and harsh shapes avoided.

One useful technique is the use of what might be called irregular hexagons. The pure geometry of squares and rectangles has a severity

The use of splay lines, or "irregular hexagons", can be useful
when deciding on the best shape for lawns and borders.

about it which is immediately reduced when diagonal splay-lines are introduced. I believe it was Rudolf Steiner who said that the right-angle produces tension in the viewer, and for this reason the few buildings he designed depart from the usual architectural geometry and contain splays and curves in every dimension. It is interesting that as soon as one departs from the right angle the eye becomes quite tolerant of deviations from exact geometry, and the angles of the splay lines can vary from each other considerably without being at all noticeable. This can be useful when the geometry of the design has to be bent round some obstacle which makes exact execution of a basically geometrical idea impossible. A further practical advantage which the use of hexagons or octagons has over curves, is that the straight edges do make it easier to mow the lawn.

If the lawn slopes across the line of sight, every effort should be made to correct it, because the garden will never look right while there is this side-slipping effect. If the lawn is made level this may make the

A garden which slips sideways will never look right. The lawn should be made as level as possible even if it increases the slope of the borders.

soil in the borders slope even more, but if they are planted with shrubs, or perhaps with evergreen ground cover at the front, the fact that they slope will hardly be noticed, and if taller shrubs or small trees are planted on the lower side this will help to balance the heights on the two sides.

When the garden slopes away from the house, along the line of sight, this is less of a problem than if the slope runs across the line of sight. A slight slope is something to be welcomed, because it will give opportunity for a few shallow steps; these are always an attractive feature and can be handled in a great variety of interesting ways. Where possible the lawn should be level, as I have said, and on sloping sites this can be arranged by breaking the lawn into sections with a bank between each. The bank should then be planted with low shrubs, and

A sloping garden broken into a series of level lawns and planted
banks.

a few steps can link the level of one lawn with the level of the next.
On steeply sloping sites the problem is more difficult. The first priority
is to have a level area immediately outside the house, whether a lawn
or a terrace; it can be one or two steps down from the house, but that
is all. To make an absolutely level lawn further down the garden may

Even in a steeply-sloping garden a level area is desirable,
particularly near the house.

require too high a retaining wall and a slight slope may be unavoidable.
If retaining walls exceed two feet (60cm) in height, they become rather
oppressive, and any wall higher than about ten inches (25cm) ought to
have a bed in front of it, so that a line of planting can soften the hard
line of the wall. Another factor which militates against the ideal level
lawn on such sites is the existing positions and heights of boundary
fences, and the need to retain the existing relationship of the level in
your own garden with that of your neighbour's.

One technique that is often useful in this kind of situation is to use

High retaining walls can look rather severe, but planting can be used to soften the effect.

large rockery stones embedded into a bank to stabilize it. This makes it possible for the bank to be much steeper — 45° or even more; the so-called "angle of repose" of soil on its own would normally form a much shallower slope than this. Having created this "rockery-bank" there is no need to plant it as a rockery with little alpine plants. Small shrubs will be much more satisfactory — for two reasons: they will be

A "rockery-bank", densely planted with evergreen shrubs which hides the stones.

big enough to hide the untidy jumble of stones propping up the bank, and their roots will also be strong enough to stabilize the bank.

Sometimes the ground rises, rather than falls, as seen from the house. If this is only slight it is no disadvantage, since if one does make a series of shallow steps there will at least be a good view of them. It is difficult, however, if the contours are steep, since to look out on sharply rising ground and see hardly any sky gives an oppressive feeling. In some cases the only satisfactory solution is to remove some of the soil entirely from the garden, and have it taken away by lorry. By reducing the level of the ground particularly near the house, the eye is given some breathing space, as it were, before the contours start to have an enclosing effect on the garden. The levels of the boundaries will probably have to be retained, so the centre of the garden midway between the boundaries will be the best place to remove the soil.

The line where the lawn meets the border is one of the most important in the garden, and when the positions of such lines have been decided the design of the garden is almost complete. It is also a labour-intensive line in most gardens, requiring edge-clipping every time the lawn is cut. To eliminate this work and to emphasize the line visually, it is a good idea to have an edging strip. This can be built of brickwork, stone, pre-cast pavings or even timber, but brickwork is particularly suitable since the size of a standard brick, just under nine inches (22cm) is ideal for the purpose. The bricks should be laid on edge and either bedded onto concrete or simply laid on sand. An edging strip not only provides a neat edge to the lawn, but also eliminates the awkward step between the grass and border. Another significant advantage is that the planting can come right to the edge of the border and overhang the edging-strip, and so do away with the awkward few inches of bare soil at the front of the border which have to be weeded with great frequency because of their prominence. A brick edging strip is not particularly cheap, of course, and I have used some quite attractive concrete setts in some schemes, but naturally they are only suitable for straight lines, whereas bricks can be taken round a curve if it is not too tight a radius. Another solution, which is much cheaper, is a timber edging strip. This is not often seen in this country but as long as it is treated with preservative and stained it should last many years. A timber member such as a six inch by two inch (150 x 50cm) board can be used, laid flat and adequately fixed to other short lengths of timber set into the ground. Needless to say, this is another method which can only be used if the edge of the border is straight. Any kind of edging, whether timber or masonry, should be set about an inch (2.5cm) below the level of the grass so that the edge is cut properly by the mower.

0   5   10   15

When we look out from the house the first six or eight feet (2m)
of the garden is scarcely visible.

In a very small garden, or "backyard" situation it may be impractical
to have grass, but even if one has paving or gravel the same principles
can be applied. A certain amount of clear space is needed in every
garden, uncluttered by planting or garden features and in a roughly
central position. One should consider any items with height (such as
plants) as things with which to surround that space and not as separate
objects to be dotted around at random.

To be effective any important element in the garden picture has to
be some distance away from the windows of the house, even if the
window sill is low, because the eye tends to look past the first few feet
of the garden. Plants under the window sill, and the first six or eight
feet of the garden, are virtually ignored as we look out, and the area
of greatest impact is a zone immediately opposite the window, between
twenty and forty feet (6–12m) out from it. The effect of most plants at
a distance of more than fifty feet is small, and most flowers become too
small at that distance to have any impact.

As a general rule, a border designed to display plants effectively has
to be placed so that it roughly faces the house, somewhere between
thirty and sixty feet (10–20m) from it. I say "roughly faces" because
borders are seen to greater advantage if they are viewed along their

55

length rather than at 90° and, because of this, some kind of diagonal or curving line can be more successful.

Occasionally one comes across an older house where the garden at the back has been made at basement level rather than the level of the living rooms, because of the nature of the contours. In cases like this, when one looks down at the garden from the main windows of the house with something of a bird's-eye-view, the plan of the garden suddenly takes on more importance for its sake as a visible pattern, rather than for the features it generates. Some recognizable formal and symmetrical pattern can be an attractive solution in such situations. Of course, there is a limit to the number of "general rules" that can be made, and in the end one must get out there and try something. To mark out one's ideas first with pegs or bamboo canes is often a good idea so that the shapes and positions of the various elements can be viewed from all relevant angles.

In a very small plot, the tendency of the eye to overlook the first few feet of the garden means that one's efforts must be concentrated more or less against the back fence, and it is only those things that have height that will contribute much to the picture. In such cases it becomes irrelevant to pay too much attention to the ground plan, and the garden has to be designed more as "an elevation", (an architectural term which refers to a drawing of the façade of a building, or of what is seen of the building on a particular vertical plane). If, therefore, a border along the rear boundary of a courtyard garden is treated as an elevation, the arrangement of the plants as vertical elements becomes the dominant factor. In a later chapter we shall discuss both the visual qualities of plants and the way they can be grouped, but in the meantime there are several other components of the garden picture to which we must give our attention.

8

Focal Points and Framing

In our effort to create a rewarding garden picture, let us go a stage further and discover what it is that makes a satisfactory composition. A study of great paintings of the past, or even of successful photographs, can be a useful aid in this endeavour.

It may seem slightly obvious to point out that a painting is usually a painting *of* something. Of course there are some modern paintings which can only be described as paintings of paint, but even so there is often a prime area of interest: something in particular has interested the painter which might be described as the Main Subject, to steal a term from musical theory, and there are related zones of interest (Second Subjects) and the remaining parts of the picture play a subservient or a supporting rôle to these. The whole ensemble forms a coherent pattern, which, as we say, "hangs together". This can be seen clearly for instance in some of the common themes of the Italian Renaissance painters, such as the Madonna and Child. Although some painters introduce St John or other figures such as Joseph and Elizabeth, and other painters depict a complex setting of rocks, trees, steps, and so on, while others pay special attention to the clothing or drapery, all these are subsidiary to the main subject which is the child held by his mother. In other traditional religious themes of a more complicated nature, such as the Last Supper or Christ Clearing the Temple, which are full of people, the great painters always succeed in focusing attention on the central figure. The centre of interest in a landscape painting may not seem so obvious. It may consist of a cluster of objects or, as in some scenes by Claude Lorrain, it may even be the brightly lit horizon. Alternatively, there may be a figure or group of figures in the foreground to catch the eye, or it may be a building in the middle distance which is picked out in greater detail than the more generalized greenery or distant haze surrounding it.

If we study photographs of great gardens to see how photographers have contrived to make their subject look as interesting as possible, we find that very rarely does the picture consist of a general view of plants alone. Either the house to which the garden belongs or some kind of garden ornament seems to creep in to the picture. It seems that to make a good photograph of a general view of a garden, more than just plants is needed. Photographs of Hidcote, for example, are almost invariably of the upper part of the garden, with its variety of "architectural" features, such as the little pointed-roofed pavilions, the elaborate topiary, the pool or the pleached hornbeams and hardly ever of the looser "natural" areas such as the stream garden or the area confusingly called "Westonbirt". Gardens such as Leonardslee or Exbury which consist entirely of plants in a naturalistic setting do not seem to photograph well. The photographer is forced to take close-ups of flowers or of plant associations which give little idea of the garden as a whole.

In small gardens, therefore, one way to make a good "picture" is to create some kind of centre-of-interest. Around it can be grouped subservient elements which will help to make something of it. The centrepiece need only be a garden seat, a vase, a flight of two or three steps, or a pool, but in a small garden this can be enough. Such features provide something for the eye to alight upon. Plants on their own tend to form an amorphous mass, with one rounded leafy shape following another, and for this reason the juxtaposition of masonry or carefully-chosen garden furniture provides immediate contrast. There is no need for this feature to have an exactly central or obvious position directly opposite the window; on the contrary somewhere slightly to one side, a "throw-away" position, can be more effective in gardens which are informal in style. To accompany such a feature, one can add strongly shaped plants to emphasize the effect. Pointed conifers have already been mentioned, or any other dominant plants can be used whose shape or colour makes them stand out from the usual run – yuccas and phormiums for example. To create a focal point, or an area of strong design interest with these plants alone is more difficult, but it is possible.

The contrasting juxtaposition of a tall fastigiate tree with a horizontal one, for example, is very striking: combinations such as *Juniperus* 'Hibernica' with *Cotoneaster horizontalis*, or on a larger scale *Chamaecyparis lawsoniana* 'Fletcheri' with *Juniperus* 'Pfitzeriana'; or *Taxus baccata* 'Fastigiata' with *Taxus baccata* 'Dovastonii Aurea'. But such effects can be overdone, and too many strong shapes can become distracting and produce a restless effect. In the larger and most prominent elements in the garden it is best to avoid too many contrasting shapes and outlines and too much variation of foliage. The larger the element the more important it is to ensure that it fits in with the overall unity of the scheme.

Planting things in pairs tends to emphasize that a design effect is intended – an effect which may be called "framing". You can frame an object in this way simply by the use of a pair of striking plants, one each side of something, to draw attention to it, and the same technique can also be used to frame an opening. When there is a way through from one part of the garden to another, the transition can be emphasized by this means.

But framing doesn't have to be symmetrical, it can be created by almost any two objects, but the effect will be clearer if there is some balance in visual weight between the two elements which provide the framing. This is another design element which is often seen in paintings and photographs. A distant and widespread landscape which looks impressive to the eye may look nothing in a photograph until it is framed by trees. One photographer I heard of used to take huge branches of foliage with him on his trips in case there were no convenient trees when he got on location, and an assistant would be employed to hold the branches up at an appropriate angle.

Ways of framing an opening are too numerous to list exhaustively, but can include openings in clipped yew, the arches of a pergola, wrought-iron gates and pairs of pillars – all of which are fairly formal. Alternatively a path may merely squeeze between two large shrubs in a more informal manner. Another attractive idea is to plant two trees together so that their branches form an archway.

It is important to consider what is seen through the opening once it is formed. If there is an item worthy of being made a focal point can it be seen clearly through the opening? When you look through the opening, is there some unwanted object in the view which needs screening?

If, as I have suggested, we wish to give prime consideration to the view of the garden from the house, we may want to create some kind of framing where it can be appreciated from the window. Such framing elements will need to be somewhere in the region of ten feet (2.5m) away from the window to be effective. One can build something, such as a frame of timber, for example, and grow climbing plants on it; or alternatively one can use plants which are predominantly stems and branches, such as *Rhus typhina* or *Aralia elata*, whose foliage all occurs at the top, allowing one to see through them at low level. These are just two ideas: there must by many more ways of framing the view of the garden, as seen from the house.

In small gardens the idea of division between one area and another can be suggested by low level planting, without an actual division which would be too enclosing, and beds can be brought forward like pincers to separate one area of the lawn from another (see page 50).

To create some kind of interest, or simply to provide some kind of object to contrast with the horticultural material, one can go in for features of a more elaborate kind, but these have to be chosen with care. Statues are fine for grand and great gardens, but it seems to me that it is doubtful whether a classical statue is suitable for the garden of a modern suburban house. On the other hand if you can afford a good piece of modern sculpture you are unlikely to be living in a small modern house! Some decorative items are produced in such enormous numbers that one becomes tired of seeing them, and very old and second-hand items usually turn out to be too expensive for most of us. If you decide to buy something new it can look rather raw, and one way to make it look ancient and weather-worn is to adopt the old method used to encourage the growth of mosses and lichens on tiled roofs and give them a more "aged" look. The secret is to paint the object in question with cow-dung and water; however if you don't relish this, I am told that milk is nearly as effective.

Unfortunately there are very few good garden ornaments produced in this country at a price ordinary people can afford. In Italy there is a wide range of terracotta ornaments, which are preferable in some ways to the nasty grey concrete stuff produced over here. Quite a lot of people, dare I say it, like garden gnomes, and others argue in their support that a gnome is no more out of place in a suburban garden than a replica of the Venus de Milo. Others think gnomes are the epitome of Bad Taste, though some reserve that distinction for the rose 'Super Star'.

The safe answer to the "feature" problem is to use some functional kind of item such as a garden seat or a pair of vases or tubs and, instead of putting such items in an obscure corner they can be made an integral part of the design. Another interesting possibility not often explored is the use of "found art". Sometimes an extraordinary flinty boulder or chunk of rock can look more interesting than any piece of sculpture that one is likely to be able to afford. Pieces of tree trunk washed in by the tide and discovered on the seashore are other examples of objects which have been used in this way. But it is important to be bold and go for something of a reasonable size; the kind of chunk of stone that can be lifted into the boot of a car will probably be too small to look effective.

Perhaps the most rewarding of all garden features is a pool. A pool is a never-failing point of interest for garden visitors: it seems to draw people to it like a magnet. The best small pools are made with concrete and masonry. I am sure I need not tell readers of this book never to buy one of those dreadful pre-formed plastic affairs of amorphous shape. Pools of irregular outline made with a plastic sheet are usually a disaster as well. However carefully they are made you can inevitably see the plastic at some point, and an assortment of rocks placed round the pool to keep the plastic in place always looks a terrible mess. I prefer to make a masonry or concrete pool of definite shape. A simple circle or square can be very effective, but if the situation demands there is a great variety of other shapes, such as half-circles, hexagons, octagons and so on which can be used. The shape and size needs to relate to the position of the pool in the garden. If the pool has a central, dominant position its shape should certainly be regular and it should be impressively large to justify its position. A smaller pool can be situated in the corner of a paved terrace or sitting area, where it can be seen at any time of year without walking on damp grass. It is better not to have a pool under trees; because of the nuisance caused by fallen leaves which will clog it up after a few years. A sunny position is far better, where the sparkle and reflectiveness of the water will show up to maximum advantage, especially if you have a fountain.

The cool sound of water has a particularly pleasant quality on hot summer afternoons and for this reason a fountain is always worth considering. It is worthwhile being bold with fountains. Avoid the cheapest pump and a timid-looking, fine-spraying head, and go instead for a big pump which will cope with a whole group of single jets which will look really impressive; or alternatively choose one (or several) of the proprietary foaming heads which are so much more effective than the weak trickles one usually sees.

There is no need for a pool to be unnecessarily deep, and it certainly should have "shelves" of varying height along its edges to provide places for water plants. It is worth doing some homework before the pool is made to discover which plants you wish to include, since every water-plant has its own requirements regarding depth of water. It is wisest to exercise some restraint with water-lilies and other plants that cover the surface of the water: there is no point in making a pool if the surface of the water becomes smothered in greenery. A good guide is to restrict water-lilies to no more than a quarter of the surface area. In small pools this means having only one plant, or perhaps none at all.

Fish are always an attraction, ordinary goldfish are best, and don't forget the water snails without which no pool will be healthy and free from algae.

CHAPTER 9

Backgrounds and Foregrounds

As we continue our search to discover ways to create a pleasing garden picture we must give some further thought to that unobtrusive part of any picture provided by the background. Many painters have been quite content for a portrait to have a completely plain, dark background. Any object of significance in a painting, whether the main one or some much less important item, has to show to advantage, but if its background is distracting this will not happen. Amateur photographers are often reminded to make sure they do not get telegraph poles or spiky bushes apparently growing out of peoples' heads, by thoughtless positioning of the subject. In the garden, if we want a focal point to be set off to advantage the background must be suitably restrained, and the same rule also applies to plants of special floral value. In the days of herbaceous borders the ideal background was a yew hedge: smooth dark green provided the perfect foil for the flowers. Although herbaceous borders are mostly a thing of the past the same principle applies. Many of the plants which I suggested for screening or for clothing the boundaries with greenery are ideal for this purpose: ivies, pyracanthas, cotoneasters, hollies, *Itea ilicifolia* and so on.

But there are several other fairly dark evergreens of medium size which would make a foil either to stone-work or to the brightly coloured flowers of herbaceous plants. One of my favourites is *Choisya ternata*, which is sometimes called Mexican Orange Blossom. Its habit of growth is good, and its foliage is glossy and is that ideal, dark green colour which is perfect for backgrounds. The white flowers are an added bonus and come early in the summer. If choisyas look a little bedraggled after a really hard winter they soon perk up and produce healthy new foliage. An even darker green is offered by *Viburnum tinus* another first class evergreen, with dense foliage which is ideal for background planting. Its flat heads of white flowers appear, conveniently enough, during the winter months, followed by small blue berries. Hilliers of Winchester currently list a form called 'Purpureum', which is presumably even darker, but I have not seen it. *Viburnum cinnamomifolium* is another admirable foliage plant; its dark green leaves are large and closely resemble the more common *Viburnum davidii*, though they are not quite so leathery. *V. davidii* is too short for our present purpose, but *Viburnum cinnamomifolium* grows quite tall in mild districts – it is unlikely to flourish in very cold or exposed gardens.

The leaves of *Osmanthus delavayi* are quite small in comparison, and their dark green colour tends towards an olive shade. In April it is covered with small white flowers which are pleasantly scented. *Osmanthus armatus* is also worth growing as a background plant, but is rarely seen; it is a dense, holly-like shrub with scented flowers in the autumn. *Osmanthus (Osmarea) burkwoodii* is a more common hybrid which has some similarity to *Osmanthus delavayii*, but with larger leaves and equally fragrant flowers.

Arbutus unedo, the Strawberry Tree, could have been mentioned when we were discussing small evergreen trees such as *Phillyrea latifolia* and *Ligustrum lucidum*, since it eventually becomes a small tree. Its leafy foliage is wholly admirable, and ideally suitable as a background. One remarkable thing about this Arbutus is that the flowers and fruits (the "strawberries") appear on the plant simultaneously, from September onwards. It is fairly slow growing and so stays looking shrubby for many years. Once it reaches tree size, however, one notices that the trunk has very attractive reddish brown bark. *Arbutus × andrachnoides* is equally attractive but is not commonly available; *A. andrachne* is only suitable for the south and west.

There is some similarity in leaf-shape and colour between an Arbutus and the Bay Laurel, *Laurus nobilis*. This is the plant whose leaves are used in cooking as a flavouring. Although it eventually reaches tree dimensions it remains bushy in outline, clothed in good foliage down to the ground; it is not suitable for the very coldest districts.

Another shrub with dark green foliage, suitable for making an evergreen foil to other plants, is *Ligustrum japonicum*, the Japanese Privet. This has dense olive green foliage which is more like that of a Camellia than ordinary privet; it has large white panicles of privet flowers in August. *Phillyrea decora* (sometimes called *Osmanthus decorus*) also has leaves which are ideally dark and glossy. *Elaeagnus × ebbingei* is another attractive evergreen, but its colour is a greyer green than the shrubs previously described. It has good, dense habit.

Another important element in our picture is the foreground. Anyone who has done some landscape photography will be familiar with this problem. A large, featureless expanse of fields, moorland or tarmac at the bottom of the picture can ruin what seemed to be a splendid view. What "framing" does for the sides of the picture, a good foreground does for the bottom line. Care is needed, though, to strike the right balance. Too little or no foreground will make the picture look bare and bleak, but too much foreground interest will distract from the main subject of the picture. As with framing, some photographers cheat by taking their foreground material around with them and one sometimes finds on visiting a famous garden that the photographs one has seen in books must have been taken by the photographer standing in the middle of a herbaceous border simply to get in some pretty foreground.

When we consider the various components of a garden picture that have been discussed, I suppose the element that needs a foreground most is the lawn. As seen from the house, a large lawn can easily seem disproportionate compared with the borders that surround it, but the addition of some carefully placed foreground planting will help to create a more balanced picture. As we have noted, plants which are immediately below the windows of the house are too low to come into the line of vision. In my own garden I have created a border about ten feet (3m) away from the house and parallel to it, and this is just far enough out to be seen if you stand by the window indoors. In some gardens there is a terrace or patio immediately outside the house, and a border between the terrace and the lawn can be used to create some foreground interest. Plants for a border such as this need to be chosen with special care, because their shape will be seen distinctly, silhouetted against the plain background of the lawn. Things to avoid are untidy herbaceous plants that lean awkwardly in odd directions, or hybrid tea roses whose pruned outline is so ugly during the winter. Instead one should plant neat shrubs with tidy habit: bun-shaped conifers, for example, like *Chamaecyparis lawsoniana* 'Minima Glauca' or *Thuja plicata* 'Rogersii' could be considered. Skimmias, sarcococcas and most of the small-leaved *Hebe* species would all be ideally suitable, but the choice is wide; *Viburnum davidii* and *Hosta sieboldiana* are amongst the plants in my "foreground border". For a more startling effect, one can take advantage of the strong silhouettes of yuccas or other spiky plants such as *Iris pallida dalmatica*.

On a more detailed level, the plants along the front edge of the border can also be considered as a foreground or as a kind of base-line to the larger and more decorative flowering plants in the border. Because of their position at the front, they are quite prominent and need to be chosen with care. It is so easy to create a front-line which is untidy and restless, with shapes and outlines of every description, and this only distracts from other more important elements further back in the border. A good solution is to plant long bands of neat, low plants such as *Dianthus, Hebe* 'Pagei' or helianthemums and to have about a five-foot run (1.5m) of one kind at a time, and then between the groups, taller plants (such as the blue grass *Helictotrichon sempervirens*) can break forward occasionally as a contrast.

Where front-line plants meet a gravel path or paving, one can choose kinds which lean forward onto the path in an elegant manner. Catmint, *Nepeta × faasenii (N. mussinii)* does this and so does *Artemisia nutans* (in silvery filigree) and *Othonnopsis cheirifolia,* an unusual grey succulent-like plant with yellow flowers, and leaves shaped rather like cats' tongues. *Euphorbia myrsinites* is another suitable grey-leaved plant which puts up a marvellous show early in the year of slightly greenish-yellow heads. *Alchemilla mollis* always looks good against paving or gravel, especially when its foliage is fresh and new in the spring. By the end of September, though, it begins to lose its good looks. *Geranium renardii,* with neat greyish green leaves and greyish-white veined flowers is another attractive choice, while for a shady path *Geranium macrorrhizum* is always keen to grow forward and mask the hard line of the edge of paving. I think the form I grow is slightly shorter than some – it is called 'Ingwersen's Variety', and has pale pink flowers.

For a sunny position, sedums and thymes both like to creep forward and rest their foliage on the hot paving. I particularly like *Sedum* 'Purple Carpet' which actually has red foliage rather than purple. I believe this is a form of *Sedum spurium,* of which there are several other good forms including 'Dragon's Blood' and 'Green Mantle'. *Sedum stolonifera* and *S. sarmentosum* are also creepers-forward, and *S. caticolum* and *kamschaticum* 'Variegatum' both have pretty foliage to recommend them. There are many varieties of Thyme available, which are appropriate to our purpose. They are invariably scented. *Thymus drucei* 'Coccineus Major' has good, brightly coloured flowers: *T.* 'Silver Posie' and 'Golden King' are taller and have the attraction of variegated leaves.

There are several silver plants which are good with paving. *Cerastium tomentosum* is too vigorous to be recommended, but its close relative *Cerastium columnae* is just as pretty a colour and is a more restrained grower. *Tanacetum densum* 'Amanum', (sometimes listed as *Chrysanthemum haradjani*) has finely cut leaves which someone has aptly described as being liked curled woolly feathers: this is another keen creeper-forward. *Anthemis cupaniana,* a relative of Chamomile, is also suitable and has white daisy flowers to recommend it, as well as a good "mat" of tangled silvery foliage.

Another silvery mat-forming plant I grow is *Veronica cinerea* which

65

has the attraction of blue flowers – a smaller plant altogether than *Anthemis cupaniana*, only about three inches (7.5cm) high. All these silvery plants that like hot dry paving also like full exposure to sun and well-drained soil conditions. But good mat formers don't have to be silver: *Iberis sempervirens*, Perennial Candytuft, for instance is about six inches (15cm) high and has leaves that are as dark green as any of the shrubs mentioned in the first part of this chapter. Its flowers appear quite early in spring and are of an astonishing Persil whiteness. *Parahebe cataractae* is another green-leafed shrublet, with white flowers – this time of a more delicate and retiring kind. With helianthemums you can have the choice of green or grey foliage, and also a wide choice of flower colours. 'Wisley Primrose' is one good variety; 'Rhodanthe Carneum' is a nice soft pink; 'Ben Afflick' is a hot orange, and there are good whites, dark reds and doubles available too.

Any of these plants could be used as a front-line to a border. But there may be places where we need something taller to associate with paving. Rosemary is a very useful plant, but beside paving it is better to avoid the form 'Miss Jessop's Upright' which is usually offered these days, and use the older, ordinary sprawling kind, or else the brighter and better 'Benenden Blue' which grows at Sissinghurst. Jackman's Blue Rue, Santolina, and the various kinds of sage (culinary, purple, or variegated) all revel in heat, and are pleased to rest their stems on warm dry paving. They are an indispensable part of any garden. Most members of the *Phlomis* family are also suitable: *Phlomis fruticosa* is the most commonly seen, but I much prefer *Phlomis chrysophylla* which has the most refined silvery foliage imaginable.

When a border is bounded by grass, the front edge is more difficult to treat than a border edged by paving. A small patch of bare earth between the plants and the grass has little to commend it: it has to be constantly weeded and creates an edge which has to be cut every time the lawn is mown. The possibility of using an edging strip has already been discussed, but there may be places where this is not suitable, especially as one gets further away from the house into a more natural setting. One way to avoid having a grass edge is to select edging plants which can be mown right up to. If the right plants are chosen a rotary mower can reach under their overhanging stems or branches without causing them any damage, and in this way the need for edging is eliminated. With large shrubs it is easy enough to carry out this idea and the choice of possibilities is wide: a shrub like *Viburnum plicatum* 'Mariesii' is ideal, with its strictly horizontal branches, and in a large garden this works well since there is scope for a good number of such shrubs but in a small garden the larger shrubs mostly need to be placed in the background, otherwise the garden will be dwarfed by them.

The ideal plants for this front edge range in height from about nine inches to eighteen inches (22–45cm) and hold their branches out in such a way that a "Flymo" type of mower can reach in underneath. Herbaceous plants are not suitable, their stems are too fragile and they are not tough enough to prevent the grass encroaching under them, getting entangled in their roots and spreading into the border. The creeping and mat-forming plants we have discussed are not suitable either since they will lie directly on the grass and leave no gap underneath for the mower.

Shrubby potentillas are a good example of what we are looking for, and their flowers range in colour from white to yellow and pale orange. Plant breeders are trying hard to produce pinks and reds – but not wholly successfully so far. *Potentilla arbuscula* is one of the best, the flowers are a good butter yellow colour and like most potentillas it blooms over a long period. I grow a plant in exactly the way I describe at the edge of the lawn. It is a little over two feet tall (60cm); 'Elizabeth' is a similar variety, but is taller. Potentillas do best in a sunny position, and I am told they flower for a longer period if they are on rich soil. There are innumerable varieties of yellow potentillas, some of which have silvery foliage, such as 'Beesii'. *Potentilla dahurica* 'Manchu' (which used to be called *P. mandschurica*) is a good short white, while 'Day Dawn' is peach pink; 'Tangerine' and 'Sunset' are almost orange. Potentillas are not plants for a prominent position because their appearance in the winter is so poor. The leaves turn brown but remain on the plant, giving it a rather bedraggled look: but they are floriferous enough in summer to be worth a place in the garden somewhere.

There are a large number of dwarf shrubs suitable for edging borders in this way. Of flowering shrubs, ornamental brooms would be a good choice: for example *Cytisus* × *kewensis* in creamy yellow, or *Cytisus* 'Allgold' in bright yellow. The shorter members of the *Cistus* family are well worth trying, although they are not suitable for very cold parts of the country. One of the hardiest is *Cistus* 'Silver Pink', a particularly beautiful variety; *C.* × *corbariensis* is white, though pink in bud; and *Cistus* 'Pat' is white with maroon blotches. Evergreen azaleas could also be used in this way. They smother themselves with flowers almost to the point of vulgarity, and the colours tend to be too bright for polite society as well. If I am forced to choose azaleas, I prefer to select the chaste 'Palestrina' in pure white; or 'Iro-hayama' which is one of the few whose colours could be called subtle – white with a pinkish mauve edging; or 'Atlanta' in lilac-pink. The usual, vivid, crashing colours of

'Hinodegiri', 'Hatsugiri', 'Vuyk's Scarlet' or 'John Cairns' should be used with great restraint, certainly not in combination with each other, and preferably not at all.

For evergreen shrubs which can be mown up to, one could try *Viburnum davidii, Lonicera pileata, Euonymus fortunei* 'Silver Queen', *Berberis verruculosa, Cotoneaster conspicuus* 'Decorus' or any of the genera *Sarcococca* or *Skimmia*. These are all excellent ground-cover shrubs: but only the *Berberis* has flowers of any great note. For grey foliage one could select *Salix lananta* 'Stuartii' or the dainty-leafed *Dorycnium hirsutum*. Of the many prostrate or semi-prostrate conifers which could be used there is *Juniperus confertus, Juniperus* × *media* 'Sulphur Spray', or any dwarf forms of *Pinus sylvestris* or *P. mugo*.

But before we go too far with our plans, and get too involved in the details, there are several practical considerations which must not be forgotten.

10

Routes and Paths

A garden has to be workable as well as good to look at, and when we come to consider ways in which we can make the garden convenient to use we find that most of the practical ways in which we use the garden concern movement: what is needed in many instances is a convenient route from one place to another. Some routes will obviously be used more heavily than others, and if there are no paved paths this will soon show up when the grass begins to wear thin in places. Grass will only take a certain amount of wear – if it is trodden on too often it just fades away and before long there will be a bare patch. Grass also gets very wet during the winter months and is not very pleasant to walk on unless we have suitable footwear. If, however, we create paths of hard-surfaced materials they become a very strong element in the design of the garden, being so clearly visible, and thus visual and practical needs have to be carefully balanced.

On the practical side, dry routes from the kitchen door to the garage or the bicycle shed, to the dustbin and to the compost-heap (if you have one) are all highly desirable. If there is a terrace or sitting area it may require a path leading to it, if it isn't immediately outside the house. For some housewives the position of the washing-line is an item of great importance. I am reliably informed that there is no substitute for a good blow in the fresh air, even in these days of tumble-driers, and this is the reason why some gardens have those nasty concrete paths running down them – as straight as a bullet and about as deadly in their effect on the design of the garden. Rotary clothes lines are not objects of beauty either, but they do make a long path unnecessary. If the garden has a vegetable plot, maybe the clothes line can go there, but most gardens need what might be called a service area. There are a lot of things any garden has to have in it which are not at all beautiful, and it is a good idea to devote a part of the garden to dustbins, space for potting-up, a compost-heap, to say nothing of coal-bunkers, wood storage, and a garden shed. Screened off from view, an area such as this will also need a dry route leading to it.

Visually, a path leads the eye on and invites exploration, and for this reason the larger the garden is the more important the parts become. If the garden contains more than one space, and becomes something to explore, the paths become a crucial part of the design. Finding one's way around a large garden ought to be straightforward – the path should simply lead you on. This is particularly important in gardens which are open to the public, and in view of the large number of private gardens which are opened these days, I will make a few simple remarks on this subject.

One of the most important things for the visitor is the entrance. This is the "big moment", as it were, when visitors are most susceptible to being impressed. This fact was understood perfectly by architects in the past, and not only did they make the position of the front entrance of a building crystal clear by devices such as a huge portico with columns or a massive flight of steps, but once you got inside the entrance hall was often the most lavishly decorated room in the house.

It always seems unfortunate to me when the way into a garden cannot be as originally intended. Most gardens have been designed to fit the house they belong to and the natural way to approach the garden is from the house itself. I remember visiting Orchardleigh House, near Frome in Somerset, on a day when it was not open to the public. It is large, Victorian and chateau-like, and the impression it made on me to enter this house of "stately" proportions by the front door was so different from being directed to a horrid little wooden shed-cum-ticket-office, and led round the back of some out-houses to approach a garden by a devious route. Instead, the owner, Mr Duckworth, led me through the house into his blue drawing-room on the south side, where the windows looked out on the lovely sun-lit, terraced gardens with park-land beyond. But this came as a surprise, there had been no hint of these gardens from the front entrance. We stepped down onto the terrace gardens from the drawing-room, exactly as intended. Of course this kind of arrangement is often not possible. Where houses are lived in, the owner cannot be expected to have large numbers of people trooping through the sitting-room, but when the house is also open to the public it does seem highly desirable. At Hidcote, for example, it would be so much more satisfactory if one could approach the gardens from the house, and plunge straight into the delights of the Old Garden, before being led along the 'axis' to the Stilt Garden. Instead, the visitor enters the imposing Theatre Lawn from a yard, but immediately one must dive off to the left and ignore the Theatre Lawn in order to get back to the Old Garden and start in the right place. At Sissinghurst, on the other hand, the archway enables us to approach the garden exactly as intended, in a proper, dignified manner. But having made our entrance, let us consider our route.

Paths should lead somewhere. It should be possible to see every part of the garden in sensible sequence, and to know you have done so, without getting lost or disorientated. But how many gardens are like this? One of the good things about Silk Wood, which adjoins Westonbirt Arboretum in Gloucestershire is that it is a simple circular walk which you can follow in a relaxed manner, admiring the planting as you go. Westonbirt itself is so confusing that one must clutch a plan in one hand and consult it at every junction. Left? Right? Have we missed the Acer Glade? Should we back-track? In other gardens, including some well-known ones in Surrey, we find that wide, important paths lead off into the potting-sheds, side paths twist and wind until the visitor has lost all sense of direction, while other paths turn out to be complete dead ends. The model of perfection is Stourhead in Wiltshire, where a single path with only one or two detours leads the visitor around a "circular" route, and from it every part of the landscape garden can be appreciated. At every turn of the path, emerging from flowering shrubs, a new view appears. There is endless variety, but firmly, with seeming artlessness, the path leads you on and lands you safely back where you started.

In this respect it is interesting to compare the gardens at Sissinghurst with those at Hidcote. The presence of the tower at Sissinghurst, which can be seen peeping over the greenery from many parts of the garden, acts as a point of reference to which the visitor can relate. Secondly, there are fewer compartments than at Hidcote, about half as many in fact; and thirdly the geometry of the whole is simpler and visitors are never allowed to become disorientated on their way.

Even in small gardens the positions of paths should be decided carefully. They are always expensive to make; and so they may as well be clear and rational rather than wayward and confusing, though it must be admitted that this confusion is sometimes the result of a garden being made in stages and not planned in its entirety from the beginning.

The way one moves through the garden gives scope for some of the most exciting of all design effects. If one space is narrow, dark and enclosed and an opening leads suddenly to a brightly-lit wide view over the countryside, the effect is called "surprise". As one cynic has rightly pointed out it can hardly be a surprise the second time one experiences it, and I suppose "sequential contrast" might have been a more accurate label. Of course, contrasts of character need not be quite as dramatic. Hidcote offers several marvellous sequences of spaces, the finest being the route to the Stilt Garden which has been mentioned already. We start in the Old Garden with its profusion of flowers. This leads into the Circle, and directly to the Red Borders; at the far end we reach a flight of steps between the two pavilions and we find ourselves in the Stilt Garden with its clipped hornbeams. Beyond these is an open gateway which provides a wide view over open countryside. Each space has its own character, and each leads into the next in a smooth transition.

The relevance of some of these remarks to small or suburban gardens may at first seem little. But in my view as soon as a garden is large enough to contain several differentiated areas, the way these relate to one another is something worthy of great attention. A clear and logical route from one section of the garden to the next is always desirable, and yet the possibilities for contrast of mood and variety of interest are almost unlimited.

The width of paths depends on the scale of the garden. A "one-person path" is about two foot six inches wide (75cm), but for two people to walk together, you need about five feet (1.5m). In small town gardens there is no room for such generosity, but in medium-size and large gardens it is pleasant to be able to show a visitor the garden in comfort, and walking single-file is not convenient. The larger the garden, the larger the paths can afford to be. At Versailles the vast *allées* were designed to cope with the huge *entourage* of courtiers belonging to the ·royal party.

Generally speaking a wide path always looks more important than a narrow one, so that in large gardens it is easier to find one's way if the route to be followed looks the most important. In which case there can be a kind of hierarchy of paths, with generous widths for main paths, and narrower dimensions for minor pathways within a "compart-ment", for paths leading to short detours off the main route, and for short cuts made for the convenience of the gardener and his wheelbarrow.

The cheapest path, I suppose, is a grass path and in many situations this is perfectly suitable. However, as I have already remarked, grass will only take a certain amount of wear. Originally many parts of Sissinghurst had grass paths, which was fine when it was privately owned and visitors came in small numbers, but when the visitors began to exceed 50,000 a year, grass would no longer stand up to the endless trampling of feet and the grass had to be replaced by brick paving — with a resultant change of character. In some National Trust gardens it is only the fact that they close two or three days a week that saves the grass from giving up. Although grass paths are cheap initially, the cost in man-hours to maintain them is quite high, especially if they have to be edged as well as mown, fed, watered and weeded.

A gravel path is less expensive than brick or concrete paving, and has the advantage of being softer underfoot and less harsh to the eye. Some care is required in preparing a gravel path, and a well-compacted base of free-draining material is needed under it, otherwise it will degenerate to a muddy track after a few years. It is also advisable to choose the surface material with care and discover what different kinds of gravel are available from your local sand and gravel merchant. It is usually worthwhile getting some samples and looking at them where they are to go, to make sure they look right. The kind of gravel available varies from one area to another and in some areas it is better to pay a little extra for a product which is superior to the usual local one. For example, the limestone chippings available in the Cotswolds are quite unpleasant; they are an unattractive yellow colour, and dirt and mud seems to cling to them most tenaciously.

Neither brick nor stone paving are particularly cheap, but some types of concrete paving made to simulate stone are quite acceptable if handled with care. The best way to use such paving successfully is to have it cut into a much greater variety of shapes and sizes than it normally comes in from the manufacturer. The usual "give-away" of mass-produced paving slabs is that they only come in one or two different sizes, which give a monotonous and mechanical appearance. However, if you have about half the slabs cut in two, some in half, others a quarter and three-quarters, and so on, this makes a wide variety of sizes which is much more pleasing. Smaller slabs look better in a small-scale garden in any case. When it gets this complicated it is advisable to draw out a detailed paving layout to a scale of 1:20 beforehand – and make sure the layer can read plans accurately!

Brick paving can be extremely attractive, but avoid coloured concrete bricks which are now used extensively by local authorities for pedestrian precincts: they look much too mechanical. Instead pay a little extra for what the brickworks call a "multi" which will have some variation of colour and texture, and ensure that it is either meant to be a paving brick, or else a brick of engineering quality, which means it will withstand frost without crumbling. Bricks lend themselves to a wide variety of interesting patterns, such as herring-bone and basket weave, and for large areas more complicated patterns can be designed. Again it has to be carefully worked out beforehand on paper if it is at all complicated.

York stone, the classic material for garden paving, is out of reach for most people nowadays because of its price. One can get smaller stone which is suitable for crazy paving, but I don't often recommend this, mainly because its surface is usually too irregular. This means that it tends to hold water in small puddles here and there, and it may also have lumps and bumps which are dangerous to walk on: it is so easy to trip and fall. However, some types of stone such as Cornish slate are quite smooth enough and can be used in this way, if you don't mind the "crazy" pattern.

In theory, a very attractive surface can be obtained from in-situ concrete if it is brushed hard before it dries completely, because this exposes the aggregate (the coarse stones) in the concrete. But this is not a skill commonly available amongst layers of paving, it seems; however, keen do-it-yourselfers will find this a technique well worth experimenting with. One example of the way this can be used is to have a tartan grid pattern of brick paviors and fill the square spaces in between with the exposed-aggregate in-situ concrete.

Asphalt is another possibility, but most gardeners are prejudiced against it, no doubt because they associate it with public pavements and paths in municipal parks. But there is nothing intrinsically wrong with it; it weathers to a harmless grey colour, it is smooth, dry and ideal for children to ride their tricycles on.

There are several other materials that can be used for paths. In America, timber is used quite extensively but in this country it gets too slippery to be safe, and is best avoided. In woodland areas I have seen shredded bark used successfully, and I even heard of one gardener who lived near a pine wood who made his paths of fallen pine needles, a solution which was both cheap and unusual, but these can also be slippery.

Steps in the garden should be welcomed as an opportunity for an attractive design feature. Some people feel so strongly about the benefit of changes in level in a garden that they think it is worth getting a mechanical digger in to change the levels even in a perfectly flat site, for the sake of the variety it introduces. Outdoor steps should be much more "gracious" than stairs indoors; in other words the "rise" (the vertical part) should be less, and the "going" (the part you put your foot on) should be much more generous. Fifteen inches (38cm) should be an absolute minimum for the "going" and eighteen inches or two feet (45–60cm) is preferable. A rise of four inches (10cm) is about right in most situations – if it is any shallower someone may trip because they didn't notice the step. And for the same reason steps should always be in groups of three or more: one odd step on its own is rather dangerous.

The finest steps used to be made of solid stone – but who can afford such a luxury these days? Concrete or "reconstructed-stone" paving slabs are not nearly so pleasing used for steps because the rough edges are exposed. I think brick steps are preferable to steps of concrete paving slabs and they have a neater appearance. Exposed-aggregate concrete cast in-situ is another possibility worth considering. In woodland or naturalistic settings timber risers can be effectively used in conjunction with gravel or even grass paths.

Wide flights of steps look much more attractive than narrow ones and one should try to be as generous as possible with steps that are looked at from in front.

There is unlimited scope for inventiveness in the layout of steps, but of course the style of a flight of steps has to be related to the rest of the garden. Formal gardens require formal steps; naturalistic gardens need something more irregular and casual. It is sufficient in most cases to allow the steps to die away into an adjoining bank; there is no need to build a flanking wall, but ground cover plants adjoining the steps will mask the junction between steps and slope.

A selection of plans showing flights of steps, some formal (*on the left*) and some informal in style (*on the right*).

11

Plant Shapes

When it comes to the design of the planted areas, there are two factors to be considered before we start to fill them up with pleasant flowers or even coloured foliage. If we imagine for a moment that the only photographs we shall be allowed to take of our borders will be black and white ones, certain other elements in the picture will come out more clearly than the flowers. The flowers will probably show up only if they are white or pale yellow, and this means that the shapes of the plants and the lines and outlines provided by the particular way each one grows will suddenly become more important, and so will the kind of texture created by the foliage of the plant. The leaves of some plants are smooth and shiny, others are rough and leathery; some are held stiffly, others are thin and drooping. Factors like these give some plants a quite distinctive presence in the garden, while others, such as many herbaceous plants, produce such an 'average' mass of greenery as to be hardly noticeable when not in bloom.

The distinct and definite outline of conifers has already been remarked on in Chapter 6. However, some shrubs and trees lend them-selves to clipping and can be given definite shape with the aid of shears. The traditional subjects for this treatment are Yew and Box, and they are ideally suitable for the purpose. There are other possibilities should you wish to depart from the well-tried and tested path. *Berberis darwinii* and *B. stenophylla* for instance do not mind being trimmed. They both reach at least five feet (1.5m) but they will only produce good flowers if the clipping is left till flowering is over. The Japanese clip their evergreen azaleas quite successfully into neat rotund mounds which still manage to bloom in spite of this treatment.

If you like the idea of clipped coloured foliage there are better possibilities than the ubiquitous yellow privet of suburbia. *Lonicera* 'Baggesen's Gold' is ideal, and for something taller *Cupressus macro-*

carpa 'Gold Crest' is suitable for all but the coldest areas. For "clipp-able" shrubs in other colours, *Berberis thunbergii* 'Atropurpurea' and *Prunus cerasifera* 'Pissardii' are probably the best purples. For vari-egated foliage, Holly is the traditional choice, although I suspect *Elae-agnus pungens* 'Maculata' would be just as good if the thought of prickly hedge clippings doesn't appeal to you. For grey foliage, *Euca-lyptus gunnii* is evergreen, and has been discussed earlier; *Hippophae rhamnoides*, Sea Buckthorn, also clips well but is prone to suckering; while for something lower *Atriplex halimus*, Tree Purslane, would be good to try. Lavender is often seen clipped, but has the drawback of being rather small; it also has flowers on long stalks which tend to destroy the shape one wishes to impose on it. If you like blue foliage the best subject is surely *Cupressus glabra* 'Conica' sometimes seen listed as *Cupressus arizonica* 'Conica'. This conifer is planted to excess by the Italians, and having seen the obtrusive effect of hedges of this blue colour on the countryside I have come to dislike this species; the dark green of their native cypress is so much more pleasing in the landscape. Similarly our own yew never looks out of place in the English countryside. One can weary of too much colour. Some plants which are traditionally clipped, such as beech and hornbeam, provide their own variation of colour during the course of the year: fresh green in spring, deep green in mid-summer, bronze in autumn and winter. If these can be used, then why not others such as *Acer campestre* or *Liquidambar styraciflua* (Sweet Gum) which have good autumn colour?

Trimming of deciduous shrubs should, as a general rule, be carried out in March or August, for evergreens in April or August, though vigorous shrubs such as *Lonicera* 'Baggesen's Gold' will need trimming several times a year. Clipped domes and hedges belong in gardens of formal style and the scope for extensive schemes of topiary in average or small gardens is rather limited, but possible nevertheless. Many yew hedges in old gardens are as much as six feet (2m) wide, but they can be kept to two feet (60cm) with regular clipping.

In less formal settings plants which have definite shape of their own without clipping are preferable, and are certainly more labour-saving. There are various possibilities: domes, and shapes approximating to domes; vertical columns; prostrate carpets; spikes; and also various plants which have a shape or type of growth all of their own, such as *Juniperus chinensis* 'Kaizuka' the so-called Hollywood Juniper.

For a plant of pointed, columnar shape a conifer is the obvious choice. The ideal, to which all others are striving, is without doubt *Cupressus sempervirens*, the Italian Cypress. There is no other conifer with such an elegantly pointed tip, and its dark green colour is perfect, especially in the strong sunlight of the Mediterranean. It has been assumed by many people that *Cupressus sempervirens* is not hardy in this country, but the thorough surveys of Alan Mitchell have shown that mature and healthy specimens exist not only in Somerset but also in East Lothian, where frosts must be as severe as anywhere in Britain. It appears that it is only susceptible to frost damage when it is young, and that it can be grown in many areas if one is prepared to give it some protection until it reaches a height of six feet or so (2m). The way to do this is to put four stout stakes round it, slightly higher than the plant, and during frosty weather drape two layers of sacking over it. This may seem a bother, but of course it all depends how much you want to grow the ideal plant for your purpose. It is surprising how much effort dedicated gardeners will devote to getting the results they want. To be on the safe side *Cupressus sempervirens* should be planted in its position when quite small – older specimens resent disturbance.

My second choice is still not one of the many *Chamaecyparis* varieties, but instead I recommend the Incense Cedar *Calocedrus decurrens* (occasionally listed as *Libocedrus decurrens*). This has good dark foliage, which is glossier than the Italian Cypress, and this is an advantage in this country. Its shape is perfectly regular, but the tip is not tapered and pointed like *Cupressus sempervirens*, but rounded. It is also much taller, and liable to reach a hundred feet (30m) after many years, whereas an Italian cypress in this country is unlikely to exceed forty feet (12.5m).

The best form of *Chamaecyparis lawsoniana*, in my view, is one of the oldest which appeared in 1855: its correct name is 'Erecta' but it is more often called 'Erecta Viridis'. Its great quality is the richness of its glossy, green foliage; it is no dwarf, (there were some huge ones by the main lawn at Bodnant in North Wales) and it can reach seventy-five feet (25m) eventually but it does this very slowly. Its shape can be spoilt by snow and like many conifers the foliage may die back locally if other plants press in too closely. It is usually many-stemmed and as a result its shape is broader than the two preceding species and can be a little irregular; it comes to a rather blunt point at the top.

Another variety of *lawsoniana* which is quite good is 'Fletcheri', which tops out at about forty feet (13m) after very many years. The foliage is feathery and juvenile, grey-green in summer with bluish bronze tints in the winter. The shape of 'Fletcheri' can be even broader than 'Erecta' and more irregular, with several pointed tops at different heights within an overall conical shape – you see how far we have departed already from our ideal "pencil-like" outline.

'Ellwoodii' is a little bluer, and is so common that, like Forsythia and Laburnum, one gets tired of it. The texture is not quite so pleasing as 'Fletcheri' and it is just as broad. 'Columnaris' is narrower but I personally object to its blue colour. 'Allumii' is a slightly preferable blue-green colour, but the broad 'plates' or sprays of leaves, held so stiffly are not nearly so pleasing as 'Fletcheri'. Another attempt at a substitute for the Italian cypress is *C. lawsoniana* 'Pottenii'. The foliage is a good green with a nice texture, but so many specimens seem to suffer from die-back that it cannot be recommended. 'Kilmacurragh' is sometimes recommended but is not specially attractive when young. Avoid the odd 'Wisselii', sometimes offered, unless you want a curiosity.

There are several possibilities in the Juniper family such as *Juniperis communis* 'Hibernica', which is the smallest pencil-shaped conifer so far, reaching twenty feet (7m) or so at the most. It can be good when it is happy: in one exposed garden on cold clay where I planted it it has not been very successful. Another variety which has become available only recently is *Juniperus scopulorum* 'Blue Heaven'; this may be tougher and has such a nice texture I can forgive its tinge of blue! Don't be tempted by the much-offered 'Skyrocket': its strongly vertical branches look quite unpleasant, like cat's fur which has been brushed up the wrong way. *Juniperus virginiana* 'Canaertii' and *Juniperus drupacea*, the Syrian Juniper, are both said to be good, but they are both rarities, and I have not seen either of them. The best *Thuja* for our purpose is probably *Thuja plicata* 'Fastigiata', but this makes quite a large specimen.

A garden can only take a small number of pointed conifers, and they should be planted for conscious effect, not scattered around at whim. There should certainly not be too many kinds: preferably only one kind or perhaps two. There is no need for your garden to be a trial ground for conifers; let Wisley or Bedgebury Pinetum do that for you.

Of the innumerable golden varieties the best for a small garden are *Taxus baccata* 'Standishii', a slow-growing and narrow form of the English Yew; and *Thuja orientalis* 'Conspicua', which is not so narrow, but a pleasing shade of yellow. The best of the Lawson varieties is perhaps 'Dutch Gold' – again a fairly broad variety, but eventually as tall as one would need in a small garden.

Other pointed or column-like trees are available and almost all such forms are selected "deviants" of trees which normally grow in the traditional manner. Not many of these erect varieties are wholly attractive: the usual gracefulness of a deciduous tree is spoiled if it starts making all its branches reach heavenwards in a "hands-up" position. Some of the best varieties are too big for a small garden in any case, such as *Quercus robur* 'Fastigiata', the so-called Cypress Oak and a Beech, *Fagus sylvatica* 'Dawyck'.

Prunus 'Amanogawa' is one of the most commonly seen in small gardens, but it has little to recommend it. One can hardly call it a tree, there is so little of it, and the flowers are such a watery pink. There are other possibilities for verticality such as *Gleditsia triacanthos* 'Elegantissima', *Malus* 'Van Eseltine', *Prunus sargentii* 'Rancho' and *Pyrus communis* 'Beech Hill', and it is best to have a look and decide whether you like these or not.

Amongst the large range of dwarf conifers there are many examples of shrubs with a dome-like outline, or, as they are described by some people, plants which are "bun-shaped". *Chamaecyparis lawsoniana* 'Minima Glauca' is a good example; it is not in fact particularly glaucous. Although it is slow growing, it can reach three feet (1m) or more after ten years. *Chamaecyparis lawsoniana* 'Gimbornii' is very similar, but eventually smaller and has more dense foliage. If you should need something larger, *Thuja occidentalis* 'Woodwardii' usually reaches five or six feet (about 2m), in a rich green colour, and a similar kind of foliage. For much harder-looking foliage of quite a different texture, one could choose a dwarf variety of *Picea abies* (the tree normally used for Christmas trees) called 'Clanbrassiliana'. This also reaches over six feet (2m) in mid-green. Another *Picea* gives us an astonishing blue colour: this is *P. pungens* 'Globosa', which eventually reaches three or four feet (about 1.5m). This colour looks good with silver foliage and any shade of green. But to contrast it with yellow conifers is too violent a contrast to my sensitive eye, and only creates a restless effect. *Abies balsamea* 'Hudsonia' repeats the texture of 'Clanbrassiliana' and is a rather more pleasant colour, with glossy leaves; this makes a smaller "bun" reaching about two foot six inches (75cm) in height.

Some conifers change their colour during the seasons and one of these is *Thuja orientalis* 'Juniperoides', occasionally listed as *Thuja o.* 'Decussata'. It has a soft appearance, and its outline is rather less regular than those we have mentioned so far; its colour is greyish green in summer, turning to various attractive purplish shades in the autumn and winter. The shape can be damaged by the weight of snow, however, which should be removed with a brush as soon as possible. It reaches about three foot six inches (1m). 'Rosedalis' is another variety of *Thuja orientalis* which changes colour, perhaps nearer to a sphere than a dome. In winter it has a purplish-grey colour, but the new shoots in spring are almost yellow, fading to an attractive pale shade of green in the summer. The variety has a soft appearance because of its juvenile foliage. *Thuja occidentalis* 'Danica' is a much smaller dome, about eighteen inches (45cm) high, with the usual adult foliage, dark green in summer, bronze in winter. For a yellow "dome" I recommend a conifer of a fairly restrained colour: *Thuja plicata* 'Rogersii'. The inner part of the foliage is dark green, while all the tips are yellow, and in cold weather the plant takes on a bronze appearance. It eventually reaches about three foot six inches (1m).

The shape of *Thuja occidentalis* 'Rheingold' is not exactly a dome, but like a few other varieties, its shape could be described as being rather like the flame of a candle, and the colour is a bit like that as well; yellow, with a tinge of copper or orange to the edge. This is surely one of the best, small, yellow conifers in existence.

To the uninitiated, *Hebe cupressoides* looks as if it ought to be a conifer. However, it occasionally has small flowers of a blueish-white colour that stud the branches – something which never happens to a conifer. *Hebe cupressoides* is perhaps more of an irregular globe than a dome in its shape. It usually reaches about three feet (1m), but there is also a dwarf form called 'Boughton Dome' with much denser foliage, which is about one foot (30cm) or less in height. Several other hebes are roughly 'bun-shaped': *Hebe albicans* has attractive pale foliage and white flowers, but the effect of the plant is spoilt in the late summer by the dead flowers which remain on the plant for several weeks after flowering is over. *Hebe rakaiensis* is similar, reaching about eighteen inches (45cm), but of a good, dense, apple-green foliage. It is still listed by some nurseries as *H. subalpina*. I have not grown it myself so I cannot say if it has the same fault as *albicans*. *Hebe brachysiphon* is much bigger, and again of globe-like shape, with tough-looking, dark green leaves, densely clothing the branches. It is often planted in seaside towns, but is perfectly hardy in other areas.

At least two *Berberis* species are roughly dome-shaped. *B. thunbergii* 'Atropurpurea Nana' has reddish foliage and an altogether neat appearance, about a foot (30cm) high, while *Berberis candidula* can reach two feet (60cm), an attractive evergreen species with yellow flowers in spring.

Skimmias are a good example of plants with a distinctive, rounded outline which deserve to be planted as specimens rather than to be jostled by other shrubs whose branches will only spoil the effect of the neatly arranged foliage. The evergreen leaves are a good glossy green, and the flowers and fruits are as neatly positioned as the leaves. But with skimmias one must have both male and female plants for pollination to take place, otherwise there will be no berries on the female plants. One of the best females is *Skimmia* 'Nymans', and the recommended male to accompany this is *Skimmia* 'Ruby Dome', sometimes listed as

'MacPenny's Male'. Skimmias are greedy feeders and soon starve if conditions are too poor or too dry, and in such cases watering and additional nutrients provide the answer. Several varieties prefer acid soil and go yellow and sickly on limy soil but a dose now and again of Epsom Salts (magnesium sulphate) (1 tablespoonful to a gallon) should cure this.

An effective way to display a plant of distinctive outline is to surround it with prostrate plants which cover the ground to a height of only a few inches. There is a wide range of such subjects, many of which provide good weed-proof cover at the same time. Amongst shrubs an ideal example is *Cotoneaster dammeri*, an extraordinary plant similar in many ways to other cotoneasters, but born without the necessary strength to lift its branches off the ground even an inch. Evergreen, and berry-bearing in the autumn, it spreads steadily, eventually covering a wide area.

Some prostrate spreaders root as they go, so that each new piece becomes self-supporting. There are two good carpeters which are like this, both of which are supposed to be lime-hating: they are *Arctostaphylos uva-ursi* and *Gaultheria procumbens*. However, the Gaultheria has survived so far in my garden which has traces of lime in it. Both have dark, glossy leaves with a purplish tinge to them, grow four to five inches high (10–12cm) and have red fruits in the autumn. The *Arctostaphylos* is less commonly seen.

Pachysandra terminalis is another leafy-textured carpeter, but a little taller, at about nine inches high (23cm). On moist soil, slightly on the acid side, it will give permanent evergreen cover spreading gradually over an indefinitely wide area. For small areas it is not prostrate enough to have the carpet-like appearance which it has when planted on a large scale.

Hebe pinguifolia 'Pagei', however, is lime tolerant, and has pretty, pale, grey-blue leaves which are neat and evergreen; but to make a carpet it must be planted at fifteen or eighteen inch centres (40–45cm), since the spread of one plant on its own is limited.

But for the ideal carpet, with real plain-carpet texture we must turn again to the range of dwarf conifers. The best selection is to be found in the genus *Juniperus*, and perhaps the best of all is *J. sabina* 'Tamariscifolia' whose horizontal branches of good grey-green foliage overlap one another in the neatest possible way. But there are several other good varieties, such as *Juniperus communis* 'Repanda', *J. communis* 'Hornibrookii', and *Juniperus procumbens* 'Nana'. Perhaps the most prostrate of all are varieties of *Juniperus horizontalis* such as 'Douglasii' and 'Bar Harbour', but these are slightly less tidy growers, sending out long, pointed, trailing branches; however, once full "wall-to-wall" cover of the space concerned has taken place, this is of no account. If you like colours other than green, *Juniperus communis* 'Depressa Aurea' is a good yellow, although it does turn bronze in the winter; and *Juniperus horizontalis* has the forms 'Glauca' and 'Montana' for lovers of blue conifer foliage.

There are no other shrubs to match the smooth carpet texture of conifers, and certainly nothing as good amongst perennials. *Vinca minor*, the Lesser Periwinkle, is a shrub though it could easily be mistaken for a perennial. It is a highly accommodating evergreen plant that will grow almost anywhere and tolerates dense shade. Rooting as it goes it produces a carpet of leafy stems, about six inches high or more (15–20cm), and it, of course, scores over conifers by having flowers, either of the pretty periwinkle blue, or, if you care to hunt them out in the gardens of enthusiasts, in white, in plum-purple, in double blue, and even double purple. The plant I grow under the north wall of my house is the variegated form 'Aureovariegata'.

For something smaller to give a flatter, more carpet-like appearance, the range of alpines offer several possibilities. Sedums and thymes, that were suggested for growing alongside paving, are suitable for this purpose as well, and other species to swell the list include *Sedum spathulifolium purpureum* and *S. spathulifolium* 'Cappa Blanca', which are only about an inch high (2.5cm) and make a good carpet of neat rosettes in a sunny, well-drained situation. *Thymus herba-barona* which smells of caraway, is suitable for southern districts. The genus *Acaena* also offers pretty foliage less than an inch high, including some varieties with blue or copper-coloured leaves. Most of these acaenas are quite aggressive and not suitable for mixing with alpine plants of a more delicate nature. But with most of these very small plants one cannot expect to get perfect cover for a large area without an occasional bare or brown patch here and there.

The kind of alpine which catalogues say is "too vigorous for the rockery" is the type most likely to give us the effect we are looking for. *Dryas octopetala* for example soon spreads itself where there is reasonable drainage. *Polygonum affine* 'Donald Lowndes' and 'Darjeeling Red' both have pink flower spikes and are good for places where sedums and thymes are not suitable, i.e. richer, damper soil. For sun or shade, the rosettes of London Pride, *Saxifraga umbrosa*, are quite pleasing, and its tiny pink flowers on their tall stems provide additional interest. *Potentilla alba* will also tolerate shade; it has pretty, grey-green, five-fingered foliage, and roots as it goes. Some of the best carpeters for cool shade come from the genus *Lamium;* but beware, they are extremely vigorous. *Lamium galeobdolon* 'Variegatum' has prettily marked leaves, and even prettier is *Lamium maculatum* 'Aureum', which has bright yellowy-green markings. But it is no good planting *L. m.* 'Aureum' in dry shade, I have discovered, for my own plant has died.

There are other shapes, too, besides columns, domes and prostrate carpets, and these are explored in the next chapter.

CHAPTER
12

Habit

There are good and bad habits, as everyone knows, but I suppose that
when we speak of the habit of a plant we are using the term in its more
old-fashioned sense of dress (as in a monk's habit) and what we are
referring to is the way a plant is "clothed" in its foliage. Many worthwhile plants do not necessarily have a particular shape or outline, but
nevertheless they have a distinctive manner of growing which is easily
recognizable. Every plant has its own habit in fact and, although it may
be hard to describe, it can still be an important factor in identifying a
plant once one is familiar with it. For instance we may initially learn
to recognize an ash tree by its black buds or its leaves, but it is not
long before we can identify one several hundred yards away simply by
the characteristic curve of its outer branches or, in other words, its
habit. Once we are familiar with the character of a plant and appreciate
its particular habit we can place it in the garden in a way that will
show it off to best effect. Perhaps the classic example is *Cotoneaster
horizontalis*, a very common but worthy plant; no doubt its elementary
recognizability has been the main reason for its ubiquity.

The Hollywood Juniper, *Juniperus chinensis* 'Kaizuka', provides
another instance of a plant of immediate distinction. It develops an
irregular sculptural shape of good green foliage, as a result of the way
its stiff branches grow out at forty-five degrees or more to the horizontal
plane, and they even twist a bit at the same time especially at the ends.
This is just the kind of plant which looks best in isolation, surrounded
only by a low-level carpeting plant, which offers no competition to the
strong, jagged shape.

One whole group of plants which is unlike any other is the whipcord
group of hebes. These seem to be either greatly admired or else hated,
as is the case with most things (or people) of definite character. Some
dismiss them as being like horticultural sea-weed; others collect every

possible species. I must admit that although I disliked them at first, I now have not only *Hebe armstrongii* (or *H. ochracea*), perhaps the best and certainly the most well known, but also *Hebe coarctica, H. salicornioides, H. propingua major* and recently *Hebe laingii*, each of these is distinct (to the enthusiast) and worthwhile. Whipcord hebes resemble dwarf conifers, perhaps, more than anything else, but of course they do have flowers, though not very startling ones.

I suppose the greatest possible contrast to the shrubs of strongly rounded shape that we have discussed is provided by spiky plants, and the finest examples of these are provided by the *Yucca* family. In my experience the best species are *Yucca gloriosa* and *Y. recurvifolia;* when well suited these eventually become large plants, with startling clusters of stiff, sword-like leaves. The impact of a mature plant is wholly sculptural, and creates a distinctly exotic atmosphere; such plants look as though they belong to hotter, sunnier countries than our own, as of course they do: the sandy, coastal districts of South Carolina and Georgia, USA. *Yucca recurvifolia* may be distinguished from *gloriosa* by its long leaves which are not so stiff, and the outer ones are usually bent back. The spines of most yuccas are quite vicious, so take care. When they bloom their splendour is complete, as the tall flower spikes of creamy-white bells are a perfect match for the dramatic foliage. Yuccas like sunny positions on well-drained soil. On cold clay it may be worth making a raised bed: the additional height can only increase their impact in the garden. *Yucca filamentosa* is also good but it is usually smaller; on the other hand I find the limper leaves of *Y. flaccida* are less pleasing.

The spiky effect of phormiums is nearly as remarkable as that of yuccas. However, the spikes of phormiums all spring from ground-level and are not grouped in clusters of rosettes in the way that makes a large Yucca a design in itself; nor are there such attractive panicles of flowers. There are many variegated forms available these days, (such as 'Yellow Wave' and 'Dazzler') many of which have been developed in New Zealand, where phormiums come from, but the species, *Phormium tenax,* is itself a perfectly good plant which has the advantage of being larger and more hardy than many of these fancy varieties. It also holds its stems rigidly, while some of the stripy and red-streaked forms curve over at the tip which is less pleasing. The basic variations of *Phormium tenax* 'Purpureum' and 'Variegata', however, are as good as the species. *Phormium cookianum* (also listed as *P. colensoi*) is also good, but shorter, but I cannot get my own plant to flower, even though it is by a south-facing wall. Phormiums do not object to damp so long as they are not too cold at the same time. An occasional good soaking in the summer helps to increase the size of the plant.

There are several species of perennial plants which have sharply vertical foliage, and although they are by no means in the same class as the yuccas and phormiums, they are useful for providing variety in the border. Irises of various kinds give us just this kind of break from the usual mounds of foliage. The ordinary iris, *Iris germanica*, has quite good foliage, but by August it begins to look a bit tatty. If you particularly want to grow irises for their foliage, choose *Iris pallida dalmatica;* and this is no hardship since it has beautiful, pale blue flowers, just as good as many a *germanica* variety. *Iris sibirica* has masses of good pointed green leaves as well as blue flowers, and is good either by the waterside or in the border, but the leaves tend to lean over in the autumn and flatten neighbouring plants. *Iris* 'Ochraurea' *(I. ochroleuca × I. aurea)* has slightly better leaves, about three feet (1m) high, with creamy yellow flowers. For a shady border one could choose *Iris foetidissima;* in this species the berries are more prominent than its flowers and the foliage is evergreen.

There are other perennials which are spiky and evergreen, such as the South American eryngiums, sometimes called Sea Holly. There are several species but one of the most reliable is *Eryngium eburneum* (sometimes listed as *E. paniculatum,* or *E. bromeliifolium*): the olive-green leaves arch slightly but gracefully and are edged with fine teeth, making a plant about eighteen inches to two foot high (45–60cm), until the flowers come on amazing airy sprays that reach up to five feet (150cm) or more, with heads like small green teasles. There are several other interesting species, such as *E. lassauxii,* which can be seen at Oxford Botanic Garden.

Curtonus paniculatus has sheaves of vertical foliage and so do the related *Crocosmia* hybrids such as 'Bressingham Blaze' and 'Vulcan', which are shorter; but the foliage of kniphofias and *Hemerocallis* is of less value having a more grass-like effect.

Some herbaceous plants have prominent flower "spikes". *Eremurus* species, the fox-tail lilies, are surely the most dramatic examples, on stems reaching up to six feet (2m), in white, pale pink or yellow. They need some care but are so astonishing in their appearance they make it worth the effort. Other perennials with spiky flowers are perhaps too numerous to mention, but cimicifugas, kniphofias and the well-known delphiniums are all large enough for their flower spikes to show up strongly in the border.

Some plants make a spike, or at least a strongly vertical element, in themselves – like the familiar wild foxglove, for instance. There are two other particularly fine, statuesque examples which deserve a mention: verbascums and *Onopordum acanthium*. Some verbascums have big, woolly, grey leaves and yellow flowers on woolly stems, and reach six feet or so (2m). Their English names include 'Mullein' (pronounced mullin), 'Adam's Flannel' and the 'Hag-taper', so take your pick.

Onopordums can be safely called Scotch Thistles, and become great gaunt, skeleton-like shapes, as high as a man, with large, grey leaves and stems and large thistle flowers. They are biennial. Seeds sown in the earlier summer of one year will produce plants to bloom (and die) the following year. Sometimes they self-sow themselves, which can be useful. I remember a charming association of onopordums and *Rosa rubrifolia* at the Vine House, near Bristol, a delightful study in pink and grey.

In complete contrast to all this verticality, there are some plants which hold their branches in a distinctly horizontal manner. The Pfitzer junipers are well-known examples of this habit. *Juniperus* × *media* 'Pfitzeriana' and 'Pfitzeriana Aurea' form a series of evergreen layers; but these are far from being dwarf conifers, and are more useful to the landscape architect than to the gardener, giving excellent ground cover and gradually spreading in all directions to a diameter of twenty-five feet (8m), when suited, and up to six feet (2m) high. *Juniperus* × *media* 'Hetzii' and *J.* 'Grey Owl' are blue and grey equivalents and are almost as vigorous. However Pfitzer junipers can be seen quite commonly in suburban gardens, often getting uncomfortably big for their position and squashing adjoining shrubs – but then we don't have to make the same mistake.

Cornus controversa 'Variegata' on the other hand is perfectly suited for an average garden, and makes a tall shrub and eventually a small tree. The horizontality of its branches is most remarkable: they form a series of tiers one above the other, often with a clear gap of many inches between each layer. The variegations are an attractive silvery shade. However, it is difficult to propagate, I am told, and this makes it expensive and, as a result, rare. There are few other plants to rival the sensational horizontals of this Cornus, but there is a well-known Viburnum whose branches do form distinct tiers: *Viburnum plicatum* 'Mariesii'. The horizontal effect is most noticeable in May when the shrub is looking its best, in full flower, with the branches lined with the white lace-cap flowers.

A more common kind of habit, at least amongst shrubs, is for the branches to hang in long, arching sprays. A good example is *Genista tenera* 'Golden Showers' (sometimes listed as *G. cinerea*), which to me is a kind of Broom but apparently boasts an English name of its own: the

Ashy Woadwaxen. This tall shrub has pendant sprays of thin branches (characteristic of brooms) which are held in an elegant arching manner. In late June and July they are covered in bright yellow flowers.

Elegance of habit is not a quality possessed by many members of the genus *Berberis*, but one of the few that has this quality is *Berberis stenophylla*. Like many of its relatives it is prickly, and in the spring large numbers of small yellow flowers appear along the many arching branches of evergreen foliage. It is a garden hybrid partly derived from *Berberis darwinii*, and although *darwinii* has brighter flowers and more glossy foliage, the gracefulness of *stenophylla* has made it a well-known shrub.

Buddleia alternifolia is at first sight quite distinct from the common buddleias that grow almost like weeds. It makes a tall, dense, deciduous shrub or with some encouragement a small tree, and in June it is a remarkable sight when the pale mauve flowers appear clustered all down the length of the long thread-like stems that hang gracefully around the bush.

The 'Filifera' varieties of *Chamaecyparis pisifera* are quite distinct: they all possess thin strands of foliage which hang down in a thread-like manner in all directions. A mature specimen of 'Filifera' has the outline of an egg-cosy – in other words it is too tall to fit into our category of dome-like plants. But the texture is curiously hair-like making it look, with some imagination, like the back of a huge, green wig. 'Filifera Nana' is smaller and could have safely gone into the list of dome-shaped plants. 'Filifera' itself can eventually reach ten feet (3m) but 'Filifera Aurea', in bright yellow, is a little slower.

Plants like these; spiky, horizontal, arching and so on, are just a few examples to tempt us to look at plants for what they are visually, and as a whole, and so prevent the garden becoming a collection of amorphous shrubs of featureless greenery whose presence is only tolerated for fifty weeks for the sake of two weeks of flowers.

For a plant to show its characteristic habit it must be left to itself, on the principle that Nature is a good designer on its own. Pruning, in my opinion, should be kept to an absolute minimum. If shrubs have been planted intelligently in the first place there will be no need to attack beautiful growing things with saws, shears and pruners and create the scenes of devastation that some parks departments and garden owners indulge in. No, if a plant is too big for its position, dig it out and plant something smaller; or, if it is a plant you especially cherish dig out the plants next to it. Pruning should be done purely on an aesthetic basis. You should stand back as you do when arranging cut flowers and, using secateurs, cut out a stray stem or branch low down where the cut will not show, taking care that the shape of the shrub or tree will be enhanced in the process. Some reduction in the number of plants in a garden becomes inevitable as the garden matures and each plant gets bigger. I remember visiting one large garden in Dorset where the lady owner didn't believe in any pruning whatsoever with the result that in places it was quite difficult to fight our way through the jungle. Overcrowding of trees is particularly common in old gardens, with the result that one can hardly appreciate the characteristic habit of any one specimen.

Some people choose a tree for the garden because of its flowers; others look for coloured foliage, but to me one of the most important things is whether the tree has an elegant shape and a pleasing habit. This is what one has to live with all the year round: flowers, however, impressive, are transitory. One only has to think of *Prunus* 'Kanzan', that well-known suburb-dweller. Its floral display is certainly second to none; and its canopy of candy-floss pink seen against a blue sky on a spring day is quite an amazing sight. But the shape of the tree, and the way it holds its branches out like a half-opened umbrella is actually most ugly, and for that reason I would never plant one, preferring the more elegant lines of *Prunus* 'Shimidsu' or *P.* 'Shirotae'.

In general I do not care for trees which are horticultural forms selected either for their erect or for their weeping habit. In this respect Nature seems to me to have been a perfectly good designer of trees without any interference from men trying to improve on her efforts. When you compare many weeping trees with a normal version of their species they appear like hideously disabled offspring. Compare the natural airy grace of our native Silver Birch, *Betula pendula*, with that poor hump-backed cripple *Betula pendula* 'Youngii'. The weeping form of the Atlantic Cedar, *Cedrus atlantica* 'Glauca Pendula' with its foolishly dangling threads is another travesty of the original. The same goes for *Fagus sylvatica* 'Pendula': it lacks all the magnificence and beauty of an ordinary wild beech tree, and is fit only to be converted into firewood. *Larix kaempferi* 'Pendula', the Weeping Japanese Larch; *Morus alba* 'Pendula', the Weeping Mulberry; *Prunus* 'Kiku-shidare', sometimes called Cheal's Weeping Cherry and *Prunus subhirtella* 'Pendula Rosea': are varieties that disfigure the garden. And yet species which are born weepers (poor souls) manage to do it gracefully – think of *Picea breweriana*, for instance, Brewer's Weeping Spruce.

Some people choose their trees for the sake of their bark and one might be tempted to choose *Betula ermanii*, for its pink-tinged creamy white bark, or *Betula costata* for its bright white bark, and yet neither of these approaches the "ordinary" birch *Betula pendula* for graceful-ness of habit.

In the case of small trees, one is to a certain extent up against the nursery trade. Most small trees do not naturally produce dead straight trunks six feet high (2m) and then suddenly burgeon out into bushy growth on top of a stalk: they are much more likely to branch out lower down, and they look much more natural if they do. In such cases it is better to buy a young tree than a so-called standard which has been regimented to the six foot trunk specification. It will be cheaper anyway, and will not require an ugly stake. Of course it will be smaller to start with, but it will catch up eventually. Another way round this, which can look very effective, is to plant two, or better still three, plants as close together as possible so that the result looks like a multi-stemmed plant – which is quite common in nature but not usually permitted in horticulture – and if one or two of these trunks lean out a little, that will help to increase the naturalistic effect.

The sculptural effect of having several stems is something which is shown up in silhouette, and there are several small trees which are particularly remarkable in this way. *Rhus typhina*, the Sumach tree, for example is often seen in suburban front gardens; this is another plant with instantly recognizable habit. The leaves are handsome and very large considering the size of the tree (which is small) and colour well in the autumn. Some people find its tendency to sucker can be annoying, and another slight disadvantage is that it is rather late coming into leaf in the spring. I grow an attractive form of it called 'Laciniata' with finely cut, ferny leaves.

Aralia elata, has a similar tendency to *Rhus typhina*, to produce several twisted stems which hold a vaguely umbrella-like canopy of leaves overhead. It is a curious plant, which may need a little help to develop into an elegant specimen. Like the Rhus, it is hardly more than a shrub in size, but because of its bare stems (they are too thin to call trunks) one is forced to call it a tree. Some impression of its character may be gained from the fact that a closely related and similar species *Aralia chinensis* is known as the Devil's Walking Stick, because of the contorted shape of its perilously thorned stems.

Cercis siliquastrum, the Judas Tree, like an incorrigible child, refuses to adopt the standard lollipop-on-stick format that trees are supposed to have, and instead tends to lean out one way or another somewhat dangerously, and certainly likes to branch out near the base. In May the bare branches are wreathed in pink flowers. It prefers some warmth and does better in the sunnier south. Unfortunately 'habit' is one of those things that hardly gets mentioned in most books, and the fact that a Judas Tree grows in a totally different way from a flowering cherry is something you have to learn from observation: Hillier's Manual doesn't mention it; Bean tells you it can be picturesque, a fact I suspect he copied it from William Robinson who uses exactly the same word; but neither tell you wherein this picturesque-ness lies.

Some examples of trees of elegant habit are *Catalpa bignonioides, Koelreuteria paniculata, Gleditsia triacanthos, Sorbus folgneri, Aesculus californica, Cercidiphyllum japonicum, Pinus sylvestris, Pinus pinea,* and of course there are many others.

This book is not of encyclopaedic proportions and every plant and tree of good habit cannot be listed: but by observation readers will find them for themselves.

Mixed planting softens the boundary wall in this suburban garden.

Trees, a stained timber trellis, and a border of yellow, lime-green and white flowers all helping to clothe the boundary. Note the brick edging to the border.

A romantic profusion of plant growth masks the boundary and even an old shed.
Plants include aquilegias and *Hosta fortunei* 'Albopicta'.

An architectural solution. The stained timber fence is ornamental in its own right.
Note the strongly articulated and contrasting plant shapes. Garden at Chelsea
Flower Show, designed by Preben Jackobsen.

A simple ornament terminates the view down the path. The blue Ceanothus is part of the boundary planting.

Contrasting textures at White Barn House, including veratrums, hostas, alstroemerias and campanulas.

Framing. A substantial pergola, clad with vines and roses, frames the view of a herbaceous walk at The Priory, Kemerton, Worcestershire.

A pool and a statue flanked by Irish yews form a feature in this garden.

The lawn winds its way out of sight in the author's garden.

A jungle of contrasting textures and shapes clothes a boundary wall in the author's garden. Plants include Artemisia 'Powis Castle' and the rose 'Wilhelm'.

A winding grass path, with oriental poppies, *Euphorbia griffithii* and *Iris sibirica*, in a suburban garden.

Contrasting shapes and textures. *Kniphofia uvaria* and *Acanthus mollis*.

A path winds out of sight beyond the pool of unusual shape.

Brick steps and dwarf walls of random stonework are a feature of this garden, which (as the above) was designed by the author.

An attractive sitting area at Essex House, Badminton.

A profusion of pink pelargoniums transforms this small terrace.

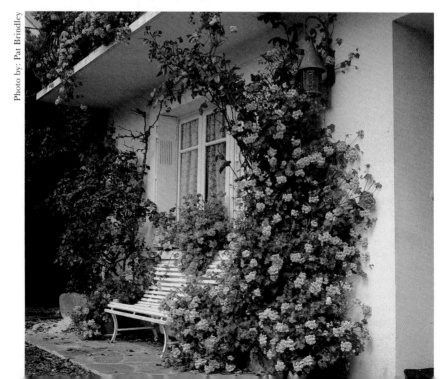

13

Plant Textures

Many excellent plants do not have a definite shape or even a specially noticeable kind of habit and yet they are valuable, even when not in flower, because of the quality of their texture. Rough, smooth; coarse, fine; heavy, light; these are the kind of words we use for textures, and these are words to describe how the eye imagines the hand would feel if it touched the object in question. In plants, these effects are created partly by the surface quality of the leaves themselves, and partly by the massed effect of the leaves together on the plant. Intensity of colour comes into this as well; for example, the dark tone of many evergreens emphasizes the heaviness of texture, while pale green or silvery foliage in other plants emphasizes their lightness of texture.

The foliage of the shrub *Colutea arborescens*, Bladder Senna, is quite a pale green colour, and this is part of the general effect of airy lightness which the plant possesses. The fact that it will grow almost anywhere, has yellow flowers over a long period and also has curious, air-filled seed-pods which can be popped by children, are additional attractions, but what I mainly want to draw attention to now is its pleasing texture of lacy, open greenery.

The texture of several plants is best described as feathery: *Salix elaeagnus* is one, for example, with few attractions apart from its pretty grey-green texture and its good habit, although it does have catkins. Occasionally it is listed (incorrectly) as *Salix rosmarinifolia*, and this refers to the way the linear leaves cluster thickly along the stem. This particular willow is not a tree, but a medium-to-large shrub, usually wider than it is tall. All the members of the genus *Tamarix* or Tamarisk also have feathery foliage, but the best for garden purposes is probably *Tamarix pentandra*, a large shrub or small tree which blooms in late summer and early autumn, when it becomes a mass of rosy pink, the flowers being even more feathery than the foliage. This is one of those plants whose habit can be a bit ungainly and some tidying up or pruning may be necessary to improve matters. As it blooms on new shoots this will also encourage flowering.

Finely-cut foliage usually tends to produce this feathery kind of texture, and some plant varieties have been specially selected for this quality, and acquire names like 'Asplenifolia' (which means 'fern-like') or 'Laciniata' (which means 'cut into narrow lobes'). A good example is *Sorbus aucuparia* 'Asplenifolia' a cut-leaf version of the native Rowan, or Mountain Ash. Another is *Rhus typhina* 'Laciniata', a selected form of the Stag's-horn Sumach.

But on the whole it is easier to discover examples of light feathery textures amongst herbaceous plants. Some of the finest examples are in the genus *Artemisia*. I grew *Artemisia arborescens* for several years, a magnificent silvery shrub about four feet high, with soft filigree foliage on elegant stems; but then an extra hard winter killed it dead, as they say. Now I grow *Artemisia* 'Powis Castle' instead, a hybrid which is both shorter, and hardier, and has woodier stems. It is very silvery, but not quite as light and airy as *A. arborescens*. I also have *Artemisia canescens* which also has silver filigree foliage, of a rather curly kind but this is only about nine inches high (22cm).

The genus *Corydalis* offers a charming group of long-flowering plants mostly less than a foot high (30cm), all with dainty, pale green leaves. *Corydalis lutea* grows like a weed on walls and in shady corners, but there are others with white, pink or even blue flowers. *C. ochroleuca* is doing a good job in my garden, colonizing bare patches in an area of dry shade.

The various delicate textures of astilbes, dicentras, Gypsophila, thalictrums, Fennel or even *Gillenia trifoliata* have each their own special qualities and are all worthy additions to the border and contrast admirably with more heavy-weight subjects.

Some plants have a texture which can be only described as woolly. *Stachys olympica* (or *Stachys lanata*), Lamb's Ears, is a well-known example. *Ballota pseudodictamnus* is another, a sub-shrub of unique character, about eighteen inches high (45cm) with small rounded or vaguely heart-shaped leaves of greenish white, each one as soft as felt.

"Woolly" is the wrong word for the unusual leaves of *Hydrangea sargentiana*, nor is "velvety" exactly right. They give the appearance of being soft and slightly limp, like pieces of pale green cloth but when you feel them they are quite bristly and firm. This shrub needs protection from winds to prevent the leaves getting battered and brown at the edges, but when well-grown it makes a beautiful specimen plant, of attractive habit.

Grassy plants also provide a distinct textural contrast. There are many good smallish grasses that have variegated leaves, such as *Molinia caerulea* 'Variegata', *Hakonechloa macra* 'Aureola' and *Dactylis glomerata* 'Variegata', all of which I have grown. For more dramatic impact something taller is needed, and the best of the tall ornamental grasses is probably *Miscanthus sinensis* 'Silber Feder', which is six feet (2m) high, with elegantly arching leaves and first class flower-heads which have given it its name. Lyme grass, *Elymus arenarius*, is a beautiful blue grass with lovely arching leaves which I grow next to *Artemisia* 'Powis Castle'. It is incorrigibly invasive and one has to pull at least half of it out quite regularly. Gertrude Jekyll used to grow it in her famous long border – but then she had gardeners to do the job for her.

For heavier, denser textures of quite a different character from the textures we have considered so far in this chapter, we must turn once again to evergreen shrubs. This kind of texture can be effective as a background as we have seen, but it can be overdone. Large collections of rhododendrons, for instance, become quite gloomy out of season if not mixed with other contrasting lighter-textured shrubs. In fact the number of rhododendrons suitable for the average garden is quite small, and unfortunately those with excellent foliage as well as good flowers are mostly the giants of the genus, such as *Rhododendron macabeanum* or the extraordinary *R. sinogrande*. One of the qualities that makes some species of rhododendrons particularly interesting is their attractive new growth which appears covered in a woolly substance called indumentum. This is usually a buff, brownish or off-white colour; one of the smaller species which has this feature is *Rhodendendron bureavii*, a fairly slow-growing species, with thick leathery leaves, which appear at first covered in reddish-brown indumentum. The flowers are pinkish-white. Other smaller species which have this attractive feature are *R. haematodes*, with bright red flowers; and *R. makinoi* and *R. yakushim-anum*, both with pink flowers.

The sheer brilliance of colour of many rhododendrons can be too much of a good thing, and those vivid pinks in particular tend to make everything else in the garden look insipid. There are two rhododendrons which I have recommended from time to time, both of which have restrained colours which can be coped with; both tend to be slightly taller than they are wide – a useful feature for smaller gardens, but not common in rhododendrons. *R. augustinii* has a delicacy of habit and delicate flowers as well; they are lavender blue colour, and are spread all over the bush rather than appearing in massive trusses. *R.* 'Purple Splendour', however, has more of the traditional rhododendron appearance, but the flowers are a rich but retiring shade of violet with a black throat, which is perfect for a background shrub.

For those whose gardens are on alkaline soil where rhododendrons will not grow, there are several possible alternative shrubs which provide a similar kind of heavy and dark, evergreen texture, but none will have the same amazing displays of coloured flowers that rhododendrons have. The leaves of *Viburnum rhytidophyllum* are rather more leathery and grainy than those of rhododendrons, but their shape is similar and so is the way they are grouped. The outline of the shrub as a whole, as a huge dome of foliage, is far too large, however, for the average garden. Its flowers are a disappointment, not even outstanding amongst viburnums.

Daphniphyllum macropodum is another large shrub, though a slow-growing one, and its leaves are even better than most rhododendrons, making it one of the finest hardy shrubs to be grown for the sake of its foliage. The flowers are of no great significance. One would hardly guess that this shrub is closely related to the genus *Euphorbia*.

A fig tree makes an excellent background plant, especially if grown against a south-facing wall, as it does in my garden. It is not evergreen, but it looks as though it is. Its big, uniquely-shaped leaves have the coarse texture of glass paper, and on the tree make a great shadowy mass of dark, olive-green. The figs hardly ever ripen in this country, though it helps to grow it against a sunny wall. But I like it for two associational, non-visual reasons: it reminds me of holidays by the Mediterranean, and also of the garden where I lived as a child.

Several worthwhile shrubs with dark, dense foliage are also prickly. The genus *Berberis*, and the closely related *Mahonia*, provide several first-rate shrubs in this category. *Berberis julianae* and *B. gagnepainii* are both a dark green, spiny mass and both have much smaller leaves than the shrubs just discussed, though the leaves of *B. julianae* are relatively large for a Berberis – but that isn't saying much. Mahonia leaves are on quite a different scale. *Mahonia aquifolium* makes a rounded bush about three feet high (1m) which spreads slowly by suckering, but the larger, more stiffly-held leaves of *M. japonica* and *M. × media* 'Charity' give the plants a more sculptured appearance and it is a pity to let other shrubs crowd in around them to spoil this effect. *M. aquifolium* 'Moseri', *M. × media* 'Lionel Fortescue' and *M.* 'Undulata' are all worth growing. They each have good yellow flowers in winter or spring, which in the case of *Mahonia japonica* and *M. × media* 'Lionel Fortescue' are deliciously scented of lily-of-the-valley and this is an added attraction to some of the most magnificent foliage plants one can grow.

There is a pair of outstanding herbaceous plants in this dark-green, prickly category: these are *Acanthus mollis* and *Acanthus spinosus*, and, as you can guess from the names, *spinosus* is much more prickly than *mollis*. Although the foliage is fairly tall, at about eighteen inches (45cm), it is good enough to deserve a position at the front of the border where it can be seen to advantage, as a mass of densely packed, arching, dark green leaves: deeply toothed in both species, but edged with spiny prickles in *spinosus*. The prickly pinky-mauve flower spikes are unlike anything else, and are a perfect match for the foliage, reaching up to four feet (1.5m) or more. These are ideal "feature" plants to break a long band of edging-plants at the front edge of the planting bed. On light soil they can be invasive, but I find *mollis* is no problem on the fairly heavy loam in my garden.

Bold foliage, created by large leaves of distinct shape, creates its own distinct texture. Perhaps the biggest undivided leaves of any shrub are those of *Fatsia japonica*, and the shape of these glossy, evergreen leaves is described as palmate – in other words they are like the palms of a huge green hand about twelve or fifteen inches (30–38cm) across, with about nine pointed "fingers" radiating out like the points of a star. The overall effect is of a plant that ought to be growing in the tropics rather than in England, and yet in spite of this it prefers mild, moist, shaded positions rather than a hot one. In a position it likes it makes a large bush up to fifteen feet high (5m) but it is usually much less than this.

× *Fatshedra lizei* is closely related; and, by the way (as gardening is a very serious subject) you mustn't refer to this plant as "Fat-headed Lizzy"! The leaves are like smaller versions of *Fatsia* leaves, but the plant has an unusual habit which can be difficult to cope with: the branches flop forward but then arch upwards to a vertical position, so things planted in front of this shrub usually have to be moved once it begins to spread out. It is perfectly happy in total shade.

Admirers of bold foliage whose soil is unsuitable for rhododendrons should also consider the merits of the many varieties of *Aucuba japonica*, an underrated and neglected species. There are plain green varieties as well as the common Spotted Laurel whose usual habitat is the front gardens of big Victorian houses: 'Salicifolia', for example, has good berries, and is fairly easily obtainable; and it is pretty obvious where you can buy the variety 'Hillieri', another all-green, berry-bearing variety.

There are several good perennials with bold foliage, but the really outstanding genera are *Bergenia*, *Hosta*, *Macleaya* and *Rodgersia*. Of these, only bergenias are evergreen, and this makes them the most valuable, although not the most beautiful. There are many different varieties. I have tried several of them and the best foliage plants seem to be *Bergenia* 'Sunningdale' and *B. cordifolia* 'Purpurea' because of the cheerful effect of the red leaves during the winter. But I do find the magenta flowers rather a bilious colour and for this reason I think 'Silverlicht' is a pleasanter plant as a whole, with its lovely white flowers tinged with pink. Bergenias are indispensable front-liners for the borders of any garden, especially against paving or gravel, and the rounded leaves, like big green flaps, provide the ideal contrast to those feathery textures or spiky shapes which we have already considered.

The most beautiful hardy herbaceous foliage, it could be argued, can be found in the genus *Hosta*. The most amazing of all are the blue-leafed kinds, and *Hosta sieboldiana* in particular. An ever-increasing range of new varieties of *Hosta* is now being produced, some only available in small numbers, and some of these may prove to be of outstanding quality, but in the meantime *H.s. elegans* appears to be the best variety easily obtainable at the moment. Each leaf has marvellous shape, excellent colour, is firm and fleshy with a smooth, but veined texture. These appear in great clumps of overlapping foliage. In summer the white flower spikes appear, overtopping the foliage, but these should be cut away as soon as they begin to look tatty. Variegated and yellow forms of *sieboldiana* have been raised. The variegated form is fairly easily obtainable and is named 'Frances Williams', but this is not very pleasing: there are so many better variegated hostas than this. The highly desirable all-gold form is still scarce. There are also smaller, blue-leaved hostas which are good, such as *Hosta tokudama*, and these are worth trying.

The best variegated Hosta is *Hosta ventricosa* 'Variegata'. The heart-shaped leaves are a good size, and have pleasing cream-coloured markings on a dark olive-green base. The colour of the flowers is a remarkable deep shade of mauve as hostas go. Other excellent vari-egated forms include 'Thomas Hogg', *Hosta fortunei* 'Albo-picta' and 'Kabitan' which is probably a form of *H. lancifolia*. Plain green hostas are less remarkable, but still desirable: for instance *Hosta ventricosa* itself and *H.* 'Honeybells' are as good as any.

Hostas are best grown at the front of the border, as specimens, where the full beauty of the shape of the clump can be appreciated. Mass-plantings under trees never seem to me to be so attractive; one can have too much of a thing and the drips from the trees, along with dead leaves and fallen twigs, do the hostas no good at all. The biggest enemies of hostas are slugs and snails. Where these are a menace it is essential to prevent them eating the young shoots as they emerge, otherwise the plant will be ruined for a whole season.

Macleaya cordata is a much taller plant. It sends up stems about six or seven feet (2m) high with most unusual, large leaves, soft green above, off-white underneath, but shaped by a series of irregular rounded lobes, giving the leaf a wiggly outline, like the shape of some Polynesian island. The stems are topped by plume-like flowers which are less important than the foliage. It makes a good plant for the back of the border, between shrubs, or even on their own in a place where the beauty of the whole plant can be seen down to ground level.

Rodgersias to the uninitiated resemble horse-chestnut leaves which have lost their way and have started a life of their own growing straight out of the ground. No wonder then that one species is called *Rodgersia aesculifolia* considering *Aesculus* is the botanical Latin for a Horse-Chestnut. *Rodgersia podophylla* is perhaps a better species, with a bronzy tint to the leaves, and *R. pinnata* is also good. *Rodgersia tabularis* is different, it has almost circular leaves (like round tables, I suppose, according to its name) but to me more like a poor man's lotus leaf. All rodgersias like moist soil, and begin to look sick if not watered during dry spells.

Such is a selection of textural effects created by the foliage of garden plants. Shape, habit, texture, we have considered, and we can now move on to the much more popular subject of colour in the garden.

CHAPTER

14

Colour and Arrangement

The twentieth century gardener has at hand an incredible range of material: we are almost spoilt for choice when we come to select plants to fill our beds and borders. Some impression of these has already been given in the last few chapters. How then can we put them together? It is rather like knowing about the instruments of the orchestra; the sounds they make, the timbre and range of each, but how do we get them to play, in Eliot's words, "in complete consort, dancing together"?

We expect a piece of music to have a certain unity of character. We don't expect it to start as a serenade for strings and end as a serenade for brass. Of course in a large-scale work there is room for greater diversity than in a short piece: a symphony, for instance, can happily contain both a funeral march and a *scherzo* (which originally meant a "jest") but we expect both to be integrated into a larger pattern. Similarly, in a large garden there is greater scope for diversity of style than there is in a small one, but nevertheless we expect some kind of overall consistency. It is disturbing if we find such radical juxtapositions of style, as we do for example at Compton Acres in Dorset where we go straight from an Italian garden to a Japanese garden, and in a few steps are whisked from one continent to another. Some people argue that gardens tell us something about the personality of their owners, and it seems to me preferable to show a positive and consistent character rather than appear to be some kind of schizophrenic who takes on a different personality at unexpected moments.

Disjointedness, inconsistency, and the presence of elements which are alien to the scheme show up even more obviously in a small garden, and this relates not only to the lines and shapes of the layout but also to the planting. If we think again of our musical analogy, one way in which a piece of music establishes some kind of unity is by repetition. In classical music, not only are long sections repeated, but also small

100

fragments of melody reappear in varied forms, and clusters of notes or "motifs" are often repeated within a melodic line.

Repetition, therefore, is one way of imposing some kind of unity of character on the garden. This need be no disadvantage: on the contrary there is a good argument for discovering which plants do really well in your garden and planting plenty of them. Don't treat your garden as a trial ground, and plant ten each of twenty different kinds of daffodil, for instance. It is better to wait and do some garden-visiting in daffodil time, to decide which you like best and then plant two hundred of them: it will be much more impressive and less messy.

But the effect of daffodils is ephemeral, and other elements have a more permanent and dominant presence in the garden; but the same principles can be applied. Supposing our plot is quite large, we might decide that there is room for about ten trees, as long as they are not too large or shade-producing. Consider the difference in effect of ten silver birches, for instance, grouped naturalistically, and the effect of ten all-different trees: one *Prunus*, one *Malus*, one *Robinia*, one Birch, one Judas Tree and so on. With the ten birch trees the unity of the whole will be stressed, but with ten different trees the concept of variety is stressed, and these two aspects have to be held in balance: too much variety will become restless; too little variety will be boring. The larger the plant the more powerful is the effect; in other words our choice of trees, large shrubs, and plants of dominant shape will be critical, and some repetition is desirable to give the scheme coherence. For example, I think the effect of five identical *Prunus* varieties (flowering cherries) is likely to be far more powerful than five different ones, all flowering at slightly different times, and the repetition of a plant of dominant shape or distinct habit will give special character to a garden, making it a particular kind of garden and not just a plant collection. Repetition can be local, that is the identical plants can be grouped together, or, for a different effect, they can be scattered at intervals around the garden. Another idea is to repeat an association of two or three plants in various places in the garden.

The way a group of plants all of one kind should be placed in the garden depends on our style. Rows, lines, avenues and hedges speak of geometry and belong to a formal style of gardening. In a more free, naturalistic style, planting should be in scatterings, clusters or drifts. When large numbers of one species are being planted in a natural manner – whether it is bulbs in grass, or trees on a hillside – particular care should be taken to ensure that there are no three units in line with each other, because this will show up its artificiality. It also helps if a cluster or drift is made up of an odd number of plants. Even numbers begin to look like pairs, and might suggest formality, and so three, five or seven in a group seems more natural.

The use of strongly-shaped plants needs care: if every plant shouts for attention, it gets a bit like Manhattan – a congested jungle of shapes. Earlier cities had a more sophisticated skyline: for every dominant building (whether the Duomo, the Palazzo Vecchio, or a slender campanile) there were dozens of examples of pleasant but unobtrusive street facades which did not rise above the conventional number of storeys. So for every dominant plant there will be many sub-dominants and less remarkable "fillers", to fill the gaps with greenery and flowers in their season.

But even with "filler" plants it is better to have groups of several plants of a kind. A border where many of the elements are rounded "blobs" of colour or green is not so satisfying as one where some of the elements are long narrow bands, parallel with the front of the border. Some people call them "sausage-shaped" clumps, a name which Gertrude Jekyll, the inventor of this idea, would hardly have approved of I'm sure.

The average gardener cares little for form, elegance of habit or subtle textures; what he wants is colour and plenty of it. And even amongst more discriminating gardeners colour possesses a far greater fascination that the more basic elements of form. The appeal of "technicolor" compared with the "silver screen", and the possibilities of colour TV compared with black-and-white are evidence of the same phenomenon in other fields. And I for one could never see the sense in publishing books about paintings where most of the plates are black and white.

But this demand for colour was not a feature of every style of gardening: before the plant introductions of the nineteenth century, and the work of plant-breeders in the twentieth, the possibility of a glut of colour simply did not exist. This is why gardens planted only with the plants available in 1650, or 1750, or some other original date when a historic garden was first made, usually turn out to be a disappointment to our modern eyes. The gardens of Renaissance Italy and the French gardens of the *Grand Siècle* did not pretend to any great concern for floral colour; for them coloured gravel was quite sufficient to enliven a scene where the main features were the beauty of stonework and the intricacies of clipped Box. Such an environment, in any case, formed a perfect background for people, and the beautifully arrayed ladies of the court of the time must have been as lovely as any flower; whereas today the photographer has to avoid all those other ghastly camera-clutching tourists when visiting an historic garden, otherwise their orange anoraks or Coca-Cola T-shirts will ruin the picture.

Flowers formed no part, either, of the English Landscape school whose broad brush-strokes of native green depicted too vast a canvas to take specks of any other colour into account. But sometimes there was a pleasure-ground, or a "close-walk" planted on a much smaller scale where flowering shrubs had a place. The enclosed gardens of Tudor and Stuart times were also on quite a small scale, where flowers could be appreciated at close-quarters and in detail.

The average garden of today is small in scale as well, but before we start to study the beauty of individual flowers in detail, some consideration must be given to the more general effects of colour in the garden; and the view of the garden from the windows of the house is once again a good place to begin. What is immediately apparent is that some flowers are much more easily visible from a distance than others. The beautiful rose 'Guinée', for example, is a rich, dark red, wonderful on close inspection, but from a distance of fifteen feet (5m) scarcely visible at all. This is because it is such a dark shade of red that it reflects very little light. Many subtle and un-obvious colours appear to contain grey or black pigment, such as sage-greens, mustards, maroons and so on. Some colours contain white (in which case they are pastel shades). These colours are much more reflective and flowers of pastel shades usually show up well in the garden.

The degree to which a colour is free of black or white pigment is called its intensity. In other words the purer the colour the greater its intensity: it is neither darkened by containing black pigment nor weakened by added white pigment. One might think, therefore, that the most intense colours would be the ones which show up most brightly in the garden but this is not so because different colours have what are described as different tonal values, which I will explain in a moment.

The part of a colour which can be considered in isolation, without added black, white or grey, is known as the hue. There are three primary colours or hues: red, yellow and blue, and by mixing pigments of these three hues further hues – the secondary colours – appear, which are green, orange and violet, and further intermediate hues can also be described by such names as violet-blue, blue-green and so on. But not all these pure hues appear equally bright to the eye, and the relative lightness or darkness of the hues themselves (containing no added greyness) is known as the tone. Yellow is the lightest in tone while violet is the darkest. Hue, tone and intensity, therefore, are the three main dimensions of any colour, but in practice there are several other factors which have to be taken into account.

One complication is the way texture affects colours, especially as seen from a distance. For instance, rough, coarse textures tend to appear darker than they really are and this is because the shadows that are cast onto the surface give it the appearance of a colour containing a certain amount of blackness. Shiny foliage, on the other hand, often contains highlights and sparkle, to relieve what may be otherwise a very dark colour.

Colours also possess "temperature". The coolest in appearance are the blue and lavender shades, while the reds are the "hot" end of the range. This characteristic affects the atmosphere or mood created by certain colours – imagine for instance how the introduction of a row of stone vases filled with scarlet geraniums would immediately alter the mood of an area which previously consisted only of dark evergreens. Yellow flowers of bright, primary yellow are cheerful almost to the point of brashness; purples and deep reds are rich and sumptuous, and so on.

A curious effect, well known to photographers, is the way cool colours apparently recede and hot colours seem to advance. Those scarlet geraniums, for instance, will seem almost to leap out of a photograph. Blue flowers on the other hand seem to hardly show up at all and the photographer has to use a special filter if he wants to do justice to them. This is not just that there is something wrong with the balance of the average colour film, it is something which can be confirmed by the naked eye, and our old position at the window looking into the garden is a good place to confirm this fact. In Nature, any object tends to lose its colour as it becomes more distant because of the effect of the atmosphere. Distant hills on the horizon appear as various shades of blue-grey even though we know perfectly well they are covered in green grass and green trees, and it maybe that when the eye sees a blue-grey object it immediately assumes it is a distant one.

What we know about the behaviour of colours can be put to use when we make a garden. For instance, if we plant blue or grey foliage at the far end of the garden we shall increase the apparent distance and make the garden seem longer. The garden I designed for the Chelsea Flower Show in 1983 was a text-book example of such effects. It was a very small plot even by Chelsea standards; only twenty feet wide and forty feet long (6m x 12m) and it consisted of three roughly oval spaces. The nearest was planted with brightly coloured subjects including some with yellow foliage and some with brilliant orange flowers such as geums. The second oval in the middle distance was planted with soft green foliage (including alchemillas) fairly delicate coloured variegated plants, together with restrained flowers (such as *Euphorbia palustris* in greenish-yellow); the third oval which was furthest away was backed with silvery trees (including the Willow-leafed Pear, *Pyrus salicifolia*

'Pendula' with *Senecio* and *Stachys olympica* (*S. lanata*) at low level, combined with blue flowers such as irises and violas. All this combined to create the illusion of a much longer garden than it really was.

Quite the opposite effect occurs when an evergreen such as an Azalea comes into bloom at the far end of a garden: the normally reticent dark green suddenly becomes the focus of attention as a result of the brilliance of the flowers, and the mass of colour seems to jump out at you in a tiresome way, creating a foreshortening effect.

Very brilliant colours are often a problem in the garden, and although this is something many people feel instinctively, there are good reasons why it is so. The brilliance may be due to the intensity of colour, to the "hotness" of the colour temperature or the inherent lightness of tone of the particular hue. A big splash of brilliance tends to have a devaluing effect on the rest of the flowers in the garden, making them look either insipid and colourless or else dull and sombre. Brilliance, of course, is a relative term, and the apparent brilliance of a group of flowers can be enhanced or decreased by careful choice of its neighbours, and the greater the contrast the more the intensity of colour will be enhanced.

Every hue has its opposite number called the complementary colour, and a device called the colour wheel shows which the complementary hue is for each colour. Yellow, for example, is complementary to violet, blue to orange, and so on, and in fact the complementary colour for any hue can be discovered by a simple experiment: you stare steadily at a brightly lit object (such as a red button on a pale background) for about a minute and then look away at a white piece of paper, and a coloured after-image will appear, which will not be red, but the complementary colour, green. This complementary colour always provides the greatest possible contrast for any particular hue. One reason why scarlet geraniums appear so brilliant is that the green colour of most garden foliage is the complementary hue to the orange-red of the flowers. No doubt the same geraniums against a background of coloured autumnal foliage would not appear nearly so startling.

We can apply this effect usefully in several ways. For example, some people might think that the flower heads of the bushy herbaceous *Euphorbia palustris* do not contrast enough with the surrounding foliage, because there is so much lime-green in their shade of yellow. However, I grow the violet-coloured cranesbill *Geranium sylvaticum* 'Mayflower' next to it, a plant of similar height, whose flowers are of a colour which is almost opposite to yellow-green in the colour wheel. The effect of this contrast is unusual and most pleasing, since neither flower is vivid in itself.

On the other hand, if one possesses a rather virulent orange Azalea, which sticks out a mile in the garden scene, one can either dig it up (probably the best solution) or you can plant beside it other azaleas of pale apricot, or creamy yellow, and further away there could be cream shades and primrose yellows, so that a succession of related hues is created leading the eye up to the offending vivid colour by degrees, and thus reducing the shock effect.

Another problem with flowers of intense colour is that if there is not a generous amount of them, they appear as annoying little blobs of brightness which disturb the otherwise limited tonal range of the scene. If one is going in for a startling effect it has to be done boldly, as if you really mean it. Bold masses of any colour, in fact, have a more pleasing effect than little dots or blobs here and there, and this means with many plants that one must have several of them in a group to make an effective display.

Some form of control over the colours in the garden seems to me to be desirable. If flowers are planted at random some terrible clashes can occur. If you are keen on perennials and want to cram in as many as possible it is quite easy to find by midsummer that you have put the Bergamot *Monarda* 'Cambridge Scarlet' in between Purple Loosestrife, *Lythrum* 'Robert' on one side and the orange Day-Lily *Hemerocallis* 'Burning Daylight' on the other: I know because I did it once myself, and it looked quite appalling.

Perhaps the simplest scheme of all to prevent clashes is to keep the oranges away from the pinks. A very common example of this clash, which can be seen regularly in other people's front gardens in spring, is *Berberis stenophylla* or *B. darwinii*, both of which have orange flowers, next to a pink flowering cherry. This always looks unpleasant. No one would put orange and pink together when choosing wallpaper and paint, nor when deciding what to wear, so it is surprising that people tolerate it in their gardens. If we adopt a policy of separating these two colours, our flowers will tend to form themselves into two groups: the creams, yellows, maroons and browns will go with the more "difficult" orange hues; and in another group the magentas, purples, and lavenders will successfully blend with the "problematic" pinks. The blues belong most happily in this second group, but being reticent by nature, as we have seen, they can also be included in the first group as well, where they associate pleasantly with pastel shades such as pale yellow. White also seems to fit into either group. But even a general scheme likes this needs care. The various shades of pink, for instance, can clash amongst themselves. Many pinks have a tinge of blue in them and these look wrong with other pink shades which contain a hint of yellow – the so-called salmon-pinks. Most pink perennials are on the blue-ish side, except for pink day-lilies, which still contain a lot of yellow. Many modern roses have a yellowish tinge, while the older ones more often have a tiny hint of blue.

Some gardeners with plenty of space like to be much more drastic and go for schemes of only one colour – or rather one colour plus green – and white usually seems to be the favourite choice. But in a small garden it seems a pity to restrict oneself quite so severely. To adopt a range of related hues, such as a pink-purple-blue scheme seems far more interesting to me. This colour range is particularly effective in September when the Michaelmas daisies, and other related *Aster* species are in bloom. A lovely group could be made, for example, with blue *Aster × frikartii* 'Mönch', the rich violet *Aster amellus* 'Nocturne', and, in pink, *Aster amellus* 'Sonia' or *A. novii-angliae* 'September Ruby'. Amongst these one could plant the taller fuchsias and especially the delightful *Fuchsia magellanica* 'Versicolor'. *Physostegia virginiana* 'Vivid' would fit in well, in deepest rose pink, and so would *Lobelia × vedrariensis* with its extraordinary royal purple spikes, and late blue aconites, such as *Aconitum carmichaelii* 'Kelmscott'. To all these rich colours one could add silvery flowers and foliage such as *Anaphalis triplinervis;* Japanese anemones in pink or white cannot be omitted either. The list is endless.

But there are other ways of selecting colours besides choosing related hues. One could, for example, have a border of pastel shades: pale yellow, pale blue, pale pink with pale grey foliage, a subtle but satisfying combination. Imagine for instance a mid-summer border of perennials such as the pale yellow *Achillea* 'Moonshine' with its flat heads and silver foliage, grouped with the soft pink *Geranium endressii;* for pastel blues there are widely different possibilities such as the thistley *Eryngium planum*, the unusual pale lavender *Phlox* 'Prospero' or the well-known catmint, *Nepeta × faasenii* (*N. mussinii*). *Anthemis* 'E. C. Buxton' is another soft yellow, which has daisy-like flowers in midsummer, while *Astrantia* varieties will also blend well with our scheme, with their greenish-white or greenish-pink stars, sometimes called Hattie's Pin Cushion.

Alternatively, one could go to the other extreme and have only intense or "hot" colours, the fieriest oranges, brightest yellows, the scarlets and deepest blues. But colourful schemes like this can only be obtained by having an extensive range of perennials, or else by planting bedding plants or annuals. Bedding plants are probably best for strong colours and they do have a very long flowering period, but of course there is a certain amount of labour involved in planting them out, and there is either the expense of buying the plants or else the bother or raising them.

But as well as these visual considerations, of colour, shape, texture and arrangement, there are horticultural requirements which also have to be satisfied in our planting schemes. First we must turn to the practical problem of the way we and the rest of the family actually use the garden.

PART
3
LIVING
·IN THE·
GARDEN

CHAPTER
15

Terraces

In the heat of summer we can sit out on the lawn, sipping tea perhaps, in the grassy shade of an old apple tree. But hot summer's days are rather elusive and on days when we do have time to sit in the garden, the grass is usually a bit too damp for comfort, and an area of hard paving makes a much more satisfactory place to sit. The most convenient place for this paved area is immediately outside the house, but it is better not to decide on the position until we are familiar with the aspect of the garden and have studied the local micro-climate for a while.

First we must find out if the hottest and sunniest place in the garden is what suits every member of the household, or whether some shade is desirable for the hottest days. There is a big difference between the "dappled" shade of a tree and the total shade cast by a building, and for this reason, if the garden side of the house faces north or east it is better to have the area of paving some distance away from the house so that it is not in complete shade on summer evenings. The amount of shade cast by the house is even more in spring and autumn, so to get the benefit of those freak warm days that come early or late in the year, the paved area may need to be even further away than one might at first assume. It could be argued that when the position of the sitting area is not obvious, it may well be worth waiting twelve months to decide exactly where the best place is. As a general rule, in suburban gardens of usual shape and size, when the garden side of the house faces north the sitting area should be on the right-hand side as you look out from the house; and when the house faces east it should be on the left-hand side, some distance from the house in both cases.

To make the most of warm days out of season, we must not only choose a sunny position but also a sheltered one, especially in rural situations and exposed sites. A masonry wall behind the terrace can make a big difference by absorbing heat from the sun and reflecting it back like a storage-heater. We are lucky to have a high brick wall on two sides of our town garden and on a sunny summer's day it is surprising how hot the bricks in the south-facing wall feel if you put your hand on them. Where the house faces south, and the terrace is immediately outside it, the house itself will provide shelter, but in exposed positions a second wall at right-angles will give added protection on windy days. In some situations the wind has a habit of getting funnelled between two objects and causes an uncomfortable draught, and one has to discover by observation which is the best place for a screen or for additional planting, in order to break the force of the wind and create a sheltered area.

The size of the sitting area needs to be reasonably generous, but not so vast that it begins to look like a concrete prairie. If it is only for the use of the household it is easy to calculate how many people will want to use it at any one time. In a small town garden, about ten by ten feet (3m x 3m) is almost adequate, while in larger gardens a rectangle of paving bigger than sixteen by twenty feet (5 x 6m) begins to look a bit dreary. To give a grander look, more in proportion with a larger house, one can extend the paving further but break it with spaces for plants, and whether this is done in a regular, geometrical way or an irregular, a-symmetrical way will depend on the style of the garden. But by leaving out odd stones one can make room for a few shrubs that associate well with paving, such as the ones mentioned in Chapter 9. Suitable alpines can be grown in smaller gaps. But if you do plant in paving make sure you leave a good-sized, roughly rectangular-shaped area of usable space.

Paving must be laid evenly: rocky tables or wobbly chairs are a real nuisance. The surface should not be exactly flat, however, but laid with a slight fall in one direction so that the rain is encouraged to run off and puddles are avoided. The more irregular the surface (and some kinds of paving can be quite uneven) the greater the fall required, but a good rule of thumb is for a drop in level of one inch in every five feet (1cm in 60cm).

It is wise to keep the joints between pavings quite wide: this is because sizes of both slabs and bricks vary considerably, even if they are mass-produced, and if you push them tight together with a hair-line joint, every inaccuracy and every deviation from the purely rectangular will show up plainly. A wide joint allows a tolerance and gives margin for error.

The remarks made earlier about various kinds of paving apply as much to sitting areas as they do to paths. In view of the greater area involved a few additional observations may be made. Complete randomness of pattern I do not admire very much, and it can present some difficulties. It can certainly be used for crazy paving, but if one is using rectangular elements such as concrete pavings of a variety of sizes one must stick to this rectangular discipline; sudden slanting deviations will look most ugly. It makes life simpler for the layer if the joints run through in one direction and all the randomness occurs in the joints

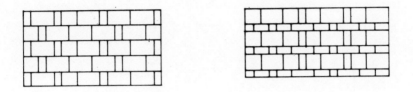

In these examples the joints in the paving in one direction run through, but are random in the other direction.

which run in the other direction. When the joints run through one direction, as I suggested, it is best if the joints run across the line of sight when seen from an important viewpoint. If the eye can run down joints, as along a line that disappears into the distance, it will soon spot any irregularities, such as deviations from straightness or variations in the widths of the joints. But if the continuous lines run across and all the lines in the other direction are staggered any discrepancies will be undetectable.

In some irregularly shaped gardens the main view down the garden may not be at right angles to the house but slightly on the diagonal, and in this case it may be better for the joint lines of paving to relate to the main axis or vista rather than to the geometry of the house.

Patterns can be created by the use of two paving materials. Alternate bands of bricks and slabs is just one example. Another solution is to have panels of brickwork consisting of 4, 8, 16 or 24 bricks which together make up the size of a slab, occuring every so often within the pattern. This random kind of pattern has a style which is informal, and avoids the feeling that too much self-conscious effort has gone into the design. Geometrical patterns, on the other hand, are suited to formal gardens, where they provide an added mathematical intricacy to the pattern of the overall design.

Lutyens and other architects of the Edwardian period often used roofing tiles to create paving patterns. They were laid on their edge so

113

In this garden the main lines of the paving do not line up with the house, but are at right-angles to the line of vision down the garden.

Randomly occurring panels of brickwork amongst paving slabs of larger size.

114

that only the narrow thickness of the tile was seen. They were not used to cover large areas, but rather to create a pattern, often being laid in long bands, whose width was formed by three or four tiles. They were usually combined with brickwork, with which they blend well, or else with natural stone. Nowadays, small clay roof tiles are not used so much in building, (interlocking concrete tiles being much cheaper) but flat clay tiles are still available, and sometimes old ones can be found when a house is re-roofed; of course it takes a bit more effort for the workmen to carry them down intact, rather than flinging them into a skip from roof-level which smashes them to pieces.

Granite setts are another attractive material which can be used in small quantities to create patterns in paving. They are easily available but rather expensive.

Slabs, or panels of brickwork, can be combined with a formless material such as gravel or cobbles, and this can be useful in awkward, non-geometrical situations, where there is a bend to cope with or a slope as well as a bend. Loose pebbles can have their uses too, and

Paving slabs set amongst cobbles or gravel: a useful idea in non-geometrical situations.

115

make a pleasing textural contrast with paving. They are particularly suitable for masking a junction between paving and a dwarf wall,

The use of cobbles to make complex slab-cutting unnecessary at awkward junctions.

making complicated cutting of slabs unnecessary. A gap left in paving for a specimen plant can be filled with pebbles instead of an underplanting of ground cover. Pebbles are particularly suitable for placing under plants which are "stemmy" and not clothed in foliage right down to the base.

We can exphasize the effects we wish to create by the way we treat the edges of the paving. One can make the formal and geometrical elements more obvious by creating a strong line at the edge, or alternatively, the line can be deliberately blurred and made indistinct, which produces a more naturalistic, unplanned-looking effect. For example, where paving meets planting, it can stop with a ragged edge, and the slabs can be used as they come. One can plant things along the edge that will sprawl and flop onto the paving, and so create a soft effect, where the paving just seems to blend into the planting. The opposite approach is to emphasize the distinction between the two by finishing the paving off with a special row of slabs that create a definite line which will contribute to the geometry of the whole design. There is a similar effect when there is an edging strip between the lawn and the planting bed. At the junction where the slabs, bricks or other kinds of paving meet the grass a sharp line is created, and if a lawn of definite shape is intended this line can be used to emphasize the intended shape.

In this design the shapes of both the paved area and the lawn are sharply articulated by a row of slabs around the perimeter, creating a very clear-cut effect.

This emphasis of distinctions is called in designer's jargon "articulation". A shape may be described as "strongly articulated", in which case it is clear cut and shows up plainly. When a paved area meets a lawn a sharp line may appear, and this may be a desirable feature which fits in with the design, or it may seem too harsh and artificial. To soften this hard line, there are several things that may be done. One is to contrive to make the line irregular and stepped rather than straight. Another is to use planting to soften the line, either as a bed between the paving and the lawn, or else as isolated specimen plantings, some of which can be within the paved area itself. A further idea is to have a few stepping-stone slabs in the grass to break the line.

However, if strong lines and distinct shapes are our intention, there

117

The soft effect of irregularly-edged paving and a lawn of indefinite,
naturalistic outline.

are several ways of doing this besides creating a series of separate
rectangles, or any other shape. One way is to overlap shapes, so that
the shape is not complete, but the mind, as it were, supplies the rest.

If the terrace or sitting area is immediately outside the house, it is

The use of overlapped-squares in the design of a garden.

118

a good idea not to bring the paving right up to the building (except of course at doorways) because of the harsh effect this will create where the two hard surfaces meet. A narrow border two or three feet wide (60–100cm) between the house walls and the paving will allow you to plant a range of pleasant, softening greenery. Evergreens can be specially appropriate. I remember once noticing how good *Choisya ternata* looked with its dark green foliage, against the golden stonework of Montacute House in Somerset. Under the walls of my own house I have a short green-and-gold border with not only *Choisya ternata*, but also the Myrtle (*Myrtus communis*), *Arundinaria fortunei* 'Variegata', *Salvia officinalis* 'Icterina', *Symphoricarpus orbiculatus* 'Variegatus', Bowles' Golden Grass (*Milium effusum* 'Aureum'), *Helleborus corsicus*, bergenias, *Hosta fortuneii* 'Albo-picta' and so on. Plants like *Myrtus communis* which need a sheltered position, are particularly suitable for a border against the walls of the house.

New and perhaps harsh-looking paving can also be softened by placing pots or tubs on it in suitable places. It usually looks more impressive to have large pots rather than small ones and they do have an advantage of not needing to be watered so often, since they contain more soil. Twelve to eighteen inch terracotta pots are ideal, and plain ones look almost as good as the ones decorated with swags and scrolls and cost a lot less. Avoid pots made to simulate classical stoneware unless you have an eighteenth century house or a Neo-Georgian villa to match them; and imitation plastic pots always look what they are – plastic. Some glazed pots from the Far East have come on the market recently, which are rather attractive, but a bit on the expensive side.

It is sensible to make the plants match the pots in scale. Small or floppy plants in huge pots will look completely out of scale, and similarly large plants in small pots will not only look top-heavy but will require frequent watering.

The range of plants suitable for pots is extremely wide. In the spring they can be filled with tulips and forget-me-nots, and later on they can overflow with petunias, geraniums (i.e. pelargoniums) and grey-leafed *Helichrysum petiolatum*. A different approach would be to use slightly exotic plants which can be taken into a conservatory, (or even indoors perhaps) during the frost-prone months. Here are some examples: *Agapanthus umbellatus*, *Hibiscus rosa-sinensis*, *Melianthus major*, cycads, *Plumbago capensis*, bougainvilleas, or spiky plants such as agaves, *Beschorneria yuccoides*, phormiums and yuccas.

Evergreens in pots have the advantage of looking good all the year round. The traditional subject for this is the rather tender Bay Tree, *Laurus nobilis*, but there are many other choices. Dwarf conifers are not suitable, because they die so easily if they get too dry. Box, *Euonymus fortunei* 'Silver Queen', × *Fatshedera lizei, Fatsia japonica, Hebe cupressoides*, sarcococcas, or *Viburnum tinus* are all worthwhile possibilities, and for larger pots or "Versailles" tubs, one of the bamboos could be tried, such as *Arundinaria mureliae*.

If you go away for several weeks in the summer, watering can be a problem. Having lost quite a lot of good plants in this way in the past myself, I have now planted an old sink, and some other containers, entirely with drought-tolerant subjects such as house-leeks (*Sempervivums*) and sedums, an arrangement which seems to work well.

We noticed earlier (in Chapter 10) that steps and changes of level help to create interest in a garden, by breaking up the flatness of the plot. This can also be done by creating raised beds. It is surprising how effective these can be, even if they are only a few inches above the surrounding level of grass or paving. A height of about nine inches (22cm) may be quite enough to create a good effect. A raised bed within a planted area, however, can afford to be much higher: roughly eighteen inches (45cm) seems to be a good average. There are several horticultural advantages when you do this. Small, neatly-designed raised beds can provide good homes for treasured alpines and small plants that like perfect drainage, or special soil conditions; and this has the advantage of being a much more orderly arrangement than the usual chaotic rockery. There are some good rectangular beds in a corner of the Savill Gardens, I remember; they are surrounded by paving which means you can get right up close to your favourite tiny plant and appreciate its beauty in detail. Larger beds are also able to offer homes for plants which like good drainage, which may be appropriate if the rest of the garden consists of heavy clay, or they can be filled with acid soil if your garden is alkaline. For deep rooting plants, however, the new soil must go down to adequate depth, otherwise the plants will only do well while they are young: when the roots discover the limy soil underneath the plant will begin to look rather sick and chlorotic.

The materials we choose to make these raised beds will depend on what has been used elsewhere in the garden, and it must relate also to our overall style. The possibilities include masonry walls, of brick or stone, with or without a coping; dry-stone walling, in areas where it is appropriate; and timber. In this country raised beds made with timber are usually formed with larch poles placed vertically, with one end sunk well into the ground. But in the north-western States of the USA where timber is plentiful, sawn or planed timber is often used not only to make "decks", which are boarded patios, appropriate on steeply sloping

A raised bed made with rows of larch poles.

A raised bed made with sawn and planed timbers.

sites, but it is also used to make carpenter-made raised beds. If these are backed with a damp-proof membrane, such as heavy-grade poly-thene, the timber will last well, and they certainly lend themselves to careful and neat detailing, and can be finished with a flat board on top – the timber equivalent of a coping stone. Timber used in this way must be treated with a preservative, and there are several decorative stains on the market, offering a wide range of colours, under trade names such as Sadolins and Hickson's Decor.

Raised beds at the side of the plot can be useful to give additional height and to help to create a framing effect: but unless you have a good wall as a boundary, they will naturally need a "back" as well as the other three sides.

A useful device, where a raised bed is constructed of masonry and adjoins a paved sitting area, is to have a wide coping-stone along one stretch of it, so that it can double up as a place to sit. This kind of permanent seat avoids the "clutter" effect of garden furniture which tends to hang about looking useless half the year; and alternatively it avoids the chore of having to get a deck-chair from a shed. A coping

121

A permanent seat formed from a dwarf wall which surrounds a
raised bed.

wide enough to sit on should be about twenty four inches (60cm) wide,
and needs to be about fifteen inches (38 cm) high to the top, above the
paving level.

CHAPTER
16

Work and Leisure in the Garden

Some people are great sun-lovers, and can take all the sunshine we are likely to get in this country. Others find this uncomfortable, and soon retire into the shade. It is easy enough to create an area of shade, and with a little skill it can be engineered to fall on the paved area to a greater or lesser extent during the course of the day. For example one can plant a tree, or trees, preferably not dense, leafy ones but airy, light-filtering ones.

Alternatively, one can build a pergola. The best place for this may not be immediately over the paving because the sun is hardly ever directly overhead in this country, but sends its rays at an angle of about fourty-five degrees or less to the horizontal. Towards evening, and in spring and autumn, the angle of the sun will be quite low, and as there is no sense in creating shade which will only be cast against the wall behind the terrace, it may be worth going to the trouble of doing some kind of mock-up before you start to build the pergola. A pergola can be a very attractive addition to the garden when well designed. The simple "rustic" arrangements one sees in Italy, where vines are trained over a rather basic and light-weight construction of wires and poles alongside a picturesque cottage, seem to be more desirable than the over-designed affairs made of heavy planks that one sometimes sees in this country. A free-standing pergola needs to be of a reasonable length, otherwise it will appear ill-proportioned. It should be at least twice as long as it is high, or else it will look spindly, like a card-table; and as seven foot (2.1m) is the minimum height; it needs to be at least fourteen feet long (4.2m). If the pergola is attached to part of the house or some other building this may not be important, since it then can appear as merely an extension of the building or as a kind of canopy.

No pergola looks its best until some sort of plant growth softens it by scrambling over it in an irregular manner; vines and some of the

123

other climbing plants mentioned in Chapter 5 would be suitable. But the classic plant for a pergola is a Wisteria, whose foliage has a marvellously picturesque quality even when the attractive flowers are not in bloom. It is important to buy a named variety or at least a species from a reliable supplier. Some nurserymen raise wisterias from seed, but these are the ones to avoid because they are unreliable. The two species most commonly seen are the Japanese Wisteria, W. *floribunda* and the Chinese W. *sinensis;* these are distinguishable by the fact that *floribunda* has more than thirteen leaflets, while *sinensis* has fewer than thirteen; W. *sinensis* is also much taller and will climb to tops of tall trees. There are white forms of both species as well as the usual mauve colour, and W. *floribunda* 'Violacea Plena', and W. *sinensis* 'Black Dragon' are a particularly dark violet-purple colour. The most amazing of all is W. *floribunda* 'Macrobotrys', where the long, pendant flowers (or racemes, as they are called), can reach an almost incredible length of three feet (1m).

Screen walls need discrete treatment; those frightful "Californian" screen blocks made of concrete should be avoided at all cost. If bricks are used, they should be hand-made: it is well worth paying the extra cost for the sake of the way they weather down to a pleasing "mellow" texture.

A timber screen can be almost as effective as a masonry one because of the way it filters the wind and slows it down, whereas a solid masonry wall forces the wind over the top and can cause down-draughts and eddies. A good wind-filtering screen can be made by fixing timber slats on alternate sides of the uprights, but if the screen is for visual purposes one can be more inventive. However, a simple grid can be very effective, and avoids any idea of trying too hard. Simple timber members of rectangular section, say four by two inches (100 x 50mm) or three by one and a half inches (75 x 38mm) can be used, with the narrow dimension on the face of the screen; the grid is made by half-joints in the timbers, and the size of the grid can be determined by the amount of screening required.

It is useful to remember that the closer a screen comes to the viewer the more effectively it will hide the things that lie beyond it. A six foot (2m) high screen at the far end of the garden may not be nearly tall enough, but a screen of the same height brought half way up the garden may be quite adequate to hide the offending object that lies somewhere in the distance.

One stage further than a pergola is a summer-house. A building in the garden tends to dominate everthing else and for this reason the design needs to be considered with extreme care. Avoid one of those

A screen made up of a simple open framework of timber members,
an ideal support for climbers.

timber buildings which can be bought "off the shelf", and are really glorified sheds, usually with green felt roofs. There are a few attractive summer-houses on the market (such as the ones made by a firm by the name of Machin), but on the whole it is better to have a summer-house purpose-built and tailor-made to your needs, though of course it will be more expensive. As always, it is sensible for the design to be appropriate to the style of the house itself. But if the house has no style or character to speak of, which is often the case, it may be tempting to indulge in a little fantasy and design something whimsical or exotic. Almost anything well-designed or carefully detailed would be an improvement on the insipidness of many estate houses of the 1950s.

Avoid an obvious position for a summer-house. A location immediately facing the house, for example, with the house and the summer-house staring at each other, tends to be rather tiresome. A summer-house placed diagonally, or tucked into an unexpected sunny corner is more likely to be successful.

It is easy for keen gardening adults to forget that the garden belongs to the children too. I don't mean that the garden has to be stuffed with swings, slides, rubber tyres hung from trees, sandpits and so on: if the garden has all these it will be no fun going on a trip to the park. In any case, sand-pits tend to become the regular haunt of the neighbours' cats – with disastrous results. More important is to consider the needs of the bike- or trike-riding members of the household and to allow space for ball games. The ideal surface for bikes and trikes is hard and smooth – its not so much' fun on wet grass or on soft gravel. A width of about two foot six inches (1m) is desirable, with passing places at intervals. Corners should be easily negotiable, with splays or curves: nobody wants to have to get off their trike and lift it round a ninety degree corner, nor is it fun for a seven-year-old to fall off his bike at a sharp corner and land on top of *Acanthus spinosus*. In any case Dad will be furious, and it won't improve the Acanthus. If you think this attention to children is going too far, I would recommend some of the admirable gardens designed by Thomas Church in California, such as the one for Mr and Mrs Littlefield designed in 1952, which contains large areas of "black top" (i.e. tarmac) for bike-riding and ball-games, and the corners of the lawn are all splayed and radiused to prevent wear by corner-cutting trike-riders and toy-car drivers.

When there are children in the house, it is also desirable to have a lawn of reasonable shape and size to suit ball games and other games like Grandmother's Footsteps. Having made an elegant but rather narrow, serpentine lawn in our own garden when the children were quite small, we now find it is quite difficult to play French cricket (to say nothing of the ordinary kind) without the ball disappearing regularly into the penstemons, or whatever.

Keen gardeners will be tempted to buy a greenhouse, but be warned, these can easily generate a lot of work. Of course they are useful, especially to the vegetable gardener, and to those who raise annuals and bedding plants. They also provide a warmer place for pottering about with pots and propagation during the colder months. They are handy, too, as a place to keep those sick-looking house plants before they are either fit to bring back inside, or otherwise throw away. But do remember that to maintain the garden and a greenhouse, too, may require rather more hours than you have to spare.

Temperature control is usually the major problem. So often green-houses are too cold in the winter, unless you can stand a good deal extra on your heating bill, and too hot in summer because of inadequate ventilation. A sophisticated, electronic temperature-control system is really the desirable thing to make a greenhouse worthwhile, with auto-matic opening of lights and so on.

Unless you have an uncommonly good one, a greenhouse is not an object of beauty, and in my opinion they should be invisible from the drawing room windows. But in spite of this *diktat* it should also be as near to the house as possible, so that it is easily accessible during bad weather, and convenient for anyone who wants to pop out and check the marrows on frosty spring nights. The desire to screen the greenhouse from sight on the one hand and the need for maximum sunshine to fall on the glass, on the other, are likely to be in conflict with each other: so it seems in that case you may have to decide which is most important, the greenhouse or the garden. Personally I think a greenhouse should be considered as a protection from the worst of the weather, rather than a means of obtaining the highest temperature; and I would be prepared to tolerate a little shade.

If there is a service area this may also be the place for the greenhouse to go. Most gardens need what might be described as a back-stage area. When the tulips or the roses are behaving like star performers against a background of permanent evergreen stage-scenery, there will always be other things to attend to which are muddly and untidy, and which are best screened from view. If you sow seeds, or take cuttings which sit around in pots in or out of a cold-frame, this is very rewarding and interesting, but it isn't neat or nice to look at. Similarly, bonfires and compost heaps need to go somewhere, if you have them. In very small gardens it is sometimes better to put all your garden rubbish in black plastic sacks and give them to the refuse collectors, or if they won't take them, you may have to drive to your local council "tip" with the bags yourself. It may be bad ecology but, in my opinion, life isn't long enough for fiddling about turning over compost heaps.

Garden sheds can be just as much a problem as a greenhouse. If you find you need a garden shed it should not be put down the bottom of the garden where it will be in full view from the house. Instead it should be brought up, nearer the house where it can be placed to one side of the garden, somewhere near the garage perhaps or even right beside it, out of the field of vision from the drawing room windows. It is a mystery why house-builders do not provide storage for lawnmowers, bicycles and garden tools as an integral part of the house. After all almost everyone has these things.

The size of most gardens in towns or in the suburbs is so small that one should always try to make the most of what area there is. A long view from the house to the furthest boundary is always desirable, and it is a mistake to block off the bottom half of the garden either with a vegetable garden or some kind of service area. There are various solutions to this problem, and one which is commonly adopted is to split the vegetable plot in two with a fairly wide path, so that anyone looking from the house can see right down to the far end. It is obviously a nice touch to provide some kind of feature to terminate the vista, to show that you mean what you are doing and that it is not just an accidental path between cabbages. To make sure the rows of cabbages or lettuces are not seen, one can, for instance, have a row of cordoned apple trees down each side of the path, or you could go one better if you are a keen fruit-grower and have a fruit-arch, which can be a very attractive feature. Or, if fruit doesn't interest you, a row of standard roses on each side could look most impressive in the summer months, cascading with bloom, but not getting in the way of the vegetables.

A second solution is to create a vista or sight-line on the diagonal, and this can be appropriate if it takes advantage of irregularities in the shape of the plot. The vegetable garden can be hidden by a series of staggered timber screens, and access obtained between two of the screens. The temptation to provide a statue, vase, seat or something to finish the thing off may be too hard to resist, but to show that the vista can be terminated in other ways a second variation is shown. Here a grass path winds mysteriously out of sight leaving the eye to wonder where this shadowy path might lead – actually to the vegetable patch.

In these plans a diagonal sight-line takes advantage of the maximum depth of plot. The vegetable garden is hidden by a series of screens.

In this formal design, the vegetables are in neat box-edged beds,
at the far end of the garden.

Sometimes irregularities in plot-shapes produce a garden which is
wider at the front than at the back, in which case it may be an asset
to have the vegetables and herbs near the house where they can be
picked freshly for dinner without the effort of putting on boots and
trailing down the garden, probably in the rain.

A third way to grow vegetables is to accept them as garden plants
and to grow them in neat plots surrounded by dwarf box hedges. This

129

is appropriate when the rest of the garden is in the same formal manner of geometrical beds edged with Box. The classic example of this, where it has been done in the grand manner, is Villandry, not far from Tours in France. On a smaller scale Rosemary Verey is creating an interesting example of the genre at Barnsley House, near Cirencester. In this style, the neat rows of parsley, radishes, sprouts or whatever it may be, are accepted for what they are; the straight-lines become part of the overall pattern, but the untidiness, if any, is partly hidden, and partly contained by the box hedges.

The cottage-garden style must also be mentioned here. Without being unfair, it seems to me that in cottage-gardens the traditional priorities are reversed. Instead of vegetables seen as something which must be tucked away out of sight, the whole garden is seen as a kitchen garden, or as an allotment or smallholding, into which ornamental plants have come, first of all as a bonus, but later taking over large sections of the garden. No doubt the pre-1914 gardeners who worked at the Big House used to acquire spare plants from time to time and put them in their own gardens, which until then had been entirely devoted to growing food. In this way, it came about that rows of Madonna lilies would flourish next to a row of peas, and rows of runner-beans would consort with rows of gladioli. Paths in cottage gardens are usually straight, or almost straight, giving easy access to various parts of the plot which are treated rather like a filing cabinet of plants, where artichokes or asters are slotted in wherever seems handy on the day when they have to be planted out. Of course this is all very charming, especially in a rural, cottage setting, but to me it is the gardening equivalent of cramming a fistful of disparate flowers into a jam jar. With flower arrangement a more sophisticated appearance is achieved by carefully arranging the flowers one by one, with thought and taste.

The arrangement of plants in the garden has already been discussed but what of the flowers themselves? Which ones shall we choose to adorn the carefully arranged setting that we have created for them? There are many treasures that can be pored over, many which repay close inspection, and many others whose blooms are beautiful but fleeting; instead of filling the garden with such things it is better to consider how we can create an effective floral display which will last as long as possible, and offer something for every season of the year. This is the subject of the final section of this book.

STEP-BY-STEP PLAN OF A GARDEN DESIGN

◄ The bare plot, whose only features
are the perimeter fence and an
unwanted view of a neighbour's
building.

POSITION
FOR THE
SITTING AREA

AREA OF

SHADOW

SERVICE
AREA

nce we have discovered which parts ►
the garden are in shadow, the best
position for the sitting area can be
found, and the most suitable place
for a service area decided.

POSITION OF THE
LATE AFTERNOON SUN

◀ The offending building is screened by trees, and the boundaries are softened with greenery. A screen hides the service area.

Possible shapes for the lawn and the ▶ borders are identified. A further area of paving by the house is added.

◀ The paving patterns are decided on. The shape of the lawn is finalised and additional trees are planted.

LAWN

SITTING AREA

SERVICE AREA

BORDERS

LAWN

PAVING

The borders are planted up, two ▶ ornamental vases are added and also some seats.

SERVICE AREA

LAWN

133

The finished garden.

PART
4

PLANTING
· FOR ·
PLEASURE

CHAPTER
17

Floral Display

What we all long for is a garden where the climate is mild, where there are no late frosts, no cruel March winds, a sheltered, sunny plot with fertile, workable, loamy soil. Here we would have a fair chance to succeed, we feel, without the constant uphill battle against Nature. But no-one ever confesses to owning such a plot: gardeners prefer instead to tell you of their problems, so that their successes will seem so much greater.

To fill our spaces in this ideal garden we demand ideal plants. The ideal plant is one that blooms unfailingly for about six months, never looks tatty, needs no staking, no pruning, no dead-heading, and comes up every year. Of course, such plants don't exist. I suppose the nearest one can get to a really long display is to use bedding plants, but many gardeners feel that somehow this is cheating. They would rather have a bedraggled plant that had had an honest struggle through a whole twelve months in the garden, than an invasion of over-cheerful, fair-weather friends who will only have to be taken out when the cold weather comes. But I suspect the main reason why people object to bedding plants is that they think they have to be used in stiff, regimented lines with brilliant and clashing colours, because this is the way they have always seen it done. In fact there is no reason why bedding plants cannot be planted with as much sensitivity as perennials or shrubs. There is nothing about a bedding plant which forces you to make the garden look like the trooping of the colour; on the contrary, a far better result will be obtained if you forget about geometry altogether, and arrange the plants in rounded groups, in drifts, or in "sausage-shaped" clumps. And with a little effort one can even impose some discipline on the colour scheme by taking the advice given in Chapter 14.

"Begonia" is a dirty word to many gardeners simply because of the garish and tasteless way they are often used, but there is nothing intrinsically bad about a Begonia in itself. Of course we shall find the horticultural trade ranged against us: seed merchants go out of their way to offer bedding plants in mixed colours, which are never described as "a range of delicate shades of pink" for instance, but always "an eyecatching mixture of pink, orange, scarlet, rose-red and white", guaranteed, and your money back if they don't clash violently. But it is possible to find seeds of the little fibrous-rooted *Begonia semperflorens*, for example, offered in pale pink on its own, such as some F1 hybrids offered by Suttons, which are called 'Pink Avalanche' and 'Frilly Pink'. Even the larger-flowered tuberous *Begonia tuberhybrida*, which some gardeners dismiss as gross and vulgar, can be obtained in a delicate shell-pink if you look out carefully for them; there is one called 'Picotee Rose', for example, available in tuber form from Suttons, which is creamy-white edged in rose pink, a very pretty combination. But seed merchants really expect you to go for something like 'Fiesta Mixed', with the inevitable horrendous colour combinations. Of course there are many other plants suitable for bedding besides begonias, but there are few which give such an unfailingly continuous display, irrespective of the weather, from June to November.

For a colour scheme based on shades of pink, crimson or purple, there are bedding plants such as fuchsias, the pink-flowered, ivy-leafed pelargoniums, petunias or *Verbena rigidus* (*V. venosa*), which is really a tender perennial. There are also several foliage plants which blend well with these such as the silver *Senecio cineraria* and *S. leucostachys*, or the red-leafed *Iresine herbstii* and ornamental Beetroot. *Salvia horminum* is also good – sometimes called 'Clary'. This can be safely raised from mixed seeds and has pink, blue or white bracts in attractive pastel shades.

There is a good selection of both blue and white flowered bedding plants. These can be used in almost any colour scheme and will help to tone down the brightness of some of the other colours. These include the scented *Heliotrope* also known as 'Cherry Pie', in violet-blue; *Ageratum*, which is mauve and rather dwarf; and blue lobelias. *Salvia farinacea*, with violet-blue spikes, is good; it is really a tender perennial.

If we decide to go for a scheme of yellows, oranges and scarlets, this will have all the brilliance that one associates with bedding plants. The idea that anyone might only want a cream colour or a primrose yellow does not seem to have occurred to those who develop bedding plants. However, someone has had the wit to raise a fascinating green *Zinnia* appropriately called 'Envy', with flower-arrangers in mind, and there is also a lime-green tobacco plant both of which could give some relief to the brashness of the yellows and oranges of such plants as

Tagetes, Calendula, Rudbeckia, scarlet geraniums (pelargoniums) and cannas. Contributing to this colour range one could use the purple-leaved version of the Castor-oil Plant, *Ricinus communis* 'Gibsonii' and *Chrysanthemum parthenium* 'Aureum'. Of course it goes without saying that on no account should one be able to see a bed with a pink-based colour scheme and a bed of the orange-based colours at the same time from any point. In a small garden it is definitely either-or.

Several other good performers are harder to find in single colour strains, and the kind of colour mixes of *Impatiens* or zinnias usually offered are more than my squeamish eye can take. One has to draw the line somewhere: I cannot imagine myself using the post-office red *Salvia splendens* under any circumstance; to me they seem too much like the ultimate, universal, computer-designed, plastic plant. There is a purple variety, but it is scarcely ever seen.

Even if one agrees that desirable colour schemes can be devised with bedding plants and that they can be grouped in a sensitive, semi-naturalistic manner, there remains the labour of raising the plants from seed, potting them on, planting them out, the need for a greenhouse, and so on; or alternatively the cost of purchasing the plants. This is certainly enough to dissuade me from using them. In any case there is no room for bedding plants in my own garden, because it's already stuffed to overflowing with perennials. Fortunately, however, there are one or two herbaceous plants which approach bedding plants for continuity of bloom.

Fuchsias, for instance, can be grown as perennials, but unfortunately many of them are only on the borderline of hardiness, and that is why they are often used as bedding plants. Because of their woody stems they should really be classed as shrubs, but as they are often cut to the ground by frosts in many areas, it is more convenient to think of them as herbaceous. In spite of being susceptible to frosts they are quite content with cool conditions, and don't do well in a hot, dry position. They flourish in sea-side areas and can be seen growing as hedges near the coast, even in Scotland and Northern Ireland where summer temperatures don't rise very high. In colder areas, such as the Home Counties, one must choose the hardiest kinds, and further north some kind of protection may be necessary, such as covering the crowns with grit during the winter. Another problem with northern gardens is that fuchsias need a reasonably long growing period before they come into bloom; and this is why they do best where the stems are not killed right to the base but retain their sap through the winter. It is a mistake to remove the dead-looking stems in the autumn: they should be allowed to remain to protect the plant. Once the spring frosts are over they can be cut down to encourage vigorous new growth.

The hardiest and most vigorous kind is the common Fuchsia, *F. magellanica* 'Riccartonii', but there are several more decorative varieties, such as 'Corallina', 'Chillerton Beauty', 'Lena', 'Madame Cornelisen' and 'Mrs Popple', all beautiful and worth trying. 'Versicolor' is particularly pleasing, with soft grey-green and pink variegations to its leaves. Where a border is edged with paving, dwarf fuchsias such as 'Tom Thumb' or 'Alice Hofmann' can be used. Grown well, fuchsias can give a continuous display from July until the November frosts.

Perhaps the next best thing in perennials for continuity of colour is a Penstemon. Like fuchsias, penstemons need a fairly mild climate, but unlike them they prefer drier, well-drained soil conditions. There are at least two reliably hardy varieties, both of which are very pretty: 'Evelyn', which is about twelve to eighteen inches high (30–45cm) with rose-pink flowers, and 'Garnet', about two feet high (60cm), and wine-red in colour. Both should bloom from June to October. Penstemon flowers appear on vertical spikes, each flower being tubular, like a mini-foxglove of rich colour. The foliage is evergreen except in the worst winters. There are many other lovely varieties well worth growing, all of which are hardy except in that once-in-twenty-years frost. I am particularly fond of 'Pennington Gem' a delicate pink and white concoction. Others are 'Hidcote Pink', 'Schoenholzeri', 'Sour Grapes', 'Catherine de la Mare' and 'White Bedder'.

Few perennials approach this degree of continuity, but I should like to put in a word for one or two other favourites which are worthy of a special mention. Most long-flowering subjects have their long run from mid-summer until autumn, but not the euphorbias which choose instead the first six months of the year. You can call them spurges if you prefer. *Euphorbia characias* and *E. wulfenii* (which are similar) seem to spend the winter poised for bloom and I can only agree with the words of E. A. Bowles, writing in 1915, "*Euphorbia wulfenii* also gives us constant pleasure in Winter by the daily changing tints of red and purple, green and gold that appear on its terminal flowering heads". The "flowers" usually open fully some time in March, last until May and fade away gradually in June. These euphorbias are extremely distinctive: not only do they have excellent bluish evergreen foliage, but the flower-heads are rounded and globular, in a most desirable shade of limy yellow. *Euphorbia polychroma* has a long spring season too, but does not start to look interesting until March. *E. nicaeensis* has a long season but is later, roughly May to August.

Two perennials which are not strictly-speaking Michaelmas daisies but closely related to them, are in bloom for many weeks, from July to October. These are *Aster × frikartii* 'Mönch' and *Aster thomsonii* 'Nanus' both have delightful, lavender-blue, daisy flowers, an asset to any garden. *Aster* 'Flora's Delight' is similar but more of a lilac-blue shade.

When we turn to the range of shrubs and look for plants which we value because of their long period of floral display we find that there are comparatively few in this category: the average shrub blooms for a couple of weeks in May, usefully enough, between the bulbs of early spring and the perennials and roses of high summer. One of the few long-lasting and summer-flowering shrubs is *Lavatera olbia* 'Rosea', which forms a rounded, rather open bush about five feet high (1.2m), and is covered with bright pink mallow flowers from June to October. It likes a sunny, well-drained situation.

But in a contest for continuity of floral display roses are the easy winners. Although some of the older roses are repeat-flowering, for real continuity one must use the more modern hybrid tea roses and floribundas, and there is a vast range of these. To select a few from the overwhelming array of varieties might seem a rather daunting task, but if we decide what we want to avoid and what we really require it does help. For myself, I want to avoid brash, crude colours; I dislike leggy, upright growth which produces beautiful flowers on an ugly bush; and I am looking for continuity and for fragrance.

A few words of warning are necessary for anyone who wants to spend some time and trouble selecting roses. Firstly, you should never believe a nurseryman's catalogue, nor is it wise to choose roses from photographs, particularly if they are of one bloom on its own: these photos are quite simply liars, which cannot be relied upon either for colour, for shape, or any other quality. Rose Shows are not worth a visit for this purpose either, nor should rose displays at the Royal Horticultural Society shows, nor at the Chelsea Flower Show be believed for one moment. The art of showing roses produces some wonderful displays which can be extremely beautiful in themselves, and although it tells you what the rose can look like when grown in perfect conditions, and then picked at that brief moment when the buds have half-opened, it does not give you any idea whether the rose in question will look any good when grown in the average garden. To do this one must visit gardens and even then gardens such as the excellent one at St Albans, belonging to the Royal National Rose Society cannot be taken as a wholly reliable guide; it is a marvellous display of an enormous range of varieties, and there you can see what a rose would be like in an ideal world; but you do have to remember that the roses at the RNRS gardens have all been fed, watered, pruned and sprayed by a team of dedicated experts and, what is more, the gardeners go round every day snipping off the dead or dying blooms. I know for certain that a rose in my garden cannot hope to receive either such expertise or such constant attention. I may remember to prune the roses at the right moment, but I may not.

I remember admiring 'Iced Ginger' several times on show benches for its unusual colour, but when I eventually saw a bed of it in real life, at Queen Mary's Rose Garden, Regents Park, it looked a complete disaster. But on the same day, under the same weather conditions and cultivated to the same standard, the floribunda, 'Southampton' was looking marvellous. 'Southampton' is described as apricot-orange in the catalogues, which sounds appalling, but in reality the colour is much more subtle than that and also much paler in tone than the catalogues would suggest. It has an excellent scent and withstands bad weather well. The firm who raised 'Southampton' also raised 'Elizabeth Harkness' another rose of even more restrained colour; this is a hybrid tea rose, creamy-buff tinged with shades of pink and amber, and fairly bushy in habit.

The well-known hybrid tea rose 'Peace' is also of subtle colouring, creamy-white with pale yellow and pink tints. I find it astonishing that so many illustrations of this rose show it half-open and looking decidedly yellow, when its characteristic feature is the huge, domed, paeony-like shape of its fully opened flowers. Its bushy habit is another point in its favour. One of the best of the early descendants of 'Peace' (or 'Mme A. Meilland' as it was named by the man who raised it) is 'Michèle Meilland', which is pearly pink in colour.

A good shrubby floribunda in this colour-range is 'Chanelle', which is creamy-buff and shell pink, and of medium height. Among pink floribundas, I have tried one called 'Abundance' (raised by Gandy) which is good. 'Sonatina' (Sanday 1982) can also be recommended. 'Märchenland', which means Fairy-tale-land, is a rose raised in Germany in 1951, a robust pink floribunda which will form a shrub four feet high (1.2m) if allowed. Another good pink floribunda from Germany is 'August Seebauer', raised by the famous grower Kordes in 1950, the man who eight years later produced the more famous 'Iceberg'. This is the finest of all white floribundas, and like others in this selection will adopt a rounded, shrubby shape. If we ignore the beauty of individual flowers and consider only garden effect a good case could be made for 'Iceberg' as the finest of all modern roses. Its tendency to produce a few odd pink petals now and again is to me an added attraction rather than a defect.

142

In 1959 Kordes raised an excellent deep crimson floribunda called 'Lilli Marlene'; the healthy foliage is a coppery colour and the blooms are particularly weather-proof. For a deep, rich pink floribunda, there is 'The Sunday Times' which is a compact variety, of spreading habit, raised by McGredy in 1971.

A whole class of roses which have been largely forgotten are the polyanthas, which were first developed in the 1880s but have mostly been superseded by the floribundas. Most polyanthas are low-growing and spreading; they produce large clusters of small blooms, like those of rambling roses, and bloom more or less continuously during the summer and autumn. One of the best of these early varieties is 'Marie Pavié', raised in 1888, with blush-white double flowers on a twiggy but almost thornless bush. A typically dwarf variety is 'Baby Faurax', of 1924, fragrant, whose double flowers, however, are remarkable for their lavender-purple colour, claimed sometimes as the nearest thing to a blue rose. Its habit is not very graceful but it is interesting because of its unusual colour. 'Yvonne Rabier' is a taller polyantha, raised in France in 1910, still well worth growing, and still appearing in the catalogues. The flowers are white, double and excellently scented.

'The Fairy', raised in 1932, is sometimes classed as a modern shrub rose; and its little, double, soft-pink flowers appear in midsummer when other roses are getting past their best. It is usually quite short, with a spreading habit. A slight revival of interest in the polyanthas during recent years may be due to the appearance of some new ones, of which the best is 'Yesterday', in delicate shades of pink, with single rambler-like flowers, another variety raised by Harkness.

Some roses defy classification, and one of these is the charming old variety 'Gruss an Aachen', raised in 1909, which can be seen at Hidcote. Sometimes it is classed with the polyanthas, sometimes with the hybrid teas, or else as a floribunda born before its time. Its colour is flesh pink, fading to cream, with double flowers and healthy foliage on a neat bush.

Shortness in roses can be a virtue, because any gawkiness of growth is thereby avoided. Amongst the better modern floribundas there are several which are quite short such as 'Allgold', which is a thoroughly reliable, clear yellow; 'Tip Top', in deep pink, is about eighteen inches high (45 cm); 'Marlena' is a crimson rose, of the same height, with nearly single flowers.

Roses with single flowers are rarely seen, but there are several charming older varieties of hybrid teas, some of which may be seen at Sissinghurst. 'Mrs Oakley Fisher', 1921, which may be grown as a shrub up to six feet high (2m), with flowers of a soft coppery buff-yellow; 'Ellen Willmott', 1936, an exquisite shade of palest lilac-pink; 'White Wings', 1947, with amazing crimson anthers contrasting with the white petals; and 'Dainty Maid', 1938, clear pink with yellow anthers.

For gracefulness of habit and subtlety of colour the shrub roses have many advantages over the modern hybrid teas and floribundas. But for our present purpose, there are comparatively few which give a continuous display. Some are recurrent, which means they have a second season of flower, others have one main burst of bloom with a trickle of flowers to follow. Even as I write, at the end of November, I have roses in bloom in my garden, one of which is a hybrid musk called 'Moonlight', but a small cluster of bloom in a corner of a large shrub can hardly be called a display. Of the various classes of shrub roses, there are several which offer flowers with some kind of continuity, but these are discussed in Chapter 19.

One problem with roses is that they don't like being crowded and jostled amongst other plants. I have tried putting them with herbaceous plants, but they don't perform well like that. Shrub roses of a height of three and a half feet (1m) or more can cope, but not the smaller modern roses. My 'Iceberg' hates being wedged against *Euphorbia characias*. Roses really prefer a bed on their own. This can look all right in the summer especially if the roses are fairly close together, but in the winter it leaves a lot of bare earth showing which is undesirable. It exposes the ugly pruned stems, and the soil has to be weeded if it isn't planted. Roses will accept very low growing plants growing round them, and almost prostrate ones such as ajugas; *Waldsteinia ternata* and acaenas are suitable, and so are the less vigorous members of the genus *Lamium*. Some of the dwarf campanulas have the advantage of blooming at the same time as the roses, such as the common *Campanula portenschlagiana*, *C. poscharskyana* or the pinkish *C.* 'Lisduggan'. Slightly taller but appropriate in some situations are *Saxifraga umbrosa*, well known as London Pride, and the charming Viola, *V. cornuta*, in blue or white. The self-seeding, but unassuming little purple-leafed Violet, *Viola labradorica* is also useful.

The edges of rose beds need careful treatment. Some varieties, as we have seen, are bushy, or low growing, and may "touch down" gracefully to ground level. But these tend to be the exception in modern roses, and most have their ankles and knees showing in a most unseemly manner. A range of edging plants is needed to remedy this, and perhaps the most useful of all is Catmint, *Nepeta* × *faasenii* (*N. mussinii*), whose gentle shade of lavender blends so perfectly with the pastel pinks and subtle apricot colours that I admire in roses. Other useful plants

144

for this purpose are pinks (*Dianthus* varieties), especially the Allwoodii kinds, *Alchemilla mollis*, helianthemums, *Parahebe cataractae, Stachys lanata, Artemisia canescens* and *Hebe pinguifolia* 'Pagei'. The smaller kinds of *Hosta*, and the smaller cranesbill geraniums such as *G. sanguineum* 'Album' or *G. dalmaticum*, pink or white, are also suitable. If something taller is needed beside a really "leggy" hybrid tea rose, the culinary sage, *Salvia officinalis* would be ideal, or its purple variety 'Purpurascens'. Vita Sackville-West used to grow irises along the edges of her rose borders at Sissinghurst, as old photographs show, and it looked most effective.

In gardens where the style is appropriate it is hard to improve on Box as an edging to rose borders: it is neat, simple to maintain and the rich green colour makes a good foil to the roses.

18

The Floral Year: from Winter to Spring

Although there are some plants, as we have seen, which have a long period of floral display, one of the great attractions of gardening in this country is that every season of the year has its own floral attractions. In some areas of the world this is not so. In the Amazon basin, they tell me, one day is so much like the next that to some of the Indian tribes the concept of a year is quite unknown – with strange results, such as not knowing how old anyone is. However, in this country, despite the vagaries of the English weather, the passing of the seasons is inescapably noticeable and no-one is more conscious of this than the gardener.

Some keen gardeners keep a diary of what is in bloom at every stage of the year, and make notes of any alterations that they think are necessary, so that they won't forget later on. It is not a bad idea to discover what does best in your garden at each stage and then plant plenty of it. A diary can be a good way of doing this, because when you look back (on that cold October day) and find that in May, for example, you had written "more tulips, at least three times as many as we have already" you will just have time to take the appropriate action, rush out and buy some. The aim, therefore, is to create a succession of interest and colour.

During the winter we need plenty of evergreen foliage, rather than flowers. It is true that there are some deciduous shrubs that bloom during the winter, but it seems a mistake to me to fill up too much of a small garden with large plants that struggle to produce a few timid blooms during the cold weather, when the space could more profitably be used by things which do really well later on. The sight of a winter-flowering cherry or a big, shrubby Viburnum braving the blast on a bitterly cold day gives me the shivers. In a small suburban garden where there isn't room for many trees it makes better sense to plant a May-flowering cherry that will be really impressive when it flowers. My own solution has been to put a few winter-flowering plants around the front door. Here they can be seen and enjoyed: if I had put them at the far end of the garden no-one would ever see them.

The new season begins with snowdrops, whose delightful and artless flowers might justly if cornily be described as the harbingers of spring. It would be hard to have too many snowdrops, and a note in our diaries to plant a hundred or so next autumn would help to cheer the garden up at the moment when it needs it most. There are various fancy forms available, doubles, and larger forms, but there seems little point in planting these unless they are the same price as the ordinary ones. To me a snowdrop is a snowdrop, though to snowdrop enthusiasts there are apparently 101 forms.

The two outstanding winter-flowering shrubs are both too big for the average garden. One is *Hamamelis mollis* 'Pallida', a form of the Chinese Witch Hazel, which has strange, spidery flowers of bright yellow, from December to March, a lovely sight on a mild winter's day. Unfortunately this *Hamamelis* is liable to be six feet (2m) high and twelve feet (4m) across; it prefers to be planted in shade. The flowers are well scented, but for outstanding winter frangrance we must turn to our second shrub, the Wintersweet. The most strongly scented form is the species, *Chimonanthus praecox* which is a completely unremarkable shrub apart from its fragrance, which is reminiscent of violets. It is best appreciated by picking the flowers and bringing them indoors. Unfortunately it can take up to seven years to flower and even in bloom this shrub is not exciting in appearance, although the form 'Luteus' is definitely an improvement. Wintersweet is usually about seven feet (2m) high and as much across and I suggest that a good way to counteract its uninteresting appearance in summer is to induce a clematis or a sweet pea to climb through it.

A much more suitable shrub for a small garden is the little-known evergreen *Ribes laurifolium*, a member of the currant family, a fact you would hardly guess from its appearance. It is a fairly dwarf shrub, with large, leathery leaves; the greenish-white flowers normally appear in February or at least by March. Other excellent winter-flowering evergreens have been mentioned in earlier chapters, such as *Viburnum tinus* and *Mahonia japonica*, and so has the indispensable Winter Jasmine, *Jasminum nudiflorum*.

After the snowdrops, the crocuses. There are many species and named varieties, none of which are seen commonly – though this may be because not much garden visiting is done at crocus time. The first thing to do is to forget all about those bright yellow or chubby purple crocuses, usually imported from Holland, and offered by a well-known chain-store and others. Look out instead for *Crocus tomasinianus* (known to their friends as "Tommies"). If you see one called 'Whitewell Purple', this is a form of *Crocus tomasinianus* and worth getting. The "Tommies" are not only elegant and refined, in delicate shades of silky lavender blue with prominent orange stamens, but they also increase generously both by self-sown seeds and by offsets, making a marvellous mauve carpet. "Tommies" are suitable for most garden soils, and are quite happy naturalized in grass. The named forms of *Crocus chrysanthus* are also worth growing, such as 'Blue Pearl', 'Cream Beauty' and 'Princess Beatrix'.

There cannot be a garden too small to contain a few hellebores. The Christmas Rose, *Helleborus niger*, is for some strange reason better known than the related but far superior Lenten Rose, *Helleborus orientalis*. It is one of the greatest pleasures of the garden during the early spring to see the progress of the hellebores. There are several species which deserve a place in every garden but the best for sheer beauty are the named forms of *Helleborus orientalis*, or else the so far un-named special selections offered by Helen Ballard of Colwall, Worcestershire. Lenten roses are usually apple-blossom pink, but these marvellous selected forms come in pure white, pale yellow, maroon, and, extraordinarily, even in slate grey; all highly desirable and increasing, especially if well-fed, to larger and more floriferous clumps every year, usually at least fifteen inches (35cm) high. The foliage is evergreen but it does sometimes look a bit the worse for wear after the winter; in which case the worst leaves can be cut off with secateurs. Hellebores are perfectly happy·in shade and make good companions for ferns.

Helleborus corsicus, the Corsican Hellebore, is also evergreen and a most refined plant. It makes a larger plant than the Lenten Rose, almost bushy in style; its beautiful three-fingered leaves have prickly edges, and the flowers are of pale Chartreuse green. *Helleborus foetidus* is a British native and, in spite of being poisonous, is another asset to the garden in early spring, with its pale green bells overtopping the dark green foliage. There is an improved form called 'Wester Flisk'.

Hellebores will tolerate complete shade under the north wall of a house, but our next plant must be given the sunniest position, ideally at the base of a wall. This is *Iris unguicularis* (some people still call it by its older, 19th-century name, *Iris stylosa*). It produces an untidy sheaf of grassy leaves about eighteen inches high (45cm) amongst which the immaculate and intensely lavender-blue flowers appear – not usually before March in my garden, but some people are lucky and have them from September onwards during mild spells. The flowers are scented and good for picking, and the hotter, drier and poorer the soil the happier your plant will be. There is a white form, but I cannot get mine to flower, or even to increase.

Winter flowering heathers, however, do genuinely flower both sides of Christmas which few plants do, outside of mild and favoured districts. *Erica herbacea* (formerly known as *E. carnea*) has several worthwhile varieties. The best is without doubt 'Springwood White'. Others are 'Vivelli' and 'Anne Sparkes', the golden form of 'Vivelli' which has very pretty foliage. Heathers are difficult to place in the garden, and in my view one should avoid "going over the top" and becoming a heather addict. One or two heathers tucked in here and there are better than huge masses of them which will be a blank later on. They do like an open, sunny position, such as they are accustomed to on their native moors.

A sunny situation also suits *Euphorbia rigida*, the brightest star in my garden in February. It is supposed to bloom in January, but it doesn't. It seems to need a warm autumn to encourage it to produce its blooms, which are bright lime-yellow, fading as the weeks go by to a dull orange shade. The foliage in itself is beautiful, a study in silvery grey which in winter becomes flushed with pink, having some similarity to the better known *Euphorbia myrsinites*, but superior to it in several ways, such as the elegant way the stems curve upwards at the ends, instead of being prostrate.

There are many small treasures worth growing at this time of year, but in our search for an effective display, we must pass over the quiet attractions of pulmonarias, coloured primroses or *Hacquetia epipactis*. The soul of spring is encapsulated, not in these horticultural delights, but rather in a crowd, or shall we say a "drift" of golden daffodils. The ideal way to grow them is in grass, and this is easy enough to arrange in a large garden; but in a small garden areas of rough grass tend to look tatty and one is more or less forced to grow daffodils in the border. The problem that results from this is to know what to do with the foliage, which on no account should be cut away until it has withered, because that seriously weakens the bulbs. It will help if we avoid the large, over-bred hybrids of garden origin, since these tend to have the tallest foliage. Gertrude Jekyll's suggestion was to plant daffodils in a border of ferns, so that the new fronds hide the daffodil foliage. This idea can be extended by the use of other herbaceous plants whose new growth appears just at the same time as the daffodil leaves are flopping about looking untidy. Of course, one must not go to the extreme of entirely submerging the daffodil leaves in foliage because they must be exposed to a certain amount of sunlight in order to feed the bulb ready for next year's flowering. But the leaves will be less of a nuisance if we choose the smaller, less refined kinds, which I think look more attractive in any case. To me, a Daffodil should look like an innocent young country girl, not an obese Hollywood star. So avoid the usual run of 'King Alfred', 'Carlton' or 'Ice Follies' and particularly horrors such as 'Home Fires', 'Eddy Canzony' or 'Rowallane'. Avoid mixed narcissi for naturalizing as well, since these will surely contain a selection of undesirable varieties.

It is hard to think of anything prettier than our own native Daffodil or Lent Lily, *Narcissus pseudonarcissus*, particularly for naturalizing in grass or in lightly shaded woodland. It likes rich, slightly moist conditions and appears in April. There is a charming nineteenth century variety still available, called 'W. P. Milner' which is a more delicate sulphur-yellow colour, about ten inches (26cm) high.

Jonquils also possess an artless grace, and have scent as well to recommend them, but as they come from Spain, Majorca and North Africa, it is to be expected that they do like a warm position. The flowers of *Narcissus jonquilla* are small, golden yellow, with small cups, and appear in late April, four or five on a twelve inch (30cm) stem, above the dark, rush-like leaves. There are several excellent hybrids with *N. triandrus*, which is itself a pretty species, especially the form *albus*, often called Angels' Tears. Two exceptional varieties with yellow flowers are 'April Tears' whose slightly pendant flowers are about four to a stem, and eight inches (20cm) high, and 'Hawera' which opens at the end of March, with about three flowers to a stem and approximately nine inches (23cm) high. 'Trevithian' is another good yellow jonquil hybrid, which is suitable for naturalizing in grass. Closer to *N. triandrus* is the lovely, tall, white 'Thalia' about sixteen inches high (40cm).

The outer petals of *Narcissus cyclamineus* are curved back, in E. A. Bowles's words: "like the ears of a kicking horse". It soon begins to spread and seed itself when it is happy in a slightly damp situation that it likes. There are several pleasant varieties, the earliest of which is 'February Gold', which is fifteen inches high (38cm); 'Charity May' in lemon yellow, twelve inches (30cm): and 'Jack Snipe', yellow and white, eight inches (30cm).

The Poet's Narcissus, *Narcissus poeticus*, does not bloom until May. It is well-known in the commonly available varieties 'Actaea' and 'Pheasant Eye', which are white, with a yellow eye edged with red, and although they are slightly less graceful than the wild forms, they are much more reliable and vigorous. There are also one or two delicious varieites with a green eye, such as 'Cushendall', which was raised, not surprisingly, in Northern Ireland.

For a good display, always buy daffodils by the hundred, and only plant one or two kinds in any one area. When buying in quantities it is sensible to obtain them from a wholesaler who will supply them much more cheaply than garden centres, and also cheaper than firms which issue those glossy, coloured (and tempting) bulb catalogues. Daffodil bulbs should be planted in July or August.

It is easy to be stingy with bulbs. Once you have seen a small "pool" of the wonderful blue *Anemone blanda atrocoerulea*, you promise yourself a hundred or so more of them, but of course unless you write a note in your diary you probably forget. This is a marvellous little plant and a carpet of *Anemone blanda* looks quite miraculous. It is said to prefer full sun and dislikes growing in grass, but Margery Fish grew it at East Lambrook naturalized in grass under a sycamore tree, so it can be done.

There are several other dwarf bulbs which will increase easily, almost too fast for comfort: *Chionodoxa luciliae*, the starry blue Glory of the Snow; *Ipheion uniflorum*, in palest blue; and the white shining Star of Bethlehem, *Ornithogalum umbellatum*.

It is easy to make the garden colourful at this time of year with purple *Aubrieta*, white *Arabis*, or yellow *Alyssum*, but if these take up too much space it may leave a lot of blank greenery later on. I have not yet managed to have too many tulips, however, and I strongly recommend that you don't fill up the garden with spring-flowering shrubs that garden centres tempt you with, but spend the money the previous September instead, on tulips.

The old way to use tulips was the municipal method, treating them as bedding plants. They can look lovely with wallflowers or forget-me-nots, and in this case it is best to use late-flowering varieties; but you don't have to plant them in regimental rows, in fact I think you should go out of your way to avoid getting all those dead-straight stalks in line with each other.

But life is not long enough for the labour of lifting tulip bulbs and dusting them, and putting them all back in again later. Most people want tulips that can safely be left in the ground. If you do this, make sure you plant them deeply, four inches (10cm) is enough. Remove the dead leaves and stems when they have faded (if you leave them to rot it may spread disease) and apply bone meal or a general fertilizer each spring. The best tulips to treat in this way are certain of the species, the *fosterana* and *kaufmanniana* hybrids, the Darwin hybrids and the so-called Cottage tulips. Almost all tulips like well-drained soil, and if your garden is on heavy clay, the area should be thoroughly dug over, adding very generous amounts of grit. A sheltered, sunny position is also desirable; otherwise strong winds will blow the petals away almost before the flowers have had a chance to open.

For those who dislike the stiff "soldiers on parade" look of tulips, the one to go for is *Tulipa turkestanica*, an early flowering species with slender stems about twelve inches high (30cm) which lean in all directions. There can be up to seven flowers to a stem; white, with cream and green markings. Other species tulips worth trying are *T. batalinii*, which is yellow, and *T. clusiana*, sometimes called the Lady Tulip, which is white with a broad pink streak, an elegant grower. *Tulipa sprengeri*, another non-traditional-looking tulip, is reliably perennial and even seeds itself where it is happy; the flowers are mahogany red, and don't appear until the end of May. *Tulipa saxatilis* has naturalized itself at the chalky garden of the late Sir Frederick Stern at Highdown, near Worthing. This is a tulip with lilac-pink flowers which spreads by underground stolons. It likes a hot baking in the summer – a common feature of tulips, and particularly applicable to some of the other worthwhile species tulips, such as *celsiana*, *primulina*, *eichleri*, *ophanidea*, and the related *hageri* and *whittallii*.

Tulipa kaufmanniana is variable, but is always short, about six inches (15cm), April-flowering, and creamy-white with slight pink or red markings on the outside. Some of the varieties are brilliantly bi-coloured and are no improvement on the species. Perhaps the best is 'Fritz Kreisler' (sometimes called 'Yolanda'), a fantasy in pink and pale apricot.

The *fosterana* hybrids are also April-flowering, and about fifteen inches high, but like *kaufmanniana* they open very wide. The white 'Purissima' is particularly lovely, at first creamy-yellow, but getting white as it opens, like a great chalice. 'Madame Lefeber', is brilliant scarlet, and an amazing splash of colour so early in the year. 'Orange Emperor' blends more easily with daffodil colours. All need protection from the wind to help them retain their precariously cantilevered petals for as long as possible.

For a traditional-looking Tulip, robust enough to be left in the ground all the year, we should choose from the Cottage tulips or the confusingly named Darwin hybrids. The older class of Darwin tulips were bred with *Tulipa fosterana* to produce the Darwin hybrids, and although these make good garden plants they only seem to be available at present in the most brilliant yellows, oranges and scarlets. A typical example is the recent 'Flaming Gold', a butter-yellow tulip with red flashes. This group starts to flower at about the end of April.

For more subtle colours we must turn to the Cottage tulips, and these bloom in May. Good examples are 'Chappaqua' a deep mauvypink; 'Palestrina' salmon-pink, tinged with green; or 'Mirella' in various shades of salmon-pink; all of the traditional tulip shape. Most amazing of all are the 'Viridiflora' tulips, which are generously streaked with green and some have highly irregular petals which make a pleasing change from the sleek, egg-shaped blooms that are traditional: 'Artist' is terracotta and green, becoming more green as it ages; 'Golden Artist' is yellow and green, 'Pimpernel' is red and green with bizarre, reflexed petals; and 'Angel' is cream and green. For some reason these strange flowers look far better in the garden than they do on the show bench but, in spite of this, the flower arrangers dote on them.

As we reach the month of May, the time for flowering shrubs arrives; and so does the time for the garden centres to make their big kill, when they sell their flowering shrubs by the thousand. The secret of buying from garden centres is to have a list of what you want before you go, and not to come back with anything that isn't on your list. We have already discussed quite a selection of shrubs that flower in May, in previous chapters: *Viburnum plicatum* 'Mariesii', for example and *Ceanothus* 'Delight' and *C.* × *veitchianus*, skimmias, and *Choisya ternata*. But the most floriferous of all are the azaleas. The evergreen kinds have been discussed already but the deciduous ones are considered by some to be even more beautiful, and it is certainly easier to find acceptable pastel colours which will blend into the garden scheme without being so brilliant that everything else pales into insignificance. Some of the oranges and reds available are just as undesirable as the vicious pinks of the evergreen azaleas. But on the other hand some of the creams, pale yellows and pale pinks are very lovely. 'Daviesii' has apricot pink buds which open to creamy-yellow flushed with deeper yellow, and 'Narcissiflora' is pale lemon with a darker centre, both remarkable for the delightful fragrance. 'Persil', as you would expect is white, though with a yellow flare; 'Silver Slipper' is pink in bud opening to cream flowers marked with yellow. 'Irene Koster' is pale pink with a tinge of yellow, and like 'Daviesii', this has excellent autumn colour. All azaleas require lime-free soil, and there is nothing which will make a comparable display on limy soils.

Gardeners who cannot grow azaleas will find viburnums (sometimes suggested) a poor substitute. Weigelas offer slightly more, since some of them have the additional interest of coloured leaves. *Weigela florida* 'Variegata' makes a most delicate picture with its pale pink flowers amongst the soft green and cream foliage. The leaves of *W. florida* 'Foliis Purpureis' are really closer to brown than purple, which makes this a most unusual combination when the deep pink flowers are in bloom. This is quite a small shrub. *Weigela hortensis* 'Looymansii

Aurea' has light yellow foliage and pink flowers; it is best in part shade. One scarcely ever sees the pretty, white-flowered weigelas: 'Avalanche', 'Mont Blanc' and *Weigela hortensis* 'Nivea'.

The next star player in this non-stop garden performance is the *Iris*. There are countless colours available, particularly from specialists like Kelways of Langport, Somerset, who have an enchanting stand every year at the Chelsea Flower Show. Everyone has their own favourite: my own is the pale silvery-blue 'Jane Philips', a wonderful though indescribable colour. My wife prefers 'Party Dress', in a pastel apricot colour with frilly petals and a vivid orange beard, not a very strong grower. The tallest of the tall bearded varieties should be avoided: once they exceed about three feet (1m) they begin to look out of proportion, and are easily shaken about by the rough winds of May. Kelways, for instance, offer a good range of intermediate irises of medium height. I have a good one called 'Magic' which is mahogany red. The very dwarf irises, such as 'Green Spot' are hardly worth growing as their flowering period is so short.

The older varieties, whose "falls" (the lower part of the flower) actually fall, are to be preferred to the modern ones which "flare" – i.e. have been bred by misguided hybridists for the show bench, with falls which are almost horizontal. Irises usually multiply well. I have managed to cram about twenty kinds into my town garden, although one or two of these, I confess, were obtained by cheekily knocking on the doors of complete strangers and asking for a small piece from the huge clump I could see in their front gardens.

In theory the paeonies are a little later than the irises, but sometimes the weather plays havoc with the timetable. There are countless hybrids of amazing beauty. The singles such as 'White Wings', 'Sir Edward Elgar' (maroon) 'Globe of Light' (pale rose with a gold centre), and 'Her Majesty' (red with a yellow centre) are all highly desirable. but then so are the doubles, like 'Sarah Bernhardt' (pink), 'Felix Crousse' (red) or 'Cornelia Shaylor' (pinkish white). The only problem with paeonies is that in a tremendous downpour of rain (the June "drop") they can be ruined, but their flowers are so lovely they deserve a place in any garden.

CHAPTER 19

The Floral Year: from Summer to Autumn

By the time June arrives it is quite easy to make the garden colourful. Many herbaceous plants are already coming out. The admirable dicentras and euphorbias are in full spate, and so are the delightful *Geum rivale* varieties 'Leonard's Variety' (coppery pink) and 'Lionel Cox' (pale yellow).

The smaller kinds of cranesbill geraniums are particularly good. "I have one rule in gardening", Margery Fish once wrote, "when in doubt, plant *Geranium endressii*". The cheery pink flowers of this cranesbill seem to go on for weeks, with another season later on, especially if they are cut down after flowering: 'Wargrave Pink' is a good form. G. 'Johnson's Blue' is a beautiful colour but has a briefer season, some gardeners say they are able to get it to repeat. It looks splendid with the yellow rose 'Golden Wings'. The double forms of the wild Meadow Cranesbill G. *pratense*, are both charming, in two shades of blue, 'Plenum Caeruleum' (light blue) and 'Plenum Violaceum' (deep violet-blue). The dwarfer *Geranium* varieties include such delights as the blue G. *himalayense* 'Birch Double', G. 'Kashmir White', G. 'Russell Prichard' (purply-red) and *wallichianum* 'Buxton's Variety', and there are many more, much loved by addicts like me, and all providing several weeks of colour.

Then there are astrantias, monardas, and *Salvia superba*, all garden-worthy perennials, not to mention our old friend *Alchemilla mollis*. But June is really a month for roses, and although we talked about the hybrid teas and floribundas we cannot ignore the shrub roses, since these are surely the finest of all flowering shrubs. They have scent, colour, elegance, and atmosphere – what else do we want?

Many of them are a bit too large for the small garden, but nevertheless the choice is wide. It is fashionable to admire the old-fashioned roses, the Gallicas, Albas, Damasks, Centifolias and Moss roses, but it has to be admitted that in a small garden one is probably better off with more modern shrub roses, when we take into account factors such as tendency to attack by mildew, the strength of stems to hold up heavy blooms, ability of the flowers to withstand rain, quality of foliage, and so on. The most satisfactory group of old roses is probably the Albas, because of their healthy, grey-green foliage. One of the Alba roses, 'Celeste' (or 'Celestial') is one of the finest of all the old roses, but 'Félicité Parmentier' (1836), 'Madame Legras de St. Germain' (1846) and 'Semi-plena' are all good. Of the other classes, 'Madame Hardy' (Damask, 1832) and 'Fantin Latour' (Centifolia) are both outstanding roses. But all are pale pink or white, and if we want a rose of a darker colouring we would do well to choose 'Cardinal Richelieu' (Gallica 1840) which has fragrant flowers of a rich purple colour.

Between these old roses which are mostly pre-1850, and the hybrid musks of the 1920s, came the Bourbon roses and the hybrid perpetuals. Some of these such as 'Paul Neyron', turn out to have amazing flowers on ungainly bushes, and many others are plagued by blackspot. The word "perpetual" in this case means that there is a second flowering in the autumn, but often on long, new, awkward-looking shoots. They are not perpetual in the way modern roses are, but it was a significant advance at the time. The best of these Victorian roses are, I suggest, 'Souvenir de la Malmaison' (Bourbon, 1843), 'Boule de Neige' (Bourbon, 1867) 'Reine des Violettes' (Hybrid Perpetual, 1860), 'Mrs John Laing' (Hybrid Perpetual, 1887) and 'Frau Karl Druschki' (H.P./H.T. 1901). Another good rose belonging to this period is 'Alister Stella Gray' (Noisette, 1894), often described as a climber, but in my garden it forms a rounded shrub with the most remarkable small, pale-apricot buds. An odd spray of flowers in December is not unusual.

There is probably no genetic connection but visually at any rate it seems a short step from 'Alister Stella Gray' to the hybrid musks. Most of these were raised by the Reverend Joseph Pemberton, and they make quite large shrubs of elegant foliage, well covered in fragrant flowers in midsummer, with many recurrent sprays later. The flowers are slightly loose and blousy, having a resemblance to some floribundas, but with more of what Herrick called "a sweet disorder in the dress" – 'Buff Beauty' (1939) is probably the best of all with 'Cornelia' (1925), 'Felicia' (1928), 'Francesca' (1922) and 'Penelope' (1924) having each its own charm. 'Thisbe' (1918) is smaller, while 'Vanity' (1920) is probably the largest.

The rugosas form a most distinct group of roses, mainly because of their luxuriant, bright green foliage. They are extremely tough and disease-free and are perhaps the most shrub-like of all roses. Unlike so many roses they manage to look attractive even when not in flower. Although *Rosa rugosa* was introduced as early as 1796, most of the important hybrids did not appear until the period 1890–1920. Their tendency to repeat makes them particularly valuable, and they also have the additional interest of large hips – large enough to look remarkably like small tomatoes in some cases. 'Agnes' (yellow, 1922), 'Frau Dagmar Hastrup' (pink, 1901) 'Rosaraie de l'Haÿ' (crimson, 1901), and 'Alba' (white) are all excellent plants. 'Sarah van Fleet' (pink, 1926) is suitable for larger gardens.

Many of the wild rose species are extremely beautiful, but many are far too large for the average garden and most flower once only. Amongst the smaller ones a good display can be obtained from 'Golden Chersonese' (yellow, 1963) a hybrid of *Rosa ecae*, and *R. villosa duplex* (pink). *Rosa rubrifolia* should be grown wherever possible for the sake of its excellent mauve-grey foliage. *Rosa elegantula (farreri) persetosa* and *R. woodsii fendleri* have an airy grace and delicacy, but neither are exactly small plants, and neither is 'Complicata', a charming pink rose, which must confusingly be described as a species hybrid of unknown origin, since it does not fit conveniently into any of the other rose classes. Maybe 'Complicata' refers to its genetics, since its appearance is one of simple charm. *Rosa virginiana* is smaller and has the best autumn colours of any rose. Those with larger gardens will want to find room for *Rosa californica plena, R. moyesii* 'Geranium' or *R. Canary Bird'*, which are all bigger plants, reaching eight feet (3m) or more.

Several outstanding modern shrub roses are only once-blooming, but are so impressive that they must be mentioned: 'Nevada' (white 1927), 'Marguerite Hilling' (pink, 1959) 'Frühlingsgold' (yellow, 1937) and 'Fritz Nobis' (pink, 1940), but it must be confessed they take up a tremendous amount of space – about six feet (2m) in each direction in fact – considering their display only lasts about three weeks. For continuous performance we must turn to splendid roses such 'Aloha' (pink, 1949), 'Golden Wings' (yellow, 1956), 'Karl Förster' (white, 1931), 'München' (dark red, 1940) or 'Lavender Lassie' (pink, 1959).

The so-called English roses raised by David Austin are still relatively new, and it is probably too soon to assess them fully, but from what I have seen they promise well. The aim is to produce shrubs with the fragrance and charm of the old roses but with healthy foliage and continuity of bloom. Whether these criteria are met remains to be proved, but the following should be mentioned, though I have not seen all of them growing in gardens: 'Red Coat' (crimson, 1973), 'Dapple Dawn' (pink, 1983), 'Graham Thomas' (yellow, 1983), 'Mary Rose' (pink, 1983), 'Heritage' (pale pink, 1984) and 'Belle Story' (pale pink, 1984).

The summer flowering shrubs, in general, do not excel themselves in the way the spring flowering ones do. Of those which flower at the same time as the roses, the genus *Philadelphus* is probably the best, commonly called 'Mock Orange'. Most species are outstanding for their powerful fragrance. Of the many named varieties 'Belle Etoile' and 'Sybille' are both excellent, and suitable for smaller gardens. Many other summer flowering shrubs have been mentioned already in this book, for other reasons. Cistuses, *Colutea arborescens*, Lavender and potentillas are all worth-while, but perhaps only the potentillas have a floral display of any great note. Later on come the sorbarias, *Eucryphia* 'Nymansay', *Tamarix pentandra* (all of which we have mentioned before) and so do some of the *Hydrangea* species. The common florists' Hydrangea and similar lace-cap varieties are worth growing on acid soil near the coast where they flourish and are a beautiful blue colour. On alkaline soil they turn a rather unpleasant shade of pink, and inland they seem to me to sulk and look sickly.

For floral display later in the summer the *viticella* Clematis varieties, which we discovered were ideal for covering our boundary walls and fences, will give as splendid a display as we could wish, in a profusion of the most delicious colours – blue, purple, crimson, dark red and white.

Lilies, like several other garden plants (such as roses, daffodils, hellebores and auriculas), are so special that some people get hooked on them. Certainly, many of them need a good deal more cossetting than I am prepared to give them, and they are unlikely to do well in the kind of mixed borders where everything has to fend for itself. But there are a few that will look after themselves and even increase, given the right, lightly-shaded, woodland environment. In a corner of the gardens of St John's College, Cambridge, once landscaped by Lancelot Brown, there is a colony of several hundred plants of *Lilium martagon* growing quite happily. Elsewhere, *Lilium szovitsianum*, *L. pardalinum* and *L. superbum* have been known to establish themselves in semi-wild conditions. They have chosen places where they can rest undisturbed under leaf-mould – very different conditions from the borders of the average suburban garden.

The two best lilies for small gardens are the Madonna Lily, *Lilium candidum*, and the Regal Lily, *Lilium regale*. A good way to cultivate lilies is to grow them in eight inch (20cm) pots which can be sunk into the ground in the appropriate place in the garden a few weeks before they flower. With this method they can be given good drainage, and at least they will be safe from jabbing trowels when they are dormant, and from nibbling slugs when their shoots first appear.

There could be no greater contrast between the cultivation of lilies and the cultivation of day lilies (*Hemerocallis*). As their name would lead you to suppose they are genuine members of the Lily family, *Liliaceae*, but they are very easy to grow: you simply "plant 'em and forget 'em". Of course their flowers aren't quite as special as those of *Lilium regale*, but they are good nevertheless, and bloom over a long period.

I have at least a dozen different varieties of Day Lily in my garden, ranging from the most delicate shell pink to deepest maroon, and from orangey-red to primrose yellow. Few of them have names because I bought several of them from a specialist nursery which sold off its stock unlabelled when it closed. Although I have too many for the size of the garden I cannot bring myself to part with any of them. The first to appear is *Hemerocallis flava* (not to be confused with *H. fulva*) which was known at one time by the prettier name of *Hemerocallis lilioaspho-delus;* it is a beautiful pale yellow colour and is pleasantly scented. What I really covet is a white variety, but the hybridists have not managed to raise one yet. They are quite easy to grow from seed, and even to breed by hand pollination (it must be easy because I've done it myself); and the results can be just as good as the named ones you pay for. To name any particular variety would be unfair, but I will mention that the double variety 'Kwanso Flore Pleno' lacks the elegance of the usual single flowers.

The advantages of day lilies are legion: they make excellent ground cover, they spread but not aggressively, they are fragrant, they will grow in full sun or light shade and in any soil that is not too dry. Of course, as each individual flower lasts only for a day, they are no good for picking. However, in compensation, I am told that you can actually eat the petals, either fresh or dried, in salads, but I confess I haven't tried it yet.

What other perennials are there to continue our succession of floral display? We must discount the teeny-weenies, the poor-doers and those that are interesting but not decorative. My own *bête-noir* in this last category is *Geranium sessiliflorum* 'Nigricans', a small cranesbill with prettily shaped leaves of the dingiest brown. My friends in the Hardy Plant Society adore it, but, honestly, from three feet away it is indistinguishable from bare earth.

There is another member of the Lily family which will give us flowers as startling as we could wish for, the red hot pokers. As they come in many more shades than red it may be more convenient to use the Latin name: *Kniphofia*, but as they were named after a certain Herr Kniphof from Germany, we ought to pronounce the "k" and also remember to pronounce the "p" and the "h" separately. If you prefer it you can always call them "pokers".

They come in red, orange, yellow, cream and even green. Personally I like least the common, bi-coloured red and yellow varieties. They vary in height from six feet (2m) to eighteen inches (45cm) and flower at various times between June and September depending on the species. They like full sun, and like other South African species they appreciate some moisture in the summer, but dislike being cold, wet and water-logged in the winter. The answer to these seemingly impossible require-ments seems to be to put them in a sunny and fairly dry position, and then give them a good soaking occasionally during the summer. It is probably arbitrary to suggest a few names, but 'Prince Igor' is orange-red and six feet high (2m); 'Maid of Orleans' is creamy-white and about three and a half feet (1m); 'Green Jade' is green, about three and a half feet (1m); *Kniphofia rooperi* (sometimes listed as 'C. M. Prichard') is a chunky burnt-orange colour, four feet (1.2m); 'Bressingham Flame' is one of the slighter, more graceful kinds, orange, two feet (60cm).

Other delightful perennials that flower in July and August include *Achillea* 'Gold Plate', erigerons, heleniums, *Echinops ruthenicus* and phloxes. Pale pink, white and deep purple (such as 'Vintage Wine') make good colours for phloxes, but avoid the more virulent pinks and orange-reds. The genus *Agapanthus*, another member of the *Liliaceae*, comes in various delightful shades of blue. Like kniphofias they come from South Africa and like warm conditions, but otherwise their needs are similar. The traditional way to grow them was in big terracotta pots, and if your garden is on damp clay, or is north of Birmingham, this is probably a good idea: the pots can then be given frost protection during the winter. The best varieties for the border are 'Profusion' and the 'Headbourne Hybrids'.

Aster × *frikartii* 'Mönch' and varieties of *Aster amellus* have already been recommended, but the Michaelmas daisies themselves, *Aster novi-belgii* varieties, are hardly worth growing in a small garden. There are some lovely colours, but they last for such a short period and suffer so much from mildew that I have let most of mine go. Some of the other species have a charm of their own and the best of these seems to me to be *Aster cordifolius* 'Silver Queen' which is healthy, graceful and turns from white to pink after it has been in bloom for a while.

In the yellow and orange colour range, rudbeckias perform well and are reliably perennial. *Rudbeckia fulgida* 'Goldsturm' is a good variety, yellow with a black centre, a feature which has prompted the name

'Black-eyed Susan' for such rudbeckias. There are others with green centres or double flowers, but these tend to be too tall and willowy for small gardens. *Curtonus paniculatus* in orange-red and the *Crocosmia* varieties in orange, yellow and bronze have already been referred to, in connection with their sheaves of pointed leaves.

In September the pink and white Japanese anemones are in flower, of which there are excellent named forms such as *Anemone japonica* 'September Charm' (pink) and *A. hybrida* 'Honorine Jobert' (white). Just because these are easy to grow and spread themselves is no reason for despising them.

Sedum 'Autumn Joy' makes a surprisingly large clump, with deep pink heads. But the real autumnal "feel" comes with the chrysanthemums. Many varieties are not reliably perennial, but 'Clara Curtis' is good, and other similar, single varieties in a watery pink can be seen growing in old gardens. With chrysanthemums it is a bit like irises: "Ask, and it might be given unto you". The short double varieties 'Anastasia' and 'Mei-kyo', both pink, and 'Bronze Elegance' (brownish) are worth obtaining, but are not often offered for sale. To avoid losing chrysanthemums it is wise to protect them against slugs, against frost, and to divide and replant clumps every other year, in the spring.

By the end of October, when you would think the best was over, the garden can produce something really exotic if you have planted it generously with nerines. The usual colour of *Nerine bowdenii* is candy-floss pink, but other colours are available from specialist breeders. Nerines might be described as frilly pink *Agapanthus*, but shorter. Like them, they can be grown in pots where they can be given the necessary tender loving care. Grown in the border they like it hot, which means that perennials should not be allowed to crowd in over them. The bottom of a warm wall is an ideal position, where the sun can bake them during the summer.

Last of all comes the Obedient Plant, *Physostegia virginiana* 'Vivid'. Blooming so late its puce-pink colour is forgivable. Like the fuchsias and the chrysanthemums it goes on till the frost comes and finishes it off.

But in case you think that is the end, it isn't. There are other things besides flowers: there are berries and autumn leaves. Few people with small gardens will want to plant large shrubs whose only merit is their autumn colour; far better to choose trees or shrubs which will include autumn colour amongst several other attractive features. The pleasures of *Disanthus cercidifolius*, in scarlet and crimson, or *Lindera benzoin*, in bright yellow are only for the eyes of those with plenty of space.

In fact, many of the plants that have already been described because

161

of other virtues, have good autumn colour as a bonus. Amongst trees, *Acer davidii* and *A. hersii, Betula pendula, Cornus controversa, Populus tremula, Rhus typhina* and various kinds of *Prunus*, all have good leaf colour in the autumn. It is also a striking feature of several climbers, including *Parthenocissus henryana, Vitis coignetiae* and *Vitis vinifera* 'Purpurea', and shrubs too, such as *Hamamelis mollis, Rosa virginiana* and *Viburnum plicatum*.

Other good examples of dual-purpose plants are the amelanchiers which have rich autumn colouring and off-white flowers in the spring (which are best kept away from the Persil-white flowering cherries). *A. canadensis* is a large shrub while *A. lamarckii* is a small tree, and both are usually multi-stemmed. The botanical names of amelanchiers are in a state of confusion, so check that you are getting a plant of the right size.

Cornus kousa chinensis is a large shrub or, with help, a small tree, which covers itself with unusual white flowers with green centres in June; (botanically, they are called bracts, since they are really modified leaves). Later there are strawberry-like fruits and excellent colours of crimson and bronze; altogether a highly desirable plant. *Cotinus coggygria* is quite a curious shrub, whose flowers consist of whiskery plumes that have been variously described as looking like wigs or puffs of smoke: they start off fawn in colour, then turn pink and finally grey. In the autumn the leaves provide one of the most remarkable riots of colour of any shrub, and a variety called 'Flame' has been selected as especially good in this respect. There are also purple-leafed forms for coloured-foliage enthusiasts.

The Japanese maples should perhaps have been included amongst our special selection of shrubs of elegant habit. For sheer poise, right out to the finger-tips, there is nothing to beat these maples. There are countless varieties: C. Esveld of Boskoop in Holland lists a mere 157 kinds, mostly with Japanese names. But only a few are usually available. One of these, *Acer palmatum* 'Osakazuki', I have planted on the north side of our house, beside the front porch where it receives many compliments from visitors. Even in summer 'Osakazuki' has an attractive pinky tinge, while in late October it goes quite wild: a rich peony red. 'Senkaki' on the other hand goes butter yellow in the autumn. One problem with these maples is leaf-scorch, and once this has happened you are stuck with it for the season, because the plant never seems to produce replacement leaves. Whether this is due to late frosts or to drying winds I am not certain. Certainly rich moist soil, shelter, and light shade are all beneficial to young *Acer palmatum* plants. *Acer japonicum* also has some excellent varieties for autumn colour, but these

162

are even slower growing than the *palmatum* varieties. The splendours of 'Aconitifolium' and 'Vitifolium' can be seen in mature specimens at Westonbirt, but these have taken many years to reach their full size.

Perhaps the only candidate for inclusion in a small garden, solely on the basis of autumn colour, is *Euonymus alatus*, which is a smallish shrub with an even smaller form called 'Compactus'. In the autumn it turns to a most uncommon shade of pink which defies classification, but perhaps "crushed-strawberry" pink is about as close as one can get.

Some plants do both parts of their double-act at the same time: in other words, they have autumn colour and coloured fruits simultaneously. *Euonymus europaeus* 'Red Cascade' is an improved version of our native Spindle tree (which is really a large bush). If such exotic-looking berries appeared on a shrub from Sichuan or Hokkaido we should all be suitably impressed, but as it grows wild in England (and I know a good place) nobody takes as much notice as they should of these extraordinary, pink, plastic-looking fruits with their orange seeds.

Several *Crataegus* species have both berries and autumn colour and perhaps the best of these Hawthorn relations is C. × *prunifolia*, quite a small tree. But I think the genus *Sorbus* has rather more to offer us. Both the whitebeams and the mountain ashes (or rowans) are contained in this genus; none are remarkable for their flowers, but rather for their clusters of brightly coloured fruits, especially in the mountain ash types, called the Aucuparia section of the genus (after *Sorbus aucuparia*, our native Mountain Ash). The most remarkable of all is *Sorbus sargentiana*, which, as it happens, comes from Sichuan. The leaves change gradually to quite a brilliant red colour by November, and the fruits which are apparent from September onwards are scarlet, in clusters of up to five hundred at a time. The leaves are also remarkable for being the largest in the genus; they open from big sticky horse-chestnut-like buds and are bronze at first. It reaches thirty feet (9m) or more eventually.

Sorbus scalaris is a similar sized tree. The fruits are scarlet and glossy, and the autumnal leaf-colour is variously scarlet or purplish, in different locations. The foliage is attractive, being much more ferny than other mountain ashes. *Sorbus hupehensis* is distinguished by its grey-green foliage which turns to orange, often suffused with violet colours, in the autumn. Effectively contrasted with this are the clusters of fruits which in this case are white, slightly flushed with pink, and because of their colour they have the advantage of being much less popular with birds. The best for yellow fruits is probably *Sorbus esserteauiana* 'Flava', contrasting dramatically with bronzy-red autumn tints.

Sorbus folgneri in common with other whitebeams has single leaves rather than ash-like rows of leaflets, and again like the whitebeams the leaves are white underneath, and this white colouring is retained when the upper surface of the leaves takes on scarlet and orange tints in the autumn. The fruits are red. This excellent tree is still very uncommon, but may be seen at Westonbirt. It reaches thirty feet (9m) and has an elegant habit, with slender, spreading branches.

A few ornamental members of the Apple family manage to offer both fruit and autumn colours. *Malus transitoria* is one of these; its leaves turn a clear yellow in the autumn, but the large numbers of small, currant-like fruits are unfortunately yellow as well – but of course they remain after the leaves have fallen – birds permitting. The other features of this excellent but little-known tree are a good display of white flowers in the spring, and an elegant, slender habit. Other worthwhile *Malus* varieties are *Malus coronaria* 'Charlottae' and the Siberian crab apples. 'Charlottae' has semi-double, apple-blossom flowers which are fragrant and smell of violets. The crab apple fruits are not remarkable, but the leaves usually colour well in the autumn.

The best *Malus* varieties for fruits are *M. × robusta* 'Red Siberian' and 'Yellow Siberian'. There are others with larger "apples" but none borne so profusely, nor held for so long into the winter. Eventually, of course, the apples fall (as Newton discovered) and this can be a bit of a nuisance. Crab apples should therefore be planted in grass where it is easy to clear away the fallen fruit; in borders it is much more difficult. *Malus baccata* 'Mandschurica' is closely related to the Siberian crab apples, and has a lovely white floral display, and slightly larger fruits.

Many of the outstanding plants that have berries have already been included in this book for other reasons: pyracanthas, cotoneasters of various kinds and skimmias, for instance. But we have not so far mentioned, *Stranvaesia* (or *Photinia*) *davidiana*, a good, small, evergreen tree, or a large shrub if left untrained. It has good red berries, or yellow ones if you choose the variety 'Fructuluteo', and some of the old leaves turn red in the autumn. It is worth noting that stranvaesias are related closely to photinias, cotoneasters and also to pyracanthas and crab apples: they are all members of the Rose family *Rosaceae*.

The most remarkable shrubs with berries are the callicarpas and the clerodendrons. The best *Callicarpa* is *C. bodinieri giraldii* which has fruits of a very unusual mauve-lilac colour; they are generously produced in small clusters along the stems, especially if several plants grow in a group which helps fertilization. It likes rich soil and a sheltered position. The leaves change to rose-pink before falling, and there is some floral interest earlier on from the small pink flowers.

When I first saw a Clerodendron in full autumn dress, I stared at it in some disbelief – rather like the child who, seeing his first giraffe declared "There's no such animal". The berries look decidedly plastic, probably made in Hong Kong. (Actually clerodendrons do come from China and Japan.) The berry itself is a bright, un-horticultural, turquoise-blue and this is in the centre of a raspberry-red star; actually it is the calyx, which means that it is the remains of the outer part of the flower. These are held gracefully on quite a large bush. *Clerodendron trichotomum* is probably the best to choose. Berrying is improved where there are several plants. A sunny position against a warm wall is ideal.

Celastrus orbiculatus deserves a mention as a vigorous, deciduous climber, quite capable of climbing trees and scrambling over hedges. Its screening ability is good but only takes effect, of course, when it is in leaf. The berries are bright red with gold seed capsules, and, since plants of both sexes are needed to produce them, they appear more reliably if there are several plants; they last well into the winter.

The *Mahonia* × *media* varieties mentioned earlier (such as 'Charity') are normally in bloom by November. There are also several autumn-flowering crocuses which deserve a place, such as *Crocus sieberi*, and *C. laevigatus* is one of the few plants likely to be in bloom on Christmas Day.

Such is our year, which began with snowdrops and ends with Christmas, when most people are too busy buying presents to do much gardening. But appropriately I must remind you of the many excellent Holly varieties, whose berries are set off to perfection by the glossy evergreen foliage. Not many people think of Mistletoe as a garden plant, but *Viscum album*, to use its Latin name, can be encouraged to grow on an old apple tree, should you so wish, and at Christmas it has its uses.

SPECIALIST NURSERIES

The following lists are intended to provide help in locating plants. There are of course very many excellent nurseries besides these, but most of the following do at least have a more or less permanent list, and offer similar stock from year to year. However, not all will send plants by post.

ALPINES	Bressingham, Ingwersen, Robinsons, Southcombe
AZALEAS	Glendoick, Hilliers, Hydon, Slocock
BULBS	Avon Bulbs, Walter Blom & Son, Broadleigh, Carncairn Daffodils, de Jager, Kelways, van Tubergen
CLEMATIS	Fisk's, Great Dixter, Treasures
CLIMBERS	Hilliers, Marchant, Notcutts, Scott, Treasures .
CONIFERS	Barncroft, Bressingham, Hilliers, Sherrards
DAY LILIES (*Hemerocallis*)	Bressingham, Kelways
HEBES	County Park Nursery
HELLEBORES	Helen Ballard, Bressingham
HERBACEOUS PLANTS	*See* Perennials
IRISES	Bressingham, Kelways, de Jager
IVIES	Fibrex, Whitehouse Ivies
MICHAELMAS DAISIES	Allen, Bressingham
PAEONIES	David Austin, Kelways
PERENNIALS	David Austin, Bressingham, Beth Chatto, Kelways, Robinsons, Scott, Sherrards, Treasures

PINKS (*Dianthus*)	Allwood Bros.
RHODODENDRONS	Glendoick, Hilliers, Hydon, Slocock
ROSES	David Austin, Peter Beales, Gandy's, Harkness, Sanday, Scott, Treasures
SEEDS	Sutton, Thomson and Morgan
SHRUBS	Barncroft, Burncoose, Bressingham, Great Dixter, Hillier, Marchant, Notcutts, Scott, Sherrards, Treasures
TREES	Hilliers, Marchant, Notcutts, Scott, Sherrards, Treasures

ADDRESSES

Miss Allen, Belmont House, Wraxall, Nr. Bristol
Specialist in Michaelmas daisies and *Aster* species.

Allwood Bros, Clayton Nursery, Hassocks, Sussex.
Specialists in pinks and carnations

David Austin Roses, Bowling Green, Albrighton, Wolverhampton, WV7 3HB
Specialist rose grower and rose breeder (especially shrub roses) perennials, peonies.

Avon Bulbs, Bathford, Bath, BA1 8ED.
Bulb specialist.

Helen Ballard, Old Country, Mathon, Malvern, Worcs.
Specialist in *hellebores* and snowdrops.

Barncroft Nurseries, Dunwood Lane, Longsdon, Stoke-on-Trent.
Conifers and shrubs, including *skimmias*.

Peter Beales Roses, London Road, Attleborough, Norfolk, NR17 1AY.
Specialist rose grower, especially shrub roses.

Walter Blom & Son, Coombelands Nurseries, Leavesden, Watford, Herts. WD2 7BH.
Bulb specialist.

Bressingham Gardens, Bressingham, Diss, Norfolk. IP22 2AB
Perennials, shrubs, conifers.

Broadleigh Gardens, Barr House, Bishop's Hull, Taunton, Somerset.

Bulb specialist

Burncoose and Southdown Nurseries, Gwennap, Redruth, Cornwall.

General nurserymen.

Carncairn Daffodils Ltd. Carncairn Lodge, Broughs Lane, Ballymena, Co. Antrim, N. Ireland, BT43 7HF.

Daffodil specialist.

Beth Chatto, White Barn House, Elmstead Market, Colchester, Essex.

Perennials. Unusual plants.

County Park Nursery, Essex Gardens, Wingletye Lane, Hornchurch, Essex.

Hebe specialist and other unusual plants.

De Jager, Marden, Kent.

Bulb specialists.

Fibrex Nurseries Ltd. Harrey Road, Evesham, Worcs.

Specialist in ivies, pelargoniums. etc.

Fisk's Clematis Nursery, Westleton, Saxmundham, Suffolk, IP8 4PZ.

Clematis specialist.

Gandy's Roses Ltd., North Kilworth, Lutterworth, Leicestershire, LE17 6HZ

Rose grower.

Glendoick Gardens Ltd. Perth, Scotland, PH2 7NS

Specialist in *rhododendrons, azaleas,* etc.

Great Dixter Nursery, Northiam, Sussex.

Clematis, shrubs, perennials.

R. Harkness & Co. Ltd., The Rose Gardens, Hitchin, Hertfordshire, S64 0JT

Rose growers.

Hilliers Nurseries Ltd. Ampfield House, Ampfield, Romsey, Hants. SO5 9PA

Trees, shrubs, climbers, perennials.

Hydon Nurseries Ltd. Clock Barn Lane, Hydon Heath, Godalming, Surrey, GU8 4AZ

Rhododendrons, trees and shrubs.

Will Ingwersen Ltd. Birch Farm Nursery, Gravetye, East Grinstead, Sussex, RH19 4LE
> Alpine specialist

Kelways Nurseries, Langport, Somerset, TA10 9SL
> *Irises, paeonies,* bulbs, perennials.

C. J. Marchant, Keepers Hill Nursery, Wimborne, Dorset.
> Trees, shrubs.

Notcutts, Woodbridge, Suffolk, IP12 4AF
> Trees, shrubs, climbers, perennials.

Robinsons Hardy Plants, Greencourt Nurseries, Crockenhill, Swanley, Kent, BR8 8HD
> Perennials, alpines, etc.

John Sanday Roses, Over Lane, Almondsbury, Bristol, BS12 4DA
> Rose grower and breeder.

John Scott & Co. Royal Nurseries, Merriott, Somerset.
> General nurserymen.

Sherrards, The Garden Centre, Wantage Road, Donnington, Newbury, Berks. RG16 9BE
> Trees, shrubs, climbers, perennials.

Slocock Nurseries, Barr's Lane, Knaphill, Woking, Surrey, GU21 2JW
> *Rhododendrons,* trees and shrubs.

Southcombe Gardens Plant Nursery, Widecombe-in-the-Moor, Newton Abbot, Devon, TQ13 7TU
> Perennials, alpines, shrubs, etc.

Suttons Seeds, Hale Road, Torquay, Devon, TQ2 7QJ
> Seed merchants.

Thomson and Morgan, London Road, Ipswich, Suffolk.
> Seed merchants.

Treasures of Tenbury, Burford House, Tenbury Wells, Worcestershire.
> *Clematis,* trees, shrubs, roses, climbers.

van Tubergen BV, P.O. Box 74, Hull, HU9 1PQ
> Bulb specialist.

Whitehouse Ivies, Tolleshunt Knights, Maldon, CM9 8EZ
> Ivy specialist.

RECOMMENDED REFERENCE BOOKS ON PLANTS

GENERAL

The English Flower Garden, William Robinson
Reader's Digest Encyclopaedia of Garden Plants and Flowers, Roy Hay
  and Kenneth A. Becket, Eds. 1971

PLANTS

Clematis, Christopher Lloyd, 1965
Collins Guide to Bulbs, Patrick Synge, 1961
Conifers for Your Garden, Adrian Bloom, 1972
The Gardener's Book of Trees, Alan Mitchell, 1981
Hillier's Trees and Shrubs, Hillier & Sons, 1981
International Book of Trees, Hugh Johnson, 1973
Ivies, Peter Q. Rose 1980
Perennial Garden Plants (revised edition), Graham Stuart Thomas, 1982
Roses, Jack Harkness, 1978
Trees for Your Garden, Roy Lancaster, 1974

FOR SPECIAL REQUIREMENTS

The Damp Garden, Beth Chatto, 1982
The Dry Garden, Beth Chatto, 1978
Gardening on Chalk and Lime, Ronald Dyson, 1977
Gardening on Walls, Christopher Grey-Wilson and Victoria Mathews,
  1983
Plants for Ground-Cover (revised edition), Graham Stuart Thomas,
  1984
Plants for Shade, Allen Paterson, 1981
Seaside Gardening, Christine Kelway, 1962

·INDEX·

171

dreamtime

alice

dreamtime
alice

a memoir

Mandy Sayer

BALLANTINE BOOKS | NEW YORK

http://www.randomhouse.com

Library of Congress Cataloging-in-Publication Data
Sayer, Mandy, 1963–
Dreamtime Alice: a memoir / Mandy Sayer.—1st ed.
p.   cm.
ISBN 0-345-42332-1 (alk. paper)
1. Sayer, Mandy, 1963– —Childhood and youth.   2. Women novelists,
Australian—20th century—Family relationships.   3. Street entertainers—United States—
Biography.   4. Australians—Travel—United States.   5. Fathers and daughters—Australia.
6. Sayer, Mandy, 1963– —Family.   I. Title.
PR9619.3.S276Z464   1998
823—dc21
[B]   97-40378

Designed by Ann Gold

Manufactured in the United States of America

First Edition: March 1998
10 9 8 7 6 5 4 3 2 1

For my sister, Lisa, with love and gratitude

ACKNOWLEDGMENTS

I gratefully acknowledge the assistance of the Literature
Board of the Australia Council, which enabled me to
complete this book.

Excerpts of *Dreamtime Alice* have appeared, in slightly
different forms, in the following journals: *Brilliant
Corners*; *Crab Orchard Review*; *HEAT*; *Indiana Review*;
Manoa; *New Laurel Review*; *Phoenix Review*; *Smashed:
Australian Drinking Stories*.

I would like to express my gratitude to the following
readers for their criticism, and encouragement: Adam
Aitkin, Jill Hickson, Maxine Hong Kingston, Ivor Indyk,
Yusef Komunyakaa, Gaby Naher, Nerida Silva, and
Maura Stanton.

Thanks also to my sagacious editors: Bernadette Foley
in Australia and Andrea Schulz in the United States.

AUTHOR'S NOTE

The people portrayed in this book are real and the events described took place, but fictional names and descriptive detail have sometimes been used as literary devices, or to protect the privacy of certain individuals.

dreamtime

alice

prelude

In the evenings we pushed our red shopping cart along the five-minute walk from our hotel to Columbus Avenue, where crowded dining tables spilled out onto open terraces and tall mannequins in tight black dresses stared down at us through plate glass and neon. It was in New York, I decided, that we would be successful. It was there that we would work every evening until the crowds drifted away after midnight. It was there that we would have lots of glorious fun and return home with bags of money. There that we would live out the long, warm nights that would later complete the repertoire of my father's stories, a repertoire of which I longed to be a part.

If only I could have been as funny as his mate Sean Casey, who drove a car right through the front door of a hotel on his way to a gig, crawled out unscathed, and said, "Park it." If only I could have played an alto sax like Rolf Pommer, and made my father swoon and cry out as he dragged wire brushes across the skin of his snare. If only I could have been as eccentric as Frank Smith or as witty as Edwin Duff or as talented as Tony Kirby, maybe I wouldn't have had to come halfway around the world to dress each night in a set of tails and follow him into the darkness to find an empty street corner.

To merit a place in his life, I knew I had to create a grand role for myself, something that would sound good, say, after the Maxine Cabaret story.

When he was fourteen he'd creep out of his bedroom window at night and catch a train and a bus down to a nightclub called Ollie Ward's Maxine Cabaret, across the road from Centennial Park. It was 1934. The pubs all closed at six P.M. The club was full of underworld figures and Dixieland music. He fell deeply in love with the muffled sounds he heard pressing through the walls and found he could enter the building through an opening called the Sly Grog Hole. He'd hide backstage every night and listen to the music, until Ollie Ward herself, a big, matronly woman who also ran a brothel upstairs, found him cowering behind some broken bar stools and ended up giving him his first job when the regular drummer was too drunk to play. I was going to come right after that, in my white stockings and red tap shoes, up there in the Gerry Sayer Hall of Fame, along with his musician mates and flamboyant theater friends, who were always immersed in some hilarious tragedy, and who were the only people he ever really seemed to love.

5

My mother had failed him by crawling off the back of his Manx-Norton racing motorbike, hanging up her leather jacket and helmet, and wanting to get married. For three years she had sat on the back of that bike while he, always a little drunk, squeezed at the throttle and tore across the countryside toward some jam session down the coast, or careened around city street corners between gigs and backstage parties. In one particular club, my father's band would remain long after the gig had ended, when the audience had left and the doors had been locked. They played all the Charlie Parker tunes they knew. When the cleaners arrived at dawn, they were promptly sat down and made to listen until the musicians wore themselves out and headed up to the Hasty Tasty Cafe for cornflakes.

My mother mostly sat on a bar stool through all this, mostly sipping beer and learning how to smoke cigarettes, staying up all night and eating bowls of cornflakes afterward just as he did. On her eighteenth birthday he arrived at her home around midnight with an eighteen-piece band he'd recruited from the Trocadero, Australia's most prestigious ballroom. He moved all my grandmother's furniture out of the living and dining rooms into the front yard so the band could set up, and that night my mother jitterbugged barefoot from room to room while outside a heavy rain fell until dawn.

Who could resist falling in love with such bravado?

"Ol' Bet was a real trooper," I remember my father saying proudly. Whether it was skinny dipping at Coogee Beach or impromptu concerts at Darlinghurst brothels, my mother was there, in a gray satin ball gown, trying to be one of the boys. Until she popped the question and he stood her up twice at the altar. Until they set a third date and disillusioned guests stayed home. Until they finally went through with it in a ten-minute service, and my father got drunk on altar wine afterward with the ninety-two-year-old priest who married them.

So, she had failed him. They were married now. She was his wife. Things would no longer be fun.

Then she had the audacity to want children. "Children?" I can hear him whining. "Why on earth would you want children?" Normal people had children. Bank clerks had children. Postmen had children. Butchers had children. Not bohemians like him. By rights they shouldn't even have married. This was going too far. Things were getting out of hand.

Nevertheless, she produced a baby every four years until there were three of us who stood looking up to a reluctant father. We mostly saw him through a haze of smoke, perched behind a drum kit, surrounded by members of his latest band, immersed in some late-night jam session in the middle of the living room.

After my parents had finally divorced, after twenty-three years of marriage, my brother—eight years older than me—failed him by freezing up only hours before the first gig of the only band he and Gerry ever formed. It was the early seventies and they were the Black Acid Band, Live from Sydney, making their debut in Cairns. It was decided that my brother, Gene, who played "a little bit of bass," would also talk into the microphone. He would announce the tunes and make the necessary birthday calls. There was no one else. My father has a harelip and the guitar player stuttered. He was Gerry Sayer's son. He would do fine.

Talking into the microphone. This was unexpected. My brother disappeared and drank seven schooners of beer. He turned up late and couldn't get the bass strap over his head. He played everything in a different key and announced his own birthday—August 24—to a bewildered crowd.

They lost the job. But what was worse, Gene didn't want to hang around and find another. He wanted to go home, goddamn him. He was eighteen years old and he wanted to go home, back to his mediocre job driving a van and his Vegemite sandwiches at lunchtime. And after they'd driven along the two thousand miles of coastline back to Sydney in a Kombi van, after the brakes failed in Rockhampton and the windshield wipers fell off in Bundaberg, after the gears jammed in Maroochydore and the exhaust pipe fell off in Byron Bay, after the police interrogated them for suspected drug possession, and they ran out of money for more repairs, my brother vowed he would never travel again.

This was not good. He was my father's only son. He was a musician. He was just a little green around the gills. He'd catch on soon. He'd learn. Soon he'd be tearing all over the place, just as he should, playing and traveling and eating cornflakes.

But within two years my brother had married my father's twenty-five-year-old girlfriend and had become a Jehovah's Witness. He wore brown suits and lectured Gerry on the virtues of triweekly Bible study. He left regular gifts of The Truth *on my father's doorstep. Soon there were grandchildren, god-dammit. Two. Now he was a grandfather. How could Gene have done this to him? Another disappointment. Another failure. At least he still had the girls.*

My sister—four years older than me—was always considered the "normal" one of our mob, always the odd one out. She was shy. She was pale. She suffered from nose bleeds and bronchitis. She liked listening to Rick Springfield. Her great redeeming quality, however—in my father's eyes—was that she had a beautiful voice. And the greatest thing she ever did was stand up in the middle of the living room one day, when she was four years old, and sing "Pennies from Heaven" in key and with perfect pitch along with a Frank Sinatra record.

That's it! he decided. *She's a singer.* Managers were called in and auditions were arranged. There was talk of a weekly television show. Photographs. She was going to cut a record with Little Pattie.

But she's so shy, reminded my mother. *And bronchial. Better wait till she's a little older. A little healthier. Wait till she comes out of her shell a bit.*

He waited fourteen years, but she was never much interested in singing again, except to herself in a corner of our bedroom when she thought no one was listening. Over the years, gentle reminders were periodically given, the story of the time Lisa got up and sang "Pennies from Heaven" in key and with perfect pitch. But Lisa just grew farther away, into her own orbit of pop stars and surfboards and halter-neck tops, and she soon began to dull in my father's eyes.

He did, however, give her another chance one day when he unexpectedly swept into the Pitt Street women's clothing store in which she then worked. She'd already been out on her own for three years, leaving home at fifteen.

My father was going to rescue her from this dreary, work-a-day life. He was forming a new band and she would be the female singer they'd been looking for. It was all arranged. They had six nights a week booked at a club on William Street. She'd work three hours a night and triple her pay. Of course she could handle it. There was no doubt in his mind. She could sing "Pennies from Heaven" when she was four.

Unlike my brother, Lisa didn't get as far as the band room. She just nodded and said she'd think about it, that she'd have to discuss it with her boyfriend.

Her boyfriend? What did boyfriends have to do with it? This was her big opportunity. This was probably the last chance he'd have to help her out.

But her boyfriend didn't like the idea much, and she probably didn't, either. She was content with the sobriety she had now finally established for herself after fifteen years of our father's gypsy circus. She was happy with a newspaper and a cup of tea after work, a picnic at the beach on Sundays.

"The next thing you know she'll be having a baby," he sighed.

All the chips were suddenly pushed to my square. I was the last in line. And the weight of all those lost causes, the resignations, the canceled gigs, the grandchildren, would eventually rest upon me.

My parents have lived in separate cities from the time I was twelve. Five hundred miles and no letters or phone calls made me often think of Gerry. My mother couldn't afford a phone, and my father couldn't write beyond printing his own name in crooked capital letters. Once or twice over the years he must have commissioned a friend to write a letter for him, with lots of I love you's and maybe even a Miss you. The handwriting was heavy and ornate, bold loops and squiggles, maybe even that of a woman, nothing like I imagined his would be. His would be light and slanted, expansive letters sloping off to the right, long strokes crossing his t's. He'd forget sometimes to dot his i's.

I skipped two years in high school and graduated at sixteen. After one term at Melbourne State Teachers College, I transferred to the City Art Institute in Sydney, moving back to my hometown. My father lived in a bachelor flat of sorts—one large room and a kitchen—in a terrace at the edge of the harbor. He looked so skinny then. He flaunted his cocky swagger, in his black leather jacket and loose blue jeans. I suppose I moved back to reclaim a part of myself, or to excavate something lost. After his departure came my first bout of depression: years of withdrawal, no friends, periods when I was unable to talk, even to hold a brief conversation or ask a simple question. When I arrived on his doorstep he was the first person in what seemed like ages with whom I could talk. He could do a simple thing like make me laugh.

He drew me out of my sadness by taking me drinking every day. In the afternoons we'd meet at a local pub and he'd buy me round after round of Guinness and entertain me with his stories. And I'd get drunk as much on his stories as on the schooners of thick, dark alcohol.

My father secured a room for me two doors up from where he lived. Most of the time I shuttled back and forth between houses, sleeping at mine; cooking, eating, drinking, and listening to music at his. At four o'clock every afternoon, if he didn't have a gig that night, he'd tap on my window and we'd *drift down the street together, into the Hero of Waterloo Hotel to sip rum by an open fire, or to the Lord Nelson to shoot pool with the roughneck wharfies.*

But he still wasn't quite satisfied. He'd look with indifference at the collection of photographs I was to mount for an end-of-term exhibition at the college. He wasn't much interested in the short films I'd made, except, of course, the one about him. Any extra screenprints or etchings I gave him never found their way onto his wall or refrigerator door. He'd click his tongue and shake his head whenever he arrived home at ten o'clock in the morning, after a Saturday-evening gig and an all-night party, to find me laboring over a drawing assignment for the following day.

However, everything changed the afternoon I walked into his flat with a small string puppet I'd just finished making. He was sitting behind his kit of Ludwigs, playing along with "In the Mood," which was booming out of the cassette player. I knew the tune well and began dancing around the room with my puppet, making its legs kick up on the accents and glide with the melody, translating sound into movement through the flick of my hand.

Within a week he had bought a boat battery, battery charger, bright clown costumes, a red plastic nose for himself, a piece of carpet on which to set up his drums, and had us out on a wide street corner up in Sydney's red-light district, Kings Cross. He would play on a full kit along with recorded big band music. I would only have to dance with the puppet, just like I had in his room. Naturally, I was intrigued and terrified. I was seventeen years old and hadn't seen my father this excited since the day my brother brought home the second-hand Fender bass. The bass he found he couldn't play very well that fatal night in Cairns.

It wasn't long before I was taking tap lessons, making bigger puppets, and rehearsing our thirty-minute show. Each Saturday morning we packed up the car and drove to Chinatown to perform beneath the Oriental gateway at the edge of Dixon Street. Shoppers from Paddy's Market would stroll over, their bags bursting with fresh vegetables and fruit. Between shows, my father would guzzle a schooner of Guinness and slap me on the back, murmuring, "One outta three ain't bad."

Then he decided we needed some comedy, something to make the audience laugh and loosen their pockets before we passed around the hat. And soon I was dragging a piece of masonite out from behind the drums, pulling on a pair of oversized green army shorts, donning a lopsided air force cap, slipping into my new tap shoes, picking up a toy plastic rifle with a black rubber hose attached where the barrel should be, and dancing a whimsical military tap along with Glenn Miller's "St. Louis Blues March." The hose waved and bounced with my every move, and on the last note of the tune I swung my hand up to salute and almost knocked myself out with the gun. Sometimes we arrived home with as much as a hundred dollars for a morning's work. It was all decided: I was now not only a dancer but a comedian, too. No more college. Why did I want to bother with that? College was for the daughters of bank clerks and dentists. Not musicians.

"You're a performer," he declared, twirling one drumstick as he stood in the shade of the Oriental gateway. Sunlight ignited the street and children ran in circles singing "Oranges and Lemons." At that moment I didn't really know who I was; I was only conscious of the fact that I was becoming a part of my father's imagination—his stories—and that he was beaming at me from behind a fan of drumsticks like he never had before.

first

movement

"In another moment down went Alice after it,
never once considering how in the world she was
to get out again."

—Lewis Carroll, *Alice in Wonderland*

1

I had my first orgasm when I was nine years old, four days before Christmas, 1972. My parents were recently reunited after a two-year separation. The whole family had moved into my father's basement room in Victoria Street, Kings Cross. My parents had obviously fallen back in love. You could see it in the way my mother happily cooked for hours on the 1930s gas stove out in the half-lit hallway, in the bouncy walk my father had cultivated in his new yellow thongs, and in the way they'd drop onto the single bed and snuggle into the hollows of each other's bodies.

It was December, and it was hot. The woman upstairs wore no underwear. My mother used to hang wet sheets across the open window and point an old metal fan into the open fridge. The cockroaches were sluggish and wandered over the cracked linoleum in slow, aimless circles. My parents and brother drank lots of Dinner Ale from amber bottles, and when there wasn't enough money for DA we'd all drink ginger beer with vanilla ice cream, and my father always made sure he got the biggest glass.

It was so hot, in fact, that one afternoon when my brother and sister were out, my parents began squeezing each other's knees and talking about taking a siesta.

I shoved my hands into my pockets and shifted uneasily. "But I'm not tired."

"Well, just lie down," my mother coaxed, "and close your eyes."

"It sounds like a nap," I persisted. "Like what babies take."

"No," said my father. "That's what the Mexican people do. They close up their shops after lunch, see? When it's the hottest. And they lie down for a while. Even the grown-ups."

As if to demonstrate, he staggered across the room, flicking invisible beads of sweat from his brow and, after spreading his arms and stiffening, dropped like a corpse in the last stages of rigor mortis onto the crumpled mess of his bed.

I gazed at him and then at my mother sitting calmly at the table. I

15

wandered over to the green sleeping bag in the corner, which I called my Little Bed.

My parents stripped down to their underwear and got tangled up in a cotton sheet like the one that hung across the window. I lay on my back in my T-shirt and knickers and, like the good Mexican child I pretended to be, closed my eyes and listened to my parents' steady breathing. I knew they were unequivocally in love in this warm, musty-smelling nest of found things—a chair from St. Vincent's De Paul, two ceramic cups from a box left out on the street, a mirror discovered on the front veranda under Mick Fowler's pot plants. My father was a bowerbird who'd built his arched nest out of bright and shiny things, who'd executed his hurried dance until my mother glided down again and only hesitated momentarily before entering.

The bedsprings creaked. The wheels attached to the base rolled a little. Through my cracked eyelids it looked as if a small animal moved beneath the sheet, up my mother's body, across her chest. She lay perfectly still and half-formed vowels rose in her throat.

I had no mercy. I could not close my eyes completely. Every muscle of my body feigned sleep as I spied on them from the opposite corner. My father buried his face in her hair and inhaled its scent. Her fingers laced themselves around his neck and she kissed his broken nose and scarred lips. When her tongue entered him, I wondered if it got lost in the cavity that should have been the roof of his mouth, or did it only feather the periphery, gentle as his own exploratory finger?

He slid the bra straps down her shoulders and burrowed his nose between her breasts while she stroked the nape of his neck. Since my mother usually moaned a lot when she made love, I had always assumed that it tortured her to have him inside her, something like childbirth, only back-ward. But now I saw gestures and expressions accompanying that which was once, at best, a muffled sound track in a language I did not quite compre-hend, played in the darkness, in that filmy netherworld between sleeping and waking. Now I saw quite clearly the pleasure that leaked out between my mother's vowels and undulated into the room.

The sheet shrank back and fell to the floor, revealing my father's small white bum pointing to the ceiling as his knees negotiated a position between her parted legs. I remember her right breast resting slightly on her upper arm, the raised nipple looking directly back at me.

I pressed my eyes shut. There was a robin in my mother's throat, calling him in, wooing him into the gentle circle of her hips.

I am not sure when I became aware of the sweat that netted my skin, or the golden light that seemed to fill a glowing triangle between my legs, but when I opened my eyes again and saw him dropping into her over and over again, and the way she raised her mound of yellow curly hair to receive him, and the strong, hard thing that seemed to give them both so much pleasure, I cupped my hands around my pubic bone to contain the tender tingle I did not comprehend.

But the pressure of my fingers encouraged and cajoled it. My father let out short, sharp sounds like a hyperventilating child. I rolled over onto my stomach and found that merely a slight rocking of my pubic bone against my fingers allowed a singing in the pink folds of my skin.

Yet even then, as I reveled in the mysterious thrills my body manufactured, a guilty feeling hovered above me. As my father arced into her and voiced his breathless mantra of Ohs, my confused body implied that he also somehow produced the nameless sensation seething into me, that I was secretly siphoning off my mother's noisy pleasure.

But I could not stop rocking as they rocked, could not help but open myself up to their circling hips and hot sighs. It was as if every moan distilled itself into the swollen landscape between my legs, and I rocked myself harder because my father cried out he could not stop, because my mother seemed to garner so much pleasure from begging him to, because I was expected to sleep through such an unholy racket, because I was nine and confused and in love with them both, because it was hot, because it was summer, because later we would sip ginger beer and ice cream and watch the moon rise into the sky.

My father was still losing himself inside her when that muscular cup I imagined inside me overflowed and a river parted and one tributary shot down my legs and into my toes and another flooded my stomach and unformed breasts, my neck, tingled my lips, trembled inside the small veins of my eyelids. I was still shuddering when my mother's voice rose and unleashed itself into the humid air, and my father, his back arched as if he were straining to spot something on the ceiling, dipped himself into her, dropped one last time, finally planting himself there and crying like some tortured man.

I remained on my stomach and closed my eyes. I steadied my breath, surrendered to the quiet bliss humming through me.

When my father drew out and rested beside her, I buried my face in the pillow.

◼ 2 ◼

During our first few days in New York I often looked for some fantastic omen to record in my journal, to scribble on postcards headed back to Sydney. I craved something to justify having left my former life, to make that other life jealous of the huge adventure that would eventually be mine.

It was with the weight of this expectation that I developed an immediate crush on a magician Gerry and I met in the Village two days after we arrived in America. Amid the rank smell of steam that rose through the steel grilles on the sidewalks, amid the cacophony of car horns and the piping of a French horn, he was standing outside a closed pawn shop on Sixth Avenue, a slightly built man with brown curly hair and a mustache, wearing a set of black tails. It was a hot and sweaty Sunday night. Men were playing basketball in the courts across the road, and groups of people were streaming out of the nearby movie theater. I was impressed by the way the magician drew the crowd in by whispering to them, how he linked metal rings by only rubbing them together, the way his hands produced white doves and silk scarves and a rain of silver confetti. While we all stood watching, he took my hand and drew me out of the audience to assist him. He blew up an oversized white balloon and handed me a knitting needle. He whispered to me to prick it. I hesitated, looked at my father, and my father nodded. Slowly, I pressed the tip of the needle against the rubber membrane, wincing in anticipation of it bursting. But the needle penetrated easily, and was soon gliding through the magician's breath.

We'd arrived in New York on August 12, 1983, into the stultifying humidity of the last month of summer. I was twenty years old but looked a lot younger. I never wore makeup in those days. My hair was piled into its usual pompadour bun. I was wearing a black leotard and black skirt embroidered with yellow musical notes, a pair of Chinese slippers. In the early eighties, most young women my age were trying to look like Madonna or Cyndi Lauper—lipstick and big tits—but all I wanted to resemble was a nineteenth-century Gibson Girl.

As we came into Customs, my father sweated through his Victoria Bitter T-shirt. He looked like an unlucky, aging boxer who had just swung himself out of the ring at a country fair. He was sixty-three at the time, but his scarred face was framed by a helmet of blond hair. His blue eyes softened the crooked nose that had endured three breakages and numerous operations. His thumbs were hooked through the belt loops of the faded jeans he'd bought for thirty-five cents.

The city into which we descended on an airport bus was not the one whose heart pumped in my imagination. It was not the city of wide avenues and magisterial buildings, not the gleaming windowpanes of Tiffany's and Bloomingdale's. It was neither the city of Ionic columns and red-brick, Greek-revival homes, nor the manicured Victoriana of Gramercy Park. It was not large, impressive statues sculpted with old money, cathedrals of bombastic light. And when we hit Broadway—that street I'd seen incarnated in so many old musicals—the violins and drumrolls in my head reached a premature climax: garbage spilled out of tall metal cans, shirtless men wheeled metal garment racks down the sidewalk, and graffiti was scrawled over the front of a Vietnamese takeout shop.

I admit it. Our adventure had been my idea. But Gerry didn't need much encouragement. All our mates around Sydney thought we were having them on, that a bloke his age should have more sense. But each afternoon down at the pub we planned a bit more, what drums we would use and what color tap shoes I should take and the costumes we would wear. I'd been tapping for two years and thought I was pretty shit-hot because I could imitate the double paradiddles that purred out of Gerry's snare drum when he practiced.

During our planning sessions at the pub back in Sydney, the notoriety we were acquiring had seemed more appealing than the actual adventure. At one point Gerry wanted to drop the idea because he'd just scored a third night playing at the Orient Hotel. But we'd made such a song and dance of our trip that we couldn't back out. Already Sparrow and Big Jack Tatlock and his mates were smirking into their beers at the end of the bar. I was learning to drink OP rum then, just like Gerry, so I stood up in the middle of the pub, drained my glass, wiped my mouth with the back of my hand, and declared, "Well, bugger you then. I'll go alone."

That first Sunday night in the Village, I could feel sweat forming across my brow as the knitting needle penetrated the balloon. The magician's act was made more exciting by the fact that we were surrounded by people applauding and throwing money into his top hat. As the crowd drifted away, Gerry and I struck up a conversation with him—about places to perform and how to avoid the cops—and moments later the magician was offering to walk me through midtown Manhattan one afternoon and show me all the good pitches. This, I was sure, was my first fantastic omen. I secretly marveled at the way I managed to leave a man in Sydney on Friday and be going out with an exciting stranger on Tuesday.

Of course, there'd been a man I'd left behind, a man whose embrace I was escaping. He was nine years my senior, and each evening between midnight and dawn I'd wait for him to appear in the moonlight, a profile against the window I kept cracked for him. Sometimes he was so quiet he wouldn't wake me. Sometimes only an arm across my waist, lips at the back of my neck, the weight of his legs against mine would rouse me.

He was the only secret I'd kept from my father. Gerry always enjoyed the way my affairs were inevitably brief and unfulfilling, how much I was like him and didn't get "hung up with all that crap and could focus on my art."

But there was something about my visitor's breath in my ear. The man was my only secret, and I'll call him White Rabbit because he started it all by touching me in the right places, by leading me down the path of pleasure and betrayal. And without hesitation I followed. Hungry for his hands, I fell down the rabbit hole into the hot underworld of longing. Often, in the dark, I couldn't see his face, and he could have been anyone, this phantom who sat on the edge of my bed and hummed improvisations on a twelve-bar blues while Billie Holiday's voice unwound like a good dream. His drops of salty sweat would fall into my eyes as he throbbed inside me. Afterward, he'd slide out of me, tuck me in and smooth down the satin bedspread, stroke my hair, kiss the back of my ear before he left. I found myself sometimes itching for his visits, while my father slept in his single bed down the street, none the wiser.

But I had one more reason to leave Australia behind when I found out he had a pregnant girlfriend.

It was nice to be stroked and cradled and held, but White Rabbit did not make that fist of blood inside me snap the way it had that afternoon when I was nine, when I'd witnessed my parents making love. He did not make that glowing triangle of light flood every pore of my skin. In fact, no one ever had.

Sometimes I used to think I was wired up wrong. I used to lie there enjoying the caresses, the kneading of my muscles, the knotting up of legs, but whenever I felt a man's surge of warm liquid suddenly flood me, my body never flooded back, not, at least, until after whoever he was had left. It was only then that I could run my fingers across those salty lips and make my limbs tremble, make my eyelids dance.

When the magician asked if I'd like to be shown around, a fraction of me felt momentarily popular, a feeling I was often striving for but to which I was not accustomed.

Gerry, despite his permissive front, usually became somewhat resentful when I went out with men because he didn't want to be left at home alone. That night, however, he was hopping around our room, making sure I would ask the magician this or that question, that I'd make a note of every good pitch I was shown.

This was how I fell farther down the rabbit hole, following a man who could transform an egg into a rubber chicken, a pebble into a long red rose.

■   3   ■

The only two books I'd brought with me from Sydney were an Oscar Wilde biography and a tattered paperback copy of *Alice in Wonderland & Through the Looking Glass*. I'd already memorized the entire chapter of the Mad Hatter's tea party, and in the weeks to come I would often recite passages to myself as I wandered around the city. During the evenings, when we worked the streets, I'd keep it in my wooden case along with my tap shoes and feather boa; it was small enough to put into a pocket or purse. For almost a year, I would carry it with me constantly. I liked to slip my hand inside my pocket and feel its creased cover and crumbling spine, loose pages yellowing around the edges.

Somehow, I had always known subconsciously that Lewis Carroll had told Alice Liddell the story of Wonderland that day because she ignited his imagination, because through the telling he could always keep her inside that golden afternoon, because somewhere deep inside himself he loved her very much.

We'd arrived without anywhere to go. No relatives, no mattress on the floor of a friend's spare room. We didn't even have a hotel reservation. The only person we knew was an old friend of the family who'd moved to New York four years earlier. Her number had been printed in my address book under *N*. She used to baby-sit me when I was a kid and could drink a bottle of wine in one sitting while reading a paperback novel.

From the shuddering checkered cab we'd caught on 42nd, I'd already noticed Times Square throbbing away like a tawdry sideshow, the smell of tar and diesel puffing through the grates in the streets, the fragments of booming rap music escaping from passing cars, a woman banked up against a doorway by pregnant plastic bags and boxes and two open umbrellas wedged into a shopping cart.

We spent our first night in New York at a run-down hotel called the Latham, on 23rd Street. The room was painted baby-shit yellow and was dominated by two sagging twin beds. It was sixty-five dollars a night, and we could not negotiate a weekly rate. The following day, my father called the old friend of our family. When my parents were separated, my father had found her homeless in Kings Cross, a sixteen-year-old runaway from a strict Christian family. He took her in for a short while to live with him and my brother until she found a place of her own. When my parents reunited, she still lingered on the edge of our family, an honorary daughter. She'd been my brother's first casual girlfriend when they were both seventeen.

Her name was Nerida. When my father called her from the Latham Hotel she insisted that we come and stay with her at her apartment down on Rivington Street. We packed up our bags, caught a taxi downtown, and a long, wine-swilling reunion ensued. I had not seen her in ten years—half my lifetime—and was surprised to see her long, dark-brown hair cut into a pageboy, her missing front tooth replaced with a cap, to hear her voice tinged with an American accent, to notice that she was now an inch shorter than me.

What surprised me the most, however, was not that she made her living in New York as a part-time actress and part-time call girl but her immediate generosity. We had not seen her in a decade, yet she was throwing open her door to us. She was on her way to Bermuda, she said, for a two-week holiday. Sailing on a yacht with some friends. She was leaving that afternoon. But of course we would stay. It was an opportunity, she said, to reciprocate Gerry's kindness when she'd had no place to go all those years ago.

Nerida's roommate, Sandy, who was a recent *Penthouse* pinup girl, had little say in the matter. We were to stay as long as Nerida was away, and when she returned, she would help us find a place of our own.

■ **4** ■

My father had been to the States once in the seventies, but had never made it to New York. He'd played on a cruise ship that docked in San Francisco for only a couple of days, and spent all his time down at a jazz club near North Beach. The drummer in the band envied Gerry's job on the ship and Gerry envied the drummer's gig in the club. It seemed simple enough, so they swapped. Gerry played with the American band for three weeks before they got the sack. He had a passport, but no visa or work permit. Nevertheless, when the rest of the band moved to Detroit, he tagged along. For the first time in his life he saw snow. Twenty degrees below zero and something called a windchill factor. He hung out in a club where he was the only white person and got in tight with the pianist, with whom he smoked North Carolina heads in the breaks. He was running out of money and the drummer got him a gig on the sly. The patrons would complain, "Hey, what's that whitey doing up there?" To which the bandleader would reply, "He only looks white. When he plays, he's blacker than you!" Gerry soon became a part of the community, and periodically they'd move him around from gig to gig to keep the Immigration Department from catching up with him.

He must have told that story ten times down at the Hero of Waterloo pub, what a high it was to play with the band, how he was treated like a brother. Whenever Locky Jamison started to boast about the time he was a junkie in Chicago and played at the Green Mill during the fifties, Gerry would roll his false teeth around in his mouth and tell the Detroit story, and then about the time he got drunk with Louis Armstrong's drummer, Barrett Dean, and the time he sat in with the Oscar Peterson Trio.

This was where I wanted to belong, in the adventures invoked by my father's tongue. He never talked about my mother in such glowing terms, nor my pale, shy sister. The only mention my mother received was when he boasted of racing motorbikes before they were married, and what a good pillion rider she was. My sister was acknowledged briefly when he remembered the day she sang along with the Frank Sinatra record. My brother fared slightly better because he was a boy and had spent several years drinking with Gerry before he married. But I had some catching up to do.

The restless urge to move, the yearning for adventure, is manifested in the men of our family. On one side, it is said we are descended from Dr. David Livingstone, the Scottish missionary who walked the skin off his feet as he explored Africa. My connection with Livingstone is through my mother's father, who one day strode out of their Marrickville house when she was seven years old and never returned. The myth of Livingstone's presence in our family grew stronger as my grandfather's absence lengthened, that ghost who discovered Victoria Falls and got lost in the difficult geography of his own ambition and imagination.

On my father's side, we have two remittance men who were packed off from England to the colony for scandalizing the family name. (One jilted his wealthy, well-connected fiancée and married the maid.) My father's older brother Jack was perhaps the greatest wanderer of us all. I grew up with Gerry boasting about him. Sometimes I think Gerry inherited Jack's adventure stories, mimicked them and kept them alive, just as I have inherited his.

The one story my father often told about me was set on the night I was conceived. And he related it on our second day in New York, when we were down in Nerida's Bowery apartment, sitting around with a couple of her friends.

Gerry and Nerida's Australian friend, Charlie, were smoking a joint. The conversation had somehow shifted to sex, and I'd disappeared into the bathroom in order to avoid it. When I walked back into the living room, Gerry was turning purple from trying to hold in a lungful of smoke. He was clicking his fingers, as if keeping time with some blues only he could hear. I knew when he reached his fiftieth click he'd let it out and gasp for air.

When he snapped his fingers for the last time the smoke came surging out, and he remarked, "You know, the best fuck I ever had was when we made her."

He nodded at me. Everyone turned, suddenly interested in me for the first time that afternoon. I could feel myself blushing. Until then, he'd only told that story when we were alone, never to other people, never to strangers.

"A bloke down the musos' club laid some Lebanese gold on me one night. It'd just come off the ship. Top shit."

He turned to face me, too. His eyes were glazed and bloodshot from the grass, his face suddenly solemn, almost sentimental.

"I was higher than a giraffe in platform shoes when I went home that night. The plaster flowers on the bedroom ceiling kept moving about in circle eights and the light cord near the door became this red snake weaving through the air. I looked at your mother and for the first time I really saw her. She was the most beautiful woman I'd ever seen, and her skin was as smooth as a piece of silk. When I kissed her I could feel my mouth dissolving, and the blood rushing through my veins and into my groin. Before I even entered her, I already knew there was a part of you in me. My balls were pregnant with you, and when we came together, a great pair of wings fluttered through us both, and I could almost feel a part of you swimming out of me and into that part of you that was her.

"Afterward, I rested against her and said, 'Now, that's a baby.' And I was right. The next month she rang me in Woy Woy, where I was working, and told me the news."

Charlie passed the joint again, but Gerry just held it between his fingers and looked at it, as if he were examining a souvenir.

"You ask your mother about that night. She remembers." He turned to the others. "That's why I always call her my hash baby. She was born with all that good Lebanese gold in her veins. That's why she's like me."

Everyone looked at me with a bit more approval. I sat beside Gerry, imagining my blood a bright yellow, the one pinhead of golden sperm that spawned me. I had lived inside both my parents for years until that one dreamy night when flowers circled the bedroom ceiling and starlings sang at midnight.

Then I asked the obvious question, even though I already knew the answer.

"But how can you be sure it was that time and not any other?"

"I was on tour," he replied. "Only got to come home that one night before we headed out again." He dragged on the joint, and we were all silent and thoughtful, and I was relieved that no one bothered to follow up with their own best fuck stories.

■   5   ■

We only lasted the weekend at Nerida's flat. On Sunday afternoon, just hours before we met the magician in the Village, Sandy threw the Classified section of the *New York Times* into Gerry's lap and told him to start looking.

The following day, the only place we could find within our price range was an old flophouse in the West Village, right on the Hudson River. It was a brick, six-story joint called the West Jane Hotel that boasted an ominous, Gothic tower. The windows on the first floor were all boarded up. When we moved in we had to put our own lock on the door and supply our own soap, towels, and drinking cups. The toilets down the hall were choked with soggy paper and didn't work, and neither did the showers. Not surprisingly, this bathroom was for women only, so whenever I needed to take a piss or bathe, I'd have to creep up to the third floor and use the men's bathroom at the end of the hall.

Some dreadful feeling of doom stole over me each time I flung my clothes off and soaped myself down under a drizzle of warm water. I'd peer over the top of the cubicle door at the rusting steel urinal reeking of piss and vomit. The third floor, I soon found out, housed all the junkies; the manager liked to keep them all together.

But we lived on the second floor, and we had an Indian lucky charm—a round stone with a hole in it—hanging in our open window. It was supposed to protect us from theft. As I lay on my single bed across from Gerry's, it comforted me to stare at it spinning in the warm August breeze rising up off the river.

I met the magician outside the bone-white St. Patrick's Cathedral, on the corner of 51st and Fifth, on Tuesday afternoon. He was waiting in front of the carved bronze doors, dressed in jeans and a white T-shirt, minus the black tails he'd been wearing on Sunday night. His brown curly hair gleamed in the sunlight. His name was Romano. He kept giving me short, shy glances as we walked up the avenue, chatting about the act he and his three musician brothers sometimes performed on the streets.

It was the magician who showed me the city of my imagination, who swept me up out of downtown's junkie theme park replete with bursting fire hydrants, disposable syringes, empty bottles of Thunderbird, and the pervasive smell of piss. When Gerry and I were staying down on Rivington Street sirens had howled for hours, and men would follow my father and me for blocks at a time, demanding to know how much he rented me out for.

But as the magician walked me through midtown, a whole new universe unfurled. I felt small yet significant as we strolled through the shadows of church spires. A cool breeze blew through my hair. Bright flags flapped above us. On Fifth Avenue, the car horns almost sounded sweet and melodious as they piped up from several lanes of traffic. As we headed toward Central Park, we passed the bronze and mirrored Trump Tower, which rose into the sky like a looming metallic altar to the city, reflecting the granite carvings of older buildings nearby. The revolving door of Tiffany's hummed a slow rhythm. As we crossed the road, Romano took my wrist and we bobbed between rows of yellow cabs. The wide, polished windowpanes of Cartier and Bergdorf Goodman reflected our duet. There was something about Romano that *seemed* magical. Once or twice, when we hovered in the shadow of the Plaza Hotel's white marble facade, or when he pointed to the naked statue of Pomona across the street, explaining she was the Goddess of Abundance, I was sure I could see a strange greenish aura about him, something otherworldly. It was at those times I expected him to take my hand or kiss me. I wanted to touch the fingers that made silver dollars and china teacups appear in an instant. But the moment would vanish and he was back to his job as volunteer tour guide for an alien street performer.

We drifted across the road, past the line of buggies and tired horses, the hot smell of manure, and into the fecund green of Central Park. I followed Romano down a path beneath the canopy of trees. People sat on benches, eating pretzels and steaming hot dogs. Couples were lounging on the grass. A few joggers huffed past. Romano waved his hand about, indicating that this would be a good place for us to work. I nodded and breathed in the scent of blossoming wisteria, expecting him to suddenly push me against the trunk of an oak or lead me down a forgotten trail. The only time he paused, however, was when we reached the Children's Zoo and found all the cages empty. Romano explained that the zoo was being renovated. Before we turned to leave, he scored a dime bag of grass from a guy with dreadlocks woven down to the small of his back.

Back on Central Park South, he ducked into a deli and bought two cans of Budweiser, then showed me how to drink on the city streets and not get fined. He folded the edge of the brown paper bag down around the rim of one can and handed it to me. Then he did the same with his own, and we sailed down Central Park South together, taking long swallows of beer and nodding at the uniformed doormen standing on the red carpets of the Park Lane and St. Moritz.

During the afternoon, Romano indicated places that were "cool to work" along Fifth and Sixth Avenues (the paved plazas in front of the Alliance Capital Building or The Time and Life, below Sherman's statue, at the gate to Central Park), and those that were "not cool to work" (outside Trump Tower, outside churches, or anywhere near a bank).

When we reached Rockefeller Plaza and I saw the golden statue of Prometheus shining like an angel above the bright umbrellas of the garden cafe, Romano must have noticed my elated expression right away. He touched my arm and said, "No. Definitely not. You'd get arrested in thirty seconds."

Instead, he led me over to the theater district, where the traffic grew thicker and noisier, where litter seemed to reproduce itself, where a couple of men stood in our path trying to sell us silver chains that were looped around their fingers.

Romano waved them away, as if they were simply a bad thought. I followed him left into 44th Street, and we lingered outside the St. James Theatre, gazing at photographs of Tommy Tune and Twiggy, and the entire, tap-dancing cast of *My One and Only*. Romano pointed to Twiggy's stylish top hat and tails and said, "That's the kinda gear you should be wearing when you work."

I nodded quickly and told him I did wear gear like that. My tails were pink, I said, with rhinestone buttons.

Romano smiled and led me up the street, past the Shubert Theatre, and told me it was here that Gerry and I should start working, along this strip, before the nightly shows began at eight o'clock.

"Now the cops around here are pretty bad, too," he warned. "But if you can get in and out before they realize you're here, you and your dad could really clean up."

I nodded doubtfully as I hurried to keep up with him. I was hoping we might sit down somewhere, find some cozy cafe, drink another beer. But Romano was already glancing at his watch as we turned right and headed toward 42nd Street.

Around four o'clock the magician put me on a train heading back to the Village. He didn't ask for my phone number or address, but assured me that he'd come and check out my act sometime. As the train rumbled through the subterranean labyrinth, I worried about how on earth he'd ever find me, among thousands of street corners and sixteen million people.

■ 6 ■

Even though our hotel had the reputation of being little more than a flophouse for Village junkies, it did have the advantage of a kind of roof garden on top, although it didn't have any plants or chairs. I used to stand on the hot, gooey bitumen and lean on the waist-high brick wall and gaze out over the city. On a good day you could see the pale outline of the Statue of Liberty hovering above the brown surface of the river.

I hadn't danced for more than a week, and I was growing anxious, afraid I might be losing some of my technique. So on the day we moved in, I wandered through the Village, looking for a large piece of wood on which to practice. On Eighth Avenue I found a construction site and, when no one was looking, I seized a six by three sheet of plywood and began wrestling it down the street. I'd only managed to walk half a block, however, when two men suddenly appeared at my side. One was well-groomed, sporting a collar and tie and carrying a briefcase; the other was older, wearing jeans, boots, and a T-shirt with the sleeves cut off. He looked like he might have come from the very construction site where I'd pinched the wood.

I was ready to throw it down and run when one of them said, "Hey, need a hand with that?"

The men lifted the wood out of my hands and carried it back to the West Jane, up the stairs, through the foyer, into the lift, up to the sixth floor, and onto the roof, while I tottered along beside them, carrying the younger man's briefcase and navigating the course.

That afternoon, with my new dance floor installed, I took our cassette player, my tap shoes, and other theatrical accoutrements up to the roof and practiced for hours. Mingus's "Three or Four Shades of Blue" unraveled across the Lower West Side, around the roof gardens and water tanks and industrial chimneys, while nine-beat riffs and cramp rolls fluttered out between my feet and the wood. Each phrase became an escaping bird, like the wings that had fanned through my parents when I was conceived, spiraling up into the silhouetted syringe shapes of Manhattan's skyline.

■   7   ■

The day after I'd danced on the roof of the hotel, I was sitting on the A train heading uptown, dressed in my pink tails with gold trim and large rhinestone buttons, a white silk top hat, and white fishnet stockings. Gerry stood beside me, clutching a pole, a side drum wedged between his feet, drum stands leaning against my legs. We were on our way to the theater district to give our gala premiere performance in New York. Even though we'd been working on the streets of Sydney for two years, I was still gripped with stage fright. What if the Americans didn't like us? What if my feet betrayed me and I found I couldn't dance? What if the cops discovered us, as Romano had warned, and hauled us down to the nearest station?

I swallowed and folded my arms. The train was roaring and shaking. Lights flickered on and off. Suddenly, a man with long dreadlocks jumped out of his seat across from us, holding a dented saxophone in his hands.

"You're all my prisoners!" he cried. "You can't escape!"

His lips found the mouthpiece, his knees bent, and soon he was honking and screeching his way through "I've Got the World on a String," pausing every few measures to take a breath and yell, "Nobody move! I've got you captive!"

I was a little afraid and glanced at Gerry for a cue on how to handle the situation. He was just standing there, grinning at the man, clicking his fingers and bobbing up and down like a fan who'd just met up with John Coltrane. No one else was moving or even taking any notice of him. They either stared at the graffiti on the walls or hid behind books or newspapers.

The horn whined between registers, punctuated by the sound of Gerry's clapping. I was just about to step on Gerry's foot to shut him up when the man stopped in the middle of a run and yelled, "OK! That's enough for you bastards! Pearls before swines! Now feed me, swines! Feed me!"

His hand shot out. Everyone ignored him. The suited man next to me shifted in his seat, and a punk sporting a green-and-blond mohawk blew a pink bubble until it burst across his face. A teenage boy held out a half-eaten apple. A quarter was tossed into the air. The train slowed down. A dull voice droned over the intercom, 42nd Street, Times Square. Gerry started going through his pockets, but the man with the saxophone was already receding into the crowd on the platform. I caught a glimpse of one ropy dreadlock flipping in the air before he disappeared into the train opposite, heading downtown.

We picked up our gear and struggled to alight. The doors closed on me in an abrupt embrace, then quickly let me go. As we climbed the stairs, Gerry dropped his drum stands, and I tore my stockings when I paused to help him pick them up.

We weren't sure which exit to take, and ended up walking down a long passage reeking of stale urine and diesel. Black, gritty discs of hardened chewing gum dotted the steps up to Times Square. Outside, a few people in front of us drifted into a three-card monte game, which was being conducted by a man behind an upturned cardboard box; Gerry and I crossed the street and plunged into the glow of red neon. The stench of roasting chestnuts blended with the smell of fried onions wafting from a corner hot dog stand. Naked women pouted down at us from photographs and posters outside strip joints.

Gerry cleared his throat. "*This* is where the magician told us to come?"

I shook my head. "Not here. Up the road a bit."

We walked two blocks and made a left at 44th. I half-expected Romano to be there, waiting, but the street was empty. We found a spot across the road from the Shubert Theatre in front of the *New York Times* building.

Smooth bricks paved the driveway to the building and looked like they'd be perfect to tap on.

I opened my wooden box, uncapped my water bottle, and took a sip. Gerry began setting up his stands. I took another sip. Gerry unzipped his side-drum case. I sipped again. He slid the drum into place. I realized I was shaking. Gerry paused and winked at me. I secretly hoped it might start raining, and that we could get back on the A train and go downtown as fast as the man with the saxophone.

I noticed a security guard a few yards away, who was quietly eyeing us.

"Oh, excuse me." I rushed toward him. "Are we allowed to do this here? We won't be bothering you, will we? Or blocking traffic?"

Part of me—a big part of me—wanted him to say yes. Yes, we would be blocking traffic. Yes, he'd be sure to call the police if we made any noise around here.

"Oh, no! You're just fine where you are." He dug his hands into his pockets and grinned. "In fact, I'm looking forward to the show."

I nodded briefly and backed away. People were beginning to drift down the street on their way to the theaters.

I asked Gerry, "Do I look all right?" I suddenly felt foolish in my pink tails and fishnet stockings.

He stopped tuning his drum. "Course! You look fine."

I fingered the tear in my stockings.

"You look fine," he repeated. "Gas. No worries."

I tried to reassure myself by going over what Romano had told me, how we could clean up working this pitch as long as we could hit it before eight o'clock and run before the cops arrived.

"Ready?" Gerry executed a drumroll. I pulled on my tap shoes and stretched my calves. A small crowd had gathered around us. Gerry placed the tip bucket out in front and pressed the Play button on the cassette player.

"Dippermouth Blues" burst onto the street, Louis Armstrong's optimistic horn marching through the introduction. I closed my eyes and surrendered to the cadence of blue notes, the street, Gerry's back beats, what we had come to do. Thoughts of running surrendered to movement and sound. My taps hit the bricks, merging with Louis's trumpet solo. I found myself adding accents by gently kicking the wooden case. Triplet turns. Cramp rolls in counterpoint to Gerry's ride cymbal. A flourish of riffs that rode the melody and drove us into the chorus.

The crowd swayed back and forth. As I danced, I caught glimpses of tortoiseshell combs, French curls, false eyelashes, a tiara, orange lipstick, a birthmark in the shape of New Zealand on a man's right cheek. Gerry's face was flushed and swollen in that undressed moment of play. All the rhythms came together in the growl of a double-stroke roll and ended with a double turn.

Dizzy with applause and the sound of money falling into our bucket, we launched into a boogie-woogie number, while a current—a golden momentum—circled between us and the audience.

My feet were carrying me. Soon I found myself feeling ashamed of my fear, as if I'd been finally released into the warm evening of bright lights and perfume. My eyes closed again and I was back on the roof of the West Jane Hotel, back on a six-story stage, listening to my rhythms merging with the city's syncopation, each beat marrying me to my father and to this peculiar new world.

A black hand dropped in a fistful of bills. A woman in a beaded gown tossed a large silver coin. Even the security guard danced about and threw in a dollar. We had to make the most of the time we had left before the crowd disappeared into the theaters. A man in a blue suit checked his watch and motioned his wife away. Her red beehive grew smaller as she wobbled on high heels down the block.

I'd just finished executing a series of wings when I looked around to see Gerry playing down the sides of his stands, onto the bricks, and hitting everything in his path—a few paradiddles on my wooden box, accents on the door of the *New York Times* building, a delicate roll on a woman's thick gold bangle. Soon he was trading fours with me while banging on some guy's briefcase. He was beating the devil out of the leather handle when I glanced up and saw, standing at the edge of the crowd, two chestnut horses with a policeman mounted on each. When Gerry caught a glimpse of them, he straightened, turned, and skulked back to his spot behind the drums.

I drew in a deep breath and wove my way through the crowd toward them. The feeling of doom that overcame me whenever I showered in the men's bathroom returned. The horses snorted. The policemen and I eyed one another.

The one to my left tilted his cap up slightly and announced, "I've got something for you."

I winced, glanced back at Gerry. "A ticket?"

"You bet!"

"It's worth fifty smackeroos," added the other. I bit my lip and struggled to keep the smile on my face. Stupid, I told myself. Should have left sooner. Shouldn't have come at all. They'll haul us down to the police station. They'll confiscate our passports. They'll deport us within forty-eight hours.

I could feel the corners of my mouth beginning to droop. The cop on the left grinned and passed down the ticket. His horse snorted again, and somewhere in the distance an ambulance howled.

I glanced at the ticket. It was black and white and shiny, with a perforated line.

"Some guy just came up and gave it to us," said the cop on my right. "Well, neither of us can get off duty tonight, so we thought you'd appreciate it the most."

I was dismayed. "Tonight?"

"Yeah, that show at the St. James, *My One and Only.* They've got some great tappers in that show. Ahh, Tommy Tune and, what's her name, the skinny dame with the long . . ."

"You'd better hurry," urged the cop on my left, looking at his watch. "You got two minutes."

Overcome with relief, I bounded across to Gerry and asked him if it was all right.

"Course!" He began shooing me down the street with both hands. "I'll just sit here and practice my three-stroke roll. I've almost got it down."

I thanked the policemen and went sprinting down the block, past Sardi's and the Helen Hayes Theatre, tails flapping behind me, taps echoing up and down 44th.

I burst into the marble foyer and was met by a number of frowning ushers. One hurried forward and looked as though she were planning to throw me out. But I held out my ticket as if it were a winning Lotto card, and she pursed her lips and muttered, "Right this way."

The auditorium was dark and hushed. It was at that precise moment before a show is about to start, when the lights have just dimmed but the orchestra hasn't yet begun, and a quiet anticipation hangs in the air. My taps made little clicking noises as I hurried down the aisle. Heads turned and a few women tittered. The usher pointed to an empty seat in the middle of a row and disappeared, leaving me to squeeze past knees, bags, outstretched legs. As I neared my seat, a few people started giggling.

When I finally sat down, the man on my right tapped me on the shoulder, leaned over, and whispered, "I'm so glad it was you." I was unable to see his face clearly, but he seemed fairly young, and I could smell a hint of his musky aftershave lotion. I tried to place him from the crowd, straining to remember faces and clothes, but instead found myself imagining the man he might be.

The orchestra started up, playing the introduction to "I Can't Be Bothered Now."

His fingers were warm against my palm, and he let them linger there a moment. I knew it must be the magician, who had suddenly appeared in my life, just as he'd predicted. This, surely, was my second fantastic omen. But then he cleared his throat, just as White Rabbit used to, and for an instant we were inside my unlit bedroom and this was his first caress of the evening. Soon he would stroke my hair and his breath would be on my eyelids. But then he was my father, and it was his fingers that were uncurling to squeeze mine, just as he always does when he's happy.

The curtains parted and I saw a bright flash of shoes against the stage and the sound of the orchestra began to swell. The man's hand drew back and we settled into our seats. I looked up at the ceiling, to my right and left, and felt small inside that theater, which was as mysterious and dark as an elaborate underworld.

8

I don't remember much about the show, except that it was a snappy, seductive extravaganza of drop-waisted satin dresses, patent-leather shoes, butterfly turns, Betty Boop hairstyles, cutaways, and cartwheels. There were songs, too, lyrics that carried the plot to its conclusion of nuptial bliss. It was a standard boy-meets-girl/boy-loses-girl/boy-gets-girl-back story.

My One and Only was made more amusing by the fact that the boy was Tommy Tune, who stands at around six and a half feet, and the girl was Twiggy, who barely reaches five feet in heels. During the puddle dance, the barefooted

Tommy and Twiggy splashed out rhythmic sequences across the stage. It was a beguiling, romantic duet. With each turn and hold you could see them falling in love, their affection for one another leaking out between their bodies. For a moment I forgot about studying the dance steps and found myself descending into jealousy.

I shook myself out of this reverie and focused on the steps. Yes, I admit, as I sat in the dark, madly sucking on the lime candies the man next to me continued to palm into my hand, I ignored the spiffy costumes, the subtle lighting, the set, the white gloves, the orchestra's brass section swirling in the pit—everything that conspired to flatter the dancing. I just concentrated on the steps. Not the fan of pleated satin as Twiggy turned, but the turn itself. Not the perfect hand and head movements of the Barbershop Quartet as they crooned above the footlights, but their staccato wings and low trenches, their jazzed time steps and half-time breaks. And as my tongue smoothed the edges of each hard sweet, I told myself, I can do that . . . I can do that, too.

Relief tingled in my stomach like a hot meal. Before the intermission lights had even come up I bounded out of the auditorium. I ran back up the street, every muscle charged to perform another set before the second act began. I jumped on and off my wooden case and babbled on about the show, and when my father asked me about the dancing, I boasted shamelessly that I hadn't seen a thing I couldn't do myself. I didn't mention the cartwheel, a fairly simple movement that my long limbs and weak arms could never execute. And the splits. I almost had the splits, but I could never quite get my reluctant fanny to nest comfortably on the ground. But all the tap steps—yes. All the tap steps I could do. In the hazy periphery of the streetlight's glow, my father pursed his scarred lips together, and I remember distinctly he was smiling.

There was still, however, another act. Gerry was feeling generous and expansive. He lit a cigarette and urged me back into the theater. He said he didn't mind waiting another hour. So off I went, giddy and half-tripping over myself as I hurried back to the St. James.

Later that night I remembered little of the second act. When I lay in bed, long after midnight, all I could recall above the din of my father's snoring was a kind of dancing I'd never seen before, a kind of dancing that had already entered me and would stay there for years, warm and intangible as desire.

He was an elderly black man and he had some part in the show during which he sat on a throne and imparted wisdom to the lovesick chap who'd lost his girl. The gist of it was that one must relax and take one's time. Bewildered Tommy Tune blinked his wide eyes and nodded. And then the man expressed his nugget of truth in a soft shoe so slow and succinct that I ceased to breathe and my fingers relaxed their grip on the wooden armrests of the seat. He slid and dragged gradually, perfectly, like an old lover knowing how to make all the right moves, when to touch the right spots, how to linger. I couldn't have expressed it like that back then, but I knew, as I watched his slim, lanky limbs swim in slow motion through yellow light, that I was foolish to assume that my technique, all my fast, slick time-steps, my double breaks, my fifteen single wings in a row on my right foot—eleven on the left—that all this postpubescent showing-off equaled something I liked to think of as Art.

As I watched him, it was as if I were falling in love—not with the man, or the steps themselves, but with an idea, a style, a way of being.

The musical ended with Tommy winning Twiggy back, and the entire cast celebrated with a razzle-dazzle, high-stepping finale. But I was already riffling through the program, trying to find the older black man's name. I wanted what he had, not knowing then that it would take more than hours of practice to make my taps kiss the floorboards that way.

But who was the strange man sitting next to me in the theater, whose ticket I'd inherited and whose candies I'd eaten throughout the show? I couldn't help thinking it would be wonderful if he were the magician. If I were writing this as a novel, I surely would have made him so. Romano with the brown eyes and soft lisp that became more pronounced when he whispered. And we would set off down Broadway together, into each other's lives: he into my pirouettes and poems and crumpled photographs; I into his disappearing doves, his unburstable balloons, his Brooklyn accent, and warm, slender hands.

I regret to say that the stranger was not the magician. He was a particularly unremarkable man in his late thirties—prematurely balding, brown tweed jacket. So unremarkable, in fact, that his date for the evening—no doubt some gorgeous thing in whose long shadow he'd been lost for months—had stood him up at the theater. He'd had no recourse but to give the spare ticket to the two policemen.

Impatience had made me embellish this man into Romano. He was not the magician. He would never be the magician. And I, in my pink tails with the gold trim, my clown makeup, which, by the end of the show, was beginning to dry and crack at the sides of my mouth, I could never be this man's gorgeous thing. After the lights came up, we regarded each other doubtfully. I raised my hand and took his and shook it, thanking him for his generosity. Hastily we wished each other luck and left through separate exits.

The program notes listed my tap-dancing angel as Charles "Honi" Coles. For a year I would mispronounce his name as Hoan-ey, when I should have been saying Honey. But no matter. I had decided he was the man with whom I was meant to study.

When I scanned the West Jane Hotel's White Pages that night, when I called Information, when I pored over the Dancing Instruction section of the Yellow Pages, I could not find a Charles "Honi" Coles. I kept staring at his photograph in my program notes, willing him into my life. Standing between our two single beds, I tried to bend my knees more and dance closer to the ground. I practiced more slowly on the roof of the hotel, sliding my feet in smooth circles across the six by three rectangle of plywood. But it would be another year before I'd hear the echo of Honi's footsteps, another year before I'd link up with his protégées and partners.

■ 9 ■

Although we'd done well on Shubert Alley, my father was not content. He sat hunched on his bed the next morning in his beige underpants and fingered an unlit Camel Plain.

"But we made twenty-five dollars," I said, "in ten minutes." I spun around in my black skirt. "That's two dollars fifty a minute!"

"That's just it, though." He scratched his bum and sighed. "You can only work ten minutes and then it dies. No intermission mob. And they don't throw when they're coming out of the theaters. They've already copped us going in."

He frowned and lit the cigarette. He wanted to work for three hours, at night, from eight to eleven, like he was used to. Most of his gigs in Sydney had been from eight to eleven, and with good reason, too. The public is most congenial then. They've had a good feed. They're out with their friends. They want to have a bit of fun.

I knew the Village would be a good place for us, but Romano had steered me away from that idea because the cops were getting nasty down there. When I had asked where he went when the police moved him on, he mumbled, "Columbus Avenue."

"Where's that?" I persisted.

"Uptown." He nodded vaguely up Seventh Avenue.

As I stood watching my perplexed father smoking his cigarette and twirling the hairs on his chest between his thumb and forefinger, I regretted having let my afternoon with Romano amble off in the direction of Shubert Alley, Central Park, and the Plaza Hotel, all of which were pitches with limited possibilities.

"Columbus Avenue," I suddenly spouted.

"Where is it?" my father quizzed.

"Uptown."

"Can you work at night?"

"Course!"

"Eight to eleven?"

I nodded.

"Many people?"

"Heaps." Of course I was fibbing. I'd never even seen the avenue on a map.

His eyebrows rose. He drew on the cigarette, opened his mouth, and let the smoke float out in a languid spiral toward the ceiling.

It was Friday morning and it was all decided. We'd start on Columbus Avenue the following night. A Saturday evening should give us a good push, allow us to test the potential of the Upper West Side.

In the meantime, however, we had a party to go to, a little soiree to which Nerida had invited us, down on the Lower East Side.

 10

The party materialized as a seven-person affair crammed around a circular coffee table replete with Lebanese ladyfingers, Nerida's vodka cocktails, a carton of Benson & Hedges, and one and a quarter grams of uncut Colombian cocaine.

There might have been a joint circulating, which I declined. At that time, grass just transformed me into a wordless imbecile whose greatest pleasure was studying the prints her fingers left on the side of a glass. Neither did I smoke cigarettes. I'd been a vegetarian since age fourteen, and thus I nibbled away at a vine leaf that looked like an oily green prophylactic wrapped around minced meat. It was offered to me by our skinny blond host, who introduced himself as Barney.

I remember being intimidated by the cheekbones that looked like two large white knuckles protruding on both sides of Barney's face, the paint flaking off the pale blue walls, the scratches on the Patti Smith album that made the air crackle, Nerida's unraveling laughter and easy way with people, the rusting bars across the open window that looked onto an unlit lane, and the faint remains of red lipstick on the rim of the glass I was handed. My father, of course, was as comfortable as a pig in shit.

The lines were passed around on an unopened business-sized envelope from Chemical Bank. As I placed the straw just inside the rim of my right nostril and drew up the stinging powder, it seemed as if Chemical Bank itself were offering me up this sudden credit of delicious white light wheeling through my sinuses.

Some people think it was my father who had introduced me to coke, but the truth is I'd already dabbled in all sorts of drugs, and only ingested the ones that suited me, the ones that insinuated themselves into every bone and blood vessel and made me grow, like a leaf that uncurls on a film in three seconds, a stalk that shoots up in four, until it's almost a beanstalk tickling the bruised belly of a cloud. As I settled back into the fraying green overstuffed couch, I fancied I could already sense the lovely ache in my limbs that my mother had once defined as the pains of growing. Perhaps the soreness was simply the effect of dancing on bricks the night before, but I was convinced, yes, I was absolutely sure that someone would soon have to place a brick on my head to prevent me from taking up too much space in the room.

And what was Gerry talking about? The way he used to smoke hash in a cherrywood pipe during the forties while riding double-decker Sydney buses? Or was it when he used to smoke funnels? Funnels were pure hashish wrapped in marijuana leaves—as long as a cigar but shaped like a funnel; you light the large end and draw from the small.

No, no, no. Not shocking enough. It was the clear-acid story. Yes. To impress all these young shits, especially this bloke who calls himself Barney and fancies himself a dealer, Gerry would create his narrative Frankenstein, a lovely creature sewn together from old scraps of detail, an eyeball here, a fingernail there, stuffed with every anecdote and rumor he'd stockpiled over the years. He'd make them envy his collection, his specimens arranged into neat and humorous things as smooth and admirable as a sculpted white wedding cake made from leftovers in the fridge.

You can't help but love his flagrant boasting, and even though my mother does not know this story, I shall tell it now, as it has been told to me, as he told his captive audience that night between gulps of vodka and cranberry juice, and additional installments from Chemical Bank.

Gerry says that he left her; my mother says she kicked him out. But no matter. It would suffice to say that they parted ways, and he moved into a Bondi flat with a suicidal bass player named Syd Hastings. I was too young to remember his departure—only aged about two or three—but my brother and sister recall the beefy bloke named Norm who drove a delivery truck for the Resch's brewery and replaced our father on the lower end of the living room couch.

My parents' squabble, as usual, had been over drugs. My mother had taken an ounce of my father's Mullumbimbi buds into the office of her family M.D., Dr. Lionel Gregory, an overweight man in his fifties with round spectacles and overlapping front teeth. He examined the contents and sagely informed her that if her husband continued smoking this stuff he'd be dead in six months. Perhaps it was my father's sarcastic laugh that made my mother, as she says, "knot up all his shirts and undies in a flannel sheet and drop them out the bedroom window." Or perhaps it was my mother's hysteria at the prospect of his prophesied death that drove him from the Stanmore house and into the relative peace of the flat in which morose Syd Hastings plotted his quiet good-byes.

Syd Hastings was a sensitive fellow who polished his bass each day with Mr. Sheen. He was in love with a ticket collector at the State Theatre named Pamela. Syd had the half-bowed, self-effacing walk of a virgin in his twenties. He ate bowls of Campbell's chicken noodle soup every night for tea and read Proust between sets of a gig.

A weak, barely perceptible romance developed between Syd and Pamela. But make no mistake; it was a fragile thing. After three and a half weeks of Syd turning up at the matinee show, perhaps she deigned to let him buy her a cup of tea and a pink meringue. Perhaps he coaxed her to his gigs, like a boy charming a bird, hoping she'd fall in love with the music he played, especially the ballads: "Body and Soul," "Tenderly," "I'm a Fool to Love You." As his fingers slid up and down the neck of the bass, as they stroked and plucked the strings, he tried to look meaningful when he gazed at her through a curtain of blue smoke, tried to will her to imagine herself as the instrument within his embrace.

In the half-darkness, through the smoke, he fancied that he held her gaze, that from the round table at which she sat she was almost pouting her lips back at him. But what poor Syd Hastings didn't know, and what he was about to find out, was that the trombone player, a tall man in baggy pants, was standing dangerously close, and it was he who was the object of Pamela's longing gaze and pouting lips.

One night Gerry came home and found Syd Hastings kneeling on the kitchen linoleum with his head resting on the bottom rung of the gas oven. Windows were flung open, terminals shut off. An ambulance was summoned and poor Syd was carted off to the Prince of Wales Hospital.

My father could not comprehend what unfortunate cocktail of emotions could conspire to drive a man's head into the stench of an unlit oven.

"But she's only a woman," he complained from the edge of Syd's hospital bed. "Don't worry, mate. You'll find another Angela."

"*Pam*ela," Syd corrected, still groggy from the antidepressants creeping through his frontal lobe.

It was the mid-sixties, and the controversial medical gossip about America's Timothy Leary was only just reaching Australia's less conservative psychiatrists. A hip and progressive shrink prescribed a therapy for Syd that included a series of monitored acid trips in his clinic.

Syd returned home after those sessions describing angels and breathing chairs, a chat he'd had with Stravinsky, and the trails of violet light my father's hands created as he hit his practice pad.

It wasn't long before Gerry deposited himself on the Doc's leather couch, counterfeiting a melancholy face. Or was it authentic? After all, he was now separated from his wife and three children, his three-bedroom home and soundproof music room. His wife had replaced him with a truck driver and was selling off his prized record collection to all his musician mates for a dollar a pop.

"But there's nothing wrong with you," declared the doctor, who probably took Gerry for the hedonistic thrill seeker he so ardently tried to be.

"But Doc," Gerry moaned, staring at the ceiling, his voice wading through some existential void, "I want to know who I *am*. Why I'm *here*." His fingers drummed against the studded leather. "I want to know if I'm really a drummer. Or if I should be cutting hair, or selling radios door-to-door."

He suddenly sat up and swung his feet to the floor. "I want to know if I'm really a musician."

Arrested development, a midlife crisis, a deep longing and a loss he couldn't name, or maybe the desire for an inexpensive kick that he knew he could shape into an impressive yarn years later—who knows what it was that enabled Gerry to convince the shrink that he was just as desperate as his gas-gulping flatmate.

"Now this gear wasn't like that bloody blotting paper junk you kids score down behind the milk bar," he'd tell each one of his fascinated children when they reached a certain age. "This was *clear clinic acid* [his cleft palate causing him to splutter on the *cl* sounds] shot into your *arm* with a *needle!*" And he'd pause for effect and allow us a moment to imagine something as large as a foot-long horse syringe pumping a pint of transparent liquid into the crook of his left arm.

Lying on the examination table, with the wires of heart and blood pressure monitors connected to him like thin, looping umbilical cords, he died seven times. The first time he drowned. The second time he was buried alive. Then he was pierced by lightning, then crushed beneath a tree. He died the fifth time when he fell from a cliff. The sixth time his flesh began to itch, to sting, to blister. His hands caught on fire, his skin began to melt, and shock dissolved him like a spoonful of sugar in a cup of hot black tea.

Of course, every death was separated by an installment of life, during which he could breathe, collect himself, and believe the ordeal was over before it would start again. But the last time, after the earth had deconstituted him down to acid and enzymes, after she'd processed him through liver and spleen and released him into the atmosphere, he floated up and drifted through the clouds, up, up, up on through the ozone layer, the gravitational shell, a lone party balloon bobbing through the universe's dark serenity.

Finally, his feet touched solid ground, a coarse, yellowish-gray gravel with intermittent round cavities the size of merry-go-rounds. The only sign of life was an ancient woman in an oak rocking chair. She was so old her facial features were lost in a web of deep creases, like the disturbed skin that forms on the surface of boiled milk. Her hair was long and white and unbrushed, and when he stepped closer, he could see what looked like burrs and twigs tangled up in complicated knots.

"Was she God?" I always asked hopefully, wishing he'd forget that he'd told the yarn before and affirm my secret wish.

But he'd shrug and answer, "I don't know."

"Your mad grandmother who had her finger cut off?"

Another shrug and a nonchalant "I don't know who she was."

Then he would mimic the woman's scratchy, cracking voice (she apparently had an Australian accent): "You're a naughty, naughty boy!"

And she rocked grimly back and forth on her squeaking chair, shaking her head, making sucking noises with her closed mouth.

When Gerry stood in front of her, toeing the yellowish gravel and feigning confusion over this sudden reprimand, the woman shook her bony index finger and declared, "You don't belong here! What do you think you're up to, Sonny?"

He mumbled something about being curious.

"Well," she croaked, "you're not up here for long. So you just have a good look around while you can, because afterward you're going straight back down to where you came from!"

Gerry kicked at the dirt and wandered sheepishly away. He bent his knees and leapt into the air again. He glided down casually toward earth. Three years before Neil Armstrong landed on the moon, Gerry witnessed our ball-shaped planet perpetually spinning around in space. He floated down farther to get a closer look, and what he saw initiated an ache in his gut. He gazed at the matchbox-sized buildings, the dots on highways hurrying back and forth in even lines, circling, returning, the even tinier, less disciplined dots crawling willy-nilly across the landscape like a silly nest of ants bumbling over each other in hurried yet arbitrary directions. And he recognized his own humble body among them, rushing to the beach, rushing home, banging on drums, rushing to work, skittering off to the Musicians Club, drinking, purging, sleeping, eating, fighting, fasting, fucking.

"Ants," he murmured to himself.

He clicked his tongue and sighed.

Suddenly, he felt the earth's gravitational pull sucking him down, but he backstroked in the atmosphere like a desperate swimmer in a fixed race.

"No!" he yelled. "I'm not going back!"

"Oh, yes you are!" he heard the old woman croak, her voice echoing down through the Milky Way.

Gerry kicked and waded, breaststroked and freestyled, but nothing could stop his drop into insignificance. He was a sinking ship, and everything down there—his family, his car, his drums, poor Syd Hastings, the hip doctor and his harem of young nurses—everything conspired in the swell that dragged him under.

The doctor coaxed my father back into consciousness with a steaming cup of peppermint tea. The sweet aroma alone stole into the stubborn places in Gerry's head and ushered him gently back to the world.

He quaffed his brew. He took a bath. After Doc checked him over, a cab was called, because he wasn't allowed to drive for twenty-four hours.

But this is the funny thing about it. At the beginning of this story Gerry was living with suicidal Syd Hastings, by the end of it he's back with my mother. Because he had several acid trips, perhaps the end of one got tacked onto the beginning of another. He takes a taxi from Doc's Dover Heights office back to our home. He walks through the door and into the kitchen. My mother looks up from a leg of roast lamb she's baking. She kisses him on the cheek. He looks at the fat spluttering out of the hunk of roasting meat, smells the boiling string beans; maybe I'm on the floor, tugging at his shoelaces.

Then he gazes into my mother's face, like a boy discovering a small universe simply by turning over a rock.

And what did he find there? A woman in her mid-thirties with shoulder-length blond hair who looked like Lauren Bacall in the Bogie days? A woman stricken with the quiet devotion of one who, as a child, was deserted by her father?

No. He saw a pinched look between her eyes. He saw someone who worried over the twelve dollars she asked of him every week, someone who made him make promises they both knew he could never keep.

"And so I looked into those green eyes of hers," he always said, "and realized I'd married the wrong woman."

Was there ever a right one? You never know. There's a sense of finality

in his voice. This is the end of the story. After all, back then, he was ultimately just an ant, and so was she, and the drums he played and the suits he
wore, the series of ceramic ducks she hung from the living room wall, those
lace doilies she set on the mantelpiece, the artificial green Christmas tree
leaning slightly to the left next to the RCA black-and-white television; these
were simply ant paraphernalia, no more meaningful than the crumb a determined bug rolls toward its nest.

When I think of that story now, it doesn't surprise me that my mother
started drinking. Her sister once told me she initially began to consume co-
pious amounts of beer and Scotch in order to fit in with Gerry's crowd—a
mob of boozy musicians who never stopped talking about themselves, lost
to their own great noise.

She would drink my father's spirits, she would smoke his Lucky Strikes,
but she would not inhale his marijuana nor inject his clinic acid. After all, she
always said, she had three young children to raise—four if you count Gerry.

As my father ascended into the mid-heaven of hallucinogens, certain
he'd married the wrong woman, convinced that he had to lock himself inside the soundproof music room and practice drum rudiments ten hours a
day, my mother descended into the distance of drink. Of course, our clothes
were always impeccably ironed; the kitchen floor was spotless. She still
sewed our dresses and shirts from patterns she drafted on the dining room
floor, still knitted jumpers and cardigans, crocheted hats. There were always
three vegetables on our plates at tea. Bedtime was at seven-thirty, and on
this rule she never wavered.

It was just that she began to sway whenever she held me on her hip,
began dropping dishes when she washed up in the evening. And sometimes,
late at night, after I'd awakened with a fright, after I'd howled her name, after she had sleepwalked down to me, lifted me to her shoulder, folded me
into her warm, empty bed, into her body that smelled of roses and damp
earth, I could hear the sigh in her throat, could feel her hand tremble
around my waist, and knew she must be weeping.

The Patti Smith record had stopped around the time Syd Hastings had
stuck his head in the oven. Now that Gerry had finished his acid story, his
moral about the ants, a thick, almost reverential silence brooded about the
apartment.

Charlie laughed quickly and lit a cigarette. His lover, Greg, a short thin Canadian, rested his head against Charlie's shoulder. Nerida licked a sprig of mint almost dolefully. Barney just sat next to Nerida, carving the white dust on the Chemical Bank envelope into isolated lines, lines that had begun to look like a maze for the baby cockroaches crawling up the armrest of the couch.

"Well," I declared, "no ant is an island."

I beamed and looked about. I thought I was being funny or reassuring or something. My fingertips tingled. My throat hummed. My tongue was all loose and pleasant-tasting in my mouth.

Everyone looked away doubtfully. Usually I would have perished back into embarrassment and silence, and have relinquished the night to my yarn-spinning father. But that evening I could not dam the words unraveling up my spinal cord. Gerunds skipped in twos and threes. Verbs prickled my skin. Pronouns left their milky footprints between my vertebrae.

The truth is that I really didn't believe all that crap about the ants, or if I ever did, I allowed it to melt out of my life that night as easily as the ice cubes in my vodka. I was twenty years old and in New York City, and I was at the nexus of a universe of fantastic omens, all of which glinted ahead of me like a thousand Chrysler Buildings. There were suddenly too many beautiful and significant things in my life even to entertain the idea of ants: the bracelet Romano's forefinger and thumb had made around my wrist as he guided it toward the pink balloon, the triangle of light that appeared above my bed at exactly 8:17 every morning; the white satin ribbons I'd found tied to a pole on the A train and used to thread my tap shoes; the free ticket, the Broadway show; the tinny sound quarters made as they dropped into our bucket; yes, all of this was substantial and true. I'd defined it on the backs of postcards that were already on planes flying to Sydney.

■   11   ■

There's another city that festers beneath Manhattan, a dark, piss-drenched Atlantis. Warm drafts steal through tunnels. Rats fat with half-eaten hot dogs and stale pretzels barbecue themselves on the third rail. Musicians pluck tired guitars. The legless steer their squeaky wheel-chairs through corridors between platforms. Always some pinch-faced boy inscribing characters on a mutilated wall. I'd heard there was another breed of New Yorkers who'd emigrated down there, living in a network of disused tunnels, sleeping between nineteenth-century tracks and the dents in tunnel walls. Children born and schooled down there. Mice stewed on portable stoves. Old-timers with no pigmentation in their skin—eyeless, transparent fish spawned in underground caves.

These were the kinds of people who always fascinated me—misfits and outsiders. In the same way that the fictional Alice was drawn to a knight who kept falling off his horse, or a hatter who was obsessed with riddles and tea, I was drawn to characters who lived just beneath the surface of convention. When I was four I fell in love with a man who sat in a wheelchair on the corner of Parramatta Road, outside the Empire Hotel, selling newspapers. His mouth was twisted, one eye was slightly crossed, and saliva always drooled down his chin and formed a wet patch on his white cotton shirt. I nicknamed him Lurch, after the ominous butler on my favorite television show, "The Addams Family." Every afternoon, when my mother picked me up from nursery school, when we walked down Johnston Street and I caught sight of the trembling man calling "Paper, paper!" to passing pedestrians, I would break into a run until I reached the corner. I'd fling myself into his lap, calling back, "Lurch, Lurch!" and smother him with kisses.

It was back into the Manhattan subway system that Gerry and I wandered in search of Columbus Avenue. We'd awakened after only four hours' sleep and had spent the rest of the day practicing for our great Upper West Side debut. We were still feeling the effects of the coke, and rather enjoyed the sight of ourselves bungling through the turnstiles with a plywood tap board, cassette player, side drum, stands, cowbells, woodblocks, and my wooden case.

Navigating was left up to me, racing ahead of my father in my eagerness, for Gerry doesn't have much sense of direction. (Once, when I planned to part with him on 42nd Street and meet up with him again on 34th, he was convinced he'd get lost along the way.)

I bounced up the platform to find the subway map. As I stood studying its network of colored veins, out of the corner of my eye I saw a man dressed in sneakers and a woman's thigh-length jacket. I glanced at the map, then back at him, finally realizing he was standing there masturbating, as if he were at home, alone in his own bathroom. The few people nearby didn't seem to take any notice. After he finished raining onto the tracks, he looked at his right hand as if he might discover his fortune in it, then wiped it on the sleeve of his jacket.

When I'd finished inspecting the map, I returned to Gerry and told him we were catching the A train. He seemed more interested in that piece of information than my anecdote about the masturbating man. He began scatting Ellington's famous introduction to the song, and I bobbed up and down and couldn't help but sing the lyrics.

The A train didn't stop at 72nd Street, but thundered all the way up to 125th, the subway stations flashing by like frames in a film. The song was right: It *was* the quickest way to get to Harlem. I vowed to Gerry I would learn to read the maps better. We waited around for about fifteen minutes, then lugged all our gear onto the B train. By the time we emerged from the 72nd Street subway station, it was pushing half-past eight. We found ourselves marching by the Gothic spires of the Dakota, a sprawling stone apartment block that looked more like a Transylvanian castle, complete with black iron gates and a doorman with a toothy smile. I imagined John Lennon's blood on my shoes, that I was leaving red footprints along the sidewalk as we drew toward the hazy glow of Columbus Avenue.

The intersection at which we found ourselves looked promising, busy with handsome people promenading up and down, no doubt in search of the latest outdoor cafe or Japanese restaurant, taking their time, wanting to be seen by each other, gazing into boutiques boasting hundred-dollar dresses and Levis with holes already worn into the knees.

The widest corner was the one outside the Chemical Bank. As we warmed up, a crowd began to grow around us. Like the old pros we considered ourselves to be, we didn't rush in willy-nilly to entertain them, but continued to prepare ourselves for the coming night. I suppose you could call it a kind of street performer's foreplay. Gerry had his head down and allowed the triple paradiddles to escape from his snare while I turned my back to the audience and no doubt showed off with some fancy step I could never quite work into a routine.

New Yorkers simply drool over anything new. Telephones shaped like Einstein's head (the top half lifts off and you speak into his cerebellum), dresses made out of parachutes, pet iguanas you can walk on a leash, singing toothbrushes, tattooed foreskins, and cinnamon cigarettes. I don't think I'm kidding myself when I admit that the reason they hoorahed us and made airplanes out of their bills and flew them into our bucket was because we were different. A welcome change from the Italian magician on the corner of 71st. We weren't like Ralph the Button Man or the breakdancers farther up who spun on their heads and backs across flattened cardboard boxes. Had we announced ourselves, our accents would have charmed them even more, but we were naive young pups back then, and it would be quite a few months before we realized our tongues increased our earning power.

We wanted to be like them. Our act, and when I say act, I mean the act we lived as well as the literal act on the street, was an homage, a tribute to their music and dance, from Louis Armstrong to Thelonius Monk, Bill "Bojangles" Robinson to Gregory Hines. We were too green then to realize that their hoots and howls were mostly just an expression of their love of something new. The crowd up there was young and white and would probably go home that night and listen to Madonna or Billy Idol.

Someone went mad with a Polaroid and it began spitting out pictures of us on that corner. In the break the photographer gave me a damp image that would join the scores that would be taken over the following years on the streets. Slipped into a folder under the bed in which I now write, the images look like an assembly of orphans. The cities and backdrops change, but the atmospheres are consistently urban, and there was always some roving photographer with a penchant for the romantic who caught me at a tired moment between shows, slumped on my wooden case and tightening the loose taps on my shoes.

In the photograph, I'm wearing black stockings, a short-sleeved leotard, a gray and white cotton waistcoat, and a top hat. From the angle at which the photograph is taken, Gerry's right drumstick seems much longer than it could have actually been, and it looks as if he's jabbing me in the leg with it. But we are grinning, oh yes. We and the crowd are having a scandalously good time. You can almost hear the celebratory, euphoric noise pressing through the gloss of the photographic paper.

The photograph, of course, does not anticipate what happened during the next break only a few minutes later. I was taking a long pull on a bottle of water when I looked up to see four black men scowling down at me. They were all well over six feet tall, and were elevated even further by virtue of the roller skates strapped to their feet.

"This is our spot!" cried a man with a red sweatband around his head.

His mate, dressed only in a pair of shorts, skated in a wide arc across the corner as if he were marking out his territory.

"We work here every night!" added a third.

The crowd obviously didn't want to get involved and gradually drifted off.

I hugged my water bottle to my chest and meekly produced the street performer's hackneyed refrain: "But we were here first."

"This is ours," volleyed back the red headband. "We've worked here two years."

I stumbled a bit with my return. A pathetic cliché I'd heard guitar players swap in Sydney's Central Station tunnel: "But you don't own it."

Already the others were skating in circles and figure eights across the sidewalk, careening dangerously close to Gerry's snare drum, fanning us with the breeze their darting bodies created. What I now call Pitch Etiquette was ambiguous to me then, when we were just beginning to feel our way through the busker's cloudy moral universe. I felt my knees lock and took another swig of water. These were the people to whom we were trying to endear ourselves, whose history we were attempting to graft onto our own patchy ancestry of hobo uncles and remittance men. Everything would have been sublime, no doubt, if we could have just slung our arms around their shoulders and declared our love for their own Duke Ellington and performed our version of "Caravan."

But when they switched on their boom box and the sound of sirens blaring over the stutter of a drum machine unleashed itself, it occurred to me that they didn't give a shit about Ellington, or what we did or did not love. When the red sweatband shouted that they needed this particular corner because of the smooth concrete with which it was paved, it seemed like a good enough excuse to me and we packed up our gear and left.

We straggled on up the avenue, still trying to maintain the nervous optimism that had propelled us into the night. On the other side of the street we discovered the Pioneer Supermarket. The sidewalk had a few disadvantages—the lighting was minimal, the pedestrians were scarce, and there was quite a bit of litter about. But I became enamored with the place the moment I jumped onto a metal covering secured over the opening of a delivery shaft in the pavement. On it my feet transcended the loud opera of traffic, sirens, and chatter, and I experienced a sudden rush of pleasure in hearing my formerly muted riffs rise up and bounce off the third and fourth floors of the brownstones, echoing down the avenue over the ghetto blasters and car horns. I was Gene Kelly with a lamppost, Houdini with a padlock, Jesse James with a good horse and gun. I intimidated pedestrians with my gorgeous noise, matching the boom of my father's snare.

Of course, such rampant anarchy could not go unchecked for long. In less than fifteen minutes I noticed a sleek black-and-white car pulling up before us. And out stepped uniformed Sergeant Herb Browning, white-faced, pointy-nosed, thin-lipped, sucking in what was obviously a developing beer paunch.

Herb Browning would, in the coming weeks, become my Achilles' heel, the omnipotent thorn in my pirouetting side. But during that first encounter, all I could think of was the nervy, uptight ranger on the children's television show, Yogi Bear. (Gerry of course was Yogi and I was the tagalong Boo-boo. "Ah, but Mr. Ranger, sir!")

Browning was shaking his head as he walked toward us. "OK, folks," he said. "Wrap it up right now. Everyone's complaining about the noise."

I stepped off the metal covering. He looked down at my shoes and then thumbed over his shoulder at the apartments and shop fronts.

"The folks in the supermarket, too," he said. "Cashiers. Grocery boys. Even the produce assistant manager."

Gerry's eyes widened. I could tell he was going to make some sarcastic remark about produce assistants and what they could do with their cabbages. But then he must have thought the better of it, for he let the smirk drop away into a sudden half-baked solemnity.

"Well, look, Sergeant—" he said confidentially, "what's your name?"

"Browning." His face twitched as he murmured his name. "Officer Browning."

"Well, look, Officer"—Gerry inched toward him in much the same way a sinner lowers his head toward the confessional screen—"my daughter and I are just trying to earn an honest buck. And I know you've got your job to do." Gerry ventured a touch on the officer's sleeve and let his hand drop away. "It's just that, well, I wanna ask your opinion here. Maybe you can give us some advice."

Browning's eyes slowly rose to meet Gerry's. He suddenly looked about an inch or two taller, and his paunch a little less pronounced.

Gerry twirled his stick for effect. "Now, you know this town like the back of your hand."

Browning considered this and nodded quickly.

"Well, then, in your considered opinion," he continued in the tone of voice he'd use when we were kids, whenever he tried to con us into brushing his hair or tickling his back, "where would be the best place for us to go? You know, somewhere we can make a few bucks and at the same time not bother anybody? 'Cause we don't want to upset anyone. You know, we're entertainers. We just wanna make people *happy*."

The thin ridge of Browning's bottom lip quivered. Perhaps he was trying to get angry, but he couldn't quite muster it against my father's imploring look or the disappointed way I folded up my feather boa.

"Well," he raised his hand and pointed in the direction from which we'd come, down toward the Chemical Bank. "Up around here's no good. But I suppose, aah, if you was to go down the avenue, like past Seventy-second Street . . ." He waved his hand about vaguely, like a drunk Queen Elizabeth. "OK, I suppose anything from Seventieth down, you know, I could safely not notice you if you went down there."

He ventured a wink at Gerry, who returned it with a dig in the ribs and a handshake.

By the end of the evening, both Gerry and I had decided that Browning had done us a favor. The corner of 70th and Columbus, outside the closed French dry-cleaning store, was well lit, flat, rather spacious, and provided us with a steady flow of passersby walking up from Lincoln Center. Infinitely better than outside the supermarket and less pressured than the Chemical Bank, at the dry-cleaning store we finally found our niche in the city.

■   12   ■

So much of street performing has to do with coping with the urban elements: the runaway trains, the police, the complaining neighbors, the other performers, the impending rain, and the lurking thieves. Some nights are simply a gift, in which all the external impediments are in some kind of remission. You're swept along on waves of applause and laughter and generosity, you're perfectly balanced and your body surprises you with its ingenuity. Riffs at a speed and precision you once thought impossible now escape from your feet, double turns making the street spin, and all the old tunes you've rehearsed for days now seem new and fresh. Those golden nights: the residents are temporarily deaf; the cops are embroiled in more serious matters; the potential muggers are stuck on the other side of town; the other buskers decided to work the Village; the predicted rain suddenly made a left turn at Philadelphia. Everyone on Columbus has just been paid, and they're milling about, looking for something unique. Needless to say, this didn't happen very often. Some nights, before we even began work, we had to endure all the setbacks I just described. Other nights we'd be set up, ready to begin work, and thunder would crack across the sky. Yet occasionally we were able just to let the handicaps roll away like salt water off a wet suit. Once we found our spot on Columbus that first night, it was as if the avenue reshuffled and opened itself up to us. And we opened ourselves up to it. We'd placated the chief cop, ingratiated ourselves with the neighboring area, and finished up making one hundred and thirty dollars.

I soon became preoccupied with divining what peculiar combination of causes it was that conspired to produce the Good Night. I became as superstitious as the baseball player who, after a winning game, replicates his every movement the next day, wearing the same underwear and eating the same cereal in the morning. I had no control over the weather and the cops, but I figured that if I could just put myself through an elaborate ritual of preparation each afternoon, I could invent a little insurance against potential accidents and bad luck.

It began with a stretching session around four o'clock—hamstrings, calves, splits, every contortion I could imagine. After an hour or so I would stop and take a tablespoon of Brer Rabbit Blackstrap Molasses to stave off my anemia (although my father begged me not to take because it always made me fart). I'd decided that one of my leotards was luckier than the other and often wore it day after day, washing it out before I went to bed at night. From six until seven in the evening we'd shower and dress and I'd don the lucky leotard, even if it hadn't completely dried. I would then paint on my clown face, thinking of Marcel Marceau, whom I'd seen perform in Sydney in 1981. While we dressed we listened to the jazz station on the radio. I rewound the tapes as Gerry checked the rechargeable batteries. We'd pack the red shopping cart we used to call Ol' Granny, and bow to each other before we left the room.

But I'm jumping ahead here. This all happened in the Ben Franklin Hotel, which we haven't moved into yet. No, it is late August 1983, and we're still immured in the West Jane Hotel. We have encountered Herb Browning for the first time, made our debut on Columbus Avenue, and earned one hundred and thirty dollars. We've caught a taxi back to the West Jane and celebrated with four bottles of Colt 45 and have forgotten to eat. We lie back in our undies on our respective beds and muse over the evening like an old married couple.

■ **13** ■

Even though he emanated bravado, my father occasionally expressed his dismay at the aggression this city seemed to manufacture. A mere stroll through the Village would invite a barrage of people demanding cigarettes, quarters, matches. A woman in a raincoat and mismatched shoes followed me back to the hotel one afternoon, screaming, "Whore! You fucking whore! You goddamn fucking slut!"

One evening on Christopher Street we saw an overweight woman shove a man through the plateglass window of a leather bondage shop.

Sometimes my father's vulnerability leaked out. Late one night, that first weekend we were staying at Nerida's, he'd arrived home, white and trembling, after a jaunt out to the bars of the Lower East Side with Charlie. They'd been traipsing down Rivington Street, tipsy and laughing over some prank or other, when four police cars careened up onto the pavement. A bevy of cops leapt out and brandished their guns, screaming, *"Hit the ground!"* Evidently, a stake-out was taking place right inside the apartment building they happened to be passing at that moment, and poor Gerry and Charlie, their stomachs hitting the gravelly sidewalk, were trapped between the cars and the building.

One Sunday morning in early September my father finally lost his cool. It was a stinking hot day, and we'd already worked up a sweat by the time we'd carried all our gear from the Columbus Circle subway station along Central Park South to the park's entrance at Fifth Avenue. There was plenty of room, which, in my inexperience, I preferred. (It took me weeks of working the streets before I understood that too much space could be a liability. It enables the audience to hang back, making it difficult to connect with them; also, they became timid about stepping forward and throwing money into the hat.)

We started up at around eleven, as the sightseers began to flow out of the Ritz Carlton, the Pierre, and the Sherry Netherland Hotel. Across the street was the Plaza, ornate and gleaming in the dewy sunlight. During our breaks I used to get a kick out of scurrying into the plush foyer of the Plaza in my costume and makeup, past all the posh people sipping from china cups in the tearoom, and bursting into the marble rest room to have a wee. After refilling my water bottle at the sink, I always made a point of leaving a tip in one of the crystal saucers discreetly positioned below the beveled mirrors.

It was hot and the crowd hung back, and between tunes Gerry would sip from a large warm bottle of Colt 45 concealed in a brown paper bag. By midafternoon I was sweating through my makeup and had to touch it up and pat on extra talcum powder. That day, too, I was breaking in a new pair of shoes. They were white leather, with a tiny heel, which disconcerted me a little, as both my street and tap shoes had always been flat. By the time we were working up decent crowds—the postluncheon mob—the right shoe was cutting into my heel. And as people pressed dollar bills into the hands of children, nudging the little tots toward us, blood was seeping into my white fishnets. But from this I culled a certain kind of perverse pleasure. I was so involved with the show, with charming these inquisitive strangers, that I simply glanced down at the soiled heel of my stockings and felt nothing.

Gerry was restless after finishing his bottle and worried about getting sunburned. (His equally fair-skinned brother had died of skin cancer during the seventies.) So we decided to move into the shade. He grabbed one side of the tap board and I the other. As we were dropping it beneath a tree, Gerry noticed a man snatch our bucket and run down the path into the park.

Maybe it was the Sunday Gerry gave up smoking; perhaps that's why his nerves were so raw. Since I had my back to the bucket, I was bewildered to watch my father grab his cowbell stand and go sprinting into Central Park, screaming, "You fucking mongrel!"

In his red and white waistcoat and plastic clown nose, he was running beneath the trees and holding up high, like an Olympian sporting the mighty javelin, the metal stand with the cowbell bobbing on its elasticized cord at the end.

The crowds were impeding the progress of the thief, and suddenly he did a U-turn and ran back. He collided with a group of confused, camera-happy Japanese, which turned the predicament to Gerry's advantage. He wove through the crowd, gaining on the bludger with our money, and all the time yelling "You bloody mug! Stop, you thieving bastard!" while people stood about dumbly, probably wondering if this was part of the act.

Gerry finally cornered the man in front of a hot dog stand not far from where the bucket had originally stood. He raised the drum stand above his head. "If you don't hand it over," he yelled, his face all red and puffy, the cords in his neck bulging, "I'll fuckin' kill you. I'll crack your fuckin' skull open!"

It was as if the entire corner held its breath. The confused Japanese, the kids, the ice cream–eating couples, the passing breakdancers, the hot dog man, everyone tensed and fixed their eyes on the mad old bloke in the clown costume about to brain another mad bloke in dirty jeans and an inside-out T-shirt.

If pushed a moment farther Gerry probably *would* have decked the guy. This was my father, the man who'd declared himself a pacifist during the Second World War, who'd been thrown in jail at a time when it was very unfashionable. The thief just stood there cradling the bucket and staring back into Gerry's eyes as if he were hypnotized, not making another move to run, yet not offering it up, either.

Finally, with his free hand—the other still raised with the threatening cowbell—Gerry reached out and snatched the bucket. For a moment he looked surprised at his apparent success, glanced into the bucket, then back at the stunned thief.

My father paused, then lowered the weapon. He leaned in closer to the man. "Now piss off," he said, suddenly sounding cocky. The man crumpled away and disappeared behind the hot dog stand, and my father, now rosy with triumph, almost swaggered back to where I stood beside the tap board.

"You gotta be tough with these blokes," he declared, handing me the bucket. "You gotta let 'em know who's boss."

He mopped up the perspiration on his face with the bottom of his waistcoat, then begged a cigarette from a nearby teenager, lit it, and inhaled a mouthful into his lungs.

When we began performing again ten minutes later, Gerry was gazing into the sky, as if he were still marveling at his one uncharacteristically dangerous deed. I could already hear him fashioning a yarn around the first time we performed in Central Park: *I was sixty-three, remember, and there I was chasing this young bloke through the park with a drum stand. I mean, he could've had a gun or something. But that's what New York does to you. It makes you like that.*

Sunlight made diamond shapes through the trees as we played through the afternoon. We lost ourselves in all the old show tunes: "Charleston," "Five-Foot-Two, Eyes of Blue," "Putting on the Ritz," "How Ya Gonna Keep 'em Down on the Farm After They've Seen Paree?" The cornier the better: "In the Mood," "Ain't She Sweet?" "Bye Bye Blackbird." They loved all that old stuff. And oh, yes, we piled it on. We iced that cake with wide eyes and grins and exaggerated gestures. As he played, Gerry could raise his eyebrows into a frown and make his scalp slip back and forth over his skull in time with the accents he hit on the cowbell. Occasionally he'd throw down the sticks and jump onto the tap board and, pretending to be older and less flexible than he actually was, kick out an improvised soft shoe while I snatched up the fallen sticks and imitated him playing the drums, moving scalp and all.

It was after one such diversion that I looked up into the crowd and saw Romano hovering between two women on roller skates. He had his tails folded neatly across his forearm. He wasn't hiding, yet it seemed as if he didn't want to be noticed. For a few moments I stopped breathing and colored. Sipped my water. Smoothed the creases of my waistcoat. I was frantically trying to anticipate the next tune on the tape: "Cabaret"? "Sunny Side of the Street"? "The Sheik of Araby"? I tightened the bow on my tap shoe, chewed the insides of my cheeks, ignored the wound on my right heel. I had to impress him. I had to be worthy of the afternoon he'd donated when he'd shown me around. My dancing had to awe him as much as his disappearing doves and unburstable balloons had awed me.

I cringed when I heard the introduction to "Don't Get Around Much Anymore." It was a slower, less energetic tune than the others; one that was no doubt included to give me a reprieve between the up-tempo numbers. The trouble wasn't so much the tune, but my sudden stiffening and the self-conscious, awkward form my steps assumed, the forced smile that seemed engraved on my face. I could not look at him as my legs scissored the air like a mechanical doll's. I forgot to breathe. I was trying to convince myself that we didn't look ridiculous. I tried not to stare at my feet, but couldn't raise my head in case I caught what I suspected might be his disappointed eye. Shadows whirled about. I tried to redeem myself with a double turn, but I lost my balance on the last quarter and stumbled into a pullback. When I accidently glanced at him he was looking at his watch. The two women nearby were beginning to skate away, and I secretly cursed him for suddenly appearing like a ghost at this ungodly moment.

By the time the number ended, about half the crowd had evaporated and Gerry decided we needed a break. He turned the cassette player off and bummed another cigarette from a tourist who was circling us, snapping photos.

I turned my back on the drifting audience and, still pretending I hadn't noticed Romano, busied myself with rummaging through my wooden case, as if I needed to lay my hands on some extremely important item. I bowed my head, extracting objects and throwing them back in again until I heard Romano's distinctly Brooklyn voice declare, "Now, why don't you folks get a real job?" When I looked up, I found him grinning down at me as if he'd just seen Bojangles himself dancing up and down a flight of stairs.

Butterflies swarmed through my stomach. I stood up and floundered about for some witty remark with which to reply, but as I gulped back my nervousness, Gerry shook his hand and leapt straight into his first recounting of the incident with the drum stand.

As I watched Romano nod at the spontaneous scaffolding Gerry erected around his story (. . . and then I had him by the throat . . .) I suddenly felt swollen with all the things I wanted to tell him myself, about Shubert Alley and the free ticket and the Broadway show and our stint on Columbus Avenue, but Gerry just kept talking. After hearing the triumphant climax and denouement, Romano laughed and clapped Gerry on the back. Then, before I'd had a chance to utter anything, he was lost to the august green of the park in order to do a show of his own.

For days I'd rehearsed the moment at which we might meet again and the witty sentences that would spring from my mouth and woo this ephemeral magician. I had myself spouting any number of amusing anecdotes and sage observations. In my fantasy, my clown makeup was far from the patchy, sweaty face I wore that day. It was fresh and perfect and utterly became me. Or else I ran into him on the way home from swimming a mile in the YMCA pool and my face was flushed and healthy.

At night, as I lay listening to my father snore, I had dreams about us teaming up with Romano and his musician brothers and forming some kind of traveling medicine show; pulling into small towns along the Mississippi and setting up in the main street. Gerry marching up and down with his snare strapped around his shoulders, drumming up a crowd. And Romano and I would make love in meadows and caravans and cotton fields, against the smooth boughs of willow trees, the hollow of a dried-up creek, until that cup inside me would overflow and flood the parched earth of my senses, just like it had when I was nine.

As I sat on my wooden case, sipping water, I suddenly felt the pain gnawing at my right heel. White Rabbit insinuated himself into my consciousness, too, and the memory of those long summer nights during which he cradled me in the dark pooled into the throb spreading up my ankle. It was Saturday night back in Sydney, and if I hadn't left I would have been down at the Marble Bar, dancing to Mike Hallam and his Hot Six. I'd be wearing my umbrella dress (a skirt I'd made from the nylon covering of a broken golf umbrella) and twirling about in front of the horns until the bright colors fanning out made me look like a spinning top. And White Rabbit would meet me after midnight, crawling through the space of my open window. He'd stroke all the euphoric energy from me until I was as still and receptive as a viola string.

"Wanna do another show?" Gerry flicked the cigarette butt away.

I glanced at the waning sun and the few people standing about us like grazing sheep, waiting for us to do something amusing.

"My foot hurts a bit," I said, not wanting to sound too pathetic. I'd grown up hearing him brag about his resilient mates, about the show going on in spite of bad luck and bullet wounds. There was the brilliant yet alcoholic saxophone player Frank Smith, who once strolled up to the center of a big-band stage, played one chorus of a solo, paused, crept back into the brass section, vomited into the wide bell of the baritone sax, wiped his mouth with the back of his hand, then walked back to the front microphone and completed his solo. Then there was Reg Robinson, who went on happily strumming the changes in "Cherokee" after he'd gashed his forehead running through a plateglass partition in his haste to get back onstage in time for the opening of the second set. My father harbored a deep admiration for such stoicism and managed to ape it quite convincingly when news of his mother's death arrived when he was forty-one years old.

This is a story my mother tells, not Gerry, because it isn't funny and because it illustrates the kind of man she found so difficult to love.

Gerry had invited all of his mates over for a jam session one weekday afternoon. The house shuddered with sixteenth notes and the brazen vitality of young men trying to distinguish themselves. The windowpanes rattled with Charlie Parker and Monk imitations, the crotchet triplets booming out of my father's bass drum and the high hat sizzling against the backbeats.

My mother was in the kitchen (where else?) when the telegram arrived:

Mum just passed away.—Joan

Both my mother and father had sisters named Joan, and Mum's immediate response was to hold the yellow paper in her shaking hands and begin to choke at the words staring back at her. She would have sobbed on for hours, for days, wondering where so much warm, salty liquid came from, if she hadn't then realized that it was Gerry's mother who'd been ill, Gerry's Joan who'd gone down to visit her at her home on the south coast.

My mother waited until the band wound itself out of the last chorus of "Scrapple from the Apple," brushed away the dew forming in her eyes, opened the lounge room door, and beckoned Gerry from his circle of boozy camaraderie.

He breezed into the dining room, almost walking on his toes, his last drum solo ringing in his ears. She couldn't look at him as she rested a hand on his shoulder and handed him the telegram.

She says he only glanced at it briefly, then he dropped the telegram onto the table and said, "Oh, well. She was old anyway."

He shrugged off her hand, closed the living room door behind him, and started belting out the introduction to Lee Morgan's "The Sidewinder."

How could I hold up the next performance with my bleeding heel, with the homesickness that made the sun hotter, the traffic noisier, and my need to pee again even more urgent? Nothing seemed to hurt or sadden him. He couldn't understand why Syd Hastings would want to stick his head in an oven. When Gerry lost a gig or a woman, he usually celebrated. He dabbed straight whiskey on his weeping skin cancers, and drank down his nightly vitamins with beer.

I stood up unsteadily. I wondered if Romano was secretly spying on me through the bushes, or whether he was lost in the paths which snaked through the park. Or whether he, like me, was daunted by the effort it took to drum up yet another crowd.

I did not want to disappoint my father. I did not want him to think I'd give up as easily as my older brother and sister. I retied my shoes. I yanked the bottom of my leotard out of the crack in my bum. I began to tap out the beginning of "St. Louis Blues" for the fifth time that day.

■ 14 ■

The magician did appear again later that afternoon. He'd obviously made a few dollars: I could tell by the buoyant walk, how his fingers jingled the coins in his pockets.

Gerry entertained him with the Shubert Alley story while we packed up. It seemed as if he were waiting for something, the way he kept nodding and responding to Gerry but allowed his eyes to stray over to me. I busied myself with drums and cases and screwdrivers. In spite of my fatigue, my heart began racing and small, delicious thrills rippled up my spine.

"And then," said Gerry, "I started banging on some guy's briefcase!"

Romano nodded and laughed. We were all packed up and ready to go by the time Gerry had that nice copper handing me the ticket to the Broadway show. The magician staggered back a few steps at the punch line and dropped into a sort of vaudeville turn. Then he grinned at me, shaking his head. It was those sorts of responses that charmed me, and charmed Gerry, too. And when Romano's face suddenly became animated, and he said, very quickly, "Hey, you wanna have coffee?" and his eyes danced back and forth between Gerry and me, we both blurted out, "Yeah, OK."

My father sat between us in the checkered cab back to the hotel, smoking a cigarette and quizzing Romano about how cold it gets in winter. Anyone would have thought Gerry had never spent those three months in

Detroit, the way he paled under Romano's descriptions of twenty-degree weather and advice on thermal underwear.

"Yeah, but I stayed inside all the time in Detroit," he insisted. "Cab to work. Cab home. Never went out, let alone trying to earn a few quid every day on some street corner."

I was beginning to realize we were a couple of tropical birds, lost on a headwind, flying too far north. It was now apparent that we'd been fools to have arrived in New York in the middle of August. We should have come in May, the beginning of the season, and worked the entire summer. Romano said that no one performed on the streets in winter, except a few hardy guitar players who migrated down to the subway stations until the weather finally broke.

Our Great Future was looking decidedly bleak as Gerry paid the driver and we all clambered out. Premonitions of snowstorms and polar winds were temporarily postponed as the three of us sat on my father's bed and counted up the money. I could see Romano was suitably impressed: one hundred and thirty-eight dollars.

"No, no," he assured Gerry, raising his eyebrows, his head caught in a series of quick nods. "A hundred and thirty-eight. Three hours. That's *good*, man. That's very decent."

Later that night, Gerry and I would speculate on how much Romano had earned in the park. Gerry was inclined to believe that he hadn't done as well as us; I wasn't so sure; I thought he was being modest and wanted to encourage us.

After a quick shower, we strolled through the Village, past psychic readers, bondage stores, and gourmet delis, until Romano decided on an Italian cafe with meringues and chocolate-dipped biscotti in the window.

Since the afternoon he'd shown me around, I'd spent several afternoons and evenings wandering through the Village by myself, hoping to run into him and make it seem accidental. I kept gravitating back to the doorway where I'd first encountered him whispering to his audience, rubbing metal rings until they linked. But he was never there when I looked, only in my imagination, in the enormous hopes I conjured.

Now he was sitting opposite me and we all had fluffy cappuccinos and Romano was biting into a huge piece of pecan pie and offering me some, and I, too shy to eat his food, said no.

Gerry was back to the subject of wintering and wondered aloud if we, too, could descend into the subways for three or four months.

Romano shook his head and wiped his mouth with a napkin. "You guys wouldn't last thirty seconds down there. Too loud! The cops'd haul you in."

Gerry's face dropped and he tried to mask his disappointment with a few sips of coffee. "Well, what do you do?"

Romano shrugged. "My brothers and me, we get indoor work. They have their own band and they back up my act."

I was sure Gerry was going to ask him if they needed a drummer and a tap dancer in the show, but Romano kept talking.

"But this year"—he grinned and gestured in such a way that the teaspoon in his hand disappeared—"we're heading south. New Orleans—"

"—the land of dreams," I spouted, remembering the words to a song.

He leaned across the table and took my wrist and made the spoon appear out of the sleeve of my blouse. I smiled back at him and nodded at the spoon. "Is that hard?"

Romano shrugged. "Just takes a lot of practice. Just like anything else."

"New Orleans, eh?" said Gerry.

"For example," Romano continued, twirling the spoon between his fingers like a baton, "I could teach you how to dance with a cane—you know, a whole routine—without you ever actually holding it. The cane floats magically beneath your open palms."

"Really?" I said. "You could teach me that?" Romano shrugged one shoulder again. "Of course. But"—he pointed the spoon at me—"it'd take at least ninety hours of practice."

"Of course," I agreed.

"Are you flying south?" asked Gerry. "I mean, in an airplane?"

Romano shook his head. "Going to pack up the van. Drive down."

I was thinking about the ninety hours of practice, some of which would surely have to be in Romano's presence. I was convinced any moment now he was going to invite me back to his Brooklyn home, and my hands began to fidget with the spoon he'd placed between us.

"New Orleans," mused Gerry. "I always wanted to go to New Orleans."

"Me, too," I added. "Louis Armstrong."

"King Oliver," said Gerry.

"All that voodoo hoodoo." I was positively drunk on the cane idea and the ride down to New Orleans with Romano and his brothers. I must

confess I forget now who it actually was that suggested we all go south together. Romano said two more people wouldn't make much difference, and
we could share the gas. I was beginning to believe that if you could just visualize something distinctly enough, your imagination could coerce it into
existence. Was he a mind reader, too? Had he seen the meadows and dry
riverbeds I'd invented during my solitary moments? The love scenes in
caves and the wide boughs of trees?

When we parted outside the Italian cafe and he looked into my eyes
and squeezed my hands, it certainly seemed so. And when Gerry and I
turned to walk back to the hotel, there in the twilight it seemed as if I carried a small part of him away with me.

And I let myself believe that he carried a small part of me away with
him, too: the scent of my skin, or a fragment of my laughter; something of
me that affirmed him, that opened itself up to his soft lisp and smooth
hands.

■ 15 ■

When Nerida found out we were paying five hundred a month for
a sleazy room in the West Jane Hotel, she concluded we were being ripped
off and wouldn't stand for it. She asked me over to her place one morning and we dressed not as well-heeled visitors to Manhattan but like a
couple of tough chicks who knew their way around Alphabet City. Nerida
spent half the morning on the phone, working her way through the Yellow
Pages, calling up every hotel in order to compare the weekly rates. Once
she'd developed a short list, we donned our leather caps and started
walking.

It's funny the things you save. I still have the yellow leaves of paper she
scribbled on in pencil that day. They are stuck in a journal I had made before I left Sydney in 1983. I'd covered the journal with part of the gray satin
that was once my bedspread. According to the sheets of paper, we looked at
thirteen hotels that day, with rents ranging from forty-five dollars a week at
the Pioneer to one hundred and twenty a week at the Ben Franklin. We
walked through the humidity all afternoon. Nerida told me to let her do the
talking with her bunged-on American accent: If the clerks realized we were

Australian the price would automatically rise. Gerry stayed at home because two young women had a better chance at a good deal than a young woman and elderly man. Nerida knew all the tricks. By the end of the day, we were sitting up in a cocktail bar on Broadway and toasting the new digs on West 72nd Street. The room was sunny and spacious, boasting blue carpet, two double beds, an en-suite bathroom, and a communal kitchen. It was almost luxurious after a month at the spartan West Jane and, in a stroke of spirited negotiating, Nerida had talked the clerk of the Ben Franklin Hotel down to one hundred and five dollars a week.

■ 16 ■

By mid-September we had moved into our new residence on the Upper West Side and had fallen into a regular performing routine. Sunday afternoons were spent in Central Park, beneath a huge oak along the way to the Children's Zoo. In the evenings, however, from Tuesday to Saturday, we pushed our red shopping cart along the five-minute walk from our hotel to Columbus Avenue.

During those weeks producers and agents were always lurking about, with their dog-eared cards and promises: they were bringing down a camera crew to film us next week; they could get us on Johnny Carson; they were going to line us up a gig as the warm-up act for Tiny Tim. Almost every week there'd be some middle-aged man in a belted spy coat, smoking cigarettes and talking big. Gerry would get excited between acts and smoke the man's fags and quiz him on the heights to which he could propel us. I might have been sucked in a couple of times by one or two particularly convincing characters who had an unusual facility for verbs. ("I'm going to *excavate* you from this street corner and *enshrine* you in the great palace of stardom to which you both belong!") For the most part, however, I remained guarded and aloof. I didn't want some big oaf bumbling in and spoiling what I thought was in some ways already complete. I never considered busking as the bottom rung of a towering ladder toward fame and fortune. I spent many a break between shows explaining this to concerned audience members, who thought we were too good to be on the street. I was happy to be a part of an almost-extinct tradition that dated back to the Middle Ages. I was a minstrel, a troubadour. Had I been born in medieval times, I would have been a court jester. I saw their faces knot into incomprehension: Surely we could get on that TV show, "Starsearch"; they were always looking for new talent. That led to The Big Time, it was said.

My relative indifference to The Big Time was not, in the beginning, so clearly defined. It only manifested itself in small ways, in my slight, protective gestures toward preserving the act. I wanted to maintain the uncompromising, zany quality, and feared that it would be diluted if aspirations toward stardom ever lodged themselves within us.

One night I found a note in our bucket, asking us to drop off our CVs at the address below. I scrutinized the thin, spidery handwriting and was annoyed. No more information other than the one question (without a question mark) and the address. Annoyance gave way to suspicion. His office was on 42nd Street. Did he presume, because I was working on the street, that I was some desperate, penniless waif who was all too willing to peel off her leotard and have a series of warm fingers slide dollar bills between her skin and a fluorescent G-string?

"Just calm down," said Gerry. "He's seen our act. Maybe he likes it. Maybe he's an agent and wants to book us in somewhere."

We sat in our room and stared at the note. We didn't even know what a CV was. In Australia Gerry had always secured gigs through his reputation. We each turned the note over in our hands. I ended up tearing a page out of my journal and writing him a note back:

To Whom It May Concern,
Today you saw me and my father performing outside the library.
You left a note in our bucket because you wanted to see our CVs.
Before we send you our CVs, we would like to know why you
want to see them, and what you plan to do with them once you
get them.

I signed it and printed our addresss at the bottom, but we never heard from him again.

There were times in the following month when I wished I hadn't been so suspicious. Winter was already prowling around corners at night and goosing my skin between shows. Gerry found a woolen scarf in the foyer of the hotel and began wearing it. Gusts of wind would come sweeping up Columbus Avenue and scare away the meager, shivering crowds.

Whenever we ran into Romano on the street, we'd prod him with questions about the ride south to New Orleans. We wanted dates and routes. We wanted to look at maps. We flirted for a brief time with the idea of buying sleeping bags. But Romano's eyes always retained some vague, solitary distance. Whenever I mentioned the dancing cane, he'd just nod and say he'd call me. I kept tearing bits of my journal out and writing down my number and pressing them into his hand. He seemed so different from the enthusiastic trickster we'd had coffee with a month ago, as if he were carrying some invisible weight that only expressed itself in his downturned mouth and rounded shoulders.

Gerry reckoned it was because he smoked too much dope. But I was sure it was because he didn't like me anymore. I berated myself for being too young, too shy, too plain, too whatever it was that might have made him so reticent toward me. And I harangued the impulse which needed that dancing cane, that magician so much.

■   17   ■

When I was a child, I loved to read fiction. By the time I was eight, however, I had turned to biographies of famous composers: Mozart, Beethoven, Chopin. Initially, I thought it might please my father. But Gerry expressed enthusiasm only for Beethoven ("Now, he was one wild cat"), so I continued to read them out of fascination and humility.

By that time I had begun to scribble music in the margins of my notebooks. They were simple tunes, melodies that occasionally piped through my head. I wouldn't begin to write prose for another year, but had been jotting down stanzas of rhymed couplets since I was six. The temporal economy of crotchets and quavers enchanted me as much as an unusual verb or a demanding rhyme scheme. Back then, it was all music, even the words. Each syllable was the deep, clean beat of a drum. There were no instruments in the house except for the Aulos student recorder I was learning to play with twenty-four other kids at school.

The instrument I had always longed to learn had been sold when I was five, along with all the furniture and our Stanmore house. Perhaps I devoured the biographies of composers in order to compensate for the loss of the piano I would never learn to play. The seven-dollar recorder was a disappointing substitute, even though I was using it to compose my first melodic lines and had been asked to play a solo in the school Christmas pageant.

Sometimes I think I continued to read the biographies in order to torture myself. Beethoven began playing the piano at the age of four and had made his musical debut at seven. Chopin was a mere toddler when he began playing duets with his older sister; by the time he was eight he'd penned his first composition, Polonaise in G minor. Mozart had performed for the Viennese Court by the time he was six and afterward had kissed the Empress Maria Theresa. Two years later he was hanging out with Bach and composing his first symphonies. And all I could show for my eight years on earth was a folder of short, formal poems and a few simple melodies that had been inscribed on the backs of electricity bills and brown paper bags. I was practically half-grown and had not produced one sonata or symphony. In spite of the way my parents hugged me and ruffled my hair whenever I showed them a new tune or rhyming verse, I felt unable to compare myself to anyone other than the classical masters and the looming precedents they set two or three centuries ago.

Perhaps it was through writing, too, that I culled attention from the two confused and preoccupied adults who had made me. My mother often fussed over my poems and read them aloud to the family, for I was too shy and the words always locked in my throat. My father didn't cluck quite as much when I proffered up my first attempts at musical composition. I would never actually *play* the melodies, but would show them, like the poems, as they appeared on a scrap of paper. My father was more impressed when I kept perfect time on the cowbell, or imitated his crotchet triplets with my knife at the breakfast table.

But mostly I submerged myself in the sanctuary of words and sounds in order to steal myself away from loneliness. Even though I knew, in spite of everything, that I was loved, the lives of my parents were circumscribed by a kind of chaos that demanded a good deal of their attention. They were also laboring under the weight of their own difficult beginnings and unfulfilled expectations. My brother and sister seemed so much older than me and, like some overlooked weed in the corner of the backyard, I was often left to take root in solitude and produce my own peculiar flowers.

In my father's absence, I abandoned my recorder and my dream of becoming a pianist and composer. Without him, there was no oil in that engine to keep it softly humming. Instead, the pistons in my mind began to pulse on words alone, producing a poem a day, and one or two stories a week. I relinquished myself to what has become a lifelong tussle with language and imagery. It would be another eight years before the abandoned machinery of my musical life would be discovered again, there in my teenage feet, when I was reunited with the heartbeat that was my father.

■ 18 ■

At three o'clock sharp every afternoon, from the solitude of our room, we'd hear a trumpet's moan descending a minor scale. Someone upstairs or across the alley, perhaps. We never saw the player's face, only listened to the slow, deliberate articulation of time through the muted tones and intervals. I'd be stretching out by then, between the bed and the table, while Gerry practiced in a corner opposite, his drumsticks purring against the rubber pad in a low double-stroke roll. The first few notes came to us each day almost as a relief, one of the few things in our lives we could count on; an announcement that somewhere very close by we had a kind of comrade who was trying just as hard.

Money wasn't the problem. At least not back then. We worked on Columbus Avenue from eight to eleven and each night brought home about one hundred and twenty dollars. Time wasn't a problem. Every day except Sundays I had to myself, and I often wandered around the Upper West Side, watching people or looking in shop windows. Sometimes I'd catch the subway down to Chelsea and swim laps for nearly half an hour in the YMCA's tiny indoor swimming pool, until some official blew a whistle and told me to get out. I went through a period during which I'd make a beeline from our hotel to the New York Library for the Performing Arts to watch rare footage of early black tap dancers, or to sink into a chair with old books about the theater. Living with Gerry wasn't the problem. Our room was large and bright, with high ceilings and one big window.

What was really bothering me was the cop who'd moved us down from the supermarket that night. Nearly every evening, while I was dancing, I'd look up and see him staring at me from his police car parked across the road. His reputation kept wafting back to us like a bad smell, riding on the headwinds of Columbus Avenue's sweeping gossip.

One night Romano was passing by our corner on his way up to do a show, and I unintentionally ensnared his attention by mentioning the devoted policeman. When neither Gerry nor I could remember his name, Romano demanded, "What does he look like?"

"Well, he's a little tubby," I replied. "Early forties. Fair skin and—"

"A long nose?"

"Yeah!"

Romano groaned. I asked him what was wrong. He crossed his arms and glanced up and down Columbus.

"Herb Browning."

"Yeah, that's right. That's his name," said Gerry.

Romano lowered his voice. "You're both going to have to watch him. He's a fruit salad."

"Really?" said Gerry. "He was pretty nice to us that night."

"Don't mess with that potato." Romano shook his head.

"Of course," added Gerry. "I worked him over with my famous charm."

"He'll throw someone in jail just for looking at him the wrong way," Romano went on. "Fuckin' maniac. One minute he's cool and offering you a cigarette and the next minute he's busting everyone along the avenue—the vendors, too—and hauling off everyone's equipment for evidence."

The self-satisfied smirk dropped away from Gerry's face. "Really?"

Romano sighed. "I told you. He's unpredictable. Can't trust him. Schizo. Whenever he's on this street—look up and see for yourself—Ralph the Button Man, me, the roller-skating team, the cello player, the balloon blower, the woman who sells the jewelry, we all pack up and go home. It's safer that way, you know?"

Before he left, Romano gave us a stern warning to stay on our toes. But when I grinned, rose up on the balls of my feet, and clicked my heels together like a German soldier, I couldn't make him laugh.

19

One night when it rained and we couldn't work, Gerry and I bought a map of the United States and sat staring at the black dot of New Orleans and the tiny islands of the Florida Keys that dribbled into the Gulf of

Mexico. The word on the street was that Key West was another warm nest for wintering. Performers were rumored to set up shop on the wharves at sunset and compete with each other for the roving, sunburned tourists. My finger kept drumming against the blue gulf as big as my hand. I was attracted to Key West because I knew Ernest Hemingway and Tennessee Williams had lived there. But Williams had also lived in New Orleans, and I was anxious to ride that tram up and down Desire Street. Our fingers traced the roads and highways Romano's van might take in its passage south. Gerry lowered his head and breathed over the mythic cities he'd heard incarnated in jazz and blues lyrics: Kansas City, Memphis, St. Louis. But New Orleans loomed largest of all.

The trumpet that played every afternoon always finished at six o'clock with Thelonious Monk's "Mysterioso," struggling through the changes before ending with that familiar little trill on a high note. As if an alarm had gone off, Gerry would put down his sticks and begin to arrange our equipment while I stood up and dressed. I was already starting to feel tired and weak from dancing and performing three hours a night, and before we left our hotel at seven I would swallow an extra two tablespoonfuls of molasses.

After Romano had given us the lowdown, we didn't see Herb Browning for two or three nights. In fact, we'd almost forgotten about him. Gerry reckoned Romano smoked too much dope and that even an unleashed poodle would make him paranoid. But this is what happened the next time Browning's police car pulled up at our curb.

We had a decent crowd, and were finishing up the last number of our show. Gerry was twirling his sticks and I was getting ready to take off my hat and pass it around. When we saw the car, I glanced at Gerry and he nodded at me to keep going. He continued playing with one hand while leaning over and turning down the cassette player with the other.

After we finished the show and the crowd had dwindled, the police car was still parked in front of us, silent and imposing. Suddenly, three honks were emitted. Gerry took a swig of his Colt 45 and burped.

"Go and see what he wants now."

"No way," I replied. "You're the father."

"Nah. You're good at that sort of thing."

"Bull! What happened to that famous charm?"

"Sshhh! He'll hear you." He took another gulp of beer.

The car horn bleated another three times.

"Go on," persisted Gerry, giving me a gentle shove. "Just go over and butter him up a bit."

I remember wanting to stomp on Gerry's foot at that moment, but instead resigned myself to walking across to the police car and peering through the open window.

"Is everything all right?" I forced a smile. "Is it too loud? Would you like us to—"

"Oh, no, no, no." Browning tilted his cap up and grinned back at me. I felt the muscles in my stomach relaxing a little.

"I just wanted to come and thank you."

"*Thank* me?"

"For being so nice when I asked you two to move that night. You know, respecting me and everything. Anyway, the name's Herb"—his open hand reached out the window—"Herb Browning."

I shook his hand and mumbled something about not minding having to move. I was starting to think Gerry was right about Romano smoking too much dope.

"I'm sorry I had to kick you off Seventy-second, it's just that—"

"I understand," I said, imitating my father. "You were just doing your job."

Browning's face lit up. "That's right! You know, nobody understands that! Hey, where you from? England?"

I glanced back at Gerry, hesitating.

"Or Australia?"

I nodded.

"Really? Australia?" Browning's voice began to waver with excitement.

"Yes."

He straightened and leaned out the window.

"Oh, I've always wanted to go there. The beaches. The sun. You know, in winter, when it's snowing, I often buy this newspaper, and on page three they always have a big picture of a beautiful Australian girl lying on a sunny beach, with a great figure and only the bottom of her bikini on! That always makes me want to go to Australia."

I edged back from him, wanting to get away before I heard any more.

"Yes, well. I have to be getting back to work."

"OK," he nodded. "And thanks again."

"Sure."

"Hey," he called as I turned away, "what did you say your name was?"

I hesitated again. "Alice," I replied. "My name's Alice."

■ 20 ■

When I was a child, I not only read biographies; I frequently escaped my own life by hiding inside the plots of novels and short stories. My favorite was *Alice in Wonderland & Through the Looking Glass*. Whenever life got tough, I would hide in bed and dream myself into landscapes lush with talking flowers and riddle-telling hares.

By the time I was ten, after my father had left, my mother took a lover who was violent and unpredictable, and I retreated farther into my imaginative world—the only one over which I had any control. For three years, this man balled his fists and aimed. He could push my mother's head through a plateglass window; he could pull her hair out in clumps; he could drive my teenage sister from the house for good. He could make my nose bleed, twist my arm up my back, but he could not divest me of my imagination, which sustained me through the fractured life I awakened to each morning.

One hot day I had to wear a sweater to school so no one would see my bruised arms, but it didn't matter because I knew when I arrived home I would change into a blue dress, slip through the looking glass, and be able to tell the Mad Hatter all about it.

Books were to me what alcohol was to my mother, a balm, a secret anesthetic.

That night after we arrived home, Gerry, as usual, stripped down to his underpants, cracked open a bottle of Colt 45, and began counting out the evening's take. I knelt on the floor, opened my box, took out my pink feather boa, and wrapped it around my neck. I reached for my copy of *Alice in Wonderland*. I stood up, the bright feathers swaying luxuriously.

"You talk to him next time," I said. "It's your turn."

But Gerry didn't reply. Just took a swig from the bottle and went on counting.

We'd never had much trouble with the police in Australia. When we did it was always Gerry who dashed over and smoothed everything out, always he who thought of something either witty or charming to say to get us out of trouble. Up on Columbus, I remember longing for my gregarious father who took care of everything. But here in this foreign country he was content to remain behind the drums, content with the familiarity of his contrapuntal rhythms and the bottle of Colt 45 at his feet.

■ 21 ■

The next evening a tall man in a tweed overcoat and black glasses hurried out of the straying crowd as I passed around the hat.

"Now tell me," he said, "what country are you from? You're not American, are you?"

"No," I confessed, and admitted my nationality.

The man grinned and nudged his friend, a shorter guy in a zipped-up black leather jacket. "I knew it!" He beamed at his friend. "I just knew it."

I folded my arms self-consciously. I looked down at my shoes. "How? How did you know that?"

He pointed to my right armpit. "No American dancer would let the hair grow under her arms like that."

"Or her legs," his friend added. "They're too—you know—" he rose to his toes and fluttered his eyelids briefly. I suspected in this gesture there was some sort of veiled compliment, but nonetheless felt a little bruised by their abrupt appraisal.

It had nothing to do with being Australian, however. I did not shave my legs or under my arms because I did not want to look too womanly. The only makeup I wore was the pantomime mask I painted on each night. For my mother's beauty had always been her undoing. Being beautiful meant that she attracted the wrong men, men who neglected her or beat her or drove her to drink. It caused ulcers to grow in her shrunken stomach, took away her appetite, made her the focus of too much attention as we walked down the street together. In my adolescent mind, to emphasize your beauty was to court disaster, and I already felt as if I had dated disaster too long or, rather, had chaperoned my mother's dates and had witnessed what could happen.

"She should go down and audition for *Forty-second Street*," the taller one decided. His name was Mitch. I remember because a note I once received from him is still stuck in one of my journals.

"Yes," his friend agreed, "she should."

I wasn't sure if they were having me on. "I'm not good enough for that."

"You are! Yes you are!" they both chorused, clucking like two stage mothers, patting me on the shoulder and smiling. I'm not sure why, but I relaxed and trusted them. In spite of their crack about the hair under my arms, I appreciated their forthrightness, which, in my mind, distinguished them from the middle-aged men in belted spy coats who kept landing on us like flies. These two didn't even have a card between them. They were a couple of actors who lived nearby and had been checking out my dancing all week.

Mitch and his sidekick were the kind of people who liked to pick fluff balls off my woolen waistcoat and offer advice in muted tones. Mitch was a good friend of the casting director. He'd mention my name before the audition. A role in *42nd Street* would allow me to get a green card. The pay was between five and six hundred a week. Less work. More pay. Security.

"I think you should go down there and have a go," said Gerry, back in our room. "Sling 'em a few of your double wings." He took a swig of beer and burped. "Save us packing up and pissing off for the winter. And who knows, by next April, you might be a big star!"

I tried to detect a hint of facetiousness in his expression, but he just raised the quart of Colt 45 to his mouth.

I felt both excited and ambivalent. Auditioning for a Broadway show, *42nd Street*, at that. Mitch had given me the lowdown: I'd just have to learn a simple tap combination and sing a song. *Sing a song!* a voice inside me wailed. I suddenly knew how my brother felt that moment he was told he'd have to talk into the microphone. Given the choice between packing up and pissing off for the winter and singing a song in front of a scrutinizing man who scribbled what I imagined would be menacing comments in a notebook, I would have no doubt chosen the former.

"You'll shit it in," assured Gerry. "You know the words to 'Pennies from Heaven' don't you? Just hop up and sing that. They'll love it."

"Pennies from Heaven." Those dreaded lyrics my sister had once sung.

"Go on, try it," said Gerry. "They're not expecting Judy Garland. They just wanna know if you can carry a tune."

He raised his eyebrows and nodded.

I stood up from my bed. I cleared my throat. I clasped my hands in front of me. Swallowing, I just stood there. Nothing would emerge from my throat. I opened my mouth, drew in a deep breath, but somehow allowed it to escape before my voice could marry itself to the exhalation.

"Whatsa matter?" said Gerry.

I fidgeted with a button on my blouse and shrugged.

"Can you remember the words? How it starts off?"

I nodded and swallowed again.

"Well, sing. Go on, just sing the bloody thing."

I looked up from the floor and stared out the window. I drew in a deep breath and allowed a voice to leak out of me in a tentative, half-musical monologue.

"Hang on, hang on—" Gerry waved a drumstick at me. "You're taking liberties."

"Well, why shouldn't I?"

"With the time," he said. "You can't take liberties with the time."

"I was improvising," I said. "I was playing with it."

He shook his head gruffly. "Well, you can't. You can't play with it. You've got to play *within* it."

"What's the difference?"

"The difference"—he shook his drumstick at me as if it were a schoolmaster's cane—"the difference between the difference is the difference!"

I pursed my lips and frowned. It was one of his sayings, gleaned from an alcoholic sax player. It was supposed to be profound.

"Well, I told you," I said. "I told you I haven't got a voice."

"Now, look," Gerry went on. "I'll keep time on the practice pad and you listen to me as you sing. That way you won't get lost."

He counted me in, but I began a fraction too late. My father was exasperated by the fact that my timing was impeccable when I tap danced and intolerable when I sang. He counted me in again. I closed my eyes and tried to sound like Frank Sinatra. Gerry had once told me Frank had learned his

distinctive timing and placement from the trombonist Tommy Dorsey. . . .
He was connected with the Mafia. . . . He was married to Rita Hayworth. . . .
Or was it Mia Farrow . . . ?

"Hang on." Gerry waved the stick at me again.

I'd lost my place in the song.

"Maybe you should write the words down."

I shook my head. "It's all right. I was just, I was just thinking about the
timing and forgot."

"Well, the timing's better. Just try to relax a bit more. You're too
uptight."

I unclenched my hands and did a few knee bends. I made a mental
note to relax. I nudged Frank Sinatra's biographical details from my mind.

"OK," I said. "I'm calm now."

And he counted me in again.

■   **22**   ■

My father sailed through his first audition. The English bandleader
Abe Romaine was so condescending, Gerry forgot how nervous he was, how
much his hands were shaking. He was auditioning for the eighteen-piece orchestra at the Trocadero, the most sumptuous dance hall in Australia. The
revolving stage had a cut-glass back wall shaped like a giant shell. The
sprung dance floor alone measured over fourteen thousand square feet. It
was made of tallow wood set in rubber and could accommodate up to two
thousand people.

Romaine glanced at young, skinny Gerry up behind the drums and
took him for an ignorant kid from the mountains who could not read music
and was wasting his time. Romaine kept calling Gerry "Son" in front of the
older musicians and auditionees, until Gerry grew so humiliated that he
ended up playing all the set arrangements—the four-bar drum introduction
to "Song of India," the Buddy Rich fills on "One Night Stand," all the fills
on "In a Persian Market"—without even glancing at the charts. In preparation for the audition, he'd worn out seventeen gramophone needles playing
the songs over and over again, until he could mimic the American drummers note for note.

I'd grown up with the cadences of that story swirling throughout my childhood. It is still in my ears now as I write—Gerry demanding to be paid for the full rehearsal; Gerry telling the important English bandleader he really didn't care whether he got the job or not. Romaine pulling ten bob out of his own pocket to pay him. And when he was finally offered the job, how he declared he couldn't start the following Thursday because of a previous commitment.

"I want to give my band up in Katoomba enough time to get the right replacement for me," he declared.

Abe looked prickled, as if he were about to kick the bass drum in. But the bandleader knew it had to be Gerry's way or no way. He nodded briefly and told the rest of the drummers to go home.

◼ 23 ◼

It was after ten the next night when I noticed a paddy wagon circling our block, prowling around the corner every few minutes. We were nearing the end of one of our most popular numbers, "Money Makes the World Go Around," when the paddy wagon slid into the curb and stopped. I couldn't see a face at the window and continued dancing until the music ended. After taking off my top hat, I made my usual spiel—"Just remember, folks, no donation is too small. . . . Just fold it up, and drop it in . . ."—while eyeing the paddy wagon.

I tipped the money into the wooden case and pointedly looked at Gerry.

You take care of it, he mouthed, making a shooing motion with his hand. I had expected him to do something like this and reluctantly crept over to the wagon. A window suddenly rolled down and Browning's filmy gray eyes stared out at me.

"Hi!" he said. "How's business?"

"Is anything wrong?" I crossed my arms in front of me. "Are we too loud?"

"Oh, no. No, it's fine. No complaints." Herb wriggled in his seat and moved closer to the window. "I just wanted to catch your show. You're a pretty good dancer." He looked me up and down. "Gee, ya must have pretty strong legs. All that work you do every night. You must be in pretty good shape."

I shrugged and looked away, not knowing what to say or how to prevent what was coming.

He craned his neck out the window. "Do you ever go to discos?"

"No."

"Why not?"

"Oh, I don't know." I glanced back at Gerry. He was pretending to be busy tuning his snare. "Not my thing, really."

"Ever been to Studio Fifty-four?"

"No."

"You've heard of it, haven't you?"

"Um . . . I think so."

"See, you can't just get into a club like that. You have to know someone. You have to be with someone important." His voice lowered to a confidential murmur. "I go there all the time."

I took a small step backward.

"So what about it? What's say you and me go out dancing one night?"

I shook my head. "I don't think so."

"Come on, Alice. Have a little fun."

"It's just that, well . . ." I tried desperately to think of an excuse. "I dance every night as it is. You know, it's my living."

"What about dinner, then? I know this nice French restaurant right around the corner from where you live."

"From where I *live*? How do you know where I—"

"Oh, I just happened to be driving along Seventy-second last night after you finished up here, and you went into the Ben Franklin Hotel."

I was backing away from him by then.

"So what about dinner? Or lunch? What about lunch?"

"I'll . . . Let me . . ." His eyes were gleaming like a cat's in the darkness as my voice trailed off into an unfinished sentence.

I returned to my father's side. I felt foolish for not being able to come up with some smart excuse.

"See you soon, Alice," he called as he pulled away from the curb. "See you real soon."

When we arrived back at the hotel that night I spooned more molasses onto my tongue, hoping the extra iron could replenish me, could make my voice soar out of my timid lungs. I wanted my father to tell me what to do. I wanted to go home. The thick, sugary molasses slid down my throat.

One spoonful. Then another. It would make me feel better. I peeled off my waistcoat, tailcoat, and shirt, still warm and wet with sweat. I waited for the anticipated lift in energy, but instead was up all night, charging through the darkness between my bed and the bathroom with an interminable case of the runs.

■ 24 ■

The next afternoon, the trumpet's slow, controlled moan penetrated our room and I knew I didn't want to go back outside. The breathy squealing on the higher notes made me cringe. Instead of stretching out, I followed Alice's adventures across the Queen's croquet lawn. Gerry was in the corner, practicing, a thick book of music propped on a stand.

It was early October and each night the streets were getting colder. I lay in my bed thinking about how, in Australia, spring was breaking open and jasmine would be blossoming out of my windowbox, while here in New York the trees and grass would wilt and turn brown until they were eventually covered in snow.

I flipped through my book as the trumpet skipped up and down octaves in triads. Alice looked so pretty in her blue dress and white apron.

Gerry put down his sticks and stood up and stretched. "You all right?"

I didn't look up from the Cheshire Cat. "Yeah," I said vaguely.

I could feel his eyes upon me. "You sure?"

I didn't answer, just turned the page, not knowing what to say.

"Is it that bloody stupid copper that's bugging you?"

I put down the book. "What do *you* think?"

"Look, I've told you not to worry about him. What can he do?"

"What can he *do*? You heard what Romano said."

"Don't worry about him." Gerry smirked and lit a cigarette. "Just tell him you're gay."

I pulled the covers up around my neck. "He followed us home the other night. Romano says the guy's a bloody nut. And you're carrying on like it's Prince Charles asking me out to the ball!"

"I don't have a magic wand. I can't make him go away." He sank back into his corner and began banging on his rubber pad.

My brother, sister, and I had always loved him for having that kind of reaction whenever he was expected to assume authority. His indifference exasperated my mother. He didn't seem to mind when my brother wanted to leave school at fourteen. He didn't mind when my sister went away for the weekend with her boyfriend. He didn't mind sharing his joints with us and our friends when we were teenagers. He didn't even seem to mind too much when a man pulled up in front of our house twice a week in a dark blue Porsche and took my mother out.

I rested my head on the pillow and watched him practice his inverted paradiddles, remembering stories of his childhood. Not the funny, extravagant ones, but those of his harelip and cleft palate, how he spent the first eight years of his life in Camperdown Children's Hospital. Stories of scores of unsuccessful operations. Dr. Wade and Nurse Watkins became his surrogate parents. After so many operations, he'd developed a resistance to ether and would wake up on the operating table in the middle of a procedure, only to have a large gray mask descend upon him and knock him out once more. In 1925, the inside of his nose was sewn with gold wire. He said he'd had no close friends in the hospital, and his favorite thing to do was to ride on the heavy lawn mower with the hospital gardener and inhale the delicious scent of freshly cut grass.

His sister once told me that Gerry had been an unusually nervous child, that after he came home from the hospital he'd often cry. His older brothers would lay bets on who could make him bawl first.

Even though he'd had no formal education in the hospital, his parents enrolled him in the third grade at the local school. Naturally, he floundered. All his peers could read and write by then, knew their multiplication tables, natural science. He was two or three years behind the others; no one thought to put him back to first grade. What was worse, for him, was that he talked differently from everyone else. The other children teased him about his speech impediment: Why don't you talk through your mouth instead of your nose? He usually punched these boys out. The school reported his misconduct to his parents, and when Gerry arrived home in the afternoons his father would demand to know why he fought so much. But my father could never admit why; he'd rather get a belting than admit why. He'd just stand there, with fists balled, ashamed to hear the sound of his own queer, breathy voice, just as I was when Gerry stood me in the middle of our room and told me to just open my mouth and sing.

As he bowed his head, Gerry picked up the tempo of the inverted paradiddles. I wondered how the transformation from the nervous, angry child to the cocky musician had come about. I knew he'd bought his first kit of drums when he was ten and was playing professionally within four years. I knew he'd never fully recovered from his difficult start at school. I knew that what he had lacked academically and socially he more than made up for musically: He'd studied percussion for ten years at the Sydney Conservatorium. I knew he'd gone on to play in the most prestigious big bands and bebop quintets, was rated as one of Australia's best drummers from the late forties into the fifties. I'd seen all the yellowing newspaper clippings in the thick scrapbook his sister had kept. Gerry on the front page of *Tempo* magazine, 1948, his sticks a blur across the drum kit, his head thrown back, laughing.

Somehow, at that moment, it wasn't hard to imagine how he'd become such an obsessive person, inventing himself with eight-hour-a-day practice sessions and heavy drinking each night. There is an oval, sepia-toned photograph hanging on my living room wall as I write. For years it sat in the bottom drawer of his wardrobe. It is a portrait of my father when he was two years old. He is wearing a worn hospital shirt, his hair a crown of blond curls, a pair of sad eyes looking away from the camera, and barely a hint of an early scar forking up above his top lip.

The trumpet began winding up a chromatic scale. My father took down a double-stroke roll. If I could be Alice, I thought, I could be a child again, growing smaller and smaller, as easy as guzzling from a bottle labeled "Drink Me." But Gerry would always be detached. He'd worked so hard to develop it. He hated being a father. The most I could hope for was a friend.

When was it that I knew I couldn't audition? Was it when I realized I didn't know in which key I should sing "Pennies from Heaven"? Was it when I surmised that they wouldn't even let me audition without having a green card? No, I think it was in the bathroom, when I gazed at the underarm hair Mitch had pointed to that night. It came away quickly under the blade of my father's razor. I was grooming myself into a woman, into the specter of my mother, even though I had already ditched the high-heeled tap shoes that had made my heels bleed. I was back to my flat reds with the bows, my lucky leotard with the fraying seams.

These were my two choices: shave the armpits, put on lipstick and rouge, brush out my hair, and sing "Pennies from Heaven" in the wrong key and return home with a comparatively unremarkable audition story; or return to the rainy corner on Columbus Avenue and anticipate the coming winter and Herb Browning's nightly visits.

I walked out of the bathroom and held my arms up over my head. "Look," I said to Gerry, "I'm bleeding."

He stopped tapping on the practice pad and glanced at my nicks and cuts. "You're not used to it," he said.

I nodded and dropped my arms.

"Don't worry," he continued. "That's just baby skin under there. It'll toughen up."

I returned to the bathroom and shoved a wad of toilet paper into each armpit. A buzzer suddenly sounded in our room, indicating that we had a telephone call to answer.

"You get it," called Gerry.

I kept the toilet paper clamped against my skin and walked out into the hall. Finally, I realized, my magician was calling me, that we were going to do a little mutual conjuring at last. I thought of the dancing cane, the journey down south, how we'd lie in a cotton field together, how he'd collapse me with his urgent hands and make my blood sing.

The telephone was three doors down. I picked up the receiver. "Hello?"

"Hi, Alice?"

My stomach tightened and I stopped breathing. I wanted to hang up but the receiver seemed frozen in my hand.

"Are you there?"

A weak voice crept out of me. "Yes."

"This is Herb. Herb Browning."

I wondered how he'd found out my room number. I hadn't told him my last name. I wondered how he'd described me to the clerk at the front desk, and why he was so interested in a woman whose real face he'd never seen.

"Yes?"

"Now listen. I'm down here in the lobby. Just downstairs. Why don't you come down here and we'll go out for lunch somewhere?"

"It's—" I tried to think of an excuse, "a little late for lunch."

"Oh, come on. Just for a couple of hours. It's my day off. Just a drink or something."

I made myself take a deep breath. I tried to picture what Herb might look like out of uniform, what he was wearing, if he had any hair underneath his cap. He emerged in my mind in brown corduroys, plaid shirt, and brown loafers. Everything was brown.

"Um, it's a little inconvenient for me at the moment, Herb."

"Well, how about tomorrow?"

I strained to think of something. Anything. A lie.

"Herb?"

"Yeah?"

"I might as well level with you."

I heard his sigh through the earpiece. "What?"

I bit my lip and forced it out. "It's my father."

Herb cleared his throat. "Yeah?"

"It's just that he"—I switched the receiver to my other ear—"that he's . . . you know . . . that he's very, um, very . . . protective when it comes to his daughters."

"Protective?"

"He's old-fashioned. Herb, I'm sorry. My father won't let me go out with you."

I heard his breath grow heavy against the receiver. I was scared he'd do something crazy, like take the elevator up to our floor and interrogate us both.

"All right," he finally said. "You don't have to say any more. So I guess I'll see you later. I'll see you on Columbus."

I pictured him about to drop the receiver in its cradle and began to relax.

"Oh, and you know what?" he added, his voice turning mean, almost a low growl. "I know your name. I mean your *real* name." He snorted dismissively. "I know it ain't *Alice*."

The phone clicked and he was finally gone. I crept back to our room, feeling nervous, yet relieved.

"Who was it?" Gerry's eyes didn't move from the sheet music.

I flopped back down on my bed. "Officer Browning."

Gerry shook his head briefly. "Did you get rid of him?"

"Yeah."

"What did you say?"

"I said"—I rolled over to look at him—"I said I was gay."

He laughed again, hitting the rubber pad harder. "Did he go for it?"

"Yep."

"I told you he'd go for it, didn't I?"

"Yep."

"Didn't I tell you that'd work?"

I nodded and rested my chin in my hands. "Yes, you did. You sure did."

Gerry grinned and turned his page of music. Upstairs, the trumpet ventured into "Mysterioso" again, a resonating moan sneaking through the changes, sounding better than yesterday, a big improvement on last week. The tone was thicker, fatter, surging up octaves and riding the flatted notes as far as time would allow before triple tonguing down to the end of the chorus and the eventual, inevitable silence.

second

movement

■ 1 ■

It was rumored that New Orleans was obsessed with two things: pleasure and making money. A rich mixture of French, Creole, and black culture, she is America's eccentric old aunt partying on at the tail end of the Mississippi River. I'd heard she boasted the longest social calendar and the shortest life span, the best food and one of the highest crime rates in the country.

She's called the Crescent City because she sits on a quarter-moon curve in the river and was built on a swamp, six feet below sea level. The French called it the Floating Island; the English christened it the Wet Grave. I could still feel the swamp's haunting presence, especially when I gazed down the streets, flat as billiard tables, or when I saw the aboveground graves that looked like a village of tiny marble and stone houses, replete with Greek columns and slanted roofs, angel statues and gardens.

The only part of the city that acknowledges the twentieth century is the business district, which begins at Canal Street and stretches into the next few blocks. I found the rest of New Orleans to be caught in a kind of time warp, somewhere between Reconstruction and the nostalgic afterglow of the now-destroyed red-light district, Storyville. In the oldest part of the city, the French Quarter, two-hundred-year-old shotgun houses huddled against one another. I remember the main streets of the Quarter boasting larger, more sophisticated, eighteenth-century dwellings. They were built of stone, three or four stories high. Louvered shutters yawned open onto narrow streets. Extravagant verandas sprawled over the pavement, ornamented with iron lace and French doors, lush plants and the occasional tropical bird.

It was rumored to be a xenophobic place. I read in the newspaper about a ninety-one-year-old woman who died in the Tenth Ward never having ventured out of it. She had only experienced the infamously decadent French Quarter, less than a mile away, through what her neighbors had told her and what she saw on TV. Similarly, those in the French Quarter—a lost herd of impoverished artists, waiters, buskers, strippers, musicians, tarot card readers, shoe shiners, and hustlers (aptly christened the Quarter

Rats)—rarely ventured beyond the right-angled boundaries of Esplanade and North Rampart Street.

The city's two obsessions, pleasure and making money, have become grafted onto one another, conjoined like Siamese twins sharing the same spine, one set of limbs writhing in some Calinda dance, the other simultaneously counting gold coins and sipping coffee. But make no mistake, the pleasure side is stronger, dragging its twin all over town, from opium den to fish fry to jazz joint, shimmying and hucklebucking until the money runs out.

2

It was into this dervish of Mardi Gras beads and brass bands that my father and I descended on October 21, 1983. Perhaps already sensing the pulse beat of the French Quarter, Gerry bought a fifth of vodka before we boarded the plane. Or maybe we tossed down one drink after another in relief and celebration of the fact that we had survived three months on the streets of New York City, that we had made good money and were escaping with a profit.

Whatever it was, we staggered off the plane with only two fingers left in the bottle, and my father muttering, "New Orleans, the land of dreams." I called around for a hotel while Gerry sat on the sidewalk, singing to himself. I suppose we were feeling extravagant after all the hard work in Manhattan.

Suddenly we found ourselves sitting in a long black airport limousine. I don't remember much about the drive, but I do recall that the chauffeur was kind enough to carry both Gerry and his luggage up the path to our suite in the Hansel and Gretel Hotel.

After we'd paid and tipped, Gerry lay prostrate on one of the beds for only five minutes before springing up and declaring that we should go out on the town. I think both of us had been too intimidated to suggest such a thing in New York, but here in New Orleans we would make up for lost good times, and we danced out onto Burgundy Street.

We knew nothing of the crime rate, nothing of the murder figures. It was late evening, and we wove down one of the most dangerous streets in the Quarter, admiring the quaint shotgun houses and the flashing lights that illuminated the gate to Armstrong Park.

We entered the first bar we came to, which looked as if it had been salvaged from a western movie: sawdust on the wooden floors, a high bar and stools, "Stand by Your Man" crooning from the jukebox. More vodka was consumed. It was a while before I realized I was the only woman there. Suddenly we were surrounded by a tribe of convivial young men, who were hooting and laughing at Gerry's jokes. He bought them a round, and in between toasts we found ourselves snorting from their bottle of amyl nitrate and rolling around in the sawdust in rushes of ecstatic laughter.

We should have gone back to the hotel after that, but no, the Swamp Boogie Queen had us in her clutches. The tribe of men swept us down St. Peter's Street and onto Bourbon. Music blared from every corner: Dixieland, rhythm and blues, soul. An elderly black man, dressed in a suit and a red bowler hat, sat in the huge open window of a bar and played a honky-tonk piano. Excited revelers swarmed up and down the street, gulping from pint-sized go-cups of beer. Someone dressed up in a chicken suit was handing out pamphlets. And a team of football players second-lined down the middle of the road, bobbing sequined umbrellas above their heads. The only other thing I remember about that night was that we ended up in another gay bar full of bare-chested men in tight jeans. It was smoky and crowded. Donna Summer blared through the PA system. And a man I was talking to about Judy Garland, who had a pair of ruby slippers tattooed above his left nipple, suddenly pulled me into his arms, stuck his tongue in my mouth, and kissed me until my knees buckled and my arms fell limp.

It was an apt introduction to the lusty city. I don't remember the man's face, nor how Gerry and I made it back to the hotel that night, or even the names of the jovial gentlemen whose amyl nitrate we continued to inhale during our sojourn through the Quarter. I do, however, recall the recriminating hangover that followed the next day, and how Gerry arose from the previous night comparatively unscathed, a little puffy around the eyes, a smudge of red lipstick on one cheek, while I could barely lift my head from the pillow even though I was convinced I was ready to spew.

■ 3 ■

During the two years my father and I spent in America performing, we lived in twelve different places. We moved more often than that, however, leaving and eventually returning to the same crummy hotel or boarding-house. As time passed, the rooms grew smaller, danker, and cheaper, and our definition of a livable space became more flexible.

But back then we were pampered and naive gypsies. On our first day in the city we were out in the Quarter, grueling hangovers and all, trying to find an apartment. The Crescent City was not only slower and more intimate than New York, she was also cheaper and more available. Instead of a room costing between four and five hundred a month, the French Quarter Realty gave us keys to empty two-bedroom apartments that fetched only around three hundred and fifty a month.

After tramping through the heat and dust all day, dehydrated and nursing a headache, I became enamored of a nineteenth-century apartment on Ursuline Street. It was on the second floor of a building painted yellow and the living room French doors opened onto a small veranda overlooking the street. As I skipped beneath the high ceilings, I was already dreaming about having my own room again.

Gerry was more hesitant. He turned in small circles, biting his bottom lip. He thought we'd better play it safe and not fork out a security deposit, that we shouldn't get tied up in a lease until we found out how much money we could make down here. I probably began to pout. We had over four thousand dollars in the bank, and if we'd been a hit in New York, surely we could make it in this little town.

The stern, overweight woman in the French Quarter Realty was not so easily convinced, however. After glancing at our lease application, she drew on her menthol and began shaking her head. No one, she said, would rent us an apartment with no references, no social security number, and no dis-cernible income. Neither my wide eyes and pleading nor my wad of trav-eler's checks could convince her otherwise.

I wandered about dolefully after that. But I think my father was secretly happy. He has a peculiar aversion to gas bills and garbage nights. Since his final separation from my mother, he's always lived in single rooms. He envisages domesticity as a huge bureaucracy of security deposits, shopping days, and lawn mowing. He prefers to let the grass grow and eat out. I didn't go in for all that domestic stuff myself, but I longed for my own room, nothing fancy, just a small space into which I could occasionally disappear.

■   4   ■

A fifty-dollar-a-week room on the first floor of the Rebel Arms was the antithesis of what I had in mind: one lumpy bed in a corner, a murky brown carpet pockmarked with cigarette burns, a few bits of forlorn furniture, imitation-wood paneling on the wall.

We first encountered the owners—two fat, bearded brothers decked out in biker gear—as they stood on a bright green imitation lawn that was unrolled across their courtyard. They were drinking cans of Dixie beer. I remember a pregnant woman wandering around, too, a half-clad urchin at her feet. She was also drinking Dixie, and smoking Marlboro Lights. She was the wife of one of the brothers, but I always forgot which. Sometimes I wondered if they shared her, if they were gradually breeding an empire of Rebels to fill their half-empty building.

The Dixie-swilling bikers didn't demand references or a deposit. They didn't bother with leases or social security numbers. They were indifferent to the fact that we held no steady job. They were happy with the fifty dollars cash-in-hand, and elated when Gerry told them not to bother with a receipt.

Our room sat directly above a noisy, late-night bar called Bonaparte's Retreat, for which the New Orleanian pianist, Dr. John, wrote and recorded a song. I don't remember the lyrics very well, but I do recall that "meet" rhymes with "Retreat" and the chorus is about all the significant people one could encounter there. We met two important people there during our first week in the Crescent City. The first was Leonard, and the second was my father's future wife.

■ **5** ■

Leonard was a divorcé who lived in a former slave quarter on Royal Street and smoked a lot of dope. He was in his mid-forties and worked in the Public Service. His wife had left him for a woman, to whom, after several years, she was still happily attached. Leonard had never quite recovered from this desertion, and his instability occasionally arose and surprised us. He had an ongoing vendetta against his female boss, who was sensitive to odors and who'd complained once about a slight smell emanating from Leonard's running shoes. The next day he pirated my bottle of molasses so he could guzzle it and taunt her all day with his farts. He'd done a lot of research and could fake the conditions of one illness so well that he could convince an unsuspecting doctor to give him a prescription for his favorite drug, codeine. The ultimate irony in Leonard's life was that his former job had been at a local hospital, assessing whether newly admitted psychiatric patients should be committed.

Apart from these occasional lapses in behavior, Leonard was a generous and devoted friend. We met him on our second night in New Orleans, after we'd called into Bonaparte's for a drink to dull our hangovers. It wasn't long before Leonard invited us back to his place for a joint. He was enticing to Gerry because he had a great record collection and really strong grass. I liked him more than most of my father's friends because he read contemporary poetry and played Scrabble; he lent me novels and took me to the art museum; he made us cafe au lait with rum and Kahlua and nutmeg.

■ **6** ■

To get into Leonard's place, you had to unlock an iron gate and walk through a stone passageway that opened into a leafy courtyard. Banana leaves, lush elephant ears, and windmill palms formed a swaying canopy overhead. Velvety moss crept across the brick wall. On your left, double French doors opened inward. The living room was just big enough to accommodate a three-person couch, a coffee table, a TV, and speakers. If you were taller than five-foot-three you couldn't stand up straight because Leonard had a wooden loft on stilts planted in the center of the room. This was where Leonard slept, on a queen-sized mattress that completely filled the upstairs space. A ladder rested in the doorway of the adjoining kitchenette. As you walked in, you noticed a narrow hallway to the right, which led to the tiny bathroom. The walls had been chipped back to their original eighteenth-century brick. For a place so small, the ceiling was unusually high, about twelve feet or so, though the effect was diminished by the loft.

Two or three slaves would have lived here up until the Civil War. It would have been just big enough for them to lie lengthwise on the floor to sleep. Yet for all its ambivalent history, Leonard's home was cozy. It was a cubbyhole filled with music, lined with books, and accessorized with cold bottles of imported beer and the loose joints he rolled.

We enjoyed ourselves so much that night that we didn't leave until four or five in the morning. As we walked back to the hotel along the foggy streets, dawn was already pressing through the oleanders and bougainvillea, the century-old live oaks along Armstrong Park, and we were content in that misty netherworld of creole cottages and iron lace, Venetian glass and casement windows. We could live here, we decided. We could live here and be happy.

■   7   ■

Our opening night on Bourbon Street was both auspicious and disappointing. After we had lodged ourselves in our room at the Rebel Arms, we decided to make our debut the following evening, a Thursday night. Bourbon Street is the mecca for Southern tourists; several blocks are closed off to make the bars, restaurants, strip joints, and clubs more accessible. I hadn't been up there since our first night, and therefore hadn't sussed out an appropriate pitch. Already I was into the New Orleanian tradition of taking things as they came.

Around six-thirty I slammed the iron gate of the Rebel Arms behind us and we made our way down Decatur Street, dressed in our costumes, pushing our gear. The smell of boiling crawfish from the restaurant next door hung in the air. It was Happy Hour, and tourists tipsy on Hurricanes and Piña Coladas were spilling out onto the street from Tujagues, Bonaparte's Retreat, and Molly's. We turned into a European-style town square named after Andrew Jackson, the general who'd mustered Kentucky sharpshooters and Gulf pirates back in 1814 and defended New Orleans against the British. The square was flanked by two impressive nineteenth-century buildings called the Pontalba Apartments. A manicured park sat between them. St. Louis Cathedral presided at the head. Street artists were packing up their portraits of Elvis and Dolly Parton and pushing their studios-on-wheels homewards. Near the corner of the upper Pontalba, outside a popular cafe, I recognized a magician from New York who'd worked every night only a block away from us. He wore a bowler hat, white shirt, red waistcoat, and black pants. I knew he was Italian, and that his name was Grimaldi. He had a two-day growth and wide, expressive eyes. When we passed, he was entertaining a crowd of children with a series of silk scarves he was pulling out of an elderly man's ear. We briefly waved to each other before Gerry and I turned into St. Peter's Street.

New Orleans at that time was preparing for the 1984 World's Fair, and all the sidewalks and roads were being dug up and repaved in anticipation of the swarms of tourists who'd be flashing money and tipping big. I guided our cart around holes in the street and piles of dirt and temporary wooden walkways. Lines were forming outside Pat O'Brien's Bar and Preservation Hall, yet the Dixieland music blaring from Bourbon Street stole our attention.

You don't have to be in New Orleans very long before you notice something peculiar. Even though blacks and whites seem to live in apparent harmony, there's an uneasiness that lurks beneath all the red beans and rice and second-line dancing. I'd sensed it in the way black waiters averted their eyes when they served me, and the quiet anonymity of aging shoe-shine men.

The intersection of Bourbon and St. Peter's Streets was a microcosm of New Orleanian race relations. Murphy Campo's group, an all-white band, was luring tourists into the Maison Bourbon with a raucous rendition of "South Rampart Street Parade," while Wallace Davenport's Quintet, an all-black band, played "Basin Street" in a club directly opposite called Crazy Shirley's. The windows and doors of the clubs were thrown open, and in the middle of the road, where the two antithetical tunes clashed, tourists clustered with their go-cups of beer, glancing into both places as if they were watching a tennis match. As we passed, I noticed that the Maison Bourbon was almost full, while Crazy Shirley's had only a handful of people at a table

in one corner. Most of the tourists were from neighboring states on their annual vacation—I could tell from the cowboy hats and the breathless melody
of their Southern accents as they called their children. They probably knew
that New Orleans was the birthplace of jazz; some of them even wore
T-shirts that proclaimed it. They no doubt felt compelled to go out and
listen to some, but they didn't seem to want to hear it from the very people
who'd created it.

Gerry and I decided to set up about halfway down the block, away
from all that racket, outside the Court of Two Sisters. The Quarter was a tap
dancer's paradise back then; every few yards there'd be a hole in the road
with a large sheet of plywood slung over it. I took off down the block,
jumped on a couple of sheets, and did a quick sound check, but the wood
was a bit dead. The third or fourth one I came across hadn't been rained on
too much and emitted loud, crisp responses to my double shuffles. I
dragged it up and dropped it beside Gerry's side drum. Fortunately, by that
time, the two bands up the road were taking a break, and Bourbon Street
was unusually quiet.

Already we were attracting a sizable audience—the tourists who hadn't
committed themselves to either the Maison Bourbon or Crazy Shirley's
drifted down and stood about us. A few ducked into the Court of Two
Sisters and refreshed their go-cups. Kids sat cross-legged in front of the tap
board. Leonard peddled up on his red bicycle and stood a few feet away.

Gerry was eager to begin, but I wasn't ready. Somehow, whenever I got
nervous, one of my taps would suddenly loosen. I sat on my wooden case
and tightened it with a screwdriver. Looking up at Gerry, in his red-and-
white striped waistcoat, I noticed he looked just like every other guy on the
street corners here, selling Lucky Dogs from portable stands.

I stood up and dropped the screwdriver in the case. "OK," I declared,
"let her rip."

He placed the tip bucket out in front of us. We launched into a version
of "Sweet Georgia Brown." We hadn't finished the first chorus when I noticed that the crowd was clapping in time with the music. A guy in a ten-
gallon hat and hobnailed boots threw back his head and cried out at the
sky like a hyena. Mothers lifted their younger kids onto their hips and
swayed back and forth to the beat Gerry kept on his woodblock. Suddenly
elated, I found myself in an orbit of syncopated turns, digging accents into
the plywood. People at the back were craning their heads and pushing

forward. We finished off with a double spin and a final *ding* on the cowbell and, while the crowd applauded and threw money, headed straight into "St. Louis Blues."

A few people stacked bricks together and sat on them, their chins resting on their knees. Gerry was rocking from side to side, grooving on a Latin feel, while I counterpointed with a combination of Spanish steps.

When I next looked down, I saw a collage of small black faces pushing toward me. They were all boys, probably between six and twelve. They elbowed and wove between the tourists to get a better look at the strange new act on Bourbon Street. One kid shot between a man's parted legs. A few of them just sat on the ground and studied my feet. They all held cardboard boxes, were dressed in cut-off jeans or shorts. Only a couple wore shirts, while the rest sat about bare-chested, their thin arms and torsos coated in a fine veil of sweat and dust. I noticed they, too, wore tap shoes, or rather, heavy leather walking shoes with taps hammered onto the soles.

After about twenty minutes, when we finally took a break, one boy, who looked about eight years old, jumped up and rushed onto the tap board. He wore a crumpled old fedora, and his shoes seemed to be about three sizes too big.

"Who taught you to do dat?" he burst out. "Shirley Temple?"

Gerry and I glanced at each other and laughed. Shirley was probably the only other white female he'd ever seen tap.

"What's your name?" I asked.

He gazed at the rhinestone buttons on my tail coat. "Pee Wee."

"You tap, Pee Wee?"

He nodded quickly and launched into a rapid triplet step, hopping on his left foot and shuffling with his right. One of his taps was dangling off his shoe, and the nails he'd hammered into the sole were protruding through the leather upper. I smiled at him and nodded back as the step grew faster and faster.

"Oh, man!" shouted another boy from behind, a little taller than Pee Wee. "I can do that." He, too, jumped on the plywood and shuffled his right foot furiously.

"You can't do shit," cried another, as he leapt on beside Pee Wee.

"Oh, yeah? Watch this!"

Suddenly there were about six or seven boys on the board, hammering their taps into the wood, jumping and hopping and spinning. Amused,

Gerry and I stepped back to watch. Dust rose around their bobbing torsos and waving limbs as they willed their feet to move faster and faster.

After a few minutes, they wore themselves out; they seemed obsessed with the competition of it. Several of the older boys ran off down the street, still arguing over who was the best. Pee Wee and another little boy, who tapped with bottle tops nailed to his tennis shoes, stayed behind.

"Come on, Pops," cried Pee Wee. "Lemme beat your drum!"

Gerry passed over the sticks and Pee Wee began an enthusiastic, if irregular, rhythm on the snare and cowbell, while the other boy hit the woodblock with his fingers. Gerry shrugged and laughed, and took a swig of the beer some stranger handed him.

After reclaiming the drum and plywood, we began our second set, and over the next half hour, the crowds swelled and receded like waves. As dusk settled in, a pale half moon eyed us through drifting clouds and a few street-lights and neon signs blinked on. The familiar chink of quarters and dimes falling into our bucket formed a backbeat to the silent flight of dollar notes and the rhythms we willed to the night.

It was just after eight o'clock when we were finishing up " The Sheik of Araby." The audience formed a ring around us and Gerry was singing along with the tape. Then he suddenly took off on a woodblock solo and gave me a four-bar break as I kicked out my final steps.

"I love you all!" he cried to the applauding audience, with that certain gesture the Queen bestows on her screaming fans. I picked up the bucket and began passing it around. People rooted about in their pockets and purses. I made my way through to the back of the crowd and was suddenly standing face-to-face with a burly, unimpressed copper.

"Do you know what time it is?" he demanded.

"No," I said, hugging the bucket. "But that guy there has a watch." I nodded to a thin man dressed up in a green tu-tu and mask.

The cop didn't take his eyes off me. "It's after eight o'clock!"

I nodded again and turned away, determined to ensnare the rest of the drifting crowd. But the copper followed me. "Do you know what that means?"

A woman dropped a handful of change into the bucket. I swiveled around and looked him up and down. "You're going to turn into a pumpkin."

The woman snickered as she turned away. The cop's face reddened. "Look, Missy"—he rested his hands on his hips—"I'll have none of that insolence from you." Sweat rolled down his face. He took his hat off and ran his fingers through what was left of his thinning hair. "No one performs on Bourbon Street after eight o'clock. You got that?"

I paused and glanced at Gerry. "But we've only been out here an hour."

"I don't care if you've only been out here five minutes. You do one more of those damn jigs and I'll drag you both down to the station."

I frowned and noticed the crowds making their way up Bourbon Street, looking for some action. "But why?" I asked. "We're not bothering anyone."

"Look," he finally exploded. "You wanna get in the paddy wagon right now? It's parked just round the corner! I've got strict instructions to clear all you idiots off of Bourbon Street by eight o'clock. Now git!"

I turned and slunk back to the tap board. Gerry glanced at me morosely and began putting away his snare. The cop wandered a little farther up the block, but continued to loiter about until we were all packed up. A few nights later I figured out why he made us move on. At eight o'clock, most of Bourbon Street's indoor entertainment began, and the clubs and bars didn't want any competition.

We were just about to head home when I noticed Pee Wee and the kid who sucked his thumb. They were hurrying an elderly black man up the street toward us, tugging on the sleeves of his coat.

"Here she is!" cried Pee Wee as they advanced upon us.

"She the one!" yelled the other.

The man they had wedged between them was barely five feet tall. He was dressed in a plaid swallow-tailed jacket; the matching trousers had been altered so they looked too short. He had a long gray mustache, a trimmed beard, and a panama hat sitting regally upon his head.

"This here Porkchop," announced Pee Wee.

"She good, man. She dance good!" cried the boy with the bottle tops as he continued to tug on Porkchop's sleeve.

I grinned and shook his hand and introduced myself. He looked strangely familiar.

"Show him how you do it, Shirley Temple!" demanded Pee Wee. "Go on. Do it!"

The copper still had his eye on us from farther down the street, so I didn't dare put my shoes on again. Instead, between the cries and demands of the kids, I began chatting with the old man, and found out that he used to travel around the world with the Harlem Globetrotters as their tiny, tap-dancing mascot, and used to perform to their theme song, "Sweet Georgia Brown."

His voice was soft and dignified, a striking contrast to the rambunctious kids at his side. "I started out here on Bourbon, too," he said. "I not only tapped, but I did acrobatics. Cartwheels, handstands, the lot. My wife used to collect the money in a cake tin." He laughed to himself. "Now I just work the clubs." He nodded at Crazy Shirley's.

Porkchop paused and looked up and down the street. "See all these kids out dancing?" He rested his hands on the heads of the boys. "Well, I taught them. I taught them all."

I smiled at him and nodded. The band from the Maison Bourbon started up a noisy rendition of "When the Saints Go Marching In." Across the street a midget dressed in a dinner suit appeared in front of Sammy's Seafood Restaurant and began coaxing customers inside to sample the best shrimp in the Quarter. A third boy hurried up and sat on the curb and tried to nail a tap to his shoe with a heavy brick.

Porkchop smiled back at me and tipped his hat.

As he was walking off, I heard Pee Wee say, "Yeah, Porkchop. She's a good tapper. She ain't bad. But you still the best, man. You the best of all."

8

How many of us have taken a lover because he reminds us of someone else? Something about the way he gazes at his hands, or yawns without parting his lips. Perhaps it's only that square chin, or the high, definite cheekbones, or a small gap between the front teeth, and all of a sudden you want to touch the smooth hairless skin on the back of his neck and run one finger down his spine.

In New York, Grimaldi and I hadn't taken much notice of one another. We just nodded and exchanged greetings; once or twice he gave us his corner for the night when he knocked off early. But the next time I bumped into him in Jackson Square, he was between shows, and we stood on the steps of the cafe. He began spinning a silver dollar between his fingertips and talked about himself. Occasionally, he'd stop and touch my sleeve and tell me he liked me. He spoke with a rolling Italian cadence and gestured with the spry, quick movements of a commedia dell'arte clown. Years of animated expressions had etched their way into his forehead and around his eyes. He sipped house red from a water glass and smoked Lucky Strikes.

Grimaldi told me he'd acquired much of his magic from an old couple back in Genoa. He explained that he and his sister had been in America three years. They worked the summer season in New York and wintered in New Orleans, like us. While we were chatting, his sister came looking for him. I recognized her as the slim, diminutive beauty who would set up a stand outside St. Louis Cathedral and read palms and tarot cards for money. I was touched by the way Grimaldi tousled her short black hair and told her he'd bring home some fried chicken and beer. I wondered whether he was lonely, too, traveling and living with a relative who provided companionship but could never satisfy those small needs that hummed beneath the skin at night. I watched her tiny frame grow smaller down St. Peter's Street, the way she almost tiptoed off the curb and up the other side. Then Grimaldi flashed a white mouse in front of my face and made it vanish into his mouth.

9

Street performers never work Monday nights because everyone else is broke and stays home. Monday night is the night you take off to party, to visit, to dance. It is the end of your working week, your Friday night, your play day. It was for these reasons that Grimaldi and I rendezvoused at the same cafe the following evening. Our hands kept brushing against one another across the table as we sipped our wine.

Suddenly he dropped a crumpled five-dollar note on the table and swept me outside. Mist was rising around the lampposts in Jackson Square. The wet gray slate was gleaming. I could hear the clopping hooves of buggy-ride horses in the distance, and snatches of Dixieland music filtering down from Bourbon Street. Grimaldi took my hand and led me quickly through the Quarter's foggy, narrow streets. We both hurried, as if it were all predestined, skipping over puddles and taking shortcuts through cobbled lanes. Occasionally, I could sense his pulse fluttering through the grip of my hand, or perhaps it was my own. When we turned into Dauphine Street, where his van was parked, I nervously hugged myself, opened my mouth, and tasted the salty air.

My father had looked a little bruised when, earlier in the day, I'd announced that I'd be spending the evening with Grimaldi. He sat on the balcony and drank a can of Foster's while I dressed. When he walked through the room on his way to the toilet, we caught each other's gaze in the cracked mirror, but he looked away quickly, trying to steal back the disappointed expression he'd allowed to escape.

He wouldn't, however, be abandoned in that awful room with the imitation-wood paneling and the plastic strip clustered with dead flies. Before I could kiss him good night, he grabbed his wallet and disappeared down to Bonaparte's Retreat, where, he said, he would sink a couple of quiet beers.

When I was a kid, a man in a blue Porsche used to pick my mother up a couple of times a week and take her out to dinner. He was a leftover from my parents' penultimate separation, someone who filled the void my father had created. When my mother and father reunited again after two years, the man with the blue Porsche was still hanging around. He was slim, in his mid-fifties, with a graying pencil mustache. He would have looked distinguished if he hadn't persisted in wearing Bermuda shorts and long socks held up by elastic bands. Was my mother trying to entice Gerry into displaying even an iota of jealousy? It never worked. We kids used to watch her unpin her rollers and put on lipstick. As they drove away together, we and our father used to stand at the window and laugh at the nervous goose in the Bermuda shorts who was ten years younger than Gerry and already bald.

We'll call him Max. My mother always encouraged me to talk to him because she knew I loved writing and reading, and Max was a very important reporter for the *Daily Telegraph*. But I mistrusted Max and his newspaper reporting. How could my mother confuse the poetry and stories that erupted out of me that summer with what he did, the daily sports report?

One night Max decided he could no longer tolerate my father's indifference to the fact that his wife was so flagrantly unfaithful. We were living in the two basement rooms on Victoria Street, Kings Cross, at the time. After he dropped my mother home, she walked into the front room, where we all slept, and went to bed. Max, however, pulled a few bottles of beer from the cooler he always kept stashed in the boot of his car. He knew that my father had a gig in Wollongong six nights a week and didn't get home until after one A.M. So he sat himself on the green vinyl beanbag in the back room and started drinking.

This was one of the many periods in my father's life when he wasn't drinking. Or smoking. He was purging. He was on the proverbial wagon. Though I suspect he was smoking the odd secret joint when my mother was out.

I know how the rest of this story goes because the next morning my father laughed about it over breakfast. He told us that he had arrived home sometime around two and noticed light beaming through a crack in the back door. He found Max hunched in the beanbag with several empty beer bottles at his feet. When he called Gerry a swine and tried to stand up, Max fell over sideways and bumped his head on the fan. He dragged himself up again with the aid of the coffee table. He called our basement rooms a slum not fit for dogs to piss in, and wondered aloud what kind of a man my father really was. He wanted to go out to the backyard and settle it once and for all.

Gerry complained the next morning that he had the work of the world getting rid of Max, who either kept parking his bum on the bed, or standing up and taking ill-timed, boozy swings. My father was more intent on folding down his sheet and fluffing up his pillow than being drawn into some protracted fight.

His nonchalance was rewarded. After breakfast my mother walked over to the red phone across the street and told Max she loved living in a slum and that this summer back with her husband had been her happiest in years. I know because she returned from the phone box and told us what had happened.

We all had a good laugh after that and decided a second pot of tea was in order. Max was never heard from again.

As I pinned my hair up in front of the cracked mirror I wished Gerry could have been as casual toward me and Grimaldi.

■ 10 ■

Grimaldi took wide, cavalier turns all the way uptown. He sat back in his seat and drove the big red van as if it were a dodgem car, not worrying about the streetcar he'd just missed grazing or the red light he ran up near Audubon Zoo. I had no idea where we were going, but gripped the dashboard and allowed myself to be taken.

He pulled up at a bright pink mansion, with two neon flamingos grazing on the front lawn. Inside, he ordered wine and we sat at a round table while he ate and ate: jambalaya, corn bread, collard greens, pigs' feet. He ate quickly and copiously, urging me between bites to order something. But I was too excited for food, and didn't want him trying to pay for my dinner. As soon as Grimaldi had consumed his last bite, he dropped more crumpled dollar bills on the table and we left as quickly as we'd arrived.

The place Grimaldi took me to after the Pink Flamingo was called the Maple Leaf. It had a high wooden bar and an antique, tarnished mirror filled the wall behind it. We sat on tall stools and ordered more wine and listened to the zydeco music piping through the speakers.

Suddenly, in the middle of our chat about favorite colors, Grimaldi had another fit of restlessness. He offered to show me the garden in the courtyard. He took my hand and led me outside. The stone-paved patio was sparsely lit, but I could see the pale silhouettes of ginger blossoms and an arbor draped with moonflower vines, whose large white flowers only opened and released their delicious scent at night. Grimaldi mentioned this as his arms encircled my waist, right before our lips met, so that when I inhaled and tasted the wine on his tongue, I also drank in their gorgeous perfume.

■ 11 ■

It was the first time since we'd been in America that I'd left Gerry alone for the evening. While I was drinking wine with Grimaldi, while I was careening uptown in his red van, while I was kissing him in the courtyard of the Maple Leaf Bar, Gerry was wandering around the Quarter, drunk, spending all kinds of money on a woman he'd picked up in Bonaparte's Retreat.

I don't know what time it was when Grimaldi dropped me back at the Rebel Arms that night, but I remember it was pretty late. Upstairs, I found the room as I had left it: The bed was still made and Gerry was nowhere in sight. I figured he was just having a late session with Leonard. I took a shower then lay on the left-hand side of the bed, waiting for his footsteps on the landing. I fell asleep imagining them, and was only vaguely conscious of his arrival when the bedsprings creaked and he nestled his face into the back of my neck.

The next morning, we sipped takeout coffee on the veranda off our room. Gerry reclined in the decomposing armchair. I sat on a milk crate with my back to the sun. The conversation went something like this:

"So what's she like?"

"She's perfect. There'll be no worries with her."

"How old?"

"Oh, probably mid-forties."

"And she's not married or attached or anything like that?"

Gerry shook his head. "Divorced. Lots of bloody kids, though. Seven, I think."

"Hmm . . . She's not a nut or anything, is she? I mean, she'll have to have her wits about her."

"Don't worry. She'll do fine."

I stared sullenly into my coffee. "Where did you say you met her?"

"Bonaparte's. Look, she's really a very nice lady. Down-to-earth. I just walked in last night and there she was, sitting by herself."

"How much does she want?"

"Two hundred."

"That's all? How come she only wants two hundred?"

"Well, if you stopped butting in and let me finish—"

"OK, sorry. Go on."

Gerry leaned forward and lit a cigarette. "So I walk into Bonaparte's, and there she is, sitting by herself at the end of the bar. And I look at her and think, here's the girl for me. So I order a beer and sit down next to her. After a couple of minutes, I turn to her and look into those blue eyes and say, 'Darling, I'm a jazz musician from Australia and my visa's running out. If I give you two hundred bucks, will you marry me?' "

She was a very nice lady, he kept assuring me. She was pretty. She had nice blue eyes. And smart, too. She was a very intelligent woman. She knew all the right places to eat and all the jazz joints in town. And she composed music! he boasted. At one club they were in, Gerry was patting out rhythms against his knees and she was supposedly writing down what he was playing on the white tablecloth. How lucky could he be? And she only wanted two hundred. She didn't mind helping out an old musician in need.

I tried to relax and enjoy the sunlight sinking into my back. Just another one of Gerry's manic fads. Across the road a band was setting up on the sheltered patio of the Mediterranean Cafe. Buggies rumbled by, drawn by dray horses wearing large sunglasses and hats. Below, in Bonaparte's, the jukebox boomed. But I couldn't fight off my unhappiness. I sat hunched on the milk crate and finished my coffee. It was not only Gerry in whom I was disappointed, not only his evening I wished had never happened.

After they'd spent several glorious and tender minutes kissing and touching each other in the pungent, shadowy garden, Grimaldi took Alice's hand and led her back through the bar, around the corner, and down an unlit street to his van. Inside, he closed most of the red gingham curtains except for the ones at the back, which allowed the faint light from the crescent moon to linger on the upholstery. They stood bowed over in the back and undressed quickly. There was a wooden storage cupboard about two feet high that filled the last quarter of the van. They were both thin, and as she lay down on the cupboard and Grimaldi lowered himself against her, his jutting hipbones met hers. He dipped into her quickly. Her legs were still hanging off the side of the cupboard, and she twisted around and raised her knees so she could lie straight. Grimaldi rested most of his weight on his locked arms planted firmly on either side of her shoulders, as he ground her lower back against the cupboard. She tried to breathe and circle her hips in rhythm with his, but her spine dug into the wood when she moved. She felt trapped beneath his insistent pursuit of his own pleasure. Finally, Alice stopped trying to participate and lay still and let him throb away inside her. It would be better next time, she assured herself. In Grimaldi's bed they could be more exploratory, have time and room to discover one another's bodies and desires. The moonlight caught beads of his sweat as they formed on his curly black chest hair. She was hoping he would whisper something or dust the backs of her ears with kisses as he had only a few minutes before in the garden. But he just kept driving the small of her back into the wood.

It wasn't long before he seemed to run out of energy. He pulled away and sat with his head resting in his hands. Too much wine, she thought, and hoped he would take her back to his place, where they could be more comfortable and start over. She knew he didn't live with his sister in just one room, like she and her father. They had a double-story cottage on Burgundy Street, with rooms of their own. She hoped he would take her there, where they could doze in each other's arms.

But instead he backhanded her twice, threw her clothes in her face, and told her to get dressed.

■ 12 ■

Why was sex so often disappointing? I had no stories to explain this, to help me make sense of that void. It was still only when I was alone, when I closed my eyes and ran my fingers across my hips, that I could rock myself until those waves rippled up my spine and made my eyelids dance.

When Grimaldi slapped me in the van that night, a string snapped within me, jerking me back to my childhood bedroom, where my mother's young lover once punched me over and over, until blood filled my nose and bruises rose above my unformed breasts. His hands were never soft with me, even when he'd creep into my room at night to try to stick his tongue into my mouth.

But even by then, by the time I was eleven, I knew that love, that sex, was not supposed to hurt this way. It wasn't supposed to make you ache. The only reason I knew this was because of that time I'd witnessed the slow-drag of my parents' lovemaking, the urgent choreography of their limbs, and the glowing light that had filled my body as I lay there on the floor.

Gerry didn't have one tale about disappointment. Except maybe the one about the acid trip and the ants, and that wasn't really the same as what I was going through. The rest of his stories all brimmed with victory.

My father first had sex when he was twelve, though at the time, he says, he didn't know what he was doing. There was a fourteen-year-old girl who lived up the road named Gloria Lovelace. Gloria was tall and willowy for her age, and you could always see a flourish of white lace just below her hemline.

It was said that Gloria knew things, like how you could get the chain back on your bicycle without dirtying your hands, and the basics of aerodynamics. She knew the names of all the plants and flowers in the area. One day she showed him as they went for a walk. Gloria would point with her long, sun-browned finger and say, "freesia, banksia, hibiscus." Gerry would nod, but didn't repeat them, afraid his breathy voice would sound strange following her lyrical articulation.

She knew the native trees, too: eucalypt, ghost gum, stringybark, bloodwood. They walked farther into the scrub. On a small hill ahead of them was one solitary tree.

"That's a peppercorn!" Gloria shouted. "Race you to it!" And she shot off ahead, so that when Gerry chased her, he saw the shape of her long thighs and how her calves flexed as she sprinted up the hill. When they reached the tree, they collapsed beside one another and looked up at the leafy branches netting the sky. She didn't rest her hand on his, or nestle her head into the crook of his arm. There was nothing tentative about Gloria. She suddenly stood up and unbuttoned her cotton dress. Gerry lay with his hands behind his head. He wanted to ask her what she was doing, but he was too reticent. Her small breasts barely filled the petticoat's lacy cups. She had narrow, square hips, and her tanned skin was brown against the white silk. She didn't take the petticoat off completely, but hiked it up over her hips to reveal a pair of yellow undies, which she lowered.

"This is what I look like," she said, the triangle of fine blond hair facing him. She looked just like a boy, Gerry thought, but with no thing.

It was almost as if she'd read his mind, for she sat on her dress and parted her raised knees. Suddenly a whole rosy universe unburied itself. Gerry sat up and looked closer. Did his sisters possess such slim, beautiful ridges, such ribbons of flesh, which seemed to open like a flower?

It was obligatory now. She didn't have to ask or tell him. He colored a little as his fingers trembled at the button of his shorts. He felt awkward, so much younger than she. The shorts dropped and shackled his ankles. He paused for a moment, still gazing at her, at the furtive pink flesh that looked as tender as the underside of his tongue, at her face, at her green eyes, the way she gazed back and gently nodded. He pulled his white cotton undies down past his knees and stood still, her gaze holding him. He was scared to look down, at what he might find there, where it felt so hard and glowing.

She beckoned him with one hand, as if she wanted a closer look. He went to take a step and, forgetting the shorts around his ankles, suddenly stumbled. He broke the fall with his hands and when he looked up he found himself facing it, the way it was opening itself up to him, that universe which smelled of the sea and shells and the oysters his father ate on Sundays.

What did she want him to do? Touch it? Kiss it? He could feel perspiration beading his brow. They had never kissed. They had never held hands. He went to stand, but before he could plant his feet on the ground she had his cock in her hand and within seconds he was inside her, lost within that warm mouth that was already rising and falling beneath him. She never said a word, not one instructive phrase about what they were doing. He knew why, though: It felt good—better than when he touched himself in the bath, or under the covers at night. He rose and fell instinctively, in rhythm with those narrow, boyish hips. He rested his head against one small, lace-covered breast. He could hear her breath singing harder against his ear. His mouth was dry. He never realized how much of himself he could fit inside another human being. He could feel his balls humming, and the way she danced his cock around inside her, in circles and spirals, and short, sharp thrusts.

"Until all of a sudden," my father always says, "my whole body erupted, and a string of butterflies flew out of my arse."

They were not moths or bees. They were butterflies. They were purple and yellow, they were large and alluring, and the first time he made love, they were fluttering out of my father's arse.

Was my mother's initiation story so perfect and fulfilling? I shall never know. She's demure about such things, stricken with a silence that for me transforms her inner life into a foreign country, so mysterious and unattainable. When I asked her once, she told me she was a virgin until she married. My father says that's crap, that they made love on the couch in my grandmother's kitchen and in a weekend shack in the bush.

Sometimes I want to hold her and shake the stories from her like silver coins from a money box. I'd keep shaking and coaxing out even the one-cent pieces—those small details that, over time, accumulate into something big. Were there butterflies gliding out of her? Did it hurt? Who was he and did she love him? Was she able to reconcile her rosy infatuation with the perfunctory thrusts of a boy who didn't quite know what else to do?

I shall never know. She is shut up tight. The antithesis of my verbose father. She was a virgin till her honeymoon. She has no past to speak of.

■ 13 ■

The only woman in our family who seemed to have sex was my maternal great grandmother. Her name was Ellen. There were lots of stories about her: she was a suffragette back in England; she'd painted graffiti on the steps of Buckingham Palace; she'd helped Emmaline Pankhurst plot the bombing of some government building.

Ellen was eighty-three years old when Gran found her one day at her bedroom mirror, pinning violets to her hat.

"Why are you doing that?"

"I'm meeting Mr. Stanton," Ellen replied. "You know, the gentleman from the bingo tournament."

She was to meet him down at the bus shelter a few blocks away, just for a little chat, to fill in an hour or two before lunch. Mr. Stanton was ninety-four. Ellen didn't get many opportunities to make friends with people older than herself.

Gran was glad to see she'd found a friend and kissed Ellen's cheek before she left. The cluster of violets drooped over the brim of her hat like a veil.

When Ellen didn't return for lunch Gran grew anxious and ran down to the bus shelter, but it was empty. She walked the nearby streets of Marrickville, but returned home alone. She waited in the front room for the rest of the afternoon, staring out the window.

At sunset she saw a paddy wagon pull up in front of the house. Two cops crawled from the driver's seat and walked around to open the back door. Ellen looked small and frail as they lifted her out. The side of her skirt was soiled. Mud was caked to her boots. The wilting violets trailed in a mess down to her shoulder.

She and Mr. Stanton had taken a bus to the Royal National Park and had asked the driver to drop them off at an unofficial stop. Hand in hand, they walked a disused path toward a creek they could hear gurgling in the distance. Perhaps he kissed her the moment the bus was out of sight.

Perhaps it had been more than twenty years since she'd felt a man inside her. His hands were softer than those of her two dead husbands. When he unfastened her corset perhaps it was only then that her breasts had ever met the sun.

They made a bed of maidenhair fern. She was happy to be held by a man again. Over the years her body had felt life come and go as quickly as the beating wings of a fruit bat, and this would be one of her last stolen moments. But as cicadas chorused, as his sweat dropped onto her forehead, as her hips rose to meet his and she listened to the heavy gasps and groans she mistook for pleasure, his muscles stiffened; he held his breath, and his weight was suddenly twice as heavy.

Later she would imagine his heart as a small, fist-shaped grenade, and the sudden gripping of his buttocks by her finely wrinkled fingers as the one fatal movement that flicked the pin inside him.

The funeral was four days later. The Stanton family forbade Ellen's presence at the wake.

She took to her room after that, rarely moved from her bed. I'm not sure what drove her there. Disappointment? Shock? Old age? Perhaps it was desire, and the way it gnaws away at you from the inside when it isn't satisfied.

▪ 14 ▪

I lost my virginity carelessly, unhappily. Like most seventeen-year-old girls, I didn't like doing it, but wanted to have done it.

He had some stupid nickname like Raven. He was a bit of a hustler, used to deal dope and bet on racehorses. He often wormed his way into the spontaneous Sunday-night parties in my father's kitchen. At that time, I was still living in Melbourne and used to visit Gerry in his two-room apartment in Sydney every month.

One day Gerry and I dropped some acid and spent the day riding ferries all over Sydney Harbor and eating ice cream. By early evening, Gerry was exhausted and fell into a deep sleep on his single bed while I watched television. It wasn't long before Raven was banging on the door. Gerry slept through the knocking, and our ensuing conversation.

"So you did some acid," said Raven, leaning in the doorway to the kitchen.

I nodded quickly. I always felt uncomfortable in his presence.

"You know what's really good on acid?"

I didn't take my eyes off the television screen. I shook my head.

He played with the small change in his pocket. "Fucking."

I swallowed. My father was only a few feet away, sleeping.

"Ever tried it?"

"No," I confessed. Over the sound of the TV I tried to explain that I was no longer tripping. It had worn off. It was very mild stuff, anyway. By then Raven was trying to unbuckle my overalls, squeeze my breasts, and lodge his beery tongue in my mouth.

I did not like him. I did not even respect him. So I wonder now why I allowed him to push me to the floor behind the armchairs in my father's room. There was a moment, I think, when it was easier to surrender.

He flipped his cock out of his fly as if he were going to take a piss. Expecting to be confronted with some monstrous thing that might hurt me, I was surprised to see a knot of flesh almost as small and narrow as my middle finger. And when he stuck it in, I felt nothing: no pain, no pleasure. He jerked away on top of me, and I lay there, indifferent. Around the corner of the armchair I could see my father's head nestled into his feather pillow, lost in sleep. I was fairly confident he wouldn't wake up, and as Raven kept up his short thrusts, I was simply preoccupied with the thought that it was all over, this sex thing, and all the teenage anticipation leading up to its enactment. All I could think about was how boring it was, how boring Raven was with his thin junkie's body.

Raven must have been bored, too, for his cock grew limp and he suddenly pulled it out and zipped up his jeans.

At the door, he abruptly swung around and said, "Listen, little lady. You're going to have to learn how to fuck."

He let the door slam behind him, and Gerry slept on. I stood facing the big white wooden door and said, "So are you."

But he didn't hear. He was gone. My father turned over and eased into a gentle snore.

■   15   ■

Gerry is often attacked by ridiculous obsessions. But they usually go into remission as fast as they claim him. He kept raving on that morning about how he could get his green card, which most Australian musicians at that time would have cut off at least one finger for, and how it would enable him to score gigs playing in clubs. It was as if that simple laminated piece of cardboard could induct him into the brotherhood of American Jazz, could even make him a better musician.

My mother had told me about his obsessions when I was a child, and how the spontaneous and irrational activities grew into a kind of pattern she eventually learned to anticipate. Once, he suddenly quit his job at the Trocadero and disappeared for six months. When he surfaced again he was bubbling over with stories about how he'd become a powder monkey in the Snowy Mountains region of New South Wales. His job was simple enough: He just had to be lowered by a rope along the mountains in order to wedge sticks of gelignite into allotted holes. She said he usually dropped these fads when he grew weary of them, whether it was scrap metal dealing, ten-day fasts, or his famous gambling system.

I didn't say much, but waited for this Marilyn thing to die down. A couple of days later he made arrangements for us to meet.

"Why do I have to get to know her?" I said. "I'm not the one marrying her."

But Gerry would not tolerate any resistance: I was going to meet her; I was going to like her; and we were all going to get along famously.

"But it's just a business deal," I said. "What's all this love and friendship crap?"

"It's not all love and friendship," he said defensively. "It's just that I think you'll really like her. She's very intelligent. She's a real good kid."

I was about to say he probably knew next to nothing about her: He had met her in a bar and they had got plastered together. What could he know? What, indeed, could he remember?

But I didn't. I didn't say a word. Just nodded when he told me to meet him in Bonaparte's.

Gerry was sitting alone at the bar when I walked in.

"I thought she was going to be here at four-thirty."

"She is here." Gerry waved at the barman. "She's just taking a leak. She's dying to meet you."

I pulled up a stool and sat down.

"Don't worry," he said. "She's really nice. Pretty, too. Yeah, a real pretty face."

I ordered an orange juice. "Pretty, huh?"

"Yeah. Blue eyes. She's perfect."

As I took a sip of juice I turned to see what looked like a mountain of blue denim, capped with a mop of frizzy red hair, squeezing through the doorway of the women's toilet.

"You must be Gerry's da-au-u-ghter!" A high, Southern drawl echoed through the bar as she lumbered toward me with her arms outstretched.

I stood up and ducked the bear hug, and instead took one of her soft, plump hands and shook it. Her eyes blinked frenetically, as if she had some kind of nervous disorder. She wore lots of mascara, with black particles clinging to each lash. As her mouth broke into a grin, I noticed her lipstick was painted on crookedly. I looked closely at her eyes. Gerry was right: They were quite pretty. But they were not blue; they were hazel, with tiny flecks of gray.

Marilyn Hampton chain-smoked Virginia Slims and would continually burst into high, nervous giggles that made her extra weight momentarily tremble. I sat on my stool, fascinated, watching it jiggle beneath her tight denim shirt every time Gerry cracked a joke. She often laughed before the punch line, and Gerry would have to pause and say, Not yet, not yet.

While my father was buying she drank double Scotches on the rocks. She'd devoured two bowls of complimentary peanuts before I'd finished my juice. I couldn't get much information out of her—she was cagey with details. She came from somewhere in California (doubtful considering that accent). She was divorced. She had five grown children, none of whom lived in New Orleans. She lived outside the Quarter, on Chartres Street. She didn't seem to work, or have any discernible income. When I asked her, subtly I thought, what she did with her time, she just laughed and drained her glass and said she was an amateur surgeon, that she liked dissecting things.

Ambivalence made me rise from my stool and go to the toilet even though I didn't need to pee. I kept reminding myself that none of this would have happened if I hadn't gone out with Grimaldi. It was as if I were being punished, or taught a lesson. I sat on the toilet and dropped my chin in my hands, wondering how long I could hide in there before it would seem impolite.

■ 16 ■

When I wasn't thinking about Gerry's impending marriage, I was worrying about how we were going to make it through the winter with that eight o'clock curfew. And when I wasn't thinking about that, I wondered about Grimaldi.

In spite of what had happened, I still wanted him. The woman that I am now as I write wouldn't want a man like that, but that girl Alice surely did. She made excuses for his behavior—he'd been drunk and had not meant to hurt her. After she'd dressed in the van that night, he'd taken her to a cafe and they'd drunk coffee. I remember they talked about milk, about how he didn't trust what they put in nondairy creamers. He didn't kiss her when he dropped her off at the Rebel Arms, but she didn't kiss him, either.

Winter crept down the cobbled lanes of the Quarter. During the day, Alice walked wider circles around the square, hoping to run into Grimaldi. She sat on benches not too far from the corner on which he worked. She forgot about that other magician she'd been crazy for, the one in New York who always asked for her telephone number but never called. She liked to listen to the crowds clapping Grimaldi on. She was being cool. She might have nodded at him from a distance on her way to the supermarket. She might have paused and chatted to his friends, a group of New York magicians who often hung out in the Pontalba Cafe. But she wasn't interested in any of those other magicians. She would talk to them so that Grimaldi might venture over between shows and join in. Maybe he did once or twice, but he always managed to avoid her eyes, and would withdraw before the departure of the others threatened to leave the two alone.

After about a week of lingering about, I was happy when Gerry gave me a legitimate reason to go and secure Grimaldi's attention. Gerry had questions about the immigration procedure, and Grimaldi was the only person we knew in New Orleans who'd received a green card via a phony marriage.

I went looking for him on a Sunday morning. The square was quickly filling up with brass bands, portrait artists, jugglers, and fire-eaters. Kokomo Joe had his kit of upturned garbage cans and cake tins set up outside the museum. A few of the boys from Bourbon Street were skittering about with their oversized tap shoes. Lothario was working Grimaldi's corner, but would probably give it up as soon as Grimaldi arrived. The magicians had an understanding. I'm not sure what it was, but they never seemed to fight over pitches the way the rest of us were inclined to do. In fact, they were all quite chummy.

I was dawdling about outside the Pontalba Cafe when I noticed Grimaldi's sister rushing by. The wooden sign that advertised her skills and fees as a psychic, and the folding stool upon which she sat, were secured to a metal travel cart, which she pulled toward her pitch on the steps of the cathedral. When she saw me, she swung off her path and hurried over.

"Have you seen Grimaldi?" she asked. The tension in her face betrayed bad news. Her knuckles were white around the handle of the cart.

I shook my head. We both scanned the square, hoping to catch a glimpse of the black bowler hat, the checkered waistcoat. I wondered if Grimaldi had ever mentioned me to her, had ever talked of me at home. Perhaps that's why she'd expected me to know where he was.

I touched her shoulder. "If I see him, I'll send him over."

She smiled, nodded quickly, and hurried off. She was as thin as he, with the same spry, fast movements.

When Lothario finished his show, he turned and skipped up the steps of the Pontalba and ordered a coffee.

"Where's Grimaldi?" I asked. And then, so I didn't appear to be the lovesick lass that I was, added, "His sister's looking for him."

I nodded at the cathedral steps, where she was unfolding her stool.

Lothario looked over and snorted. "Is that what he told you?"

I tried to steady my voice, to prevent my face from coloring. "What do you mean?"

Lothario was trying not to smirk. He wrapped a napkin around his latte and took a sip. "Grimaldi doesn't have a sister. Angelina's his wife."

"Oh," I said, trying to seem only mildly interested. "You mean the one he married to get his green card?"

"Angelina? Of course not. Angelina's Italian. You're talking about Denise. She lives in New Jersey. She did it for nothing. Angelina's his real wife. They come from the same town."

My fists were balled inside my pockets and my stomach was tight but I made sure my face remained impassive.

"Well," I said. "Don't forget, if you see him—" I was scared Grimaldi might turn up right then, "tell him Angelina, that it's very important; tell him she's looking for him."

I turned and tried to walk away casually, to take slow steps, to pause by the brass band and Kokomo Joe, not to keep glancing back. As I wandered through Jackson Square, I tried to slow my heartbeat by taking deep breaths.

The anger that must have been there, stirring in my limbs, only manifested itself in my hands, which I tried to steady by clasping them together into one unbroken fist.

■ 17 ■

Our success in New York had made us a little cocky. Frank Sinatra kept crooning in our heads, "If I can make it there, I can make it anywhere," and we quoted him often. Yet New Orleans, with her eight o'clock curfew on Bourbon Street, proved to be a slippery challenger. We investigated all the possible alternatives. We tried afternoons in Jackson Square, where there were no curfews and a steady stream of tourists. But it was hard to find a place amongst the jugglers, fire-eaters, balloon blowers, bluegrass trios, break dancers, puppeteers, and stilt walkers. There was even a guy who played melodies by rubbing the rims of champagne glasses filled with varying amounts of water. The Rebirth Brass Band thought nothing of setting up beside us. Our rhythms were lost to the cacophony of tubas and trombones and the rehearsed cries from Uri the Unicyclist. We tried moving across the square, outside Cafe Du Monde, where the terrace tables provided a captive audience. I leapt onto the raised foot-wide lip of the fountain and happily tapped my way around it. But the noise of the falling water drowned me out, and I think the customers assumed that the entertainment was provided by the cafe, for it never occurred to them to throw money.

We soon came to the conclusion that day shows weren't worth the effort we had to put into them, and we returned to the slim pickings of Bourbon's six-to-eight shift.

Our regular pitch was outside the Royal Sonesta Hotel, which was paved with smooth bricks that precluded the need for a tap board. The other advantage was that it was only a few blocks up from Canal Street. Consequently, when eager tourists spilled out of their hotels and onto Bourbon, we were the first act they would encounter. An added bonus was the chance that a guest at the hotel might lean out of a window and drop dollar bills, watching me run back and forth with the upturned hat.

The crowds didn't really start thickening until after seven, however. By eight o'clock they usually had enough booze in them to warm up and clap, and even throw some money. Having to stop abruptly at eight and pack up was frustrating. If that copper didn't pounce on us right on the hour, Gerry would occasionally put his watch back ten minutes and we'd play over, and if we were caught out Gerry could hold up his left wrist and feign confusion.

It soon became clear that we had to find a spot very close to Bourbon Street where we could perform later at night: We had gone from making between seven and eight hundred dollars a week in New York to about one hundred and fifty in New Orleans.

Our first strategy, after we knocked off at eight, was to move around the corner from Bourbon and set up on St. Peter's Street, outside the popular Pat O'Brien's. It was a zoo back there: dug-up pavements, drunken revelers tripping over makeshift footpaths, blinking lanterns signaling wet cement, tipsy men in Bermuda shorts wrapping themselves up in fluorescent tape marked "caution." It was just our thing. By nine-thirty or ten, that Southern reserve had dropped away, and everyone careened about in their feathered and sequined Mardi Gras masks, dancing and throwing money. They loved to scream "Faster! Faster!" as I hammered out my triple-time shuffle. We were even stealing crowds from Murphy Campo, whose band was still screeching away in the nearby Masion Bourbon. The line outside Pat O'Brien's began to dissolve: It was cheaper and more fun to buy a beer and hang out on the bulldozed street. Shoe-shine boys worked the crowd as they two-stepped about.

It wasn't long before the club and bar managers called the police. I remember a long and heated argument with the cop we'd met on our first night. He was suddenly trying to bend the eight o'clock Bourbon Street curfew around the corner and down St. Peter's Street to where we worked. When he finally came to the conclusion that he couldn't get us on the ordinance argument, he began inventing new charges against us: interfering with the flow of traffic; disturbing the peace; and public drinking from an illegal container. (My father was slurping Budweiser out of a can instead of a go-cup.)

Gerry crushed the empty beer can between his hands and we packed up once again.

■   18   ■

My father had paid Marilyn half the promised two hundred dollars, had invested time and money in numerous lunches and happy hours, and had loaned her twenty-four bucks before she announced she was three months' pregnant.

I sat him down in our room and counseled him, told him to drop all this marriage nonsense while he could, but Gerry was unperturbed. He was convinced a burgeoning child would look good on paper down at the immigration office, would speed up the process of his green card application.

"But once you're married," I wailed, "you'll be legally responsible for the kid."

"But it's not *my* kid. I've never even kissed her."

"Try that line of reasoning at the child welfare office," I volleyed back. "After she slaps a paternity suit on you. You'll be paying maintenance every month until you're what? Eighty-two years old?"

Gerry sunk a little in his seat and stared at the floor. No one knew who the real father was, not even Marilyn. Or if she did, she was feigning ignorance.

"But I've already paid her half the money!"

"So what? A lousy hundred bucks. Cut your losses and keep going."

He pursed his lips and drummed his fingers against the side table. I thought I had him halfway persuaded, but he apparently had some other course of action percolating in his mind, another scheme that he thought would allow him his cake and the gorging of it, too.

My father and Leonard did all the plotting over three joints and two cups of coffee and rum. At work, when his supervisor wasn't watching, Leonard used one of the computers to design and print out an apocryphal letterhead: *Leonard J. Cabot, Attorney of Law,* with some impressive uptown address and two telephone numbers. A couple of days later Leonard donned his three-piece suit, trimmed his beard, and dusted off his leather briefcase. During his lunch hour he met Gerry and Marilyn in a coffee shop on Canal Street.

"Good afternoon," he said seriously. "I'm Leonard J. Cabot, Mr. Sayer's lawyer."

He ordered a coffee for himself and flipped back the brass lock on his briefcase. He'd typed up the document in triplicate at work. I can't remember the exact wording, even though they'd roped me in to composing it. ("You're good with words. Go on! Make something up . . .") But it basically said that a Mr. G. Sayer was not financially responsible for any children who might be incurred by a Mrs. M. Sayer (née Hampton) after they were married. The document, purred Leonard in his low lawyer's voice, was a prenuptial agreement, very common these days.

The aim of the exercise, from my father's point of view, was to see how Marilyn would react. If she were trying to con him into supporting her child, she'd get all huffy and refuse to sign. That's at least the argument he used with me when I reminded him that the document wasn't legal. ("As long as she *thinks* she's signed a legal agreement, that's the main thing.")

Well, the unfortunate part of it was that she had no qualms at all.

"Didn't bat an eyelid," Gerry later gloated.

She hastily took the black-and-gold fountain pen Leonard produced from his pocket and scribbled her signature beside her typed name.

◼ 19 ◼

I tried to distance myself from both the prewedding bustle and Grimaldi by dating the handsome blond dwarf who worked as a doorman for Sammy's Seafood Restaurant on Bourbon Street.

He had a sharp wit and used to laugh a lot. Even though he was only three-foot-four, he cut quite a dashing figure in his black suit and white bow tie. His name was William. He had a fine, heart-shaped face, brown eyes, and straight white teeth. When he wasn't working he wore jeans and sneakers and was light and energetic on his feet. He had a well-proportioned, muscular body. He used to invite me around to his apartment on his nights off, when he was entertaining friends, and he would serve strong margaritas and jambalaya.

After William's friends left, I used to bathe in his tub. Sometimes he would pop in and squeeze washcloths of hot water down my back. Later I would recline into his white beanbag in the living room, and he would crawl onto my lap and we'd make love to the sound of footsteps and laughter only a few feet away, on the other side of the closed shutters.

I enjoyed his company, but there on his beanbag, that fist of light still did not snap within me, my blood did not sing through my veins. And afterward, even though he'd wrap his tiny arms around me, I'd feel lonely.

■   **20**   ■

My strongest memories of William are centered on the night he took me to the circus. Having had links with that business, he was able to secure two free tickets when the Big Top came to Armstrong Park in November 1983. In a suit and tie, he looked remarkably distinguished, and I tried to match his elegance with a long black velvet evening gown that I'd been carting around for three months but hadn't had the opportunity to wear. I crowned it with an equally unworn black hat, complete with feathers and veil.

He met me in front of the Rebel Arms and took my hand. I was pushing five-eleven in my black patent-leather shoes, but we promenaded down St. Phillip Street together, toward Armstrong Park.

At the circus, we had second-row seats, and he snuggled up into the crook of my arm. Acrobats flipped on the backs of ponies and tu-tued baby elephants danced. A strong man lost his arm inside a lion's mouth and with two fingers extracted a supposed tooth. Sequined trapezists arced and spun above us, barely catching one another by the wrists and ankles, and all the time smiling and triumphant. I whispered to William my childhood longing to be a trapeze artist. He laughed and said he'd try and pull some strings with the ringmaster.

But when the clowns burst out, my stomach began to sink. There was one in patched baggy pants and suspenders who was only slightly taller than William. The little bloke was having trouble mounting a Shetland pony. Whenever he managed to sling himself onto its back, he'd slip head-first over the other side. Crashing cymbals punctuated his every fall. The pony stood there, indifferent, almost deadpan. The clown tried jumping on backward, stood on his hands and wrapped his legs around the pony's neck, even tried to get the poor animal to lower itself to the floor. Children squealed and adults roared. It was just occurring to me how cruel all this conviviality was when a handful of unaccompanied boys in the next row noticed William curled up next to me. I can't remember their exact words, but they began jeering him. They pointed their grubby fingers. William gripped the velvet of my dress and almost cowered. He responded with rehearsed comebacks, but his voice wavered in anger, and this seemed only to encourage the prepubescent brats. They called him Shorty and Midge and wondered aloud about the size of his genitalia, until I stood up and threatened to kick their arses right around the Big Top if they didn't shut up.

■   **21**   ■

Why is the pursuit of pleasure such a nasty business? When I was five, my parents took my sister and me to Luna Park. After vomiting on the Octopus, my bronchial sister clung to my mother, and for the rest of the afternoon, those two explored the comparatively subdued features of the River Caves and the merry-go-round. Conversely, my father and I marched up to the Big Dipper—front carriage—and after the terrifying thrill was over, all I wanted to know was whether we could go on it again. I was even more infatuated with the Wild Mouse, and reveled in the sharp thrusts and hairpin turns, the screams escaping from my own mouth, the wind in my hair, the knowledge that at any moment the carriage might be derailed and we'd go sailing over a sixty-foot drop. Even my father complained that the Wild Mouse was too dangerous as he rubbed at the bruises purpling his forearms. But I was secretly triumphant, and I hadn't yet started kindergarten.

I suppose that's the reason William and I eventually drifted apart: He liked me; he was attentive and easygoing. I enjoyed his company, too. But he wasn't unobtainable the way Romano and Grimaldi had been. If I asked him to, he dropped by. If he said he'd meet me after work, he was always there, before I'd had a chance to untie my shoes.

Even though Grimaldi had hurt her that night, Alice had to torture herself a little longer with him.

■   22   ■

After having sifted through all the clauses and sections and bylaws of my father's immigration papers, I took pleasure in noticing that Gerry was beginning to panic. I'd discovered that in order for the papers to be processed, he needed to produce divorce documents to prove the end of his marriage to my mother. However, he could produce no such thing. He'd lost the documents when he was touring in 1976, and he reckoned it would take too long to write away and obtain a copy.

So, once again, I was sent in search of Grimaldi. This time I found him in Jackson Square and, with a solemn expression, asked him to talk to my father about a serious and rather delicate matter.

Grimaldi was fond of my father, and nodded and followed me back to the Rebel Arms. I walked a little ahead of him, still annoyed by his lies and the way he'd behaved toward both me and his wife, but not completely beyond caving in under a kind word or the suggestion of a quiet drink.

Any weak hopes I had for a reconciliation were doused once we reached our room, however. After my father explained his predicament, Grimaldi just shrugged and waved a blasé hand.

"I marry girl in New York. We no get along. I go across state line. Ten miles. I marry another girl in New Jersey." He laughed and spun his silver dollar between his fingers. "No divorce from first girl in New York. They no check. I marry girl in New Jersey. Six month later, I want green card. But second wife not U.S. citizen. I drive across state line again. North Carolina. I marry girl there. Still no divorce from first or second girl. They no check. I say no married before. Boom-boom! We marry. I get my card. Easy! Easy! Just say you no married before. No marry, no need divorce paper."

My magician was a trigamist, and I was sure he wasn't counting his marriage to Angelina when he ran through his nuptial catalog. I remembered one of his mates had told me they'd married in Italy, that she'd only joined him in New York after he'd received his permanent residence, and that she was still an illegal alien.

As he told his story, he threw me quick, sidelong glances. And I— I was the apotheosis of composure, stock-still except for my nodding, my smiling at the cheek of him, as if nothing had happened between us. I squashed the shock of it down some place deep, thanked him for his counsel, and promised never to repeat what he'd just told us.

But as I showed him out, I couldn't resist asking after his sister.

"I'm feeling kind of confused," I said. "I think I'll ask her to read my cards."

Grimaldi suddenly stiffened. For the first time he dropped his silver dollar, and I took pleasure in seeing it spin and roll down the concrete passageway.

"Angelina is sick," he said, running after the coin. "She no work today." He lost his hat as he ran and it plopped into a puddle left by one of the landlord's boxers.

He retrieved his coin and hat and quickly nodded a good-bye. I smiled to myself as I watched him hurrying down Decatur Street like a nervous thief, almost tripping on the curb as he crossed St. Phillip.

23

After our aborted stint on St. Peter's Street, any hopes we'd had of working on Bourbon after eight o'clock were dashed. We were still averaging only twenty or thirty dollars a night for those meager hours between six and eight. Afterward we'd trudge home, bathe, and then walk over to Leonard's place to forget about it all. At that time, we weren't making enough money to cover our expenses, and every Monday morning, when the rent was due, I'd have to walk down to the bank and draw it out from our New York profit.

We tried one more alternative before we gave up and began working days.

He was nicknamed Spinner, because if things were going badly and crowds were thin he could put down his clarinet and draw a sudden audience by executing a series of backflips across Jackson Square. Looking at him, you'd never think he had it in him. He was short and on the tubby side, and if he wasn't playing his clarinet, he usually had his mouth full of something else: strong black coffee, a cigarette, a chocolate croissant.

We initially met Spinner in Molly's Irish Pub on the night of our first Thanksgiving Day. It had been a rather depressing celebration for us. We weren't quite sure for what the Americans were being thankful. All we knew was that it was a day on which even the most independent person became disturbingly familial. Leonard flew back to California to spend a few days with his mother. William disappeared into Metairie. The streets of the Quarter were empty and the sky was solemn and overcast.

Holidays are not particularly joyous occasions for street performers. We're usually on the road, away from our families, living in some cheap flat or room, or in the back of a van or car. Except on New Year's Eve, we can't work. And in America the loneliness is perpetuated by the fact that the major holidays fall in the dead of winter.

With our closer friends out of town, we weren't invited to anyone's house to tuck into turkey and cranberry sauce before an open fire. Instead, it was an avocado each from the A&P, and a ferry ride across the desolate Mississippi to Algiers. The streets were empty as we walked along them, waiting for something to happen.

Nothing much did. And we ended up in Molly's Irish Pub that night, drinking mugs of flat beer with the other itinerant musicians and performers who had nowhere else to go. A lot of the local musos were bored and had formed a Dixieland band for the evening, playing for tips and drinks. There were about nine or ten in the group. Most were half-drunk and didn't care if the drummer dragged or if the trombone was out of tune. They played all the old New Orleans standards, and even managed to make the ballads sound bawdy and pleasantly rude.

This is where we first found Spinner, standing in the pair of oversized black tails he'd found in the garbage can outside a witchcraft shop on St. Phillip Street. During the break, he bragged loudly about his discovery in his cultivated Southern drawl, and when he found out I was a tap dancer, demanded that I go home and bring back my shoes.

24

What sustained me during those days was not the prospect of "breaking into show business," nor the hope of meeting a man I could love, but the quiet knowledge that I was now lingering on the edge of my father's stories. I wasn't exactly a protagonist, but listening to him yarn to Leonard about our months in New York, I found myself occupying a minor subplot of his life. This alone created a little sense out of the chaos of my twentieth year.

I was beginning to become aware of this around the time we began working with Spinner. One morning in particular rises above the hours and days of performing, all the scores of times Spinner played "Muskrat Ramble" exactly the same way, note-for-note, breath-for-breath. It was a weekday morning, and instead of going straight to Jackson Square, Spinner decided we should hit the Moonwalk first and catch the tourists who wandered along to get a closer view of the river.

The Moonwalk is a raised area of the levy paved with gray slate and garnered with bougainvillea. It makes a good lookout point, especially at night. It is supposed to be the New Orleanian Lovers' Lane.

It didn't look particularly beguiling at ten o'clock in the morning, but we were there for sustenance, not romance. We set up quickly, close to the ramp up which the anticipated tourists would flock. By ten-fifteen we'd only earned a dollar from a Japanese couple, and that was because they'd wished to be photographed—the woman blowing into Spinner's clarinet and the man pretending to beat the shit out of Gerry's drum.

My father dug his hands in his pockets and kept gazing out over the river. He leaned against a railing and, if I didn't know him better, I'd say he looked wistful. I wandered up beside him and gazed out too, watching a tiny tugboat drag a rusting carrier ship upstream.

"I remember when I was about eighteen," he said. "I went to the State Theatre in Sydney and saw this movie called *Syncopation*. It was the life story of Rex Stewart, a trumpet player. I saw it about a dozen times, you know?"

Gerry smiled, still gazing out over the water.

"King Oliver played the cornet in the movie. His band would jam on a riverboat right here on the Mississippi. There were never any white people on board. It had a low ceiling and red-and-white checkered tablecloths. The lights were turned down and on the tables were beer and wine bottles with burning candles stuck in them. The King would play the blues, you know, real slow. And sometimes, sometimes while they were playing, he'd cut the band off and give the dancers four bars. During the breaks, you could hear their feet dragging across the floor all in time together, all in rhythm. Then King'd bring the band in, moaning and wailing through his horn. King was different from Louie, he was more blues, more soul.

"Anyway, in the movie, young Rex Stewart's mother wants Rex to go to college and play 'the good white man's music.' So Rex goes along, but he can't understand all the theory—he just gets confused. It doesn't mean anything to him. So he starts sneaking out at night, you know—he's only a kid—and he goes down to the riverboat to listen to King Oliver. One night he takes his trumpet with him and sits in the front row with it, looking up at King. So, of course, King Oliver asks Rex to come up and play with him. Before they start, King whispers to Rex, 'Now listen, you just follow me.' And it became a regular thing. And King becomes Rex's teacher."

We both watched the tugboat chugging against the current. Spinner was sitting on the other side of the Moonwalk, smoking a cigarette, not listening.

"After a while," continued Gerry, "his mother gets suspicious, see, and follows Rex down there one night. When she sees that he goes to the riverboat she goes berserk and abuses King Oliver for leading Rex astray. She says, 'I want Rex to grow up to play the white man's music, not the devil's music. Who do you think you are, doing this to my boy?'

"And King Oliver, he was real cool, and he says to her, 'Once in a while, the great Lord above drops a tiny spark into somebody. If you mess with it, that spark can get snapped out: one, two, three—' " Gerry clicked his fingers in quick succession. " 'But if you leave it alone, it's going to grow into a great big ball of fire, giving off so much heat that after that boy dies, folks'll still be able to sit around that fire and keep warm.' "

Gerry's voice dropped, his imitation of a deep-throated American accent softening. " 'Now you leave little Rex with me, and I'll watch over that fire of his.' "

My father paused for a moment, resting his arms against the railing, and he relaxed into his normal speaking voice. "And after Rex grew up and became famous," he went on, "one night he had his trumpet and was sitting out in his backyard with King Oliver, and he says, 'I wanna blow a star, King. I wanna blow a star out of the sky, just for you.' "

There was silence, a stillness haunting the river, like it, too, was listening to my father. Even the tugboat slowed down and nodded in the current. Standing there beside him, I remembered the story well. And other things, too. Like how he taught me to listen. Some nights at home the lights would be turned out, candles lit, and the living room would be charged with music. He'd begin by playing Benny Goodman; then, as the night progressed, he'd work on up through the big bands, Count Basie, Ellington, and then onto Coltrane, Miles, Mingus, and Dolphy. He used to do it in increments so the more modern or avant-garde music sounded natural and necessary rather than an isolated peculiarity. He'd work himself up into a boozy trance, squeeze my hand, and hiss, "Listen, listen . . . See, they play in the cracks. The cracks. You hear that?" Then he'd start patting out rhythms on my head or scatting drum phrases into the darkness.

Somehow, standing on the Moonwalk that morning, the Rex Stewart story sounded different. The river before me was *the* river, the river upon which everything had begun.

We looked around to see a small crowd of people gathered near us.

"OK," called Spinner, dropping his cigarette. "Let's get started. 'Basin Street.' "

He counted us in, and off we went, into the blues. Spinner's tone didn't sound too bad that morning, and Gerry was driving a snarling, growling press roll out of his snare that sounded as if he were warning the audience to watch out for him. He continued to gaze out over the river as he played, and after hitting the cowbell for the first time, he abruptly turned away from it and nodded to me.

I slipped into my solo easily: two bars straight tempo, two bars doubling. I closed my eyes, and the checkered tablecloths rose up to meet me. Gerry was giving me two-bar stops. There was suddenly a crowd shuffling around in the dark. What was I doing? Triplets? Double shuffles? Syncopated wings? I was doubling the tempo all the way by then, Gerry playing underneath me, coaxing me on. The candles were burning, the people were dancing. Sweat beaded my hairline, and gorgeous flatted fifths oscillated into falling stars, slow moans, the way my father used to scat. . . .

I spun around and Spinner came in with the chorus. My father let out a triumphant cry and the audience cheered. And I was suddenly flushed and self-conscious, barely able to recall the patterns that had freed themselves against the Moonwalk's slate, only the way I'd imagined those couples slow-dragging against the Mississippi's rhythm.

We continued to perform as money flowed into Gerry's side-drum case. In between tunes, we paused as the tourists shouldered their way in front of one another to get a snap of the "real live New Orleans jazz band" playing traditional music on the street. As long as Gerry and I kept our mouths shut, they didn't know the difference, and as Spinner was from Kansas City, we let him do all the talking.

"*Ladies and gentlemen!*" he bellowed, raising his clarinet above his head. *"This is . . . the Toulouse Street On-the-Lam Street Band! Featuring the Thunder from Down-Under Tap Dance Revue!"*

He swept an expansive hand in a spiral above his head. "Now don't push or shove," he cautioned, picking up the side-drum case, "unless you have bills."

He then began the introduction to "Fidgety Feet." Gerry and I joined in, and the tourists kept snapping photos until the calliope on the riverboat not far away from us suddenly chimed out the melody of "Way Down Yonder in New Orleans." It was a loud, piping sound, something like an amplified jewelry box, and it completely drowned us out.

"Oh, this always happens," Spinner said as he shook saliva from his clarinet. "At eleven o'clock, on the dot. You can set your watch by it, that calliope goes off and plays for half an hour."

We decided to pack up and move to Jackson Square. The audience meandered off toward the river. Gerry dismantled his side drum. Spinner lit another cigarette and I slipped off my shoes.

The three of us drifted back down the stone ramp toward Cafe Du Monde. The sound of the out-of-tune calliope grew fainter than memory. And all I could hear was a slow blues, a walking bass line, and just within earshot, the breathy melody of my father's voice, and how, later that night, he'd describe to Leonard the way we'd just performed.

■ 25 ■

The walls of the witchcraft shop were uneven and pockmarked with what looked like several cheap paint jobs. At that time, it was a dark yellow color. A wooden balcony on the second story shaded the sidewalk, though the entire building seemed to sit in constant shadow. It was even darker inside. The only illumination came from the trembling flames of three beeswax candles in a black candelabra propped on the glass counter. I squinted, and could discern the outlines of bottles along the shelves. They were filled with herbs and powders and were labeled by someone with a fine, willowy hand. A colony of gris-gris dolls lay on a table, their hand-sewn limbs almost bursting with some secret, potent stuffing. They were not unlike the rag dolls of my childhood: embroidered faces, woolen hair. There were lots of trinkets on display, too: metal rings, stones, plaster statuettes of saints, votive candles. A few small skulls sat grinning from a shelf above a bejeweled iron crucifix.

When I took a second glance at the candelabra I noticed for the first time two men dressed in black who were perched behind the counter.

"Come on over and meet everyone!" bawled Spinner.

Gerry and I crept toward them.

"This is Thomas." Spinner gestured to the man on his left. He was the older of the two and his hair and beard were beginning to gray. "And this is Pete." The man on the right was so overweight the buttons on his black shirt threatened to bust off as he raised one leg to cross it. Pete's black hair was slicked back with Brylcream, but the series of dark ringlets that fell around the nape of his neck had been spared. His white, perspiring skin was gleaming in the candlelight.

Thomas folded his arms across his chest and scrutinized us. After a few awkward moments, he suddenly barked, "So you wanna room?"

Gerry nodded. I couldn't help staring at the jungle of Spanish moss that hung in ghostly tendrils above their heads.

"Where you from, kid?" he snapped at me.

My gaze dropped down to Thomas. His eyes looked as if they contained no iris, just big black pupils within yellowy balls.

"Australia."

"Long way from home. Watcha doin' here?"

"Busking. Gerry and I are busking." I swallowed, then added, "On Bourbon Street."

"He your father?" Thomas jerked his head toward Gerry.

I wondered why he was asking me all the questions. Everyone else always spoke to Gerry. I clasped my hands together and nodded back at him.

"Then why do you call him Gerry?"

"Because," I said without thinking, "because that's his name."

"Oh," Thomas smiled and turned to Pete, "we got a real Einstein here. Don't let the sailor suit fool yer."

Pete just sat there like a straight man, grinning and nodding his head.

Thomas narrowed his eyes and regarded us for a few more moments. "I got one room out the back. It's on this side." He jerked his head across his left shoulder. "Right next to my apartment."

He rose from his stool and almost glared down at us. "This is my special side. I only keep people I like on my special side. The other side"—

he pointed his finger to his right—"is where I put all the animals. The crazy, rowdy bunch. I figure if I keep 'em all together, they won't bother me and other normal people who live on this side."

Thomas paused and his mouth almost twisted into a smile. "So you're pretty lucky, huh?"

I sucked on my bottom lip and stared at a collection of feathers displayed in a fan shape within the glass box. I wasn't sure if I wanted to be considered normal by a man dressed in black with a five-pointed star hanging around his neck, sitting in front of a shelf of glass canisters marked Powdered Tahitian Mandrake Root.

"You bet," said Gerry, nudging me.

"Yeah," I added. "Can we have a look at the room?"

"Sure." Thomas turned and hollered through an open door that led into his apartment. "Have you got the keys to the vacant room?"

A woman's voice filtered back, "No, they're with all the others."

Thomas began fumbling about behind the counter. After a few moments, the woman appeared in the doorway. She was tall, and I could see she was self-conscious of her height by the way her shoulders curved inward and by her slightly bowed head. She wore a long, unadorned white dress, a bit like a Christmas angel. I half-expected to see some cardboard wings sprinkled with glitter flapping at her shoulder blades. If her blond hair had been shorter she could have passed as a kind of cosmic Princess Di.

Thomas finally found the keys. He stood up, sucked in his gut, and pulled up his trousers.

"This here's Athena. We run the shop together. She's the High Priestess of this area."

"Really?" exclaimed Gerry, barely containing the mocking edge to his voice. "Well, I'm pleased to meet you."

Athena stared back warily and nodded, unsure if Gerry was being facetious.

We followed Thomas through the store and onto the street. Between the shop and the adjacent gay bar was a tiny gate barely big enough for a grown person to fit through. I had to duck my head, and we walked single file into a long dark passageway with galvanized pipes running along the walls. The ominous feel of the passage was relieved by the strong sunlight at the end that drew us into a large paved courtyard. A two-story structure on the left adjoined the rear of the shop, with a flight of wooden stairs along the side. Another structure at the end of the courtyard looked as if it had been divided into two apartments. Everything had been painted the same murky yellow with green trim. We followed Thomas to a door underneath the stairs. He undid the padlock, pushed the door back, and Gerry and I stepped inside.

The room had been painted bright pink. Brown linoleum was cracking and splitting beneath our feet. The ceiling was so low I could raise my arm and touch it with the tips of my fingers.

But the most imposing characteristic of this room was the Eye. Painted in the middle of the front wall was a five-pointed star, a couple of feet in diameter, and in its center was one large, imploring, black and blue eye that seemed to follow me wherever I moved. I tried to ignore it, but it looked right into me, an X-ray machine searching for some accumulated tally of sins.

Gerry leaned against one wall. He didn't even seem to notice the eye. "How much you want in advance?"

Thomas shrugged. "Just a week."

"OK," said Gerry.

Spinner was thrilled at the prospect of us all being neighbors. When we stepped out into the courtyard, I asked him the location of his room.

"On the other side," he replied. "Wanna come over for a cup of coffee?"

"No thanks," I said. "I've got to go back to the Arms and pack."

◼ 26 ◼

Since our rent was due at the Rebel Arms, we moved into the pink room that same afternoon. One of our walls connected with Thomas and Athena's apartment; the opposite one adjoined the room of a small skinny man named Renoir. Between his room and ours was a doorway blocked only by a sheet of imitation-wood paneling. On our first night there, I awakened to the sound of moans pressing through the blocked doorway. After I rested my head against the paneling for a few minutes, I was convinced he was making love to an imaginary woman. No one responded to his "baby, baby, baby's." There was no sigh, no muffled groan, no answer when he hissed, "Do you like it there, baby? Do you like it?"

I became intrigued, and dragged a pillow and blanket off my bed and made myself a little nest beside the paneling. After a while, he seemed to grow impatient with the absent woman's silence. He began grunting, "Fuck you, fuck you." I could even hear his breath breaking into short, sharp pants. His voice rose and I could clearly hear him crying, "Take that, you bitch," and his fist thumping at a pillow. In my mind, Grimaldi slapped me again, and I felt the sting of his hand on my cheek. I heard something hit the wall and shatter, and the man finally wailed like a banshee. I glanced across at Gerry, who slept on impassively. After the wailing stopped, I heard the man go out into the courtyard. When he didn't return, I rubbed my cheek, curled back into bed, and fell asleep.

In time, we met the rest of our neighbors: a gay couple upstairs; a transsexual, Terry, and her lover, Daryl; and a Vietnam vet named Byron. We only saw Byron when he clumped down the stairs for his morning evacuation in the communal bathroom. He refused to come to happy hour with us at Bonaparte's Retreat because, he maintained, the Vietcong were in there, waiting for him.

These were the normal people to whose side of the witchcraft shop we'd been assigned. When I went to write my mother a letter, to let her know our new address, I was suddenly overwhelmed with all the things I could not tell her. I could not tell her the real circumstances under which we were living. I could not tell her about Romano, about Grimaldi, about my loneliness. I could not tell her we had snorted amyl nitrate on our first night in New Orleans, that my father was preparing to marry another woman in order to get his green card.

Instead, like my father, I embellished the good things and left out the bad. My embroidery didn't make me feel too guilty. Actually, my mother is a great "don't tell" advocate herself. She allowed my sister and me to feed stray animals over the years as long as we didn't tell our father, who thought that three children were difficult enough without further complicating his life with pets. Once, when I was ten, and we were on our way to visit my mother's mother, she gave us one of her sternest warnings, "Now, when we get to Granny's, don't tell her your father and I are back together again. You know she has a bad heart."

I smiled and doodled in the margin.

"Don't forget to tell her about Bourbon Street," said Gerry. "And the black kids. You know, the Shirley Temple bit."

We were sitting in one of the doorways that faced the courtyard, trying to catch the morning sun. I nodded and edged away from him, wanting to keep my notebook private.

Suddenly, the green doors we were leaning against swung inward, and Gerry and I dropped backward and found ourselves at the feet of Pete, the assistant warlock.

"Good morning, fine people!" he declared.

I stood up and let him through into the courtyard.

"Isn't it a fine day?" Pete's chubby hand gestured at the sky. He reminded me of an actor in an amateur play. His movements were stiff, and his comments seemed more like rehearsed dialogue than casual small talk. Instead of the imposing warlock Thomas seemed to be, Pete looked more like a kind of fallen Friar Tuck in a high school production of *Robin Hood*.

"So you live back here, too?" said Gerry, squinting up at him.

"Yes," Pete nodded. "No excuse for being late for work!"

"So you really believe in all this witchcraft stuff?"

"Oh, yes!" Pete's eyes widened. "I let the spirit guide me. The spirit governs everything. I have to ask the spirit before I can go through the mirror, you know."

I stopped doodling and looked up. "The mirror?"

"Yes, I have my mirror in there." He nodded at the closed doors of his apartment. "I can go through it any time I want."

"Where do you go?"

"Any place I like!"

As I nodded, he lit up a Kool and rolled back onto his heels.

"We have this strange star painted on the wall of our room," I said, "with a big eye in the middle of it. Who'd ever paint a thing like that?"

Pete drew on his cigarette. "I painted it." He was looking exceedingly proud of himself, or was acting out some kind of manufactured pride, I couldn't tell which. "I was living in that room last year. The five-pointed star is a symbol."

"So what's the eye got to do with it?"

"The eye"—he widened and rolled his own eyes, taking a practiced, theatrical pause—"the eye represents the spirit."

"The same spirit that helps you through the mirror?"

"Yes, there's only one. The spirit sees many things."

I nodded. I wanted to ask him if the spirit could help me get through the mirror. Or, rather, *back* through the mirror, back into the familiar world that had once been mine.

"The people on this side," I whispered to Gerry after Pete had left, "Thomas reckons they're the normal ones. The crazy and rowdy bunch are on the other side."

"Maybe he got them mixed up," said Gerry.

"But Thomas lives on this side."

Gerry didn't take his eyes off Byron's door. "That's what I mean."

"Spinner," I said. "He lives on the other side."

"Well, maybe they're all bloody mad."

"Except us," I said.

"We're just passing through," said Gerry. "Until things pick up a bit."

I nodded and went back to my letter.

Gerry and I are making—I chewed on the pen again—*lots of new friends.*

I signed off at the bottom and went off in search of a stamp.

27

Over those first few weeks behind the witchcraft shop, we became increasingly intimate with its inhabitants, and after a while they and their antics didn't seem quite so peculiar. Renoir spent the better part of each day in the courtyard, rooting about with his potted plants and herbs. I was relieved to find that the imaginary woman was quite an aloof lover, and only returned to his room on the odd occasion. Byron mostly kept to his room, no doubt hiding from the predatory Vietcong. Terry and Daryl lived next to Pete. They reminded me of a 1950s heterosexual couple: Terry was all housework and plastic rollers and fingernail polish, and Daryl was all motorbikes and six-packs of Dixie. The gay couple seemed to be a bit more balanced. They were waiters at a local restaurant, and on their days off would invite us up for vodka and Diet Sprite (the boys were always watching their weight). Thomas usually kept to himself, but occasionally he'd pop up for some of our vodka and a drag on a secret joint. Athena, the high priestess, was even more distant, and could barely even crack a smile when we barreled into the shop each morning to pick up our mail.

But Pete more than made up for their reserve. He was always popping over with cans of beer and his crystal balls and tarot cards. It seemed to me that he wanted desperately to belong to the cult, and culture, of witchcraft, but wasn't yet quite accepted. Consequently, he seized any opportunity to display his abilities. And Gerry and I, both amused by his role-playing and genuinely interested in the occult, allowed him to rehearse and refine his expertise on us.

I was raised with ghosts. They were always there, lurking about the upright piano and watching me as I slept. They wrote notes to my parents on the big sheets of butcher paper that were spread across the living room floor each night. They spoke through mediums. They told my mother she was Chinese in a previous life, that my father was a drummer in the German army and died when he was thrown down a well. My parents clicked their tongues and nodded knowingly. I was so young then that I took it all very literally, and when other kids asked me where our family came from, I always answered Germany and China.

Every night after tea, the butcher paper carpeted the living room floor; my parents gripped the ballpoint that lost itself in the extravagant penmanship of the afterworld, the bold, unwieldy loops and squiggles, purgatory's cursive letters. Ghosts apparently didn't possess the force to lift the pen at the end of each word, and their sentences were one long, unbroken river of letters around which we would crowd, attempting to decipher. This was the way I learned to read, not from the alphabet other kids had hanging on their bedroom doors, nor from bedtime stories, but from our excited attempts to translate what I thought of then as monologues from heaven.

Eventhoughyourfatherleftyouheisstillaliveandthinksaboutyou, some kindhearted spirit once wrote to my mother. It got so that my parents wouldn't purchase a toaster or visit a relative without first consulting one of the resident ghosts. And there were many in that big Stanmore house. One had a penchant for Ella Fitzgerald and demanded my father play her records. I used to lie in bed at night and listen to them creaking up and down the hall, and occasionally felt their breath on my forehead. The ghosts weren't always right in their advice, but I sensed even then that their presence was benevolent. One was even with me during my first traumatic day at school, guiding me through the intricacies of tracing and play lunch, numbers up to ten, the cool stares of conspiratorial older kids, first- and second-graders who wore the right kind of school shoes and made a point of using local argot I didn't quite understand. There was definitely a presence about, no farther than an arm's length away, that drew me toward a couple of other odd kids who also thought kindergarten terribly overrated, and with whom I could commiserate and play. In class, I found myself stricken with silence when I knew the answers to the teacher's droning questions, and it was that anonymous force that finally pushed my hand up and allowed me the pleasure of my own voice.

It was my mother, I think, who attracted the mediums and ghosts. Men, both living and dead, flocked about her beauty like moths around a light bulb—that bouquet of blond curls, the high cheekbones and sad green eyes, all of which had been imprinted on her by a statuesque father, the first man to desert her. Sometimes I think they were clamoring to fill the space he left, which widened when she married a man with the same name, face, and detachment as her absent father.

Perhaps spirits only appear to those who are haunted by loss and absence. For the first four years of her marriage, my mother tried desperately to fall pregnant, but my father's desire was attuned to both the moon and her body, and he only felt himself swelling toward her during the first and fourth quarter. For fifty-six moons she felt the tide inside her dragging itself down, and the first flower of blood that appeared against the silk of her underwear each month made her mourn for a presence she'd never known. Even her younger sister, who had married two and a half years after her, had been able to produce a son. She'd fallen pregnant in the seventh week of her marriage.

Her sister lovingly shared the child. My mother rehearsed the role for which she was preparing. She knitted lemon-colored matinee jackets. She pushed the white wicker carriage up and down Parramatta Road, pausing in front of shop windows long enough for strangers to stop and coo over the blue-eyed baby.

The boy thrived under the warm glow of so much attention. My aunt, too, was glad for the relief my mother provided, for her son was not yet twelve months old when she realized she was pregnant again.

The second pregnancy must have been a blow to my mother, who was four years older and had been married so much longer. I can imagine her now, buying lavender lingerie and perming her hair. But still nothing happened—her womb never lost a second in its interminable ticking toward the end of each month. And for this I think my father was secretly grateful.

My aunt was well into her second trimester when the infant child fell ill. At first, the rash that rose into his pale skin seemed like one of those standard allergic reactions to which children are prone. It was difficult to keep an eighteen-month-old in bed all day, but they wrapped him up and wiped his nose and fed him vegetable soup.

By the following Tuesday, when my mother next visited, the child was already dead. He'd passed away suddenly only the night before in Camperdown Childrens Hospital, from a second allergic reaction to his medication. The mysterious red welts that the doctors could not explain still marked the child as he lay on one of the morgue's white sheets.

Gerry drove the old MG down from the mountains on the day of the funeral. The white casket was as small as an enameled toy box. When they lifted it out, it looked as if it could be blown away by the wind sweeping through Rookwood Cemetery.

My parents returned to Katoomba the next morning. Gerry was still parking the car as my mother walked dolefully up the stairs of her building. She was halfway up the second flight when the old woman who lived in number three shot out of her flat. The woman usually kept to herself, but that day, when they met on the landing, she directly called my mother's name and touched her arm.

"Don't worry over that child you've lost," she soothed, resting one hand against my mother's cheek. "He'll be back soon. Just don't you worry."

And then she was gone. She disappeared into her flat as fast as she'd shot out of it. My mother stood unsteadily on the landing and held onto the banister. Twenty-three days later her doctor confirmed she was pregnant. Thirty-two weeks later she bore her first child.

Having been raised in the shadow of the afterworld, I settled rather comfortably into the practices and paraphernalia of the witchcraft shop. I made a point of befriending the eye painted on the wall of our room, and would often sit staring back into it whenever I felt sad or confused. Pete read my tarot cards one night, and the whole reading pivoted around the card of The Magician, which appeared in an apparently significant place in the pattern of cards on the Formica table, a place not far from the salt and pepper shakers that indicated my symbolic future. Pete predicted a long and fruitful union with the man represented by the figure on the card, who was swathed in a red robe, his arms raised into some potent gesture. He looked like a clean-shaven Jesus. When I pressed for more details, Pete couldn't tell me if I'd met the man yet, or if he remained in the ambiguous months ahead. My stomach widened into a series of small thrills, and I silently speculated on who he might be. The Magician . . . the magician . . . a long union with the magician . . . I quickly dismissed William and Spinner—and even Grimaldi, whose profession was nicely aligned with the card.

It would have to be Romano, I decided. Romano, the whisperer, the urban wanderer, the illusion keeper. I remembered the way he'd touched the small of my back as we'd crossed Fifth Avenue, and I began counting the weeks till our return to New York.

Pete had piqued our interest in the future with the tarot reading, and when he invited us in the following evening, for a reading from his crystal ball, we couldn't help ourselves. The smooth crystal was about the size of a naval orange, and Pete kept it wrapped in a purple silk handkerchief. He let me hold it for a moment, then briskly swept it out of my hands and told me not to look into it. In the crystal's cloudy universe I had expected to see a scene from some point in my own life, actors in period costume perform-ing a script that was yet to be written, enacting a future moment of euphoria or fear.

Pete sat us down at his kitchen table and lit the clean wick of a new red candle. A heavy, full-length mirror was propped against one wall, and re-flected a circling mobile Pete had made out of finger-sized plastic dolls and metal crucifixes. Beside the mirror was an altar: a black lacquer cabinet with candles, bowls, and an incense burner on top. A crucifix and skull hung above, along with various feathers and tendrils of Spanish moss.

Pete sat down and went to work. Still swaddled in the purple silk, the crystal ball lay in the curve of his hand and he began to rub it with the cloth as if he were polishing a piece of silver. When my eyes strayed toward it, he reminded me not to gaze into the ball. He continued to rub. Gerry took a swig of beer and burped.

Suddenly Pete stiffened and his eyes rolled back in his head for a moment. I sat with my hands under my thighs and wondered how long he'd re-hearsed that movement in the full-length mirror. His voice then assumed a ghostly, soprano quality as he gazed into the ball.

"*I see children,*" said the voice. "*I see children and I see sadness. I see a house falling down.*"

I rested my elbows on the table and leaned forward. The voice coming from Pete was not his own. It was not quite a man's and not quite a woman's.

"*I see a scalpel. I see a drum. I see the shy man he used to be.*"

Gerry straightened up at the mention of himself and momentarily for-got to swallow his mouthful of beer.

"*I see you both growing older. . . . I see a wedding. . . . I see a small boy wearing a hat—a checkered cap. I see his small hands holding a lacquer box. I am seeing your father's death. Your father is dying. . . . I am seeing your father lifting away. I see the boy in the cap growing older. I see the box is shrinking as his hands develop. I see the man in the cap fathering. . . . The man in the cap is fathering your father. The man in the cap is returning your father to you. And you're an old woman now. And you're holding that child, you're rocking him back and forth and you know it's him—you know that infant is your fa-ther. . . . Even though you're an old woman now, you're an old woman who's begun to notice the reaper's breath on the bathroom mirror. . . .*"

Pete paused and batted his eyelids. His chest rose with one long in-halation and his eyes rolled sideways. I stole a glance at a part of the ball where the purple silk had fallen back, but saw only a flickering pink light buried in its glassy depths. I looked at Gerry, whose face had blanched to the color of pale eggshells. My hand crept across the table toward him. Without looking, he took it in his and held it carefully, as if it, too, were a crystal ball whose secrets forbade his gaze.

The pink limbs of Pete's mobile circled overhead. The thought of los-ing, of living without, and regaining my father years later made me dizzy, even though I was sitting down.

Pete wouldn't reveal any other details about Gerry's departure—no cause, no year. I wondered how long I would have to live with his absence before I'd recognize him contained within the bruised, purplish skin of a newborn. What would his calling card be? A gaze? A gurgle? An unformed upper lip that would make him wary of language, of his family, of his own breathy voice? Would I discover him in his developing obsession for the sounds he'd later find he could raise from upturned pots and cake tins? Would episodes from my father's childhood emerge and reenact themselves? Would he grow up to father me once more, and on and on, this old act of love, this story of ours, transcending the casket's trajectory?

The possibilities were intriguing and terrifying. I had not until then considered my father's death. I had not anticipated children, let alone grandchildren. But now it suddenly seemed necessary, a duty, to extend my father's existence, or more precisely, the life we had together, our union.

When Pete positioned me in front of the full-length mirror that night, I stood still and gazed into myself, those two pupils dilated by darkness and desire. A shadow trembled on the wall, and the room began to breathe. I raised my arms and relinquished myself to the glass, not Narcissus's cold blue lake, nor the Queen's conversational mirror, for I knew that shadow in the background was my father, and he was watching, watching me watch myself momentarily surpass the silence and anonymity of that half-lit, temporal room.

■ 28 ■

Who knows what Marilyn Hampton did with the mysterious child she claimed was growing inside her? Did she terminate the fatherless fetus, or was it lost on one of her walks down Royal Street? Sometimes I think she simply erased it with a bad thought, a flick of the tongue. Gerry reckoned she'd concocted the baby between double Scotches and mugs of beer, that it was easy to get rid of a child who only lived in the imagination.

All we know is that one morning, when she and Gerry walked the half-mile down to City Hall to obtain their marriage license, she claimed to be fetus-free. She was vague and ambiguous: "There's no baby anymore." And Gerry, uncomfortable discussing the mysteries of the female body, let alone the female mind, said nothing.

The City Hall waiting room was jammed with couples all awaiting the State's approving stamp. They took a ticket and Marilyn began filling out a set of forms. Gerry noticed that they were by far the oldest couple in the room, and took pleasure in the incongruity of it all.

It wasn't long, however, before Marilyn's behavior began reducing

Gerry's glow of self-satisfaction. Later he would tell me that he suspected Marilyn's past was a tad shady.

"I reckon she's on the run," he said, nodding knowingly. "She's terrified of coppers. Whenever a pig walked past us down there, she froze up faster than a packet of peas."

Later that night Gerry and I would lie awake in bed and speculate on what magnificent crime she could have committed to make her cower so.

Over an hour passed before their number was finally called. Gerry gave the woman on the other side of the counter one of his most magnanimous grins and slid across the paperwork. After glancing through it, the woman looked up and requested their birth certificates.

"I had mine in my wallet," Gerry told me later. "But when I raced over to Marilyn, I found out she didn't even have a *copy* of hers."

I asked him where she was born.

"I dunno," he groaned. "California, I think. Anyway, it'd take ages to write away and get a copy of it."

My father returned to the counter with only one certificate and the woman firmly shook her head. All Gerry could think of was the hundred and fifty dollars he'd already given Marilyn, of the visa that was gradually expiring in his passport, of the green card he so desperately desired.

"So I pull this woman aside," he later boasted. "I pull her aside and I whisper in her ear, 'Listen, Miss. I know you have rules to abide by. But can't you make an exception here? You see'—and I move real close to her, and I lower my voice—'*you see, she's pregnant.*' And this woman's eyes widen, and she glances over at Marilyn, who always looks about eight months' pregnant anyway, and she whispers back to me, 'Oh, I see what you mean, sir. Listen, you go 'cross the river. To Algiers. There's a man who'll marry you right away. No certificates, nothing. Just pay him fifty dollars.'"

She wrote the directions to the Algiers courthouse on the back of a used envelope and quickly slipped it across the counter with the paperwork.

When I asked him about the date of the big day, Gerry just shrugged and said, "Well, I would've gone over today, but I didn't have the cash on me."

I rested on my bed and pressed my face into a pillow. I tried to imagine Marilyn raising a gun or wielding a predatory knife. But it was hard to impose violence or malice on those chubby, nervous hands. Instead, I suspected some benign and surreptitious act. I could see her lifting chocolates from a display and slipping them into her pocket. I could see her strolling out of a department store wearing a new coat. I could see her plowing through the limit on her credit card in one afternoon and slipping across the state line before she received the first bill. I could imagine her raising her feet to the abortionist's stirrups. I could even imagine her thinking she was pregnant, lost in some menopausal fantasy.

■   29   ■

By December 1983, our one window was covered each morning in a fine veil of frost. Gerry took to wearing his hooded parka to bed. Thomas loaned us a one-bar electric heater and a coffee machine. At night after work, if we didn't go around to Leonard's, Gerry would sit at the table, listening to jazz on WWOZ, pouring cheap rum into plastic cups of lukewarm chicory coffee. Too cold to escape to the communal entertainment of the courtyard, everyone now huddled in their rooms and only saw one another by invitation.

That was the winter we lived on avocados and raw vegetables. Our only condiments were salt and lemon juice. There were no cooking facilities in the room, and since we couldn't afford to dine out much, the salads I prepared and served on two upturned cake box lids sustained us.

As winter progressed, fewer and fewer tourists flocked to New Orleans, and those who did weren't hardy enough to dawdle about on street corners to watch dancers and drummers, to throw money. We passed the A&P supermarket every night on the way home and, while Gerry continued to push our shopping cart full of gear down Royal Street, I would shoot in and buy enough groceries to last us another twenty-four hours, counting out the change we'd only just earned.

At that time, we had about three thousand dollars in the bank, but we were slowly chipping away at it. The fountain of prosperity we'd enjoyed in the summer had slowed to a trickle by the end of the year. Those nights are still vivid in my mind; they are the ones that, twelve years later, still rise up and reenact themselves when I can't fall asleep until three or four A.M. Nights when we set up outside the Indian curry shop, when we'd dash back into the empty restaurant on our breaks. Nights when I'd linger by the stove in the kitchen to warm myself, near the scent of lemongrass and paprika. The displaced Bombay family who was going broke trying to sell chicken marsala to tourists who'd come to Bourbon Street to gorge on red beans and rice and seafood gumbo. Nights when the wind howled up from the river, when we'd perform "Lu Lu's Back in Town" over and over because it was a fast tune and kept our blood circulating. Nights when the street was virtually empty and we continued to dance and play, seemingly oblivious, refusing to be ignored by the world. Nights I'd wear that baggy pair of blue tails I'd bought at Volunteers of America for two twenty-five, because my pink pair with the rhinestone buttons had begun to rot with sweat.

If it ever got us down, we never revealed it to one another. Gerry had raised me well. I lost myself in books borrowed from Leonard's shelves; my father reclined into Leonard's dope and jazz tapes, into that fine and glorious home that I like to think of as His Past. Whenever things got tough, he would pull back into that enclosure like a tortoise into a shell. The past was his fortress, a grand old mansion that was always renovating itself with textured wallpaper and new paint jobs, and at night, after work, he would get down on his hands and knees and polish the maple floorboards of his youth. At twenty, I had no magnificent past of my own into which I could retreat, and the one I was trying to build in New Orleans was plagued with bad plumbing and faulty foundations. Who would want to reminisce about bawling in the toilet of the Indian curry shop between performances, about earning fifteen dollars a night? Instead, I became a lodger in my father's castle, running errands, assisting with the upkeep of such a sprawling, impressive structure. I was intimate with every corner of that place, the wide corners and secret passages, the doors that opened into subsequent years and consequential anecdotes, the locked parlors of his marriage, the grand ballroom in which he lost so many nights. I was hired help, the housekeeper. When he drank too much and took the wrong turn—when he forgot an important detail or neglected a certain phrase—I'd rush down that passage and point him back before he got us lost. I prompted him when he hesitated at a closed door. I polished his silverware.

Surrendering myself to the indomitable architecture of his imagination, I was his girl, his Alice.

■   **30**   ■

It was Pee Wee who taught me how to work the New Orleans streets. I have only one image of the boy. It's not more than a silhouette snapped at twilight, pinned above the desk at which I now write. He's off-center in the photo, tapping on my wooden board, his cardboard box thrown before him on the road. It must have still been warm: He wears only a pair of cut-off jeans and a black bowler hat, his thin torso glowing in the dusky light. Four strangers, dressed in light summer shirts, walk away from him in the background. Pee Wee's perfect row of white teeth highlight the picture. He's smiling into the trashy indifference of Bourbon Street. Even though the first time I met him he told me he was twelve, he was so tiny I thought he was eight. Skin as soft as the back of my ear and almost as dark as my pupils. He was smart enough to know the stereotype tourists expected, and told me once that "dressing down" made him more money.

The French Quarter was riddled with former child tap dancers who were summarily dismissed once the hormones wheeling through their bodies surfaced into muscles and facial hair. Unlike castrati singers, once their voices broke, they were not thrown into the street, for they had always been there, and there they would remain, eventually supporting wives and kids on the pittance garnered from shining shoes and smooth, good-natured hustling.

What distinguished Pee Wee from the throng of other boys skittering through the Quarter that year was his sheer love for the music he seemed to draw up from the earth. That love was something we shared but never talked about. I sensed it in the way in which he lingered at night, studying my footwork, in his eagerness to learn new steps, and in the way his fast, percussive feet embraced them. His love leaked out in slow syncopation, in his ability to ride a back beat across bar lines and choruses, untouched by the frequent great white apathy that permeated Bourbon Street.

This love, I think, was the first indication of his generosity, devoid of ego and greed. So many childhood nights on the streets would eventually bleed it from him, but back then it was still intact, and the rhythms he created—the ones he in turn shared with me—were an affirmation of all the beauty dance could be.

There was an older kid on the street, too, who was probably just a little

younger than me. He unintentionally taught me lessons, too. His name was
Hambone. He always had a big, difficult grin set in his face as he hammered
his few fast steps against Bourbon Street's bitumen. Hambone openly defied
the eight o'clock curfew, and had made a habit of throwing down his box
before groups of tourists, shuffling to a few hummed bars of "The Saints."
The key to his success was mobility and brevity. If he saw a cop looming in
the distance, he simply whisked up his box and evaporated as fast as Elli-
son's Invisible Man. Over the years, Hambone broadened his act to include
a display of amateur acrobatics. I still have a black-and-white photo of him,
somersaulting over a crouched woman outside Papa Joe's Female Imperson-
ators. His four limbs are frozen in the air, his head is ducked, the sole of his
right shoe is facing the sky. If the woman didn't crouch beneath him, he'd
look like a man dropping to his death.

Like me, Hambone defied the unofficial restriction that limited tap
dancing to prepubescent boys. And he seemed to enjoy flaunting his rebel-
lion, hustling and dancing on into the night, long after the rest of us had
knocked off and gone home.

Hambone declared his rivalry with me during our second week in the
Quarter. He suddenly appeared one night, outside the Royal Sonesta, and
his timing was impeccable: I'd invested over an hour building the crowd up
to a scraggly, hundredfold circle. Gerry and I were doing the big pay-off finale: "My Feet Can't Fail Me Now." I was about halfway through the tune
when I turned and saw Hambone swaggering into the space on the road between me and the crowd. He threw down his cardboard box. The tourists
smirked and bobbed with interest. He waved a smart, dismissive hand at me
before launching into a fast slick step.

People nudged each other, smiling, and drew closer to await my reaction. But I continued to ignore him, losing myself in an orbit of spins. I
think a few of them secretly hoped Gerry would threaten to crack Hambone
over the head with one of his drumsticks. But Gerry played on, oblivious.

A small cluster of men, nursing beers and edging forward, began toss-
ing coins into Hambone's box. Hambone clapped his hands and threw himself into another step. When he turned slightly, our eyes locked and he shot
me an audacious grin. He swept up his box and wheeled about, fleecing the
edge of the crowd as he tapped.

It was when I saw the first bill float down that my adrenaline kicked in.

I sprang off the footpath. I planted myself right beside Hambone. I dropped all the pirouettes and wings, the cutaways and double spins, all the precious patterns into which I'd trained my limbs—I dropped them all and got down to the plain hard truth: the rapid execution of simple rhythms on the rise of an uneven road.

I liked having to cut Hambone about as much as I liked living off avocados and raw vegetables: It was a depressing but necessary routine. When the tune ended and the money clattered into Gerry's side-drum case, Hambone wouldn't look at me, but continued to harangue the crowd with his cardboard box until they drifted away. He then followed them up the street, shuffling and riffing all the way to Crazy Shirley's.

Being drawn into competition annoyed me, but Hambone's challenge helped to toughen me up. He didn't return the next night, but every couple of months he'd pop up and try to overtake the act. I'd have to leap out onto the road and we'd go through the whole cutting contest again. After that first time, though, it was easy: I was learning how to keep my feet closer to the ground to develop more speed, how to appear bold and unruffled beside him.

If Hambone reduced his every movement to mere competition, Pee Wee elevated his to pure communion. In his tense expressions, I recognized the closed, meditative look of a soloing musician striving to articulate some buried melodic line. Perhaps Pee Wee was interested in me because I danced in a style unfamiliar to him. Some nights we'd steal a few minutes between shows, trading steps and snatches of stories about ourselves. His favorite number was our recording of "Sweet Georgia Brown," arranged with a Charleston beat behind it. Pee Wee liked to try out his steps against it, and during our breaks, he'd appear and demand that Gerry put it on. Soon we drifted into a casual performance together, our respective styles creating polyrhythms against the smooth bricks outside the Royal Sonesta; yet we knew enough of each other's repertoire that we could frequently come together during the chorus and execute unrehearsed, yet synchronized steps.

It had nothing to do with money. We did it just for fun, for the love of the sounds we found we could spontaneously invent. Pee Wee liked my dancing, but told me one night I didn't know shit about making money in New Orleans. He'd hovered in the background long enough to notice the audiences clapping, but only occasionally reaching into their back pockets and purses.

"You're too slow!" he wailed one evening. "You can't be waiting for them to drop something in. You got to git out there and *git* it!"

Pee Wee began to coach me in ways to extract money from tight-fisted tourists. After kicking out the final steps of every second or third number, instead of waiting for donations to be tossed into Gerry's drum case, I lifted my top hat, sprang into the crowd and passed it around quickly. Like Pee Wee and Hambone, I passed it with pluck and expectation, sometimes even having to prod the swollen bellies of unsuspecting cowboys with the rim of my upturned hat. Soliciting tips in this manner was illegal in the Crescent City, but Pee Wee never mentioned that. He only knew what needed to be done if we were to survive the Southern winter. With that extra bit of hustling our nightly take almost doubled. With that extra bit of money I bought almonds and multivitamins, and my father bought Dixie beer.

There were never many words between us, just rhythm and sweat. Some nights, when we both found ourselves surfing on the same riff, Pee Wee would slip his small hand into mine and we'd turn and face Bourbon Street together, conjoined by simultaneous phrasing, a syncopated time step or double-shuffle break, his loose, warm fingers laced into mine.

It wasn't long before the local whites began to murmur.

"Watcha doin' dancin' with that little bastard? You don't need him!"

He copped the same reaction from his own group. I'd heard the hissed put-downs and objections, the snickered criticisms, the word *trash* associated with my own name. But it all skipped off Pee Wee like a light breeze.

In spite of the civil rights movement, in spite of integration, education, and a growing interracial community, in 1983, in that city, it seemed as if not much had changed since the forties. I couldn't stop thinking about two of my favorite tap dancers, the white Eleanor Powell and the black Bill "Bojangles" Robinson. Eleanor became famous for combining her impressive ballet technique with flawless footwork. Bojangles distinguished himself with his unique stair dance, and with his close-to-the-floor style, dropping his heels during certain intervals to provide the pulse of a deep bass line. Sometimes the two dancers spontaneously teamed up at a private party and performed. Each admired the other's style and made no secret of it. But it wasn't long before their respective film companies stepped in and forbade their partnership. They would never make a musical together, nor were they allowed to perform in public. Eleanor was paired with Fred Astaire, while Bojangles was demoted to Shirley Temple's shuffling butler.

One night Pee Wee wanted to try on my red leather taps. He slid his feet into my size tens and tied them up. He coaxed out a few riffs and managed a couple of quick pull-backs. His feet were lost within those huge shoes as five-beat riffs stuttered out beneath him. Clarry the grimacing clown wandered by with a cigarette stuck between his lips. He shot Pee Wee and me a contemptuous look, muttered "Nigger," and spat a gob of mucus an inch from my bare foot. Pee Wee slipped off my shoes, tossed them to me, and pulled on his own pair. I knew then that the only things we'd let ourselves hear that night were the Dirty Dozen's bebop lines and the wedded rhythms of our feet.

■ 31 ■

A northern engineer once exclaimed, "New Orleans was built in a place God never intended a city to be built . . . six feet below sea level in the middle of a swamp, squeezed between a giant river and a huge lake. . . ." But after you've lived there for a while, you forget how much water enfolds the place, about the marsh grasses and cyprus logs, how the alligators and spider lilies linger just out of eyeshot.

We hadn't heard that the Crescent City is the recipient of more rainfall than any other major U.S. city. No one ever mentioned the sixty-four inches per year. But we knew something was wrong when, by the second week in December, water gushed into the courtyard and drowned Renoir's crop of sweet basil. Gutters overflowed and sent a steady waterfall streaming past our window. Rivers burrowed through uneven streets; those that were dug up for repaving turned to mud. I could almost see water moccasins slithering through marsh grass, sniff the stench of alligator musk riding on the wind. The river nudged the levy. Lake Pontchartrain rose.

We bided our time by trying to perform in the display window of a wax museum on Bourbon Street. For this I painted on my pantomime makeup, and we both dressed in white tailcoats. But the rain kept tourists in their hotel rooms. And instead we found ourselves entertaining the pallid wax figures of the voodoo queen, Marie Laveau—whose hands were frozen around the legs of a beheaded chicken—and her equally imposing male counterpart, Doctor John. They were an attentive audience, but we made no money.

The plans for Gerry's marriage proceeded with only slight impediments. When the appointed day arrived, the wedding had to be postponed because Marilyn overslept and didn't turn up at the witchcraft shop until after one P.M. She was apparently nursing a hangover, and made Gerry take her to the bar next door and buy her a beer.

The rain muddied my sense of purpose. My toes grew white and crinkly from their encasement in perpetually wet shoes. We both came down with colds. Having so much time on my hands made me meditate upon my future. Soon Gerry would be a legal U.S. resident, while the tourist visa in my passport would expire in eleven weeks. I wondered about the possibility of obtaining an extension. Some people said I'd cinch it, others said I'd be better off going across the border to Mexico and returning with a new visa. I even entertained the idea of marrying a U.S. citizen myself, of obtaining my own green card so Gerry and I could tease out legitimate work together.

But who would marry me? I wondered. Who would endure the bevy of blood tests and government forms for me?

Some nights we tried to defy the rain. We'd dress and pack our gear and barrel on up to Bourbon Street, ducking under awnings and verandas to avoid getting wet. We'd take shelter in the empty Indian curry shop, sit at a table at the front of the restaurant, and commiserate with the owners. While we waited for a break in the weather, Gerry would take long gulps of the cheap beer, which, over the course of the evening, began arriving free of charge. Soon we would all be getting slowly drunk, and Avi, the slim older son, would be singing Hindi love songs while my father tapped out backbeats against the edge of the table.

One night a fat Texan in a plaid sports jacket appeared. He sat at the bar, drinking go-cups of beer and eating dahl with his short, stubby fingers. He went on ordering into the night: chicken marsala, jasmine rice, green chutney, a side of yoghurt and cucumbers. When he'd scraped the last morsels from his plate, had wiped his mouth and discarded his napkin, he swiveled his huge body around to face our table and declared, "How would you two like to earn over five hundred a week clear doing your show in a Houston nightclub?"

The man's name was Harry. A mate of his owned the nightclub and was looking for new entertainment. Harry had seen us trying to make a buck on Bourbon and thought we were too good to be on the street. By this time,

Harry was seated at our table. My father offered him a cigarette and told him he'd worked with Frank Sinatra and Jerry Lee Lewis. Harry planted a Camel between his lips and told us that we were throwing ourselves away out there, that with the right break we could end up working Las Vegas.

This kind of talk went on over the next few nights. The rain persisted throughout the week, and while we were holed up inside the shop, the idea of working in a club in Houston began to sound a little more appetizing. Harry drank too much, but he seemed to have plenty of money, and wasn't above buying all five of us in the restaurant a drink.

I mentioned to him that I wasn't into any funny stuff. No soft-shoe stripteases or topless tap dancing. But the way Harry arched his indignant brows made me regret even broaching the subject. He was a gentleman, a Southern gentleman. His friend in Texas was a gentleman, too. Harry had already telephoned his friend, who was keen on the idea, but wanted to see our CVs first.

It was the second time we'd received that request, but we were still unable to meet it. We had to postpone the mailing of our curriculum vitae until we could get Leonard to type them up.

The rain's woeful rhythms accompanied us everywhere. At night, they drummed in our ears as we lay in bed. Terry's push-up bras and lace panties hung on the courtyard's clothesline for over a fortnight, flapping wetly in the wind. Byron complained of a leaking roof. Renoir made a small fortune by donning his yellow raincoat and hat and riding his bicycle through the flooded streets. He'd take orders for meals from the strippers stuck in the joints along Bourbon. Upon delivery of the food, they'd each tip him a buck or two. That's how he met Jinny, the slim blond stripper from Big Daddy's who eventually moved into Terry and Daryl's flat when they got sick of the weather and suddenly fled to Florida. In her haste, Terry forgot her wet underwear, and the day after they left I witnessed Renoir slinking up to the clothesline and briskly unpegging the soaked brassieres and knickers.

■ 32 ■

It was on one of these interminable, waterlogged days before Christmas that my father finally married Miss Marilyn Hampton. She appeared at the witchcraft shop only a few minutes late, attired for the occasion in a pair of jeans and a sweater. She had several shopping bags in tow, which made it virtually impossible for her to manage the wilting black umbrella with its one broken spoke as she hovered in the doorway of the shop. My father met her in his one suit: a tan three-piece number that made him look like a successful gambler. He'd even had his hair cut the day before. He was apparently disappointed in his fiancée's ensemble and asked if she had anything else she could change into. But Marilyn refused to change and she also refused to leave her bags at the shop. So off he went with her—bags, jeans, and all—ready to part with his fifty dollars and to share our family name.

Gerry later complained of how long it took to get there. After busing down to the Canal Street wharf, they rode the ferry across the river. When they arrived at Algiers, they caught another bus, the windshield wipers of which could barely stem the torrents of rain lashing against the glass.

After about three-quarters of an hour, the bus pulled up in the town that the woman down at City Hall had told him about. Marilyn struggled up the stairs of the courthouse with her bags while Gerry brandished the deformed umbrella. Inside, they filled out more forms. The man who was to marry them was a balding justice of the peace with a handlebar mustache and lots of gold glittering in his mouth.

Gerry confessed right away that Marilyn didn't have her birth certificate, but the JP just waved a dismissive hand, unbuckled his belt, and loosened it a notch. He seemed quite happy when Gerry then palmed him the required fifty dollars.

"Witnesses?" The JP's voice was soft and musical and unconcerned. "The marriage won't be legal without two witnesses."

"Witnesses," Gerry said. "I forgot about that. . . . You see, I've never been married before. I didn't know."

He was already dreading the thought of having to return to this provincial courthouse another day, with me and Leonard in tow.

The JP smiled and patted Gerry's shoulder. "Never mind. I'll just go downstairs and ask two of the secretaries up. But it'll cost you three dollars per secretary."

Relieved, Gerry nodded and happily palmed him a further six bucks.

The secretaries were two permed and cardiganed model citizens of rural Louisiana. They both wore knee-length wool skirts and pantyhose.

They exuded the scent of foundation powder and lipstick, two smells that still make my father's stomach turn. (He's often told me that whenever he bedded down with a woman, he always demanded that she remove her makeup first.)

"Ladies and gentlemen," announced the JP, "we are gathered here today to witness the union of"—he glanced at the form Marilyn had just filled out—"to witness the union of Marilyn Jean Hampton to, er"—he glanced at the form again—"to, to Mr. Gerard Augustus Sayer." He nodded and ran one finger across his mustache.

"If there is anyone in this room who has reason to object to this union, speak now! Speak now, my friend, or forever hold your peace."

He paused and looked about the room, as if there were a throng of guests snuffling into lace handkerchiefs. The only thing that could be heard was the sound of Marilyn sucking on a candy. Now that the two witnesses had their three dollars each, they seemed to have no objection, and the service went on unimpeded.

"Miss Marilyn Jean Hampton—" the JP took a gracious turn toward her.

"Yes?" she murmured.

"Do you take Gerard Augustus Sayer to be your lawfully wedded husband, to love, honor, and obey, in sickness and in health, for as long as ye both shall live, for ever and ever, till death you two part?"

Marilyn pursed her lips, glanced at Gerry, and nodded.

"Say I do, my dear."

"I do," she repeated in a monotone.

The JP gave her an encouraging smile and turned his attention to the groom.

"Mr. Sayer, do you take Marilyn Jean Hampton to be your lawfully wedded wife, to love and honor, in sickness and in health, for better or worse, for long as ye—"

"What about obey?" interjected Marilyn.

"I beg your pardon?"

"Obey," she persisted. "If I obey him, he should have to obey me."

Gerry cringed and shot her one of his looks.

"I mean, I mean why can't he obey me sometimes? Why can't he?"

The secretaries bowed their heads and smiled behind their raised hands.

The JP glanced at Gerry. "Mr. Sayer?"

Gerry replied with an exasperated shrug. "I don't care. Really. I'll love, honor, and obey her, in sickness and in health, until we both die. Yeah, I will. I mean, yes. Yes, *I do.*"

"Right, good." The JP folded the forms in half. "Now, Mr. Sayer, do you have the ring?"

Gerry clasped his hands in front of him and shifted. "The what?"

"The ring, Mr. Sayer. The wedding band."

Had Gerry planned it better, he could have borrowed a ring for the day, but it had been thirty-three years since he'd married my mother, and he'd forgotten such nuptial necessities.

"I, I didn't know we had to have the ring today—"

"Never mind," soothed the JP, "you can buy her one tomorrow." Then, in his most triumphant voice, he chimed, "I now pronounce you man and wife. You may kiss the bride."

Gerry hadn't anticipated having to do this, either, and was momentarily frozen at the thought of planting one on Marilyn's already pouting lips.

He folded his hands in front of him, leaned toward her, and went to peck her on the cheek, but she jerked her face around and suddenly his mouth was lost within hers, her round, substantial bosom pressing into his.

■ 33 ■

The rain pressed into the end of December and turned to ice and sleet. Shop windows brimmed with baubles and holly, ribbons and mistletoe. Canal Street's flashing lights blinked over swarming bargain hunters. Street vendors blew onto their freezing hands. Frost inched its way across cobbled lanes. Fragrant fur trees lined up in doorways and were flogged for ten bucks apiece.

Still unable to work regularly, we dreaded the festive season. We began to feel that our disappointing Thanksgiving Day was merely a dress rehearsal for the upcoming holidays. The Quarter slowly emptied itself. Leonard booked a ticket back to California. Pete disappeared on a bus heading north.

We spent our first American Christmas holed up in Leonard's slave quarter. He'd allowed us to house-sit because our room had no heat, no stove, no television, no running water. On Christmas day, I ventured out into the biting air. The frozen puddles, the icicles glistening above doorways and windows, the cutting wind, and the fine, billowing snowflakes that had always looked so enticing on television from the security of a warm Sydney living room, now made me shiver with both the cold and fear. There was no way we could make a living on streets paved with thin sheets of ice.

■ 34 ■

The distinguished Houston nightclub that Fat Harry had boasted about was a barnlike structure made of rusting aluminum built at the edge of a dust bowl parking lot. A sign above the splintered wooden door declared THE HOT POTATO! in crooked red lettering. Someone had drawn crude nipples on the os with a black marker.

When I walked in, "Truckstop Mama" was whining from the jukebox. It was fairly dark, but I could make out the figures of several hefty men slouched on stools at the bar. A couple of them wore cowboy hats. The carpet emanated a stale, smoky smell.

My knees went weak under the stares of those slouching men. Johnny Harriff took me by the arm and led me by a narrow catwalk stage still swathed in silver tinsel and spray-on snow. A long pole stood at the extreme end, as if at any moment a fireman might come bursting through the ceiling and slide down into the club.

Johnny ushered me into a tiny, windowless room divided from the bar by only a thin curtain. A cracked mirror hung on the wall. Below it, a yellowing sink was coated in cigarette ash and butts. He introduced me to a woman named Kitty, who was slipping her feet into a pair of red fishnets. Her bleached-blond hair fell around her shoulders in brittle curls. One of her front teeth was missing and she lisped when she exclaimed "Sonuvabitch!" to a hole in her stockings. This was the woman who was supposed to take care of me, who was supposed to show me the ropes.

At six A.M. on New Year's Day, Gerry had put me on a westbound plane. He'd realized at the last minute that he couldn't leave New Orleans right away. He had to lodge his immigration application, go through the interviews, and he needed to have Marilyn on hand. He persuaded me to go on ahead of him, promising that once they'd finished their interviews, he'd join me. The Harriff brothers seemed unfazed by the fact that I'd be performing alone, and sent us a telegram to the effect that Gerry could take his time.

Only days before, I'd bought a new leotard and pair of silver tap shoes with two-inch heels—thinking my red flats were too unsophisticated for a sleek Texas nightclub.

Johnny met me at the airport. He was a short, olive-skinned man with a black mustache. He drove me to the clean, vinyl-ridden suburban home he shared with his brother, Freddy. The older Harriff was a plump, aloof fellow with a fondness for low-fat chocolate ice cream and the Playboy channel on cable. He spent the entire New Year's Day immersed in the blue flicker of soft porn. Part of our agreement with the Harriff brothers, negotiated through Fat Harry, was that they would put us up in their home until we found suitable digs.

Johnny took my bags to a small room with a queen-sized bed and bland furniture made out of imitation oak. "Big enough for the both of us," he said, dropping my luggage onto the bed.

He must have noticed the mortified look on my face, for he added, "Don't worry. I'll stay on the right side of the bed; you stay on the left."

That night I lay rigid between his blue sheets, terrified that one of those nicotine-stained hands would steal below my T-shirt, that the substantial weight of Johnny Harriff might suddenly roll against me. I'd tried to insist on the plaid couch and a spare blanket, but Johnny wouldn't hear of it, maintaining that Freddy's passion for the Late, Late Shows would interrupt my slumber. I stayed awake long into the night, poised at the edge of the bed, stiff as a cadaver, swallowing at every shifted limb and turn of the head, trying to cheer myself up with thoughts of the adventure I might be on, an impending story I could later tell my father on the phone. I only relaxed and drifted away when I finally heard Johnny emit a gentle snore.

"So how do you like Texas?" said Kitty, fingering the hole in her stockings.

I murmured something about it being different.

She stood up and pulled a scarlet leotard across the curve of her butt. I watched her in the jagged double image the cracked mirror threw back into the room.

"Don't worry, honey," she said, suddenly grabbing my right breast, "you'll get used to it."

I waited until she left the room before I changed into a simple white leotard and black skirt. I buckled up my new silver tap shoes and felt a little wobbly balancing on high heels. At that time, I still wore no makeup to make me look older. Kitty burst back in with a drink in her hand, lifted the strap of my leotard and snapped it against my shoulder.

"You look like a *waitress*, girl! Whatta we gonna do with *yooou?*"

She slipped her free arm around me and led me out. A few more men had joined the ones sitting at the bar. Kitty left me standing alone in a corner while she swept up to one of them and planted herself in his lap.

I'd brought the tapes Gerry and I had been using on the street: Louis Armstrong's "Dippermouth Blues," Glenn Miller's "In the Mood," George Formby's "Fan-Dance Fanny." A plump woman in a skin-tight black dress walked past me, and I managed to detain her long enough to ask her about the sound system. But she just popped her gum at me and said, "This is whatcha do." She nodded to a throng of men leaning up against the bar. "Go over there and make yourself friendly. Get 'em to buy you drinks, see? You get a percentage of every drink someone buys you."

"But—" I protested.

"Don't worry, all girls' drinks are watered down to nothing."

"But what about the—"

"Just git over there," she ordered. "You'll dance later."

I held my breath and managed to hover at the end of the bar.

"Silver Threads and Golden Needles" began crooning out of the jukebox, and a young woman in tight denim shorts and a bikini top wandered up the stairs and stepped onto the stage. She wore lots of makeup to conceal what looked like acne-ravaged skin, and her fine brown hair fell across her face whenever she bowed her head. She gazed down at the floor and took small bobbing steps, barely moving her arms, as if she were on a discotheque dance floor with some invisible teenage boyfriend. The men at the bar continued to talk and drink. I could hear them over the music: "Gimme 'nother shot." "Godda-a-ym son-of-a-b-i-i-y-tch! Watcha goin' do that fow?"

No one turned to watch. Her worn cowboy boots remained in one place as she shifted her weight from one leg to another. Everyone ignored her, even Kitty, who was busy coiling the chest hair of her host around her index finger. The tune faded and died. The young woman lowered her head and turned away. The jukebox hummed and clicked on another record. Suddenly, as if they were mechanized, all the men put down their drinks and turned toward the stage.

One hand went up behind her back and she pulled on the fluorescent green tie of her bikini top. "It's So Easy to Fall in Love" boomed out of the speakers. She pulled on the second string knotted around her neck and the top came away. She flung it into the lap of an older bearded man who was sitting close the stage. All eyes now rested on her small white breasts, the nipples of which were raised, not from arousal, I suspected, but from January's nip in the air.

She threw herself into Linda Ronstadt's moaning chant, circling back her shoulders and pouting her lips. Someone hooted and whistled. She cupped her breasts and allowed her hands to move slowly over her ribs and waist, then threw her head back and kicked one leg out in mock pleasure. Her hips began to gyrate, as if she were trying to maintain the rhythm of a child's hula hoop. One hand found the snap of her shorts, and her fingers hesitated before she flicked it open. The zipper parted and she gave the denim a coquettish tug until the shorts dropped and fell about her ankles. She kicked them away into a corner. Her white G-string couldn't quite contain the wiry black pubic hair that sprouted up beyond the thin veneer of nylon lace. A man at the bar stuck his fingers in his mouth and emitted a piercing whistle. She spun and took a few steps back, shaking the spare weight of her breasts like a consumptive belly dancer. More howling and whistling. Skipping forward, she suddenly swung herself around the pole. When her boots touched the floor again, she wrapped her legs around the gleaming shaft of metal and rubbed herself against it.

"Go, baby, go!" yelled the bearded man by the stage, who was nursing the green bikini top in his cupped hands. He raised it to his face, turned to the rest of the men in the bar, and made much of inhaling whatever of her scent it still held, then howled like a dingo at the red light that suddenly began flashing about the stage. A cheer went up in response. The woman continued to hump the pole and allowed her face to draw up into a knot of counterfeited pleasure. Two men strolled into the bar and cried, "Hallelujah!"

As if she could no longer contain herself, she abruptly jumped back, raised her arms in surrender, and forced the triangle of white lace forward, thrusting into the air. She managed to edge her way to the side of the stage, into the waves of whistles and hoots, each thrust a little harder and faster. Her legs began buckling and she gradually lowered herself to the floor, still fucking the air as she kneeled before the forest of wide eyes. The bearded man stood up and tied her top around his head. She pulled her shoulders back and pointed her breasts at his face, her groin pulsing toward him. He glanced at the rest of the crowd and then deliberately pulled a bill from his wallet. He folded it in half, slipped it under the elastic of her G-string, and let his hand linger there a moment. With the bill secure against her skin, the young woman drew back and dropped face-up onto the floor of the stage, spreading her legs slightly, her body undulating, as if she bore the weight of the man who had endowed her with the note, until the music stopped abruptly and she froze into a rehearsed orgasm: arched back, raised groin, parted lips, a taut pink tongue licking her upper lip.

After the hollers and applause died down, Johnny walked out of the office and grabbed my arm. "Hey," he said, "you're on next."

My kneecaps did a little nervous dance. *"Me?"*

He pursed his lips and nodded.

I gripped the edge of the bar. "I can't."

"Yes, you can."

"No, I can't. I mean, I haven't got my tapes cued. And anyway, I can't dance like that."

"We don't use tapes here. All the girls dance to the jukebox."

"But *I* can't. I've got routines. They're all *rehearsed*. You know, that's the way I—"

"All the girls use the jukebox. We don't have a tape player. Just go over and pick something you like."

I swallowed and glanced about. The bar was hushed and everyone was looking at me. The man with the beard unknotted the bikini top. He handed it to the young woman as she glided into his lap.

"I don't have any change," I said.

Johnny sighed and rattled one hand about in his trouser pocket. "Here," he dropped two quarters into my hand. "But from now on, you go 'round and ask the customers for coins. I can't afford to be doing this all the time."

The bar remained hushed as I walked across the room. No one stared at me directly, but I could sense their surreptitious looks falling against my back.

The jukebox glowed with purple neon. I went down the list of titles: "You Picked a Fine Time to Leave Me, Lucille," "Yodeling Cowboy," "Love Me or Leave Me." "Blue Skies" caught my eye in the third row and I dropped the coins in and pressed the buttons.

Willie Nelson's voice was a comfort as it lilted into the darkness, a voice that seemed genuine and tangible above the hoots and whistles still ringing in my ears. I used to dance to the same tune on Sunday afternoons down at Circular Quay in Sydney, decked out in my full regalia—tails, top hat, pantomime makeup—only yards from the harbor, encircled by a crowd, listening to the ring of coins as they fell into my hat.

I smoothed down my skirt, wobbled up the stairs in my high heels, and took a tentative step into the garish red light. I stood there for a few awkward moments, stiff and self-conscious. I hung my head and forced my legs into the half-remembered routine.

My feet, encased in the unfamiliar silver pumps, betrayed all the precision I had trained into them. By the second chorus, I found that I had worked my way down the catwalk and, looking at my feet, noticed a solitary hand resting on the edge of the stage. It almost appeared to sit there alone, disembodied from a man, for the darkness of the club and the glare of the lights precluded my seeing any more. Careful not to step near it, I managed to pirouette away to the right, but when my left foot descended, it dropped against nothing but air, and I found myself falling off the edge of the stage. Perhaps it was the sudden roar of laughter throughout the bar that pushed my hands back to snatch at anything. The gleaming shaft of metal saved me, the pole which had been humped by the other dancer only a few minutes before. I grasped it between my hands and swung myself around, but no one cheered my recovery. I was just recuperating with a simple combination step when Willie's voice drifted away and the jukebox died. I was right not to expect any applause, for after I completed the combination and tagged it with a modest turn, I was left standing up there in a kind of prolonged, dumb silence.

Johnny's face was like an oasis at the edge of the stage. He was almost smiling as he beckoned me over. I hurried forward.

"That was fine," he murmured.

I could barely hear him, so I crouched and leaned forward.

"Now, for your second number," he added, almost whispering, "just slip your arms out of your leotard and roll it down to your waist."

"Huh?" I managed. Perhaps I hadn't heard him right.

"Just roll it down to your waist."

Johnny stood below me, eye-level with my breasts. The night before, he'd kept his promise and hadn't touched me, had stayed on his side of the bed, swathed in his paisley flannel pajamas. That was the promise I had expected him to try to break. Not the other one, not the understanding I'd had with him and Fat Harry from the very beginning.

"I can't."

Johnny frowned. "Of course you can."

I shook my head. Leaning out of the glare, I could see all the faces in the bar staring back at me, anticipating my second number. Since my near fall from the stage, the bar remained suspended in a kind of exalted hush. The older man kept gazing at me and stroking his beard.

Johnny rested his arms on the stage. "Honey, what harm will it do? All the other girls do it. No one's gonna hurt you."

Perspiration beaded my brow and my ankles were chafing inside those ridiculous new shoes. "My father wouldn't like it."

"Your daddy ain't here."

"I'm not used to, it's just that I can't—"

"Honey, you ain't gonna make no money acting like the Flying Nun."

I wiped my forehead and gnawed at the insides of my cheeks. I dreaded the thought of one of those bourbon-swilling buffoons breaking the silence with "Take it off, baby!!" But they all just stared, even the overweight barmaid who was enveloped in what looked like a lurid purple negligee.

I heard a sigh singing through Johnny's teeth. "OK, OK. Come down and mingle with the customers. Jesus Christ, I don't know—"

He shook his head and wandered off into the office.

I wobbled back down the stairs and dubiously looked about, preparing for the next sorry performance: mingling. I'd never been one for small talk, nor was I in the habit of planting my arse onto the laps of strangers. I wondered what they might talk about. Oil? Horses? The price of cattle? But these were urban men, or, rather, *sub*urban men, probably with wives and children and two-car garages.

A hefty guy in a ten-gallon hat waved me over and, almost glad for something to do, I followed the direction of his beckon. He was wearing jeans and a shirt, the checkered design of which would have been better suited to covering a kitchen table than the broad wasteland of his back.

"Well, now, honey"—he touched my arm lightly—"y'r a shy little one. Lemme buy you a drink. This here's mah brother, Jack, 'n' mah name's Rich. Ain't she pur'ty? Yew just sit y'rself down here, young lady, and tell us what they call yew."

I lowered myself onto the stool and didn't tell him my real name. He beckoned over the purple-clad barmaid and ordered three Jim Beam and cokes. Rich palmed her a fifty-dollar bill. She ran it up on the cash register. The drinks were eight dollars each. He tipped her ten.

"Well, now, Alice"—he took my hand in his—"ah'd like to marry yew."

I drew my hand away and shifted on my stool, which was wedged between the two brothers. I felt as if I were sandwiched between Hoss and Little Joe on "Bonanza."

"Yes-er-ree! Ah'd like to take you away from all this. You ain't married or nothin' are yew?"

"Um, engaged," I lied. "I'm getting married next week." I took a closer look at Rich's weathered face, slightly shadowed by the brim of his hat. It was furrowed with deep, premature lines and a thin, banana-shaped scar cut across the left side of his chin. It was then that I noticed his left eye, which was a pale, deathly gray, contrasting with the rich brown color of his right. The gray eye was also slightly crossed, so that when he took my hand again, it seemed as if he were keeping the brown one fixed on my face and the other on the rest of the bar.

"Well, ain't that a shame," said Jack.

Rich let his mouth droop and rested one hand on my knee.

I picked it up and placed it back in his lap. Kitty was onstage, dancing to "The Man Who Shot Liberty Valence." Since it was her first number, no one took any notice of her.

"Wah don' you take y'r clothes orf?" said Jack.

I took a sip of my drink, which tasted like sugary water despite the fact that it looked exactly the same as the other two bourbon and Cokes.

"She's shy," said Rich. "That's why ah'm goin' marry her."

"Won' make no money bein' shy!"

They both laughed and slapped their knees. It wasn't long before the music stopped and all the men put down their drinks and turned to watch Kitty.

"Honky-Tonk Woman" began blaring into the bar. Kitty turned her back and wagged her arse at the crowd. A few guys at one table began howling. She freed one arm from the sleeve of her leotard, then the other. She hugged herself, hands wildly caressing her back, as if she were locked in the wild embrace of an urgent man. Her fingers worked the leotard down her back, first revealing the shoulder blades like tiny, stunted wings, then the rib cage pressing through her skin. When she freed herself and finally swung around, Jack and Rich whistled at the white gooseflesh of her breasts divided by a tattooed knife pointing out of her cleavage.

I couldn't take it anymore, and slipped off quickly to the silence of the rest room. It was becoming a theme in life, barricading myself in women's loos when I needed a moment to myself.

For the rest of the day, Johnny tried all kinds of ways to get me to simply slip my arms out of my leotard and roll it down. Throughout the afternoon he sent various dancers over to entice me to get my gear off. One woman in black smiled like Doris Day and kept touching my shoulder. Another had a venomous whisper and kept hissing at me, "Who the *hell* do you think *you* are, swanking around like a goddamn princess!" She barely parted her teeth as she spoke. Her limp red hair fell about her face in oily tendrils. "Who the hell do you think you are?"

I continued to shake my head and, every hour or so, clambered up on the stage to dance my two respectable numbers. Early in the evening, I managed to extricate myself from the gaze of Rich Harley's one good eye. I slipped out of the club, and dashed across to the telephone box standing like a mirage on the other side of the highway. The collect call I tried to place to Gerry via Leonard's place didn't go through. The cars roared past. Soon my absence from the club would be noticed. What was Gerry doing? Buying Marilyn dinner in some Canal Street restaurant? Twilight was settling over the city. I'd have to wait until I finished work before I could get my hands on a stack of quarters and make some more phone calls.

Back in the club, Freddy Harriff appeared, nursing a bucket of Kentucky Fried Chicken. He looked at me, shook his head and said, "I dunno what all the fuss is about. You ain't even got any tits to shake."

On into the evening, the men continued to eye me from the shelter of their cowboy hats. The only money I made, apart from the two dollars an hour the Harriff brothers deigned to pay their dancers, was from the 50 percent of every watered-down drink Rich Harley bought me. I remained completely sober. Rich's one good eye grew red and shiny. He switched to tequila. I sat on my stool and watched his hands begin to perspire as some sort of rash purpled its way around his neck.

In spite of his glowing eye and sweat, he remained amicable enough, persisting in his boozy proposals of marriage and his perplexed questions about the logic of Aussie Rules. He didn't badger me to take my clothes off, and I was thinking that I could have been biding my time in worse company. But around seven-thirty, when he went to order another round, he snatched up my half-empty glass.

"I want you to take a *real* fuckin' drink," he hollered, swaying toward me.

I shifted on my stool, glancing about.

"Yew think ah don' know!" He held the glass so tightly, I thought it would shatter within his grip. His crooked eye leered closer to me. I glanced about, but no one seemed to take any notice of Rich's little turn.

"I want yew to drink a fuckin' *double*." I edged my way around the stool, trying to escape the gaze of his gray eye. "Not all this goddamn *sugar water* ah'm payin' through the nose for! D'you hear me?" he yelled. "Yew ain't gonna pull one over *me*!"

He raised the glass level with his shoulder and suddenly threw it. It shattered around my stool and flat Coke sprayed up and soaked my calves. The room went quiet and all I could hear was Rich Harley heaving against the bar, almost out of breath.

Broken glass formed a rough circle around my feet; my ankles were wet and sticky. I was trembling a little. I had the same feeling that had possessed me when I'd tried to duck the blows of my mother's lover all those years ago. I had learned early on that fighting back was not the answer—it only exacerbated the wrath of your tormentor, made him hit you even harder.

"What the fuck are you looking at?" he managed to cry out to all the people who were staring at him.

Johnny Harriff hurried up and diffused the situation. He ordered another round for Rich, took me by the hand and led me into his office.

When I left with Johnny a few minutes later, the broken glass still sat gleaming beneath the crossed legs of the dancer who had taken my place.

■ **35** ■

Johnny was wordless in the car, and made no further comment about the extent to which my leotard covered my body. In the office, before we'd left, he'd tallied up my earnings and made no fuss about paying me my thirty-six dollars, though he didn't forget to deduct the fifty cents he'd given me earlier.

Back at the house, he reclined into one of the vinyl easy chairs while I strode up to the nearby shopping center to eat a sandwich and make my phone calls. It was a relief to hear my father's voice. Before I'd had a chance to tell him the Hot Potato was a strip club, though, he began babbling on about his immigration forms and speculating about the application fee and how he was planning to post his scrapbook, and how that would convince the Harriff brothers of his standing as a famous Australian drummer, and perhaps they could use it for publicity purposes, and as soon as he got his green card we could start making some real money, and what was the club like? Was there enough room on the stage for his drums? Would he need to buy a drum mat? And what were the acoustics like? And how awful it was in New Orleans, how dead it was after New Year's Eve, how happy he'd be to get out of the place. When I could get a word in, I stopped chewing on the insides of my cheeks and answered in monosyllables. Before I'd had a chance to tell him, the last quarter had clicked away, and I was left with the recorded voice of an American woman repeating, "If you'd like to make a call, please hang up and try again."

■ **36** ■

Johnny Harriff was a man of curious contradictions. Between his polyester sheets he slept at a respectful distance, but in his scarlet-hued bar he pressured me to reveal my breasts. In his kitchen I was allowed to help myself to food, but in his office he deducted the loaned fifty cents from my pay. It was such incongruities that sustained a fraction of hope in what was promising to be a decidedly dismal future. I returned to his house in the anticipation that he might finally acquiesce and employ my father and me as legitimate entertainers.

That night I sat in the Harriff living room, while Johnny guffawed his way through repeats of "Green Acres." I kept willing the phone to ring, but it remained silent, defying me. When Eva Gabor gestured at the Manhattan skyline and pined for Park Avenue at the beginning of the evening's fourth episode, I took a shower and buried myself beneath Johnny Harriff's blue sheets.

The next morning, I prepared myself for another day at the Hot Potato, dressing in a black leotard and skirt, toting the uncomfortable high-heeled silver shoes. In the car, Johnny told me to stay away from the Harley brothers. Even though I suspected the answer, I asked him, "Why?" But he just shook his head and kept his eyes fixed on the highway.

The club was empty when we arrived, except for the barmaid, who was dressed in the same purple negligee. Johnny disappeared into his office while I sat on a chair in the looming darkness and tried to psyche myself up for another eight hours of smoke, wolf whistles, and pale, reluctant flesh.

However, my future was decided for me when, after a few hours, another woman chose not to remove her halter top at the beginning of her second number. She simply continued to twirl about in her platform shoes as if she had forgotten her duty. The red lights blinked on and off in their usual frenzy. A murmur began to rise in the bar and Jack Harley jumped up from his chair near the stage and banged on the office door. Someone yelled, "Get it off!" And a couple of soggy, balled napkins sailed up and splattered between her shoulder blades. Still, she danced on, indifferent, arcing her arms and moving counterclockwise in quarter turns. Johnny emerged from his office with his glasses perched on the tip of his nose.

What surprised me was that the defiant woman was not Kitty, who clearly hated working in the Hot Potato, nor the dancer I'd overheard complaining in the toilet, but the one with the straggly red hair who'd vilified me the day before with her menacing whispers. She was spinning into the howled objections as if she were Isadora Duncan celebrating the Greek earth.

When the song ended, and she sauntered offstage, Johnny didn't go near her. He grabbed me by the wrist instead, pulled me into his office, and sacked me.

Then he snatched up the receiver of his phone, recited his credit card number, and booked me a ticket back to New Orleans.

■ 37 ■

I arrived at Leonard's to be greeted with a banner hanging from his loft: *Welcome Home!* Leonard must have been up half the night painting it, for I hadn't called them with my news until about six o'clock the previous evening.

My father tried to veil his disappointment in imitations of Marilyn's Blanche Dubois voice, but it was easy to see he pined for a nightclub to dignify his music. Now we were back to square one: bad weather, stingy crowds, and curfews.

Fortunately, our pink room behind the witchcraft shop had not been relet—Thomas apparently couldn't find anyone suitably normal—so we moved our few belongings back in under the gaze of the gimlet blue eye.

In eleven weeks my visa would expire. I had to marry, or leave the country, or stay on as an illegal alien. I didn't have much choice but to put it all out of my mind and anticipate the upcoming celebrations of Mardi Gras.

■ 38 ■

If there was any point at which we were going to give up, it was then, at the beginning of January. In the Alpine Cafe, just off Jackson Square, we ate a five-dollar meal and, for the first and only time, talked about going home. The winter was getting us down. It would be three or four months before we could return to New York. I was pissed off about my Houston experience and had been scouring Bourbon Street, looking for Fat Harry, fantasizing about punching him in his bloated gut.

But everyone in Sydney had said, "I'll give you six months, and you'll be back." And here we were, five months later, wanting to skulk home.

Gerry buttered a piece of French bread and inched his chair toward me. He had another idea: Since we already had our return airline tickets, we could slip back into Sydney without telling anyone, nick up to Surfers Paradise—where it was warm and we could swim every day—work the streets for three or four months, and make enough money to fly back to New York in time for the summer season.

I sipped my coffee, unconvinced. It sounded like a rose-colored admission of failure. Surely I wouldn't be able to get Gerry back on a plane once he had his feet wet with the Pacific Ocean. His voice had assumed that soft, persuasive tone he'd use when he tried to slip out of a promise, like the time he attempted to bribe my sister and me with lollies instead of taking us to Luna Park.

Silly Dad. Silly Dad even to try. We girls wanted to ride the Ghost Train—with him. To spin on the Octopus—with him. Not to suck on Tarzan jubes and Big Charlies out on the balcony while our parents sat inside, drinking Scotch and listening to Count Basie.

If I ever wanted to change my mind about the Surfers Paradise offer, it was too late by the time Gerry lodged his immigration application, because along with his forms, he had to submit his passport. All month long I was edgy with anticipation. What if they traced his passport number back to Sydney and found out he had three kids? Not to mention the phony marriage and the shady, fifty-dollar wedding.

My father sipped from four-dollar flasks of rum and told me to calm down. They get hundreds of applications every week, he soothed, from Greeks, Japanese, Mexicans, Brazilians, hundreds of applications from all over the world. They don't have time to check every one. They're not going to be bothered doing that.

He poured me a cup of rum and told me to sit down. Mardi Gras was coming up soon and we were going to make a fortune, and then there'd be the jazz festival, and then it'd be time to go back to New York and really make a killing.

39

On warmer afternoons, when the sun was high in the sky and lightly baking the courtyard, Jinny the stripper would saunter out of her apartment in a G-string, unfurl a blanket beside the stairs, and lie face-up in the winter light. We had to walk around her to get to the bathroom. I'd noticed Renoir was spending a lot of time out there, fertilizing a new crop of chili peppers in a collection of punctured ice cream containers.

Jinny was two years my senior but seemed older. She had a slim, golden body that she unabashedly revealed to the sun, and to anyone who happened to walk by. I hated wandering out of the toilet and being confronted with her unself-consciousness, not to mention her smiling invitations to strip off and join her on the rug. If I wanted a bit of sun myself, I sat on Pete's doorstep and read a book.

Perhaps Jinny wasn't the smooth, assured woman I assumed her to be, for she was always trying to win the attention and admiration of absolutely everyone. Apart from her daily public disrobing, she bought Renoir a set of new flower pots. Pete became enamored with her over a box of mixed biscuits. A few flattering comments about his golden locks and my father was suddenly swooning.

■ 40 ■

One afternoon, after Jinny had disappeared into the bathroom to take a shower, Pete noticed me sitting glumly on the stairs with a closed book of poetry in my hands. I'd been glancing through Wordsworth, yet I couldn't bring myself to read another line about flowers or streams. I had to be honest. I wanted a man. Not a Grimaldi type of man. Not a Jack Harley.

Pete told me to be patient. Soon my life would deliver him. I frowned and sighed and drummed my fingers against Wordsworth.

"You don't know what it's like," I said. "The waiting."

Pete grinned and nodded knowingly. "I know more than you think."

"Can't we do something?" I said. "Something to entice him? Even kids put out beer and chips to con Santa down their chimneys."

Pete stroked his beard for a moment, led me into his apartment and up to his altar, and plucked a small bottle of oil from one shelf. It was a golden color with a tiny stone swimming about at the bottom. He told me to anoint my forehead, below my left breast, and above my belly button every day at the same time.

"And don't forget," he added, "to rub it onto the soles of your shoes."

I unscrewed the top and took a sniff. It had a pleasant lemony odor. "Which ones? The taps or my walking shoes?"

"Both," he said, lighting a red candle. "Though the taps are the most important."

■ 41 ■

"That Jinny's a nice girl," my father remarked one night as we dressed. "Pretty cluey, too."

I grunted as I rubbed the lemony oil above my navel.

"She can't believe I'm sixty-three." Gerry pulled his trousers up and tucked in his shirt. "Well, actually, I'm sixty-*four* this year."

Then he went on about her generosity, about how she split her six-pack of Old Milwaukee with him and wouldn't take a cent for it, how she offered to rent a car and drive us to New York and charge the expenses to her wallet of credit cards.

I slipped my hand under my shirt and rubbed below my left breast, then across my forehead, just as Pete had told me.

"Of course," he added, clipping on his bow tie, "she can afford to be like that. D'you know how much she makes up at that joint?"

I buttoned up my waistcoat and shook my head.

"Over a hundred bucks a night. Can you believe that? Five hundred bucks a week, just for shaking her tits in the right direction."

He laughed and shook his head.

"Shit, I wish *I* was a chick."

I tipped some more oil onto my palm and began rubbing it into the soles of my taps. "They have male dancers, too."

"Yeah, but not wrinkly old farts like me."

"No one believes you're sixty-three," I volleyed back, working the oil into the leather of the second shoe. "Look at all that gorgeous blond hair."

"Yeah, but I'm not camp enough for them. It's the camp blokes they want."

"Well, it's too bad, eh?" I said, massaging one toe tap with my thumb.

Gerry pursed his lips and gave me a long stare. "What in the fuck are you doing?"

I worked the yellow liquid around the edges. "Tap shoes are just like cars," I said. "And gates. They all require a little maintenance."

42

Our dismal nights back out on the street fertilized Gerry's interest in Jinny and Big Daddy's. During the afternoons, he made a habit of sunning himself on the stairs and chatting with her. One day she passed around color photographs of herself snapped while she'd been performing, though there didn't seem to be much dancing going on. Tassled pasties the size of silver dollars were glued over her nipples, and a lamé G-string didn't quite cover the triangle of her trimmed pubic hair. In many of the photos she seemed to be merely bending over, her hip thrusting toward the outstretched hand of a man, who was about to pluck the elastic of her G-string and slip a note against her skin.

When Gerry passed them to me, I nodded and managed to produce a vague smile, though I inwardly fumed at his admiration of Jinny, and the way she made her living. *Five hundred bucks a week*—it was the mantra that followed me whenever we had a particularly bad night on Bourbon Street. *Cash in the hand. Clear!*

One rainy night I grew tired of arguing with Gerry about the ingenuity of Jinny's vocation. He kept talking her up. Up and up. All that money. All that cash.

I couldn't believe my father was trying to persuade me to play a part for which I was clearly unsuited, to audition for a role I'd spent my whole life trying to avoid. Did he know me at all? I wondered.

Any protective shield I still hoped he might brandish between his daughter and the world dissolved that night. My father became another Johnny, another Grimaldi, another man to resist.

43

There are various ways to resist what seems to be the inevitable, and Alice knew all the covert ones. When her father persuaded her simply to accompany him to Big Daddy's, she pinned her hair up under a checked cap. She took pleasure in dressing like a boy, like one of the urchins who swung around corner lampposts in the Quarter: Wearing one of her father's sweaters, a pair of jeans. Though she didn't forget to anoint her sneakers with Pete's lemony oil.

"Haven't you got any lipstick or something?" her father asked as they were leaving.

"I thought you didn't like lipstick."

"I don't like the taste of it, the smell of it," he said. "But it looks all right."

"I don't have any," she said. "Only the clown makeup."

"Don't worry about it." He shrugged and closed the door.

The manager of the club met them in a pokey office in the back of the building. His skin was sallow beneath the bare lightbulb and he habitually raised his hand to his forehead as if to conceal his prematurely receding hairline.

The father did all the talking in his smooth Australian accent. Alice sat mute beside him, receiving the perfunctory glances of the manager. Her father's voice was a river swirling about the man's head: We were good friends of Jinny's. Jinny had seen Alice dance and thought she'd fit right into Big Daddy's. Alice was a very fine dancer, and had just returned from an engagement in Houston.

The man's gaze grew longer. A line of ants marched across a corner of his desk and into the creamy yellow universe of an abandoned custard tart.

Alice had performed all over the world, the voice went on—Sydney, New York, London. And Alice is so different. A stripper who *tap dances*. All the way from Australia. Think about it. It's different, see?

The father offered the man a Camel and lit one up for himself. The manager reclined in his seat and smoked. Another line of ants formed, snaking back across the desk and down one leg, carrying the remains of the tart crumb by crumb away to some secret nest. Music palpitated through the office walls, a deep electric bass. Alice hunched into her chair, one ankle crossed over the other, her eyes avoiding the balding man. She found herself recalling that story her father used to tell, about how he was tripping on acid, floating on the edge of the earth's atmosphere, how the thousands of people down on the surface of the planet looked like ants crawling over a carcass. The ants were symbolic of something, she recalled. Insignificance. Meaninglessness. Though she was sure this scene in her life meant something.

"Got any hair up under that hat?" he asked, flicking his ash onto the carpet.

"Course!" said the father. "Course she does."

He lifted the cap from her head and revealed the messy bun. He told her to take out the pins, and she did, letting her unbrushed hair fall down her back and around her shoulders.

Gerry waved his cigarette. "Of course, it looks better when it's all done up. When it's combed and everything."

He passed her the cap and she placed it back on her head.

The manager flicked his ash again, rubbed his shrinking hairline, but Alice only felt her stomach loosen, only began to breathe again when he finally sighed and said he didn't have any openings at the moment. It was only then that her fingers loosened their grip from the arms of the chair, allowing themselves to extend across the desk to engage the man in a parting handshake.

◾ 44 ◾

I was relieved to return to the January streets, to the bricks worn smooth by my nightly dance steps, to my duets with Pee Wee, to my cutting contests with Hambone, to the ring of coins, to the game we played with the cops, to the mercy of the rain clouds—it was all familiar and comparatively benign after my aborted stint in the strip clubs. I was free again to pirouette on pavements, to cutaway on curbs. I was free to dress in oversized tails and a striped waistcoat, red satin breeches, a bowler hat. I was also back within my father's gaze, where he must see and watch me every night, every night beside him, he and I.

I was, however, still disappointed in the role he expected me to assume. I did not want to be in a story about Big Daddy's Strip Club. But instead of confronting him, I sat on my disappointment. I squashed it down beneath the heel of my shoe and remained silent. I blew it through a straw, into the bubbles erupting through my lemonade. On my days off I placed a paper-thin wafer of acid on my tongue and waited for my jaw to lock, for the colors to begin whirring between the ginger blossoms hanging over the courtyard fence. I drifted around the Quarter, watching moonflower vines riot in the trees. I began swimming two miles a day in a pool that had been sunken into the courtyard of a gay bar called Menifee's.

Back and forth. Back and forth. Men would drape their arms about each other and, slowly getting drunk, gaze at me through the plateglass window all afternoon. When I'd finally crawl from the pool, one or two would stagger into the courtyard and try to persuade me to swim the English Channel.

I dressed myself in secondhand clothes bought from Volunteers of America. A Chinese straw hat. Silk pajama pants. While Gerry was over at Leonard's place, smoking dope and listening to music, I chose to walk alone. I frequently ended up under an umbrella in the empty courtyard of Pat O'Brien's, watching the rain glisten within an orb of electric light, while I sipped a cheap cocktail called a Rainbow.

■ 45 ■

Toward the end of January, my father and Marilyn were summoned to the Immigration offices for their long-awaited interview. Once he had endured this, Gerry surmised, his green card would be in the mail.

The only preconceptions we had of immigration interviews were gleaned from Nerida's anecdotes about turning up to the New York office with her black drag-queen fiancé. But apart from a couple of funny stories, Gerry had no idea what to expect when he arrived with Marilyn. Probably just a quick chat and the signing of a few papers. The taking of photographs and two sets of fingerprints.

The office doors opened at seven-thirty, and they were the first in line. They took a ticket and then proceeded to wait another hour and a half before an officer was ready to see them. When their number was finally called, they were led down a hall by a middle-aged black man in a gray suit. They reached his office. The man raised his hand at Gerry and told him he'd see the lady first.

Gerry bided his time with a few cigarettes. He leaned against the door, but could hear nothing through the thick wood. He took a leak, returned. When Marilyn finally emerged from the office, he heard the man call, "I'll see you now, Mr. Sayer."

But just as Gerry went to walk in, Marilyn grabbed him and pulled him aside.

"I told him we met on a cruise ship," she whispered quickly. "That you were playing drums on it and I was taking a holiday. We live, we live in an apartment on Royal Street"—she threw a quick glance over her shoulder—"number five thirty-one. We pay four hundred a month."

Gerry could see, through the ajar door, the officer's head, bowed over some paperwork on his desk. Marilyn's grip tightened around his arm.

"You proposed to me one morning while we were making love. And oh, don't forget, we've got green carpet in the living room and dining room, but in the bedroom it's all red."

Before Gerry had set foot in the office, he'd already forgotten the number of the house in which he was supposed to be living. Why hadn't she simply stated the address that was all over their forms, his actual address behind the witchcraft shop? Why hadn't she simply told him they'd met in Bonaparte's Retreat, as it had happened?

He had no time to contemplate these questions, for the officer behind the desk had many of his own: What was the name of the cruise ship on which they had met? What religion was Marilyn? Does she have an inward or outward belly button? What kind of birth control do they use? Do they keep the bread in the kitchen cupboard or the fridge? What brand of soap do they buy? Does Marilyn have any scars, and if so, where? Who introduced them? Does Marilyn use tampons or sanitary pads?

Gerry blundered and waffled his way through. Marilyn had been only able to tell him a fraction of the answers. What he didn't know, he made up, sometimes simply saying the first thing that flew into his head. Thus, Marilyn suddenly became a lapsed Roman Catholic with a six-inch scar beneath her inny belly button. And the supposed bathroom ended up being red, for in his haste he'd mixed it up with his wife's lascivious bedroom.

The interview was long and exhausting. Gerry tried to light a cigarette, but the officer told him there'd be no smoking in his office. The questions kept firing: What side of the bed does he sleep on? What does Marilyn eat for breakfast? Where did they spend last Christmas?

When it was finally over, Gerry staggered out, relieved, yet craving a double shot of something strong. He lit up a Camel, wondering what would happen next. Either they'd start shooting photographs for his file and green card, or two security guards would sidle up and take him into custody. He was just nodding to Marilyn, ready to adjourn to the waiting room for coffee, when the officer's voice boomed again, calling Marilyn back in for a second interview.

It went on like that all day. Interview upon subsequent interview. Question upon question. Until, by late afternoon, they had embroidered each other with magnificent and contradictory lies. For herself, Marilyn spontaneously elaborated on the romance that had burgeoned on the Love Boat, the man behind the kit of drums with whom she'd fallen in love. Gerry narrated a marriage defined by boiled eggs and shopping days, as if his proposal had been prompted by boredom more than anything else.

At the end of the day, the officer who'd replaced the black man after lunch rubber-stamped the application and told Gerry it would be three to six months before he'd be posted the results. In the meantime, he wasn't allowed to leave the country.

The officer led them downstairs, where Gerry was permitted to apply for a social security number. While his application was pending, the card on which the number was printed allowed Gerry to work legally in the United States. Since Marilyn had forgotten her own number and had lost her card, and since she had a new surname, while she was waiting around for Gerry, she reapplied for a number herself.

When the cards were issued she held hers up and kissed it.

Gerry was a bit bewildered by this gesture, until he remembered she was terrified of policemen.

"Marilyn Jean Sayer," she declared. "A whole new identity!"

He winced and glanced about, hoping no one had heard. He slung an arm around her shoulders and hurried her toward the door.

46

I was in the courtyard when I heard the cocky click of his boots against the cement. I was stretching, trying to cajole my legs into a split, when he emerged from the passage. He was holding the card up like a trophy.

"I got it! I got it!" He waved the card about and half-ran toward our room. I rose and followed. He was already pouring out two cups of rum.

As he undressed, he told me the whole story, from the Love Boat to Marilyn's new identity. After he'd stripped down to his undies, he swigged at his rum and held the card up and danced about the room, shaking his arms and swinging his bum from side to side, until he tripped over his discarded boots and fell backward onto my bed.

I picked up the dropped card and studied it.

"Gerry, even though this card is green, it's not a *green card*."

He settled himself against my pillow. "Whaddya mean? It's green, isn't it?"

"Yeah, and it's blue, too."

"So?"

"So what I'm saying is, it's just a temporary work permit until they figure out if you and Marilyn are for real or not. That's why they said three to six months. They'll have to check the information you gave them before they'll let you become an American."

Gerry sat up and hugged his knees. "I know that—"

"The *real* green card," I continued, remembering the one Nerida had shown me, "the real one has your photo on it and your date of birth and social security number, and on the back are all these secret numbers and codes. And it's laminated. And it's not green. That's just a *symbol*—like giving you the green light."

"Well, I'll get that eventually," he sulked, "in a few months. And anyway," he continued, gesturing at me to pass him his rum, "I can work legally in the States now. You'll have to write back to Sydney and tell everyone about it."

I nodded, but thought we should keep the tale to ourselves. I returned to the courtyard, dropped into a split, and tried to coax my crotch to flatten itself against the cement.

■ 47 ■

One night after work, as I pushed the cart up the passage leading to the courtyard, I saw a cluster of suitcases and boxes, a few sticks of furniture, plastic laundry bags brimming with clothes, and a large figure looming on the stairs.

"Marilyn?" I called.

The figure shifted on the stairs.

"*Marilyn!*" exclaimed Gerry. "What on earth—"

"Oh, thank God you're finally home!" She stood up and rushed toward Gerry.

He pushed back her fawning hands. "What're you doing here?"

"I've been evicted from my apartment! The landlord kicked me out. He tossed my things onto the street. Everything. Even my nice new pajamas with all the holes in the right places and my underwear and all. And I thought, well, since we were married and everything, it'd be OK if I—"

Gerry raised one hand, as if he were stopping traffic. "Now, hang on a minute—"

"I came home and everything was out on the street, and I thought, What am I going to do now? Where am I—"

"Marilyn!" barked Gerry. "Look, we've only got a tiny room between us, with two single beds. So if you think you're gonna move in, you've got another think coming." He nodded at her mountain of luggage. "Half of all that shit wouldn't even fit in there."

"But I thought, since we were—"

"How'd you get in here, anyway?"

Marilyn's voice became all sulky. "I banged on the gate for about twenty minutes and finally a man came down and let me in."

Gerry was about to make some smart-arsed reply when I hopped between them, hoping to abort the brewing domestic battle.

"Listen, Marilyn," I said, lowering my voice, trying to keep it calm, "I'm sorry you've been evicted, and I know you're in a jam. But the simple fact is that if you move in with us, we'll all get kicked out. Thomas won't stand for it. He's very strict about that sort of thing."

Thankfully it was true. We'd heard about people on the other side being asked to leave over the occasional sharing of rent.

"Oh, that's right," agreed Gerry. "He'd hit the roof. Isn't there anyone else you can stay with?"

"Well"—she threw a forlorn gaze at her bags and suitcases—"I guess I could call Dot. At least she could pick me up in her car." She glanced at our tip bucket in the shopping cart. "Does anyone have a quarter?"

■   48   ■

Even though my skin remained perpetually lubricated, and in spite of my having tracked oil throughout our room—not to mention the streaks I'd left on the footpath outside the Royal Sonesta—I had not yet attracted the man. Day after day I'd followed Pete's instructions to the letter, anointing myself at the same time every day, just before we left to go out to work, yet nothing much had changed.

When I expressed my disappointment, Pete told me to be patient, that the universe takes time to shuffle the aspects into place.

"Isn't there something else you could give me?" I half-whispered in the shop one morning. "Something stronger?"

He sighed. The candle flame made his looming shadow tremble against the curtain of Spanish moss.

"Have you thought about doing your hair different? Maybe combing it out and—"

My eyes grew wide. "What's wrong with my hair?"

"Nothing! I just thought that maybe—"

I glanced in the mirror hanging above the crucifix jewelry. My face was still there, below the careless blond pompadour, framed by loose strands and tendrils.

"Look," he added quickly, glancing at his watch. "Meet me tonight. At midnight. Just bang on my door and I'll be ready."

"Ready for what?"

A group of tourists wandered into the shop and began examining the books and amulets.

Pete squeezed around the counter and lowered his voice. "Never mind. Just bring along one thing."

"What?"

He glanced about, as if he were a spy about to reveal a code. "Tonight, when you go out to dance, wear a T-shirt beneath your clothes. Try and sweat through it as much as you can. When you come over afterward, bring it with you."

■　49　■

The first thing I noticed when I walked into Pete's place that night was the smell of rose incense. Smoke billowed up from the burner and coiled around the room. He'd placed fresh jasmine in a vase on the altar, a bowl of dirt, and a teacup of water.

I had the sweaty T-shirt in my hands. I was a little reluctant to give it up, since I wasn't sure what he was going to use it for. He told me to kneel beside him in front of the altar, which I did. He crossed himself and took two red candles from his altar cabinet, rubbed them with oil, popped them in their holders, and lit them.

"How long will this take?" I asked, shifting my legs.

He plopped down beside me and grinned. He took another bottle from his cabinet, tipped a little oil onto his fingers, and with it drew a cross on his forehead. Lifting the T-shirt, he pressed his face into it, and inhaled.

After a minute of silent contemplation, of simply staring into one candle flame, he spread the T-shirt in front of us on the floor. Then he rooted around in his cabinet and pulled out a pair of scissors. He began mumbling again, working his way into some sort of chant, though I couldn't understand what it was because it seemed to be in Latin.

The mantra grew louder as he began cutting into the cloth. He didn't cut in a straight line, but curved around here and there until the shape of a human figure began to emerge within the shirt's white cotton. It looked like a featureless gingerbread man—parted arms and legs, a rather large head. When the cutout was complete, Pete lifted it up and placed it on his lap. He'd simultaneously cut the front and back of the shirt, so there were actually two figures resting against his knees.

He rummaged through the cabinet again and pulled out a ball of yellow wool, some buttons, cotton, and a packet of needles. Within ten minutes, he'd stitched the two pieces of material together, leaving a gap at the head about an inch long.

All the while he was humming and chanting in Latin. It reminded me of the Catholic Church, except that I'd never encountered a priest who got a kick out of sacrificing soiled T-shirts. Every now and then, my name would spring from his tongue and fill the air between so many foreign words.

Suddenly, he snatched up the scissors again and turned. Before I could protest, he'd already snipped off a lock of hair that had fallen away from my bun. He stuffed it into the opening at the head of the doll. He then proceeded to fill the doll with a red feather, a few crushed leaves, three pinches of the dirt from the bowl on the altar, a handful of berries, some dried flowers, two stones the size of my thumbnail, and some Spanish moss.

Lastly, he held the doll up to me and told me to spit into it, which I did, then he sewed up the opening and mumbled my name again.

Next, he sewed two green buttons onto the head. The only other distinguishing feature he added were about nine or ten strands of yellow wool to the top, where the opening had been. Then he drew the ends of them together and knotted them to the doll's crown—it was my pompadour, and those buttons were my wide green eyes.

Pete's chanting rose again as he passed the doll through the flame of each candle. Its shadow yawned up and danced across the walls. He sprinkled water on the head and between the legs, passed the body through the smoking incense. Then he placed it in my lap. It was my gris-gris, my mojo, my charm. I picked her up and held her to my chest. She smelled of roses and sweat, the scent my mother used to exude when I was a toddler, when she folded me into her empty bed.

50

The next morning, Gerry and I were sitting in our room, drinking tea, when Thomas's shadow fell across the doorway and he suddenly appeared before us.

"Gerry, there was a friend of yours just in the shop."

"Yeah? Who was it?"

Thomas crossed his arms. "She just left a message for you. Meet her in the bar next door."

Gerry groaned. "What was her name?"

Thomas shrugged.

"What time?"

"All she said was you better get in there right away."

Gerry sighed. "OK, thanks Thomas."

Thomas nodded and disappeared.

"What the fuck does she want now?" Gerry slurped down the rest of his tea.

I drained my cup and asked him if he wanted me to come with him.

"Yeah, you'd better," he replied, sliding into his thongs.

It was fairly dark when we walked into the bar, but I soon made out Marilyn's frame. She'd plonked herself on a stool and was chatting with the heavyset woman who sat next to her.

"Well, Marilyn?" announced Gerry.

Both women spun around. Marilyn was trembling; she looked as if she'd received some bad news, or was about to impart some. Her companion just glared at Gerry. She was older than Marilyn, and the hard living she'd endured was firmly etched into the powdered creases of her face. Her thick makeup didn't entirely erase the scars embedded in her right cheek, nor the way her mouth tended to grimace into a tight knot of contempt. She smelled of gin and menthol cigarettes.

"H-hello, Gerry," Marilyn ventured weakly.

"You shut up, Marilyn," her companion barked, "and let me do the talking."

Marilyn nodded and sipped her drink.

Gerry turned. "And what do *you* have to say?"

The woman scowled. "Plenty! I got plenty to say to you." She slammed her glass on the bar and straightened up. "First of all: Who the hell do you think you are? You've cheated Marilyn out of a big chunk of money that's rightfully hers!"

"What are you talking about?"

"Two hundred lousy bucks. You might be able to pull one over on Marilyn here, but you can't fool me! You and I both know that the going rate is two *grand* and even that's cheap!"

Marilyn wilted a little on her stool and turned her face away.

"And who do you think you are?" he volleyed back. "Marilyn's mother? She and I had a deal, and quite frankly, she was *glad* to get two hundred bucks."

"Listen, Buster," the woman hissed through her teeth. "I'm not taking any shit from *you*. You *owe* her. And I'm gonna make sure she gets it."

"And what do you get out of it?"

"Satisfaction," she said, grabbing Gerry's arm. "Satisfaction in seeing slime like you squirm."

I was already squirming, edging away from her as subtly as possible.

Gerry looked at Marilyn and sighed. "And I thought I could trust you—"

"You just shut your goddamn face," her companion hissed to him. "Now, I'm gonna tell you what Marilyn needs right now. This morning she needs exactly one hundred and thirty-five dollars. Get it."

"What?!"

"I said, *Get it*. Get it right now or else I'll go over to the pay phone, call up Immigration, and tell them that this marriage is a complete hoax and you and your goddamn daughter will be arrested and deported back to Australia within seven days!"

Back in our room, I flopped onto my bed and groaned. I couldn't stop thinking of my mother. Sure, this marriage to Marilyn was purely for the sake of convenience, but when I'd straightened Gerry's preinterview tie, guilt settled into my stomach. My mother haunted me in that room, her presence always coalescing out of the wide blue eye painted on the wall. I was sure the blackmail we were being subjected to was a form of punishment, that some ghost or angel associated with my mother was acting on her behalf.

"I knew something like this would happen," I said, not looking at my father.

Gerry was more philosophical: "Everything would've been fine if she hadn't met up with that bloody Dragon Lady. Marilyn's not a bad kid, you know? It's that stupid woman putting ideas into her head."

"What are you going to do?"

Gerry shrugged and sat at the table. "What *can* I do? I've gone too far to have this thing screwed up now. The Immigration people said that we could be called in for more interviews at any time."

"The trouble is," I said, rolling onto my back, "that if you give them the hundred and thirty-five now, who knows how much they'll want next week? Or next month? Hell, it could go on for years."

"Well, I can't back out on this immigration thing now!" He poured the dregs of the rum flask into his teacup. "I'll get into all kinds of trouble!"

"I know," I said. "That's what I tried to tell you weeks ago."

"Look, let's cut the lecture." He ingested the rum with one quick slug. "Just hotfoot it down to the bank and draw out a hundred and thirty-five bucks."

51

I noticed him on the way back from Canal Street, after I'd withdrawn the Dragon Lady's ransom. He was in the Square, juggling eight bowling pins. He was so tall he looked as though he was wearing stilts inside those baggy, black-and-white striped pants. He was as tall as his partner was short. The little bloke wore shorts and suspenders and would have been around the five-foot mark.

They were new in town and everyone in the square was talking about them. They were a pretty slick act. It was rumored they came from Boston. They were pulling bigger crowds than anyone in the Quarter.

It was the tall one who'd caught my eye. In spite of his height, his thin limbs exuded a certain grace as he conjured patterns in the air with burning torches or machetes. He had shoulder-length black hair and high cheekbones and even though he projected a deep, theatrical voice across the square, he had about him a kind of winning shyness that sat well on top of his immense talent for wielding many dangerous objects at once.

But I couldn't linger too long that afternoon. Marilyn and the Dragon Lady were still in the bar, and my father was waiting anxiously for the money.

When I returned, Gerry was sitting on the wooden stairs, sharing a joint with Renoir. I palmed the money into Gerry's hand, and he swayed a little as he stood up and slipped it into his back pocket. His face was flushed and I could see that his eyes were watering behind his thick, yellow glasses. He held onto the banister and walked unsteadily down the steps. His head was bowed, and he suddenly looked tentative and fragile, as if he were battling some furtive illness.

I watched him amble down the alleyway in his green cords and thongs. His jeans were loose and baggy around his hips and the hems kept getting caught beneath his heels as he walked.

I swallowed and leaned against the stairs. I held out my hand to Renoir, who had begun singing "Me and Bobby McGee."

"Give us a toke," I said.

He handed the joint over. I raised it to my mouth and drew in a lungful. I could taste my father on the cardboard filter, a warm breath wheeling through my sinuses.

52

Over the next few days, I saw the juggler once or twice in passing. But not a week had passed before I noticed him hovering in the shadows of

Bourbon Street, watching me dance. He was standing on the other side of the road. I pretended not to notice, but suddenly my steps became more intricate and my arms coordinated themselves into spontaneous and exalted flights. As I spun and glided, my feet sang out their consonants, multiplying them into a secret language I was inventing just for him.

When eight o'clock tolled and we knocked off, my father crossed to the Indian curry shop to take a leak. He was looking a little more relaxed since he'd handed the money over to the Dragon Lady. We'd not seen either of them for days, and assumed they'd pulled that stunt because one of them had had an urgent debt.

The tall juggler was still leaning into the shadows of the street. I began to pack up, waiting for him to come over, but he just stood there, hesitating at the edge of the sidewalk. I sat on my wooden case and untied my shoes. He glanced into the Court of Two Sisters, as if he were contemplating buying a beer. He wasn't wearing the striped pants he performed in, but a cloth pair with a drawstring, and a denim jacket. Whenever our eyes met, he'd quickly look away.

It wasn't until Gerry emerged from the shop that he turned and walked off, hands in pockets, shoulders slightly hunched. I watched his back grow smaller as he meandered down Bourbon Street. And just as Gerry was urging me to hurry along, I was sure I saw the juggler swing around again and glance at me one last time.

The next day, as I wandered through the square on my way to the A&P supermarket, there he was again, catching his minute partner from behind when the little bloke keeled over from the size of the enormous balloon he was blowing up. The smaller one was a nerdy-looking straight-man to the tall one's spectacular juggling and smooth good looks. I lingered on the edge of the crowd, admiring the ease with which he wheeled about on an elevated unicycle, the way his slim, graceful hands managed to juggle a knife, a cabbage, and a Ping-Pong ball. And I couldn't help wondering how those hands might touch me, how they might cup the curve of a bare hip or breast.

The following night, just before eight, I looked up and saw the juggler again, standing on the other side of the street. He was sipping self-consciously from a go-cup of beer and holding me in that same long gaze. People milled about, taking photos and throwing money, but he just stood in the one spot. With every step, I felt as if I were binding him to me, to every shuffle and pull-back and double wing, every double turn and cramp roll.

We stopped, as usual, at eight o'clock. Gerry miraculously disappeared again, and for that I was grateful. The tall juggler and I finally regarded one another from opposite sides of the street without the nervous averting of eyes.

I took a long swig of water and eventually summoned the courage to walk across the road and offer a sheepish hello. I prattled on a bit about the quality of his show, how funny he was, and how well he and his partner worked together. He shrugged self-deprecatingly and threw me back a few compliments, and couldn't seem to decide which hand he should hold his beer in. His eyes were wide and serious. His free hand kept arcing up and he'd rest his index finger against his lips, as if he were thinking something profound.

When a lull rose between us, and we noticed my father walking out of the curry shop, he suddenly blurted out, "Hey, d'you like dancing?"

I must have looked incredulous, for he quickly added, "I mean . . . you know . . . when you're not working. Just for fun."

I nodded. He told me about this new music that was spreading through New Orleans. It was played with a piano accordion and a washboard. It had come out of the bayous and the backwoods of Louisiana. It was supposed to be great to dance to.

Ordinarily, the thought of dancing to a washboard and piano accordion did not excite me. But he had those wide, serious eyes, and my father was standing impatiently by the cart, waiting for me to return, so he could zip down to the A&P and buy his six-pack of generic beer.

We hastily arranged to meet the following night—a Monday—at Molly's Bar on Toulouse Street.

We bade farewell with a few quick nods, and he raised his cup and said, "Cheers."

■ 53 ■

The morning after my encounter with the juggler, Gerry and I rose at about eleven and decided to treat ourselves to a five-dollar fish dinner at the Alpine Cafe. All the street performers and artists ate there, but we only dined at the cafe when we couldn't bear to look at another avocado or raw carrot. The fish was battered and deep fried, served with thick french fries, collard greens, and all the bread and butter you could eat. Sometimes we'd wait as long as we could before walking over there, so that the lunch would stretch on into the night and preclude the need for another meal.

But that day we did not wait. We both woke up starving. After our second cup of coffee out in the courtyard, we let ourselves through the gate and began heading toward Jackson Square.

We were approaching the square when I looked up and saw Marilyn and the Dragon Lady turning the corner. Marilyn still had her plastic bags in tow, and her companion was lugging a big, bloated shoulder bag. Gerry groaned and I grabbed his arm and yanked it, wanting to run into the sanctuary of Tujague's Bar.

"I'm not hiding from those two old tarts." He shook his arm free. "Anyway, it's not like they don't know where we live."

He sucked on his Camel defiantly then flicked the butt into the gutter. We paced toward them, and they toward us. It was like a duel, but in reverse. Gerry nodded at a distance of five or six paces. "Morning, ladies." He tipped an imaginary hat at them and mustered a smile.

The Dragon Lady's eyes widened, and I let out a sigh, thinking that we would pass unscathed.

But right when I went to step around Marilyn, she dropped her bags and I tripped on a plastic container that came rolling out of one of them.

Marilyn cried out and went running after the container, which seemed to be filled with tiny objects that were rattling about inside. She was chasing it along the gutter, when it got caught between the heavy hooves of a buggy horse trotting down Decatur.

"*My medicine!*" she howled, as the container bounced between the horse's legs. The buggy driver yelled at her to get back, but all she could do was scream, "*My medicine! My medicine!*"

The horse whinnied and veered into the adjoining lane. A car horn sounded and we heard a screech of tires. One of the buggy passengers began yelling. The driver spanked the air with his crop, trying to drive Marilyn back. But by then the container was lost beneath the buggy, and the next thing I saw was the lid bursting off and an explosion of round, colored pellets flying through the air.

Marilyn accidentally rammed herself into a parked Chevy as she dashed to recover the container. She dropped to the road and just sat there, surrounded by the small, gaudy nuggets.

Her companion didn't waste a moment. "See what your stupid kid did now?"

She grabbed the top of Gerry's shirt and twisted it into her fist.

"We need another payment, Buster. *Tomorrow.* Another hundred," said the Dragon Lady. "Two fifty-dollar bills."

They were caught in a tussle with one another. If they hadn't been grimacing, it might have looked as though they were bound up in the intricate footwork of some bawdy waltz.

"I haven't *got* any more," my father pleaded.

"Well, you better *find* some. Else Immigration's gonna throw you and your klutzy kid in the clink!"

Marilyn was busy collecting the pellets that had sprayed out over the road, oblivious to the passing traffic.

"I'll be waiting for you tomorrow in the bar. Four o'clock. Be there."

Then she suddenly turned and barked, "Come on, Marilyn!" And my father's wife picked herself up, cradling the plastic container, and ran after the Dragon Lady.

I walked over to the gutter and picked up one of Marilyn's so-called tablets. It was round and red, the width of my thumbnail. I broke it in half. Instead of finding powder inside it I discovered hard chocolate. It was an M&M.

"Should we go to the bank before or after lunch?" I asked.

Gerry smoothed down his shirt and pocketed a button that had been ripped off during the altercation. He was wide-eyed and pale. He straightened his glasses.

"They're both fucking insane," he said. "Mad as cut snakes."

54

The juggler was halfway through a mug of beer when I walked into Molly's exactly ten minutes late. I ordered a Dixie, sat down beside him, and we slipped into the preliminary small talk. His stage name was Bruno and his partner's was Boofhead. I swallowed my beer and laughed. Bruno and Boofhead—it seemed so perfect. They were a Boston-based duo and had made a stack of money working one of the malls there over the summer. Boofhead was a professionally trained actor, and this was his first foray onto the street. Bruno, however, had always worked the streets, even while he was growing up in California.

Boofhead had not come to New Orleans voluntarily: It had taken Bruno's most forceful powers of persuasion to pry his partner from the only city in which he thought he could live. Because they'd enjoyed such a successful stint over the summer, Bruno had been keen to continue working with Boofhead, but the weather had prevented them from staying up north.

After weeks of hearing Bruno talk up the virtues of Mardi Gras, not the least of which was the minor fortune to be made, Boofhead had packed his bags, kissed his girlfriend good-bye, and boarded a southbound jet. Bruno, on the other hand, had driven his dark blue VW beetle through nine states alone, dozing at the side of the road whenever he needed a rest.

Now they were sharing an uptown apartment, on Carrollton, and waiting for Mardi Gras to begin.

While we slowly drank our second beer, I narrated my own tale of Australia and New York, a similarly profitable summer, my father's marriage to Marilyn, our little universe behind the witchcraft shop. I neglected to tell him about the blackmailing business. I didn't want to scare him off.

When we drained our mugs and left Molly's, I was conscious of the fact that my outing with Grimaldi had begun in the same way: a couple of drinks on a Monday night, a walk through the Quarter to a vehicle, a drive uptown. But, I told myself, Bruno was as shy and self-effacing as Grimaldi was bold and cavalier. There'd be no quick bump in the back of a van with him. Besides, Bruno drove a VW Beetle and could only just sit up straight in the driver's seat, let alone fit into the back, on top of me, in pursuit of a quickie.

I was a little mortified, however, when he drove to Oak Street and parked across the road from the Maple Leaf. It wasn't long before I was sitting up at the bar, just as I had with Grimaldi. In the adjoining room an R&B band boomed away, played with the aid of a washboard and a piano accordion.

It sounded lusty and seductive. Nothing like the accordions I'd heard in Australia, nor the rickety scratches made by board players in corny Dixieland bands. This kind of music could have accompanied a voodoo ceremony, or a snake dancer. Couples wove and gyrated around the pulsing bass line.

The Dixie beer was cool and pleasant and I could feel the tension in my neck begin to melt. Bruno's head bobbed in time with the music and he drank quickly, supplicating his nervousness with long swallows. In spite of my perpetual desire to touch his dark hair, to lay one hand against the back of his neck, I contained myself and didn't ask him to dance.

The black man at the microphone sang about a woman who got into his blood and made him do crazy things, "Like walking off of buildings, thinking he's got wings."

Everyone at the bar smiled and nodded knowingly. Bruno swayed in his seat and ordered another round. In the adjoining room, an overalled man buried his face in his partner's cleavage and kissed her so deeply she fell to her knees with laughter, and he went down with her, tumbling onto the floor amid cheers from their fellow dancers.

After several more mugs of Dixie, we clambered back into Bruno's Beetle. Since we were so close, he said, he'd show me where he and Boofhead lived. He steered us through the rising mist along St. Charles Avenue. Towering live oaks formed a canopy overhead and an olive-green streetcar rumbled along beside us. Bruno continued to hum one of the tunes we'd just heard as he sat hunched over the steering wheel.

Soon he pulled up outside a large wooden house. He and Boofhead occupied the second-floor apartment. We sat in the dark, chatting away, our tongues loosened by the beer. I wondered if he'd muster the courage to invite me up. His hands remained on the steering wheel and only moved when he wanted to make a point or to run his fingers through his hair.

When a pause fell between us, I swallowed and gazed out at the thick, crooked arms of the oaks holding up the indigo sky, the stars, the winking pattern of Orion and Canis Major. Then I leaned across the gearstick and kissed him. I kissed him gently, briefly. Then I drew back into my own seat and waited for an answer.

■ 55 ■

Bruno seemed to like the fact that I made the first move, for he smiled shyly, took my hand, and led me up to his apartment. When he flicked on the light, I found myself in a front room overlooking the shiny silver strips of the streetcar tracks. A polished hardwood floor glowed beneath my feet, and I couldn't resist patting out a few soft rhythms against it as I turned away from the window.

Bruno said he'd be back in a minute and disappeared into a dark hallway. The fifteen-foot ceiling loomed above me. I leaned on the mantelpiece and surveyed the room. There wasn't much furniture, just his mattress in one corner, and a folding chair over which he draped his clothes. His four-foot high unicycle stood by the door, and nearby, on the floor, his clubs and balls and firesticks lay in a nest in the open mouth of an unzipped nylon bag.

It occurred to me that I should do something provocative in his absence: undress, perhaps, and lie on his mattress with his colored balls balanced on strategic parts of my body. Or, with the aid of the mantelpiece, I could attempt to mount the unicycle and hazard a naked ride across to his bed. I was surveying the clubs, imagining some game in which he'd have to remove a piece of his clothing for every time he dropped one, but since he was so good at juggling, I'd have to keep adding items to his repertoire until they eventually overwhelmed him.

I was still imagining the possibilities when he walked back into the room in a pair of blue underpants and flicked off the light. Then I felt his big hands on my waist and my mouth was suddenly wet with the earthy taste of his breath.

I awoke to find Boofhead padding across the hardwood floor in his Nikes, and it was only then that I realized Bruno chose to sleep in the living room. Decked out in a gray jogging suit, Boofhead looked like an athletic leprechaun as he hurried by the bed, trying not to notice that Bruno's long limbs were around the body of an unknown woman. Fortunately, we were entwined in a white sheet and bedspread, and the blushing Boofhead was spared the embarrassment of witnessing more than a bared leg or shoulder.

Boofhead let himself through the door and closed it quietly. Bruno sighed and shifted, but did not awaken.

It was a relief to be held by a warm body, to feel a knee nestled into the crook of my leg, a chin against the hollow of my neck. Even though Bruno's hands had eventually grown shy, even though his cock had grown limp inside me, I still enjoyed the pageant of sensation that had paraded beneath my skin long after he had left me and drifted into sleep. It was pleasant to wake up with a hand on my breast and sunlight flooding that spartan room.

56

Since Gerry and I didn't have a phone, whenever Bruno wanted to see me he drove over in his Beetle and stood at the gate. There was no bell or buzzer on the street and so, instead of bothering Thomas to let him in, Bruno would stick the bell of a long blue plastic horn through a small opening in the gate and blow. Suddenly, what sounded like a giant's loud fart would echo up the passage, and I'd rush out of the pink room, barefooted, half-dressed, my heart hammering against a taut piano string of desire.

Sometimes we'd eat oysters down in the corner restaurant, or hit happy hour at Tujague's or Molly's. Sometimes it was crawfish gumbo at Buster Holmes's, or Piña Coladas at Bonaparte's. Occasionally, we'd drive straight back to his place and I'd watch him rehearse routines with Boofhead, and I'd roll about on their mahogany floor, laughing.

Sometimes we'd make love in the long iron bath, or on his mattress in the front room, amid the clusters of balls and rubber chickens and collapsible top hats. I loved all of Bruno's paraphernalia, his firesticks and unicycles, his machetes and Mardi Gras beads, his velvet-lined prop case, the water pistol, the toy handcuffs, the disappearing bouquet of artificial daisies.

One night we ate a dozen oysters and Bruno said he'd marry me so I could get my green card. "No need to go to Mexico," he announced. "We could do it right here."

Our cheeks were hot from several pints of beer in that steamy cafe of boiling crawfish. After we paid the bill, he slung one long arm around me and we swept out onto the street. It was close to midnight and the pavements were bare except for the mist that seemed to rise like the breath of one hundred ghosts. We passed my street and followed the slight curve in the river. Farther on, the shell of the abandoned Jax Brewery stood against an ebony sky. We walked between piles of discarded lumber and sheet metal, a hill of crumbling bricks. Suddenly, Bruno pushed me down onto the bonnet of a rusting car, but I shoved him off. We wrestled each other through the darkness toward the back of the brewery, until I glimpsed the gleaming metal ribbons of two old railway tracks. The Mississippi murmured over the rise of the levy. I dropped onto the tracks, my neck against one, the backs of my knees against the other. As I glimpsed the phantom moon my magician fell like a blanket and bound me to his sorcerous limbs.

■   57   ■

The revelry leading up to Mardi Gras was growing. Sequined masks winked lewdly in the moonlight. Purple and yellow streamers flourished across walls. Drag queens paraded up and down Decatur Street, lost in drunken dress rehearsals, flaunting feathered capes; glittery, seven-inch heels; and headdresses made out of a hundred inflated condoms. Brass bands sprouted on corners overnight, practicing the Mardi Gras theme. Bonaparte's Retreat concocted a new cocktail: the Fat Tuesday Blues, composed of vodka, tequila, lime juice, lemonade, crushed ice, blue food coloring, and a sprig of mint. Balloons filled restaurants. Fringed parasols swayed down the streets. The galleries along Royal Street boasted paintings of masked clowns and bejeweled Zulu kings.

Carnival was the oasis in every Quarter Rat's financial desert. We were not the only ones struggling through the winter—every shopkeeper and proprietor and musician and shoe-shine boy strained toward Mardi Gras like salmon swimming upstream. Parade routes were advertised and there was much gossip and speculation about this year's floats. Over a million people were expected to hit the streets.

That was the time, I remember, when everyone was practicing. Bruno's juggler friend arrived from Colorado and began bedding down on the dining room floor. His specialties were whips and lassos, and he used to wear a cowboy hat and boots with spurs. He could place the end of a carrot in your mouth and, with one definitive crack, chop off the first two inches, leaving you trembling with an orange stump between your lips.

Gerry and I were working on a new routine, too. It was comprised of tap and drums, without the aid of recorded music. It was a kind of rhythmic dueling banjos. On our days off, we would take all the furniture out of our room so I'd have more space to move around in. Gerry insisted on recording every run-through. Then we'd play it back and he'd point out all the mistakes, the sluggish accents, the increasing tempo. He'd rewind the tape and we'd start all over again, and he'd tell me to dance lighter, or to vary my breaks a little more.

This would often go on for hours. Whenever we'd take a break, I used to stagger into the courtyard and flop onto my mattress. Gerry would stay in the room, setting his metronome and putting his ear to the tape recorder's speaker.

■ 58 ■

Two days into Mardi Gras, however, I was left wondering for whom we were rehearsing. Instead of throngs of fascinated spectators, herds of drunken tourists stampeded up and down Bourbon Street, tipping beer over Gerry's side drum and yelling at me to take it all off. Brass bands frequently drowned us out. Instead of sequined floats and Carnival Kings, we witnessed men pissing against the walls of nightclubs and women standing on second-story balconies baring their breasts to the hooting masses. One topless lass on the sidewalk even tottered forward in her pink stilettos and vomited at my feet.

That was the night we knocked off early and bought a fifth of rum and some Piña Colada mix. We sat on a bench in Jackson Square, watching the fireworks bloom in the sky and trying desperately to get drunk. When I commented on the futility of all our hours of practice, Gerry slid an arm around me and patted my shoulder.

"We're not rehearsing for these idiots," he said. "That'd be like feeding strawberries to pigs. No, when we get back to New York we're gunna make a killing. All those indoor gigs we're gunna have next winter."

Then he poured some more rum, and was suddenly inventing a magnificent story for us both. He had us working in clubs and theaters, on a cruise ship, even doing a spot on David Letterman. We could work in the subway stations until we had our first break. I sipped my drink, rubbed my shivering arms, and couldn't help feeling as if I were in a movie with Mickey Rooney.

■   59   ■

In the four months we knew each other, the only time Bruno and I left the New Orleans city limits was on the occasion of my twenty-first birthday.

St. Valentine's Day, 1984. It was a chilly, cloudy morning in the South's last month of winter. It was the day, with all its original and romantic associations, that I sensed our affair could not last.

None of us had much money, so it was decided we should celebrate my induction into adulthood by packing the car with provisions and driving into the woods to have a picnic. My companions on this day, my benevolent role models, the tribal elders initiating me into this great ceremony of Mature Life, this sanctified state of grown-up-hood, were a five-foot-one frustrated Errol Flynn called Boofhead, a towering juggler who couldn't make love with the lights on, and my hungover father in a pair of studded cowboy boots he'd found in the garbage outside the bondage shop on St. Phillip Street.

The problem was that we had no destination. Gerry and I never ventured much beyond Canal Street's invisible border. Boofhead had never jogged farther than the terminal where the streetcar tracks ran out on Carrollton. Bruno only traced a regular route between Uptown and the Quarter.

He decided to drive east, toward the bayous and canopies of Spanish moss, but at a vital intersection of Napolean Avenue, we found the crossroads clotted with cars, trapped behind the debris of what looked like a head-on collision.

Bruno swung the car up over the median strip and headed back the other way. My father had already begun sipping from one of the flagons of red we'd just bought at the A&P. Boofhead sat in the backseat beside him, head tilted back, jaw extended, and gulping at the air like a starved guppy. It was all part of his chin-tightening regime.

So Bruno nosed the car south and headed toward the river. We followed the curve of the levee for a while. But when he finally pulled up and we clambered out not fifty yards from the Canal Street Ferry Terminal, we gave each other disappointed looks. The river was low and shit-colored, and a man in a pair of brown house slippers was asleep under the cabbage tree palms.

When we got back in the car, Bruno began gnawing at his bottom lip and absently steered the car uptown, along his usual route. I was feeling stupid as I sat there beside him, sweating and knotting my fingers together in the silence. I was wearing an Edwardian silk blouse the color of egg yolk, with layers of cream lace stitched around the neck and bodice. The skirt looked a little Spanish, I suppose. I'd made it from the leg of a wide pair of bell-bottoms. The pants, cast-offs from a former Sydney teen talent queen, had two ruffles of yellow satin stitched around the bottom. Now they rested about three inches above my knee, and sat there, almost mocking.

"Where did you get that outfit?" Boofhead had asked when they'd pulled up outside the witchcraft shop earlier.

His tone had been warm, almost friendly. Suddenly my fingers were running across the lace and I was telling him about my dubious inheritance from the teen talent queen, how I got two skirts from one pair of pants. As we climbed in the car, I continued to prattle on about my tailoring expertise, the dress I'd converted from a Colombian coffee bean sack. The multi-colored skirt that appeared after I'd snapped off the metal spokes of a golf umbrella. As I fastened my seat belt, I detailed how I'd hemmed and threaded the waist with ribbon, assuming he found it all mildly amusing, until I glanced in the rearview mirror and saw the smirk on his face. Had his original inquiry been motivated by sarcasm, too? How long would he have let me rattle on about the fashion potential of discarded fishing nets and parachutes before he'd reveal his incredulity, his judgment of me as a mere dingbat?

I sat next to Bruno in the shuddering car and wished I'd worn something plainer. After all, it was only a picnic, and in the woods, at that.

Bruno hunched over the steering wheel and kept his eyes nailed to the road. The prodigious fumes released by Gerry's furtive gulps of wine filled the car. Boofhead was busy doing eye exercises, glaring from left to right, up and down. For a while there, his eyes rolled along a diagonal plane as we idled in front of a red light, as if he were checking to see if his right temple and left jaw were still intact.

Bruno turned the radio on, and the billowing howls of Ellington's "Creole Love Call" filled the car. I closed my eyes and breathed it in, suppressing the desire to unknot the bow at my side and rip the troublesome skirt to shreds.

We hit a bump in the road and, when I opened my eyes, I found Bruno steering us onto a long, concrete bridge. His hands, the way he held the steering wheel, the way he slowly changed gears, betrayed a sudden sense of purpose.

I straightened, clapped my hands together, and declared, "Oh, Master, where dost thou take me?" (It was a mixed impersonation: something between Shakespeare's Ophelia and Barbara Eden's Jeannie.)

But Bruno just grinned and stared straight ahead. "This is the longest bridge in the world," he said. "Twenty-four miles."

And then the green road sign rose up before us: Mandeville—24.

The bridge over which we winged was called The Causeway. With every mile we covered, Lake Pontchartrain's beguiling green shimmered farther into the car, implacable and serene, a watery silver aura humming toward the horizon. And there were small breaks in the cloud formations as narrow as my finger, where fine shafts of biblical light yawned down to the water.

Boofhead stopped biting at the ravaged stumps of his fingernails and Gerry finally burped and screwed the top back on the flagon. Bruno's VW propelled us on and on. Over the miles, the Causeway seemed to rise imperceptibly. Toward the middle of the bridge, I looked around and could barely see the shore we'd left behind. Just water, inexorable green water swelling against every horizon. Periodically, a sign would appear, reporting how far we still had to go.

When distant shapes began to form, a knot of sadness loosened within me. It was my big day, and we had driven across the longest bridge in the world to celebrate it in a town whose name beheld my own, at least phonetically.

Bruno swung the car off the bridge and turned right. Little black kids in shorts were crowded around a huge puddle, sailing what looked like handcrafted boats made out of Popsicle sticks and paper. Bruno scoured the side of the road, trying to find a clearing through the bare oaks and tall Judas trees.

Things were not looking good, however. Dead foliage and scrub clung to the earth between the road and the water, and the leaning magnolias looked haughty and imposing.

Gerry sighed and started drinking again. Red dust formed a fine veil across the bottom of the windshield. Boofhead suggested in a deadpan voice that we should all sing a song. " 'Ten Green Bottles,' " he said, "or 'Do the Hokey-Pokey with Me.' "

No one responded. Bruno just straightened and changed gears. Gerry, melancholy and half-pissed by now, murmured, "I'm just a fucking jazz drummer, not a singer. Why do bands these days always advertise for drummers who can *sing*? I said to this one bloke, I said, 'Listen mate, I'm a drummer born with a harelip, I'm flat-out *talking*.' "

Bruno smiled briefly. A chain-link fence, about twelve feet high and choked at the top by coils of barbed wire, appeared on our left, divulging, perhaps, the promise of a clearing or a grassy knoll. Bruno leaned on the accelerator and followed the long, impervious fence around the curves of the road.

I wondered what was behind such a barrier, and why it was so high. Through the fence's steel web, I saw nothing but wilting honeysuckle and ivy.

Soon a sign appeared on top of the wasteland of gray wire: TRESPASSERS WILL BE PROSECUTED. The place was looking more and more intriguing and formidable. Bruno continued to trace its trajectory into the Gothic wilderness of Louisiana. I folded my hands and made an effort to hope, to feel confident in God's great design: I was twenty-one; it was St. Valentine's Day; and both the man who fathered me and the one with whom I thought I was in love were right here with me. But I couldn't stop thinking of my mother alone and asleep in her double bed on the other side of the world, dozing against the heat of the last month of Australia's summer, the humidity into which I was born.

I was drawn from my meditation by the sudden appearance of cut grass, of a manicured lawn rolling like a wide green carpet toward the edge of the lake. There were two picnic benches and a solitary wire garbage can.

Bruno swung a hard right and we followed the gravel path up to the lake, close to the concrete levee. We crawled from the Beetle and stretched. Gerry staggered over to the nearest bench and crowned it with the now somewhat-diminished jug of deep red plonk. Boofhead announced he was starving and whisked the picnic basket—a cardboard box stamped Dixie—from the open trunk of the car.

Bruno cubed cheese with his Swiss army knife, and Boofhead was soon relishing his appointed task: tearing up a breadstick over half his size into manageable, bite-sized pieces.

It was only after I'd poured the wine and we'd all sat down together that I noticed a sign on the other side of the street, above a pair of heavy iron gates. Bruno had driven us to the family reserve in front of the Louisiana Southeast Hospital for the Insane.

My indomitable father was the only person in our quartet who felt duty-bound to clown about and make this miserable afternoon bristle with the conviviality for which it was intended. Gerry burped and farted and told the story about how he passed out on his father's boat after drinking two flagons of port, and woke up two days later on a beach off Newcastle. And then the one about his teetotaling Irish Catholic mother, who reluctantly began to imbibe one glass of the same Ruby Red port, upon her doctor's instructions, before she retired at night. The prescription was to soothe her nerves and cure her chronic insomnia. Clara, the ginger brunette who never missed a Sunday mass, ingested her medication each evening with a mouthful of guilt: Drink was a demon masquerading as a demigod. Still, she swallowed her one snifter of Ruby Red before she crawled into bed at night, and soon the devil went to work inside her, drawing down her eyelids and inviting her into the sanctity of her own dreams. Over the weeks, if she were feeling particularly restless, she sometimes took two drinks instead of one. And if she occasionally snuck a mouthful while she was baking bread or ironing, it was only because she had eight children practicing either violin or piano throughout the day in the living room. And that little bugger Gerry banging on cake tins in the backyard.

But her hairdresser husband, Aub, knew things were getting out of hand one day when he came home and found her swaying as she divided herself between the two tasks of chopping vegetables for soup and grating Sunlight soap for the boiler that was washing his uniforms. Not only did she sway, not only did she break out in a bawling rendition of "Amazing Grace," when Aub returned to the kitchen after his evening bath, he found handfuls of yellow shavings melting into the chicken broth, and what must have been half the backyard's spinach and carrot crop floating about with his white coats and cotton underwear in ravaged, irregular pieces.

"And then Aub went tearing down to the doctor's joint and abused the shit out of him," said Gerry, smacking his lips and grinning. I wondered if it occurred to him that he was now cradling the neck of a flagon not too unlike the large bottle of Ruby Red that had caused his family so much consternation almost sixty years ago.

"Told the quack he'd reduced his God-fearing wife to a hopeless boozer who couldn't get through the Lord's prayer at night without hiccuping!"

Bruno smiled and Boofhead erupted with a chuckle. Sometime during the monologue, Gerry's plastic cup had blown off the table and was skittering across the buffalo grass toward the solemn iron gates of the asylum.

Gerry took a swig from the flagon, wiped his mouth, and laughed. " 'But Mr. Sayer,' said the doctor, 'I told her to drink two *fingers* of port, not two *bottles*.' "

It was at times like this that I loved my father, that I was conscious of the loving. How he was sticking to the edict of the Show Must Go On in spite of the hollow theater of that day and the solemn house to which he was playing. His mother was one of the few female characters who was secure in his bawdy comedy, the rollicking, circuitous story he was still plotting throughout his sixty-fourth year.

That afternoon he was a man with a mission, ensuring the flagon continued to circle, and that we might all laugh, just a little, on this supposedly significant day.

I knew Boofhead was succumbing to Gerry's incantations when he stood up, tottered a few feet toward the lake, and collapsed onto the grass with a big, goofy grin on his face. Bruno sat across from me and swallowed mouthfuls of water for every sip of wine, unable to relinquish himself to my father's ribald magic.

I abandoned my cup and began, like Gerry, to swig from the flagon directly whenever it was passed to me. The more I drank, the more I wondered about Bruno's possible motivations and intentions. Had he driven me here deliberately? Was it some perverse joke, this picnicking outside the insane asylum? Did he know it was here all along?

I realized that he'd hoped for the bayous or a spot by the river, but I wrestled with the possible subtexts of the afternoon, and Bruno's disturbing gift for metaphor.

I uncapped the second flagon and wandered across to the levee. I kicked off my shoes, sat down, and dangled my black-stockinged feet in the lake. The water was cool. I lifted the flagon and swallowed a mouthful of wine: It wasn't Ruby Red port, but it was close enough.

■   60   ■

I don't remember if we had birthday cake and nodding candle flames. Surely I would have bought one of those inexpensive pies with a rope of imitation cream around the edge, or a jam roll from the day-old table at the A&P. The only sweet thing I can recall about that afternoon, however, was Gerry's herculean effort to make us laugh.

Occasionally, I thought that perhaps Bruno and I should not have talked of marriage, even if it was only a union of convenience, a favor between friends. You weren't supposed to marry someone you were dating, but someone who was gay, or a stranger, someone you paid a fee to and didn't care about very much.

It wouldn't be until four years later, back in Sydney, that I would comprehend it, that the last troublesome piece of the puzzle would slide into place. Bruno had kept secrets in his early courting of me, which is probably why, sitting outside the asylum that day under a cloud of confusion, I slowly and deliberately got drunk.

The drive back to New Orleans was uneventful. Bruno dropped us off in the Quarter on the corner of Decatur and St. Phillip. Before I slammed the door, I looked into his eyes.

I willed my voice to be as casual as possible. "Will I see you tonight?"

But Bruno just looked at his hands and shook his head, said he was tired.

Gerry and I waited until the Beetle had shot off toward Canal Street before we crossed the road.

■   61   ■

My disappointment was soon dulled by more pressing matters. The next morning, the fifteenth, I was awakened by the sound of knocking. I leapt up and pulled on a long T-shirt. When I opened the door, Thomas was standing there with an envelope.

"Some chick just dropped this off," he said. "Thought it might be important."

"Thanks, Thomas." I took the envelope and nodded. It was a plain white business envelope, sealed.

I shut the door quickly and switched on the light. Gerry began stirring within the thick folds of his gray army blanket.

I tore the envelope open. The writing paper seemed curiously scented. Hairspray, perhaps. Or cheap perfume.

I smoothed out the page against the table.

YOU'RE WIFE NEEDS THIS WEEKS HOUSEKEEPING MONEY, it said, in slightly crooked lettering, SEAPORT 4 OCLOK.

It was this third demand that propelled Gerry out of bed and sent him pacing through the room. For some reason, he hadn't expected it, as if they'd be happy with a couple of extra hundred dollars and a few free drinks.

"All we're doing is working for those two nuts every night. You know that? Hundred dollars here . . . hundred dollars there. . . . Hell, we're like a couple of hookers paying pimp money without getting any of the protection!"

Only five weeks had passed since Gerry and Marilyn's immigration interview. It would be at least another seven before he'd know the results. In the meantime, it was imperative that Marilyn not contact the authorities. Still, in the four and a half months we'd been in New Orleans, our bank balance had diminished by half, and we were only averaging about one hundred and fifty a week on the street. At this rate, I calculated, as I poured ground coffee into a filter, we'd be completely broke within three months.

I wandered outside with the glass jug and filled it in the bathroom. If only Gerry hadn't surrendered his passport, I mused, we could pack up and be on a plane back to Sydney tomorrow.

I walked inside, poured the water into the mouth of the machine, and placed the jug on the sizzling hot plate. Gerry was sitting on the edge of his mattress, staring at his cigarette as if it might reveal a solution.

In spite of three cups of coffee, my father, the incorrigible wheeler-dealer, could not come up with a plan.

He wondered out loud about what his brother Jack would do. Jack once won the toss of a coin and ended up having an entire barber shop in Darwin signed over to him. Or Ernie, the brother who'd swaggered home one day after the races with three suitcases full of cash. Or Dolphy, who became a rapid millionaire by selling and buying real estate he never actually saw.

This blackmail story was turning out to be the first one in my father's bulging catalog that was not very funny, that was in fact becoming nothing short of a disaster. What made it worse was that this was one of the few yarns that had allowed me a minor role in its unfolding melodrama. I was the straightener of preinterview ties, the money-runner, and secret-keeper.

I had no control over my father's behavior, the only power I had was invested in my literacy: The bank account was in my name and only I had legal access to its funds. Gerry had insisted upon this arrangement because of his lifelong difficulty with the rigors of reading and writing.

I sat on a chair squarely in front of him. "When you meet them this afternoon," I said, "tell them the bank account is in my name. Tell them I refuse to give you more money."

"But what if they call up Immigration?"

"Try it," I said. "Try it and see what happens."

Gerry shrugged. "All right," he said. "I'll give it a go. But I don't reckon it's gunna make much difference."

That night, after he returned from his rendezvous at the Seaport Bar and Restaurant, he wasn't swaggering with victory, nor dragging his feet with disappointment. He dropped half a dozen cans of beer on the table and plopped himself into a chair.

"Well?" I said, pulling one from its plastic holder. "Did you tell them?"

He pulled out a can for himself and flicked back the aluminum ring. "Yep."

"And?" I cracked a can and cupped my lips around the opening.

"They said," he murmured, running a hand through his hair, "they said they'd be looking for you."

62

It happened a few times that week. I'd be walking down Royal Street, or cutting through the square, and I'd see them in the distance, lumbering along the footpath. My eyesight was impeccable back then—I could spot a cop five blocks away—and if I saw two women heading my way, I'd suddenly duck into a bookstore and hide behind the Local History section, or conceal myself behind the sequined gold and purple robes of a Mardi Gras shop.

We had to make a couple of other adjustments during this time. It was important, for example, that Thomas, Pete, and Athena be briefed on the current situation. Without going into details, Gerry asked them to tell anyone who came looking for us that we had gone back to New York. Of course, the witches were puzzled, but agreed.

We also had to make changes to our work routine. We decided that we had to perform at random times in unlikely places. Thus, the Moonwalk received us a few mornings that week; a tiled corner of Royal Street was graced with our presence between ten and midnight, and we once had a disappointing matinee down on Canal Street, playing to a stream of indifferent shoppers.

One night the sky opened up and it began to rain, and we were spared another evening of slim pickings and sneaky routes through the Quarter. Gerry pulled on his cowboy boots and clumped up to the A&P, returning half-drenched with a flask of rum and a six-pack of generic beer. On his way through the courtyard, he ran into Pete, and soon the three of us were in a conference of idle chatter, sipping rum and chasing it with that dreadful, bitter ale.

We were into our second lot of shots when Pete assumed a serious air, folded his hands on the table, looked directly at me, and said, "I don't mean to pry . . . but is everything all right with you folks?"

"Yeah," I said, sipping quickly. "Why?"

"Oh, I don't know . . . You don't seem your lively selves."

"We're not doing well on the street this week," said Gerry. "Too bloody cold."

"That's no good." Pete stroked his beard thoughtfully. Gerry drained his Marmite jar of rum and stared morosely at the table. A dull silence descended into the room.

"But that's not the only thing," he finally admitted.

Pete perked up in his chair. "Oh?"

Gerry sighed and splashed some more rum into the jar. "I guess I can trust you." He took a couple of quick sips. "I have to talk to somebody." He scooted his chair closer to the table and rested his arms on its fading red Formica.

He related the whole sordid tale, the desire for his green card, the wedding, the interviews down at Immigration. When Pete asked how the interviews went, Gerry said, "Well, I reckon everything's OK, but I won't know for sure for another two months."

"So what's the problem?"

Gerry cracked another can and told him about the blackmailing.

Pete's eyes narrowed. "What's the name of the woman?"

"She didn't say. But the woman I married, her name is Marilyn."

"Marilyn!" A frown formed on Pete's face. "What does she look like?"

"Well," Gerry mused, "she's got short red hair. She's about forty-five. And she's real . . ."

"Overweight," I said, glancing quickly at Pete's enormous belly.

Pete's face suddenly reddened and he butted out his Kool and drew another from his pack.

"What?" said Gerry. "Do you know her?"

Pete was struggling with a matchbook, trying to ignite the strip of stubborn cardboard between his fingers, but all he could raise was a series of spluttering sparks.

"*Know* her? Pardon me, but to tell the truth, she's a smidgen gone upstairs!"

"Really?" I said, almost mocking.

"Yes! Neurotic!" Pete abandoned his original match and tore out another. "Hooked on pills. Valium. She'll take five Valiums and chase them with gin. I've seen her 'round at Bonaparte's."

Gerry looked as if he were cemented to his seat, the way he just sat there staring at Pete.

"She comes into the shop all the time. . . . *Wait a minute!*"

He suddenly slammed the matchbook on the table, and his eyes almost grew as wide as the one painted on the wall above us.

"What?" Gerry and I chimed together.

"A couple of weeks ago Marilyn and her friend—Dot, they call her—they came into the shop and I remember Dot saying to me, 'Listen, I wanna get some dough out of a guy, got something for that?' And I said, 'Sure,' and I mixed up some money-drawing powder and sold her two green candles. Lord, if I'd known it was intended for you I wouldn't have sold them to her."

Gerry was still rigid in his chair, but his lower jaw had dropped a little and I could see his upper denture was loose in his mouth, slightly sinking away from his receding gum.

"But it only works if she *touches* you with the powder. Has she touched you at all?"

Gerry finally closed his mouth and thought for a moment.

"Yeah, she did," I piped up. "In the bar. She grabbed hold of your arm, remember?"

He nodded. His face was swollen and pink.

"Don't worry!" announced Pete, suddenly cheerful, snatching up his matches. "I have a secret formula that can reverse the powder. It'll all back-fire on her, you'll see!"

And he leapt out of his chair, as if in some satirical impersonation of Superman bursting out of a telephone booth. He struck the match against the book and a flame finally flashed between his fingers as he lit his cigarette.

■ 63 ■

While Pete was busy mixing up the antidote to the money-drawing powder, the gris-gris doll that had drawn Bruno to me seemed to lose her potency. After my birthday, it was never the same. Long silences welled up between us as we lay on his mattress, until I could no longer stand his dis-tance and would almost run from his apartment. There were things he was uncomfortable about: the squalor in which Gerry and I lived behind the witchcraft shop; Boofhead's understated disapproval of our affair. My visa was about to expire and, sensing his ambivalence about helping me get le-gal, I decided we shouldn't marry.

Life was further complicated when I sprained my right foot. It hap-pened on the first clear day after a week of continual rain. None of us had been able to work and we'd all gone a bit mad cooped up inside for so long. The storms finally stopped one Saturday morning. I awoke to find the court-yard glistening with dew and Renoir's water-logged plants nodding into the sunlight. Gerry didn't like working mornings, but I adored it. I dressed in some ordinary street clothes, grabbed my shoes, and skipped outside. Jackson Square was already full of magicians and portrait painters, break dancers and clowns. Ruthie the Duck Lady was roller skating through the crowds in what looked like an old taffeta bridesmaid's dress.

A Dixieland quintet had set up in one corner of the square, and the washboard player, Harold, invited me to join in. I tied on my shoes and leapt into the ring the audience formed around them, distilling my frustra-tion into the fast, slick patterns I struck against the gray slate. The music was bawdy and seductive, great trumpet howls and a trombone's wicked wailing. The rhythm of the washboard tickled each tune along, allowing me to improvise on top of it, in the spaces old Harold deliberately left for me.

The sun was shining and I was dancing again, shedding the anxiety that had wrapped itself around me for weeks like a fine, translucent caul. By the time the band had knocked off at one o'clock, I was hungry for more. The musicians divided the take and gave me eleven bucks. I went darting through the square and leapt into a performance with Mr. Dobbs, a friend who dressed in a three-piece suit and bowler hat and sang old show tunes while playing the ukulele. We went through his entire repertoire that afternoon: "Yes Sir, That's My Baby," "Shine," "I Wish I Could Shimmy Like My Sister Kate." I had long since pulled off my black sweater and was wheeling about on the slate steps outside St. Louis Cathedral. Bruno and Boofhead were working farther down, in Grimaldi's usual spot. Grimaldi wasn't around, and they were sharing it with Lothario. I could see the perfect arcs Bruno's machetes made in the air above the crowd. And it was these beautiful patterns that spurred me on, the distant kaleidoscope of his colored balls, the orange streaks of his firesticks.

By the time Gerry and I had set up on Bourbon Street that night, I had already been tapping for five and a half hours on the hard pavement of Jackson Square. Still, I felt pretty good. Excited, actually. Earlier, during one of his breaks, Bruno had asked me out. A band was playing on a steamboat and he thought I might like to go out dancing. The prospect of sashaying with my juggler on *The Natchez* as it chugged up the Mississippi appealed to my romantic disposition. My heart did not flinch at so much overtime that day, relentlessly pumping, hour after hour, under the strain of protracted mania. By eight o'clock that evening, however, when Gerry began packing up, my right foot began to ache.

It started as a slow burn along the top of my toes and gradually spread into the ligaments between the metatarsal bones. By the time we arrived home, I was limping. I'd had foot trouble before, back in Sydney. I once consulted a therapeutic masseur and was told that if I didn't quit dancing on the street I'd get varicose veins and that the prolonged pressure on my back would cause the vertebrae in my spine to weld together.

I took a shower and rubbed Ben-Gay into my swelling flesh. I slipped a belated shock-absorber into each of my shoes and kissed my father good-bye. I hobbled down the passageway to meet Bruno. Nothing, not even a stubborn foot, was going to stop me from being happy.

The riverboat was like a floating ballroom: high ceilings, pillars, a wooden dance floor, all bobbing imperceptibly in and out of the currents of the Mississippi. When Bruno's arms encircled my waist and he began to sway, to guide me across the polished wood, my right foot throbbed inside the pumps I was wearing. I kept pressing my face into his chest so he wouldn't see my pained expression.

■ 64 ■

It wasn't until the next morning that I realized the extent to which I'd punished myself. When I got up, my foot was swollen into a bruised mound of blue flesh, and when I put my weight on it, the pain was so great I fell back on the bed. I secretly cursed Marilyn and the Dragon Lady. They probably made a gris-gris in my image, burned some candles, and suddenly cut off my right foot with a pair of garden shears, or hammered it over and over with the heel of a shoe. It certainly felt as if I were being pounded by some heavy object.

For the next few weeks I could barely walk. Sometimes I could get up and hobble across to the table to make a cup of coffee, but that was all. Gerry, of course, couldn't do the act on his own. So we spent many miserable days holed up in our room, waiting for my foot to heal.

This gave my father plenty of time to ruminate. He mostly sat, moving his dentures around in his mouth. He was now responsible for buying and preparing food. I remember we ate a lot of day-old iced buns and take-out cheese Po-Boys. I often lay in my bed, rereading my Wilde and Carroll, trying to figure out what wild demon had driven me to dance for hours on end.

One morning I dragged myself out of bed, slipped on a pair of shoes, and decided to try and limp down the passageway and out to the shop to see if we had any mail. I thought a little walk might toughen up my muscles. Gerry was still asleep, so I didn't have him telling me to sit down and rest. I held onto the wall for support until I reached the gate and unlocked it. I had just slammed it shut when they appeared, Marilyn and the Dragon Lady, moving like two huge phantoms through the doorway.

The latter seized my shoulders and pressed me up against the wall. "Listen," she hissed through her clenched teeth. "No more fucking around. We'll be at the Seaport at five o'clock. Bring three hundred dollars or I'll be reporting you both to the authorities first thing tomorrow morning."

"I've sprained my foot," I replied weakly. "I can't get down to the bank."

"Get a cab!" she volleyed back, suddenly releasing me.

But my back remained against the wall until they'd both lumbered off together and into the bar next door.

■ **65** ■

Gerry's brilliant plan hit him in an epiphanic moment over coffee. Perhaps it was the new blend we were trying, Cafe Bustello, or our switch from honey to white sugar. Or maybe it was the effect of all the feather-shaking and chicken-bone-grinding that was going on in Pete's apartment every night.

Gerry ran over to Leonard's before he went to meet them. I thought he just wanted to have a quick joint in order to calm his nerves. But apparently he had to consult his so-called lawyer about some legal technicality.

When Gerry walked into the Seaport that afternoon he found Marilyn sitting up at the bar, sucking on an oyster shell; the Dragon Lady was beside her, draining one glass of red wine and about to start on another. Like us, the two women often dropped in for happy hour because the drinks were two-for-one, and if you ate enough complimentary hors d'oeuvres, you didn't have to worry about buying dinner.

"Well, look who's here!" said Gerry, helping himself to one of Marilyn's oysters.

"It's about time you showed up." The Dragon Lady started on her second glass.

He let the oyster slip down his throat. "Yes, it is about time I showed up."

"Got the three hundred?"

He licked his lips and smiled. "Have I got the three hundred?" He laughed quickly and shook his head. "No darling, I've got something better, much better than that."

The Dragon Lady puffed on her menthol and frowned. Marilyn, bless her heart, held out her plate and offered Gerry another oyster.

"I made an appointment to see my lawyer today," he continued, helping himself. "Remember my lawyer, Marilyn?"

She thought for a moment and nodded.

"You see"—Gerry lowered his voice and leaned in close to them—"not only does he have a contract on file stating that I'm not in any way financially responsible for my wife, Marilyn—"

"You signed a *contract*?" said the Dragon Lady.

Marilyn produced another miserable nod.

"You idiot!"

"As I was saying," said Gerry, "not only does he have that contract on file, he also advised me that if you intend to alert Immigration about our phony marriage, the worst thing that's going to happen to me is that I'll get a free trip back to Australia. But your dear friend Marilyn, the American citizen, she'll be sentenced to three years, *hard labor*, for her part in the whole thing. So listen, dear"—he began rooting around in his pocket—"do us all a favor and make the call. And I know you're pretty broke, so here"—he tossed a coin onto the bar—"let me give you a quarter."

▧ 66 ▧

We never heard from Marilyn and the Dragon Lady again. Occasionally I'd see them lurking around the Quarter, but they never approached me.

In the weeks that followed, I kept trying to coax my right foot into action. Sometimes I'd make it around the corner to Sydney's Grocery and back, but it took a lot of effort, and my foot was too swollen even to fit into my tap shoe.

I felt like an ugly sister who had just missed out on her Prince. Sometimes I'd call Bruno from the pay phone in Sydney's and ask him out for lunch or a beer, but he was always getting his car fixed or practicing a new routine. The nights we did see each other, Boofhead was always with him.

Most of the time, I was holed up in our room, putting on weight and driving myself crazy trying to figure out what was wrong between us. After the second week of my convalescence, Gerry and I began to panic because we had absolutely no income and didn't want to keep dipping into what little savings we had left. So Gerry got a job washing dishes around at Cafe S'Bisa on Decatur. They paid him two dollars an hour and a meal each night. They wouldn't let him take cigarette breaks and he had to wash the kitchen out after everyone else had gone home. At the end of the week, they gave him the sack because they said he was too old for the position and wasn't scrubbing the pots fast enough.

So much for the day job. We both went back to staring at my purple foot, almost willing it to heal. I soaked it in Epsom salts. I massaged it with Ben-Gay. I wrapped it in bandages. I even tried talking to it in a soft and apologetic voice.

Since the marriage with Bruno was definitely off, I had to do something about my visa. I caught a cab to the Immigration Department early one morning and was second in line when the doors opened at seven-thirty. I limped in and took a ticket. I had my shtick all rehearsed: I needed an extension so that I could go back to New York and study dance for six months.

The officer turned my application down. I began to beg, to plead, but the man was adamant. He explained that I had entered the country on a tourist visa, not a student visa. A tourist visa could not be extended for study, or vice versa. He didn't make the rules, he only enforced them. He closed my passport and promptly slid it back across the counter and called the next number.

When I hobbled into our room later that morning, I woke Gerry up and told him the news. I was already making plans to slip off to Mexico for a few days, or to marry Leonard. But Gerry just shook his head and pulled on his corduroy jeans.

"All you have to do," he said, "is go back in there in a couple of days. When they ask you why you want an extension, just tell 'em you wanna travel a bit more. Tell 'em you wanna see Disneyland or some other bullshit thing, you know, what everyone else goes to see. The Grand bloody Canyon or something."

"I *can't*," I said. "I've already told them I want to study dance. They'll know I'm lying."

"They won't remember *you*. They see hundreds of people and passports every day."

"But what if I get the same guy again?"

Gerry gave me an incredulous look. "How many people were serving at the counter?"

I thought for a moment. "Four, I think."

"Well, there you go. The odds are on your side. You probably won't get the same guy, anyway. Just wear different sorts of clothes and do your hair another way."

My father was determined to teach me the importance of bravado, and he was ready to pack me off to Immigration the following morning. But I decided to wait, in case I encountered the same officer.

A few days later saw me up at six-thirty again. I brushed my hair out from its pompadour bun, donned a man's suede hat borrowed from Leonard, dressed in a pair of jodhpurs and a zip-up cardigan. My foot was still tumid and throbbing, and so I cabbed it to the office. When my number was called, I heard the same dour voice I'd confronted three mornings ago. I pulled the hat brim down over my forehead and walked up to the counter, trying desperately not to limp. I'd already filled out the extension application, had blathered on in blue ink about wanting to visit Disneyland and Hollywood and Beverly Hills, touristy places Gerry and I would never have wanted to see. I tried smiling at the man then looking away as I slid across my passport and form.

The man hazarded a half-grin and asked how I was doing. As he glanced over my application, I rested my weight on my good foot and bemoaned the fact that I'd never ridden the giant roller coaster or seen Mickey Mouse in person. I waited for signs of recognition to surface on his face, but there were none as far as I could see. I continued to elaborate on my imagined itinerary: Marilyn Monroe's house, Sunset Boulevard, a guided tour through MGM. And then on to Seattle to stand on top of the highest building in the world, and how that was so very important to me and my trip to stand on top of the tallest building in the world and be able to take a photograph because Australia doesn't have any really tall buildings you know it's just a colony and Oh how wonderful it would be to be able to tell my friends back home that I've been inside Disney's Magic Kingdom . . .

The man just sat there grinning and nodding. He stamped a six-month extension into my passport and told me to have a good time.

■ 67 ■

It wasn't until early April that the swelling went down and I could finally slip into my shoes and manage an awkward shuffle. By that time, we only had about fifteen hundred left in the bank. Sometimes I caught myself wishing we had been deported, that some man in a uniform would simply escort us to the airport.

Once my foot had begun to heal, however, Gerry was suddenly brimming with hope. We would return to New York for the summer season and really make a killing. We would work from May right through to late autumn, and by then, who knows? We'd probably be able to score some indoor gigs to take us through next winter instead of coming back to New Orleans.

He began counting down the days until our intended departure. We decided not to hang around for the jazz festival the following month, and booked two airline tickets for the second week in May.

My comeback on the street was slow and arduous. I kept my foot wrapped in an Ace bandage and a smile plastered on my face. My tendons burned, however, and every few numbers, I'd have to take a break. Gerry would do a solo on the woodblock and bang out counterrhythms against the metal drum stands.

One night we decided to have a drink and something to eat at the Seaport before work. I was just lifting some raw broccoli onto my plate when I looked up to see Boofhead standing beside me. He was with a short, slim woman wearing lots of makeup and high-heeled sandals. He asked me if I'd seen Bruno. He'd missed all the Sunday performances and hadn't come home last night. I shrugged and said I didn't know where he was. Boofhead almost seemed to be enjoying Bruno's mysterious absence, or rather, he enjoyed telling me about it.

After we'd eaten our fill of bean dip and nachos, Gerry and I walked a block down Bourbon and set up. I tightened my bandage and slipped on my shoes. There were hardly any tourists around, but we started playing anyway. We'd only been at it about fifteen minutes when I looked down the street to see Bruno half-dancing toward us with a tall, fair woman on his arm. In his free hand he held a go-cup. He looked more like a Mardi Gras reveler than my self-effacing juggler. He was headed straight toward us, bumping and grinding to our music. By the time he reached us, the song had ended and he just stood in front of us with the grinning woman.

I leaned over and turned the cassette player off. "This is Kathy," he announced. I could tell he was a bit drunk by the way he held her arm and swayed. "Kathy is a singer. A brilliant, beautiful singer."

I regarded her and shook her hand. She looked a little bit like me, but older, perhaps in her early thirties. She was also heavier. She smiled and seemed friendly enough. She obviously didn't know that Bruno and I had been seeing one another. Within seconds I had made a virtual study of her, trying to ascertain what it was that made her more desirable to Bruno than me. She wore makeup, had a suntan (how did she manage it in April?), and she curled her long blond hair.

I wasn't going to let Bruno see me disappointed. I made myself smile at her. He knew the hours I worked on Bourbon Street and had obviously planned this supposed chance encounter.

"You kids have a good time," I chimed, throwing my hands up in the air and bustling them away. "Has Bruno showed you," I joked, "what he can do with his balls?" Kathy threw her head back and laughed.

Bruno shot me a quick look and slipped his arm around her waist. They went sashaying up Bourbon Street together and eventually disappeared into Sammy's Seafood. As Bruno was walking in, William, my tiny ex-lover, was walking out, about to assume his nightly position in the restaurant's gateway. There was a peculiar moment when they both paused and eyed one another. The top of William's head was level with the middle of Bruno's thigh. They looked as though they could have formed a sideshow together. America's tallest and shortest man.

When Bruno and Kathy entered the restaurant, I turned and switched on the cassette player. And I danced and danced on my throbbing foot because I was finally free of all of Bruno's uncertainty, because the neon light across the road had just blinked on, because we didn't have to worry about Marilyn and the Dragon Lady anymore, because it was the middle of spring, because I was twenty-one, because my father was still playing beside me. I spun through the air because, with Bruno, my dance had not ended: I was still looking for love, for my magician, still looking for someone who could open me like fruit.

■   68   ■

The last time I saw Bruno was the morning I found a series of pans set out in the courtyard. There were ten of them, standing in a row beside the fence. I noticed them on my way to the toilet. Some were cake tins, some were saucepans. There was even a black-handled frying pan.

Bruno ducked over to the witchcraft shop between performances to return the shopping cart he'd borrowed and a notepad I had left at his place. He blew his horn through the hole in the gate, and I went dashing past the pans, and down the passageway to meet him. He pressed the notepad into my hands and told me that he and Boofhead were leaving for Boston the following week. I nodded—bravely, I thought—and mentioned we were off to New York in two days. There were no addresses exchanged, no contact phone numbers. He just leaned down, kissed me quickly on the lips, and went sprinting up the street.

I dropped the notepad into the trolley and wheeled it up the passage. It wasn't until later I noticed Bruno's small, cryptic handwriting at the back of the pad. It was a letter he'd begun to someone called Jude. It detailed the trouble he'd had with his car repairs, the difficulty of working with Boof-head, an Australian woman he'd been seeing. I sat down on a chair and kept reading. The Australian woman had asked him to drive down to Mexico and marry her. She'd be paying for the trip, and they'd only be marrying so she could get her green card. It was just a marriage of convenience—he wasn't in love or anything. Jude, wrote Bruno, I miss you. I wish you were here. I wish I could see you again.

He hadn't finished the letter. It wasn't signed, or dated. I sat in the pink room and wondered if he'd accidentally returned my notepad with his writing concealed in the back, or if it had been intentional. Who was Jude and why was she no longer a part of Bruno's life? He'd never mentioned old girlfriends before.

Years later, back in Sydney, I met a juggler from California. I found out he was an old friend of Bruno's. He told me I was the spitting image of Bruno's former fiancée. Same hair, same face, same body shape. She'd bro-ken it off with him in order to study filmmaking in New York City.

■ 69 ■

The night before our departure, Jinny and the witches got together and threw us a party in the courtyard. Two dozen cans of Old Milwaukee and a cauldron of spiced red beans. We drank prodigiously, made speeches, gave away furniture, tore up my old tap board, and got three hours' sleep.

Well into the evening, I noticed the ten empty pans were still standing in a row beside the brick fence.

"What are they for?" I asked Pete, who was busy tucking into a bowl of guacamole.

"The pots?"

I nodded.

"The first rain in May." He seized another corn chip and shoveled in more dip.

"Yeah," I said, "what's it about?"

"We collect the first rain in May for lots of our spells. It's a great healer, and brings luck."

"What if it doesn't rain in May?" I asked. "Is your magic stuffed for the rest of the year?"

"It always rains in May," said Pete. "It's the last month of spring."

■ 70 ■

My father had such a fantastic story about tripping on acid, I suppose I wanted one of my own. I had always loved the way he'd described his seven deaths, the breathing trees, the way his body had melted like a ball of soft wax. The acid I'd done before had never been very strong, had only allowed me to see rippling sidewalks and pale blue rain.

We were awakened by Leonard at seven sharp. He was looming in the open doorway with his backpack slung over one shoulder. "Where's all the furniture?" he demanded.

I crawled out of bed and threw him a pillow to sit on. After switching on the coffee machine, I stumbled out to the bathroom to fill the jug.

On my way back I noticed Mr. Dobbs strolling across the courtyard.

He'd offered to drive us out to the airport in his black mini-bus. "Good morning, Ladies and Gentlemen, Boys and Girls," he announced, as if he were in Jackson Square, performing to a group of tourists.

I noticed the bottoms of the pans along the fence were glimmering with a quarter-inch of water. It must have rained heavily while we slept.

Dobbs followed me back into our room. I sat him on a pillow next to Leonard and shook Gerry awake. "Come on," I urged. "You haven't even packed!"

His face still crumpled with sleep, he groaned and reached for his glasses. We had an eight-thirty flight, and it was already well past seven. But Gerry just scratched his head and asked me what happened to all the furniture.

"You gave it away, remember? Jinny got the table. Pete got the chairs. And Renoir made off with the bookshelf." I poured some coffee and passed him a cup. "You even gave Thomas your shirt."

Gerry looked down at his naked torso. "Not the checked one with the green buttons."

"Yep."

"That was my favorite."

I nodded. "You said, 'Tom, Tom, me old mate. I'd give you anything. Anything. Even the shirt off me own back!' He was pretty tickled when you ripped it off and slung it over his shoulder."

Gerry pursed his lips and sipped his coffee. His clothes and socks were strewn around the room.

When Dobbs went to the toilet, Leonard pulled some tissue paper from his pocket, unfolded it, and proffered the paper-thin wafer as small as a postage stamp. It was a bit like a psychedelic Holy Communion, I suppose. Gerry halved it and passed me my portion and we said Cheers to each other and drank down our respective wafers with coffee.

While we were packing, Leonard took his leave, promising to visit us in New York and wishing us a good trip. Mr. Dobbs tapped on his watch and dutifully sat on Gerry's suitcase while he struggled with the lock.

My head was pounding as I carried our equipment down the passage for the last time and deposited it in the back of Dobbs's van. I felt a bit nauseous and began to sweat. Gerry and Dobbs followed with the bags and drums. We turned in the keys to Thomas, who was sitting happily behind the glass counter, wearing Gerry's shirt.

Before we left, however, I announced that I had forgotten something. I went limping up the passageway and into the empty courtyard. When I was sure no one was looking, I pulled off my right shoe and the accompanying bandages. I lifted my foot and placed it in one of the tins, allowing the medicinal magic of the First Rain in May to seep into my swollen flesh.

We piled into the van and Dobbs took off, glancing at his watch and hoping to make good time.

It wasn't until we were out of the Quarter and on the expressway that I noticed trails of colored light whirring past my window. I looked across at Dobbs and noticed that he had transformed himself into a pointy-eared demon. His beard had thickened and had turned a shiny black color. His fingernails were suddenly an inch long. I frowned and moved a little closer. Beneath the brim of his hat were the buds of two little horns pressing through the skin just below his hairline.

I blinked and withdrew into my own seat. Dobbs hit the accelerator and swerved between lanes, trying to overtake a semitrailer packed with live pigs. We were almost level with the truck's cabin when the road veered to the right and the trailer shot ahead of us, and I found myself sitting only a few inches from the squealing mass of next week's ham and bacon.

Dobbs pressed down harder and soon we were racing the pigs down a straightaway, neck and neck with the cabin.

"This van's got wings," was my father's only comment. I looked out the window and saw that we had lifted off the road and were now cruising about two feet above the lane. Dobbs was our demon pilot, steering us toward premature death and the fat logbook of our sins.

My stomach turned again and I gripped the dashboard as Dobbs finally overtook the semi. I was starting to feel like a pig myself, all desperate and sweaty. I wanted to ask Gerry how he felt, but when I opened my mouth, all that came out was a pathetic squeal.

By the time Dobbs swerved into the airport carpark, his horns had receded and the long nails had vanished, but silver rain was pelting down from the heavens. When I clambered from the van, it made my skin shimmer and ripple. I stood there, fascinated by the fluid texture of my arm. Dobbs pulled our gear from the backseat and told me to hurry up.

I picked up my tote bag and slung it over my shoulder. Gerry was in charge of the red shopping cart; he had his suitcase wedged inside it, and all his drum stands. Dobbs dashed ahead of us. It was as if he were inventing a spontaneous obstacle course, the way he darted through revolving doors, around columns, and zigzagged between groups of people. I was running second in the race and Gerry was keeping up a steady last.

Bounding onto an escalator, Dobbs dropped the suitcase he'd been carrying and turned. "Come on, Gerry," he bawled in a tour-guide voice, "keep up with the group!"

I was a few steps below Dobbs. My jaw had locked and colors were spiraling through the air like bright streamers. I was wondering how Gerry was going to get the shopping cart onto the escalator. Dobbs and I looked down to see how he was faring. He actually maneuvered the cart onto one of the rising steps quite well. As he stood behind it, he rested his hand on one hip and smirked, looking proud of himself.

Dobbs stepped off at the top and scurried ahead, looking for the TWA counter. I called to him to wait for Gerry, and we both stopped and turned. We saw the top of the red cart rise up first, then Gerry's head. He was looking dreamily at the ceiling. Right then the wheels jammed against the ridge into which the steps were collapsing, and Gerry, still on a lower stair, keeping a firm grip on the cart, continued to rise, so that the cart eventually toppled forward and he went somersaulting over the top and landed on his back.

Dobbs and I ran to help him. As we were lifting him to his feet, two men in suits hurried up to us.

"Where do you think you're going?" asked one, as Gerry struggled to shove his suitcase back into the cart.

"You can't leave!" exclaimed the other.

For a moment I thought they were going to flash their badges and cart us off to Security, or the police station.

"Where are you going?" the first one persisted.

Maybe they were from Immigration. Maybe Marilyn had called them after all.

"Nowhere," I said weakly. Ribbons of golden light were circling above the man's head.

"New York," declared Dobbs.

"You guys can't leave New Orleans," one of the men persisted. They were right behind us, swinging their briefcases.

I noticed Gerry was pale and sweating as much as me.

"We're on the City Council," added the other.

I was just about to swing around and confess to the drugs swilling around in my bloodstream, to working without a green card, when the first one said, "We've seen you two on Bourbon Street. Great act! This city really needs people like you. Just don't stay away too long!"

And then they were gone, and Dobbs was bustling us up to the counter.

An attendant in a red suit flashed her professional smile at me and said something, but I couldn't understand what. It was as if she spoke in another language. I was starting to feel sick again, and dumped my bag on the ground. Gerry nudged me and began pawing through a pocket in my shoulder bag. He pulled out a few papers and finally dumped two crumpled and coffee-stained tickets on the counter.

Miss TWA screwed up her nose at the weathered specimens and reluctantly picked them up.

"What is your destination today?"

Gerry and I just stared at her. All I could think of were the larger implications of her question. The big existential angst. I mean, where were Gerry and I really headed? How was this story about us going to finally end?

"My God," she exclaimed, looking at the tickets. "Flight 603 to La Guardia. If you hurry you just might make it."

She dragged our luggage onto the scales and gave me a pen and some tags to fill out.

I fidgeted with the pen. Dobbs was urging me to hurry up. But I couldn't remember my own name, and when I thought about my address, I realized I didn't have one. We no longer lived behind the witchcraft shop, and we had no home in New York.

Miss TWA pressed our tickets into my hand and garbled something about gates and time. She waved me away and pulled the untagged luggage through to the nearby conveyer belt.

Dobbs rushed us across the purple carpet. The thought of having to leave him at the security checkpoint terrified me. How were we going to cope without him? How were we going to move to New York City when I couldn't even remember my own name?

"What gate are you leaving from?" he asked.

I glanced up at the digital Departures board. The white lettering and numbers were displayed clearly enough, but to me they appeared to be in some foreign language, some obscure series of hieroglyphs.

"Shit," I said. "I can't remember."

I kept staring at the board, realizing that I could no longer read, that the chemicals wheeling about in my cerebellum had reduced me to an infantile preliteracy.

Dobbs was already running back to the TWA counter to check on the gate number. Gerry's shirt was wet with perspiration, and his face had a distinct green tinge about it.

"Ten B!" Dobbs shouted, jogging up behind us.

After a couple of quick hugs, I dumped my shoulder bag on the wide rubber belt of the X-ray machine and let it disappear. Dobbs pushed us through the security checkpoint and then he suddenly vanished.

I collected my bag and scurried down to the departing plane. An attendant shouted, "Sayer?" which sounded vaguely familiar. Gerry nodded and the man unlocked the door of the plane and bustled us inside. Because the flight was so crowded, we couldn't sit together. Being isolated from my father added to my anxiety. I was placed in a row between two middle-aged women. In the window seat sat a white woman engaged in embroidery. The one on my left was black and had her head bowed over a paperback. I glanced at the open page, but still could not decipher the characters.

I tried to fasten my seat belt, but couldn't quite get the metal to click into its socket. The white woman noticed my struggle. She lay the embroidery on her lap, took the two pieces out of my hands, and within a moment I was safely locked into my seat.

She gave me a benevolent smile and went back to her needlework. Gerry was sitting directly in front of me.

The plane took off smoothly. After the mad ride with Dobbs and the pig trailer along the expressway, cruising inside a 747 was a comparative joy. I still felt gratitude toward the embroidery woman for her help, and asked her where she was headed.

"Germany," she replied, somewhat surprised, as if I should have already known. "To visit my daughter and grandchildren."

I gripped the armrests and stared at the back of Gerry's head. I wanted to tell her that she was on the wrong plane, that this was a New York flight, but I couldn't muster the words. How disappointed she would be when we touched down at La Guardia and instead of seeing her grandkids, she'd be greeted by unregistered taxi drivers hustling for fares.

The FASTEN-YOUR-SEAT BELT NO-SMOKING sign blinked off and a collective sigh sang throughout the plane. Metal clicked and cigarette lighters coughed.

I turned to the black woman, who was peering down the aisle. "Where are you off to today?" I thought this would be a subtle way to alert the poor, misdirected grandmother on my right that she was on the wrong flight.

"Berlin," she replied, glancing at her book and flipping a page.

A burning sensation, like hot molten lead, began twisting in my stomach. I glanced out the window, at the electric-pink clouds. Below, the countryside looked like a green chessboard, and I couldn't help feeling like a pawn, or one of the ants my father had witnessed almost eighteen years ago.

third
movement

"I would believe only in a God who could dance."

—Nietzsche, *Thus Spoke Zarathustra*

■ 1 ■

I see it now. In my mind, I return to that flat square of bitumen on 34th Street. I see the uneven pavement and weeds struggling through the cracks. The young men congregating below the fire escape with their tiny plastic bags of coke. I see the unlit neon sign, the corner where my father talked his way out of a knife wound to his gut.

It is only a midtown parking lot now, but in 1984 a deteriorating four-story hotel stood on one side of it, between Eighth and Ninth Avenues. In 1994, when my husband and I took a trip back to New York, we caught the A train downtown, and for the first time in ten years I walked the path Gerry and I used to trace each night on our way home from Columbus Avenue.

My husband and I rounded the corner to 34th. I had a camera and planned to photograph the building in which my father and I had lost so many nights, practicing our routines in that small room with the ugly green wallpaper, paying our rent each week with four hundred rolled quarters. My husband and I passed the 1950s bar where Gerry and I used to drink. But when we reached the site, the hotel was gone. I stood there, holding his hand, glancing up and down the street, straining to remember the crumbling brick walls, the staircase leading up to the glass double doors, the store in the basement that sold candy and eventually expanded into second-hand goods (it wasn't until we'd lived there a couple of months that I found out the candy and the recycled junk were a front for a numbers racket).

"That's where it was," I said. "It was there." I pointed to a corner of the carpark. My husband took the camera and stood me beside the unlit neon sign, before the ghost-walls of the Penn View. He shot an entire roll of black-and-white. The next week I would send the photos to my father in Sydney, so he'd be able to witness our vanished past, and through that sudden loss, could recall it.

Mostly I remember the aging German prostitute. She comes back to me over and over. Her bulging belly, the rounded shoulders. Her sharp, irregular teeth, the scar that pearled down the side of her right cheek like a tattoo gone wrong. She always stood in the same place, to the left of the ho-tel's entrance, nursing a beer can hidden inside a brown paper bag, sipping through a plastic straw. Gerry and I were impressed by her efficiency: She'd walk into the foyer with a man on her arm, and no more than ten minutes later she'd emerge from the room next to ours, buttoning up her dress and assuming her position on the street once more.

As I stood there, watching my husband gaze at me through the lens of the Canon, I wondered where the German prostitute was standing now, or if she were standing at all. She'd had an unusual name, like Alma, or Aggie. And she was the saddest woman I've ever known.

■   2   ■

It was Gerry who set me straight about the flight path of the plane we'd boarded in New Orleans. In my confusion, I'd begun to sweat, and had managed to unbuckle my seat belt and squeeze past the knees of the plump black woman.

"Gerry!" I hissed from behind the beverage cart. He didn't seem to hear me. I leaned over the lemonade cans and packets of pretzels. "Dad?" I found myself calling. "Dad, can you come here?"

He looked around, frowning. It was as if someone had called him a bastard, or had accused him of some misdeed. He sighed and negotiated his way past the man next to him and had to crawl over the armrest to get by the cart.

"What?" He stood there with his hands shoved in his pockets.

I looked around, scared that we might be overheard. The walls of the cabin were shifting, as if they were made of some fine fabric, sheets of silk billowing in the breeze created from the breath of the chattering passengers.

"Not here." I turned around and made my way down the aisle. As I walked, I could hear snatches of German, those tough, throaty syllables. The strange thing was that I was sure I could understand them, or at least in-tuit their meaning. A suited woman blabbering on to a man next to her was telling him about the virtues of cheese, and he was saying, *"Nein, nein,"* and shaking his head. Two businessmen farther on sipped mixed drinks and chatted away about mag wheels. Even though I'd only learned twenty words of German when I was twelve, and could no longer read English, I was sure about the mag wheels and the men's ensuing dialogue about differentials and brake pads.

I found a private spot near the toilets at the back of the cabin.

"Dad," I whispered, leaning toward him. I had momentarily forgotten his distaste for the word. "We're on the wrong plane."

Gerry frowned and sighed again. Every pore in his face seemed to be breathing on its own. "What are you talking about?"

"This flight," I murmured, glancing about, "this flight's headed for Berlin. You know," I continued, "Germany."

His pores exhaled, inhaled. His broken nose looked like a craggy rock formation on his face. A river of sweat formed along one of the horizontal lines of his brow.

"Is it legal to perform on the streets of Berlin?" I wondered aloud. "Maybe we'll need a permit. At least on the East side. Unless we do a little propaganda," I rattled on, "some theater to further the socialist cause. That big wall, you know, the acoustics'd be pretty good."

My father just stared at me with wide eyes. They looked all yellow and sickly through the thick lenses of his glasses.

"Yeah," he said, wiping his brow. "This plane's going to Berlin, *but it's stopping in New York first!*"

Then he turned, noticing that the beverage cart was well past his row and heading toward First Class. "Arh, shit," he muttered, running after it. "Now I've missed my honey-roasted peanuts."

By the time the plane landed two hours later, I could read again. Colored lights still burned through the air, however, and I could feel the shifting gears of my internal organs as they respectively digested food and pumped blood and manufactured cells.

"Jesus," I whispered as we made our way through the airport to collect our luggage. "I'll never do that again."

My father just smiled and slung an arm around my shoulder. "Most people are content to fly while sitting in their seats. With their seat belts fastened. But you and I"—he gave me a conspiratorial pat on the shoulder—"you and I have got to get out and tap dance on the wing."

■ **3** ■

We rode a bus into town and caught a cab from 42nd Street down to the Bowery. It was still cool in New York and I shivered inside my black leotard. We were on our way back to Nerida's. Gerry had called her from New Orleans and asked if we could stay until we found a place of our own. She was no longer living with the buxom Sandy, who had been kicked out after failing to pay some bills while Nerida was in Europe.

We were allowed to stay at the Rivington Street flat again under the condition that we were in good health and could work around the exigencies of her other roommates. Charlie and Greg had taken Sandy's place, and they had particular problems that they were trying to help each other through. Charlie was trying to kick booze; Nerida was trying to kick smack; and Greg was struggling to overcome the tuberculosis he'd contracted during the winter. Nerida had returned from England to find them holed up in their apartment on Avenue C with no heat (the landlord had cut it off because everyone in the building was on a rent strike).

It had been nine months since our last cab ride down to the Bowery. In that time it had completely transformed itself: There were no drunks lurching about on the pavement, no broken glass, no dealers and hookers hovering in unlit doorways. Dusk was settling in, and a curious violet light imbued the uneven pavement with a certain diminutive majesty.

When Nerida opened the door I felt like a lost child falling into the wide arms of her mother. She was a little heavier, a little rounder, and it felt good to be folded into her warmth. She told us that dinner was ready and helped us up with our bags.

While our last welcome into her home had been fueled by carafes of wine, bottles of Pernod, a bag of grass, and exotic deserts, nine months later we were ushered into a monastic sobriety. The renovations had been completed, and the lumber that had formerly lain strewn throughout the rooms was now reincarnated into angular shelves, a built-in bed-base, and, by the windows, a huge desk the shape of an isosceles triangle.

Everything now had its place, including the consumptive-looking Greg. He sat in a butterfly chair by the kerosene heater, swathed in a thick maroon dressing gown. His cheekbones pressed through the withered flesh of his face. He'd always been thin, but now he was positively emaciated.

Greg's partner, Charlie, greeted us swinging a soup ladle. He was still as jolly as ever, happy to be cooking dinner. The three of them were on a strict macrobiotic diet to help them through their various illnesses. Within moments, Charlie was doling up egg drop soup, brown rice, and slices of organic, corn-fed chicken, and pouring bancha tea.

After Gerry had made the call from New Orleans and found out about Greg's TB, he'd convinced me that we wouldn't be vulnerable to the disease because we were too healthy. "You have to be really run-down to get it these days," he said. "Practically on your last legs." Even so, Nerida had devised a system to subvert the dangerous microorganisms. All of Greg's utensils—everything from his teaspoon to his toothbrush—were isolated from the others and marked with an orange sticker. As if to test the truth of my father's claims, I sat next to Greg in the butterfly chair. I sat huddled against the wool of his robe, my arm nestled around his waist.

My right foot was still mummified inside a sweaty bandage reeking of Ben-Gay and Epsom salts. During my convalescence, I had put on weight, and each morning was a minor torture as I gazed at the peculiar roundness of my hips reflected in Nerida's full-length mirror.

I was becoming more womanly and I hated it. With the added weight, my breasts bloomed, and the long, lithe body that had been mine was slowly being claimed by hormones and my increasingly sluggish metabolism. The black skirt with the embroidered musical notes, which had looked so charming only six months ago, now looked silly and childish hanging over the curve of my expanding arse. Even the clown mask now appeared to be just that—a mask, something behind which that uncomfortable woman was hiding. Who was she, I wondered, and why did she conceal herself behind greasepaint and the wide brim of a top hat?

Being a woman brought all sorts of problems. Recently, in New Orleans, I'd been approached a few times, and asked, "How much?" as if our busking were a front for more lascivious solicitation.

As my breasts and belly swelled that spring, I tried to beat them back with skipped meals and hours of dancing, with the mile-wide circles I ran around the Lower East Side on our one day off.

■   **4**   ■

Nerida wasn't turning tricks anymore and had a good job working as a madam in a brothel. All she had to do was answer the phones and match clients with suitable women. I suppose you could have called her a consultant or a matchmaker, but Ned isn't one for euphemisms, and she liked the sound of Madam, which conjured up images of red-light districts, honky-tonk pianos, and champagne.

Alma the German prostitute didn't have it so good. She didn't have a pimp and had to work cheap because younger and prettier women were edging onto the block.

We ended up at the Penn View after a solid week of looking for a hotel room with a weekly rate of no more than one hundred dollars. We'd tried to get back into the Ben Franklin Hotel, but during the winter the building had been converted to condominiums, and unless we could come up with two hundred thousand dollars, they weren't interested in talking to us. I called the Capital Hall Hotel on West 87th, the Elton on East 26th, the Kenmore on East 23rd, the Sahara on East 14th. On through the phone book—the Terminal, the Vigilant, the Yale. I even tried the Chelsea, where everyone from Dylan Thomas to Brett Whiteley had stayed. I dreamed of my own creative flowering in the hotel that boasted of having been the home of so many others. But Mr. Bard at the Chelsea had no openings, and prices there were well above our meager budget.

We walked miles around Manhattan, hoping for a vacancy. It wasn't the TB that Gerry was worried about. No, he was in a hurry to move out of Nerida's apartment because she'd declared it an alcohol-free zone. He liked staying there more last year, when the Pernod flowed and everyone wasn't creeping around looking half dead. The whole thing was giving him the willies. Sometimes, at night, he would pop out and sink a couple of rums in a local bar, or buy a few cans of beer and sit in the park with the dealers, quietly sipping and watching the transactions take place near the swings.

I remember calling the Penn View from a public phone booth on the Upper West Side. After days of tramping around, of scouring newspapers and following up obscure leads, my foot was throbbing and I was desperate to find a place to live. A high-pitched voice piped through the receiver, saying that, yes, they had a vacancy, and the price, well, the price was negotiable, depending on how long I needed the room, and how many people I'd be sharing with.

A bus ride down Ninth Avenue took us to 34th Street, and it wasn't long before the Penn View appeared, a four-story brownstone with a cracked glass door and cardboard boxes out the front filled with junk from the basement store. And Alma was there, dressed in a tight gray skirt, standing by the steps, sipping her beer through a plastic straw.

She gave us the once-over as Gerry pushed on the door. We stepped inside and up the stairs to the foyer. The place smelled weird, of stale cigarette smoke and cheap detergent, not unlike an Australian pub early on a Sunday morning. The linoleum tiles were chipped and worn. One solitary lightbulb hung from the ceiling. We saw ourselves amid the squalor when we turned toward the front desk and caught our reflections trapped in the full-length mirror hanging near the stairs. Imitation-wood paneling formed the backdrop, along with a garbage can brimming with balled paper, polystyrene McDonald's boxes, and crushed cans of Coke.

"Can I help you?" cried the ghostly, feminine voice I had heard on the phone.

A thin, aging black man sat behind a barred counter with an unlit cigarette butt between his lips. It was as if he had forgotten it was there.

Gerry swept up to the counter. "I was wondering if you had any accommodation?"

"One room. You want it for the whole afternoon, or just for an hour?"

Gerry straightened and let go of the bars. "No, no. You don't understand. This is my daughter."

The man glanced at me and took the butt out of his mouth. "Right."

"We're looking for permanent accommodation, you see. We're looking for somewhere to *live*."

The man eyed me again, leaned closer to Gerry. "You from England?"

Gerry shook his head. "Look, we really need a room."

"We-e-ell," he whined, looking at his ledger. "I don't usually have permanents on this floor. It's not very—you know—it's not like we"—he shrugged and waved the butt about—"you've got the girl and all—"

"How much?" said Gerry. "How much a week?"

The man stood up, drew out a huge cluster of keys, unlocked the gate, and let himself out. He led us down a narrow hall on the same floor.

The stained yellow carpet was blemished with cigarette burns and the charred remains of discarded matchsticks. The man was slightly hunched, and as I walked behind him, I noticed that he had a flashlight in his back pocket. There was nothing unusual in this, except that it was switched on and the glowing bulb protruding from his trousers seemed to spotlight his every move.

He stopped in front of room one twelve, and unlocked the door.

I crept in after Gerry. It was small and dark and narrow, barely enough room for a three-quarter bed, a sink, a side table, and one chair. Striped, dark-green wallpaper echoed the hotel's cage motif. A closed window overlooked the bottom of the fire escape and the uneven parking lot; through it I could hear the shouts of teenage boys and the dull monotone of a boom box spitting out rap.

"How much you want a week?" asked Gerry.

"Hundred and twenty dollars."

"How 'bout a hundred?"

The man shrugged. "OK."

I opened the window and leaned out, unable to visualize myself in such a seedy place. It certainly was no Chelsea, no literary and artistic Algonquin.

The man told us he'd let us think about it and he and his spotlight disappeared.

"One bed," I murmured.

Gerry tried to sound optimistic. "It's pretty central to everything."

"It's small. A single room."

"All this closet space!" he added, opening a nearby door.

"I can't stand this wallpaper. It feels like it's closing in on me."

Gerry did a little dance inside the walk-in closet. "Only a hundred bucks a week! That's our price. Did you see the way I talked him down from one-twenty? Did you see that?"

I sat on the bed and fidgeted with the buckle of my bag. He must have noticed my disconsolation, for he walked over, sat beside me, and slipped an arm across my rounded shoulders.

"We'll just stay here for a week or two, until we can find something better." He patted my arm and ran a hand across my hair. "Now I'll go and fix up old Aunty at the desk and we can move in this afternoon."

I was reluctant to leave the domesticity of Nerida's apartment, the warm smells of convalescence. It was a peculiarly feminine atmosphere for which I longed. I loved the aroma of Charlie's stir-fried vegetables, and the comforting scent of the kerosene heater. Nerida would press herbal poultices against Greg's rib cage. She would come home from work at the same time each night and bring us little presents: magazines, fruit, a secondhand book or two.

If Greg was trying to kick TB, and Nerida was trying to kick smack, and Charlie was trying to kick booze, what was I trying to kick? My foot still pulsed when I ran around the East Village and, no matter how much I rubbed and soaked, it remained red and swollen. Perhaps I was trying to kick the punishment I persisted in inflicting upon myself.

Whatever it was, any possible cure was forestalled when we packed up a taxi with all our gear and moved into the Penn View that May afternoon. I found a syringe under the bed, and on my way to the shops a young man stopped me in the carpark and asked me how much for a blow job.

 5

After we moved our gear in, we went out and had a couple of drinks and a bowl of spaghetti at the bar on the other side of the parking lot. When we returned, Alma was still standing out in front. I passed her and opened the glass door, and she shot me a sad look, not unlike a pet who wants to come in out of the cold. It hurt to leave her there.

When we walked into the foyer, we were greeted by a small party of black men, all of whom were standing around the Coke machine, sipping dark Bacardi from plastic cups.

"Here they are!" announced a well-built man in track suit pants and a pale-blue T-shirt. He had a trimmed mustache and a shaved head that glowed under the bare lightbulb.

The other men let out a chorus of cheers.

"Man, we've been waiting for you guys for ages!" said the shaved one. He glanced at me and hurried forward to shake Gerry's hand. "Fred told us all about you. Australia, right? Father and daughter. Street performers. Man, that's too much!"

Already he was pouring Bacardi into two plastic cups. He topped them up with Coke and handed them to us. An elderly man sat on a stool, a cigar wedged between his lips. His name, we soon found out, was Pop and he originally hailed from New Orleans. A younger guy with a pot belly and a leather cap on his head was introduced as Ricky, and a thin, middle-aged one was named Willis.

The gregarious man with the shaved head was named Earl. He smoked More, a brand of long, thin cigars with filters. "Man, I knew some great Aussies in 'Nam. Jesus, those suckers could fight!"

I sipped my drink and leaned against the Coke machine. This, I thought, was why Gerry was in such hurry to get out of Nerida's place. It wasn't just the alcohol ban he was trying to escape, but also the kind of conversation to be had with two homosexuals and two women.

"Is that right?" he replied, accepting one of Earl's filter-tipped cigars and its accompanying match. "Well, I tell you what, mate, I met some unreal black guys in Detroit when I was playing there. Treated me like a brother! Got me gigs, found me a place to live. The whole bit, you know?"

Earl laughed loudly, but all the time he was looking past Gerry's shoulder, eyeing me.

"And I'd be playing drums in this all-black club, and some of the guys in the audience would hassle the bandleader, saying stuff like, 'Hey, what's that whitey doing up there?' And the bandleader would say, 'Man he only looks white, when he plays, he's blacker than you!'"

The quartet of men burst out laughing. Earl walked toward me and dropped some quarters into the machine. Two cans of Coke came clunking out.

"You've got an honest face," he said. "Just like a Quaker girl."

I shrugged and stared at the floor. He looked like a boxer, but I didn't tell him so.

"Whatever you do," he added, confidentially, "stay away from the fourth floor."

"Why?" I asked, my curiosity peaking. Fred had told me the same thing as we were moving in.

"Just don't go up there," he repeated.

Earl turned away and, like an actor returning to the stage after a brief respite, declared, "Those *Aussies*, man!" I noticed he was one of the few Americans I'd met who pronounced the word correctly. "Shee-it, what they couldn't do with a gun ain't nobody's business! And ambushes! Ambushes, man—forget it!"

That was when Gerry launched into his own war stories, even though he'd never been in the army. He was jailed for six months for refusing to fight. When he returned home, his brother, the captain, the hero, disowned him.

"But I tell you one thing," Gerry continued, lowering his voice, "I tell you what, I wasn't the one who was messed up. My hands never shook and I never heard explosions in the middle of the night. And I didn't have to pour half a bottle of Scotch on my cornflakes every morning."

Earl shook his head. "Yeah, I know all about that one. I was a Green Beret. Man, they had me doing all kinds o' shit. Parachuting. Ambushing. My nerves are shot, man. I got my green pills and my purple pills and my Bacardi. 'Nam was a shit hole. The only good thing about it was R and R. I'd get my butt into Hong Kong, a nice hotel, call up my favorite mama-san. Ohhh, shit. A sauna, a massage—"

"Yeah, we know what comes next, son," said Pop.

"C'mon, old man," cried Ricky. "You wouldn't even remember how!"

They all began laughing.

"Shh!" cautioned Pop, glancing at me. "No talkin' like that in front of the girl."

My father and the circle of men regarded me. I was still sitting on the milk crate, trying to think of something smart to say, something to divest them of their perception of me as an innocent underling. But I couldn't think of anything, and just grinned stupidly and held out my cup for more rum.

Earl smiled widely and freshened up my drink. At that moment the front door swung in and Alma appeared with a disheveled, middle-aged man on her arm. She stood at the counter and nudged the man. He nodded and began shelling some bills into Fred's hand. Alma snatched up a pen and reached in under the bars to slide the ledger through. She scribbled in it and took the man's arm again.

Fred palmed her a key, and she led the man past us and down the hall.

I leaned back and noticed that they stopped in front of the room next to ours. Alma unlocked the door and hurried the man inside.

▦ 6 ▦

Women, I suppose, have their own war stories. Stories they keep to themselves, stories that don't get celebrated in pubs and marches and over boozy two-up games. My mother was only eight when the Second World War broke out. She was a poor kid growing up in a rough part of Sydney. My grandmother, Florence—or Dolly, as everyone called her—had been deserted by her husband only a year before, and was suddenly left with four children to support. Throughout the war she did what she had always done, packed up the wicker pram with detergents and brushes and wheeled the buggy from door-to-door through Marrickville, asking people if she could scrub their floors. My mother's earliest memories are of this difficult ritual, being bundled up as a toddler into the pram, nestling under a flannel blanket along with the mops and cleaning rags. The footpaths gleaming with rainwater. The lush smell of soap. The bruises that purpled her mother's knees. The songs they sang together as they traced corners and ventured through the front gates of haughty, Victorian homes: "Sister Suzie," "My Blue Heaven," "A Slow Boat to China."

When my grandfather left them and fled to Tasmania only months before the outbreak of the war, Gran invested in more soap and sponges and went into battle against hunger and poverty, a mop in one hand, a duster in the other. Her allies were marshalled in the community. The couple in the fruit shop gave her left-over produce every Saturday afternoon. The butcher slipped her cuts. She washed out the nearby bakery twice a week, and loaves of fresh bread miraculously appeared on her doorstep each morning.

One of my earliest memories is the weekly visit to my grandmother's house, the same house in which my mother was conceived, the one in which she was raised. My ritual then was to go through the family photo album. But there were no pictures of the mysterious man who'd left them. I'd received descriptions from my grandmother, whose heart had softened over the years into lily-scented nostalgia. "He was gorgeous," she'd say. "Your mother got her looks from him. Tall, lean. A beautiful head of blond hair. And dance! You should have seen him on a dance floor . . ."

Jerry Partridge had come from a wealthy Scottish/Irish family that disapproved of his marriage to my working-class grandmother. They'd met on the dance floor at the Albert Palais in 1924. Dolly was eighteen years old and had worked in a textile factory from the time she was twelve. Yet she'd distinguished herself at the Albert Palais and had become a championship ballroom dancer. Jerry's family thought he was wasting his life with a common woman who was just trying to trick him into marriage.

The last time I saw Dolly alive I was telling her about my own husband, whom she never met. But she sat on the edge of her bed and patted my shoulder. The final image she left me with was a description of how she and her older sisters flew out of their house after tea each night, escaping the strict eye of their mother (the one who ended up half-naked in the National Park thirty-three years later with a dead Mr. Stanton still inside her). The sisters used to run across the street and, before walking the half-mile to the ballroom, would gaze at their reflections in the glowing Arnott's Biscuit sign and quickly apply red lipstick.

For years, these fragments of feminine history never seemed quite as significant as a story about an adventurous uncle who saved a whole battalion in Europe, or a father who wasted away in jail for refusing the draft, or a mysterious grandfather who suddenly vanished one day and was never seen again.

As I sat on the milk crate in the Penn View Hotel, I still labored under that misconception. But now, as I write, twelve years later, as the women in my family know that I am writing, telling the stories, that I am making them mine, I know who possessed the most tenacity during those long and arduous years.

■ 7 ■

During our stint down south, everything on Columbus Avenue had turned Japanese. Sushi bars had sprung up through the winter; calligraphic signs decorated boutiques; even the mannequins were Asian. All we needed to do was don some satin kimonos and we would have fitted right in.

I was still dreading the thought of running into Herb Browning again. I tried to assure myself that if, in the space of six months, Nerida could kick her habit, Charlie could stop drinking, and the avenue could transform itself into Little Tokyo, Officer Browning could well be stationed on the other side of town, chasing dealers and thieves, especially if the culprits wore high heels and liked dancing at Studio 54.

Gerry and I began working on the corner of 71st the night after we'd moved into the Penn View. It was Grimaldi's old pitch. He'd willed it to us before we'd left New Orleans because he was staying down there to work at the World's Fair. Since it was so early in the season, and still fairly chilly, there weren't many other performers out, and soon we were enjoying hundred-dollar nights and magnanimous applause again. We would have earned even more if hadn't been for my foot, which ached and ballooned inside my shoe if I stayed on it too long. Every few numbers, I'd have to take a break.

After a few nights the manager of the clothing store got sick of our noise and complained about losing business. She preferred the silent magic of Grimaldi's hands to our boisterous productions. We moved way down the avenue, to the corner of Broadway and 65th, across the road from Lincoln Center. The pedestrian flow there was fairly steady, and we could always pick up some fast cash when the well-to-do patrons poured out of the concert halls after an evening with Pavarotti or Wynton Marsalis.

It was on that corner, outside yet another branch of Chemical Bank, that some lost threads of the previous year returned and knotted themselves around me.

The mystery of Romano's mixed messages the year before—his seeming attraction to and nonchalance about me—was solved late one May evening when the sky was clear and the temperature was up to the sixties. He appeared while we were taking a break outside the bank. He was wearing the same black tails and jeans. I could tell he was very stoned—the whites of his eyes were bloodshot and the pupils were dilated into big black saucers. His voice was soft and dreamy, and he couldn't stop talking about Jesus and the Glory of God. With his characteristic lisp, he told me he was going to quit the street and go back into plumbing. He'd stayed in New York throughout the winter, and in my absence had apparently been Born Again. Perhaps the rebirth was mired in complications, however, for he was obviously still smoking a lot of dope.

About ten minutes after he'd drifted up Columbus in order to do a show, a very pregnant dark-haired woman came barreling around the corner. She introduced herself as Anna. She had olive skin, like Romano, and shared his deep, Brooklyn accent.

"You seen Romano?" she said. "You know. The magic man?"

I nodded and pointed up the avenue.

"You his sister?" I asked, trying to detain her.

She laughed and swung her hair about. "If I was, we'd be havin' some kind of sheep-child here!" She pointed to her huge belly and grinned.

My foot began throbbing again and I slipped off my shoe. "When are you due?" I asked.

"Next week!" she said happily. "We're gonna have us a little girl."

"Congratulations!" I lifted my foot and rubbed it. "Got a name picked out?"

"Collette," she declared.

"Collette," I repeated. It was one of my favorite names, ever since I'd begun reading her books at fifteen.

Anna smiled and bade me good-bye, striding up Columbus in search of the stoned father of her child. As I sat on the footpath and unrolled my bandage, I counted back the months and realized I'd met Romano in the same month that Anna had conceived. No wonder, I thought; no wonder he'd backed out of our New Orleans plans, his offer to teach me the cane trick, his quiet overtures toward me in those early autumn weeks.

A framed photograph stands on my Victorian bookshelf as I write. My mother is seven and her brother is ten. They are perched on a piano stool in a studio, ankles crossed, their feet not reaching the carpeted floor. My mother's short blond hair is curled and tied with a ribbon. She's staring into the camera, her left hand opening like a flower on her lap, as if, in her own ethereal way, she's requesting that something be placed there.

On the day that photograph was taken, Dolly had dressed the four children in their best clothes and they'd caught a tram into the city. My grandfather was working at the General Post Office then, eking out a living sorting mail. My mother remembers posing for the photographer in the studio, how still she had to sit for the eye of the enormous camera. Afterward, Dolly took the children to Hyde Park, where they sat in the shade of the evergreens and ate ham and pickle sandwiches. The boys ran circles around the fountain. Dolly nursed the drowsy three-year-old. My mother stood up and pretended to walk a tightrope, her arms planing out to the sides, placing the heel of one patent-leather shoe against the toe of another. She'd almost reached the paved path when she looked up and saw the profile of her beloved father in the distance.

"Look!" she cried back to Dolly, pointing. "There's Dad!"

Dolly jumped up and walked across to the path, gazing in the direction at which the youngster gestured. In her excitement, my mother had failed to notice that her tall and handsome father had his arm wrapped around the waist of an auburn-haired woman.

For how many years did she try to put those three words back in her mouth, to curl that index finger and slip it into the pocket of her silk dress? The moment Dolly saw the other woman was the beginning of the end, the beginning of nights when he'd come home drunk and fall into bed, and she'd stab him with hat pins or douse him with boiling water.

Still, the mysterious woman lingered on, her face appearing on the wet surfaces of the kitchen floors Dolly scrubbed each day. She scoured and rubbed, trying to erase the auburn hair and blue eyes, but no amount of lye and disinfectant could make her go away. Her husband, Jerry, stayed out later and later, resigned to be hanged for a pound as much as a penny.

"I didn't mean to dob him in," my mother once told me. "At first, I didn't even notice the other woman in the park. I was just happy, you know, I was just glad to see my father."

It was as if she were apologizing to his ghost, calling him back, still wanting to protect him from the sharp points of Dolly's hat pins.

I didn't exactly want to stick a hat pin into Romano, but I was disappointed in his lack of forthrightness. I wouldn't have minded holding one of his white doves above his head and allowing it to crap on his curly brown hair. Why hadn't he just told me he had a girlfriend, and a pregnant one, at that? Why give me those long, silent gazes, keep telling me he was going to call, plan a trip together down to New Orleans? I was mad at myself for having wasted so many hours dreaming about all the places in which we could have made love, the magnolia-scented fields, against the boughs of willow trees. I'd been naive enough to make him my Magician, the one who'd appeared in the tarot reading months ago.

Meanwhile, I was growing plump. I could see my reflection in the windows of passing cars as I danced, and it horrified me to glimpse my widening hips and the two breasts pressing through my worn leotard. When we weren't working, I took to wearing a red Santa Claus jacket to disguise my developing curves—the fluffy white trim hung a few inches above my knees and, apart from rendering me androgynous, kept me warm during the chilly spring days.

Occasionally, I'd see Romano wandering the streets, still obsessed with Jesus. I noticed he never mentioned anything to me about Anna, nor the daughter that surely must have been born by now. It gave me a certain covert pleasure to appear indifferent to his presence, and to resist the temptation to prolong any conversation he started up.

My story, I was beginning to realize, was the story of my mother and her mother and her mother before that, and the prospect of its continuity terrified me. If this is what being a woman meant, I'd rather be a child, an Alice.

8

After that first night in the foyer of the Penn View, my father and Earl became fast friends. We used to finish work on Columbus at eleven P.M., catch the bus down Ninth Avenue, and be home by eleven-thirty. I'd barely have enough time to strip off my sweat-soaked clothes and change before there was a knock at the door. Gerry would open it and Earl would be standing there, almost sheepishly, dressed in what he used to call his "slumming gear"—running shoes, a tracksuit, and a baseball cap. He'd always bring an offering—a couple of bottles of Colt 45, a joint, or enough coke for a couple of lines each, as if, in order to enter our room, he felt obliged to pay a toll.

We only had one chair and Gerry always got it. I used to perch at the end of the bed and Earl would sit on the floor with his back resting against the closet door. We'd switch on the radio and listen to the twenty-four-hour jazz station, Coltrane and Mingus and Roland Kirk providing a fiery sound track to the burgeoning friendship between the two men.

Earl's life was like some kind of Robert Johnson blues song. He used to sip beer and rake up the coke on the little hand mirror I gazed into when I touched up my clown makeup on the street. He'd rave on about the golden life he'd once enjoyed: the house he'd owned on Coney Island; the Cadillac he used to drive; his former wife and two teenage daughters. But the good life, I noticed, was always in past tense. As the night wore on, however, it often skipped into the future, when next year's tax return would arrive in the mail, or some unnamed friend would pay him back some money.

Gerry was enamored of Earl because he fit into Gerry's narrow concept of African-American manhood, a stereotype with which he had always identified and had often tried to ape—the streetwise, substance-abusing, my-woman-done-left-me kind of guy.

"You remind me," Gerry would often say, after the third line of coke and the fourth bottle of beer, "you remind me of the black mates I had in Detroit. They took me home, fed me, got me a gig down in a place called the Panther Room, with an all-black band."

Earl would laugh on cue and they'd slap each other's backs. Like me, like all of us now, he'd heard the story before. But Earl always enjoyed the comparison.

Gerry never seemed to notice that Earl's eyes would glaze over whenever he'd swoon into a soliloquy about the significance of Miles Davis's recording of the album *Milestones*, or about how, in the late forties, J. J. Johnson transformed the way in which the trombone was played. My father couldn't fathom a world in which all black people didn't have or care for rhythm. It didn't occur to him that his own Australian daughter might appreciate the music he loved more than this urban African-American. I knew Miles had begun his modal approach on *Milestones* and had abandoned the traditional songlike structure by the time he recorded "Kind of Blue," but Earl wasn't sure what instrument Duke Ellington played and thought post-bop was some kind of boxing technique.

Nevertheless, Gerry related to Earl as a finger-popping, palm-slapping brother, akin to the Detroit musicians who had rescued him from frostbite and poverty. And Gerry reminded Earl of the daredevil Aussie soldiers who'd saved his arse a couple of times in Vietnam. It didn't seem to matter that the only gun my father had ever brandished was the green plastic water pistol I used to play with as a kid.

■ 9 ■

One night when we were working opposite Lincoln Center a young couple walked past me and stopped. Gerry and I were taking a break, as my foot had begun to ache. He'd disappeared into a store across the road in search of a bottle of Colt 45. I was sitting on the sidewalk, rewrapping my Ace bandage.

"We tap dance on the street, too," announced the woman, who was not much older than me.

"Down in the Village," added the guy. He had Asian-American features and was as slim as his partner. "You should dance on a board," he said. "The concrete's not good for your feet."

"I know," I said, shrugging. "But it's too much to cart around. You know, on the bus and everything."

"Who's your favorite tap dancer?" asked the woman. She was standing close to me by now, looking at my shoes. I felt like a kid at a new school, being auditioned by a couple of potential new friends in a corner of the playground. At any moment I expected them to ask me what my father did and if my mother was pretty.

"Coles," I said, without hesitating. "Hoaney Coles."

"Honey," corrected the woman. "Like on toast, you know?"

I told them about seeing him dance in *My One and Only*, and my inability to track him down in order to take lessons.

The woman shook her head. "He doesn't teach anymore, but one of his partners does. His name's Cookie Cook. That's who we learn from every week."

She wrote down the address of the school on the back of a supermarket receipt. The class went from seven to eight-thirty, she told me, on Monday nights, and only cost four dollars a session.

■ 10 ■

It was in early June that we decided to get a refund on our return airline tickets to Sydney. They expired in the second week of August and, now that we were back in New York and making good money, we didn't want to go home. We were gripped by a certain anxious excitement as we walked up Fifth Avenue toward the airline office. Burning bridges is always a bit of a cheap thrill, especially when you get money in return. The woman at Japan Airlines wrote us out a check for eight hundred dollars, which made me feel both good and bad. It was good to have some extra cash, but the loss of the escape route back home meant that we really had to make it as an act.

As the mateship between Earl and Gerry developed, I felt more and more left out. It was all war stories and antiwar stories, ex-wife tales, the glory days of their youth. At least in New Orleans, while Gerry got stoned and raved on and patted out rhythms against his knees, Leonard and I could play Scrabble or I could flick through his large books on Matisse and Kandinsky.

The only way Earl could let me into his world was as a narrowly defined woman, someone to be pursued, to be had. After a couple of weeks, I came to recognize his persistent insinuation into our lives, his camaraderie with my father, as a thinly disguised project to bed me down eventually. It was a familiar plot of which I had grown weary. Gerry was always oblivious to the fact that I was female; that, in the eyes of his friends, I was not simply an honorary son. Sometimes I wonder how many devotees Gerry would have attracted over the years if I hadn't been lingering on the edge of his life in my red tap shoes and laddered stockings.

It wasn't that I disliked Earl or found him unattractive. His training as a Green Beret had honed his body into a fine muscular sculpture, and his dark skin often assumed a glowing violet hue in the candlelight of our room. The problem was that the only thing we had in common was my father and our shared predilection for the dreamy world that could be induced by chemical substances. After the first few nights, I grew bored with his mythologizing of the Vietnam War, the way he reveled in the moribund details of military strategy, his renditions of grenading and parachuting expeditions. Even though he'd been a victim of his own country's political ineptitude, he seemed unable to grasp the moral subtleties of such a history, and I could not love a man who celebrated so much violence. He was not my kind of man and, in spite of how much he pursued me, I was not his kind of woman.

Still, my father held court between us, spinning his stories and sniffing coke into his broken nose through a rolled-up dollar bill.

I distanced myself from the decadence that was beginning to define my life by developing what I liked to think of as my Art. The Monday night following my meeting with the tap dancers on Columbus, I tossed my shoes into a plastic bag and walked almost twenty blocks up Eighth Avenue to the Clarke Center of Performing Arts.

The studios were on the second floor, and in the hallways between them, people stretched and limbered up. Muscular legs pointed into the air and arms were poised above heads like the long necks of swans. I paid my four dollars at the office and made my way toward the doorway at which the receptionist had pointed, past lean young women in Capezio chiffon skirts and Lycra leotards. I felt like an imposter, an urchin among princesses. It had always amazed me how ballerinas all managed to look alike. I'm not referring just to their thin bodies and the little buns on the backs of their heads. It's as if they're all spawned by the same gene pool, an inbred family forever reproducing aristocratic profiles and pale, consumptive-looking skin.

I'd had to endure their sense of superiority, and my feelings of inferiority, on the street. There must have been some sort of balletic extravaganza on at Lincoln Center at the time, for while we performed on the corner outside Chemical Bank, girls a few years younger than me would pour down the steps from the Center and across the road at around ten every night. They'd still have their hair plastered back into tight buns, faces glittering with makeup. Some wore pale pink leotards beneath designer jeans. Others would be caught in the embrace of doting mothers. Fathers were frequently at their sides, wearing tailored suits and cuff links that glinted in the glow of the streetlights. They were all repairing, I imagined, to the Russian Tea Room or the Plaza Hotel for a postperformance supper.

I crept into the studio. It was exactly seven-thirty, and I was hoping my punctuality would put me in good stead with my prospective teacher. I glanced about quickly, looking for the couple who had encouraged me to come, but they hadn't yet arrived. There were three or four dancers rehearsing steps before the mirrors, and an elderly black man wandering between them. He was probably older than my father and was about my height. I noticed he was tubby around the waist and had a furrowed look set into his face.

I approached him a little shyly, introduced myself, and started babbling on about how I'd met his students, how long I had waited to study this style of tap. Perhaps it was my broad Australian accent, or the stupid-looking white cotton skirt I was wearing—it was elasticized at the waist and was decorated with horizontal colored stripes—for he simply regarded me non-committally, turned to the mirror, and executed a step I remember to this day. Unlike my former teachers, he did not count the step out or break it down into parts. When he completed the sequence, he stopped and turned. It was like being given a peeled boiled egg without any silverware and having to swallow it whole. I hurriedly kicked off my walking shoes, pulled on my taps, and asked him to do it again. He pursed his lips, sighed, and launched into it once more. Then, without looking back to see if I had grasped the finer intricacies of the pattern, he walked off to the other side of the room.

Maybe that was his way of sorting the wheat from the chaff, of scaring off uncommitted students. I had a pretty good ear then, and the step wasn't too difficult. After watching another student execute it at a slower tempo, I was soon making the right sounds and moves. I had barely mastered the step before he was back again, throwing something a little harder at me. This time I didn't get the benefit of a second viewing, and had to stand at the back of the room, studying the footwork of my peers.

The class seemed to be divided in half: On the left side of the room he was training a couple of dancers in a more complicated routine, while on the right—where I was—the sequences were challenging but obviously less demanding.

After perfecting the first chorus in twenty or so minutes I was feeling pretty good. I joined in with the others at the front of the room, where we ran through the routine together. As time went on, more and more students drifted into the studio and joined in, until there were nearly two dozen of us hoofing away in front of the mirror. The sequences Cookie demonstrated were not as slow and smooth as the ones I'd seen Coles perform, but the footwork was much closer to the floor than anything I'd danced before, and considerably more complex.

With that first choreographic installment came a tenuous sense of be-longing. I had been dancing alone for so long I had forgotten the nervous joy that could be garnered from being a part of a bigger rhythm. There was perhaps no greater thrill for me than to be a little cog in the great synco-pated machinery of a chorus line, one of eighteen people all trapped within time's collective push. Now I had something to go home and tell my father about. I was flushed with satisfaction and leaned against the wall, mopping my brow. It was better than sex, I was thinking, and lasted a hell of a lot longer.

But my infatuation with the new routine was promptly aborted when the door swung open and admitted the two dancers I'd met on the street. They smiled and waved at me as they crossed the room.

Cookie stood up from his chair in the corner and herded the two groups together. The second group knew our routine and suddenly the whole class was executing it as one. The two latecomers joined in up front. When Cookie counted us in the second time, he'd almost doubled the tempo, and I got lost. I wiped my brow again and moved to the back of the room. Even though I was not the only one who was toe-tied by the tempo, Cookie didn't bother running us through it again. He simply stood in front of the mirror, adding five-beat riffs juxtaposed against a scuffing phrase while his students crowded about his reflection.

It took me a good deal longer to acquire this step, especially at the speed at which he danced it, and I wouldn't begin to master it for days. My feet tried to grind out the breathless punctuation of Cookie's rhythmic language. But by that time his taps were prattling on about something else, fast-talking to the floor, caught in some blues I could not comprehend.

In a regular tap class you might learn a few new steps, and if you're lucky you can get through a sixteen-bar chorus of new material, but the choreography needs to be fairly straightforward and the tempo not too fast. In the hour and a half that was Cookie's first lesson, however, I had an entirely new routine and style thrown at me, chorus upon chorus of complicated patterns, of eleven-beat riffs and syncopated, single-footed wings, spanking Suzie-Q's and permutating pull-backs.

If I could call tap my secret language, it was as if I had been mumbling some crude pidgin talk that had barely sustained me through the years. So many nights, so many years dancing against concrete pavements had reduced my technique to a few heavy-footed and flashy steps that grabbed people's attention on a busy street and prompted them to throw money. There was, I suddenly realized, little art in what I'd been articulating, for subtlety on the street was a distinct liability.

I walked out of that class as stunned as a zombie, my mind numbed by rhythmic overload. In my hunger, I had grasped the rudiments of some of the harder steps farther into the routine and, scared that I would forget them by the time I got home, kept replaying them over and over in my head, counting them out, singing them to myself. I walked down Eighth Avenue and, every block or so, stopped and went over one or two of the steps to make sure they'd not escaped me.

When I arrived at the hotel, Gerry and Earl were in our room, drinking Colt 45 straight from the bottle. They asked me how my lesson went. I threw down my bag and began tapping my feet against the carpet, all the new sequences and steps, but it was, as Gerry would say, like taking a shower with an overcoat on. It was obvious I needed somewhere to practice— a hard, smooth surface—or else the future lessons would be pointless.

My father stood up and said it looked pretty good. He slipped some money into his back pocket, and said he'd be back in a minute. He was going down to the Korean deli on Eighth Avenue to buy another two bottles and a pack of cigarettes. He hadn't been gone longer than thirty seconds when Earl reached out and pulled me down on the bed and tried to plant his beery lips on mine.

■　　11　　■

I no longer slept with my father in the lumpy double bed—he had a tendency to snore and the mattress sagged in the middle. I always ended up squashed at the edge, trying to escape his expansive arms and noisy inhalations. Poised there in the dark, I often found myself staring out the open window at the fire escape, listening to sirens howl over the city, and imagining the tawdry acts that had been committed where we lay.

Instead, I fashioned a little nest in the narrow entrance of our room. Between the two walls and the bottom of Gerry's bed, there was just enough space for me to spread a single sheet on the floor. A pillow went down at the top and a second sheet and army blanket completed the improvised boudoir. The locked door became my headboard, and when I couldn't sleep at night, I could lean up against it and read in the dancing candlelight.

It was there that I awakened the morning after my first lesson, with the sounds of the new rhythmic patterns repeating themselves in my head. They were like the antibodies of some syncopated virus burning through my brain, some feverish infection.

The following morning, I was utterly preoccupied with the new dance patterns and, in the back of my mind, troubled by Earl's growing advances.

After he'd dragged me down on the bed, I'd pushed him away. I kept saying, No, trying to draw away from his hands. I could smell the faint odor of cigarettes on his breath, and the deep scent of the cocoa butter that he smoothed into his skin after he showered each night. When I regained my balance, he sat at the edge of the bed like a boy, gazing into my eyes and holding onto the hem of my skirt.

"Don't," I said, my voice wavering, "don't do that again."

I took hold of my hem and snatched it away. I left the room and hung about in the foyer with Fred until my father returned. I knew it would be useless to tell him about the incident: Earl was his best mate, his brother, just like the guys in Detroit.

My father was still unconscious on the bed, under the fading blue chenille bedspread. I grabbed some change and slipped out of the room. Instead of ruminating about my problem with Earl, as I walked down the hall and through the foyer, I instead made myself concentrate on solving the problem of having nowhere to practice. I was halfway down the stairs, on my way to the shop to buy milk, when it occurred to me that there might actually be some space in the hotel itself, an empty storeroom or unused suite.

I knew it would be pointless to ask Fred. He was a crusty old bugger. I'd had to beg him for a set of extra sheets when I'd decided to defect from the lumpy bed and Gerry. I'd seen him turn away strung-out junkies when they were ten or twenty cents short of the five dollars it cost to hit up in the bathroom.

I jogged back up the steps and smiled at him as I hurried past the cage.

Earl's room was on the first floor. It was the same size as ours, but was in better condition. I walked down the hallway, hoping to find a door that was ajar or an empty room, some space that wasn't covered by the yellow carpet.

I had no luck on the first floor, and repeated my search on the second. There I was met with the same ominous closed doors. At the end of the hallway on the third floor, I found what looked like an unused bathroom: spiderwebs netted the dusty toilet bowl and the hardened pellets of some kind of animal droppings were calcifying in the sink.

I returned to the stairwell and continued to climb. I came to the landing of the fourth floor and paused. The layout of this floor varied from the others: one hallway veered down the length of the hotel, while another traced its breadth. The shorter hall was wide, almost as big as the foyer, and was littered with old newspapers, soft drink cans, and the discarded cartons of takeout food. The only light came through the cracked windowpanes, where dust motes swam in the air above faded gray linoleum.

In spite of the warnings of Earl and Fred, the absence of the awful carpet tempted me into this forbidden netherworld. I would be careful, I told myself. I would tread lightly and tentatively, so that a loose floorboard or rotting beam would not break beneath my weight.

I made my way down the hall, then turned left and tiptoed into the half-light of a narrow passage. Broken glass crunched under my feet and I found myself walking straight into the translucent curtain of a spiderweb.

I was peering into a dank parlor of discarded sheets and empty cans of Mountain Dew when a mangy tabby cat sprang out of one corner with its orange fur on end, hissing. I froze, bound to the creature by its fixed, hypnotic stare. In that moment I noticed how thin and hungry the cat looked, her striped coat reduced to a motley garment by chunks of missing fur. Claws brandished, she hissed and spat, as if I were some unsuspecting dog who'd wandered into the wrong lair. I extended one hand to quiet the distraught creature, when suddenly the sheets shifted and a thin, bony arm rose up out of the quagmire of filthy cotton, followed by a hollow, unshaven face. He had the same starved look in his eyes as the cat, the pupils reduced to shallow black pinholes. Saliva dribbled out between his parted lips. I expected him to sit up or grab my ankle with that bony hand and demand to know what I was doing here. But he seemed unable to move; his wrist dropped against a crushed soda can and he simply left it there. The cat was still hissing and spitting, her back arched and her tail undulating above like a furry, hypnotic snake. I shifted to the side a little, and it was only then that I noticed it, the discarded syringe lying within the folds of yellowing cotton, the carnation of blood drying on the sheet.

I raised my hand to my mouth and backed away, but as I was turning to retrace my steps I saw another body on the floor in the room opposite, between the beams left standing by a demolished wall. This one was still as a corpse, and the only clue to the life that was in him was the blanket's slight movement in concert with his faltering breath.

By this time I was holding my own breath as I hurried back down the passage. I was on my toes, trying not to make a sound. The cat ran up behind me and quickly skittered past. I recoiled sideways and stumbled against a broken chair, sending a number of empty bottles clanging about my feet.

The noise was answered with a loud groan from somewhere else on the floor. Afraid I'd be met by the outstretched hands of a strung-out madman, I regained my balance and followed the cat's swift trajectory around the corner into the wider hall, hurrying through the stench of urine and the eerie, primordial light.

As I ran past the windows, however, my right foot hit a floorboard and at that moment I heard a beam creak and felt the rotting wood collapse beneath me, swallowing up my bandaged limb, as if I were sinking into some premature, shallow grave.

■ 12 ■

If the Penn View could not provide me with a floor to practice on, I decided, then I would provide one myself. In his own peculiar way, my father had taught me the virtue of stubbornness, and I was not going to give up until I secured that space for myself.

After I'd pulled my foot from the murky underworld of electrical wiring and pipes, I walked down the stairs, through the foyer, and out onto 34th Street. I headed toward Ninth Avenue, where, five generations ago, Hell's Kitchen had sprawled over block after block and into the twentieth century. Years later, it was still no paradise. Shabby, empty shop-fronts sat behind rusting iron bars and crooked security doors.

I discovered a huge metal industrial door lying amid discarded furniture on a vacant lot near one such row of shops. I lifted one corner from its muddy plot and pushed it up on its side. I tapped my fingertip against the metal and listened to the hollow ring.

It would do, I told myself. It would do just fine.

■ 13 ■

The metal door could just be squeezed into the space between the closet, the sink, and the end of Gerry's bed. When I made up my little nest at night, I had to lift it and lean it against the wall because it took up most of my sleeping area. Even though it was not wood, and the surface emitted a tinny sort of laughter each time I danced on it, the door was wide and hard and allowed me to rehearse Cookie's repertoire of steps.

On Monday nights, which we still took off, Gerry would get out his rubber pad and sit on the bed and rehearse exercises from his *Roy Burns Drum Technique* book. When I came home from my lesson I'd find him there. I'd jump straight onto the metal door. After that first class, the lessons grew no easier, and I'd practice for hours so that the intricate rhythms would not evade me.

During that time, I was trying to win Cookie's acceptance, the way Heather and her partner had. They had told me that Cookie was eager to transmit what he knew to a younger generation. If I rented the studio myself, they said, he'd give me extra lessons and wouldn't take any money for his trouble. What they were saying, of course, was that I had to become part of the inner circle; I had to win his admiration.

Looking back on it now, I suppose I was hungry for a role model, a mentor. The more he ignored me in class, the more I wanted to impress him. I always arrived early and stayed late. When he told me to get rid of my jingle taps and buy some Capezio's, I did it the next day. When he mentioned that real hoofers only wear flat-heeled shoes, I discarded the ones with the one-inch heel and bought two pairs of men's shoes and attached the Capezio teletone taps to the soles. If Cookie had told me that my mind and my feet would sharpen up if I jumped from the eleventh floor of the Empire State Building, I would have been climbing the stairs to the appointed level and convincing myself not to look down.

■   14   ■

Everything would have been fine had it not been for the stringent New York bank regulations. Gerry and I had the check from Japan Airlines and one thousand dollars cash to deposit, but no one would take our money.

Initially, I'd tried to deposit it in the Dry Dock Bank, the branch down on Grand Street, where we'd opened an account the year before. But when I caught the subway down there—my pockets lined with bills—I found the building had burned down. After that, I went to three different banks in midtown, closer to where we lived. My attempts at depositing money, however, inevitably drew the same responses. Whether it was Chemical, Chase Manhattan, or Citibank, no one would allow me to open an account without credit cards or a driver's license.

In the meantime, we hid the check and wads of cash under the carpet of our room, in a small seam between the floorboards. Still, it made me nervous to go out at night and leave it all there. Our window had no lock, and we weren't sure who in the hotel had access to the keys to our door.

"The only thing we can do," I said to Gerry, as we walked down to the subway with our gear, "is buy a thousand dollars' worth of traveler's checks. That way, if they get stolen, at least we'll be able to have them replaced."

"But that costs money!" he objected. "One cent for every dollar. It's a rip-off."

"Yeah," I said, shifting the cassette player from one hand to another. "But it only adds up to ten dollars."

"But what about the check?" Gerry shook his head. "Nah. I got a better idea."

I dreaded asking what that idea might be. We had not yet fully recovered from Gerry's last great plan. Since his interview with Immigration six months ago, he'd heard nothing about his application. Before we'd left New Orleans, he'd informed them that he'd moved, and had given them Leonard's address. In our absence, Leonard was instructed to open all our mail and, in the event of correspondence from the Immigration office, to ring us at the hotel immediately.

By early July, the phone call still hadn't come. Ever since the blackmail affair had been resolved, Gerry was out of contact with Marilyn. Even if he'd needed to get hold of his wife in order to expedite some minor glitch in the processing of his application, it would have been impossible. The entire melodrama was now out of his hands and in the crowded lap of Fate.

I fished around in my pocket for the correct change for the subway tokens and, not looking at my father, asked him about his plan.

Gerry tried to sound all soothing and confident. "Well, I was talking to Earl last night and—"

"And what?"

"Well," continued Gerry, as we paused outside the token booth, "he was saying the easiest thing to do would be to open up a joint account with him."

I put down the equipment I was carrying, the cassette player and my wooden box. "With Earl?"

"Yeah. Don't forget, he's got a regular job and credit cards, social security number, driver's license, the lot!"

I looked at Gerry doubtfully and purchased the tokens.

"Come on," he said when I passed him one. "He'd be doing us a favor."

"Doing us a favor, or doing himself one?"

Gerry shook his head. "Earl's our friend! He wouldn't rip us off."

At that moment a downtown train roared into the station, making it impossible to talk. We picked up our gear and bungled through the turnstiles. Gerry always had trouble getting the drum stands through; inevitably one of the legs would get stuck, or the cowbell would get hooked around one of the metal arms.

Once we were safely settled at the edge of the platform, I said, "How long have we known him?"

Gerry pushed his glasses up a fraction. "Two months." He rubbed his chin for a moment and hooked his thumbs around the belt loops of his jeans. "But Earl isn't like that. I know he isn't. He's just like the guys—"

"—in Detroit," I said. "Look, don't you think the safest way to go is with traveler's checks?" I was starting to sound like an advertisement for American Express. Any moment I expected Karl Malden to jump out from behind a pylon with a microphone and camera crew.

"Nah," replied Gerry. "We need our money in the bank, where it's safe. 'Cause you gotta remember, you know, it's not just this money we've got to worry about, but all the dough we're gunna be making over the next few months."

I looked at him uneasily as our train thundered into the station. We picked up our gear, and as the carriage doors opened and the passengers flowed out onto the platform, I heard him say, "You're just like your mother. You worry too much."

▪ 15 ▪

The next afternoon, Earl met me during his lunch hour at his Citibank branch, on the corner of 34th and Seventh. During the day, he looked like a successful businessman: three-piece blue pinstripe suit, white shirt and tie; a panama hat covering his shaved head.

Opening a joint account is a bit like getting married, except that this union was really between my father and Earl, and the money was Gerry's and mine. Earl filled out all the forms, and within twenty minutes, the blue Citibank passbook was issued, with my full name and Earl's handwritten at the top, and two cash cards.

Now that our money was secure, I was free to concentrate on strengthening my weak foot, and on my aspiration to become a great dancer. It did not occur to me that these goals were in conflict with each other: The only way to become a great dancer is through diligence and practice; the only way for a bad injury to fully heal is to rest.

The metal door I'd found on the edge of Hell's Kitchen became my chamber, my studio, the one place where I could escape the city's noise, the parties that regularly erupted between Gerry and Earl, and my father's obsessive storytelling. But it wasn't all solitude. Occasionally, it would turn into a little musical soiree: Gerry would buy a few bottles of Colt 45, and the dealers and users in the carpark would crowd around our open window and watch. On these nights, Earl would often swagger in with a couple of joints and half a gram of coke, both of which invested in us a kind of euphoric desire to play, to dance, to articulate everything that lived within us.

These were the times when my father and I were closest, riding the same riffs, trapping the same accents. These were also the times when the three of us were in communion and not battling some barrier of elliptical tension. Earl would clap his hands or begin tapping rhythms of his own against the side table. I loved the way the chemicals wheeled through my sinuses, the way they drew me out of my melancholia, the way my dancing assumed a breathless precision. Perhaps we only formed a contented trio at those times because there were no stories and myths, because on coke I could transcend silence and contribute an equal share to the world's vociferous noise.

■   16   ■

I had always taken Romano at his word when he'd warned me never to attempt to work in the Village. I'd believed him when he said the cops were bad. But the residents on Columbus Avenue were still complaining, and Gerry was tired of playing on the rim of his snare. I, too, was eager for a change. So, one Sunday night, after we'd finished a long stint in Central Park and had gone home and showered and changed, Gerry and I took the subway down to Christopher Street.

It's easy to get lost in the Village, and we did that night, walking the humid, tree-lined streets, past majestic four-story houses with brass door knockers and window boxes brimming with geraniums and petunias. I found myself wanting to walk up the stairs of one of these grand residences and knock on the door. I wanted to be welcomed by a familiar face and ushered into a drawing room, or a table laid for tea.

I wanted to find a place for myself, but after tramping past the magnificent row of Greek revival homes, with their Ionic columns and peaked window lintels, past the steaming cafes, the neon lights of leather and bondage shops, the cozy bookstores, the tiny bars, the jazz joints, the only place at which we arrived was the corner of Sixth Avenue and 4th Street, where we'd first seen Romano himself making white doves appear in the doorway of a pawn shop.

We were surprised to see the crowds swarming up and down the street on a Sunday night. People were spilling out of the cinema, lingering in front of the improvised stalls that offered everything from silver puzzle rings to lacquered chopsticks to dog-eared Penguin paperbacks. Across the street, coat hangers were hooked through the wire fence of a basketball court, displaying what looked like an entire wardrobe of secondhand clothes. A guy was playing an accordion outside one of the bars, and from the plaza farther south came the strains of a string quartet.

Not two minutes had passed before we decided to overlook Romano's advice and give the Village a shot. After two years on the streets in Sydney, and almost a year on the American corners, we could almost taste the potential of a given pitch. There was money to be made here, we decided, and it was worth a calculated risk.

Unlike the marriage scam and the joint account with Earl, working Sixth Avenue was a plan that we both made quickly, without bickering or hesitation. And, like many of our experiences on the street, performing down there was fortuitous and dangerous. It was where someone tried to rob us again. It was where we were first busted. It was also the place where we were filmed for a New York television show, where we enjoyed our first break.

I don't remember much about Geoff Strate, except for his amusing name and spry amicability. A man in his mid-thirties with short, sandy-colored hair, he was a reporter on the local current affairs program, "PM Magazine." One night in July, as we were packing up near the Waverly cinema, he approached us about the possibility of doing a story on us. After so many months of virtual destitution, the offer was a bit of a thrill, and that night we caught a taxi back to the Penn View with a bottle of cheap champagne and prattled on endlessly about the heights to which our imminent television exposure would lead.

Two nights later we were approached by a woman who was interested in booking us for a surprise birthday party. Her name was Bonnie Kogan, and she had a nice camel-colored business card that I slipped into my waistcoat pocket and treasured all evening.

We were excited about the possibility of performing at a birthday in New York City. When I finally extracted Bonnie's business card from my waistcoat and summoned the courage to call her, I didn't know what to say when she inquired about our fee.

I told her we usually made a hundred dollars a night on the street. As she agreed on the price, I ran my finger across the raised lettering of her card and noticed she worked as an independent theatrical consultant. I asked her what that entailed, and she laughed and told me she gave wise counsel to various professionals in the industry. She'd barely uttered the words before I asked her if she'd be willing to barter: our performance for one consultation. Of course, I added, I'd have to ask my father first.

Bonnie was amenable to the idea and, when I got back to the Penn View, so was Gerry. He moved between the bed and the chair, the chair and the bed, in his quick, excited way.

"Maybe she can score us some more indoor gigs," he said. "That way, we won't have to go back to New Orleans for the winter."

Not returning to New Orleans had become a priority in our lives. Apart from wanting to avoid the poverty of another Southern winter, the thought of having to abort my lessons with Cookie filled me with disappointment. It would be like being a child again, having to move and start a new school and slowly make new friends, to become accustomed to an alien curriculum. I'd attended twelve public schools by the time I was fourteen: ten in Sydney, one in Adelaide, and one in Melbourne. I'd developed a certain amount of academic and social flexibility, yet my learning and friendships were always fractured and had always left me longing for something more.

We had our first and only consultation with Bonnie Kogan on a Thursday afternoon in July. She lived alone in a flashy, high-rise apartment in the West 50s. It was decorated in a contemporary fashion—parquet floors, African-print upholstery, and the odd Tibetan mask and bonsai tree.

After our stint behind the witchcraft shop, and our residency in the Penn View, her flat appeared sumptuous and spacious. I sat in one of her cane chairs, balancing a porcelain coffee cup and saucer on my knees, feeling like an imposter.

It wasn't until after Bonnie had booked us that we had realized our half-hour show would be her gift to her boyfriend. We had to arrive early at the Chinatown loft—at about seven o'clock—while he was at dinner with a couple of friends. The loft was the size of a tennis court. I remember the subtle, indirect lighting and oriental flower arrangements in tall vases, the polished hardwood floor, the long-stemmed crystal glasses brimming with a bubbly, pink elixir. Gerry and I looked like a couple of itinerant troubadours in our frayed tailcoats and scuffed shoes as we set up our equipment in the center of the room. I remember wondering why Bonnie had chosen us as her gift. As she was a theatrical consultant, she had all kinds of contacts and could have booked virtually any act in the city. It wasn't until hours later that I realized the very modesty I was ashamed of that night was what appealed to her the most. Our vaudevillian poverty was a novelty to these twenty- and thirtysomething high-flyers in their crushed velvet dresses and leather pants.

The lamps were turned off and we stood in the darkness, awaiting the sound of a key in the lock. It was hard to stop the trembling in my knees. After a few minutes, the front door swung open, the lights flashed on, and we all shouted *"Surprise!"* as arranged. Then Gerry and I plunged into our show with all the gusto we could muster. I spun and riffed my way across the yards and yards of floor space, as much as my aching foot would allow, soft-shoeing before the long windows that overlooked Wall Street's winking lights. By the second number, I was becoming aware of how much easier this was than working the streets: the audience was captive; our fee was pre-arranged; and the length of our performance was a fixed half-hour. After years of dancing on concrete and bricks, the polished wood felt smooth and generous beneath my feet, and I didn't have to fight so hard to make the sounds.

It was a pretty leisurely gig, and afterward, as we stood about helping them drink up their excess Dom Perignon, the possibility of doing other indoor work became more appealing.

Gerry and I left the luxurious loft around midnight, half-drunk on the champagne and the assurance of our big, bright future, which is why I was sitting in Bonnie's cane chair two days later, balancing a cup and saucer on my knees and trying to look relaxed.

Bonnie told us we should always have an up-to-date résumé on hand. She also made a number of other suggestions that day, such as renting a twenty-four-hour answering service instead of relying on Fred to pass on our messages; having business cards printed to hand out on the street; and making a sign to exhibit the date and time of our forthcoming television appearance. She also mentioned it would be good to wear black sweatshirts when we performed, too, with "The Thunder from Down Under" printed in white across the chest.

"That way," she said, "the crowds will know you're Australian, and that'll increase your popularity."

Her last piece of advice was to take 7 percent of our earnings each week and deposit it into a separate business account. It would cover ongoing professional expenses and fund future projects. Since she herself was self-employed, Bonnie religiously followed the 7 percent regime.

"Even if I only receive a check for a dollar and forty-eight cents," she said, "I still put seven percent into my business account."

This counsel was merely straightforward common sense, yet I'd had little experience in the professional world. My father, who'd had plenty of experience, was still lodged back somewhere in the Australian 1950s, when everyone knew his name and he secured gigs easily, through the strength of his reputation.

■   17   ■

For twelve dollars a month, we rented our own telephone service, which meant that when somebody called, an out-of-work actor answered the phone, took a message, and left it in a pigeonhole marked with our name. Twice a day I would call the service, identify my coded number, and collect the messages. Over the course of a month, we usually accumulated about fifteen dollars in pennies, and it was with these rolled-up coins that I paid our bill.

In the interests of our budget, we decided to go with simple black lettering on a white business card. "The Thunder from Down Under" was printed across the top. I'd drawn the logo with my own hand: a map of Australia with a lightning bolt piercing the center. When I gaze at it now, it looks like an amateurish rendering, something a child or a bored teenager might doodle in the margin of her history book. Nevertheless, we printed it on five hundred cards along with the number of the answering service.

Just as Bonnie had suggested, I bought black sweatshirts and had our title printed across the front in white lettering. They made us look less anachronistic, more like a couple of pale breakdancers than a vaudeville duo.

The crew of "PM Magazine" arranged to film us in the Village one Friday evening in early August. By that time, in order to diversify our audience, we worked Columbus Avenue during the week, and the Village on Friday and Saturday nights. On the weekends, we enjoyed great popularity down on Sixth Avenue, with huge, excited crowds and one-hundred-and-fifty-dollar nights.

For the filming, we were decked out in our new sweatshirts. Gerry wore a pair of jeans and I had on my black skirt with the embroidered musical notes. The crowds were enthused by the sight of cameras, and everyone, it seemed, wanted to be recorded in the act of dropping money into our hat.

We knocked off at around eleven, then Geoff interviewed us in the bagel shop around the corner. It was then, too, that my father pressed his scrapbook with the yellowing newspaper clippings from the late forties into Geoff's hands.

"Take a look at this," he said, between bites of his poppy-seed bagel. He pointed to the fading images of a smooth-faced man with a garland of golden hair, enthroned behind a kit of Premier drums. Some of the headlines read GERRY BEAT-OF-THE-DRUM SAYER and SOME LIKE IT HOT!

"That was me," he added, licking lox from his fingers. "That was me, all right."

■ 18 ■

The following Monday, Geoff Strate left a message with our service, informing us that our segment would be aired in two weeks' time. So, that day I followed Bonnie's instructions and painted a sign to hang from Gerry's woodblock stand, advertising our upcoming appearance.

If I was smiling in August, it was not because I was in love, not because I had met my magician. Yes, I was still waiting for him to appear in my path like a sudden apparition, to wrap his arms around me, to hear his breath thrum in my ear. But I was smiling in August because of the story of my father and me, which was about to be broadcast to five million viewers throughout the state of New York.

That month a few more opportunities came our way: a middle-aged woman named Silver Friedman (her real name, she assured us) approached us on Columbus Avenue. She explained that she owned the famous comedy club, Improvisation, and invited us down to do a ten-minute spot. She was not inflating the reputation of the club when she mentioned that people like Robin Williams and Richard Pryor had had their start on her stage. We arrived the following Monday, all nervous and excited. On the walls we saw a gallery of portraits—successful actors and comedians—and their affectionate inscriptions to Silver and the club itself.

When our call came, we sprung onto the small stage and performed three numbers. During the last tune, "My Feet Can't Fail Me Now," Gerry and I enacted a planned moment of madness: We lost control and allowed the rhythms to possess us like boisterous ghosts. Suddenly, we both leapt off the wooden platform. Gerry's kit was now the dinner setting of one young and startled woman. The accents stuttered out of her empty plate and sounded like the hooves of a horse galloping across a field of smooth marble. He hit the side of a wine bottle, a saucer, and managed a slight, delicate roll on the rim of a champagne glass, while I shuffled and riffed my way down the aisles in a conjured, insatiable frenzy.

Sober men in tweed jackets were soon throwing their heads back and howling at the ceiling. A party in the corner began keeping time with their knives and forks. Others clapped their hands, stamped their feet. Gerry darted from table to table like a demented waiter, hitting anything that caught his eye, coaxing rhythms from the most unlikely objects: candleholders, dessert bowls, chair legs, soup tureens, ashtrays, coffeepots, the steaming breast of an entire roasted chicken. As I spun and strutted ahead of him, the cries of the audience prompted me to leap onto the occasional empty wooden chair and kick out a few flashy and complementary riffs. My father got a big laugh when he threw down his sticks and, with his bare hands, patted out a soft rhythm against a man's bald head.

We'd tried a similar routine before, on the street, but inside a nightclub it was definitely more subversive and exciting. Gerry played the table, the walls, the doors. At one point, he dropped to his knees and played the floor while I was embroiled in an improvised routine on the steps leading back to the stage.

Occasionally, my father became overwrought—held his sticks too tight or misjudged an angle—and a glass of champagne or tumbler of wine would suddenly shatter onto the white cotton of a tablecloth. One would think the patrons or even Silver herself might raise an objection—every time I heard another breakage I inwardly winced—but the crowd just whistled and hollered for more. By the end of the night Silver appeared in the front bar of the club and extended an open invitation to us to return.

■ 19 ■

By late August, the professional advice Bonnie had given us was beginning to pay off. The business cards, the sweatshirts, the vamped-up résumés, the answering service, all these accessories were gradually uniting to open small doors into our future.

Gerry and I were developing a lucrative sideline in the surprise party business. One of the extra services we began to offer was a song composed especially for the birthday boy or girl, sung by me at the end of the show. Usually, the relative who was hiring us gave me details about the person—occupation, hobbies, idiosyncrasies—and in half an hour I'd write a chorus and several rhyming stanzas to break into after our final number. At first, the thought of having to sing filled me with trepidation. I practiced in front of Gerry, just as I had the previous year, before I'd backed out of my audition for *42nd Street*. He coached me in my phrasing and breath control, told me when I was flat, suggested that I try a different key. By the time I made my vocal debut in the apartment of an Australian couple on Riverside Drive, I was virtually belting it out.

That was the party where we had the most fun. The birthday boy's wife had booked us. Like most Australian ex-pats, she enjoyed a bit of mischief, so when I suggested that we make a surprise entrance to the party, she chuckled and said, "OK."

We arrived at about ten to eight outside their ground-floor apartment on Riverside Drive. We cased the joint, then stood around, waiting for our cue. At about five past eight, the living room window was opened, and a few minutes later, I suddenly hoisted Gerry up, and he went through headfirst like a burglar. Next, the cassette player and side drum went up, into the room, and I crawled in last, dressed in my pantomime mask and tails.

Under the circumstances, we were lucky the birthday boy didn't grab a gun and start shooting. Certainly, in America at that time, sudden trespassers were being killed for accidentally walking through the wrong door at the right time. But the chorus of laughs we got as we made our entrance signaled to the guest of honor that we were relatively benign, and by the end of the show, after he'd listened to his song and was bequeathed an empty jar of Vegemite ("We got a bit hungry on the way over"), he was beaming.

Soon we discovered a new spot on the street. It was downtown, on Broadway, right outside City Hall. The workers there were of a different caliber than the midtown crowd, executive types in tailored suits who spilled out of tall buildings and government offices in search of their tabouleh salads and canteloupe smoothies. We enjoyed setting up in front of the manicured park each morning, a backdrop of wide elms dappling the sunlight, and having the entire block and all the lunchtime crowds to ourselves.

A few opportunities caught up with us as we worked that particular spot. While we were performing one day, we were approached by a guy who offered to pay us to pack up, to move down three blocks and perform outside his restaurant. The restaurant was celebrating its gala opening, and he figured our clowning about would attract customers and create a festive ambience.

It wasn't until we'd packed up and had arrived at the restaurant that

I realized why he'd insisted on our show. The restaurant was called Ham Heaven, and we, of course, were the hams.

It was during these times, I think, that Gerry and I were at our best, when the money was guaranteed and we didn't have to hustle. Our gigs at the Improvisation club, the birthday parties, the business openings, our spot on "PM Magazine," they all bristled with energy and humor because the audience was captive. By the end of our engagement, we knew our bellies would be full for a few more days. Yet it was because we'd worked so long and hard on the street that we were able to stroll into a club or a party and completely take it over. I guess there's some truth to the cliché about hitting yourself over the head with a hammer because it feels good when you stop. When I was eleven, I was placed in an advanced reading class at school. The teacher made us turn our books upside-down and read for twenty minutes; when we were finally told to turn them back the right way, I was amazed by how quickly I could devour each page.

20

We still had a few problems, of course. I was having tiffs with Gerry about his drinking. Apart from the considerable amount of money he was spending every night, I was concerned about his health, and about his presentation during our performances on the street. We'd argued a little about it in New Orleans: My theory was that his guzzling from a large bottle of beer between numbers discouraged the crowd from throwing money. His theory was that it was bloody hot outside and no one gave a shit about what he was drinking.

To some extent, in New Orleans, this was true. But down in the Village, I'd noticed people scrutinizing Gerry's beer-swilling at the end of each show. They'd always walk off before I could pass the hat their way. Maybe it was just a coincidence, but I was sure there was a positive correlation between Gerry's drinking and our less lucrative nights.

I also suspected that the slower nights were partly my fault. I still couldn't rely on my foot to carry me through some of the flashier and faster steps. I'd have to take frequent breaks. Even though we were getting more indoor work, most of our living was still made on the street.

Perhaps, too, some of my vibrancy had been dulled after eighteen months on the corners of New York and New Orleans. Or maybe the tension between my father and me leaked out and seeped into the thinning crowds.

Also, there was no doubt about it: I was getting fat. Gerry, on the other hand, was losing weight at an alarming rate. This, coupled with his nightly boozing on the street, rendered him almost as desperate-looking as a Bowery derelict. Even stranger, we consumed exactly the same amount of food each day: one serving of boneless chicken and steamed rice from the Chinese takeout on Ninth Avenue. We used to eat half our respective servings before we went to work, and the rest when we came home. Apart from Gerry's beer, and the pints of water I had to drink each evening, we only drank coffee. Even then, Gerry took three spoonfuls of sugar in his cup while I had cut down to one.

Something else had to be done. I stopped eating boneless chicken and switched to vegetable chow mein. I began using Sweet and Low instead of sugar. On our days off, I made myself run through the humidity down to 14th Street and back to 34th. I spiced up the act with some new material, a little boogie-woogie. I attached a plastic whistle to a Mardi Gras necklace and ran up and down our block in the Village, blowing it madly, in order to rustle up a crowd without exerting myself too much.

But Gerry could never restrain himself for very long. We'd have one of our little discussions and he'd reluctantly agree not to drink while we were working, then no more than two or three nights would pass before he'd disappear during a break and quietly return with a bagged bottle in his hands. "I'll hide it behind the cassette player," he'd say. "No one'll see."

That was when the silence grew thick between us, when he played on his own and I danced on my own even though we were only a few feet apart, when I wouldn't look at him and he wouldn't look at me, when we'd return to the Penn View and he'd go straight upstairs to see Earl while I stayed down in our room and wrote a letter or read a book, or practiced some difficult steps.

Maybe I was just jealous: all of Gerry's extra beer flab seemed to be going onto my hips instead of his gut. I imagined some kind of fat-fairy flying in through our window at night while we slept and magically transporting the calories from Gerry's liver to my own. I didn't quite know what was happening to my body, or my mind, or the tenderness that had always graced the relationship between my father and me.

■   21   ■

The night that "PM Magazine" was being aired, Fred propped the portable black-and-white television up on a couple of stacked milk crates in the foyer. Earl and all the other guys—Ricky, Willis, Pop—crowded around it, sitting on stools and upturned bins. Gerry and I each had a milk crate to ourselves. Fred watched from behind the cage, leaning on the counter. Earl poured everyone Bacardi and Cokes in little plastic cups. I couldn't help thinking how much this scene was like the night we first moved in, except that now I wasn't lingering on the periphery while they waxed eloquent about war and women; I was standing in the center of a dialogue about dance and drums. And it felt good to be a part of something, even if it was only idle chatter.

The story, when it was aired, lasted exactly two minutes. It was between a segment on a Beatles convention and another on the production of the nude musical *Oh, Calcutta*. In our story, Geoff Strate plays the role of a phantom agent, a kind of television talent scout with the voice and diction of a private eye. Our piece opened with us performing down on Sixth Avenue, a throng of clapping people crowded around us, and Geoff's deep American detective voice explaining our relationship, our itinerate lives since we left Sydney a year ago. "You know what I like about the business?" he says. "Magic time. Yeah, magic time. When the low-budget acts say, 'You ain't seen nothing yet,' and then deliver the goods." The camera focuses on my father's drumming; I'm dancing in the background, and I'm beaming so brightly it almost seems fake. The Phantom Agent tells us that Gerry and I deliver the magic, that we followed the yellow brick road from Sydney to New Orleans to New York. I'm spinning around on my wooden tap board, against my father's backbeats. Geoff goes into my father's past, how he was a top jazz and big band drummer back in Australia. Pictures from the forties flash up on the screen, twenty-five-year-old Gerry behind his kit of Ludwigs at the Trocadero. Another shows him playing congas with his friend and mentor Gene Krupa in the fifties. The Phantom Agent tells us how Gerry sneered at retirement at sixty-one and joined me on the streets of Sydney. Photos of my seventeen-year-old pantomime face flash upon the screen, taken in Chinatown, where our journey first began.

Now, as I view the videotape of the show for the first time in twelve years, I notice things I wasn't aware of before. My head is often bowed as I dance, strained forward, some heavy, invisible weight on my shoulders. My father does most of the talking during the interview in the bagel shop. I stand beside him, looking a bit simple, a little dumb, actually. Grinning and nodding at my father's remarks, chewing on my bagel. I only make two statements during the segment. Referring to the "magic" we make when we perform together: "When it happens it's really beautiful." And then, at the end, I say, "There's an old saying, 'You can pick your friends, but you can't pick your relatives.' Well, he's not my father. He's my friend. Well, he *is* my father but—" And I pull a face, lost for words, and in that momentary silence, when I watch it on the television now, I see that longing for a father, a protector.

When the segment finished, the foyer exploded with Bacardi and Coke, with toasts to our imminent success. But even as I laughed and joked and allowed everyone to slap me on the back, I gulped down my drink and couldn't help glancing through the glass doors of the Penn View. Alma was still standing on the steps with her stockings rolled down to her knees, and what scared me was the fact that if we did not have some sort of professional breakthrough soon, I might end up like her.

◼ 22 ◼

The following morning I rushed out of the hotel and around the corner to the post office telephones. I called our answering service, expecting at least two or three responses to our segment. Perhaps a booking agent or a nightclub owner had rung the television station for our phone number. Perhaps a director wanted to see our CVs. Perhaps an Australian company such as Foster's Lager wanted to use us in their American advertising campaign. But the only message I received was a reminder that our monthly service fee was due.

Maybe it was too soon, I told myself. Maybe all those important people didn't awaken until midday. Maybe they were finding it hard to contact Geoff Strate. Gerry said virtually the same thing when I returned to our room and told him the news, which was no news.

We waited another day, and another. Still, there was no response. I paid our service fee and kept ringing, but in spite of the fact that the show had been broadcast to six million people, it seemed as if no one had really noticed us.

The only three things I looked forward to at that time were going to class, practicing, and doing coke. Perhaps the triple experiences had become conjoined in my psyche, since they all propelled me into some dervish of unbridled joy. Oh, I still looked forward to our great breakthrough, but it always seemed so far away.

The quality of the cocaine was like the strength of a love affair—it varied according to how much shit was mixed up with it. Some nights my blood would be crashing through my veins and I'd be dancing a blue streak across the industrial door; other nights I hardly felt anything at all.

Late one night Earl swept into our room, gushing about some uncut Colombian gear that was going in the carpark. He wanted to go halves in a deal, but Gerry and I didn't have the cash on us, and I didn't feel like walking down to the ATM on the corner of Seventh Avenue. It was then that Earl offered to go down himself and withdraw our portion from our joint account. He had his own cash card, so it was no problem.

I looked at Gerry and shrugged. I didn't want to be a nervous worrier. I didn't want to be like my mother. I didn't say anything when Gerry nodded to Earl.

The next day, I went down to the bank and checked the balance myself. When the thousand and three dollars beamed up on the screen, I felt ashamed of myself for not trusting Earl, for being so wary of him. My father was right: I worried too much; I had to learn how to go with the flow.

I was flowing pretty well on that tiny mountain of uncut coke that week. We did, however, have some professional ethics, and didn't begin snorting the stuff until after we'd arrived home from work. Then Earl would appear and Coltrane would blare and the window would be flung open, and that intoxicating white light began oscillating through my veins. It was a convenient distraction from all the waiting I was doing at that time: waiting for our breakthrough, for my magician, for a change in my relationship with my father.

It was during that week that someone crawled through the open window of our room while we slept and stole our cassette player. It was also the week in which I finally succumbed to Earl.

By Friday, however, I regretted the latter event as much as the former. If only the platonic relationship Earl and I had once shared could be restored as easily as our missing music box—all that took was an afternoon subway ride downtown and a little haggling over the price of a new Samsung.

Pleasure, I was still learning, is a painful business.

▩ 23 ▩

Alice had been abstaining from sex for a good five months before she finally gave in to Earl. She did not know why; her skin did not ache for him the way it had for Bruno, for Grimaldi, for Romano. It was a common experience that linked her, in some kind of ontological way, to so many other human beings on earth, this kind of arbitrary coupling that arises out of loneliness.

It happened during one of their coke-induced evenings. Earl kept taking her hand and pressuring her to come up to his room. Alice finally stood up, straightened her skirt, and followed him out the door. She knew he was not the magician, but she was tired of waiting for him. She gave a short wave to her father before she disappeared. She wanted him to say, Wait a minute, or Don't go, or What do you think you're doing? But he did not look up from his music.

She followed Earl up the back stairs, down the hall, and into his room, which smelled of Cocoa Butter and shaving cream. She was wordless as he guided her toward the bed and removed her clothes. There was something about his fast, urgent hands, the anonymity of the room, the strange tongue in her mouth, the sudden weight crushing down on her that made her unable to suppress the choking in her throat, the sob that began in her belly and made her tremble. It reminded her of the first time she'd had sex, only a few years before, on the floor of her father's room. Perhaps Earl thought it was pleasure that made her squeeze her eyes shut, for he pushed himself into her without hesitation and did not stop thrusting and saying her name. The deeper he went, the more it hurt. A sharp pain began gnawing away inside her, like salt in an old wound. She wanted to tell him to stop, to slow down, to pull out, but when she opened her mouth, he kissed away the cry in her throat until his back arched back and he had his spasm.

It was only when he collapsed breathless beside her, when she turned away and buried her face in the pillow, that she allowed herself to gasp.

■   24   ■

Two days later I knew there was something wrong, not only between Earl and me, but also within my body.

I suspected it was just a urinary tract infection. I'd had one once before, years ago, after the second time I'd had sex. Sometimes it's called the Honeymoon Complaint, since it often occurs after the first time a woman has sex, or after a period of abstinence.

When I walked into our room and told Earl and Gerry I couldn't piss without feeling as if my labia were on fire, Earl suggested I take some Tylenol and Gerry asked me what a labia was. I thought if I drank lots of water and waited long enough, maybe I could piss all of Earl's semen away and not have to fork out seventy bucks to see a doctor.

Drinking lots of water, however, was not a good idea. It just made me go to the toilet even more often than usual. Instead, I attempted the reverse, reducing my liquid intake to a bare minimum. I cut out beer and tea, which I knew were diuretics. I stopped smoking grass, which made me thirsty. I restrained myself when I went to slug on my bottle between shows—still hot and sweaty—telling myself to sip on the water as if it were a rare wine.

Not drinking liquids, however, was also the wrong thing to do. The flesh between my legs still burned, and soon I was suffering from dehydration: at the end of one show in Central Park during a sweltering Sunday afternoon, I turned on my heel with my upturned hat and fainted onto the pavement.

While this was unfolding over the course of a few days, my father maintained his supreme nonchalance to the fact that I had slept with his best friend and had obviously contracted some sort of sexually transmitted illness. Gerry still slapped Earl's back in exactly the same way, passed his bottle of Colt 45 with even more amicability, shared his take-out chicken. He pretended that nothing at all had transpired between us; in fact, he almost seemed to be making an effort to be overly courteous to Earl.

The only good thing about the whole affair was that it dampened, temporarily at least, Earl's more amorous moments. Whenever he lifted his arm or sent his breath toward my closed eyelids, all I had to do was reproduce the groan I let out whenever I began to urinate, and he would suddenly pull away.

◼ 25 ◼

Earl grew so frantic with my condition that he insisted on taking me over to Bellevue Hospital one morning before he went to work. I'd had only a few hours' sleep, but he bundled me into a cab on Eighth Avenue at seven-thirty in the morning.

Unsurprisingly, the diagnosis was urinary tract infection. The cure was about fourteen packets of powder, which produced a fizzy lime drink when added to water. I was instructed to take one every morning until I'd finished the prescription. After a few days, the burning in my groin diminished, and it eventually disappeared. Like most patients, I was tempted to discontinue my treatment once the symptoms had gone away, but Earl had read the instructions on the box and convinced me to use every packet it contained, which took about two weeks.

My father didn't seem very worried. Sometimes I think he disliked women's bodies and the interminable fluids they produced, all the pregnancies and periods, the lavas of lactation, ovulation's slow white leaks.

During my convalescence, we continued performing on Columbus Avenue, to do coke when we came home, to eat our one meal of Chinese food. I never missed a lesson with Cookie. I persisted with my practice on the metal door. I still waited for my magician. I wrote letters to my mother, detailing the wonderful time I was having, embroidering the hours of toil with amusing anecdotes and exaggerated possibilities.

◼ 26 ◼

One morning, a few days after I'd completed the treatment for the infection, I awoke to find myself covered in a rash. I lay on the floor of our room, looking at the pale red welts patterning my arms. I pushed back the sheet, lifted my shirt, and followed the rash's journey over my breasts, my rib cage and stomach and, almost fascinated with the way in which it virtually left no part of me untouched, how it brooded over my hipbones and left track marks along the insides of my thighs.

Suddenly I was hot and thirsty. I stood up and drank a glass of water, then another. My father was still asleep on the bed, flat on his back and snoring. It occurred to me to consult Earl. But it was eleven o'clock and Earl would now be at work, busy selling car radios or whatever it was that had enabled him to hang five *Salesman of the Month* plaques on the wall above his bed.

I figured that the probable cause was simply too many drugs. That day, I decided I would stop doing coke and drinking beer, and buy a bottle of multivitamins. I waited for Gerry to wake up, then filled one of the empty Colt 45 bottles with water and bundled myself into the bed. My skin was hot and perspiration bled out of me, as if a wound had suddenly broken, dampening the sheets and pillowcases so that by twilight Gerry had to beg another set from Fred.

Earl arrived later, all giddy and excited about a recent sale. But when he examined my limbs, he sighed heavily, refilled my water bottle, and went out and bought a packet of Tylenol. He rested his cool hand on my forehead and made me take two tablets. He disappeared upstairs to change, and when he returned he brought with him a jar of cocoa butter, which he smoothed into my skin while my father quietly sat in his chair and cracked his first bottle of beer for the night.

Nausea moved in by mid-evening, and by the time Earl and Gerry had done their first line I had vomited all over his rubber practice pad and wooden drumsticks. Earl cleaned it up and brought me a bucket. He felt my forehead again. He made me take three more Tylenol for the fever burning deep red half-moons across my brow. He squeezed out a cold washcloth in the sink and rested it against my forehead.

Around midnight, he went to change the pillowcase and sheets again. He helped me out of bed slowly, like a son guiding an infirm mother. It was at moments like these that I felt myself warming toward him. It wasn't a side effect of the fever—the tenderness I sensed within him, the grace that had been absent the night we had gone upstairs to his room, surfaced in his caretaking and eroded my defenses.

All the while, my father was stripped down to his underpants, sitting on the chair at the end of the bed, downing his Colt 45 and brushing his hair. Sometimes he patted rhythms against his knees along with the radio, for his practice pad was wet and he thought he could still smell my bile in the hard black rubber.

The next day was worse. My limbs began to ache and the rash rose up into boil-like wales. By mid-afternoon, it had erupted onto the palms of my hands and the soles of my feet. When Earl came home from work, he wanted to bundle me into a cab and take me back to Bellevue. But I cowered between my damp pillows and told him we should wait until the following day.

It was so hot that night I wore only a T-shirt and cotton undies, but modesty made me pull the sheet up over my ravaged form. Every now and then, I'd lift the sheet and look down, checking the rash's progression around my rib cage and shoulders, noticing the way it bound my feet in scarlet ridges.

Earl kept telling me to drink water, and kept refilling the bottle beside my bed. He managed to wrestle an old fan off Fred in return for a flask of brandy. He removed my top sheet and soaked it in cold water. After wringing it out, he smoothed it over me. Then he set the fan on the side table, plugged it in, and pointed the whirring blades in my direction.

It provided some relief for a couple of hours, and I half-dozed into the melancholy music that was the city's inexorable noise. But when I awoke at around ten o'clock, the sheet was stiff with dried sweat and I noticed the rash had worked its way up around my neck. That was when Earl put down his bottle of beer, dragged me out of bed, and ordered me to get dressed.

■ 27 ■

When the taxi dropped us off at Bellevue, Earl wrapped his arms around my waist and half-carried me into Emergency. Up at the main counter stood two women in white—one young, one middle-aged.

We waited for about five minutes while the nurses examined charts and talked on the phones. My bandaged foot began to throb. Earl finally slammed his fist on the counter and demanded some attention.

The older nurse leaned over the counter and examined my arms. "Looks like hives," she remarked. "Does it itch?"

"No," I replied.

"It doesn't itch?"

"No."

The nurse turned and called out to her partner. "Hey, Rita, come and have a look at this!"

"What?" the other nurse asked, sidling over. Rita was younger, with a little curl at the bottom of her shoulder-length blond hair. She glanced at my arms and then walked around the counter and examined my legs. I slipped off my shoe and showed her the deep red corrugations on the sole of my left foot.

"Hives," the nurse declared, flipping her hair over her shoulder.

"Yes," I said. "But it doesn't itch."

"Hmmm," said Rita. "Take a seat and we'll be right with you. And in the meantime," she added, passing over a handful of forms, "fill these out."

I was aching so much I could hardly sit up in my chair, let alone complete the forms. I rested my head on Earl's shoulder and held my stomach. Earl borrowed a pen and quietly read the questions to me and filled in my responses. He had to leave quite a few questions blank, however, like my U.S. visa number and my passport number and if anyone in my family has had foot and mouth disease.

When he lodged the forms with the head nurse, she glanced through them with her brisk, professional air. Not half a minute had passed before they began arguing about numbers and identification. Earl was prodding the air with his index finger and she was pursing her lips and shaking her head. I could have made an effort to listen, but by that time the walls of the cavernous Emergency Room had begun to waver, and I was sure I could see small insects crawling through the pattern of the linoleum floor tiles.

When Earl returned, I rested my head in his lap, watching the ceiling and the way in which it fluttered like a white sheet in a breeze. Sometimes he wiped my face with a handkerchief. When the ceiling stopped trembling, I turned onto my side and watched the stretchers come barreling through the Emergency Room doors. Many of the people were probably unconscious, but when I glimpsed the pallid flesh of their hollow faces, the bleeding veins, the teeth marks along their limp arms, they looked as if they were already dead.

When Earl complained to Rita about how long we'd been waiting, she just shrugged and said, "Well, you picked a bad time, honey. This is the Suicide Happy Hour. From midnight until two, anyone who's gonna do it does it now."

Earl returned and made me drink some water. Then Rita came over and let me lie down on one of the spare stretchers near the doors. This gave me a better view of the cases as they arrived. She gave me a pillow and told me she was sorry, but suicide victims take priority over others. I nodded. I was relieved to lie down and also to have something to look at, to see things I'd never seen before.

A woman, bound in a straitjacket, was thrashing around on a stretcher as they wheeled her in. She was screaming, "You cocksucking motherfuckers!" at the attendants. She managed to kick Nurse Rita's arm and tried to bite one of the doctors at her side.

After they rolled the woman off through some double doors, I drifted into a humid purgatory, watching the colors dance behind my eyelids. If I felt content dozing by the entrance of Bellevue Hospital's Emergency Room, it was only because, for a little while at least, I sensed that someone was taking care of me.

At last they put me in a room on my own. Doctors appeared and stood gazing at my rash. They were in awe of the way it patterned even my palms and the soles of my feet. They told me it looked like hives and when they asked if it itched I shook my head. One of them stuck a thermometer in my mouth and gave me a hospital gown. The other gave me a plastic cup to piss in and they both left the room.

I did what they told me to do. They knocked on the door. The thermometer was still in my mouth, but I managed to make a sound to let them know they could enter. One of them whisked away the plastic cup and vanished. I lay back down and looked at the ceiling. The overhead fluorescent light burned my skin. When I inhaled, it began to enter me. I closed my eyes and felt it filling me up. I was a balloon. I liked how soft the light made me feel.

When the doctor pulled the thermometer from my mouth, I opened my eyes, and he said that my temperature was one hundred and five. I asked him if that was bad, and he nodded and said it was.

He pushed me out into a corridor and said he'd be back soon. Someone came along and draped a sheet over me. Even though I felt as if I were badly sunburned, I was shivering. I was glad to have the sheet, but there was nothing to look at in the corridor except passing nurses.

I heard a few things, though. I was parked outside the closed door of a room. Inside the room a woman was yelling. Lots of swear words. Words like "motherfucker" and "prick" and "cocksucker." Words I sometimes thought of but never said. Words I might have yelled at Earl, at Grimaldi, at my father. Words I'd always wanted to yell at the man who'd beaten me as a child, the man who'd beaten my mother.

Suddenly, I heard glass shatter and a nurse talking about giving the woman a stronger sedative.

The woman kept saying the words over and over again—asshole, shit-face, pissbucket—and she was still saying them when a nurse finally came along and wheeled me away.

When I awoke, I found myself lying alone in the Observation Ward. My fever felt as if it had subsided a little. The walls no longer wavered, and the insects that had woven their way through the pattern in the tiles only a few hours earlier must have sprouted wings and flown away.

Meanwhile, the news of my mysterious illness was circulating throughout the hospital, and every few minutes some new intern or other would appear at the bottom of my bed, sheepishly asking if he could look at the rash. Sometimes they arrived in twos and threes. When they pulled back the sheet they'd stand almost reverentially beside the bed, gazing at the scaly texture of the great raised red welts and hazarding guesses at its cause. This made me feel kind of special, like a large jar of jelly beans, the exact number of which no one could be sure of naming.

Every half hour a nurse would take my temperature, which kept wavering between one hundred and three and four. Sometimes they made me swallow more Tylenol. I asked to see Earl, but no one seemed to know who he was. By now it was around four in the morning. I asked if I could go home soon, but was told that I couldn't. One nurse came by and took my blood pressure. He told me that phone calls were being made, that a large meeting was being arranged.

"A meeting?" I asked. "Why?"

He tapped my arm and smiled before ripping back the Velcro of the tourniquet. "You're a mystery, my dear," he said, winding the cord around his hand. "But your blood pressure," he added, winking, "your pressure *es perfecto*."

I waited for what seemed like a long time. The hospital staff came and went. I wondered about what had happened to my clothes and if I'd ever see them again. I contemplated the possibility of an escape through the X-ray room down the hall. I anticipated the perils of limping from one side of Manhattan to the other at five in the morning wearing only a white hospital gown and an Ace bandage. Mostly I just lay there in the half-light and worried about how much money all this was costing. I was a little Australian nobody without health insurance, and this was a Big American Hospital.

When Earl finally found me, he held my hand for a while and told me I was going to be all right. I asked the nurse if I could go home now, and she said, "No." I told her I couldn't pay, that I didn't have any money. The nurse said I shouldn't worry. That I should try to get some rest.

"This is a charity hospital," she declared. "Only those who can afford it are charged."

And she smiled so pleasantly that I believed her. Until Earl told me he had to go to work, and to tell them nothing about where I lived in Australia, or how I earned my living.

After he left, I was alone again. All I wanted to do was find my clothes and go home. I listened to the whir of the fan for a while. I noticed they'd plugged a drip into my arm. The bag looked like a bulging breast implant. I watched the cool solution pulsing through the plastic tubing and into my arm, and the pattern of swelling veins in my wrist.

Suddenly, I heard a woman screaming, "Cocksucking motherfuckers! Lemme outta this thing!" Then they wheeled in the woman bound in the khaki straitjacket.

"I wanna go to the bathroom!" she screamed.

Two male nurses wrestled her writhing body from the stretcher and heaved her onto the bed opposite mine.

"Can't you pricks understand? I gotta pee! Piss! Wee-wee! Do a little number on your stinkin' fuck-faces!"

"You can use a bedpan," said one of the nurses, while the other tried to contain her flailing legs.

"I don't want no fuckin' bedpan!" She swung around and spat. The huge gob of phlegm arced through the air and, as the nurse proffered up the portable throne, landed on the lapel of his white jacket.

"Fine then," he said, drawing away. "You can do without."

The two nurses left her thrashing about on the bed, still bound in the jacket. As they were leaving, the one who'd been spat on walked over and felt my forehead. I couldn't stop staring at the gob of phlegm on his jacket until he took a tissue and brushed it off.

Before he turned away, he leaned closer to me and whispered confidentially, "She's in here every month. Her boyfriend brings her in."

"Really?" I breathed, trying not to look at her.

"Every month, like clockwork, she goes mad and tries to knife him."

I glanced at her writhing about on the bed like a beached fish. "Every month?"

He nodded again and gazed at the damp spot on his lapel. "Worst case of PMS we've ever seen."

■   28   ■

It wasn't until the nurses began to move me again that I realized I hadn't seen my father in what seemed like a long time. As they wheeled me out of Observation, I begged to be discharged. But my fever was still so high that one nurse told me that if I walked out of the building right now I could drop dead. I drifted in and out of sleep. My fever continued to rise and ebb. Meal trays appeared and were swept away. Sometimes it was day and sometimes it was night. Sometimes I saw Earl sitting by my bed, and once when I awakened he was holding my hand.

During those days, if I wanted to see my father I had to dream of him. I had to pretend I was a mirror and he was looking into me. Sometimes I placed him at the bottom of the bed, or standing by the window. I invented imaginary conversations, just as I had as a child, when his absences had grown larger than my memories of him.

There were years when his presence was as transparent as dust. Years when he disappeared from the family and became little more than an anecdote. This was the man I grew to love, the one we all reinvented. The man who flew a Tiger Moth plane under the Harbour Bridge, who sold a radio to a deaf woman. The man who jumped up on the kitchen table one morning and showed us how to cha-cha. We kids would sit around and talk him back into our lives, until we could catch a glimpse of his feet springing between our cereal bowls once more, until we could see his bum wagging at our bemused mother and begin to shake with laughter.

Sometimes his work demanded that he travel, doing tours with famous people such as Frank Sinatra and Katherine Dunham. Sometimes he would disappear altogether. He'd hop on a plane and fly to Darwin, or jump a coastal fishing trawler. Maybe he couldn't stop following the ghost of his dead brother Jack. My mother would shake her head and tell us he'd be back.

It was my mother who taught me how to wait, how to endure his distance. I waited hour after hour, day after day for the doorway to frame him. But I could only make him appear when I closed my eyes.

When I opened them again, five doctors, two dermatology specialists, and sixteen interns descended upon my ward and crowded around my bed. There was a quick hello, and one of the doctors asked me if it was all right if the students observed.

"For educational purposes, of course," he said, half-chuckling.

Still sweating and in a stupor, I gazed at their wide faces. They reminded me of people on Columbus Avenue, at about eleven P.M., when they'd pause in their promenades down the block and wait for us to begin our show.

I nodded at the doctor, and he pulled the sheet back. Everyone suddenly bowed in over me as if I were a wishing well, taking in the sight of my swollen skin. They asked me to sit up and I sat up. They gazed at my back. They lifted my right foot and unrolled my bandage. They each studied my palms, my feet, one by one, taking turns. When they asked me to, I lifted my gown so they could follow the rash's tracks across my stomach and rib cage. When the doctor produced a camera and asked if they could snap a few photographs for a medical journal, in the interests of research, I shrugged and said, "If you want."

"Your face won't be in the pictures, of course," said the doctor.

I let them lift my gown and take the photos. First they went limb by limb, then finished the roll with long shots. When they asked me to, I raised my legs. When they asked me to stop, I stopped. When they suggested I turn over, I rolled onto my stomach and pressed my face into the pillow.

The official diagnosis was "allergic reaction." The doctor kept winding the film on and saying I was a rare and classic case. Someone announced that my temperature was back up to one hundred and five. I was lying naked on my stomach in front of twenty-two strangers and wondering what I was allergic to. The interns were taking notes. The doctor said it was the sulfur in some medication I'd recently taken. The diagnosis seemed unlikely to me, for I'd stopped taking the prescription days ago.

"The amount she ingested," he said, pausing between shots, as if I wasn't there, "could have killed her."

By the time the doctors and their flock of interns left, I had acquired a kind of cult status in Bellevue. As the morning wore on, new doctors and nurses would randomly drop in to view the rash, and even touch it if they asked nicely.

■ 29 ■

I'd flirted with death before. I'd invited him into my bed and allowed him to touch my secret places. He'd been following me around from the time I was born. My first memory is of him. I was two years old and saw him shooing a bee toward me as I crawled about in the back garden. The bee stung me and my whole body ballooned as a result of a severe allergic reaction. When I was three he slipped a disease into my kidneys. During my convalescence, when getting out of bed and walking could have killed me, it was he who pulled the covers back and told me I could run up and down the hallway. He dragged me down under a wave one day, and if it weren't for the stranger's hands that finally dragged me from the surf, he would have had me right then. At seven, I felt an invisible foot shoot out, and I tumbled headfirst down a flight of concrete stairs. Sudden fires raged in my bedroom in the middle of the night. One day I found a nest of little black spiders with red dots on their backs and watched them crawl over my hands and trace the pale blue rivers of my veins.

He was like an old lover I could never quite get out of my blood. Sometimes, in Bellevue, when the nurse was late making her rounds and my skin burned like strips of lean bacon, I could taste his saliva in my mouth and sense his fine smooth fingers along the inside of my thigh.

But my childhood brushes with him were a kind of foreplay for the several days I spent spiraling up and down the nautilus of my hallucinatory fever. With those days came a burning nectar between my legs and a white light that slammed me behind the eyes and left my tongue swollen and bruised.

One night I awoke and was surprised to see my mother sitting on the side of the bed. She was dressed in a white hospital gown, just like me. She was thin, almost gaunt. She raised her hand and began stroking my brow, wiping away the sweat. I closed my eyes. I wondered how my mother had found me. I realized I must be dying, otherwise why would she be here? The weight of the cotton sheet was as heavy as a wooden board. Her hand was cool against my forehead. She began running her fingers through my hair, just as she had when I was a child.

When I opened my eyes again, she held me around the chest and gently pulled me up to a sitting position. Then she took my legs and eased them out of the bed. I felt giddy, but I was drawn to the scent of my mother, that old, familiar musk.

She took me by the hand and led me out of the ward. My legs felt weak, but I made an effort to put one foot in front of the other. I followed her down a hallway, past nurses and stretchers and the doorways of other wards. No one tried to stop us. At the end of the hallway was a tiny door, only about two feet high, with a gold doorknob and lock. When we reached it, she tried to open it, but couldn't. She looked around for a moment, then lifted her white gown. Like me, she wasn't wearing any underwear. None of the passing nurses seemed to notice, and when she parted her legs and pulled a golden key out of her vagina, no one gave her a second look. She gave the key to me and motioned me toward the door. The key smelled salty, and I was conscious of the fact that it had come from the same place as me.

I pushed the key into the lock and turned it. The door swung open. I peered inside, seeing only a long, dark tunnel. I wanted to go back to my bed, but my mother persuaded me to crouch, and when I did, she nudged me into the opening. I was sure I wouldn't fit, and began to panic. My shoulders were too wide. But just as I began to pull away, the opening shifted and took me in, and moments later, I was standing in the darkness on the other side.

My mother crawled in beside me, and suddenly I felt her cold hand upon mine. She began leading me through the tunnel, and she finally broke the silence that had smothered her for years.

I've lain in hospital beds and waited, too, she said, as we walked into the darkness. *I bore you kids without him, with a stranger's hands pulling the damp heads from the opening that had once given us so much pleasure.*

She paused. The air smelled salty, as if we were approaching the ocean. I tried to make out shapes in the darkness, but could not. *Those were the days,* she continued, *when new mothers had to stay in maternity wards for a week. And there I'd lie, day after day, breast-feeding my new baby and listening to the radio. Sometimes I'd wait for your father to arrive, so that he could see the thing our desire had made. But he was always playing music when I was having children, and didn't like the smell of hospitals.*

I heard her sigh, but could not see her as we continued to walk, just felt her cold hand in mine. *Perhaps he wanted me all to himself. Children were a burden, and made him like other men. They meant he had to do normal things from time to time, like cutting hair, and selling radios door-to-door. They meant he had to say responsible things and turn the record player down after eight o'clock. Having children, you know, was as bad as having really straight parents. You always had to do the right thing.*

She squeezed my hand. *But I knew what he was really scared of. Yes, he was afraid of the responsibility, the financial strain, the way a family cut into his music. But his real fear was producing a child with a harelip and cleft palate. I tried to calm him down with reminders of modern medicine, but he still always said, "I wouldn't want anyone to suffer what I went through."*

Suddenly, her voice dropped to a half-whisper, though I didn't know why. There seemed to be no one else in the tunnel who might overhear. *When I finally fell pregnant with our first child after five years of marriage, I wept. I wept because I was happy, because I had waited so long, and I wept because your father was sad.*

The next day he drove me to a doctor in Homebush. The doctor gave me a pint of liquid to drink before I went to bed that night. The liquid was inside an old milk bottle, and was the color of custard.

My knees began to weaken, and when I slowed down, she slipped her arm around me for support.

That night, she went on, *when I climbed into bed, your father asked, "Did you drink that stuff?"*

And I said, "Yes."

"Good," he said, and turned over and went to sleep.

A week later, when I came home from the doctor, I said, "It didn't work."

"What do you mean it didn't work?" he said. "You took it, didn't you?"

"Of course I did." And I made a face. "It tasted like charcoal."

I never told him I'd taken the time to smell the stuff before I tipped it down the toilet and pulled the chain.

Your brother was born eight months later, his skin knitted into perfect crossbow lips.

I thought this was the end of the story, and was relieved. Now we could turn and go back. But my mother's grip grew tighter around me and she continued to hurry me forward through the darkness.

A year later, I had our second one. He was two months premature, but his face was perfectly formed. During the birth, I lost so much blood that I lost consciousness and had to have a transfusion. I remember there was a lot of confusion that day. Perhaps the bottles were mislabeled, or the steps to certain procedures were forgotten, because four pints of the wrong blood-type went flowing into my veins, and by the time I'd recovered twelve hours later my baby was already dead.

I wanted to stop, to go back, but she wouldn't let me. I realized I couldn't remember where I'd put the golden key. I had no pockets in the white hospital gown, and I panicked when I realized I must have left it in the lock on the other side of the door.

Your father never came near me during that week in the hospital, her voice went on. *I had to heal myself on my own. I suppose it's easy to think that he didn't care, that he was secretly glad there wasn't one more baby to clutter the house with midnight cries and the smell of piss. But when I learned I was pregnant with your sister two years later, he not only celebrated, he attended six A.M. mass at St. Bridgit's seven days a week until Lisa was born healthy and perfectly formed only four nights after Christmas.*

I was beginning to feel dizzy again and wanted to sit down and rest. She'd never talked so much before, had never been so insistent. I told her I wanted to go back, but she just squeezed my hand again and kept pulling me through the darkness.

But two kids were enough, she said. *A boy and a girl. As far as he was concerned, we'd both reproduced ourselves. Perhaps he considered himself lucky not to have had his harelip mirrored on the faces of his kids. Maybe he'd struck up a deal with God, sweet-talked an angel, or charmed an errant saint. You see, essentially your father is a gambler, and he understands probability. He knew it was possible to win two horse races in one day, but to win three was a long shot, no matter who was chalking up the odds, even that great celestial bookie in the sky.*

Right then I saw a pinhead of light in the distance, a tiny white eye looking back at us.

So, three years later, when he found out I was pregnant again, he didn't call the doctor in Homebush, but made an appointment for me with a gynecologist whose surgery overlooked Maroubra Beach.

The light was growing wider as we approached it, the smell of the ocean even stronger.

It was 1962, you see, and no one listened to jazz anymore. All the teenagers were into Jerry Lee Lewis and Buddy Holly. We sold the car. We had to take in a boarder to help pay the mortgage. Whoever gave him the number of the Maroubra gynecologist must have also mentioned the huge fee, because that week your father sold the only objects he loved: the set of Zildjian cymbals that had been hand-spun in Turkey.

The light was growing stronger, and closer, and soon I could make out her tall, thin frame. She looked years younger. Her skin was smooth and clear. Her green eyes were wide. She was no longer wearing the white hospital gown but a gray suit and a frilly white shirt. Her hair was swept up into a French curl. She was wearing makeup, but it was streaked a little, as if she had been crying.

Sometimes those cymbals come back to haunt me, she went on, as she hurried me toward the opening.

The gynecologist's fee was fifty pounds and that's what he sold them for. On the day of my appointment, he gave me the cash and extra money for the taxi. I dressed in my gray suit with the mother-of-pearl buttons. But when I arrived at the surgery, I realized I was ten minutes early.

Suddenly the light opened up to us. I looked down and realized I had lost my hospital gown and was completely naked as my mother led me out of the tunnel. We walked into the sunshine. She took me over to a rock and we sat together, overlooking the sea. Waves rose and crashed against a golden beach below, and a slight breeze blew and ruffled our hair.

So I didn't ring the bell of the house, she continued, still holding my hand, *but walked across the road and sat on a rock above the surf. All I did was watch the waves. The sunlight slanted in a peculiar way through the clouds that day, like thick ropes to heaven. I watched the columns of light. I saw the clouds shift. I saw the rhythm of new waves moving through the sea.*

Around midafternoon, I took the money out of my pocket.

She pulled something from her pocket. They were pound notes. They looked strange and foreign to me. I was lowering my head, to get a closer look, when she ripped the notes in half.

And I tore the money up, she said. *I threw it to the wind and let it fall into the surf.*

She stood up and threw the ripped notes over the cliff and we watched them flutter down to the sea like confetti.

That night, your father moved out of our bedroom and into his own room at the end of the hall. He wouldn't speak to me for three weeks.

I remained on the rock and swallowed, shivering in the wind. But when I looked down at my naked body, I noticed the rash had melted away and my flesh was as smooth as a ripe plum. My mother wrapped her arms around me. I felt the prickle of her woolen suit against my skin. *You were born on the following St. Valentine's Day, twelve pounds heavy and twenty-four inches long.*

She paused and squeezed my arm. *Even God,* she added, *enjoys a little irony.*

▨ 30 ▨

When I awoke the next morning my skin had stopped burning. The sprawling red welts had begun to sink back into my flesh like dissolving sugar. It was then that I became aware of certain things, like the pulse beat throbbing in the hollow of my neck, and the way my fingertip smelled—like an old boot—after I'd rubbed it into the tiny thimble of my belly button. It was then that I noticed the two wings of my hipbones, and felt a nerve dancing beneath my right eyebrow. For the first time in years I counted my own breaths and didn't lose track until after five hundred.

That afternoon someone brought me my clothes and I was released from my incarceration at Bellevue. My legs felt weak as I dressed. The waistband of my skirt sagged onto my hips and I realized that during my illness I had at least managed to lose some of the cumbersome weight I'd acquired over the last few months.

I had hoped that Gerry might turn up to accompany me home, but he didn't. I walked out of the hospital alone, a queer, light-headed sensation steering me down the halls and into the street. I decided to reacquaint my leg muscles with a hint of the hours of work that lay ahead: Gerry and I had not performed in a week and had lost a lot of money. I would walk the two miles from Bellevue to the Penn View—from one side of the island to the other—in order to make the nerves in my hamstrings dance.

They say when you almost lose your life, you begin to have a different relationship with it. As I walked out of Bellevue and into the sweltering heat, I was only conscious of how lost I felt, of how much my father had let me down, of how much he had let my sister, brother, and mother down. Gerry could wax lyrical about the night of my conception, but where had he been during my mother's pregnancy, and while I was being born?

I walked uptown, toward 34th. I thought about those years when he was gone. The years in which he disappeared to play music and we never heard from him. The same years that are mythologized in his outrageous and funny stories. I thought about the violent man who took my father's place in their double bed. About the blows that landed for years on my chest, my face—the bleeding noses, the bruises that swelled across my mother's eyes, the clumps of hair he ripped from her head. And as I walked and walked, I also walked into my mother's bedroom in 1974 and saw her sprawled across her bed, barely a pulse at her wrist, the empty bottles of Valium and Mogadon lying on the floor.

By that time my father had been gone eighteen months. My brother had left home the year before. My sister was spending the weekend at a girl-friend's house. The violent lover was not at home. I was eleven years old. I sat on her bed and tried to shake her awake, but her head just lolled back and forth like a doll's, her arms heavy and limp. I shook her harder, pinched her skin. I called her name over and over again, but she just lay there like a corpse, a bluish hue rising into her skin. And it was I who had to run the three blocks to the nearest telephone booth, alone, and call an ambulance.

It was her third attempt at suicide, but by far the most dangerous. After she was loaded up and driven away, she spent three days unconscious in intensive care, wired up to machines and IVs.

I tried to call my sister from the hospital. Her best friend's mother told me the two girls had packed their suitcases and had run away. My sister couldn't have known about the suicide attempt; it was merely a coincidence that she'd chosen to flee the unbearable conditions of our lives on the same day as our mother. Even so, I wouldn't see her again for six months.

Fortunately, after three days of dancing with death, my mother awakened and demanded a cigarette. Eighteen months later she would wake up again and finally leave the man for good. But by the time she had attempted her third suicide, by the time I was eleven, I was feeling utterly abandoned. And as I walked along the garbage-strewn sidewalk of 34th Street, I had exactly the same feeling again.

I wasn't conscious of it then, but after my release from Bellevue, I would become more selective about what I allowed to enter me. I would stop my physical relationship with Earl and go back to being the daughter of his best friend. I would draw away from men completely and commit myself to celibacy. I would stop eating Chinese takeout every day and move on to salads and tofu. I would stop all the drug taking, the drinking. I'd even give up coffee.

After my illness, I could not be touched. The thought of a tongue or an alien finger filled me with dread. Pleasure was a thing that made me wary, like whipped cream, or the smiles of the smooth-faced con men on the corner of 42nd and Eighth.

My healing had to begin at the bottom of the well in which I had been languishing for years. Up until then, I'd been like a seasoned drinker who dulls her hangover each morning with a quaff of the brew that caused it. Taking one man to get over another man to get over another man.

As I walked back to the Penn View, my foot still bandaged, my legs weak, dry skin flaking off me after days of fever and sweat, a kind of paralysis set in, a part of me frozen like the heart of a bird who hasn't flown south fast enough. I fixed my eyes on the horizon, where the Penn View loomed like a dark gray prison, and was numb with the realization that I had lost faith in my beautiful, difficult father.

■ 31 ■

He was sipping coffee and smoking when I walked into our room.

"Hey," he said, "you're back."

I splashed my face with some water. "Barely."

He dragged on his cigarette. "You all right now? You look OK."

I wiped myself dry and threw the towel in the sink. I didn't know what to say.

"Earl kept me up with what was going on. You know ..." Gerry shrugged, shifting in his seat.

I stared at him through the blue spiral of smoke.

"You know I hate hospitals," he said.

I grabbed some change from the table and pocketed it. I opened the door again.

"Yeah," I said. "I know."

I backed out the door, backed away from my father's neglect. I looked past him, over his shoulder, into the future. I gazed into a life without him, a kingdom in which the only gods were me and my tap shoes.

That week, on the street, I met a Colombian dancer who'd performed with Nureyev and trained people such as Billy Idol for their music videos. He stood on the corner, smiling, holding a bottle of Perrier as he watched me tap. His hair was black, his skin olive and suntanned. He was shorter than me, but his posture was so erect, his carriage so serene, I didn't notice his height at first.

Afterward, when we were packing up, he walked over and we began chatting. His teeth were white and shiny, and I remember thinking I hadn't seen anyone look so healthy in a long time. What surprised me even more was that he thought I was a good tap dancer and wanted to take lessons from me. He was primarily a ballet dancer, though he did modern and jazz, was a hotshot roller skater, and was sought after as a private trainer for many Broadway performers.

I wasn't sure if he was bullshitting or not, or why he would want to take lessons from me. I shrugged and told him I wasn't in the best condition, that I was still recovering from a sprained foot. But he insisted that he liked my style, and that he could help me with some body work to prevent future injuries. He lived just around the corner, he said, and we could work in his apartment.

We arranged for our first lesson to begin on the following Monday afternoon at two o'clock, but by Monday morning, I was having serious doubts. I had only spoken to this man for ten minutes, and now I was going to allow myself to be alone with him in his apartment for the whole afternoon. I called from the office of the Penn View and canceled, told him my foot was acting up. He sounded so genuinely disappointed, however, that we made another appointment for the following Thursday.

The hospital bill soon arrived. My four-day captivity in Bellevue, with Tylenol and a drip as my only treatment, amounted to $2,500. It seemed I received no discount for my contribution to the glossy pages of the latest dermatological journal.

Two and a half grand was about seventy-five hours of tap dancing on the street in New York, and about three hundred and seventy five hours on a New Orleans corner. It was a frightening amount of money. When Earl arrived home at six, I almost pounced on him as he walked through the door, the bill flapping in my hand.

He didn't seem too worried, though. He slung one arm around my shoulder and told me everything was going to be all right. He said he never phoned in my passport number to the hospital accounts office. He'd neglected to give them a photocopy of my U.S. visa, too. Everything was going to be fine, he said. I wouldn't have to pay the bill. There was no way the hospital could trace my existence beyond the address of the Penn View Hotel. I tried to feel relieved, but it took some effort. We had eight hundred and fifty dollars in the bank, and no return airline tickets. Gerry still hadn't received his American residency. In two months the extension on my visa would expire.

When Earl rested his hands on my hips and invited me upstairs for a joint, I shook my head. My skin suddenly felt hot and feverish again, and my stomach began to flutter. I drew away from him quickly, folded up the hospital bill, and disappeared into the dark green monotony of my own room.

That night, I was feeling so anxious, I missed my lesson with Cookie. I crawled into my father's sagging bed and listened to the dealers jostling about beneath our open window. Gerry sat with me for a while and drank a quart of Colt 45. He was glad I was getting better and told me so.

"I'd be fucked if anything happened to you," he said, ruffling my hair. I smiled weakly and looked away, feeling mildly warmed by his admission. But the sensation passed quickly, for something had happened to me. I no longer desired his schemes and stories, his anecdotes and adventures. My father finally needed me, but I no longer needed him.

32

When I awoke the next morning, I promised myself we would have a one-hundred-and-twenty-dollar night. Even though they'd been commonplace last summer, we weren't having nights like that anymore. A couple of residents on Columbus Avenue regularly complained to the police about the noise we made. Occasionally Herb Browning would turn up. Fortunately, he never asked me out again, but would always tell me to move, waving us down toward Lincoln Center.

We were also no longer considered "new." What had seemed like a unique family act twelve months ago was now the noise that began at eight o'clock. Mr. Bendeasy and his twelve-year-old niece, Juliet-the-Clown, were pulling in the crowds this year.

But tonight, I decided, the gods would be with us; the residents wouldn't complain; there'd be a lot of tourists on the street; I'd don my lucky leotard and wear my stockings backward, just like the last time we'd earned one hundred and twenty dollars on the corner of 70th.

By midafternoon, though, thick clouds were brooding in the sky, and by five o'clock, they'd darkened and drifted into one deep purple bruise.

I sat outside on the steps of the hotel and watched the sky, trying to will it to not let the first raindrop fall; then Alma suddenly leaned into my line of vision. She was standing two steps down from me, sucking up beer through a plastic straw and glaring at me. In spite of the heat, she wore a woolen skirt and a polyester turtleneck with fluff balls clustered along the seams.

"You should move away," she declared.

I nodded and glanced back up at the sky. "I won't be here long. I'm just waiting to see if it'll rain."

"You should move," she repeated, a little gruffer than before.

"If it rains," I said, "my father and I can't work. I'll be gone in ten minutes."

I figured she wanted me off the steps so her customers wouldn't assume I was soliciting, too.

But Alma shook her head. "Where you fr-r-rom again?"

Even though each syllable was articulated with the halting difficulty of a foreigner, I was fascinated by the perfect way she rolled her *r*'s.

"Australia."

"Oustr-r-r-ral-e-ea," she repeated. "Gir-rl, why don't you go home?" She gestured to the street, the stairs I was sitting on. "Is no good, this place. No good for gir-rl like you."

She shook her head and spat on the pavement. A man in khaki overalls was hovering beside a telegraph pole farther down the block.

I glanced up at the sky again. The clouds were the color of dried blood, and formed a foreboding ceiling above the pinnacle of the Empire State Building two blocks down the street.

The man had edged his way along the sidewalk, and was now eyeing us both from behind the sandwich board that advertised the rates for the carpark.

"You should move," Alma repeated.

Then the first fat raindrop landed on my face. I nodded, stood up, and climbed the stairs back into the Penn View.

■ 33 ■

There were many ways in which I wanted to move, but there was nowhere to go. I was stuck in the hotel, stuck on the street, and, now that we had sold our airline tickets, firmly stuck in America. It was this desire to move that finally motivated me to risk possible rape, robbery, and murder and turn up on the doorstep of the man I'd met on Columbus the week before.

I arrived promptly at two P.M. on a Thursday afternoon, as we had arranged. He lived in a brownstone on 69th. The elevator was old and rickety, and shuddered all the way up to the fifth floor.

I found the right door and stood before it, hesitating. The carpet was decorated with soft, musky-print flowers and the hallway smelled pleasant, the scent of honeysuckle. Not a likely abode for a madman or serial killer. I straightened my skirt. I swept the stray tendrils of my hair up into my onion knot. I took a deep breath, raised my hand, and rapped on the tall, wooden door.

Alberto Delgado was a slim, muscular man in his early thirties. His skin was the color of milky tea. His dark eyes glittered, and his black hair was slicked away from his high forehead. When I imagine him now, he looks a lot like Antonio Banderas, exuding the same kind of pouting boyishness.

Alberto's most striking quality, however, was not his handsome profile but the utter goodness of his manners. When he kissed your hand, he meant it. When he inquired after your health, he really wanted to know if anything was wrong.

Alberto was the first of hundreds of students I've had over the years. And like all good students, he taught me a lot, and not only about the mysterious underworld of my own body. He also showed me how to teach other people, and how to teach myself.

He lived in an apartment with polished hardwood floors, high ceilings, and long windows that filled the breadth of the wall overlooking the street. It was one large room with an adjoining bathroom and kitchen. Alberto slept on a queen-sized futon over by the windows. A small round kitchen table was pushed up against one wall with three folding chairs around it. The table held most of Alberto's stray paraphernalia: his Cervantes and Marquez, his *Gray's Anatomy*, the stumps of his white candles standing on Devonshire saucers, the bulging journal in which he wrote every day, his packets of sandalwood incense, a jar of face cream, and a photograph or two of himself taken by Ken Duncan.

We always began with his lesson then moved on to mine, and that first day was no different. When I kicked off my patent-leather shoes in order to tie on my taps, he suddenly grabbed my injured right foot and held it in both hands as if it were a dying pet. After so many months, the swelling had diminished and the flesh above my toes had acquired a steely hardness. But it still ached like hell toward the end of each evening. Our last hour on the street every night was an arduous pleasure: It was usually the time when the crowds thickened and cheered on Columbus; it was also the time my foot buckled under the pressure of another pull-back and wing, another series of double-time shuffles.

I still wore a withered pink Ace bandage reeking of stale menthol ointment. Alberto unclipped the hook, and slowly unrolled it, as if he were unwrapping a gift and didn't want to tear the paper.

When he finished, he tossed it away and told me I wouldn't need it anymore. Then he held in his hands the wrinkled white mummy that was my foot, pressing it here and there, rubbing his thumb against the metatarsal muscle and his palm into my modest arch. He told me then that the problem wasn't my foot, but my entire body, which had been thrown out of alignment as a consequence of hammering myself into concrete and brick pavements for years.

Alberto was a keen student, but like most good ballet dancers he was too uptight. His knees were often locked, and he unconsciously stood on the balls of his feet. He frequently tried to leap in the air instead of developing more intimacy with the wooden floor, which was now the instrument he must learn to play.

Throughout that first lesson, and during the scores that followed, I'd have to remind him to come down from that high, controlled position twenty-eight years of solid study had trained into his muscles. I showed him how to bend his knees slightly and pretend he was resting his bum on the edge of a tall stool. On that first day, I taught him exercises to loosen up his ankles, and the fundamental steps that most teachers in Australia have you practicing for about the first six months: the tap-step, the shuffle, the ball-change, the shuffle-ball-change—all two-beat steps that didn't require any heel work.

After about an hour or so, when we'd exhausted the possibilities of those four steps, we took a break and drank some mineral water. Alberto showed me his journal, which was a handmade book with cloth binding and filled with pressed violets and photographs, and the fine, small printing of his delicate hand. On subsequent visits, he would ask me to write something in it and to jot down the date. I'd rarely inscribe anything that sprang from my own tongue, but instead would quote someone else. My favorites at that time were "If one tells the truth, one is sure, sooner or later, to be found out" (Oscar Wilde) and " 'I could tell you my adventures—beginning from this morning,' said Alice a little timidly, 'but it is no good going back to yesterday, because I was different person then.' "

When my lesson began on that first day, Alberto told me to strip down to my leotard. After I'd discarded my shirt and shoes, he walked in a circle and studied my physique as if I were a piece of furniture he was considering buying.

"You're going to have to stretch," he said, eyeing my shoulders.

He pressed his hand against my bum and gently nudged it forward. Then his other hand dropped against my stomach and pushed it in a little. Suddenly, I felt an inch taller. I held the position while he took my rounded shoulders and pulled them back into a simulacrum of the broad, sinewy wings they'd been only a year and a half ago.

This was the beginning of my grueling and transcendental apprenticeship with Alberto Delgado. It was also the beginning of my first true friendship in America. He was a man who was not a mate of my father, who was not and could never be my lover, and who wanted nothing more from me than my knowledge of tap and to enjoy my company.

As Alma had said on the steps of the Penn View that day: I should move. I interpreted the statement as some kind of streetwise prophecy, a sort of mystical message from the angels I imagined tangoing in the sky. I suspected they had dropped Alberto into my life as their earthbound agent.

That first day we did a lot of floor work: stretches, holds, repetitions. Some of the exercises were familiar: I'd studied modern dance technique in Melbourne as a teenager, as well as two years of mime in Sydney. I still warmed up late each afternoon with a repertoire of stretches developed from my early training.

Up until that afternoon, I thought I was sufficiently strong and limber, but under the stress of Alberto's brusque commands, my muscles almost collapsed. There were some exercises that seemed deceptively simple when Alberto demonstrated them, like the one during which he laid on the floor, flexed every muscle in his body, raised his head so his chin touched his chest, lifted his taut legs about half an inch from the floor, and held the position for about twenty seconds.

When I attempted to do it, however, I felt as if my tendons would snap after the tenth slow count; by the fifteenth my whole being was shuddering from the pressure, and I managed to get the words out, that I couldn't hold it any longer. But he just kept counting—slowly—and in between the counts he kept muttering under his breath that I could, that I must, that I had to. He told me to breathe, to concentrate. The tight fist my body had contracted into began to shudder, as if I were holding back a concrete block that threatened to crush me if I relaxed. The nerves in my knees jumped and a hot white light burned up my thighs, devoured my stomach, and began gnawing at my waist.

When Alberto finally said, "Twenty," I dissolved onto the floor and allowed the air to rush back into my lungs. Then he passed me the water bottle and, after I'd taken a gulp, told me to lie back down and do it again.

He insisted that we meet two or three times a week, which, in addition to my Monday-night lessons with Cookie, my regular practice, and my nightly performances, seemed a little excessive. When I hesitated, however,

Alberto was firm: I would have to work very hard indeed in order to over-come the problems that had been plaguing me for years.

"Remember," he said, looking at me solemnly, "the body and the mind are like this." And he pressed his palms together in front of his chest, then allowed his fingers to drop and lace themselves together in a gesture of silent prayer.

I had not expressed my other problems to Alberto—only the physical ones—so I was surprised that he realized I was suffering from more than an injured foot. As I dressed in front of him late that afternoon, as we kissed each other's cheeks in his open doorway, a current of gratitude welled through my stomach and loosened in my throat.

▩ 34 ▩

Earl decided he wanted to rent a house in Brooklyn or Coney Island and to have us come and live with him.

Since my discharge from Bellevue, we'd gone back to being just friends. Though he had tried to make a couple of moves on me, each time I'd quietly nudged him away.

So when he suggested we share a house, I assumed it was out of friend-ship. In some ways, we'd grown closer since my hospitalization, and the concern and care with which he treated me during my illness continued. During those weeks, it was Earl who expressed the protectiveness my father avoided. It was Earl who told me to stop cutting through the carpark at night, who bought me three pairs of cotton socks, who showed me how to soak my white underwear in a bucket of diluted Clorox.

Gerry was keen on the house idea, too, and for once we were all in agreement. Earl was talking about a two-story place with three bedrooms and two bathrooms, just like he'd owned when he was married and raising his two daughters. The great plan, of course, was contingent upon his an-nual tax return, which should, he assured us, arrive in the mail any day.

I was eager to transcend the tawdriness of the Penn View, but even more important, I was desperate to escape the increasingly irate notices from the Bellevue Hospital accounts office. By the end of September, the hospital was threatening to forward the bill to a collection agency, and Gerry and I had to brief Fred and the night clerk, Ricky, on our current situation. We even confided in the owner of the hotel, Chase, a chubby, balding man in his late thirties who'd grown up in the Bronx and still lived there with his family. Oddly enough, it was Chase who seemed the most sympathetic, and it was he who instructed Fred and Ricky and Pop to play dumb if anyone came looking for us.

When I expressed my appreciation to him, Chase just shrugged and began picking his teeth with a broken matchstick.

"I been there, sweetheart, don't you worry. My wife had a complicated labor with our last kid. Those bastards down at Bellevue tried to charge us ten grand. *Ten fucking grand* for a pair of forceps and a couple o' needles."

He said he'd move to Canada before he'd write them a check, and to consider his instructions to Fred and Ricky as his little stab at socialism.

The paradox was further deepened by his reputation as a hardened slum lord. Gerry and I had always paid our rent on time, yet our punctuality was motivated more by fear than any sense of duty. We'd witnessed what happened to tenants who were even an hour late in their rent. It was Ricky's job to enter the room of a given patron when he or she was absent, clear it of all personal possessions, and dump the gear out the front of the hotel. Then he would change the locks before the tenant returned. Any possessions not claimed by the end of the day were subsumed into the sprawling merchandise of the basement junk shop and eventually sold.

I dreamed of a bigger place to live the way other young women crave popularity, or chocolate. My father and I had shared a room and the occasional bed for over a year. Sometimes, after his snoring would start up like the chorus of a drowsy cricket, when I was sure he was asleep, I'd lie in my improvised bed on the floor and dream of my magician and quietly touch myself beneath the threadbare sheet. Sometimes I could hear Alma howling away in the next room. Occasionally, muted sighs rose like octaves in a music hall, and I'd know then that one of the dealers was standing below our window, getting a blow job.

One morning my father awakened all pink and glowing. He took himself off to the shower and dressed. When he returned, I boiled the jug for my peppermint tea and his coffee, and he sat down in the chair, grinning, and smoked his first cigarette of the day.

"You'll never guess what happened to me last night," he said.

"What?"

His face was rosy, almost flushed. I thought he might be sick, that he might have vomited out the window as I slept, or suffered a mild angina.

"I had a wet dream," he declared, as if he'd just won some money on a horse.

I sat on the bed and sipped my tea. "What's a wet dream?"

I'd heard the term before, but did not know its meaning.

With a few pithy and well-chosen words, my father explained the phenomenon, and added that he hadn't experienced one in donkey's years.

"I thought I was past all that," he said, smiling at the green wallpaper. He sipped his coffee with that half-embarrassed grin set in his face and quickly crossed his legs.

I lowered the metal door onto the floor in order to begin practicing Cookie's most recent lesson. We needed a bigger place to live, I decided. There was no doubt about it.

◼ 35 ◼

I returned to Alberto's apartment twice a week to give him lessons and to surrender myself to the euphoric torture of his training. Sometimes our sessions turned into entire afternoons. He'd have me stretching and contorting myself for hours, doing back bends and sit-ups, headstands and push-ups. Double leg lifts. Slow abdominal curls. He was mostly trying to develop my solar plexus, that area deep within the belly, where one's center—one's relationship with gravity—is buried.

Every dancer knows that all movement through space must germinate from and through the center. I'd been aware of it since I'd taken my first modern dance class back in 1978. But somehow, like a good piece of unheard motherly advice, the knowledge hadn't impregnated me. My muscles hadn't quite understood that their energy wasn't being drawn from the right place.

Alberto considered it his mission in life to help me develop it. He harangued me until I committed myself to three sessions a week: Monday, Wednesday, and Friday. On Tuesday, Thursday, and Saturday, I'd awaken on the floor of our room, aching in the aftermath of so much sudden training. Fifty full-weight push-ups left my biceps raw and tender. The insides of my thighs often felt like two musical instruments with the strings tuned so tight they might snap under the touch of a finger. Other days it was my pectorals, my scapulas, or my underdeveloped gluteus maximus. But every day my abdomen throbbed, where the elusive center was buried, where Alberto worked me the hardest.

He showed me Balinese dance movements to warm up my torso. He made me drink mineral water. He corrected my posture again and again as I stretched before his gaze. He worried about my feet, my meager arches. He told me my butt wasn't strong enough and demonstrated an exercise that, when I attempted it, made me howl.

Alberto was a hard taskmaster and would not let me quit. All this pain was good pain, he told me. The kind that relieves damaged muscles, that prevents further injuries. I kept lifting my leg into the air, over and over, in time with his slow counts, trying to breathe, to continue, to put flesh on his advice.

36

It was during those first weeks with Alberto that I returned home from a lesson to find Alma standing out front with a bright blue shiner blooming around her right eye. The bruising had swollen it shut. She stood on the bottom step, her stockings still rolled down past her knees, her shoulders rounded. But she held onto her beer can. And with her good eye she watched the block, her gaze falling on each passing man.

When I picked up our mail, I received another notice from Bellevue Hospital demanding payment in full for $2,500. The amount was highlighted in pink. I folded it and slipped it into the drawer of our small table, along with the previous one. I had other things to worry about, like earning a living and regaining my health. Our indoor gigs were still sporadic—the odd birthday party or spot at the Improv—and most of our income was still gleaned from the streets.

That month I began reading *The Garden of Eden* by Jethro Kloss. In it, Kloss espouses his theory about food, the main thrust of which is the insistence upon the fresh, the natural, and the in-season.

My theory was that, in spite of my rigorous training with Alberto, there was still a lot of sulfur in my bloodstream. When Alberto told me I needed a thorough cleaning out, it was to Jethro Kloss's miracle cure that I finally surrendered myself.

Kloss spurned any substance that was even mildly stimulating. I'd already given up alcohol, coffee, and drugs, and soon tea and sugar were eliminated from my diet. Next to go were my occasional forays into chicken (I hadn't eaten red meat since I was fourteen). After a week, however, I felt my energy plummeting instead of peaking.

It was then, under Alberto's encouragement, that I embraced what I call Kloss's Final Solution: a ten-day elimination diet consisting of only fresh fruit and raw vegetables. My only liquids would be water and peppermint tea. The program was supposed to flush the body of toxins, excess acid, and mucus, to feed the bloodstream with natural vitamins and minerals.

The first couple of days were hard; there are only so many oranges and celery sticks you can eat before a deeper hunger sets in and you suddenly want to devour entire loaves of bread and slug down several cappuccinos. However, if I chose to grit my teeth and quarter another apple, it was not only because I wanted to renovate my body. By then, a strong strain of obsessive-compulsiveness was percolating in my head, so much so that I'd convinced myself that if I didn't stick to Kloss's Final Solution for the pre-scribed time, something really bad would happen.

I'd had similar experiences before. As a seven-year-old gazing into the deep end of an unheated pool, I heard a voice telling me that if I did not muster the courage to dive into the freezing water, both my parents would be killed. This voice inside me scared me so much I plunged into the pool fully clothed, yet when my mother wanted to know the reason, I could not find the words.

I could not name that force which drove me to dance for hours on a bleeding foot, or to starve myself for weeks at a time on citrus fruits and car-rots. And because I could not name it, nor explain it, the force itself as-sumed a position of power in my life.

Perhaps Alma's stoicism became my unconscious role model, for, as I continued to halve grapefruits and peel mandarins, I reminded myself that my lot was easy compared with hers. She had no friends and not much of a future. Yet she continued to stand on that bottom step every day.

I used to wonder what she thought about as she counterfeited pleasure on the other side of the wall. It only occurs to me now that people often asked me the same question on the street: What did I think about as I danced each number, and how did I keep smiling for hours on end?

◼ 37 ◼

I suppose I marveled at the way Alma could keep working in spite of her puffy and tumid black eye. She stood out in front of the hotel all day long, and did not try to conceal the wound that had been left by the hand of some faceless john. When my hamstrings ached from Alberto's unrelenting instruction, and when my entire being screamed for Chinese food or pasta or chocolate, I thought of Alma in her sagging stockings and with her muted dignity.

I'd first seen her bruised face on a Monday afternoon. By Wednesday, when I left the hotel for my lesson, I was shocked to see her other eye as black and swollen as the first. She looked more like a ring-eyed pup than a mature woman teetering on the edge of menopause. I wanted to take her hand and draw her inside, make her lie down, press an ice pack against her battered head. It was as if the culprit could not have borne the asymmetry of only one bruised eye, for it was obvious that the second blow was aimed by the same fist. What relentless devil had induced her to go back into a room with that bastard for yet another beating?

I was sure she wasn't a junkie, had never seen her scoring in the carpark or shooting up in the bathroom. She did not possess the thin, gaunt body of a regular user. As I walked toward the subway station, I gnawed on the stump of a carrot and told myself I would not weep.

◼ 38 ◼

Toward the end of October, I received yet another notice from Belle-vue, informing me that my bill had been forwarded to a collection agency. I was on my tenth day of fruit and vegetables, and was feeling distinctly light-headed. My stomach and bum were still aching from the grueling three-hour lesson I'd had the day before. I crumpled onto the bed with the notice in my hand, finally realizing the deep shit we were now in. When Gerry got out of the shower, he was more philosophical. He stood in his undies before the mirror above the sink and combed his wet hair back off his face.

"We'll just have to move," he said.

"Where?" I wailed.

He shrugged, absorbed in his hazy reflection. "Don't panic"—he tilted his head to one side and combed behind his ear—"I'll figure something out."

Nothing could hurry him out of his slow, pedantic morning ritual: the shower, the hanging of the wet towel across the windowsill, the hair-combing in front of the mirror, the first cigarette with the first cup of coffee, the second cup of coffee, a second grooming of his hair once it had dried. Then it was up to Eighth Avenue for his takeout boneless chicken and rice. Then it was eating half his lunch and saving the other half for when we arrived home at midnight after work.

But I knew we wouldn't be working tonight because we had to move.

It wasn't until Gerry had wiped the corners of his mouth with a napkin and had packed up the complement of his Chinese food for later that he finally stood up, burped, and said, "Right."

He disappeared out the door, and was gone for about a quarter of an hour. When he returned, he was still sporting his cool and casual demeanor. I secretly marveled at the way he could maintain it: I was hunched up on the bed, having premonitions of jail sentences and deportation.

"Right," he said again. He closed the door behind him and threw his cigarettes on the table. "Start packing. We're moving this arvo."

My father's plan was deceptively simple. On the other side of the carpark, facing 33rd Street, was another hotel, the Palmer, and the back of it almost adjoined the rear of the Penn View. Chase apparently owned both of them. When Gerry approached him at the front desk, it was Chase who suggested we slip into a spare room at the Palmer until the heat subsided.

The other part of the plan, Gerry told me, was telling everyone in the hotel that we're moving back to Australia. The only people who were allowed to know our real whereabouts were Chase and Earl. The rest—even Fred, Ricky, and Pop—were to be deliberately misled.

This, I surmised, was going to be a challenge, especially since we were only moving about thirty yards from the front door of the Penn View. Yet in spite of my misgivings, I was somewhat amused by my father's audacity, and there really was nowhere else we could go on such short notice.

While Chase walked Gerry over to the Palmer to show him the only vacant room he had, I turned on the radio and began packing. A melancholy tune eased out of the speakers and the wiry ruminations of a tenor saxophone filled the room. I remember being surprised by how closely the composition approximated my own nervous tension at that moment, and I began folding my clothes in time with the restrained wails buried beneath the melodic line. As the afternoon crept over the city and I shoved what few possessions I now owned into my canvas bag, I knew it was a moment that would always be with me. I made sure I heard the title when the DJ's voice interrupted the last dying notes—it was John Coltrane's "Blue Train," with Curtis Fuller on trombone. I found myself thinking there was no better sound track to this circuitous film I was beginning to recognize as my own life.

Gerry appeared in the open doorway.

"How's the room?" I asked.

"OK." He sighed and pulled his suitcase out of the closet. "Now, let's see how fast we can move this stuff before everyone in the joint realizes what we're doing."

I nodded and lugged my bag toward the door.

"And if anyone asks you where you're going," he added, "make sure you tell 'em you're going back to Australia."

I nodded again, made my way down the hall, into the foyer, past Pop, and told him I was going back to Australia. Through the front door, down the stairs, past Alma and a prospective client, and told her I was going back to Australia. Around the corner, into the carpark, past the coke dealers and hookers, and told them I was going back to Australia. Around the corner to 33rd, down a few steps, and into the Palmer Hotel.

I pressed the buzzer and the security door magically opened. A slight young black guy met me inside. He was dressed immaculately in a three-piece suit, a gold watch chain snaking out of his waistcoat pocket, and what looked like spit-shined black Italian shoes. I was intrigued by this pedantic man, who was such a striking contrast to muddle-headed Fred with his unlit cigarette butt always wedged between his lips. It wasn't until weeks later that I found out why Chase had kept Fred on for so long as head clerk: Back in 1978, he had been shot twice in the back trying to resist a gunman who wanted to make off with the Penn View's petty cash.

The suited man with his trimmed mustache introduced himself as Mervyn. He led me down a narrow hallway and into our new room. It was smaller and narrower than the one in the Penn View. A three-quarter bed was jammed in at one end, below the barred windows that overlooked the half-lot separating the backs of the two hotels.

"It's a bit of a squeeze for both of you," said Mervyn. "But, you know, this is Manhattan."

It looked even smaller once we'd moved everything in. After I'd stashed our equipment in the cemented alcove that was once a fireplace, I found there was just enough floor space for me to lie down and sleep that night.

Unlike Fred, Mervyn bluntly refused to accept one hundred dollars in rolled quarters as our first week's rent. Thus, I had to cart them down to our bank and exchange them for five twenty-dollar bills. It was around four o'clock in the afternoon. After I'd divested myself of the rolls of coins, I walked back out onto the street and was about to return to the Palmer when I decided to check our balance.

A line had formed inside the glass annex of the bank housing the automatic teller machines. It was like standing inside a huge humidifier, and I could feel the sweat patches forming under my arms and around my waist. Finally, a machine became vacant and I produced my blue card and gazed at the screen.

HELLO. WELCOME TO CITIBANK. PLEASE INSERT YOUR CARD.

I did what it told me to, and listened to the electronic hum and click.

PLEASE PUNCH IN YOUR PERSONAL IDENTITY NUMBER.

I pressed the buttons and selected the BALANCE option on the keyboard.

The screen blinked on its neon-green answer:

SIXTY-FOUR CENTS

I stared at the screen, unable to believe it. I ejected the card, inserted it again, took my time punching in the PIN number, making sure it was correct, and selected the BALANCE option once more.

SIXTY-FOUR CENTS

I tried to breathe, but my throat was locked, and I was feeling so light-headed I had to hold onto the counter of the machine. Suddenly some guy was barking at me to hurry up.

"What d'ya think it is? A fuckin' television or something?"

Another man and a woman began arguing in one corner, something about a pair of tickets, and amid the confusion, a corgi wandered into the annex and began pissing against one of the garbage bins. I walked out onto the street, hot, dazed, and a little nauseous. There had to be some mistake. Only a few weeks ago over eight hundred dollars had appeared in green lettering across the very same screen.

I made my way back into the bank and found a Customer Service telephone. As I picked up the receiver I thought of the collection agency and winced. Could they have traced me to this account so soon? Was it legal to seize funds without telling the custodian? This was America, I told myself. Anything was possible. For a moment the receiver froze in my hand.

"Hello?" A woman's voice whined through the earpiece. "Customer Service. How may I help you?"

If that were the case, I thought, the agency might have instructed the bank to notify them as soon as I identified myself and made an inquiry.

"Hello?" piped the voice again. "Customer Service!"

In my paranoia, I glanced around to see if anyone was watching me.

"Hello! How may I help you?"

I lifted the receiver, recited my PIN number, and asked for the details of any transactions in the last week.

She must not have heard me correctly, because she launched into a litany of transactions that had begun over a month ago: "September 23, thirty dollars withdrawn. September 26, fifty dollars withdrawn. October 2, twenty dollars deposited. October 8, two hundred dollars withdrawn. October 12, sixty dollars withdrawn. The 16th, two hundred dollars withdrawn. The 17th, fifty deposited. The 18th, seventy dollars withdrawn. The 20th, two hundred dollars withdrawn. October 21, seventy dollars withdrawn. Total current balance: sixty-four cents. If you wish to maintain your account, Miss, you should deposit at least another dollar within three working days."

Then she hung up. I placed the receiver back in the cradle, walked outside, and vomited behind an idling taxi.

■ 39 ■

As I walked back to the Palmer I imagined that Earl was in West Virginia by now, snorting up our eight hundred bucks. All we had to our name was the rent-money in my pocket and a little over a hundred dollars in small change.

Gerry's slightly smug attitude was somewhat dented when I told him the news. He sat in his undies, hunched over on the side of the bed, with his forearms resting on his knees. All he kept saying was, "Earl wouldn't rip us off. There's got to be an explanation."

I splashed my face with water and rinsed my mouth out in the tiny corner sink. It was nearly five o'clock by then. My father assumed responsibility for apprehending Earl. He'd wait in the foyer of the Penn View until he came home from work.

"But we're supposed to be on our way back to Australia!" I said. "Everyone'll know we're lying!"

Gerry waved me back into silence. "I'll tell 'em the plane's leaving tomorrow. Don't worry. Leave it to me."

He pulled on his jeans and sweaty T-shirt, grabbed his cigarettes, and left the room.

I sat on the bed and stared through the barred windows that faced the small lot between the hotels, where weeds and withered dandelions struggled up between the rusting cans, broken glass, McDonald's hamburger containers, empty Thunderbird bottles, and discarded syringes. I don't know how long I sat there, half-dumb, meditating on the block's abandoned paraphernalia, but when I turned around, Earl was sweeping into the room and gushing about how well I looked.

I told him to cut the crap and demanded to know what happened to our money. I even thumped him on the chest with the heel of my hand and shoved him toward the fireplace. Gerry appeared in the doorway and told me to calm down. Earl grabbed me by the arms to restrain me, held me in a tight bear hug until I stopped writhing and yelling. He grasped my shoulders and eased me back onto the bed. He sat beside me and took off his hat.

"I wanted to *invest* the bread," he said, "and then put *it* and the *profit* back into your account before you knew it was gone." He turned the hat in his hands. "I wanted it to be a surprise."

He looked up and touched my face, but I jerked it away.

"You had *no right* to—"

"I wanted you to be able to go down to the bank, put your card in, and see *three grand* appear before your eyes!"

"Yeah, right"—I began hammering my index finger against his chest— "and all I saw this afternoon, you bastard, was *sixty-four cents*! It's not even enough to keep the account open."

"Well, you would have to check your balance while I was still finalizing my investment."

"What was it?" I sprang up off the bed and began pacing the room, which was hard considering I had to turn around every three steps. Gerry was hovering in the doorway.

Earl sighed and murmured something under his breath.

"What?" I asked, swinging toward him.

"A coke deal," he repeated, looking sheepishly at the floor.

"A fucking *coke deal?*"

"Keep your voice down," said Gerry, closing the door.

"We had a slight complication and it hasn't all come through yet. Now, sweetheart"—he leapt up and grabbed me by the shoulders—"there's no way I'd jeopardize your financial security. If the deal doesn't come through, I'll replace the eight hundred. If it *does* come through, I'll replace the eight hundred *plus* the two grand profit."

Gerry collapsed onto the bed. "Thank God we got that straight."

Earl gently nudged my chin up so that my eyes met his. "I'm sorry you were shocked this afternoon. Listen, the money will be back in the bank by Thursday, deal or no deal."

After Earl left, I was still so wound up that I took two rolls of quarters from our money sack, walked up to Ninth Avenue, and bought a cheap bottle of red wine and six bottles of Colt 45. What was the point of sweating my way through this stupid life? What was the point of pushing myself so hard? You just got fucked over in the end. If you moved a little ahead in the game, there was always someone looming in the wings, ready to drag you back. There was no reason to continue my arduous sessions with Alberto, my weekly lessons with Cookie, to keep purifying my system with a strict diet of fruits and vegetables, to keep hammering myself into the ground every night on Columbus Avenue and in the Village, to keep hustling on the phone for more indoor work, to keep practicing on the metal door, to keep dreaming.

I gave the beer to my father and kept the red plonk for myself. We got pissed together quickly on the floor of our shoe-box room, and my father waxed lyrical about the good old days.

In three years' time I would move back to Sydney with my husband, and he and I would see a film in Double Bay called *Round Midnight*. It is loosely based on the lives of the jazz musicians Bud Powell and Lester Young, and stars the aging tenor sax player Dexter Gordon.

The film opens in a run-down Manhattan hotel room. An elderly musician, Hershel, is in bed, dying. Dexter is pacing the worn carpet, surrounded by garish wallpaper. He's restless, wants to move to Paris. Dexter smokes and says he has to get away from New York's snow, from these sad, raggedy-assed rooms. Hershel, in an inspired moment, leans forward and tells Dexter that he can run as far as he wants, but when he gets to Paris, there'll still be someone waiting for him at the airport, and that someone will be himself.

In Paris, Dexter battles the bottle while playing with old friends in a local club. The music's good, but he finds himself living in yet another crummy hotel room, exactly like the one from which he's just escaped. "Oh yes," he says more than once, "I'm tired of everything . . . but the music." After a stint in a mental institution, he gets clean and begins composing and recording again. But the specter of Death is always stalking. While Dexter's in Paris, his buddy Hershel dies. And when Dexter returns to New York, he finds himself back in what looks like exactly the same room in which he and Hershel had last argued.

"Is this the same room Hershel died in?" asks Dexter's Parisian friend.

Dexter pauses, and when he speaks his voice is rough and croaky with regret. "I don't know," he says, "they all look the same. Same raggedy drapes, this crummy wallpaper. They all look the same."

Within a month, Dexter is also dead.

In 1987, I would sit in the theater at Double Bay and recognize the steps down which the hookers hurry. I would recognize the iron bars around the front desk, the long mirror in the foyer before which I spent so many hours practicing. I would recognize the dim corridors, the cheap brown-and-fawn-colored paint job. The dealer hovering in the shadows. The only difference between the Penn View we lived in and the one Dexter returns to is that in the film the hotel has been tarted up a little: They'd torn down the striped green wallpaper and had replaced it with sheets printed with ferns.

But Dexter is right. The rooms are all the same. I sat in the dark theater and held my husband's hand, watching the shadows of the Penn View grow wide across the screen.

After our first night in the Palmer, after Gerry and I had gotten stinking drunk as fast as we could manage, I was awakened the next morning by a strange tickling sensation along my arms. I shifted and turned over on the floor, trying to postpone the merciless hangover I knew was stalking me.

Already my head was throbbing. If I could go back to sleep, I could stall it a little longer, along with all the problems that sat in my mind like a row of irate children.

Still, the tickling feeling persisted. I brushed my arm and shifted again. But soon I could sense it on the soles of my feet and in the curve of my left armpit. When I opened my eyes, dizzy and disoriented, I found the room moving with hundreds of tiny green caterpillars. They were crawling across the walls, the carpet; a few were even languishing on the ceiling. Some were caught in the folds of my sheet, others were trekking their way up my leg.

I looked across at the bed where Gerry lay stripped down to his undies, unconscious, below the two open windows. Scores of the furry green creatures had claimed him, were inching their way across his stomach, his chest, his shoulders. A few were caught up in his hair. One was negotiating a journey around his left earlobe, and my father, my father just kept on snoring.

■   40   ■

We lived in that room for about a month. It was a little claustrophobic, and we had to keep the windows shut at all times so the caterpillars breeding in the garbage dump outside our window didn't infiltrate it again.

We told Mervyn that if anyone came asking after us, we didn't live at the Palmer. We avoided the Penn View as much as possible. We'd heard via the grapevine that wove through the carpark that two men in suits had made inquiries about us, and Fred had told them we'd gone back to England.

Of course, our eight hundred dollars was not back in the bank by Thursday, as Earl had promised. The weekend after we'd moved into the Palmer, he sheepishly produced fifty dollars cash, and told us he'd get us the rest "as soon as possible." Our man obviously had a bad habit, but by then there was nothing we could do about it except wait and hope.

As much as I wanted to give up at that point, I couldn't. My sixty-four-year-old father was still getting out there every night, playing his drums, spinning his sticks, nary a single complaint escaping his lips. And what would giving up mean? Surrendering to the fate of all the other women on the block between Eighth and Ninth Avenues? Opening my veins up to the vast, seductive chemicals circling the city like currents of perfumed sewage?

Had Gerry not been beside me, this might have happened. It wasn't that he functioned as an overriding moral force in my life—clearly, it was quite the opposite—but at twenty-one I felt a certain grueling responsibility toward him, to ensure he didn't disappear into drink or die in my custody. After all, the great adventure we were on had been a product of my own ambition and imagination, and it just seemed too easy to relinquish myself to a life of destitution.

Of course, we've never talked about these deeper issues. When Gerry now raves about those hungry days, it is with the same invocatory tones in which he relates all his other hilarious stories. Only now, as I perch on a crag of our mutual life and look back, do I realize how much my father must have quietly suffered through his seventy-seven years to have produced so many witty yarns.

I stopped drinking again and returned to Alberto's strict instruction, Cookie's intricate tap routines, my hours with the metal door, and Jethro Kloss's Final Solution. Alberto made a list of vitamins I should be taking to supplement my diet, and I bought them and took them religiously.

By then, I'd had a taste of healthiness, and knew how good it felt. I enjoyed the way my muscles were tightening up, how much my balance was improving. I could now do a triple spin on the ball of my right foot without wavering. Because we had no money, there were no drugs to tempt me away from my daily regime. The only time we ever saw Earl was when I managed to corner him in the carpark on his way home from work in order to hit him up for a portion of the owing cash.

We also had a few other good omens to keep us going: Gerry was hustling the manager of a bar in Penn Station to see if we could work the winter there for a nominal wage and tips. Occasionally we returned to do a spot at the Improvisation club. And Alberto was pleased with my progress, with the flesh I was beginning to shed, the emerging definition of my muscles, and how much straighter I seemed to stand.

■   41   ■

The harder our lives became, the harder I became. One Friday night, while working outside the basketball courts down in the Village, we took a break and I crossed the street and bought a huge plastic cup of iced water. Making my way back across Sixth Avenue, I saw Gerry bowed over his snare, showing an interested customer the intricacies of his double-stroke roll, when I noticed a tall man snatch up our cassette player and sprint off down the block.

Gerry, still caught up in his demonstration, was oblivious to the burglary. The guy was already several lengths away. Before I had a moment to think, I had thrown my cup down and was swerving through the lanes of traffic in my tap shoes in hot pursuit of the disappearing man.

I leapt onto the pavement and began gaining on him. The tap shoes were a bit of a handicap, but he was lugging the cassette player as he ran, so I guess it was a fair race, except that he'd started with quite a lead. I didn't waste my energy yelling out—he must have heard the taps gunning away behind him—but just pushed myself to run faster and faster. The fence of the basketball court seemed to go on forever. He was keeping close to the line of trees planted beside it. There wasn't much light, but I could see his outline. Soon he would reach the corner and disappear into West 3rd Street.

When I finally caught up with him, he miraculously stopped. He stood there, clutching the cassette player and gazing down at me, almost terrified. I, too, was frozen with fear, and stared up at him. I was shocked by how tall he was—pushing six and a half feet—and by how he could have simply raised his free hand and crushed me like an aluminum can. All I knew was that if I could keep eye contact with him, everything would be all right.

"Just put it down on the ground," I said softly. "I don't want to call the cops." I tried to make my voice sound even and gentle, to not lose eye contact. "Just put it down. And you can go that way." I nodded at West 3rd Street. It felt as if I were talking down a man poised on the ledge of a tall building, or pleading with a nut toting a loaded gun. "Please," I added. "I don't want any trouble. Just give it back and we'll call it quits."

And then it happened. His knees bent, and he slowly lowered the cassette player to the ground. I picked it up and, still gazing into those large brown eyes, murmured, "Thank you."

I turned. I didn't look back. I made myself stroll down the block at a leisurely pace. When I reached our spot, Gerry was still banging on the drum, oblivious to what had just transpired. It was only when I told him what had happened that I began to tremble.

Exhibiting fear, I've found, is the worst thing you can do in a moment of danger. If you don't have any guts, you have to pretend. I'd learned this from my father and, by the time I was twenty-one, the philosophy was serving me well. After I told him the story of my chase down Sixth Avenue, Gerry shook his head and ruffled my hair. Then we placed the cassette player back behind my wooden box and began another show.

■ 42 ■

As winter began to stalk us again, we decided to try working during the day. We'd been spending over twenty dollars a week in subway and bus fares up to Columbus Avenue. It was a significant amount of money to be saved. Since we lived in midtown, we could stroll across to Macy's on the corner of 34th and Broadway and work the lunchtime crowds. During that period, we were virtually living hand-to-mouth, and only received a small installment from Earl when we were desperate to pay the rent or buy food. We spent a few hours a day on that corner, competing with a steel drummer and wiry men flogging hot Walkmans, pendant watches, and packets of patchouli incense.

After a month, a larger room became available on the third floor of the Palmer. It was three times as big as the ground-floor one, and Chase let us have it for the same price. There was room enough for me to stretch out every day without accidentally kicking my father.

We were feeling pretty hopeful until we came home one day, opened the door, and were met by a pile of plaster and splintered wood. Looking up, I could see into the room above, copper pipes circling into a sink and torn floral wallpaper. As funny as it seemed at the time, to me the collapsed ceiling was also an omen, a warning that I had better watch my back. What if it had fallen as we slept? Or as I stood at the sink, brushing my teeth?

A few days later, another strange thing happened: As we performed outside Macy's, in front of the wide display windows, a series of burglar alarms suddenly pealed out onto the street. One moment we were grooving our way through "Fan-Dance Fanny" and the next the entire block was flooded with sirens and security guards. The alarms were so loud and unrelenting I was expecting a nuclear bomb to drop out of the air. We turned off the music, and while confused shoppers stood about wondering what was going on, I took advantage of the captive audience and passed around the hat.

The security guards were still scouring the area and the alarms were still bleating across midtown when they finally apprehended their culprit: I had apparently danced a little too close to the gleaming sheets of glass, and had tripped the entire system.

When we arrived back at the Palmer that afternoon, we were met at the door by a livid Mervyn.

"I don't want *criminals* living in my hotel!" he gushed.

At first, I thought he'd heard about the Macy's alarm, that he was being facetious, and brushed past him without a comment. But Gerry stopped and squarely faced him. "What are you talking about?"

Mervyn drew in a deep breath and momentarily rose to his toes. "Just after you left this morning, two men came looking for you."

I paused in the corridor, my hand frozen around the handle of my wooden box.

"Yeah?" said Gerry. "So what?"

"They told me you owed Bellevue Hospital quite a bit of money. That you've been *breaking the law*."

By the way Mervyn was glaring at Gerry, a stranger might have thought my father was guilty of multiple war crimes.

"You didn't tell 'em we were staying here, did you?"

Mervyn gave his head an impetuous toss. "Of course I did! Do you think I'm going to implicate myself in—"

"Oh, shit, Merv"—Gerry suddenly dropped his side drum and stands—"I thought I told you that if anyone came looking for us, we don't live here. Didn't I tell you that?"

"I'm not paid to protect *criminals*!"

He seemed to relish the word. I leaned against the corridor wall, already contemplating our next move.

"This is the law we're talking about. I can't lie about a thing like this!

Now look"—he held out a slip of paper and passed it over to Gerry—
"they're going to come back tomorrow. At eleven o'clock. For a quick chat.
And I think you'd better cooperate with them. They don't look like men to
mess around with."

I took the slip of paper from Gerry. In neat black printing it read; *Mr.
Lipton. 11 am—Wednesday.*

After combing the Classified section of the *Village Voice*, we couldn't
find much accommodation within our price range. We were severely limited
in what we could pursue because we had only two hundred dollars to our
name and had to move within eighteen hours. The only listing that looked
vaguely promising was a room in a building on 32nd Street, but when we arrived, a man who lived next door told us the room was vacant because, only
a week ago, a young woman had been murdered in it.

After we left the house on 32nd, we walked up to the diner on Ninth
Avenue, drank two solemn cups of coffee each, and argued about who
should call Nerida. It was the third time in eighteenth months that we'd
been stuck for a place to live, and by now it was getting embarrassing. Gerry
argued that he'd called her the last time, from New Orleans, and the time
before, from the Latham Hotel, on the day we'd arrived in New York. He
palmed me a quarter, but I slipped it back in his pocket. "You're her
adopted father," I said. "Not me."

He sighed, shook his head, and slipped off the stool. He wasn't on the
pay phone longer than two minutes.

"All taken care of," he quietly announced when he returned. "Now
let's get back to the hotel and see how fast we can get packed up."

Since we'd moved twice in the last six weeks, it didn't take long to or-
ganize our few possessions into a couple of bags and suitcases. I did the
packing while Gerry went around to the Penn View to wait for Earl to come
home from work. He still owed us five hundred dollars, and we didn't want
him to lose track of us.

We moved our gear out of the Palmer in less than ten minutes, deliberately parading past Mervyn and shooting him looks that were, to say the
least, slightly soiled.

As we carried the last bags down the hall, Gerry couldn't resist pausing
in front of Mervyn and saying, "Tomorrow you can tell those guys that we

shot through. And don't forget," he added, half-grinning, "to thank 'em for tipping us off about when they were coming back. That was very kind of 'em. Very, very polite." And we walked out of the Palmer for the last time, leaving Mervyn as silent as the dust on the staircase.

■ 43 ■

We stayed at Nerida's with the understanding that it was just temporary, a couple of weeks at most, while we looked for another place. Since the last time we'd stayed there, Greg had grown pink and healthy, and had begun to conquer the TB that had so ravaged his body the winter before. Charlie, on the other hand, was back on the piss and drinking up to three bottles of red wine a day. And I found out by overhearing a whispered discussion that Nerida was using again. She jokingly related how she and her friends had gone bowling one day and, after shooting up in the toilet, she was so disoriented that when she aimed at the pins and swung, the ball shot off backward and knocked the club manager flying.

While we stayed at Nerida's, we continued to work, and scoured the papers each day in search of some new digs. It was the same old problem: too few places and too little money.

I kept up my tap lessons with Cookie and my sessions with Alberto. And in between, I spent hours on the wooden floor of Nerida's living room, stretching and repeating exercises over and over again, feeling my tendons lengthen, the tightening of the deep muscles of my center. By that time, Alberto had me doing seventy-five push-ups a day, and seventy-five sit-ups. One-legged demipliés. Side leg lifts. Spine rolls and back bends. The splits. Stretching my hamstrings, the insides of my thighs. He had me repeating an exercise to improve my balance: standing on one foot, I had to close my eyes and, during fourteen counts, slowly rise onto the ball and lower myself again. It sounds easy, but it took weeks to master, especially on my left side.

The more taut, balanced, and controlled I became, the better I danced. In Cookie's classes, the difficult rhythmic patterns that had confounded me four months ago now rushed out beneath my feet in a syncopated euphoria.

I had now graduated to the front row, cutting it with the best, keeping up with the ten-beat riff turns, the six-beat wings, the subtle slow-drag of the Creole time-steps.

I began to modify Cookie's choreography when I practiced and danced on the street, until I found myself improvising, pushing the accents, varying the transitions, dropping a step in a combination and adding one of my own. Sometimes I'd double the time on a down-tempo sequence, until I was making the patterns my own, uniting them with the rhythms I heard in my head, just like my father's stories, the way I now write them and make them mine.

I was gradually inventing my own language, my own voice, and soon it did not matter so much that there was no magician in my life to love me, to transform me, to make my sadness suddenly disappear. As my body lengthened, as my foot healed, as my skin began to glow, I was slowly becoming the protagonist of my own life, not the auditionee, someone else's supporting actress.

I was, to put it simply, becoming my own magician.

Once Earl met us in his lunch hour. As we walked along Sixth Avenue, he kept remarking about how much taller I looked. It seemed like an anatomical impossibility. Nevertheless, I couldn't help but shrug and agree with him. My two skirts now hung much shorter on me, and the hem of the fraying black velvet dress, which had only last year reached my toes, now barely covered my lower calves. When I stood beside Earl that day, I didn't have to gaze up. For the first time I could look him squarely in the eyes, which he confessed he found a little disconcerting.

After a week of solid searching, of combing the entire island, the only room we found for four hundred a month was a tiny one on the third floor of the Penn View. At first, I thought Gerry was mad for even contemplating going back there. But my father, with his cultivated Irish bravado, with his great love of irony and reversal, was keen to return to the lair from which we'd escaped.

"They'll never think to look for us back there," he reasoned. "They reckon we're on the run."

"But we are on the run," I reminded him.

"Exactly!" he said, slurping up a steaming mouthful of borscht.

"You'd have to be an idiot to move back to square one." He paused and grinned, a deep purple stain ringing his mouth. "And that's why we're gunna do it."

■ 44 ■

As a precautionary measure, Gerry reregistered at the Penn View under the name G. Gas. It had always been the word he'd used whenever he needed a code or pseudonym. I presumed he'd chosen it because Gas was an adjective he often liked to use. "That was gas," or "What a gas idea!" He told me, though, that it was the only word he could consistently remember, as it was made up of his initials, Gerry Augustus Sayer.

I didn't register at all. Everyone at the Penn View understood that Mr. Gas did not have a daughter. Especially Fred, who was still standing by us.

The nightly camaraderie between Earl and my father did not resume when we moved back. Earl kept to his room; we kept to ours. The weather had turned, and icy December winds stole down the avenues. Gerry took to wearing woolen gloves with the fingers cut off as he played. We continued to work the lunchtime crowds during the week, though no longer in front of Macy's. After tripping the burglar alarms, we were effectively banned from that block by the security guards. Thus, we were banished farther downtown, back to our spot outside City Hall.

My health kept blossoming, as did my friendship with Alberto. Sometimes, after our lessons, he'd take me to the theater. Or we'd sit around his table, reading and writing things in his scrapbook. Sometimes he'd introduce me to his lovers, muscular young men with good haircuts and the same chiseled features as his own.

Alberto had noticed the threadbare skirts I wore, the holes in my one sweater, the runs in my stockings. One day, after a lesson, when we'd settled down to a pot of tea, he flung open his closet and pulled out a black silk shirt, a pair of tweed pants, and a long gray overcoat. I flushed with embarrassment when he offered them to me. But he insisted they were taking up too much room in his closet and made me try them on.

I was particularly grateful for the coat, which was long enough to cover my knees, and would prove invaluable when the snow set in. The black silk felt soft and luxurious against my skin and the trousers fitted me perfectly.

In his clothes, I no longer looked like Alice, no longer the waif who used to stare back at me from the gleaming panes of shop windows. I looked more like a woman going on twenty-two, the woman I was supposed to be. The ensemble became my best outfit, and on the first date I would have with my future husband, it would be Alberto's hand-me-downs that I'd be wearing.

■   45   ■

One night we were shivering outside the dry-cleaning store on Columbus, trying to hustle up a crowd, when a young man in a suede coat walked directly up to us.

"You're not going to believe this," he said.

I gazed at him, bemused. He had a square chin and shaggy brown hair. The collar of his coat was turned up. He looked vaguely familiar.

"I live just around the corner here on Seventieth," he continued. "Almost every night on my way home I see you guys out here. I mean, you're always here and you're always making a noise . . ."

His voice trailed off and I assumed he was yet another disgruntled resident who would soon be threatening to call the police.

"Yeah," I said. "So?"

"Well," he said, "this is the funny thing. Last weekend I wanted to get out of the city, and I took a trip upstate. Do you know a little town called Woodstock?"

"Where the rock concert was," I said. "The big one."

"Where all the hippies went," added Gerry.

"Yes," he said, leaning in closer. "So I'm thinking about how nice it is to get out of the rat-race, and away from all the noise"—he eyed our cassette player and Gerry's snare—"and last Saturday morning, I walked into the town's art gallery, and what should I see?"

"What?" Gerry and I chorused.

The man shook his head and half-smiled. "A life-sized oil painting of you two hanging right in the entranceway. And you're dressed"—he gestured to my skirt with the musical notes, my hat, Gerry's shoes—"you're dressed exactly as you are now."

"Who painted it?" I asked. "There haven't been any painters around."

"They must have taken a photograph," said the man. "Or several. I couldn't believe how lifelike it was. The dry-cleaning store's in the back-ground. I said to my friend, I said, I almost expect to see myself leaning into the frame."

The man laughed to himself and hurried off. Gerry and I glanced at each other and grinned. Over the years, I have tried to track down the paint-ing, but have failed. Sometimes I still berate myself for not extracting more details from the shaggy-haired man, the artist's name, the actual address of the mysterious Woodstock art gallery. The only canvas I've ever seen us on is the one stretched across my imagination, the one I am now inscribing as I write.

■ 46 ■

Even though winter had descended upon us, even though it snowed occasionally, by mid December I was feeling so well, so tall, so lean, so inde-pendent, that I did not worry about the weather, about how we were going to make next week's rent.

In fact, by that time, we had stopped paying rent because the Penn View had been condemned and Chase was trying to kick everyone out. All the old-timers, all the prostitutes and dealers were organizing a meet-ing to protest the evictions. Gerry and I didn't really care. We couldn't af-ford to part with a hundred dollars a week, and the eviction controversy gave us a good excuse to keep our money hidden under the carpet of our room. Each night we still went out and entertained people, even when it snowed.

During December, a director named Karen Goodman approached us about being in a film she was making about street performers. She wanted to shoot us during the day, when the light was more favorable. She arranged to meet us outside City Hall but was almost an hour late. Her schedule had been thrown because the fire-eater she'd been filming earlier had forgotten his gas.

It had been raining lightly for most of the afternoon. While we were waiting, we worked under the trees, where it wasn't quite so wet.

When Karen Goodman and her crew arrived, we ran through a couple of numbers to get the sound right. We were wearing our "Thunder from Down Under" sweatshirts, and I had on the faded black skirt with the embroidered musical notes. I'd also made a pair of minstrel tights for the occasion, with the left leg black and the right one red. On my left foot I wore a red shoe, and on the right foot was a black one. Gerry, of course, wore the complement on his feet. When a passing businessman yelled out that he liked Gerry's footwear, Gerry called back that he had another pair at home just the same.

Karen filmed two numbers and interviewed us. I cannot remember the tunes, nor what we said on camera. There are only three images that keep returning to me from that afternoon, like dreams, repeating into every dark night. We never saw the film, as we lost contact with Karen when we fled to New Orleans at the beginning of a snow-choked January.

But nine years later, in 1993, a woman stopped me in a health-food co-op in Bloomington, Indiana, and, leaning over a pile of organic pumpkins, told me she'd seen my father and me on television recently. It was an hour-long program on New York street performers and we had opened the show. The declaration was no less startling than if a stranger had told me I was a bird in a previous life. I was, by then, the wife of a professor and poet, the author of two novels, and about to graduate Phi Beta Kappa from Indiana University. My father was far away from me, back in Sydney, teaching music and playing the odd gig. I remember placing my palms on the cold skin of a pumpkin and having those three images rise like ghosts and haunt me back into the past.

I am standing in the drizzle on a path that slopes down through a park toward Broadway. I am holding a red umbrella above my head. When the camera-person waves her hand, I begin to spin. I begin to pirouette down the path beneath the wet arms of the elms, the umbrella a red beacon oscillating through the rainy afternoon.

Then I am standing on a piece of plywood outside City Hall. When my father hits the drums, my feet hit the wood. But I'm not dancing some trite routine taught to me by a bored Sydney teacher, nor am I trying to ape my father's triplets against the snare. I'm not even mimicking Cookie's intricate patterns, which I'd rehearsed for hours on the metal door. As the camera hums and I gaze up Broadway into the flotilla of gray clouds, I'm only aware of how vibrant and well I feel. No longer that girl Alice, I now stand three inches taller, and my breath buries itself deep inside me. My skin is clear, my foot no longer aches. I can now feel my muscular center between my hips like a well-oiled engine. And the sounds, the sounds I am making are not

Gerry's. They are mine—my own syncopated soliloquy running like a river of words into and around the pulse-beat of my father.

Then the movie in my mind always cuts to the last shot. Gerry and I are packing up and slowly walking away, walking away together down Broadway through a light, watery mist. After about twenty yards, we turn and disappear into the darkness of the subway station. It is the one shot Karen insists on taking several times, and each time we walk back to the spot outside City Hall and unpack our gear. We stand in the drizzle and await our cue. When the camera hums and we get the wave, we pack up our drums, our taps and feather boas, and walk away together again.

c o d a

"If only the plot would leave people alone."

—Bob Perelman, *Anti-Oedipus*

Our erotic potential begins at birth, with that first breath of a mother's blood and sweat, the scent of her salt and fear. It's her molecules we first inhale. When we come close to someone, we literally enter their atmosphere. Perhaps marriages are not made in heaven, but merely in the body's subtle musk.

Families fling us into intimacy, into shared odors, a whole sensual archive of warm water and bitter tonics, inherited underwear, the balm of another's touch. The vapor your mother's hairspray makes against the window. The brittle half-moons of your father's fingernail clippings at the edge of the piano. The baking dinners, the setting custards. The bloom of your sister's breasts silhouetted against night.

And the curse's red carnation drying on a corner of her sheet. Piss diluted by shared bathwater. The traces of your mother's vomit clinging to the toilet in the morning. Yes, and her soft words, her keeping you home from school because she's lonely and likes having you around. Her fingers moving through your hair, the circles she draws on your temples, the wild perfume of her breath. The secrets against father, the stray cats. The sadness of her sagging nylons.

Your sister's virgin bangles clinking beneath her blanket. Her skin as pale as a peeled apple. Hot nights in cotton underwear. Salads and cold meatloaf stuffed with boiled eggs. Overheard arguments. Your father's false teeth grinning in a glass of water beside the sink. Your brother's first stray pubic hairs wet and wilting into the drain of the bath.

Your father coming into your room after a long gig and quietly waking you with whispers. His boozy stories there in the darkness, his somber resolutions. Healthy baby teeth loosened and pulled in order to tempt the tooth fairy for a twenty-cent piece. Losing a pea in your ear and having it pop out moldy one morning six months later. Your brother's laughter echoing through the house, his suntanned back, the way he hugs you as you both fly down a hill on his homemade billy-cart. A honky-tonk piano at two in the morning, and seeing your parents flirt with other people.

And families get sick together. The pervasive surrender to chicken pox and measles, in twos and threes, like a bacterial Noah's ark. Colds swarm you in brief quartets. You snuffle into the same hankies and get to watch "General Hospital" with your mother. Your father massaging Vicks VapoRub into your chest at night. The cups of milky tea. Rain on a corrugated roof. Seven thousand and forty-two home-cooked dinners. Twenty-one summers. Ninety-six menstrual cycles. Eighteen progressive shoe sizes. It's a bloody long ache of furtive joy.

There was something about Yusef that tasted of soil, of damp earth. He was a lick of familiarity in that strange land of corn dogs and roasting knishes. In him perhaps I recognized my mother's serene melancholia, my father's daring. In him I saw my own awkward grace, the hollow ache that prowls through your body after hours of hard work. Between his two dark nipples I found my brother's burgeoning beatitude, a sixteen-year-old boy drunk on the scent of cut grass and wisteria, a boy who could rock me like a double bass and make me sing. In him, my sister's quiet beauty, an elegance further deepened by being so unsure of itself.

In Yusef, I recognized my own lost family, and somehow he returned it to me.

For even though it was not perfect, even though it had self-destructed by the time I was ten, my family had already inducted me into sensuality, had shown me how to take love in and hold it, like nourishment, like a trace mineral, building up my bones and blood vessels, augmenting my veins, connecting my synapses, until my skin was soft and glowing and my hair shined. Until there was a single moment in my life when my body took one final breath and it all came flooding out and into someone else, someone who took me in and made my spleen surrender, the long ladder of my spine extend, someone who was not family, who was not father, nor mother, but one who was ripe and true and imperceptibly familiar.

Even though we didn't want to leave New York for the winter, we'd read the omens and knew we'd have to flee. On New Year's Eve, after we'd made one hundred and sixty dollars, after we'd packed up, a man suddenly attacked me. He grabbed the long handles of my shoulder bag and I grabbed the bag itself, dropping to the footpath and wrapping my body around it. But he wouldn't let go of the handles and began dragging me and the bag across Columbus Avenue. Gerry was taking a leak when it happened. The man kept pulling the bag and me between lanes of traffic, as if I were a toy wagon. I was *screaming at him to stop, but he wouldn't. I yelled for the cops, but of course, not one was around. If it hadn't been for the Ukrainian taxi driver who pulled up and beat the man off me, we would have lost all the money we had.*

The second omen came the following night, when my father was walking through the carpark next to the Penn View Hotel. Two men jumped him and one pulled a knife. Gerry just laughed at them and said that he'd been about to hit them up for five dollars. They finally let him go, but the two experiences left us both shaken.

All around us, things were coming to an end. The hotel had been condemned. Chase was evicting all the tenants. The snow set in for good and we still didn't have any permanent indoor work. Earl suddenly moved out of the Penn View on New Year's Eve without saying good-bye or leaving a forwarding address.

We had stopped paying rent, and we held onto the one hundred and sixty dollars that had almost been stolen.

But when we were down to below a hundred dollars, when it was so cold that we couldn't work, when we had no place to go, Gerry struck up a deal with Chase. My father offered to move out of the Penn View the following day, without any of the fuss and demands the other tenants were making: all Gerry wanted was one hundred dollars cash as a kind of compensation and we'd be on our way.

I'm not sure if Chase realized that we still owed him two weeks' rent, because he happily palmed my father the money. Suddenly our savings were bumped up to almost two hundred dollars. The cheapest one-way airfare I could get to New Orleans was one hundred and forty dollars. I booked two seats over the phone for the following day. The agent said we could pay for our tickets at the airport.

We still needed another eighty dollars to buy the tickets, and a bit extra to see us through until we could start working on Bourbon Street. It was too cold and snowy to perform that night. We thought about hocking something, but apart from our performing equipment, we didn't own anything of value.

Earl still owed us two hundred dollars. We didn't know where he lived, but I had his work number. I rang him and explained our situation and begged him for the money. He said he'd try to get it to us in the morning, before we left for the airport. I told him we had to leave by midday at the very latest and hung up.

The next day we were all packed up and ready to go by eleven A.M. We sat in the foyer of the hotel with our bags. We paced across the cracked linoleum. Through the glass doors I watched Alma shivering on the snow-covered steps, a frayed black overcoat wrapped around her, head slightly bowed.

We said good-bye to Fred, to Ricky, to Pop and Willis. By midday, Earl hadn't arrived and I began to panic. The last airport bus to get us out to JFK on time left the Port Authority at twelve-thirty. I rang his work, but he wasn't in. I asked Fred where Earl had moved to, but he shrugged and said he didn't know. We moved our bags out onto the street, hoping to see him, to receive the money and start running uptown toward the Port Authority.

Our breath made puffs of steam as we waited on the sidewalk. Suddenly I was overcome with regret for what I was leaving behind: my lessons with Cookie, my apprenticeship with Alberto, all the dreams my father and I had shared between the walls of the crumbling hotel. I hated this twist in my story, this sudden giving up.

It was ten minutes past twelve when I finally noticed Earl's panama hat bobbing through the traffic at the Eighth Avenue intersection. He strode up the street, grimacing and glancing at his watch. We picked up our bags and rushed to meet him. He gushed his apologies and handed Gerry the money. It was only one hundred and fifty dollars, but Earl said that was all he could get his hands on at such short notice. It was enough to cover the airfares and left us with a little extra cash. We didn't have time to argue with him, and our good-bye was swift: a quick hug before he disappeared up the steps of the Penn View.

Before we picked up our bags again, I could not stop myself running back and enveloping Alma in a quick embrace. "I'm moving," I whispered, and she nodded and almost smiled.

Gerry and I arrived back in New Orleans in the first week of January 1985 with sixty dollars to our name and nowhere to live. Our old standby, Leonard, offered to share his slave quarter with us until we made enough money to rent a room of our own.

It was cramped with the three of us living in a space that was a squeeze even for one person. I continued to stretch in Leonard's courtyard, on a wooden board I'd found on the street: splits, spine rolls, sit-ups, push-ups, bridges, and balancers. Every afternoon, if it wasn't raining, I'd pull on my tap shoes and practice what was turning out to be my own choreography, listening to the sounds in my head stuttering out through my feet, a sanguine syncopation.

I was happy, almost serene inside my long lean body, happy to make my own magic.

Even in New Orleans, things were coming to an end. I'd heard a rumor that my arch rival, Hambone, had been thrown in jail. In the ten months since I'd last seen Pee Wee, he had suddenly become a teenager. He'd shot up a few inches, and he'd had his two front teeth capped with gold, with stars cut into the center so the gleaming ivory shone through. He'd also toughened up a lot, was not as interested in dancing as he was in making money any way he could. It hurt to realize that soon he would join the throng of shoe-shine men snapping rags along Bourbon Street.

My father and I were there among them, in the gaudy neon glow, earning twenty dollars a night outside the Royal Sonesta Hotel. But I was already growing away, and by the following month, by my twenty-second birthday, I was only dancing to the drum that beat in my own head.

I missed my friend Alberto. I'd not had a chance to say good-bye to him before we left New York, but sometimes we'd talk on the phone. He'd tell me about his latest boyfriend and chide me if I'd hadn't done my seventy-five sit-ups that day.

Occasionally, when we performed on Royal Street, I caught a glimpse of Marilyn in the distance, walking out of the A&P. She still had her bags in tow, but the Dragon Lady was never with her. Whenever I caught her eye, she always turned away.

As I write now about all the characters of my past, as I remember Pee Wee, Hambone, Porkchop, Marilyn, and the others, it seems as if I'm looking back through glass at people who never surfaced from the underworld—that trashy, seductive wonderland of the street. In the coming decade, I would return to New Orleans about once a year with my husband, and we would sit at the window tables of cafes and bars and watch them all growing older, the children becoming heavy-drinking hustlers, the stoops settling into the bodies of the older shoe-shine men. One year we even found Porkchop standing outside Crazy Shirley's, selling autographed black-and-white photos of himself in order to pay for his funeral.

Within six months he was dead; the cancer had ravaged his liver.

My father never received his green card in the mail; in fact, he never heard from Immigration again. When he called them one day, they said they *had no record of his application, that they must have misplaced his file. In a few months' time, when he would fly back to Sydney on his own, on a ticket purchased with borrowed money, he'd have to admit his alien status to Immigration before he boarded the plane.*

I met Yusef on Mardi Gras night, at a Brazilian wedding reception. I met him in a jazz club called Snug Harbor. The groom was his next-door neighbor.

I ended up at the club reluctantly, begrudgingly. It was around ten at night. I'd been performing all day, had tap danced on Royal Street for about nine hours and wanted to collapse into bed. While Gerry and I were working, the wedding party had passed right by us—a mobile Brazilian band at the front playing a hot bossa nova, a hundredfold group of guests half-dancing behind them, and in the center, the suited groom and the bride boogying along in her white lace wedding gown.

She was Leonard's Portuguese teacher. He was among the crowd of jiving guests, following the band to the Moonwalk, where the service was to take place at eleven A.M. We waved to them all as they passed, and began performing again once the party had rounded the corner.

I was still in my top hat and tails when we returned to Leonard's. Thousands of revelers were in costume that night, and I didn't feel out of place. When I walked through the door, I found Leonard waiting for me, almost grimacing. He reminded me that I had agreed to accompany him to the wedding reception, and that we were running an hour late.

I twisted my hands. I wiped my brow. I told him I was exhausted, that I could not go out again. He frowned and fumed, told me that I had promised to accompany him. He made me feel so guilty that I finally sighed and followed him back out the door.

I met him on Fat Tuesday, 1985. New Orleans had been partying for ten days, and Mardi Gras was the greatest feast, the crowning celebration of them all before the long period of Lent.

Five days after my twenty-second birthday. Not a drop of alcohol had passed my lips for months. I was four inches taller, fourteen pounds lighter. I could tap dance for nine hours without bruising my feet. I was not looking for a man. I did not pine for a magician. As I walked in my top hat and tails down Decatur Street, I was only conscious of the fact that I would rather have been in bed, asleep.

When we entered the club, we were confronted by hundreds of gyrating guests dressed in jeweled headdresses, feathered capes, ball gowns, and sequined costumes. The club was so hot and crowded I wanted to turn around and go back home. But Leonard grabbed my sleeve and led me up the stairs.

It was packed up there, too, and for a minute we just stood about, feeling awkward. The mezzanine was lit by candles burning in colored jars on the tables. Up there, you could look down on the band and at all the guests spinning about on the dance floor. Leonard noticed an empty seat at an otherwise crowded table. He sat me down in it and introduced me to most of the people. I nodded at his acquaintances, but their names escaped me because the music was too loud.

I did not notice him immediately, but after a minute or two, the quiet, slender black man across the table caught my eye. Every time I glanced up, he was looking at me, holding me in a long gaze. His eyes were dark and elegant. His black curly hair was cropped short, and he sported a wiry goatee beard. He was wearing a short-sleeved blue shirt. I could tell he was shy by the way he kept his head slightly lowered as he looked across the table. His fingers continued to grip the stem of his wineglass between the occasional sip.

Weeks later, after he'd folded me into his arms for the first time and we finally admitted our earliest impressions of each other, he told me that he guessed I was about sixteen years old and was far too young for him. And I laughed and confessed that I thought he was a bit mad—for he didn't stop gazing at me.

If Leonard hadn't decided that he wanted to smoke a joint at that moment, maybe my story would have ended differently. If Leonard hadn't demanded that I accompany him to the wedding reception, if Gerry and I hadn't been forced back to New Orleans, if the Penn View hadn't been condemned, if we hadn't lost all our money, if I hadn't lost faith in my father, I would never have encountered that mellifluous voice, that gentle countenance.

After Leonard rolled up a three-papered joint and stood up, everyone at the table but the shy black man and me got up, too, and followed him down the stairs. Suddenly we were alone, and we both just sat there, glancing at each other. The music erupted into a syncopated dervish. It was a rhythm that smelled of sweat and longing, of swamp mist and alligator musk. I enjoyed watching how the music held him, the embrace that stole around his body and nudged his arms into uncrossing themselves, seduced his legs into a more casual position.

I never would have thought that Patrick White would finally break the ice between me and my future husband. We started off with the usual small talk: names and origins. When Yusef realized I was from Sydney, however, we fell into a discussion about White's later novels, A Fringe of Leaves, The Vivesector, *and* A Solid Mandala. *And it was then that I knew he was not crazy, and he knew I was not sixteen.*

Soon I was sitting beside him, enjoying the first hour of what would turn out to be years of exciting conversation about books, language, writing, and ideas. He'd just published his first book of poetry. He'd taught English at the University of New Orleans for three years, but was now teaching Creative Writing in the public school system.

At midnight, when the groom brought out King Cake for everyone to eat, when the band struck up a rendition of "Baila mi Gente," when Yusef stood up, took my hand and led me downstairs, we began our first tentative dance, something between a slow-drag and a cha-cha. He drew me toward him, spun me away, placed his shy hands on my waist, and gazed into my eyes again. I breathed in the earthy musk of his breath, gliding in and out of his embrace.

In the middle of March, after our second date, I sat in the front room of his shotgun house on Piety Street. I was gazing at a print in a book on the artist Romare Bearden when he suddenly turned and kissed me for the first time. And I felt my mouth dissolve, my throat opening itself up to him.

I pressed my face into his hairless chest and inhaled, drawing the scent of his sweat down deep into my belly, where my song always began. His bones, his lean, long body, almost felt fragile within the grip my limbs made around him, as if they might break if I exhaled too quickly. His skin was as smooth as a piece of vintage satin. The hands that had cut cane, picked cotton, grafted roses, wielded guns, penned scores of lyrical poems, drew long lines along my thighs, and up under my skirt, around the curve of my arse.

When he guided me toward his bed, I felt his cock swelling against my hip bone and nudged him back, running my tongue across his nipples, tasting the sea in them, the rock salt of his flesh. During this dance, this duet of ours, a sound trapped itself in his throat, and as he allowed it to escape, he willed his fingers through the swollen crevices, the wet geography between my legs.

Soon I had my tongue in his mouth again, and I drank him in, all his sadness and temerity, his silence and saliva, his breath that tasted like damp coun-

try earth. I took him in, the smooth tongue swelling with so many secrets. I took in the stories of his childhood, a boy who sold blackberries on the side of a country road, who grew up in the South during segregation, a boy whose mother had deserted him at ten. I took in the roof of his mouth, the insides of his cheeks. The slow grind of his cock against me. I took in the scent of his curly black hair as he pressed his face between my breasts, the bouquet blooming through every muscle and vein, through the glowing triangle between my legs. I took in this conjurer of words, his teeth against my nipples, his arse between my hands, the liquid darkness of the room. The loose cuffs his hands made around my wrists as he grasped them and steered me toward his bed again. I took in the force of his movements, the man who dodged grenades for a year in the jungles of Vietnam. Pressing back, I drank him in farther, the way he gently pushed me down and untied my skirt, peeled off my leotard in one fast, masterful gesture. And when he nudged himself into the warm ravine between my legs, when he entered me, my tendons gripped the strong hard thing that filled the absence, the loneliness, the legacy of my childhood. I took in his voice as it sang into my ear, the body's sleight-of-hand, desire's quick alchemy, until that muscular cup I imagined inside me finally overflowed and into someone else, swilling in currents through my stomach and breasts, until he joined me in that arabesque of blood. The bedsprings creaked, and just within earshot I heard my parents making love, the soft cries my mother used to make undulating into the room.

ABOUT THE AUTHOR

MANDY SAYER studied tap dancing with Cookie Cook and Brenda Buffalino and later joined the Bill Evans Dance Company. Her first novel, *Mood Indigo*, won *The Australian*/Vogel Award in 1989, which was followed by her second novel, *Blind Luck*. Her latest, *The Cross*, was a finalist for the Ned Kelly Award for Best First Crime Novel and has been nominated for the 1997 International IMPAC Dublin Literary Award. She has also been named one of the ten Best Young Australian Novelists by the *Sydney Morning Herald*. She received an M.A. in creative writing from Indiana University.